SAP PRESS e-books

Print or e-book, Kindle or iPad, workplace or airplane: Choose where and how to read your SAP PRESS books! You can now get all our titles as e-books, too:

- By download and online access
- For all popular devices
- And, of course, DRM-free

Convinced? Then go to www.sap-press.com and get your e-book today.

Implementing SAP S/4HANA Finance

SAP PRESS

SAP PRESS is a joint initiative of SAP and Rheinwerk Publishing. The know-how offered by SAP specialists combined with the expertise of Rheinwerk Publishing offers the reader expert books in the field. SAP PRESS features first-hand information and expert advice, and provides useful skills for professional decision-making.

SAP PRESS offers a variety of books on technical and business-related topics for the SAP user. For further information, please visit our website: www.sap-press.com.

Bala, Cacciottoli, Ryan
Consolidation with SAP S/4HANA
2018, approx. 425 pages, hardcover and e-book
www.sap-press.com/4532

Dirk Neumann, Lawrence Liang
Cash Management with SAP S/4HANA: Functionality and Implementation
2018, 477 pages, hardcover and e-book
www.sap-press.com/4479

Kathrin Schmalzing
CO-PA in SAP S/4HANA Finance: Business Processes, Functionality, and Configuration
2018, 337 pages, hardcover and e-book
www.sap-press.com/4383

Bardhan, Baumgartl, Chaadaev, Choi, Dudgeon, Lahiri, Meijerink, Worsley-Tonks
SAP S/4HANA: An Introduction (2nd Edition)
2018, 511 pages, hardcover and e-book
www.sap-press.com/4499

Anup Maheshwari

Implementing SAP S/4HANA® Finance

Rheinwerk Publishing

Editor Emily Nicholls
Copyeditor Melinda Rankin
Cover Design Graham Geary
Photo Credit iStockphoto.com/152150686/© oztasbc
Layout Design Vera Brauner
Production Marissa Fritz
Typesetting III-satz, Husby (Germany)
Printed and bound in the United States of America, on paper from sustainable sources

ISBN 978-1-4932-1619-2
© 2018 by Rheinwerk Publishing, Inc., Boston (MA)
2nd edition 2018

Library of Congress Cataloging-in-Publication Data
Names: Maheshwari, Anup, author.
Title: Implementing SAP S/4HANA finance / Anup Maheshwari.
Description: 2nd edition. | Bonn ; Boston : Rheinwerk Publishing, [2017] |
  Includes index.
Identifiers: LCCN 2017043385 (print) | LCCN 2017048457 (ebook) | ISBN
  9781493216208 (ebook) | ISBN 9781493216192 (alk. paper)
Subjects: LCSH: Accounting--Computer programs. | Business--Data
  processing--Computer programs. | SAP HANA (Electronic resource)
Classification: LCC HF5679 (ebook) | LCC HF5679 .M28 2017 (print) | DDC
  657.0285/53--dc23
LC record available at https://lccn.loc.gov/2017043385

All rights reserved. Neither this publication nor any part of it may be copied or reproduced in any form or by any means or translated into another language, without the prior consent of Rheinwerk Publishing, 2 Heritage Drive, Suite 305, Quincy, MA 02171.

Rheinwerk Publishing makes no warranties or representations with respect to the content hereof and specifically disclaims any implied warranties of merchantability or fitness for any particular purpose. Rheinwerk Publishing assumes no responsibility for any errors that may appear in this publication.

"Rheinwerk Publishing" and the Rheinwerk Publishing logo are registered trademarks of Rheinwerk Verlag GmbH, Bonn, Germany. SAP PRESS is an imprint of Rheinwerk Verlag GmbH and Rheinwerk Publishing, Inc.

All of the screenshots and graphics reproduced in this book are subject to copyright © SAP SE, Dietmar-Hopp-Allee 16, 69190 Walldorf, Germany.

SAP, the SAP logo, ABAP, Ariba, ASAP, Concur, Concur ExpenseIt, Concur TripIt, Duet, SAP Adaptive Server Enterprise, SAP Advantage Database Server, SAP Afaria, SAP ArchiveLink, SAP Ariba, SAP Business ByDesign, SAP Business Explorer, SAP BusinessObjects, SAP BusinessObjects Explorer, SAP BusinessObjects Lumira, SAP BusinessObjects Roambi, SAP BusinessObjects Web Intelligence, SAP Business One, SAP Business Workflow, SAP Crystal Reports, SAP EarlyWatch, SAP Exchange Media (SAP XM), SAP Fieldglass, SAP Fiori, SAP Global Trade Services (SAP GTS), SAP GoingLive, SAP HANA, SAP HANA Vora, SAP Hybris, SAP Jam, SAP MaxAttention, SAP MaxDB, SAP NetWeaver, SAP PartnerEdge, SAPPHIRE NOW, SAP PowerBuilder, SAP PowerDesigner, SAP R/2, SAP R/3, SAP Replication Server, SAP S/4HANA, SAP SQL Anywhere, SAP Strategic Enterprise Management (SAP SEM), SAP SuccessFactors, The Best-Run Businesses Run SAP, TwoGo are registered or unregistered trademarks of SAP SE, Walldorf, Germany.

All other products mentioned in this book are registered or unregistered trademarks of their respective companies.

Contents at a Glance

PART I Migrating to SAP S/4HANA Finance

1 Preparation 53
2 Installation and Upgrade 107
3 Preparation and Migration for General Ledger 131
4 Preparation and Migration for Asset Accounting 175
5 Preparation and Migration for Controlling 207
6 Preparation and Migration for House Bank Accounts 241
7 Data Migration 251
8 Postmigration Activities 315
9 Postmigration Testing 327

PART II Setting Up New Financials Functionality

10 SAP Cash Management 337
11 SAP BPC for SAP S/4HANA Finance 419
12 SAP Fiori Applications 465

Dear Reader,

You may have heard the adage, "If it's not broken, then don't fix it." At SAP PRESS, we operate under a slightly wordier maxim: "If it has already been an invaluable resource for thousands of readers and there's something new to say, then update it."

Last summer we published the first-ever implementation guide for SAP S/4HANA Finance, and this fall we're back at it. This second edition takes the approach lauded by reviewers of the first edition: a unique combination of step-by-step implementation instructions and insights into the way SAP S/4HANA impacts key financials processes and applications. It comes at a time when countless SAP S/4HANA Finance projects are underway or just beginning, and as consultants and IT teams draw their roadmap for the journey ahead. With new expert tips and previews of SAP S/4HANA 1709, this practical guide to migrating financials data and customizing SAP S/4HANA Finance is your comprehensive resource for the road.

What did you think about the second edition of *Implementing SAP S/4HANA Finance*? Your comments and suggestions are the most useful tools to help us make our books the best they can be. Please feel free to contact me and share any praise or criticism you may have.

Thank you for purchasing a book from SAP PRESS!

Emily Nicholls
Editor, SAP PRESS

emilyn@rheinwerk-publishing.com
www.sap-press.com
Rheinwerk Publishing · Boston, MA

Contents

Preface 21
Introduction 29

PART I Migrating to SAP S/4HANA Finance

1   Preparation   53

1.1	Check Functional Scope and Restrictions	53
1.2	Feasibility Checklist	55
1.3	The Maintenance Planner and Prechecks	63
1.4	Check Custom Coding	64
	1.4.1 Check Custom Code and Modifications	64
	1.4.2 Handling Custom-Defined Fields and Interfaces	65
1.5	Check Sizing	66
1.6	Precheck for Migration to New Asset Accounting	66
1.7	Activate Business Functions	68
	1.7.1 Activate Business Functions for Asset Accounting and Parallel Valuation	68
	1.7.2 Activate Enterprise Extension EA-FIN	71
	1.7.3 Activate Business Function FIN_AA_CI_1	72
1.8	Check and Activate New Depreciation Calculation	73
	1.8.1 Execute the Periodic Depreciation Posting Run	73
	1.8.2 Execute Year-End Closing	75
	1.8.3 Fiscal Year Change	75
1.9	Consistency Checks	76
	1.9.1 SAP ERP Financials Data Consistency Checks	76
	1.9.2 Reconciliation of the General Ledger and the Accounts Payable/Accounts Receivable Subledgers	79
	1.9.3 Reconciliation of the General Ledger with Asset Accounting	80

	1.9.4	Reconciliation of the General Ledger with Materials Management	82
	1.9.5	Reconciliation of Ledgers	84
1.10	**Perform Period-End Closing Activities**		86
	1.10.1	Copy Number Ranges	86
	1.10.2	Lock Periods in Materials Management	87
	1.10.3	Perform Closing for Periodic Asset Postings	87
	1.10.4	Execute the Periodic Depreciation Posting Run	88
	1.10.5	Verify Held Documents Status	88
	1.10.6	Carry Balances Forward to the Current Fiscal Year	89
	1.10.7	Reset Valuations for Periods in the Current Fiscal Year	91
	1.10.8	Lock Prior Periods in SAP ERP Financials and Controlling	92
	1.10.9	Batch Jobs	94
	1.10.10	Execute Report to Confirm Asset Accounting Prerequisites	94
	1.10.11	Lock Users	94
1.11	**Consistency Check before Activation of SAP S/4HANA Finance**		95
1.12	**Execute Business Reconciliation**		96
1.13	**Summary**		106

2 Installation and Upgrade   107

2.1	**Installation and Upgrade Checklist**		108
	2.1.1	SAP HANA and Minimum Versions	108
	2.1.2	Software Update Manager	110
	2.1.3	SAP HANA Live	111
	2.1.4	Administrator's Guide, Release Information Note, and Browser Support	111
	2.1.5	SAP Cash Management, Cost Objects, and Cost Object Hierarchies	112
	2.1.6	Industry Solutions and Add-Ons	112
	2.1.7	Maintenance Optimizer	113
	2.1.8	Target Stack XML and SAP NetWeaver Kernel	116
	2.1.9	Customer Code	117
	2.1.10	Data Definition Language Statement Corrections	117
2.2	**Review Data Model Changes**		117

2.3	Use the Maintenance Planner	118
2.4	Install the Related Software Component Version	120
2.5	Apply SAP Notes	121
2.6	Content Deployment with SAP HANA Application Lifecycle Management	123
2.7	Perform HANA-tization	123
	2.7.1 HANA-tization Checks	124
	2.7.2 HANA-tization Tools	125
2.8	Optimization	126
	2.8.1 Optimization Approach	126
	2.8.2 Optimization Tools	127
	2.8.3 Optimization Best Practice	128
	2.8.4 SAP HANA Modeling	128
2.9	Summary	129

3   Preparation and Migration for General Ledger   131

3.1	Activate SAP Reference Implementation Guide for Financial Accounting (New)	132
3.2	Check and Adopt Fiscal Year Variants	133
3.3	Define Currency Settings for Migration	134
3.4	Migrate General Ledger Customizing	135
3.5	Define Settings for Ledgers and Currency Types	136
3.6	Define Ledger Groups	138
3.7	Assign the Accounting Principle to the Ledger Group	140
3.8	Review the Assignment of Ledger and Company Code to Accounting Principles	141
3.9	Define the Ledger for the Controlling Version	141
3.10	Define Document Types for Postings in Controlling	142
3.11	Define Document Type Mapping for Controlling Business Transactions	143

3.12	Check and Define Default Values for Postings in Controlling	143
3.13	Define the Offsetting Account Determination Type	145
3.14	Define the Source Ledger for Migration of Balances	145
3.15	Check and Define Settings for Substitution for Cost-of-Sales Accounting	146
3.16	Check and Define Settings of Controlling Area	146
3.17	Execute Consistency Check of General Ledger Settings	147
3.18	Activate Business Functions	147
3.19	Key Changes to the General Ledger	148
	3.19.1 Architectural Impact	149
	3.19.2 Functionality Impact	156
	3.19.3 Configuration Impact	158
	3.19.4 Customer and Vendor Master Data	166
	3.19.5 Credit Management Impact	167
3.20	Key Changes to Period-End Closing	168
	3.20.1 Architectural Impact	169
	3.20.2 Functionality Impact	169
	3.20.3 Security Impact	172
3.21	Summary	173

4   Preparation and Migration for Asset Accounting   175

4.1	Prerequisites	177
4.2	Install SAP S/4HANA Finance with New Asset Accounting	177
4.3	Migrate Charts of Depreciation	178
4.4	Customization Prior to Activation	179
	4.4.1 Define Asset Balance Sheet Accounts of Parallel Valuation	179
	4.4.2 Define the Depreciation Area for a Quantity Update	180
	4.4.3 Define the Technical Clearing Account for Integrated Asset Acquisition	180
	4.4.4 Specify an Alternative Document Type for Accounting Principle-Specific Documents	182

	4.4.5	Specify Revenue Distribution for Asset Retirement	183
	4.4.6	Post Net Book Value Instead of Gain/Loss	183
	4.4.7	Check Transaction Types	184
4.5	Check Prerequisites for Activating New Asset Accounting		184
4.6	Determine Active Charts of Depreciation		185
4.7	Change Definitions of Depreciation Areas		186
4.8	Specify Transfer of Acquisition and Production Cost Values		188
4.9	Specify Transfer of Depreciation Terms		190
4.10	Activate New Asset Accounting		191
4.11	Adjust Parameters in Charts of Depreciation		192
4.12	Display Migration Log		193
4.13	Key Changes to Asset Accounting		194
	4.13.1	Architectural Impact	194
	4.13.2	Functionality Impact	195
	4.13.3	Configuration Impact	202
	4.13.4	Closing Process Impact	205
4.14	Summary		206

5   Preparation and Migration for Controlling   207

5.1	Execute SAP Business Warehouse Delta Extraction for Account-Based Profitability Analysis		208
5.2	Adapt Settings for Profitability Segment Characteristics		208
5.3	Maintain the Operating Concern		209
5.4	Activate Account-Based Profitability Analysis		210
5.5	Transport Operating Concern		211
5.6	Preparations and Migration for Material Ledger		211
5.7	Key Changes to Controlling		212
	5.7.1	Functionality Impact	213
	5.7.2	Configuration Impact	220

5.8	Key Changes to Profitability Analysis	228
	5.8.1 Architectural Impact	229
	5.8.2 Functionality Impact	230
	5.8.3 Configuration Impact	232
5.9	Key Changes to Cost Center and Profit Center Accounting	234
	5.9.1 Architectural Impact	234
	5.9.2 Functionality Impact	236
5.10	Summary	240

6 Preparation and Migration for House Bank Accounts   241

6.1	Define Number Ranges for Bank Account Technical IDs	242
6.2	Define Number Ranges for Change Requests	242
6.3	Define Settings for Bank Account Master Data	243
	6.3.1 Bank Account Types	243
	6.3.2 Define Sensitive Fields to Be Protected from Changes	244
	6.3.3 Define Import Methods for Bank Statements	246
	6.3.4 Define Signatory Groups for Payment Approvals	246
	6.3.5 Define the Signatory Groups and Approval Sequence for Approval Patterns	247
	6.3.6 Assign Approval Patterns	248
6.4	Summary	250

7 Data Migration   251

7.1	Partitioning of the Universal Journal Entry Line Items Table	252
7.2	Regenerate CDS Views and Field Mapping	253
7.3	Analyze Transactional Data	256
7.4	Display Status of Analysis of Transactional Data	257
7.5	Start and Monitor Data Migration	260

Contents

7.6	**Migration of Cost Elements**		**261**
	7.6.1	Check Consistency of G/L Accounts and Cost Elements	262
	7.6.2	Migrate Secondary Cost Elements to the Chart of Accounts	264
	7.6.3	Display Status of Migration of Cost Elements	265
	7.6.4	Migrate Default Account Assignments	266
	7.6.5	Display the Status of the Default Account Assignments Migration	267
	7.6.6	Adopt Authorizations	268
	7.6.7	Define Authorizations and Profiles	269
7.7	**Technical Check of Transaction Data**		**274**
	7.7.1	Reconcile Transactional Data	275
	7.7.2	Display Status of Technical Reconciliation of Transactional Data	276
7.8	**Material Ledger Migration**		**280**
	7.8.1	Migrate Material Ledger Master Data	280
	7.8.2	Check Material Ledger Master Data	280
	7.8.3	Migrate Material Ledger Order History	281
	7.8.4	Check Material Ledger Production Order and Purchase Order History	281
7.9	**Enrichment of Data**		**281**
	7.9.1	Enrich Transactional Data	281
	7.9.2	Display Status of Transactional Data Enrichment	282
	7.9.3	Check of Migrated Documents	283
	7.9.4	Display Status of Migrated Documents Check	284
7.10	**Migration of Line Items into New Data Structure**		**285**
	7.10.1	Migrate Accounting Documents to Universal Journal Entry Structure	286
	7.10.2	Display the Status of Document Migration to Universal Journal Entry	286
	7.10.3	Check Migration of Accounting Documents to Universal Journal Entry	287
	7.10.4	Display Status of Accounting Document Migration Check	288
7.11	**Migration of Balances**		**289**
	7.11.1	Migrate Balances	290
	7.11.2	Display Status of Migration of Balances	290
	7.11.3	Check Migration of Balances	292
	7.11.4	Display Status of Migration of Balances Check	293

7.12	Calculation of Depreciation and Totals Values	296
	7.12.1 Calculate Initial Depreciation Values	297
	7.12.2 Display Status of Calculate Initial Depreciation Values	298
	7.12.3 Check Initial Depreciation and Total Values	298
	7.12.4 Display Status of Check Initial Depreciation and Total Values	299
7.13	Migrate General Ledger Allocations	301
7.14	Migrate House Bank Accounts	304
7.15	Credit Management Migration	305
	7.15.1 Migrate Credit Management Master Data	306
	7.15.2 Display Status of Migration of Credit Management Master Data	307
	7.15.3 Migrate Credit Management Exposure	307
	7.15.4 Display Status of Credit Management Exposure Migration	307
	7.15.5 Initialize Documented Credit Decisions	307
	7.15.6 Display Status of Initialization of Documented Credit Decisions	308
	7.15.7 Reconcile Documented Credit Decisions	308
7.16	Complete the Migration	308
	7.16.1 Reconcile and Compare Migrated Data	309
	7.16.2 Set Migration to Completed	310
7.17	Migration with Near-Zero Downtime	311
	7.17.1 Near-Zero Downtime	311
	7.17.2 Restrictions on Business	312
	7.17.3 Activities on the Clone System	312
	7.17.4 Delta Migration	313
7.18	Summary	314

8   Postmigration Activities   315

8.1	Run Reconciliation Reports to Check Data Consistency	316
8.2	Validate Business Process to Ensure Successful Migration	316
8.3	Transfer Application Indexes	317
8.4	Display Status of Application Indexes Transfer	318
8.5	Fill Due Dates in FI Documents	318

8.6	Display Status of Filling Due Dates in Financial Documents	319
8.7	Fill the Offsetting Account in Financial Documents	320
8.8	Display Status of Filling Offsetting Account in Financial Documents	321
8.9	Enrichment of Balance Carryforward	322
8.10	Manual Activities for Credit Management	323
8.11	Deactivate Reconciliation Ledger	324
8.12	Summary	325

9   Postmigration Testing   327

9.1	Test SAP HANA-Optimized Report Transactions	328
9.2	Test Multidimensional Reporting Capability	328
9.3	Test Database Footprint Reduction	329
9.4	Test Intercompany Reconciliation	329
9.5	Test the New Process Redesign	330
9.6	Test Closing Improvement	331
9.7	Test the Universal Journal	331
9.8	Execute Change Management	332
9.9	Summary	332

PART II   Setting Up New Financials Functionality

10   SAP Cash Management   337

10.1	Validate Prerequisites		339
10.2	Set Up Bank Account Master Data		340
	10.2.1	Banks and House Banks	340
	10.2.2	Migrate House Bank Accounts	342
	10.2.3	Upload and Download Bank Accounts	343

15

Contents

10.3 Define the Payment Approval Process 344
- 10.3.1 Basic Settings for Approval 345
- 10.3.2 Rule Maintenance 346
- 10.3.3 Additional Criteria for Payment Grouping 347
- 10.3.4 Mark Rules for Automatic Payment 348
- 10.3.5 Specify the Signature Method for Approval Using a Simple Signature 349
- 10.3.6 Enable Signatory Control 350
- 10.3.7 Specify Settings for the Bank Statement Monitor 350

10.4 Enable SAP Business Workflow for Bank Account Management 352
- 10.4.1 Maintain Event Type Linkage 352
- 10.4.2 Define and Maintain Organizational Hierarchy 354
- 10.4.3 Define Responsibilities and Assign Users 354
- 10.4.4 Create Custom-Defined Workflows 359
- 10.4.5 Predefined Workflows 359

10.5 Create Cash Pools for Cash Concentration 363
- 10.5.1 Define Clearing Accounts for the Receiving Bank for Account Transfers 364
- 10.5.2 Define Clearing Accounts for Cross-Country Bank Account Transfers 365
- 10.5.3 Define Account Determination 365
- 10.5.4 Check Account Determination 366

10.6 Manage Cash Operations 366
- 10.6.1 Define and Assign Flow Types 368
- 10.6.2 Define Liquidity Items and Hierarchies 378
- 10.6.3 Define Planning Levels and Planning Groups 382

10.7 Load Data to One Exposure from Operations 385
- 10.7.1 Integration with Source Applications 386
- 10.7.2 Integration with Remote Systems 386

10.8 Set Up Cash Management Transaction Data 387
- 10.8.1 Activate Individual Source Applications 389
- 10.8.2 Activate Multiple Source Applications 390
- 10.8.3 Rebuild Planning Levels, Groups, and Dates in Accounting Documents 390
- 10.8.4 Insert House Bank and House Bank Account Data to Accounting Documents 391

10.8.5	Rebuild Liquidity Items in Accounting Documents	392
10.8.6	Rebuild Flow Types in Accounting Documents	393
10.8.7	Load Transaction Data into One Exposure from Operations Hub	394

10.9 Set Up SAP Liquidity Management 395

10.9.1	Install and Configure SAP BusinessObjects Business Intelligence Content	396
10.9.2	Activate SAP BusinessObjects BI Content	397
10.9.3	Install Template for Cash Flow Analysis	399
10.9.4	Generate a Planning View	401
10.9.5	Activate SAP BPC Content	401
10.9.6	Install SAP BPC Content	402

10.10 Set Up Liquidity Planning 404

10.10.1	Specify an SAP BPC Configuration Set	405
10.10.2	Create Planning Units	406
10.10.3	Activate Planning Unit Hierarchy	406
10.10.4	Currency Conversion Rules	408
10.10.5	Reference Data Sources	408
10.10.6	Exclude Liquidity Items Representing Balance Values	409
10.10.7	Liquidity Planning Types	409

10.11 Key System Changes 410

10.11.1	SAP Business Client	410
10.11.2	Functionality Impact	411
10.11.3	Security Impact	414
10.11.4	Configuration Impact	415

10.12 Summary 416

11 SAP BPC for SAP S/4HANA Finance   419

11.1 Planning Overview and Activation 420

11.1.1	Business Benefits	420
11.1.2	Applications Used by Planning	423
11.1.3	Activate Business Functions for Planning	424

11.2 Architecture 424

11.2.1	Planning Accelerators	425
11.2.2	Data Flow Architecture	426

Contents

11.3	**Authorizations**	427
11.4	**Activate Embedded SAP Business Warehouse**	431
	11.4.1 Choose SAP Business Warehouse Client	432
	11.4.2 Check SAP Business Warehouse Client Setting	432
	11.4.3 Set the SAP Business Warehouse Client	433
	11.4.4 Assign the Logical System Client	434
	11.4.5 Set SAP Business Warehouse Namespaces to Changeable	437
	11.4.6 Install the Technical SAP Business Warehouse Content	438
	11.4.7 Check Installation Status and Resolve Errors	439
	11.4.8 Check Planning Content Activation	441
11.5	**Activate the SAP BusinessObjects BI Content Bundle**	442
	11.5.1 Activate the DataSources	443
	11.5.2 Activate the Content Bundle	444
11.6	**Test the SAP Business Warehouse Installation**	449
	11.6.1 Set the User Parameter	449
	11.6.2 Test the Planning Query Installation	449
11.7	**Activate Services and Test Planning Applications**	451
	11.7.1 Check General Settings for Web Dynpro	451
	11.7.2 Run Report RSICF_SERVICE_ACTIVATION	452
	11.7.3 Activate Services for the Planning Applications	453
	11.7.4 Test the New Planning Application	454
11.8	**Planning Modeler**	456
11.9	**SAP BusinessObjects Analysis for Microsoft Office**	457
11.10	**Key System Changes**	462
11.11	**Summary**	464

12   SAP Fiori Applications   465

12.1	SAP Fiori Project Phases	466
12.2	Architecture	467
12.3	Configure SAP Fiori	469

12.4		Install SAP Fiori Apps	472
	12.4.1	Transaction and Fact Sheet Apps	472
	12.4.2	Analytical Apps	473
12.5		SAP Fiori Launchpad	473
	12.5.1	Frontend User Screen	474
	12.5.2	Backend Configuration Screen	476
	12.5.3	SAP Smart Business Key Performance Indicators	478
12.6		SAP Fiori Application and Roles	480
	12.6.1	General Ledger Accountant	480
	12.6.2	Accounts Payable Accountant	483
	12.6.3	Accounts Receivable Accountant	485
	12.6.4	Controller	488
	12.6.5	Cash Manager	493
	12.6.6	Cost Manager	495
12.7		SAP Smart Business Application and Roles	496
	12.7.1	For Accounts Payable	497
	12.7.2	For Accounts Receivable	498
	12.7.3	For Chief Financial Officers	500
	12.7.4	For Cash Management	500
12.8		Summary	501

Appendices 503

A	Central Finance	505
B	Project Plan for SAP S/4HANA Finance Migration	529
C	The Author	559

Index	561

Preface

Global competitiveness and the rapid pace of technological changes are driving organizations' IT infrastructure toward automation, simplicity, and user-driven, faster data processing. Cloud and mobile solutions with real-time transaction processing and analytical capability are tools that shift organizations toward high value creation at a reasonable cost. Not long ago, what happened last year, last quarter, or last month dictated what is likely to happen tomorrow. In this modern era of growth, decision-making by CFOs based on past activity and data can no longer be sustained.

Most enterprise-level CFOs agree that the global business environment has caused real-time decision-making to become a necessary part of business, rather than a nice-to-have feature. Technological innovations are now able to provide the necessary insight, in an accessible way, to support this requirement.

The finance functionality in SAP S/4HANA (known as SAP S/4HANA Finance) is SAP's next-generation technology created to support the new CFO agenda to remain competitive and ahead in the race. Adoption of such a groundbreaking innovation requires an organizational transformation and very strong executive sponsorship, both of which are only secured in an organization when there is a significant business case for the migration and implementation of SAP S/4HANA Finance.

Some of the key pain points that face every organization are multiple versions of the "truth," the need for better cash management, a desire to improve user experience (UX), a lack of integrated end-to-end business scenarios, an imperative to standardize and simplify business processes, and a need for better legal and managerial reporting. SAP S/4HANA helps resolve these organizational challenges with a renewed architectural design and the introduction of new and enhanced finance functionality.

About This Book

Before we get too far, let's first consider for whom this book is written, how this book is written, and what it's designed to do.

Target Audience and Objective

This book is intended for SAP FI-CO and SAP S/4HANA application consultants, SAP solution team members, application administrators, business process architects, business process owners, power users, project/program managers, delivery/team leads, IT managers, finance managers, and solution architects.

The book provides the required knowledge of SAP S/4HANA Finance and the sequence of configuration steps required to complete the migration. It will also help readers prepare for the associate-level certification (SAP Certified Application Associate—SAP S/4HANA for Financial Accounting Associates for SAP S/4HANA 1610, or C_TS4FI_1610) and begin their preparation for the professional-level certification (SAP Certified Application Professional—Financials in SAP S/4HANA 1610 for SAP ERP Finance Experts, or P_S4FIN_1610) in this space.

After reading this book, you'll know how to implement the finance functionality in SAP S/4HANA. However, we know that the completion of an implementation project is only the beginning for many readers; consequently, we take care to outline what changes arrived with SAP S/4HANA in business processes, functionality, and configuration of various financials functions. This book uses screenshots, practical examples, and real-life scenarios encountered and executed during migrations from SAP ERP 6.0 to SAP S/4HANA 1610.

To provide insight into the SAP S/4HANA financial data migration process and the new functionality from a functional perspective, this book offers the following:

- Documentation of each process step based on real-world project implementation and hands-on experience
- A set of best practices, configurations, and lessons learned during migration from SAP ERP 6.0 to SAP S/4HANA
- An overview of technical activities linked to the migration of financials data to SAP S/4HANA and installation of SAP Fiori and SAP Business Client
- A conceptual understanding of and customization information about new functionality such as SAP Cash Management and SAP BPC for SAP S/4HANA
- Information on architecture, configuration, transaction, and business process changes and their impact on the FI and CO functionality with the introduction of SAP S/4HANA
- A business case for using Central Finance as the deployment option
- A detailed project plan for a migration to SAP S/4HANA Finance

Structure of This Book

This book has been structured to follow the SAP S/4HANA financials migration lifecycle shown in Figure 1. (You should note that moving forward, when we refer to SAP

S/4HANA Finance, we're discussing the financials functionality in on-premise SAP S/4HANA—not the once-independent SAP S/4HANA Finance add-on.) To this end, the book is divided into two major parts, with multiple chapters and subsections in each part.

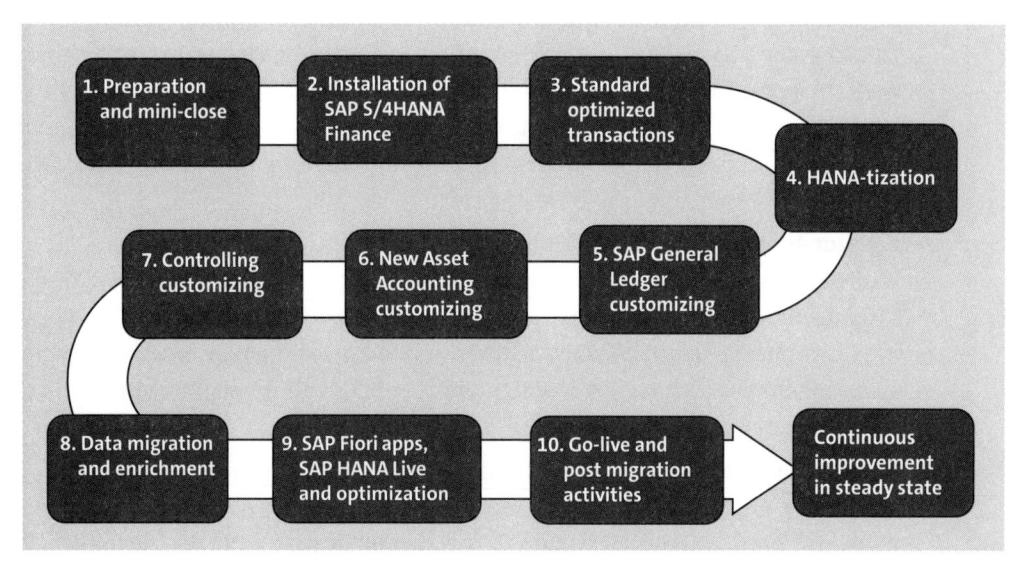

Figure 1 SAP S/4HANA Migration Roadmap

Part I provides all the project phases for a financials migration to SAP S/4HANA, along with all the Customizing steps for SAP S/4HANA Finance to work seamlessly. The migration is treated as a single migration, with each chapter divided into the various phases of a project lifecycle. Following the implementation instructions in each chapter, we dedicate some time to outlining specific changes to the relevant FI and CO business processes, when comparing SAP S/4HANA with a traditional SAP ERP implementation. Though this may sound repetitive, we include this information for readers who may not participate in the implementation project themselves, but who need to understand how the new system operates once it has been set up.

Part I contains the following chapters:

- **Chapter 1: Preparation**
  This chapter highlights the scope and restrictions of SAP S/4HANA Finance that you need to understand and analyze before starting migration activities. It includes precheck, correction of errors, and execution of financial reports to allow comparison after the migration.

Preface

- **Chapter 2: Installation and Upgrade**
  This chapter covers the technical steps and business functions that are required to either install or upgrade the existing system to SAP S/4HANA Finance. It includes creation of backup tables and SAP HANA compatibility views.

- **Chapter 3: Preparation and Migration for General Ledger**
  This chapter summarizes the configuration in General Ledger Accounting that needs to be performed in preparation for migration to SAP S/4HANA Finance. This chapter also explains the architecture, configuration, transactions, functionality, and business process changes in General Ledger Accounting with the introduction of SAP S/4HANA, including period-end closing.

- **Chapter 4: Preparation and Migration for Asset Accounting**
  With SAP S/4HANA Finance, classic Asset Accounting was replaced with new Asset Accounting, which makes this Customizing mandatory. This chapter describes the Customizing steps and activities required to enable the new functionality; it also explains the architecture, configuration, functionality, and business process changes in new Asset Accounting.

- **Chapter 5: Preparation and Migration for Controlling**
  With SAP S/4HANA Finance, the CO and FI components have been merged, eliminating the need to reconcile FI and CO. This chapter describes the key Customizing activities that need to be executed in CO and explains the major system changes that have arrived.

- **Chapter 6: Preparation and Migration for House Bank Accounts**
  This chapter provides the Customizing activities required for the migration of house bank accounts. It includes setting up the approval process for bank account opening and adjustments, setup of signatories, and the centralized review of the Bank Account Management process.

- **Chapter 7: Data Migration**
  This chapter presents the migration steps that must be completed during system downtime, including migrating line items into the new data structure, migrating and checking balances, and reconciling the migrated data.

- **Chapter 8: Postmigration Activities**
  This chapter ensures that the data is reconciled and consistent with the premigration reports and shows you how to finalize the migration to SAP S/4HANA Finance.

- **Chapter 9: Postmigration Testing**
  This chapter covers change management and plans for adaptation to the new SAP S/4HANA Finance system that an organization needs to determine to make full

use of the new transactions and functionality. It includes testing the system to make sure the functionality works without any errors.

Part II discusses all the configuration and new functionalities introduced with SAP S/4HANA Finance. Part II includes the following chapters:

- **Chapter 10: SAP Cash Management**
  SAP S/4HANA makes the classic Cash Management obsolete and the new SAP Cash Management that runs on SAP HANA mandatory. This chapter presents the Customizing activities required to enable the new SAP Cash Management and teaches readers what has changed for this financials process for bank account management, for example, and in other areas.

- **Chapter 11: SAP BPC for SAP S/4HANA Finance**
  This chapter covers the setup, configuration, and functionality provided with the embedded planning function within SAP S/4HANA Finance. It includes the integration of Microsoft Excel predefined templates, SAP Business Client, and a web client.

- **Chapter 12: SAP Fiori Applications**
  This chapter highlights the installation and the application of the various SAP Fiori apps that provide enhanced UX in terms of posting transactions and analyzing SAP Smart Business key performance indicators (KPIs) from any mobile device.

This second edition concludes with two appendices: the first introduces the business case for a Central Finance implementation, and the second lists a comprehensive project plan for migration from SAP ERP to SAP S/4HANA Finance.

New in This Edition

Let's consider the progression of software releases for SAP S/4HANA, as shown in Figure 2.

The first edition of this book, which was published in the summer of 2016, described the implementation of SAP S/4HANA Finance when it was an add-on from SAP. That book was written for SAP S/4HANA 1605.

Since then, SAP has released SAP S/4HANA 1610; rather than maintain two separate SAP S/4HANA financials products, it ceased development on the SAP S/4HANA Finance add-on and moved all its powerful, innovative functionality into the core of SAP S/4HANA. This new edition of the book is up-to-date for implementing SAP S/4HANA 1610, but it will be applicable largely to SAP's next SAP S/4HANA release, which is version 1709. (Because SAP S/4HANA 1709 has only just been released, there are no live implementations as of the time of writing in fall 2017.) So, to help readers keep an eye on upcoming developments, we've added recurring "1709 Preview" text boxes to this book to highlight key changes in that new release, in addition to the recurring "Expert Insight" text boxes that call attention to tips and tricks.

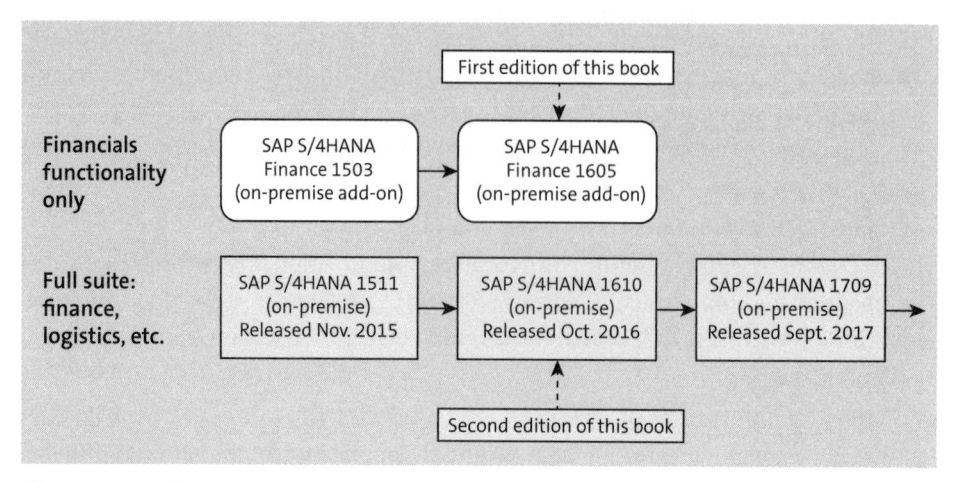

Figure 2 SAP S/4HANA Releases

Acknowledgments

I'd like to take this opportunity to thank my parents, who have always supported me with my decisions and helped me achieve my goals in life. My upbringing has been instrumental in all walks of my life and helped me to accomplish the things that I have achieved in life today. I respectfully dedicate this book to them.

I would like to convey my heartfelt thanks to Rajni, my wife, and my children, Rishab and Arush, for all their love and support, which made it possible for me to complete this book on time along with my full-time consulting career with out-of-state travel every week. There have been several occasions and weekends during which I wasn't able to provide time to my family and friends because of my engagement with and perseverance to complete this book. Without their patience and tolerance, I wouldn't have been able to write this book.

A special thanks to the team at SAP PRESS, who provided me with this opportunity and have been very supportive throughout the writing of this book. Their advice, availability, and quick responses are really appreciated.

I would also like to extend my gratitude to all my readers who took an immense interest in purchasing this book and have provided it with an overwhelming response and reviews. SAP S/4HANA Finance is quite stable now but is still under development from SAP, with new functionalities and new SAP Fiori apps being released with every new version to enhance UX and meet all the requirements of running an organization. It's taken a lot of time and effort to ensure that the quality of the second edition remains high and once again meets your expectations. I've personally executed the transactions and functionality presented in this book to ensure that it all will work in the new SAP S/4HANA Finance environment. My goal is to facilitate the process for readers who are engaged in either a greenfield implementation or migration from SAP ERP to SAP S/4HANA Finance.

Introduction

We live in an era of global competition in which organizations are facing tremendous challenges to collect information and analyze data to stay ahead of their competitors. Failure to process both structured and unstructured data in a timely manner to make decisions is no longer an option. The solution to this problem is SAP's next-generation SAP HANA database with in-memory computing power, which can process huge amounts of data for analysis in a very short time. An SAP HANA database supports columnar database tables and can move logic to the database layer through stored procedures.

SAP S/4HANA represents the next generation and latest evolution of SAP's core application platforms, designed and engineered to exploit the in-memory capabilities of the SAP HANA database. Although SAP presents SAP S/4HANA as a new platform that introduces some radical changes to the architecture of the SAP system, it isn't a completely different product requiring a system reimplementation. Instead, SAP S/4HANA builds on the proven functional base of SAP Business Suite and can be introduced in an evolutionary, gradual, and selective way into an existing SAP environment.

SAP S/4HANA is revolutionary in that it adds transactional simplicity, advanced analytics, innovation, and enhancement of functionality compared to traditional SAP ERP. SAP S/4HANA provides a complete rewrite of SAP ERP code organized by functional area and moves some application code to the database layer as stored database procedures. It provides a new data model by removing old tables, aggregate tables, and index tables to create fewer columnar-based tables and deliver a single source of truth. SAP S/4HANA is designed with an SAP Fiori integrated user experience (UX) that provides users with instant insight and works on any mobile device. It offers real-time operational analytics on the SAP ERP platform, reducing the data latency of SAP Business Warehouse (SAP BW) reporting. Via integration to the Internet of Things and business networks, SAP S/4HANA enables real-time collaboration (machine-to-machine, via SAP Ariba Network, via Concur, etc.) in the networked economy. SAP S/4HANA can be deployed using SAP Cloud Platform and the DevOps platform for extensions.

Some of the key benefits of SAP S/4HANA (discussed in detail in the section "Benefits of SAP S/4HANA Finance") include the following:

- Providing real-time reporting and a single source of truth via SAP Fiori apps, SAP HANA Live, and the Universal Journal
- Bringing many data sources from inside and outside the business into the SAP HANA platform for real insight
- Building business rules in the platform, including embedded analytics, to create new optimized and innovative business processes
- Optimizing and simplifying the business model (e.g., embedded SAP BPC for SAP S/4HANA Finance), including removal of unnecessary steps and batch processing
- Using a simplified user interface (UI) via SAP Fiori to provide real-time insights

In this introduction, we'll discuss the role of the chief financial officer (CFO), before jumping into the key benefits SAP S/4HANA provides to address the CFO's needs. We'll then provide a summary of functional changes present in SAP S/4HANA Finance and its system architecture. We'll finish with an overview of the migration process for SAP S/4HANA Finance to help you understand the whole process before you dive into the first steps in Chapter 1.

Evolution of the Chief Financial Officer

The role of the finance function continues to be delivering sustainable and superior shareholder value, but with access to a wider range of levers to make this happen. As a result, the role of the CFO today is broader and more complex than ever. Creating and maintaining efficiencies in operations is essential for the finance leadership in an organization. The CFO isn't restricted to optimizing operations such as paying the bills, closing the books, and producing financial results. Today's CFOs are expected to develop new approaches to manage their organization, produce business insights daily, spot market opportunities, and help the business with scenario planning to increase reaction times. Ultimately, they're involved in predicting changes in the business environment and driving the business to growth.

CFOs' most critical task isn't limited to measuring and monitoring the company's performance; they also must focus on business transformation and developing people with the right skills. Providing strategic input, managing enterprise risk, and integrating different sources of information to generate meaningful business insights have soared up the CFO agenda in recent years.

To address the information requirements resulting from this shift, SAP has introduced SAP S/4HANA Finance, which was its first module for transactional simplicity and advanced analytics in the new SAP S/4HANA offering. Although it does cover key functionalities such as the Universal Journal, the extension ledger, new asset accounting functionality, and an accelerated close, SAP S/4HANA Finance is all about creating a simplified UX.

> **Note**
>
> Asset Accounting didn't experience a name change with the introduction of SAP S/4HANA. To differentiate Asset Accounting in SAP S/4HANA Finance from Asset Accounting in SAP ERP Financials (FI), people often refer to Asset Accounting in SAP S/4HANA Finance as new FI-AA. Throughout this book, though, we'll refer to Asset Accounting in SAP S/4HANA Finance as new Asset Accounting, for the sake of consistency.
>
> The SAP General Ledger (G/L) is in much the same boat. It's commonly referred to as the new G/L in SAP S/4HANA Finance. Throughout this book, we'll refer to it as the new G/L.

SAP S/4HANA Finance is highly focused on the requirements to run a real-time business. Many CFOs require access to real-time financial information to better facilitate decision-making. SAP S/4HANA Finance migration works to enable this vision and help the CFO and finance function in this transformational journey by accessing real-time data and transformed business processes across the globe.

SAP S/4HANA Finance functionality caters to the evolving business requirements of the new-age finance department. It's a broad offering covering end-to-end solutions for finance, and it contains data architectural changes and a set of new functionalities that weren't part of the previous SAP Business Suite. SAP S/4HANA Finance takes full advantage of the latest in-memory and real-time capabilities of SAP HANA with a modern UX (accessible on almost any device), a simplified data model, and near-real-time reporting.

Benefits of SAP S/4HANA Finance

Table 1 describes the key performance indicators (KPIs) that a CFO considers and how SAP S/4HANA Finance provides the functionality to address these needs.

Key Performance Indicator (KPI)	SAP S/4HANA Finance Functionality
Drive integration of information across the enterprise effectively (single source of truth)	Universal Journal's virtual single operating model, seamless FI-CO integration, and real-time data across all financial dimensions
Drive enterprise cost reductions	Improved automation capabilities in nearly all areas with real-time insight into global sources, uses of cash, and elimination of batch jobs
Measure/monitor business performance	Consistent business insights and prediction capabilities across all FI value map elements; discovery and visualization tools to easily understand your data
Optimize planning, budgeting, and forecasting	SAP BPC for SAP S/4HANA Finance, deployment options—on-premise, cloud, and hybrid—integrate planning and consolidation functionality in real time
Execute continuous finance process improvements	Financial close, planning, forecasting, and budgeting processes; streamline communications with banks and automate payment workflows; integrate collaborative finance operations and fraud and audit management
Provide inputs to enterprise strategy	Extended simulation flexibility and speed through on-the-fly calculation capabilities; better business advice due to more relevant and timely insight
Develop talent in the finance organization	Use of modern UX and SAP Fiori apps and improved automation capabilities to get rid of transactional activities and free up resources for value-added tasks

Table 1 How SAP S/4HANA Finance Addresses CFO Concerns

Arguably, the largest benefit SAP S/4HANA Finance provides is its role as a source of real-time and consistent data. For example, the following key business scenarios illustrate the business value of SAP S/4HANA Finance:

- **Accounting and financial close**
  SAP S/4HANA Finance's Central Finance deployment option addresses the challenge of multiple SAP ERP systems (e.g., due to merger and acquisition) causing high total cost of ownership (TCO) and slow innovation cycles. SAP S/4HANA Finance's month-end-close business scenario addresses current long closing cycles and the desire to have reliable finance data at any time.

- **Treasury and risk management/collaborative finance operations**
  SAP S/4HANA Finance's working capital and receivables management business scenario addresses organizations' pain points of high days sales outstanding (DSO) and cash flow challenges.
- **Enterprise risk and compliance management**
  The process oversight functions of SAP S/4HANA Finance help identify areas with a high risk of fraud.
- **Financial planning and analysis**
  SAP BPC for SAP S/4HANA Finance addresses the need for dynamic planning and ambition for enterprise-wide integrated planning at the same level of granularity.

SAP S/4HANA Finance delivers an easy-to-consume yet comprehensive value package covering the complete capabilities of FI. Some additional business benefits of migrating to SAP S/4HANA Finance include the following:

- The introduction of the new Universal Journal table provides a single source of truth. Seamless integration between transactions and analytics streamlines and eliminates cycle times and data reconciliation efforts during period-end close.
- New on-the-fly and real-time reporting capabilities are available with the elimination of batch jobs during period-end finance processes such as goods receipt/invoice receipt (GR/IR) clearing, cost allocations, and FI-CO reconciliations. Speed and online availability are achieved using the in-memory functionality within SAP HANA and via the reduction of aggregation tables.
- The reconciliation between FI and CO is removed by design: the cost elements are created as G/L accounts, and all the data from CO and FI are held in a common database structure.
- Along with predictive and comparative analysis, real-time planning and forecasting are integrated within the same system to explore new what-if business scenarios for better decision-making. This functionality particularly caters to the relatively new role of the FI function to generate value through data insight and data intelligence.
- The in-memory SAP HANA database features significantly improve the execution of large reports with huge data volumes and complex computational logic within the SAP Business Suite system. This, in turn, speeds up tasks such as GR/IR clearing and cost allocations. One of the primary reasons for the improvement is that the data resides in the database layer rather than in the traditional application layer.

- New reporting and analytics capabilities for FI users with drilldown capabilities and KPI measures allow instant insight-to-action capability. Historical data now can be used for predictive analysis, with reports and dashboards available on tablets and mobile devices.
- Global statutory- and legal-compliance capabilities across multiple countries, currencies, languages, and industry solutions provide governance, controls frameworks, and continuous risk assessment for all business processes.
- Cost efficiency is improved by decreasing an organization's database size due to reducing aggregation and index tables to compatibility views, which results in a smaller data footprint and decreased storage costs.
- Most of the new SAP Fiori apps providing transactional, analytical, and fact sheet capabilities are only available via the SAP S/4HANA Finance functionality.
- The new apps within SAP S/4HANA Finance improve the UX, provide flexibility to work on mobile devices, and reduce the reliance on the data warehouse system for reporting and analysis.

Functional Changes with SAP S/4HANA Finance

On the technical side, migration to or implementation of SAP S/4HANA Finance redefines data aggregation using the in-memory capabilities of the SAP HANA database. This allows for reduction of your data footprint because calculations for financial transactions are performed on the database layer instead of the traditional application layer on an ad hoc basis.

On the functional side, Table 2 covers the major changes in SAP S/4HANA Finance.

Functionality	Business Benefits
Universal Journal	This is the single source of truth for financial information. It has a new data model that combines Controlling (CO), SAP ERP Financials (FI), Asset Accounting (AA), SAP Material Ledger (ML), Profitability Analysis (CO-PA), and other financial data into one Universal Journal entry, all represented in table ACDOCA, with full details for all components. Because all data are provided in real time from this single journal, the period-end reconciliations and financial reporting preparation efforts are reduced considerably.

Table 2 Changes in SAP S/4HANA Finance

Functional Changes with SAP S/4HANA Finance

Functionality	Business Benefits
Ad hoc and on-the-fly computational power	The new Universal Journal allows ad hoc, on-the-fly computations for converting periodic transactions from batch to real time without needing data to be replicated first to other systems such as SAP BusinessObjects Business Intelligence (SAP BusinessObjects BI). Reporting is simplified, fast, and multidimensional, making the drilldown reports almost redundant.
Accelerated month-end and year-end close	The ability to move away from batch-based and toward event-based processing enables period-end processes to be run daily or weekly. This allows organizations to get a real-time view of their profit and loss (P&L), providing the business with early visibility into emerging trends. This functionality facilitates prompt remedial action where necessary, rather than having to wait until after month end, which helps accelerate month-end activities by reducing dependency on scheduled and periodic batch jobs and tedious reconciliation efforts.
SAP BPC for SAP S/4HANA Finance for real-time integrated business planning	This is a new planning functionality in which planning data can be uploaded using Microsoft Excel, which in turn loads real-time data back to SAP ERP for reporting. It contains templates for cost center, internal order, project, profit center, cost of sales, and P&L planning.
New Asset Accounting	New Asset Accounting in SAP S/4HANA Finance replaces the classic FI-AA functionality. The simplified posting logic allows seamless integration with the Universal Journal. Due to real-time postings, there is no need to wait for the month-end depreciation run.
SAP Cash Management	This optional replacement for SAP Cash and Liquidity Management adds bank account management, short-term cash position and forecast reports, and real-time liquidity planning, which allow for working capital optimization. SAP Cash Management provides on-the-fly reporting capabilities for cash position and liquidity forecasts.

Table 2 Changes in SAP S/4HANA Finance (Cont.)

Functionality	Business Benefits
SAP Smart Business KPI reporting with SAP Fiori	These are optional replacements for many of SAP's traditional drilldown reports. The code framework used by the old reports can't be accelerated much with SAP HANA. SAP Smart Financials reporting uses the SAP Smart Business mobile UI with online KPIs and essential financial information.
Data aging	This technical change replaces SAP data archiving. The new method builds data-aging objects, creates partitions, and executes data-aging runs, thus reducing the SAP HANA memory footprint. Only operational relevant data (hot data) is loaded in the main memory; historical data (cold data) is stored on disk.
New General Ledger (new G/L)	The classic G/L functionality has been completely replaced by the new G/L. The classic G/L is only supported before the introduction of SAP S/4HANA Finance.
SAP HANA Live	SAP HANA Live, along with SAP BPC for SAP S/4HANA Finance, replaces the standard Profit Center Accounting reports. With SAP HANA Live, real-time reporting is available on actual versus plan inside SAP ERP or Excel. Historically, this reporting was performed in an external SAP BW system with a time lag for actuals.
Average balance ledger	This seldom-used functionality is no longer available in SAP S/4HANA Finance.
SAP Credit Management	SAP Credit Management is now completely covered under collaborative finance operations and receivables management.

Table 2 Changes in SAP S/4HANA Finance (Cont.)

System Architecture with SAP S/4HANA Finance

SAP S/4HANA Finance's Universal Journal architecture is comprised of a single source of truth for all accounting components, which makes reconciliation a topic of the past. The new architecture consists of the following elements:

- One single source for data in FI is provided in the form of line item table ACDOCA with full details for all components. The following are some of the Universal Journal features:

- Link on line-item level (1:1) between FI and CO
- Link from CO line items to a dimension table in CO-PA
- Enhancements of account-based CO-PA (detailed postings for cost of goods sold [COGS] and variances)
- Logical document (SAP HANA view) for analyzing the converged data
- Universal Journal entry as the reporting database, with the following features:
  - A Universal Journal entry (table ACDOCA) is used for all accounting-relevant data, but all previously used tables are still supported via compatibility views.
  - All fields are persisted in the Universal Journal entry, such as asset data, CO-PA attributes, and so on, and they can be reported from this single table.

- Accounts and cost elements are harmonized. Secondary cost elements are created and depicted as G/L accounts with the following activities:
  - G/L accounts and cost elements are merged.
  - Secondary cost elements are G/L accounts, and cost element attributes have been merged with G/L accounts.
  - Primary and secondary cost elements must be maintained at the company code level.
  - The authorization concept is adjusted.
- Simplification of reporting based on a single source of truth (e.g., replacement of SAP BusinessObjects BI reporting) allows for fast multidimensional reporting on the Universal Journal, which is possible without replicating data to a separate system. This simplification allows the following:
  - Cross-area reporting within FI on all possible dimensions for all reporting objects (cost centers, orders, projects, etc.)
  - Drilldown to all dimensions—for example, from balance sheet and P&L to a single line item
  - Profitability attributes for every P&L line item in real time
- If SAP BusinessObjects BI is in place, only a single SAP BusinessObjects BI extractor is needed instead of many extractors as used in traditional SAP ERP.
- The memory footprint is reduced by eliminating redundancy.
- Technical preparations enhance important structural capabilities of the financial solution (e.g., multi-GAAP, additional currencies).

Introduction

When SAP S/4HANA Finance is activated, the following aggregate tables of classic FI-AA are replaced with SAP HANA views with the same name:

- General Ledger Accounting's totals tables and secondary index tables, such as tables GLT0, BSIS, and BSAS, and tables FAGLFLEXT, FAGLBSIS, and FAGLBSAS, respectively
- The totals tables and application tables of Accounts Receivable (AR) and Accounts Payable (AP), such as tables KNC1, KNC3, LFC1, LFC3, BSID, BSIK, BSAD, and BSAK
- The totals tables of CO, such as table COSP and COSS

Because the views have the same name, the read access of all these tables continues as usual. Therefore, custom programs that only read these tables are expected to work as before, whereas others will need to be replaced.

Migration to SAP S/4HANA Finance

Several considerations come into play when migrating to SAP S/4HANA Finance. In this section, we'll briefly cover your path from SAP ERP to SAP Business Suite on SAP HANA and finally to SAP S/4HANA. We'll also discuss three major activities you must perform prior to your migration to SAP S/4HANA Finance: implementing the new G/L, migrating your data to the new Asset Accounting, and assessing your custom code. We'll close with a discussion of the most common deployment scenarios and the project phases your migration will go through.

Path from SAP ERP to SAP Business Suite on SAP HANA to SAP S/4HANA

Figure 3 shows the high-level technical path to get from SAP ERP 6.0 or lower to SAP Business Suite on SAP HANA, and then to SAP S/4HANA.

If an SAP ERP 6.0 system is being used with the classic G/L functionality, you need to undertake a new G/L migration project—ideally before the start of the upgrade to SAP S/4HANA Finance. This is because the classic G/L functionality is discontinued in the latest version of SAP S/4HANA Finance. In addition, during the upgrade, the new Asset Accounting needs to be enabled with the relevant enhancement packages. New SAP Cash Management, although optional, can be enabled during the upgrade or at a later stage.

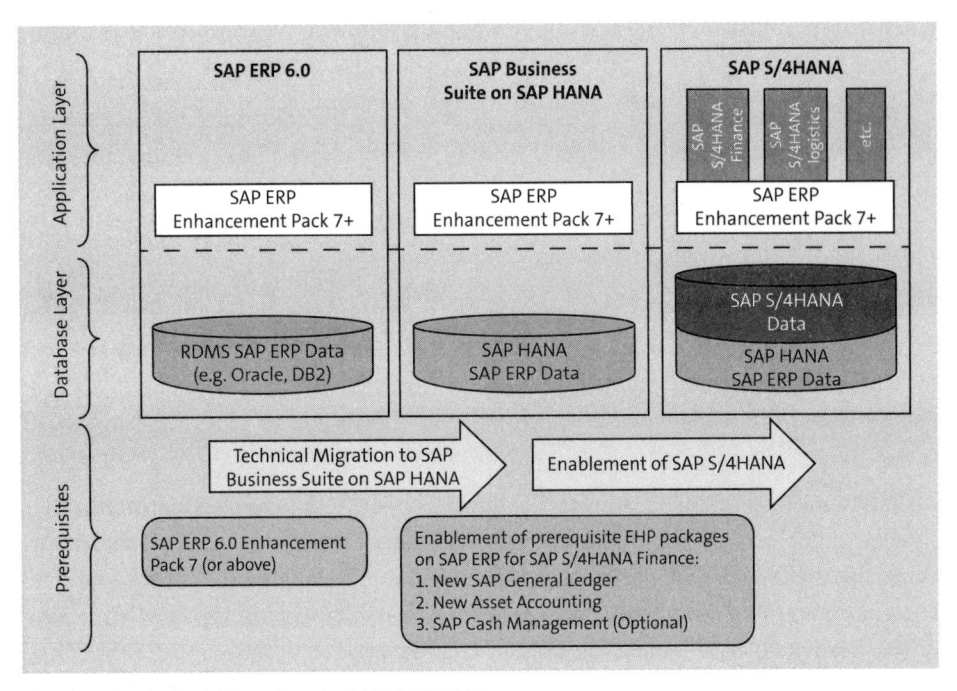

Figure 3 Technical Migration to SAP S/4HANA

You also can perform a new G/L migration together with the SAP S/4HANA Finance migration. However, this migration provides fewer functional options and features compared to separate migrations.

A new G/L enablement is an invasive change, so it needs to be planned carefully. Although a lot of the prerequisite activities (e.g., design, realization, testing, data migration) can be done before cutover, the cutover from classic G/L to new G/L must happen at the start of the new financial year. Time scales for a new G/L migration project can be in the range of 6 to 18 months depending on the volume of transactions to be migrated.

As illustrated in Figure 3, the logical progression for customers on SAP ERP 6.0 or lower and on any non-SAP HANA database is to move first to SAP Business Suite on SAP HANA (with or without the SAP S/4HANA Finance enhancement package). SAP S/4HANA is the next step. There are two approaches to this migration from an SAP ERP system running on a relational database management system (RDBMS) to the SAP S/4HANA environment:

1. **Two-step approach (EHP 7 or above upgrade followed by SAP S/4HANA migration)**
   This option is risk-averse but creates a longer overall project and higher costs.
2. **One-step approach (EHP 7 or above upgrade and SAP S/4HANA migration combined)**
   This option is a faster, more cost-effective migration, including synergies of testing, but it's admittedly a more complex project.

Under both approaches, after the upgrade and migration to either SAP Business Suite on SAP HANA or SAP S/4HANA, most of the code is expected to work as normal. However, custom code that is database-dependent may have to be remediated. An SAP check program validates noncompliant SAP HANA code as part of the migration process.

Although moving business users to the new SAP S/4HANA Finance functions is relatively straightforward and involves a change management process, the actual technical enablement of the SAP S/4HANA Finance enhancement package is very invasive. For example, the current code and Data Dictionary (DDIC) are replaced with new SAP S/4HANA Finance table structures and a new set of transactions. Note that once enabled, this can't be reversed without restoring the system. Old transactions and custom codes should still work against the old DDIC because SAP has compatibility views of old tables mapped to new tables. However, this needs thorough testing along with FI interfaces to and from the connected systems.

In the one-step approach, database migration options (DMOs) and Software Update Manager (SUM) together allow for combinations of different steps, such as a dual-stack split (SAP NetWeaver ABAP and Java stacks), a Unicode conversion, a database update of any database, an upgrade of your SAP software, and a database migration to SAP HANA. Using a shadow repository of the traditional RDBMS, the legacy database continues to run uninterrupted and remains a fallback throughout the complete process.

Several considerations must be addressed during the technical migration to SAP Business Suite on SAP HANA and ultimately to SAP S/4HANA Finance. The migration approach must be tailored to the business's requirements for service outages and project timelines.

Prior to any migration effort, the initial work on the existing system to ensure that all the prerequisites are met and that the system is in the best possible shape is of paramount importance. This initial work includes such items as the following:

- Performing data cleansing and archiving to ensure that only good and relevant data is contained in the system, thus reducing migration errors and service downtime
- Considering the correct time to migrate, which may impact period-end and year-end closing, as well as the critical period for business processing
- Ensuring the current systems are technically patched correctly to ease the initial migration work

SAP HANA is quite different in terms of its deployment to SAP compared to a traditional relational database. The SAP HANA platform usually is considered more of an appliance than a database, and, as such, requires a different set of operational and administrative processes.

SAP HANA has two basic scaling paradigms: scale-up and scale-out. With scale-up, the SAP HANA database size is limited by the size of the available, approved hardware; with scale-out, the database size is effectively limitless. However, the scale-out option is very complex in an SAP ERP deployment. Great care needs to be taken to ensure that the distribution of tables across the various SAP HANA nodes doesn't give rise to the well-known performance issues with table joins.

The potential size limitations of the scale-up option can be mitigated with the use of hot and cold storage. This function can offload infrequently accessed data from the hot SAP HANA in-memory database to the slower, disk-based cold storage. However, this isn't an automated process, and periodic routines must be configured in a similar fashion to archiving. The benefit of cold storage over archiving is that the user won't see any operational or functional difference apart from speed when accessing cold data.

Migration to SAP Business Suite on SAP HANA requires meeting several prerequisites and mandatory code changes to ensure a smooth transition to the SAP HANA platform, as well as accurate continuity of existing business processes. The ability to choose between row and column storage for custom tables requires careful design. Further adoption of SAP S/4HANA Finance will fundamentally change some of the underlying FI tables and may therefore result in significant rework of custom code and transactions.

In summary, moving to SAP S/4HANA Finance from an existing SAP ERP system running on an RDBMS requires the following steps:

1. Upgrade to SAP HANA EHP 7 (or later).
2. Migrate to SAP Business Suite on SAP HANA. Most code will work as normal, but certain custom code that is database-dependent may have to be remediated. An

SAP check program validates noncompliant SAP HANA code as part of the migration process.

3. Enable the new G/L and, if in use, the new Fixed Assets functionality and new SAP Cash Management by enabling the relevant enhancement packages. The new G/L functionality isn't dependent on the SAP HANA database and can be enabled either on SAP ERP 6.0 EHP 7+ or after migration to SAP Business Suite on SAP HANA. With the introduction of version 1709, organizations on classic G/L can also migrate to the Universal Journal with subsequent introduction of parallel ledgers and document splitting.

4. Enable SAP S/4HANA Finance to replace the current code and DDIC with new table structures. Once enabled, this can't be reversed without restoring the system. As noted previously, old transactions and custom codes against the old DDIC should still work because SAP has virtual views of old tables mapped to new tables, but testing and FI interfaces for the connected systems are required.

Key Prerequisites

The following three critical tasks need to be performed prior to migration to SAP S/4HANA Finance:

1. Implement the new G/L (recommended but not mandatory beginning with version 1709).
2. Migrate to the new Asset Accounting.
3. Assess custom code in detail.

In some cases, the migration to the new G/L and new Asset Accounting can happen during the SAP S/4HANA Finance migration. In all cases, however, a detailed assessment of these items must happen before the migration. The details of these prerequisites are illustrated in the following sections.

Implementation of the New General Ledger

SAP S/4HANA Finance is based on the new G/L concept and functionality involving multiple accounting principles and reporting at a granular level using document splitting. If a customer is on classic G/L and wants to migrate to SAP S/4HANA Finance, there are three possible approaches to this migration:

- Complete the migration to the new G/L as a separate project using the SAP General Ledger Migration Service and then undertake the migration to SAP S/4HANA Finance as a second step.
- Migrate to the new G/L while performing the SAP S/4HANA Finance migration.
- Migrate to SAP S/4HANA 1709 from classic GL and subsequently activate the parallel ledger and document splitting through configuration and the data conversion cockpit. (This would require a fiscal year change as a prerequisite step.)

When the migration to the new G/L structures is performed as part of the SAP S/4HANA migration, the following data are transferred to the new structures:

- FI documents relevant to the G/L (migration is only performed for the leading ledger)
- Balance carryforward values

However, this migration doesn't support the activation of the following new G/L functionalities after migration, if the SAP S/4HANA version is 1610 or below:

- Document splitting
- Migration from the Special Purpose Ledger to the new G/L
- New implementation of parallel accounting
- New implementation of segment reporting
- Implementation of the ledger approach of parallel accounting
- Change in chart of accounts
- Inclusion of custom fields

To implement these functionalities, the customer should first carry out a separate project migrating to the new G/L. It's important to note that for implementations of SAP S/4HANA 1709 or higher, these functionalities can be activated after SAP S/4HANA Finance is active.

Migration to New Asset Accounting

New Asset Accounting is a part of SAP S/4HANA Finance. Migration to new Asset Accounting can happen only after the new G/L migration is completed. If a completely new implementation of SAP S/4HANA Finance is being performed, new Asset Accounting must be activated.

Introduction

> **Note**
>
> Although SAP S/4HANA Finance doesn't have to be installed at the end of a year or a period, you must complete a period-end close directly before SAP S/4HANA Finance is installed.

Detail Assessment of Custom Code

Because the data model in SAP S/4HANA Finance is simplified, some of the custom objects developed may need to be reviewed and reworked. The details of the necessary changes are given in SAP Note 1976487. At a broad level, the following points need to be assessed and, if required, remediated:

- **Write access to totals tables and index tables in FI and CO**
  FI-CO index and totals tables now have the SAP HANA views with the same name. This supports read access but doesn't allow for writing/updating these tables. Therefore, all write accesses to these tables must be removed. The solutions that require these write accesses must be reviewed and rewritten.

- **Views for totals tables and index tables**
  If a customer has defined database views for a table that has been eliminated by SAP S/4HANA Finance, these views must be removed. ABAP doesn't support a view on a view. For example, if a customer has created a view called Z_BKPF_BSIS with the base tables BKPF and BSIS, in SAP S/4HANA Finance, BSIS is a view. As a result, Z_BKPF_BSIS is based on the BSIS view, which isn't supported. These views must be replaced by an Open SQL SELECT statement or a read module call.

- **Aging**
  Data archiving is replaced with data aging in SAP S/4HANA Finance. If a customer has implemented custom-defined developments for data archiving, they need to be reviewed. If SAP standard function modules are used for archiving FI documents, no adjustments are needed, and access to archived files is supported.

- **Elimination of old processes**
  As part of SAP S/4HANA Finance accelerated closing, many periodically run settlement jobs are eliminated or are obsolete. Custom enhancements to such programs or those that read settlement data from settlement runs, for example, must be revisited.

- **Performance considerations**
  Many new programs in SAP S/4HANA Finance leverage the in-memory capability

of SAP S/4HANA by having ABAP code for calculation and aggregation algorithms pushed into the database layer. Custom programs have all their algorithms still within the application layer. If the provision of real-time data for key business processes is critical to the business case, then impacted performance-intensive custom programs must be reviewed.

Deployment Options

Implementation of SAP S/4HANA Finance is undoubtedly a significant strategic decision both for IT and the business. Several deployment scenarios might be in play based on the situation and the requirements of the organization. The options include the following:

- **Greenfield implementation**
  This scenario features a fresh implementation of business processes on the SAP S/4HANA platform either because it's a new implementation or because migrating the existing implementation to SAP S/4HANA provides little benefit.

  For any greenfield SAP implementation, brand-new customers might take the view that because they're already implementing SAP, they should go all the way and get SAP S/4HANA. However, careful analysis of the organization's specific financial requirements is required to determine the components of SAP S/4HANA Finance that need to be activated, including assessing nonfunctional requirements. Here, you need to expect premigration validation checks and data fixes that require patience and persistence.

- **Upgrade and migrate**
  In this scenario, a pre-EHP 7 release of SAP ERP exists on any non-SAP HANA database, and the organization wants to move to SAP S/4HANA. For customers on SAP ERP 6.0 on a non-SAP HANA platform, the following steps are recommended:

  – Upgrade to EHP 7 or above to ensure the technical readiness of the systems whenever the organization decides to move to SAP S/4HANA.

  – In addition, given the future direction of SAP to discontinue/disable the functionality of classic G/L, implement the new G/L with SAP ERP 6.0 if it's not already in place.

  Customers should also run the SAP S/4HANA value assessment analysis on the existing system to determine the potential benefits of SAP HANA.

  Although this can be combined into a one-step approach (technical migration of the database to SAP HANA and enablement of SAP S/4HANA Finance), the

recommendation is to follow the two-step approach and keep enablement of SAP S/4HANA Finance as a separate functional release from the technical database migration. This avoids the complexities, risk, and increased downtime of combining two big changes in one production cutover window. Based on the validation of cutover downtime and possible risk, a company might combine SAP HANA migration and SAP S/4HANA Finance enablement as one project.

- **SAP HANA database migration**
  In this scenario, an organization is already on SAP ERP 6.0 EHP 7 or above (on a traditional RDBMS). Organizations on mature SAP ERP 6.0 implementations can analyze the impact of what a real-time analytical environment may bring them and how they can monetize the value of speedy availability of real-time information and create value for their organizations.

  Technically, this commits the organization to SAP's proprietary in-memory platform. Organizations need to spend time assessing the business case, including the risk of adopting the SAP HANA platform versus running the SAP Business Suite on other platforms, particularly in industries that use many other connected applications.

- **Replicate to Central Finance**
  This scenario replicates all systems, both SAP and non-SAP, into a Central Finance instance before deploying SAP S/4HANA Finance into the company's environment.

  For organizations not yet ready to upgrade their legacy systems or for organizations in which such an upgrade will be complex and time-consuming, they should go for the Central Finance deployment option. This makes it possible to benefit from SAP S/4HANA Finance without touching the existing system landscape by using Central Journal facilities to connect legacy SAP and non-SAP systems to an environment based on SAP S/4HANA Finance.

- **SAP S/4HANA Finance enablement**
  In this scenario, an organization is already running its SAP ERP system on the SAP HANA database and has the option of enabling SAP S/4HANA by installing the SAP S/4HANA Finance add-on (version 1503 or 1605) or on-premise SAP S/4HANA (version 1511, 1610, or 1709). For organizations with an existing SAP HANA footprint, the adoption of SAP S/4HANA will impact investment plans and roadmaps for all existing SAP Business Suite users.

Organizations should choose their overall SAP HANA adoption strategy—including potential migration to SAP Business Suite on SAP HANA—as a first step on the journey to SAP S/4HANA.

For those organizations that already have clarity into the business case and the roadmap for SAP HANA adoption, they should consider the benefits of a one-step SAP S/4HANA adoption, including an SAP S/4HANA Finance implementation, for cost and business risk reasons.

If an organization is already on an SAP HANA platform and is considering migrating to SAP Business Suite on SAP HANA, SAP S/4HANA Finance can provide additional benefits to support the business case, as described earlier in the section "Benefits of SAP S/4HANA Finance."

Project Phases

Migration from traditional SAP ERP to SAP S/4HANA Finance should be implemented as a project with the following phases. Each of the phases is accompanied by a figure that lists the major objectives, activities, and deliverables:

1. Preparation (Figure 4)
2. Installation (Figure 5)
3. Customizing (Figure 6)
4. Data migration (Figure 7)
5. Postmigration (Figure 8)
6. Testing (Figure 9)

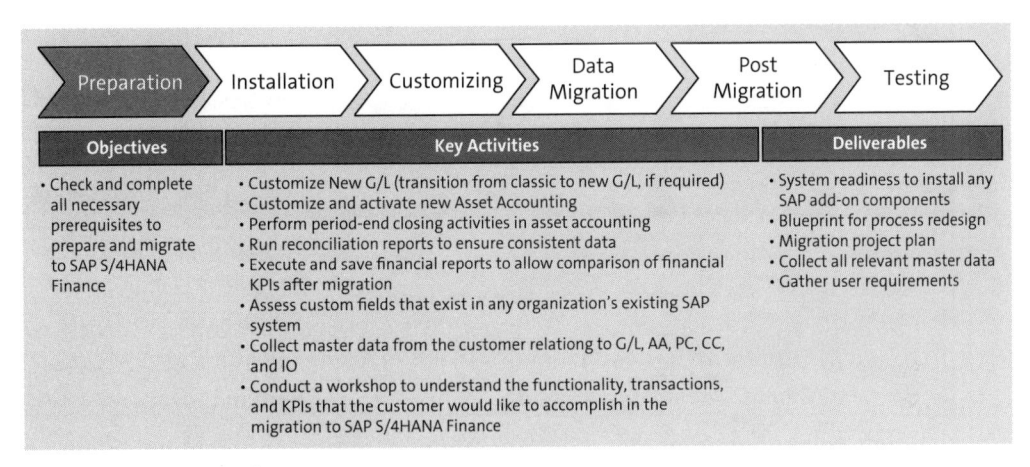

Objectives	Key Activities	Deliverables
• Check and complete all necessary prerequisites to prepare and migrate to SAP S/4HANA Finance	• Customize New G/L (transition from classic to new G/L, if required) • Customize and activate new Asset Accounting • Perform period-end closing activities in asset accounting • Run reconciliation reports to ensure consistent data • Execute and save financial reports to allow comparison of financial KPIs after migration • Assess custom fields that exist in any organization's existing SAP system • Collect master data from the customer relationg to G/L, AA, PC, CC, and IO • Conduct a workshop to understand the functionality, transactions, and KPIs that the customer would like to accomplish in the migration to SAP S/4HANA Finance	• System readiness to install any SAP add-on components • Blueprint for process redesign • Migration project plan • Collect all relevant master data • Gather user requirements

Figure 4 Preparation Phase

Introduction

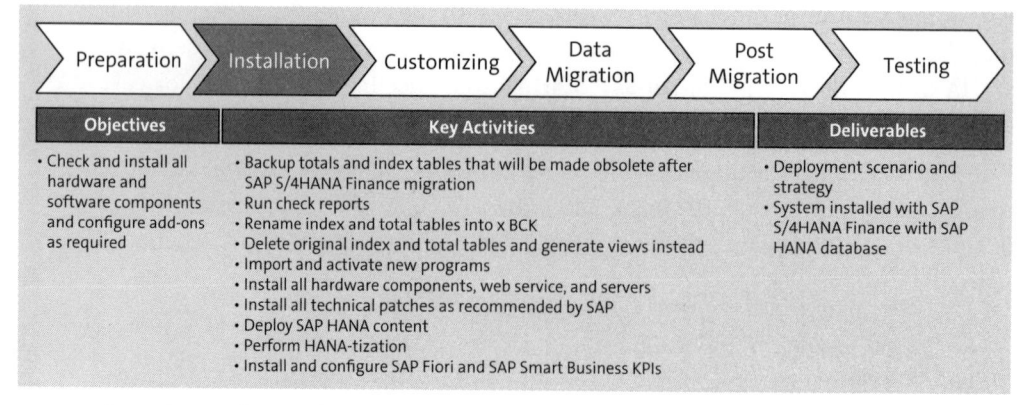

| Preparation | **Installation** | Customizing | Data Migration | Post Migration | Testing |

Objectives	Key Activities	Deliverables
• Check and install all hardware and software components and configure add-ons as required	• Backup totals and index tables that will be made obsolete after SAP S/4HANA Finance migration • Run check reports • Rename index and total tables into x BCK • Delete original index and total tables and generate views instead • Import and activate new programs • Install all hardware components, web service, and servers • Install all technical patches as recommended by SAP • Deploy SAP HANA content • Perform HANA-tization • Install and configure SAP Fiori and SAP Smart Business KPIs	• Deployment scenario and strategy • System installed with SAP S/4HANA Finance with SAP HANA database

Figure 5 Installation Phase

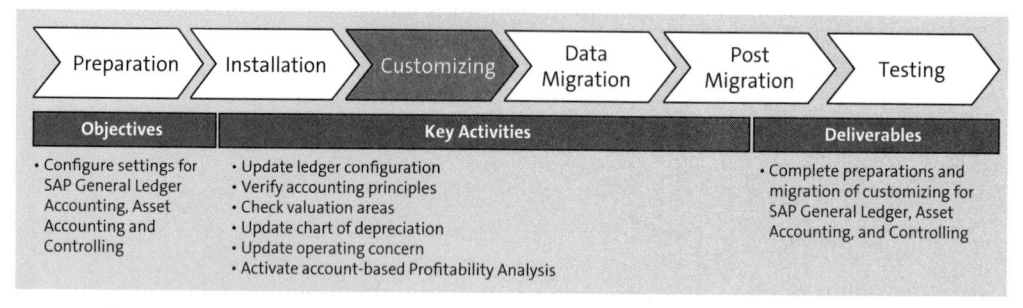

| Preparation | Installation | **Customizing** | Data Migration | Post Migration | Testing |

Objectives	Key Activities	Deliverables
• Configure settings for SAP General Ledger Accounting, Asset Accounting and Controlling	• Update ledger configuration • Verify accounting principles • Check valuation areas • Update chart of depreciation • Update operating concern • Activate account-based Profitability Analysis	• Complete preparations and migration of customizing for SAP General Ledger, Asset Accounting, and Controlling

Figure 6 Customizing Phase

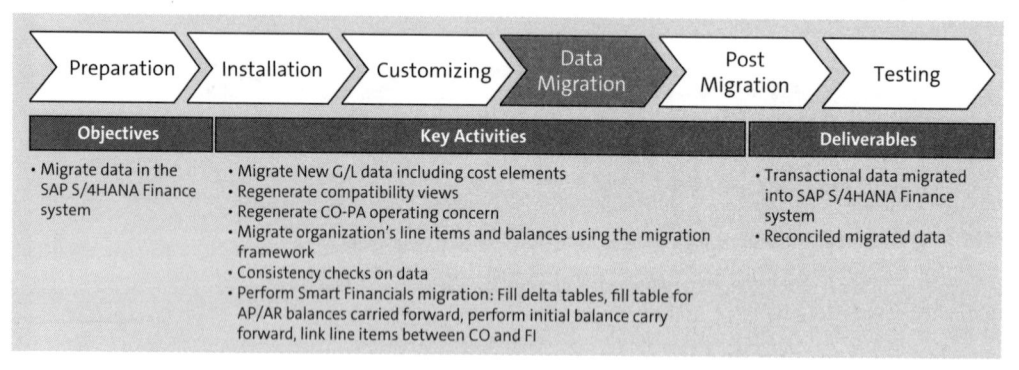

| Preparation | Installation | Customizing | **Data Migration** | Post Migration | Testing |

Objectives	Key Activities	Deliverables
• Migrate data in the SAP S/4HANA Finance system	• Migrate New G/L data including cost elements • Regenerate compatibility views • Regenerate CO-PA operating concern • Migrate organization's line items and balances using the migration framework • Consistency checks on data • Perform Smart Financials migration: Fill delta tables, fill table for AP/AR balances carried forward, perform initial balance carry forward, link line items between CO and FI	• Transactional data migrated into SAP S/4HANA Finance system • Reconciled migrated data

Figure 7 Data Migration Phase

Summary

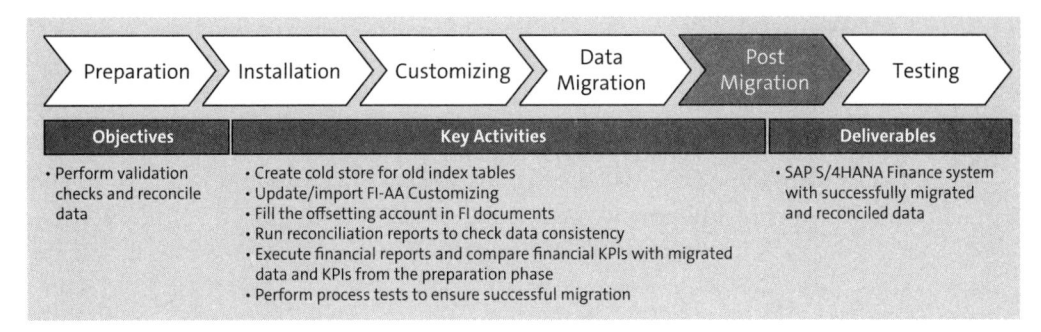

Figure 8 Postmigration Phase

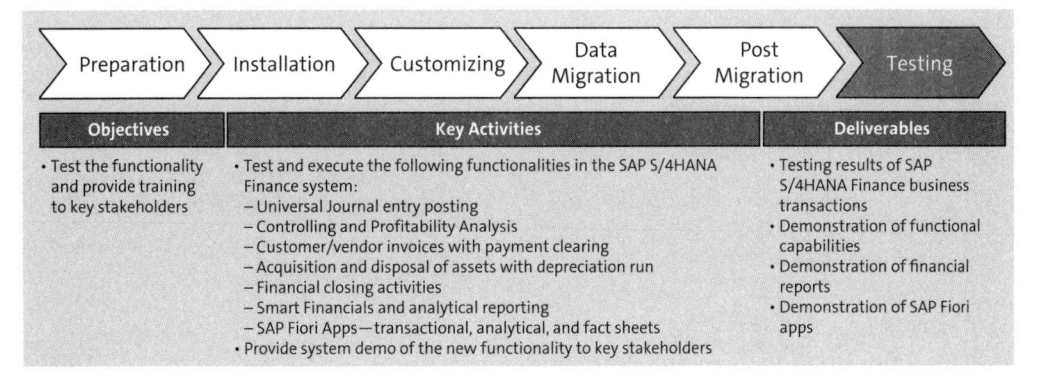

Phase	Objectives	Key Activities	Deliverables
Preparation › Installation › Customizing › Data Migration › **Post Migration** › Testing	• Perform validation checks and reconcile data	• Create cold store for old index tables • Update/import FI-AA Customizing • Fill the offsetting account in FI documents • Run reconciliation reports to check data consistency • Execute financial reports and compare financial KPIs with migrated data and KPIs from the preparation phase • Perform process tests to ensure successful migration	• SAP S/4HANA Finance system with successfully migrated and reconciled data

Figure 9 Testing Phase

Phase	Objectives	Key Activities	Deliverables
Preparation › Installation › Customizing › Data Migration › Post Migration › **Testing**	• Test the functionality and provide training to key stakeholders	• Test and execute the following functionalities in the SAP S/4HANA Finance system: – Universal Journal entry posting – Controlling and Profitability Analysis – Customer/vendor invoices with payment clearing – Acquisition and disposal of assets with depreciation run – Financial closing activities – Smart Financials and analytical reporting – SAP Fiori Apps—transactional, analytical, and fact sheets • Provide system demo of the new functionality to key stakeholders	• Testing results of SAP S/4HANA Finance business transactions • Demonstration of functional capabilities • Demonstration of financial reports • Demonstration of SAP Fiori apps

Summary

Technology is changing the world every day. Mobile and cloud solutions with real-time transaction processing and analytical capabilities are driving organizations toward high levels of value creation at a reasonable cost. Most enterprise-level CFOs agree that the changing global business environment is forcing more ad hoc decision-making, and technological innovations are now able to support it.

SAP S/4HANA is SAP's next-generation of technology created to support the CFOs of today's world. It's clear that adoption of such a groundbreaking innovation requires an organizational transformation and very strong executive sponsorship, both of which are only secured when there is significant business value to be realized by these implementations.

Introduction

The SAP HANA platform provides significant new business capabilities for customers in addition to simplification of their existing SAP landscapes, as detailed in this introduction.

Let's now move on to Part I, in which we'll walk you through each phase of the SAP S/4HANA migration. First, in Chapter 1, we'll discuss the activities you need to perform to prepare for your migration to SAP S/4HANA.

PART I
Migrating to SAP S/4HANA Finance

Chapter 1
Preparation

Before you install SAP S/4HANA Finance, you need to make sure the system is configured correctly by confirming that the required business functions have been activated and by executing precheck reports, as we'll discuss in this chapter.

As is the case in most implementation projects, the preparation phase is the most critical for an SAP S/4HANA Finance migration or installation project. The main task of this phase is to execute checks and activities prior to installing SAP S/4HANA Finance. The prechecks help you fix any errors before the migration, which reduces the time and effort required to resolve issues during or at the end of the migration process.

In this chapter, we'll discuss how to determine whether all the necessary configuration is in place and how to execute all the precheck reports before you begin your migration to SAP S/4HANA Finance.

> **Expert Insight**
> Make sure you back up the existing system along with all the Customizing settings and functionality before you install SAP S/4HANA Finance and any other components.

1.1 Check Functional Scope and Restrictions

It's prudent to familiarize yourself with all relevant SAP Notes and to read all the scoping and restrictions for the SAP S/4HANA Finance installation. The information on scoping and restrictions is relevant for organizations that need to migrate to SAP S/4HANA Finance from SAP ERP 6.0. For greenfield implementations, the SAP client comes with SAP S/4HANA Finance installed with SAP Best Practices.

1 Preparation

SAP S/4HANA Finance entails certain restrictions that can affect the usability of parallel valuation, fiscal year variants, industry solutions, enterprise extensions, and SAP add-ons. For a successful migration, you need to understand and analyze how these restrictions will affect your landscape before starting the migration activities. Some components or restrictions may require additional remediation activities before the start of the migration.

You must transition to the following applications as part of your SAP S/4HANA Finance migration:

- New General Ledger (new G/L)
- New Asset Accounting
- Controlling (CO)
- SAP Cash Management
- Real Estate Management
- Activity-based costing (ABC) using delta versions
- General cost object and cost object hierarchies
- Lease Accounting Engine (LAE) and Joint Venture Accounting (JVA)
- Balance sheet planning, reports for comparing planning data and actual data in Profit Center Accounting, and average balance ledger

> **References**
>
> The following are some useful SAP Notes on scoping and restrictions for the new functionality and release:
>
> - SAP Note 2044295: SAP Cash Management Powered by SAP HANA Requires a Separate License
> - SAP Note 2127080: Limitation on Usage of Cash Management
> - SAP Note 2165911: Integrated Business Planning for Finance (note that Integrated Business Planning for Finance is the old name for SAP BPC for S/4HANA Finance)
> - SAP Note 2081400: P&L Planning and Profit Center Planning Can Now Be Done Using Integrated Business Planning Functionality
> - SAP Note 2333141: SAP S/4HANA 1610: Restriction

We recommend that you go through the following SAP Notes before starting the SAP S/4HANA Finance migration activities:

- SAP Note 2399707: SAP Readiness Check for SAP S/4HANA
- SAP Note 2495992: SAP S/4HANA 1709 Application-Specific Notes in System Conversion/Upgrade Preparation Phase
- SAP Note 2119188: Release Scope Information for SAP S/4HANA Finance
- SAP Note 1835621: Such Errors Could Be Corrected as Per the Procedure Described in the SAP Note 1835621—FAQ: Circular Posting
- SAP Note 2153644: Overview of the Country Release Information and Limitations Concerning the Localization Functions
- SAP Note 1946054: Detailed Comparison of Transaction Codes and Reports in SAP ERP 6.0 and SAP S/4HANA Finance
- SAP Note 2103558: Compatible Add-On to ERP 6.0 for Usage with SAP S/4HANA Finance
- SAP Note 2100133: Compatible Partner and Third-Party Add-On for Usage with SAP S/4HANA Finance
- SAP Note 2269324: Compatibility Scope Matrix for SAP S/4HANA On-Premise (SAP provides certain classic ERP solutions limited rights to run on the SAP S/4HANA installation)

Let's start with the feasibility checklist.

1.2 Feasibility Checklist

One of the premigration activities is to analyze the current technical system architecture details and landscape to ensure that the technical migration to SAP S/4HANA Finance is feasible. Normally, the system review is executed using a questionnaire that helps to identify the migration scope, including any remediation activities.

The questionnaire in Table 1.1 is designed to help analyze and assess the system environment and determine whether the installation of and migration to SAP S/4HANA Finance is technically possible.

All the questions marked as high criticality need to be thoroughly reviewed with both the business and IT before the migration, whereas those of medium criticality need to be analyzed for the best possible solution. The questions with low criticality aren't showstoppers, so they can be taken up later if the business doesn't have the knowledge to address them during the preparation phase.

1 Preparation

No.	Criticality	Question	Sample Answer
System Landscape			
1.1	High	What is the database and version of the current SAP ERP system?	Oracle 11.2
1.2	High	What are the SAP applications and add-ons in your landscape (e.g., SAP ERP, SAP Business Warehouse, SAP Advanced Planning and Optimization, SAP Master Data Management, SAP Supply Chain Management, SAP Supplier Relationship Management, SAP Customer Relationship Management, etc.)?	SAP ERP, SAP BW, SAP MDM, SAP CRM
1.3	High	Which versions and enhancement package levels are your SAP components at present?	SAPKB74010 SAPKA74010 SAPKH61707...
1.4	High	Do you have database compression turned on?	No
1.5	High	What is the current operating system and version for your database server and application server?	Oracle Database 12c, WebAS 7.0
1.6	High	Is the system single stack or dual stack for ABAP/Java?	Single
1.7	Low	Do you have a preferred hardware vendor (e.g., IBM, HP, Fujitsu, Dell)?	IBM
1.8	Low	Do you have a single global instance or multiple regional instances for SAP ERP?	Single global instance
1.9	Low	Do you have a single global instance or multiple regional instances for SAP BW?	Single global instance
1.10	Low	Do you have non-SAP systems handling significant business processes? Attach system landscape diagram, if possible.	Vertex for tax reporting, warehouse management system (WMS)

Table 1.1 Questionnaire to Assess Readiness for SAP S/4HANA Finance Migration

No.	Criticality	Question	Sample Answer
1.11	High	What is the current system landscape, and what is the expected landscape (dev, testing, QA, prod)? Attach SAP ERP system landscape diagram, if possible.	Landscape description attached with the flow of data from all legacy systems
1.12	Medium	Can you share the SAP EarlyWatch Alert report?	Yes, attached
1.13	High	Are these environments on-premise or hosted by a hosting provider? If the latter, where?	On-premise
1.14	Medium	Is your system on Unicode? If not, what is the code page installed in the system?	Unicode
SAP ERP Users and Maturity			
2.1	High	How many total SAP users do you have?	5,000
2.2	High	How many total SAP ERP users do you have (split by components)?	500 FI, 500 CO, 1,000 MM, 1,000 PP, 1,000 SD, 1,000 others
2.3	Medium	How many concurrent users access SAP ERP during a peak period such as month end or quarter end?	1,000
2.4	Medium	What are the crucial business processes supported by SAP ERP?	Order planning and execution, period-end closing
2.5	Low	What is the breakdown of users by capability and maturity (operational, analytical, power users, executives)?	See attached list
2.6	Low	Who are your major information consumers, and how critical is SAP ERP for their day-to-day tasks?	Finance end users; SAP ERP is the source of all financial data, which is fed from various legacy systems

Table 1.1 Questionnaire to Assess Readiness for SAP S/4HANA Finance Migration (Cont.)

1　Preparation

No.	Criticality	Question	Sample Answer
Data Size and Growth			
3.1	High	What is the database size (in giga- or terabytes) of your production system?	4 TB
3.2	Medium	How many years of historical data do you have in your system?	Five (+ three in archive)
3.3	Low	What is your rate of growth in the past six months?	500 MB
3.4	Medium	What is your forecast for the next six months?	500 MB
3.5	Low	Are all your divisions or business processes already in SAP ERP?	No, EMEA will be rolled out in 2019
3.6	Medium	Do you have archived data in SAP ERP? Do you have a data archiving strategy?	Yes, strategy document attached
Performance Expectations			
4.1	Low	Do you have any benchmarks on performance expectations? Are response times in seconds a nice-to-have feature or a must-have behavior for your reports? Do all reports require that or only a few?	Yes, expectations attached per critical SAP ERP reports
4.2	Low	What types of queries or reports are available for your users' system, or what type do you anticipate creating (e.g., summary/aggregated reports, detailed document-level list reports [data dump style], dashboards, formatting)?	In use: Standard SAP ERP line-item and summary reports, SAP BW, SAP BusinessObjects (see list of reports attached)
General/Business Drivers			
5.1	Low	How did you hear and know about SAP S/4HANA and SAP S/4HANA Finance?	SAPPHIRE NOW
5.2	Low	Why do you want to implement SAP S/4HANA and SAP S/4HANA Finance?	Smart KPI reporting, data consistency, faster closing

Table 1.1 Questionnaire to Assess Readiness for SAP S/4HANA Finance Migration (Cont.)

1.2 Feasibility Checklist

No.	Criticality	Question	Sample Answer
5.3	Low	What do you consider some of the critical success factors for the SAP S/4HANA and SAP S/4HANA Finance implementation?	Speed, ROI, data redundancy
5.4	Low	Who is going to sponsor the SAP HANA implementation? Is it business-driven or IT-driven?	Business
5.5	Low	Do you have a future enterprise SAP HANA roadmap/architecture or vision?	Yes, attached
5.6	High	Is your intention to migrate all organizational units/companies to SAP S/4HANA Finance or to utilize a step-by-step approach?	Need support to make decision
5.7	Medium	Do you need/will you consider a proof of concept (POC) to analyze SAP S/4HANA functionality and build business case?	Yes, must start with critical functions... first phase
5.8	High	What is the planned business downtime for this migration?	Max. eight hours
SAP ERP-Specific Questions			
6.1	Medium	What modules have you implemented in SAP ERP (e.g., Sales and Distribution, Materials Management, Warehouse Management, Financial Accounting, Controlling, Production Planning, etc.)?	FI, CO, MM, SD, PP
6.2	Medium	Which enterprise extensions are currently active in your system (from Transaction SFW5)?	EA-FIN, EA-PLM, ...
6.3	High	Which industry solution is currently active in your system (e.g., aerospace and defense, automotive, banking, etc.)?	IS-Oil
6.4	High	Are you using the SAP Fiori UI or SAP GUI? Do you use any SAP Fiori apps currently?	SAP Fiori, where available by standard. Currently using some SAP Fiori apps.

Table 1.1 Questionnaire to Assess Readiness for SAP S/4HANA Finance Migration (Cont.)

No.	Criticality	Question	Sample Answer
6.5	Medium	Are you considering using the SAP Smart Business functionality?	Yes, where available
6.6	Medium	Which SAP and partner add-ons are currently installed?	SAP IS-M 617, SAP IS-U LOCIN 100, SAP EWM 9.2
6.7	High	List custom workflow, report, interface, conversion, enhancement, and form (WRICEF) objects in the existing SAP ERP system.	See attached list
6.8	High	Which components in FI and CO do you use?	FI: G/L, AP, AR, AA, SL CO: OM, PC, Profit Center Accounting, CO-PA, PS, RE-FX
6.9	Medium	Describe the finance organizational structure in the system (e.g., single or many operating concerns and controlling areas, assignment of company codes to controlling areas, etc.).	Operating concern, controlling areas per region; hierarchy attached
6.10	Low	Are there any "obsolete" organizational units in the production system (e.g., old company codes/controlling areas without recent update but with data)?	Yes, the following company codes from 2010 are inactive: ...
SAP S/4HANA Finance Questions			
7.1	High	Do you use classic G/L or new G/L?	New G/L
7.2	Medium	Which type of Profitability Analysis (CO-PA) do you use currently (costing-based or account-based)?	Account-based
7.3	High	Which type of CO-PA will you use in SAP S/4HANA Finance (if already decided)?	Account-based in parallel with costing-based
7.4	High	Do you use the ledger approach or account approach in General Ledger Accounting? List ledgers and their purpose.	Ledger approach; ledger list attached

Table 1.1 Questionnaire to Assess Readiness for SAP S/4HANA Finance Migration (Cont.)

1.2 Feasibility Checklist

No.	Criticality	Question	Sample Answer
7.5	High	If you use the new G/L with the ledger approach and FI-AA, do you use delta valuation areas?	Yes
7.6	Medium	Which characteristics are used in the new G/L? Is splitting used?	Profit center, segment; splitting used for leading ledger
7.7	High	If on the new G/L, do you have custom Z tables defined for parallel ledgers (not table FAGLFLEXT)?	Yes, table ZFAGLFLEXT for local tax accounting
7.8	High	Are there any custom fields in G/L totals tables?	Yes, list enclosed
7.9	Medium	Do you utilize shifted fiscal year for leading valuation (or of parallel valuations)?	Shifted fiscal year from June 1st for leading valuation
7.10	High	Do you use the transfer prices functionality in SAP ERP?	No
7.11	High	Do you use SAP Material Ledger (ML)? Which functions of ML do you use (e.g., parallel currencies, actual cost calculation, revaluation of stock/consumption, CO-PA revaluation, actual activity price)?	Yes: parallel currencies, actual valuation, actual cost of goods sold (COGS), CO-PA revaluation
7.12	High	Do you use multiple valuation of cost of goods manufactured (COGM) functionality?	No
7.13	High	Do you use planning functionality in SAP ERP? Are you considering using SAP BPC for SAP S/4HANA Finance functionality?	Planning on cost centers, internal orders. Plan to use SAP BPC for SAP S/4HANA Finance
7.14	High	Do you use the SAP Cash and Liquidity Management functionality with the following functions: cash position, SAP Liquidity Management for Banking, and Bank Account Management?	Yes, SAP Liquidity Management for Banking

Table 1.1 Questionnaire to Assess Readiness for SAP S/4HANA Finance Migration (Cont.)

No.	Criticality	Question	Sample Answer
7.15	Medium	Do you currently use classic Real Estate Management (RE) or Flexible Real Estate Management (RE-FX)?	RE-FX
7.16	Medium	Do you use activity-based costing (CO-OM-ABC) using delta versions?	No
7.17	Medium	Do you use general cost object and cost object hierarchies in CO?	No
7.18	Medium	Do you use FI-AA integration to LAE and JVA (business function JVA_GL_INTEGRATION)?	No
7.19	High	Do you use the balance sheet planning functionality? Do you want to keep this function?	Yes
7.20	Medium	Do you use standard SAP reports for comparing planning data and actual data in Profit Center Accounting?	Yes
7.21	Medium	Do you use P&L planning and profit center planning by profit centers?	Yes
7.22	Medium	Do you use either former budgeting functionality as part of Funds Management (component PSM-FM) or a new budget control system (PSM-FM-BCS)?	No
7.23	High	Do you use any of the following as part of Fund Accounting (components PSM-FM and PSM-FA): Cash Ledger, Cash Flow Reporting, Cash Control, or Average Daily Balance (ADB)?	No
7.24	High	Do you use SAP BW reports to report FI figures out of the SAP ERP system? List reports/extractors/data origin if possible.	Yes, report list with data extractors attached

Table 1.1 Questionnaire to Assess Readiness for SAP S/4HANA Finance Migration (Cont.)

> **References**
>
> Read the Administrator's Guide for SAP S/4HANA, On-Premise Edition 1610 at *http://help.sap.com/s4hana_op_1610_002* under **Additional Information • Administrator's Guide**.

1.3 The Maintenance Planner and Prechecks

You must use the Maintenance Planner for your conversion to SAP S/4HANA Finance; it creates the download files (add-ons, packages, database drivers, stack files, etc.) used by the Software Update Manager (SUM) to install SAP S/4HANA Finance. The Maintenance Planner checks the following:

- Whether the add-ons in the system can be used for the conversion
- Whether the activated business functions in the system can be used for the conversion
- Whether a valid file path is present (and will prevent the conversion if it's not)

After these checks are performed, the stack configuration file is created, which SUM uses for conversion to SAP S/4HANA Finance.

Before the precheck is performed, the Maintenance Planner needs to be executed because the stack.xml file is an input for the precheck report. This ensures the compatibility of the system with the conversion process, so these checks should be performed before starting SUM.

These checks provide users with all the mandatory steps for conversion to SAP S/4HANA Finance in the form of SAP Notes. To ensure accuracy, the checks are run twice in SUM during the conversion process. The precheck result provides the log that needs to be addressed before the actual conversion process. If errors are encountered during the process, the conversion is stopped. The execution of some precheck reports can be time-consuming.

> **References**
>
> For more information, see SAP Note 2182725: Delivery of the S/4 System Conversion Checks.

1.4 Check Custom Coding

The migration to SAP S/4HANA Finance creates new data structures in SAP ERP Financials (FI), with table BKPF as the header table, with table ACDOCA as the line-item table, and with read-only access compatibility views replacing existing SAP ERP 6.0 tables. You might need to adapt certain custom code to comply with the SAP S/4HANA Finance data model; otherwise, the installation of SAP S/4HANA Finance may be blocked with ABAP dictionary activation errors. The SAP Basis, technical, and development teams must perform the checks and activities detailed in the next sections in the test system to check the nondisruptive usage of the existing ABAP programs.

1.4.1 Check Custom Code and Modifications

Per SAP Note 1976487, you need to check whether you have write access to the tables in your own custom objects in the custom namespace. When you migrate to SAP S/4HANA Finance, your old tables are replaced by identically named compatibility views. During this process, the write access is changed to read access. You must change this to write access to allow changes.

You should also check if you have custom-specific views in your own objects in your custom namespace for the tables that have been removed. These views need to be replaced with an Open SQL SELECT statement or the call of a read module because the Data Dictionary (DDIC) doesn't support stack views such as database views that are based on other views.

When migrating from classic FI-AA, the batch input programs for Transaction AB01 are no longer supported in new Asset Accounting. All the existing custom-defined programs must be converted to Business Application Programming Interfaces (BAPIs) before the migration.

> **References**
>
> The following are some useful SAP Notes on migration of custom programs from a prior version of SAP to SAP S/4HANA:
>
> - SAP Note 1976487: Adjusting Custom-Specific Programs to the Simplified Data Model for SAP S/4HANA Finance
> - SAP Note 2219527: Notes about Using Views BSID, BSAD, BSIK, BSAK, BSIS, and BSAS in Custom-Defined Programs in SAP S/4HANA Finance

> - SAP Note 2221298: Notes about Using Views GLT0, FAGLFLEXT, FMGLFLEXT, PSGL-FLEXT, and JVGLFLEXT in Custom Programs in SAP S/4HANA Finance
> - SAP Note 2185026: Compatibility Views COSP, COSS, COEP, and COVP: How Can Their Use Be Optimized?
> - SAP Note 2297729: Documents which Are Posted in BKPF/ACDOCA but No Entries in BSEG/BSEG_ADD

1.4.2 Handling Custom-Defined Fields and Interfaces

Custom-defined fields, like custom codes, are minimally impacted by the SAP S/4HANA Finance migration process, whereby these custom fields are converted to the respective compatibility views so that the existing programs work without any disruption. The custom fields are created with the same-name views per the following rules and procedures:

- If a custom field exists in both table BSEG and index tables, it's automatically generated into the same-name compatibility view table so that the custom ABAP program can read the fields through these compatibility views. If the custom field exists only in the index table, it must first be included in table BSEG and filled before its conversion to compatibility views.

- If you're already using new General Ledger Accounting and have custom fields in table FAGLFLEXA, these fields are generated into the FAGLFLEXT view.

- If you've used interfaces so that the data flows from the external systems to make financial postings to General Ledger Accounting, you need to check if any adjustments are required for these interfaces to work with SAP S/4HANA Finance. You may have to activate business function FIN_GL_DISTR_SCEN_1, which enables transfer of totals and single documents in distributed systems.

- In SAP S/4HANA Finance, Application Link Enabling (ALE) scenarios currently are only partially supported. The migrated SAP S/4HANA Finance system can't receive the values for CO line items because both FI and CO line items are posted to table ACDOCA in SAP S/4HANA Finance. The CO line items can't be posted without the corresponding FI line items. The CO-related transaction data needs to be checked manually as a preparation step because SAP doesn't provide an automated check for this scenario, although it still supports the ALE scenarios for the distribution of CO master data such as cost centers or internal orders.

1 Preparation

1.5 Check Sizing

This step involves determining hardware requirements such as network bandwidth, physical memory, CPU power, and I/O capacity. Often, the sizing is determined based on the volume of the current data and the rate at which the data is expected to grow. The hardware platform, the SAP software, the system settings, and the Customizing settings based on the business processes are all factors that influence sizing. The recommended approach to compute the memory requirement for SAP HANA is to take half of the current disk-based database space, add a 20 percent contingency and buffer, and then add another 50 GB for coding, stacking, and other services. For the SAP HANA database size, the recommended approach is to use half the size that currently exists for the disk-based database.

In a live production system, this step needs to be planned carefully with the architecture team and hardware partner. Using SUM along with the Maintenance Planner is required for the installation of SAP S/4HANA Finance.

Check for and get the latest SUM release and patch level before you start the migration or installation of SAP S/4HANA Finance. Aggregate tables such as table GLT0 and application index tables such as table BSIS are deleted and replaced by the compatibility views. These views ensure that when data is retrieved from these tables, the same information is extracted from the database using these views based on the new data model structure.

> **References**
>
> Some relevant resources include the following:
>
> - SAP Note 1813548: Database Migration Option (DMO) of SUM
> - SAP Note 2117481: SAP S/4HANA Finance Release Information Notes to Apply All Important Bug Fixes
> - *http://service.sap.com/sizing*
> - *http://service.sap.com/quicksizing*

1.6 Precheck for Migration to New Asset Accounting

You must use program RASFIN_MIGR_PRECHECK when you want to migrate from classic FI-AA to new Asset Accounting in the context of migrating to SAP S/4HANA Finance. This program checks whether the prerequisites for migration to new Asset

Accounting have been successfully applied for all company codes activated in FI-AA by executing Transaction SA38 using program RASFIN_MIGR_PRECHECK, as shown in Figure 1.1.

Figure 1.1 Running Program RASFIN_MIGR_PRECHECK

The program checks whether the periodic acquisition and production cost (APC) postings have been completed for all company codes. The migration to new Asset Accounting incorporates configuration changes pertaining to the execution of periodic APC postings.

The program also checks the configuration settings to find the depreciation areas that post to the G/L periodically with automatic posting indicator BUHBKT = 2 assigned. This option for posting to the G/L no longer applies with the implementation of SAP S/4HANA Finance because depreciation areas post in real time to the G/L account. These depreciation areas must be posted using the **Depreciation Area Posts Account Balances in Real Time** option instead of the **Depreciation Periodically** option (BUHBKT = 4). After you've installed SAP S/4HANA Finance, adjustments must be made to the automatic posting indicators of the affected depreciation areas. Select the latest release to check the prerequisites before you execute the FI-AA migration, as shown in Figure 1.2.

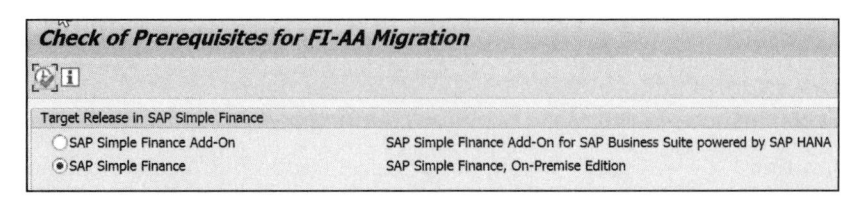

Figure 1.2 Check Prerequisites before FI-AA Migration

1   Preparation

Before you install SAP S/4HANA Finance and migrate to new Asset Accounting, use the program to check that you've complied fully with the prerequisites for new Asset Accounting. The output in Figure 1.3 appears if the system encounters no errors.

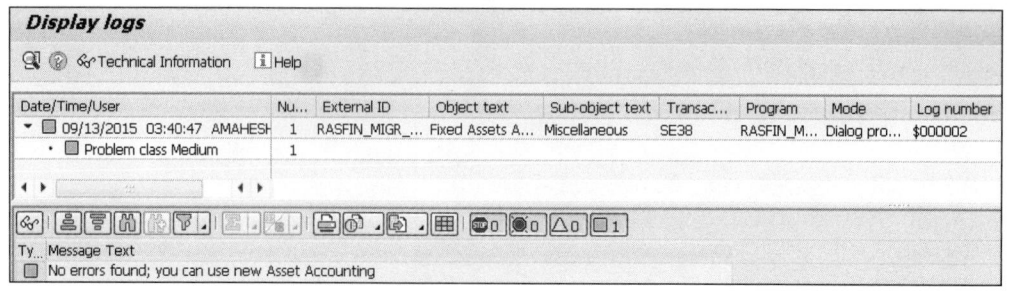

```
Display logs
    Technical Information    Help

Date/Time/User                          Nu...  External ID      Object text       Sub-object text  Transac...  Program      Mode         Log number
▼ ☐ 09/13/2015 03:40:47 AMAHESH          1     RASFIN_MIGR_...  Fixed Assets A... Miscellaneous    SE38        RASFIN_M...  Dialog pro... $000002
   • ☐ Problem class Medium              1

Ty   Message Text
   ☐  No errors found; you can use new Asset Accounting
```

Figure 1.3 Display Logs

> **Expert Insight**
>
> If you see inconsistency errors related to *assigned ledgers* in FI-GL and FI-AA, then consult SAP Note 2147666. If you see inconsistency errors related to *currencies* in FI-GL and FI-AA, then consult SAP Note 2180591.

> **References**
>
> For more information, see SAP Note 1939592: Precheck Report for Migrating to New Asset Accounting.

1.7   Activate Business Functions

Enhancement packages and business functions enable you to simplify the process of introducing and using new developments for SAP Business Suite considerably. In this section, we'll discuss the key business functions that need to be activated to migrate to SAP S/4HANA Finance.

1.7.1   Activate Business Functions for Asset Accounting and Parallel Valuation

Business function `FIN_AA_PARALLEL_VAL` supports parallel accounting. The prerequisite is that you must be using new G/L with the ledger approach for parallel accounting.

1.7 Activate Business Functions

FI-AA performs valuation-based postings to a specific ledger group or depreciation area, which eliminates the delta areas for parallel valuation.

You can activate the business function using Transaction SFW5. Click **Continue** when you encounter the security information shown in Figure 1.4.

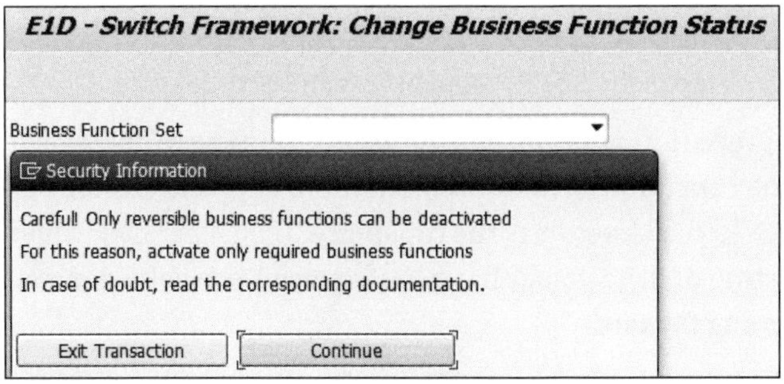

Figure 1.4 Change Business Function Status

On the **E1D—Switch Framework: Change Business Function Status** screen, select the business function **FIN_AA_PARALLEL_VAL**, as shown in Figure 1.5.

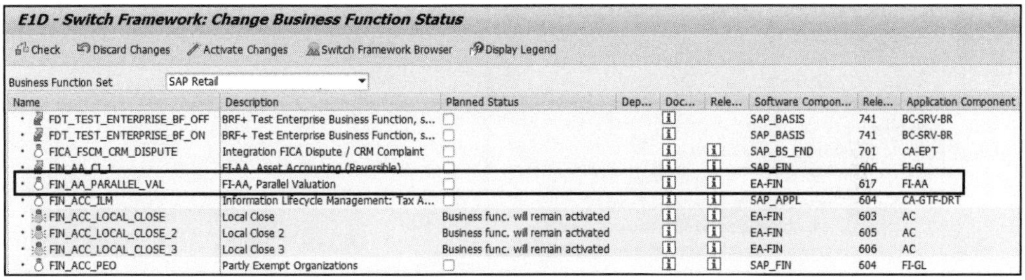

Figure 1.5 FIN_AA_PARALLEL_VAL Not Yet Activated

Then click **Activate Changes**, as shown in Figure 1.6. You'll notice that the **Planned Status** column entry will change from a null value to **Business Func. Will Remain Activated**.

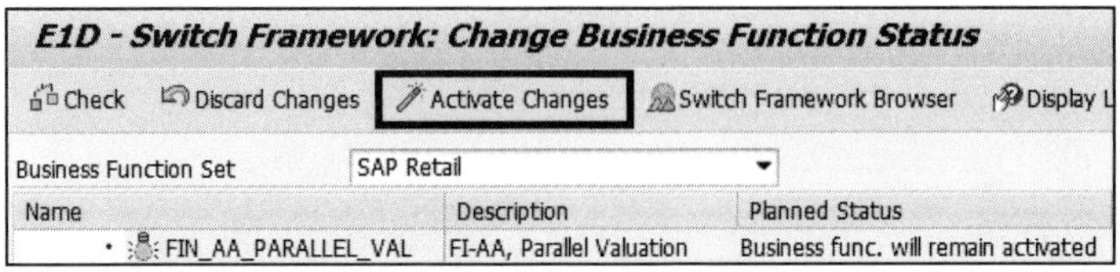

Figure 1.6 FIN_AA_PARALLEL_VAL Now Activated

1 Preparation

> **Expert Insight**
>
> Asset Accounting with an active business function and active Customizing switch is referred to in Figure 1.7 as **Asset Accounting (New)**. The older Asset Accounting is referred to as classic Asset Accounting (or classic FI-AA) to distinguish between the two.

The Customizing menu under Transaction SPRO appears, as shown in Figure 1.7.

You can now assign the depreciation areas of new Asset Accounting to the ledger groups of the G/L without the constraint of fixed assignment of depreciation area 01 to the leading ledger in the G/L. The system has the capability to post parallel values in real time. Because the posting of delta values has been replaced, the delta depreciation areas aren't required going forward.

With the activation of this business function, you can now make real-time postings for all accounting principles, such as the International Financial Reporting Standards (IFRS) or the US's generally accepted accounting principles (GAAP). The business valuations or accounting function EA-FIN (Financials Extension) needs to be activated for a new depreciation calculation.

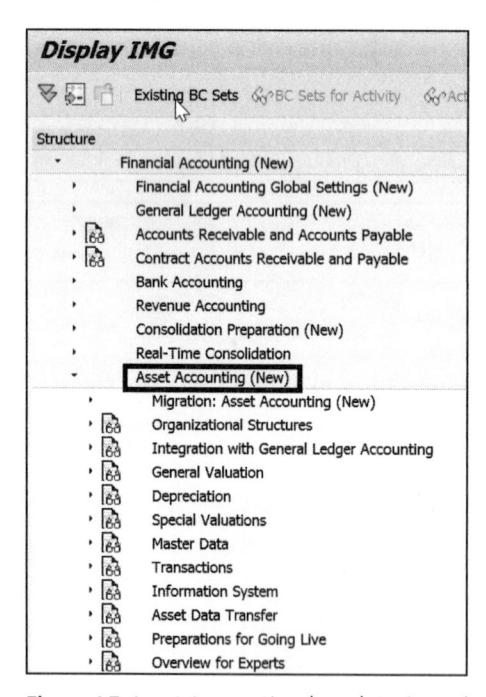

Figure 1.7 Asset Accounting (New) Activated

1.7.2 Activate Enterprise Extension EA-FIN

This generic business function provides enhancements to the areas listed in Table 1.2.

Area	Relevant Application Component
Closing	AC
Parallel accounting	FI-G/L
Accrual engine	FI-G/L-G/L-ACE
Manual accruals	FI-G/L-G/L-AAC
Provisions for awards	FI-G/L-G/L-SOA
Postprocessing the electronic bank statement	FI-BL-PT-BS, FI-BL-PT-US
Intercompany reconciliation (cross-system)	FI
Asset Accounting	FI-AA
Lease Accounting	FI-LA
Product Cost Controlling	CO-PC
Down Payment chains and progress reports	FI-AF-DPC, PS-REV-CPR
Flexible Real Estate Management	RE-FX

Table 1.2 Areas of Enhancement for Business Function EA-FIN

When this business function is activated using Transaction SFW5, as illustrated in Figure 1.8, the system activates the Business Configuration Sets (BC Sets) listed in Table 1.3.

Technical Name	Name	Description
EA-FIN-AKH	Enterprise Financials Switch for AKH	Adds the entries for component FIN to the application component hierarchy
EA-FIN-IMG	Enterprise Financials Switch for IMG	Adds the entries for component FIN to the SAP Reference IMG
EA-FIN-MENU	Enterprise Financials Switch for MENU	Adds the entries for component FIN to the SAP menu

Table 1.3 Activation of BC Sets

1   Preparation

E1D - Switch Framework: Change Business Function Status		
Check Discard Changes Activate Changes Switch Framework Browser Display Legend		
Business Function Set	SAP Retail	
Name	Description	Planned Status
▼ ISR_RETAIL	SAP Retail	
• ISR_RETAILSYSTEM	Other Enhancements for SAP Retail	Business func. will remain activated
▶ ENTERPRISE_BUSINESS_FUI	Enterprise Business Functions	
▼ ENTERPRISE_EXTENSIONS	Enterprise Extensions	
• /CUM/MAIN	Compatible Units	☐
• /SDF/WS_MON	Web Service Monitoring	☐
• EA-CP	Consumer Products	☐
• EA-DFP	DefenseForces&PublicSecurity	☐
• **EA-FIN**	**Financials Extension**	**Business func. will remain activated**
• EA-FRC	FERC: Regulatory Reporting	☐

Figure 1.8 EA-FIN Now Activated

1.7.3 Activate Business Function FIN_AA_CI_1

You can use this business function to be more flexible in the use of different fiscal year variants with parallel ledgers. After the activation of this business function, you can post depreciation to different ledger groups while using the ledger approach for parallel accounting. The individual ledgers assigned to these ledger groups can use different fiscal year variants, as long as their start and end dates are the same.

If business function FIN_AA_CI_1 using Transaction SFW5 isn't activated, the planned status is null, as shown in Figure 1.9. Thus, it needs to be activated to derive the benefits of posting depreciation to different ledger groups.

E1D - Switch Framework: Change Business Function Status		
Check Discard Changes Activate Changes Switch Framework Browser Display Legend		
Business Function Set	SAP Retail	
Name	Description	Planned Status
• **FIN_AA_CI_1**	**FI-AA, Asset Accounting (Reversible)**	☐
• FIN_AA_PARALLEL_VAL	FI-AA, Parallel Valuation	Business func. will remain activated

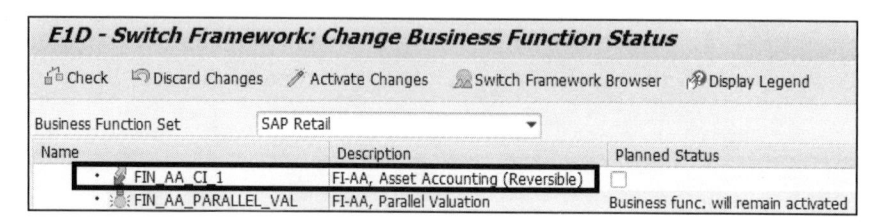

Figure 1.9 FIN_AA_CI_1 Not Yet Activated

> **References**
>
> For more information, see the following SAP Notes:
>
> - SAP Note 2240359: SAP S/4HANA—Always-Off Business Functions
> - SAP Note 2240360: SAP S/4HANA—Always-On Business Functions

1.8 Check and Activate New Depreciation Calculation

Next, you need to check if the new asset depreciation is active. Before activating the FI extension (EA-FIN), the system posts using the old depreciation calculation method; however, after this business function is activated, the system automatically switches to the new depreciation calculation.

Extension EA-FIN is activated using Transaction SFW5. To check whether the new depreciation calculation has been activated in the system, you need to execute Transaction AW01 and choose **Display Depreciation Calculation** to navigate to the fixed assets trace. Based on the new depreciation calculation, a different screen will appear. If the period interval procedure is listed in the header line of this screen, the new depreciation calculation has been activated. The new period-end process for FI-AA, including depreciation run and fiscal year change, is illustrated in the following sections.

1.8.1 Execute the Periodic Depreciation Posting Run

When you execute the periodic depreciation posting run, the calculated depreciation amounts are first compared to one another. To obtain the depreciation values with the "old" depreciation calculation, you can use Transaction AW01_AFAR (Asset Explorer: Old Depreciation Calculation). This transaction always uses the old depreciation calculation, even if the new depreciation is active.

Follow these steps if there is any problem with the new depreciation calculation:

1. Execute Transaction AW01 (Asset Explorer) for the fixed asset that has the depreciation differences. If the message states that the values of the fixed asset have changed, the depreciation for this fixed asset may not be current. In this case, the change value needs to be analyzed thoroughly. However, if the fixed asset wasn't changed and already existed before the changeover to the new depreciation calculation, the difference might be due to rounding off caused by the new depreciation calculation method.

2. In another SAP session, execute Transaction AW01_AFAR (Asset Explorer: Old Depreciation Calculation) for the same fixed asset. If the message states that the values of the fixed asset have changed, then it's obvious that the old depreciation calculation will provide a different result. You can calculate alternative values by choosing **Recalculate Depreciation**.

1 Preparation

3. After comparing the values of both the depreciation calculations, if the difference is found to be less than one integral currency unit, you may assume the cause to be a rounding difference due to the change in calculation procedure. For larger differences, the cause needs to be determined using the fixed assets trace by displaying the depreciation calculation procedure.

Use Transaction SA38 (or program FAA_DEPRECIATION_POST) to post the depreciation and interest to the G/L accounts in FI or to Cost Accounting, as shown in Figure 1.10.

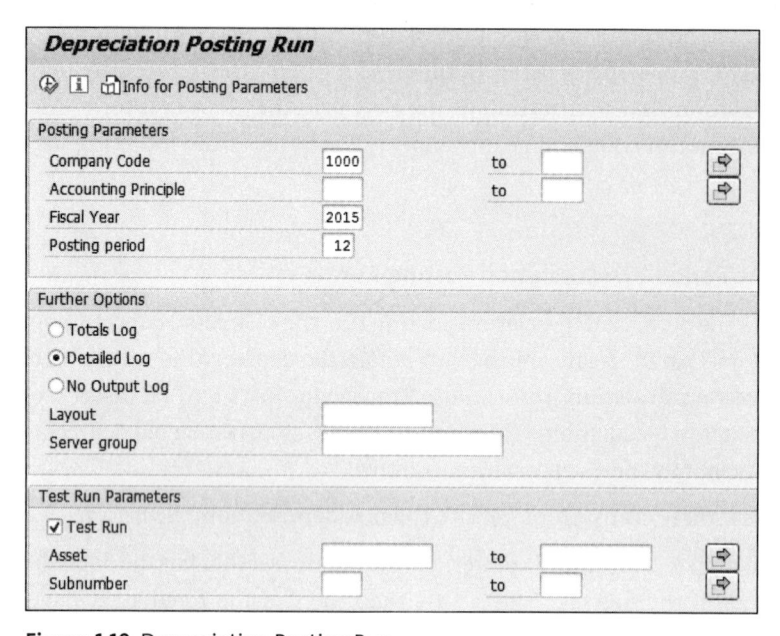

Figure 1.10 Depreciation Posting Run

After the program is run in the test run mode, and no errors are encountered, you may remove the test run check and then execute again.

> **Expert Insight**
>
> Periodic APC posting using Report RAPERB2000 is no longer necessary or supported.
>
> The update in the G/L takes place immediately instead. The indicator for posting to the G/L corresponds with the **Area Posts APC Immediately, Depreciation Periodically** option (BUHBKT = 4).

1.8.2 Execute Year-End Closing

The FI-AA fiscal year-end closing is carried out using Transaction AJAB, as illustrated in Figure 1.11. As a prerequisite, you need to ensure that all asset-related transactions have been posted for the fiscal year, the depreciation run has been executed, and the account reconciliation of AA and FI has been performed.

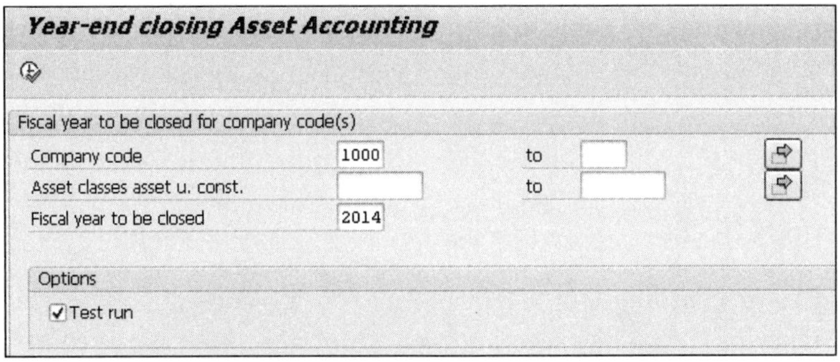

Figure 1.11 Transaction AJAB: Asset Accounting Year-End Close

1.8.3 Fiscal Year Change

The system opens a new fiscal year for a company code with the execution of the fiscal year change program. In doing so, the accumulated asset values from the previous fiscal year are carried forward to the new fiscal year. After the fiscal year change takes place, you can execute asset-related transactions and post to assets using value dates in the new fiscal year. Posting in the previous fiscal year is still allowed until the previous fiscal year is closed by running year-end closing program RAJABS00.

You can carry out the fiscal year change at any point in the new fiscal year. The FI-AA fiscal year change is carried out using Transaction AJRW, as illustrated in Figure 1.12.

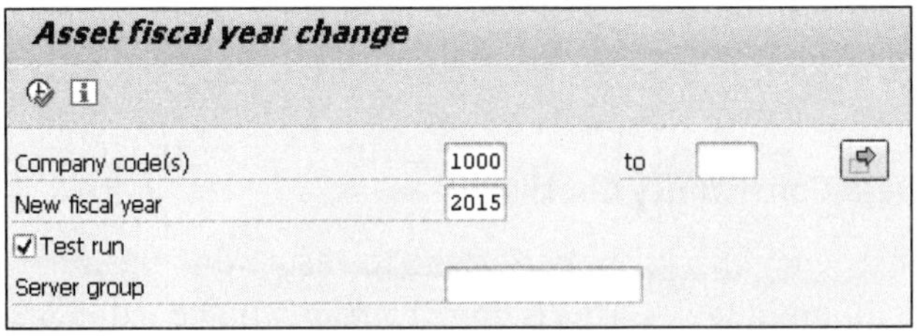

Figure 1.12 Transaction AJRW: Asset Fiscal Year Change

If you haven't carried out a fiscal year change, and you nonetheless post a transaction in the new fiscal year, the system automatically carries out a fiscal year change for the asset in question. If the fiscal year change has been made, and you post in the old fiscal year, the system automatically corrects the values for the asset in the current fiscal year and in the previous fiscal year.

The system starts the fiscal year change of FI-AA automatically with the balance carryforward to FI. The balance carryforward for the last representative ledger triggers the fiscal year change for all asset-relevant ledger groups in FI-AA as a background job.

1.9 Consistency Checks

Before migrating to or installing SAP S/4HANA Finance, it's imperative that you check the consistency of FI data by executing both financial and technical reports. Financial data reconciliation and check reports are covered in Section 1.12 of this chapter. A technical report can either be a preexisting custom-developed report or a report provided by SAP to check records from an old table to a new table.

Because SAP S/4HANA Finance introduces new architecture with fewer and new tables, data structures, and coding capabilities, you should perform consistency checks across multiple areas, including the following:

- Table indexes
- Historical and current FI-related data
- Cross-module reconciliation checks against the G/L to ensure the G/L reconciles with Accounts Payable/Accounts Receivable (AP/AR), Fixed Assets, and Materials Management (MM) against all ledgers and valuations

Perform the following activities in the test environment regardless of whether you're using classic or new General Ledger Accounting.

1.9.1 SAP ERP Financials Data Consistency Checks

During this activity, data consistency checks are performed to ensure that the financial data is consistent across different tables. This is done by comparing documents to indexes, checking documents against transactional data for all fiscal years, checking for duplicates, and identifying missing document headers (table BKPF) and line

1.9 Consistency Checks

items (table BSEG). Any difference in values and errors encountered should be corrected before moving to the next activity.

This activity is carried out using Transaction SA38 (program RFINDEX_NACC), as shown in Figure 1.13. This program checks the consistency of the document views from tables BSIS, BSAS, BSID, BSAD, BSIK, and BSAK with the line items in table BSEG.

If the test environment is a copy of the production instance, then select all the options. If the test environment has minimal transactional data, you can skip options such as **Check Clearing** and **Open Items Total**.

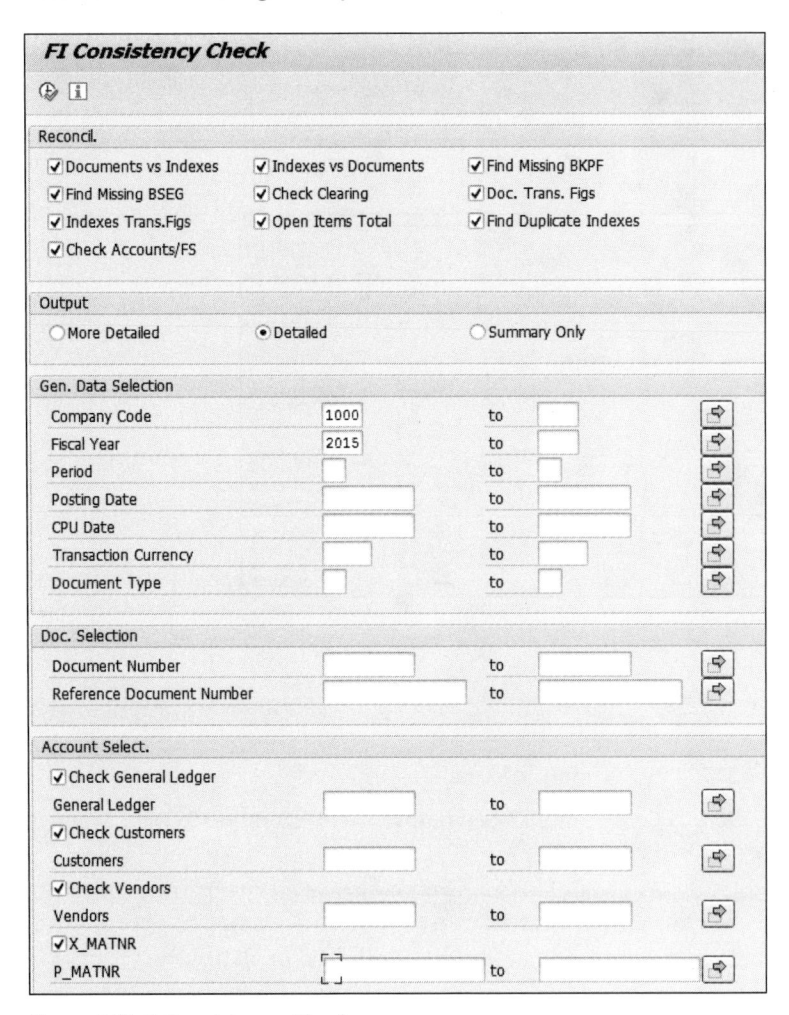

Figure 1.13 FI Consistency Check

1   Preparation

Upon execution, the report identified some differences between indexes and table GLT0 totals, as shown in Figure 1.14.

Summary of Reconciliation BSEG vs INDEX (Testmode)									
Table	BKPF	BSEG	BSIS	BSAS	BSID	BSAD	BSIK	BSAK	BSIM
Errors	0	2	0	0	0	0	0	0	0
Read	818	6,032	5,753	44	68	35	43	22	0

Summary of Reconciliation Index vs Bseg (Testmode)									
Table	BSIS	BSAS	BSID	BSAD	BSIK	BSAK	BSEG	BKPF	
Errors	2	0	0	0	0	0	0	0	
Read	5,753	47	68	35	43	25	5,971	5,971	

Summary of Clearing Check			
Table	BSAS	BSAD	BSAK
Errors found	0	0	0
Clearings checked	13	14	11
Indexes read	44	35	22

```
Company Code 1000 Smart US Company                                              Documents
Ledger 0  - HSL-Fields: Currency USD   Currency Type 10 Company code currency
Comparison Documents - KNC1 Level A                                  No Differences found

Comparison Documents - LFC1 Level A                                  No Differences found

Comparison Documents - GLT0 Level A
Account    RLDNR GJAHR GSBER PSWSL Field        Documents            GLT0         Difference

113025     0     2015        USD   TSL06_S            0.00         7,250.00        7,250.00-
                                   HSL06_S            0.00         7,250.00        7,250.00-
                                   TSL06_H      299,990.00-      307,240.00-       7,250.00
                                   HSL06_H      299,990.00-      307,240.00-       7,250.00
                                   TSL07_S       11,400.00        28,780.00       17,380.00-
                                   HSL07_S       11,400.00        28,780.00       17,380.00-
                                   TSL07_H       60,220.00-       77,600.00-      17,380.00
                                   HSL07_H       60,220.00-       77,600.00-      17,380.00

121000     0     2015        USD   TSL06_S      227,461.50       245,405.25       17,943.75-
                                   HSL06_S      227,461.50       245,405.25       17,943.75-
                                   TSL06_H       41,361.30-       59,305.05-      17,943.75
                                   HSL06_H       41,361.30-       59,305.05-      17,943.75
```

Figure 1.14 FI Consistency Check Result

> **References**
>
> See the following SAP Notes for more information:
>
> - SAP Note 1592904: FI Consistency Check in Advance of Migration to New G/L—Describes the Origin of These Differences
> - SAP Note 1835621: Correcting Inconsistency Errors—FAQ: Circular Posting

1.9.2 Reconciliation of the General Ledger and the Accounts Payable/Accounts Receivable Subledgers

This activity ensures that summary totals in G/L match the totals per AP and AR subledgers. The activity is carried out using Transaction SAPF190 (classic G/L) or Transaction FAGLF03 (new G/L), as shown in Figure 1.15.

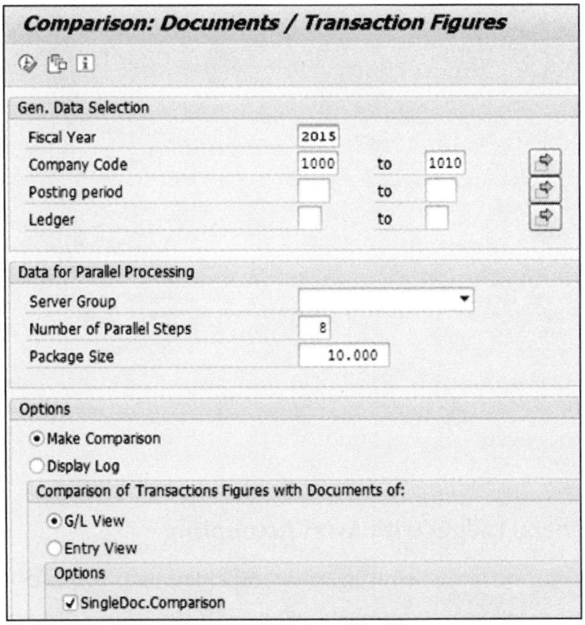

Figure 1.15 Comparison of Transaction Figures with Documents

This activity should be performed for the last fiscal year using the single document comparison option. During the execution, the system also checks Customizing for document types and number ranges, and it reports errors, if found. Possible errors include the following:

- No number ranges for specific ledgers
- No document types defined in ledgers

If no errors are encountered, the result appears as shown in Figure 1.16.

1 Preparation

Comparison of Document Transaction Figures

Differences per Ledger

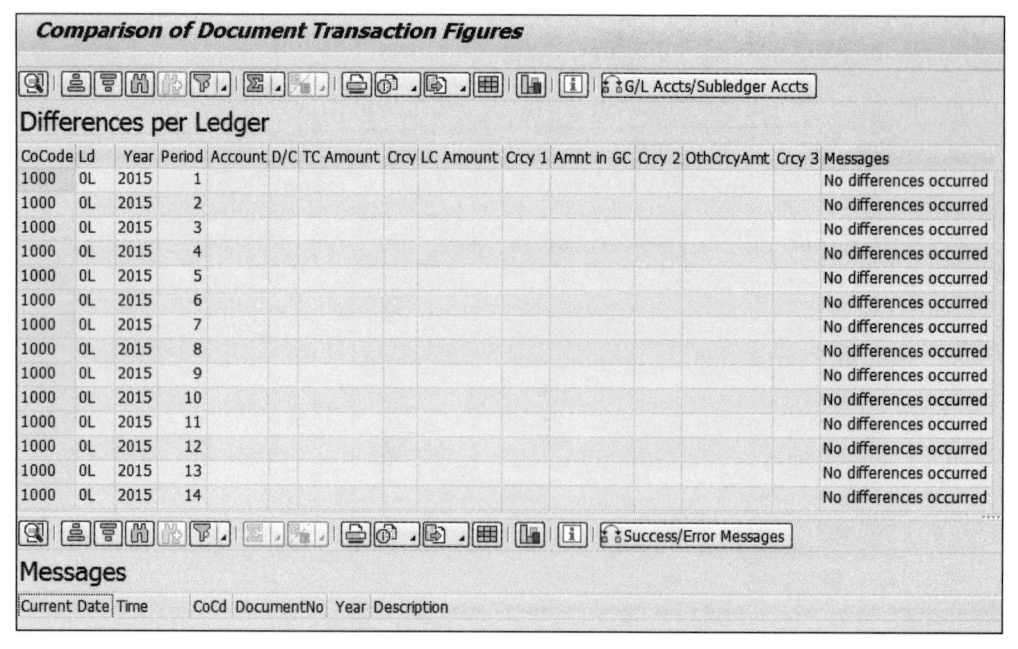

CoCode	Ld	Year	Period	Account	D/C	TC Amount	Crcy	LC Amount	Crcy 1	Amnt in GC	Crcy 2	OthCrcyAmt	Crcy 3	Messages
1000	0L	2015	1											No differences occurred
1000	0L	2015	2											No differences occurred
1000	0L	2015	3											No differences occurred
1000	0L	2015	4											No differences occurred
1000	0L	2015	5											No differences occurred
1000	0L	2015	6											No differences occurred
1000	0L	2015	7											No differences occurred
1000	0L	2015	8											No differences occurred
1000	0L	2015	9											No differences occurred
1000	0L	2015	10											No differences occurred
1000	0L	2015	11											No differences occurred
1000	0L	2015	12											No differences occurred
1000	0L	2015	13											No differences occurred
1000	0L	2015	14											No differences occurred

Messages

Current Date	Time	CoCd	DocumentNo	Year	Description

Figure 1.16 No Differences between Ledgers

1.9.3 Reconciliation of the General Ledger with Asset Accounting

The G/L and FI-AA are reconciled for both the leading and parallel ledgers. You must check and ensure that the last period closed in FI-AA matches with the last period in the G/L. Use Transaction SA38 (Program RAABST02) and select all the company codes that are active in the production environment and relevant for your organization (see Figure 1.17). This report can be used if you're using classic FI-AA or new Asset Accounting. Alternatively, you can use program RAABST01 if you're using classic FI-AA.

Reconcil. program FI-AA <-> G/L: List of accounts showing differences

Company codes	1000	to	1010
Layout			

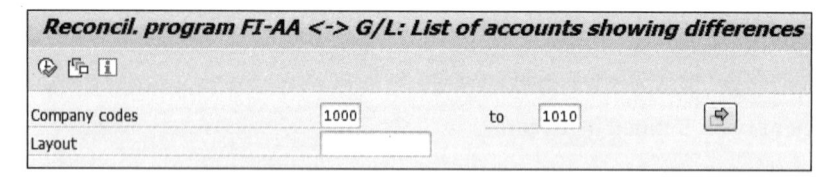

Figure 1.17 Reconciliation of FI-AA with G/L

1.9 Consistency Checks

Upon execution, the system highlights inconsistencies between FI-AA and G/L close periods, as shown in the display message in Figure 1.18.

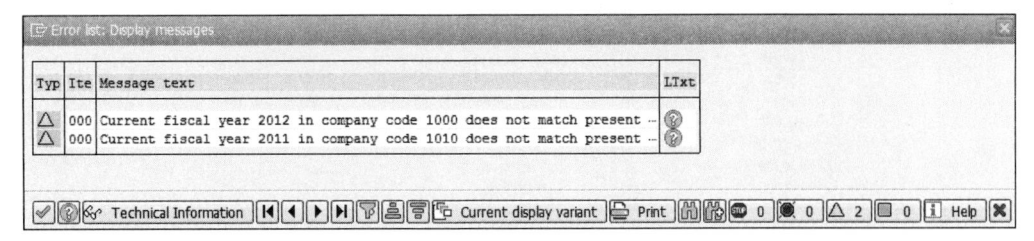

Figure 1.18 Error List for Differences between FI-AA and G/L Periods

To correct the inconsistencies, the FI-AA periodic processing and year change must be performed for the company codes in which the error was encountered. Run the following transactions (this is the usual closing procedure within FI-AA):

- Transaction AJRW (Fiscal Year Change)
- Transaction AFAB (Execute Depreciation)
- Transaction AJAB (Execute Year Closing)
- Transaction ASKB (APC Values Posting)

After execution of the closing steps for FI-AA, the consistency report must be rerun with no resulting errors, as shown in Figure 1.19.

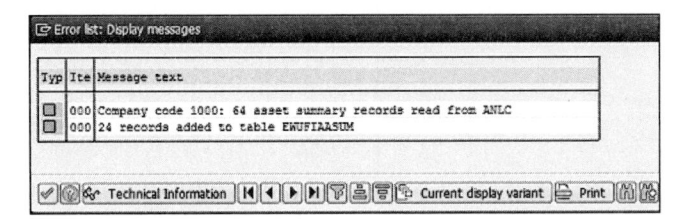

Figure 1.19 Error Message for FI-AA and G/L Reconciliation Resolved

Figure 1.20 shows that the value of assets in FI-AA is completely in sync and reconciled with the G/L.

1 Preparation

Reconcil. prog. FI-AA <-> General ledger / adjustmt posting (Analysis)

Sc	CoCd	Ld	Account	Doc.no.	Period	Year	Σ 1st LC Delta GL/AA
AS	1000	0L	160000			2015	515,260.84
			160010			2015	32,000,000.00
			160020			2015	2,024,000.00
			160040			2015	251,124.78
			160060			2015	136,260.88
			160070			2015	87,474.78
			160200			2015	1,620.00
			170000			2015	386,496.84-
			170010			2015	8,000,000.00-
			170020			2015	741,760.00-
			170040			2015	109,707.38-
			170060			2015	43,847.84-
			170070			2015	35,615.30-
			170200			2015	1,620.00-
		0L					• 25,696,693.92
							•• 25,696,693.92

Figure 1.20 Reconciled List of FI-AA with G/L

1.9.4 Reconciliation of the General Ledger with Materials Management

Simply put, the objective of this activity is to ensure that the summary totals in the G/L match the totals in the MM subledger. You can carry out this activity using Transaction SA38 (program RM07MBST and program RM07MMFI). The report must be executed for each fiscal year (current and prior year), as shown in Figure 1.21 and Figure 1.22.

MM/FI balance comparison

Database Selection
Company Code   1000   to

Functions and Layouts
⦿ Perform MM-FI Balance Comparison
Parameters for MM-FI Balance Comparison
  ⦿ Current Period
  ○ Previous Period
  ○ Previous Year
  ○ Year Before Last

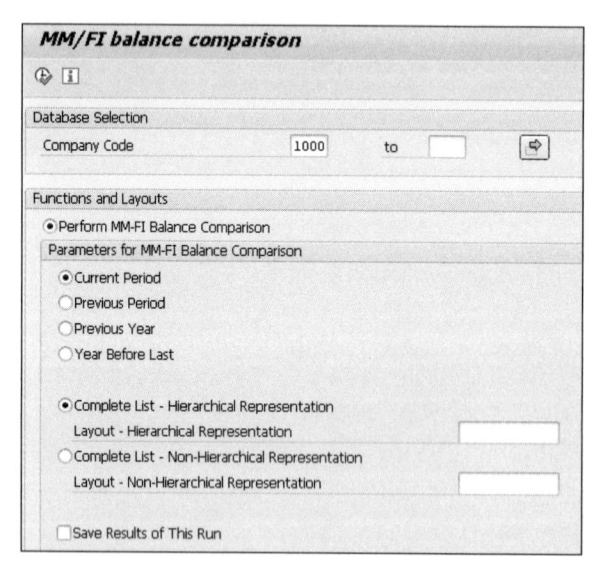

  ⦿ Complete List - Hierarchical Representation
    Layout - Hierarchical Representation
  ○ Complete List - Non-Hierarchical Representation
    Layout - Non-Hierarchical Representation

  ☐ Save Results of This Run

Figure 1.21 MM-FI Balance Comparison Using Program RM07MMFI

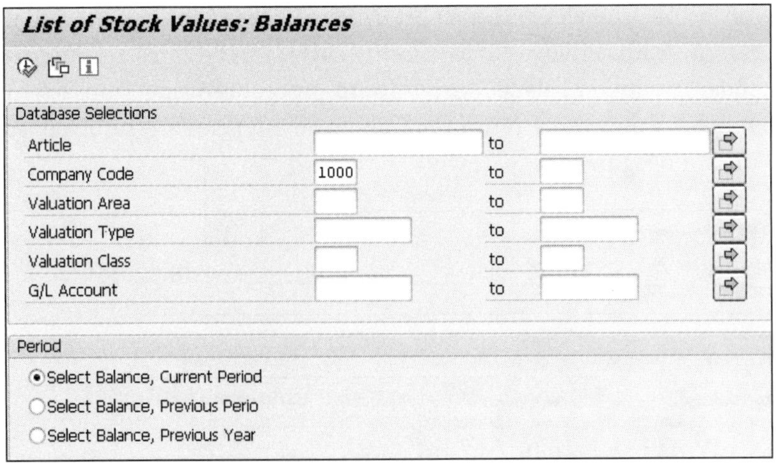

Figure 1.22 Stock Value Balances Using Program RM07MBST

You might find some inconsistencies after execution of the report, which will appear as shown in Figure 1.23 and Figure 1.24, respectively.

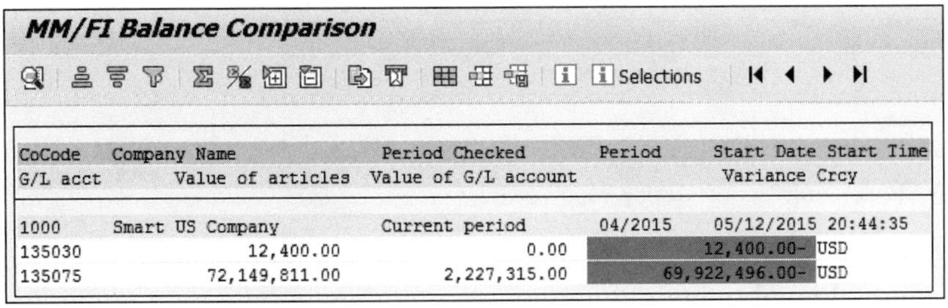

Figure 1.23 Error in MM/FI Balance

Figure 1.24 Error in Stock Value Balances

You might identify inconsistencies in this report that are linked to the nonexecution of the balance carryforward activity. These inconsistencies can be corrected by performing the standard year-end balance carryforward procedure using Transaction FAGLGVTR. The report needs to be rerun until all inconsistencies are resolved, as shown in Figure 1.25 and Figure 1.26.

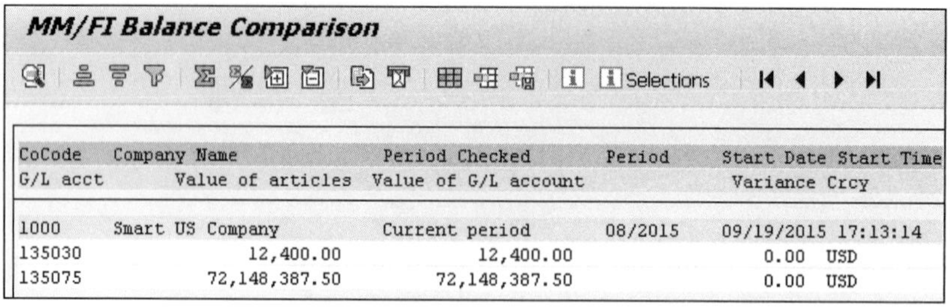

MM/FI Balance Comparison

Selections

CoCode	Company Name	Period Checked	Period	Start Date	Start Time
G/L acct	Value of articles	Value of G/L account		Variance	Crcy
1000	Smart US Company	Current period	08/2015	09/19/2015	17:13:14
135030	12,400.00	12,400.00		0.00	USD
135075	72,148,387.50	72,148,387.50		0.00	USD

Figure 1.25 MM-FI Inconsistencies Resolved

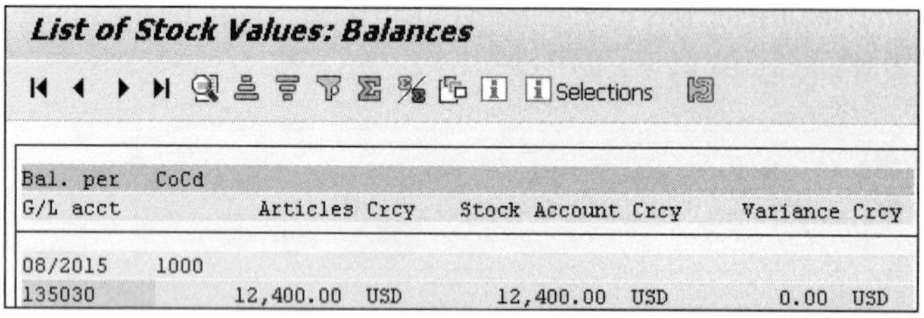

List of Stock Values: Balances

Selections

Bal. per	CoCd					
G/L acct	Articles	Crcy	Stock Account	Crcy	Variance	Crcy
08/2015	1000					
135030	12,400.00	USD	12,400.00	USD	0.00	USD

Figure 1.26 Stock Value Inconsistency Resolved

1.9.5 Reconciliation of Ledgers

If you're using the new G/L, then you must handle this activity by comparing all the ledgers and checking that they reconcile by executing Program RGUCOMP4 using Transaction SA38 or Transaction GCAC. This program compares the totals record of any two ledgers—leading, nonleading, or any other ledgers—as used for tax or management accounting purposes or with varying fiscal year variants and charts of accounts.

The ledger comparison report must be executed for each fiscal year, as shown in Figure 1.27. Upon execution, you need to ensure that no inconsistencies are found in the ledger totals (see Figure 1.28).

1.9 Consistency Checks

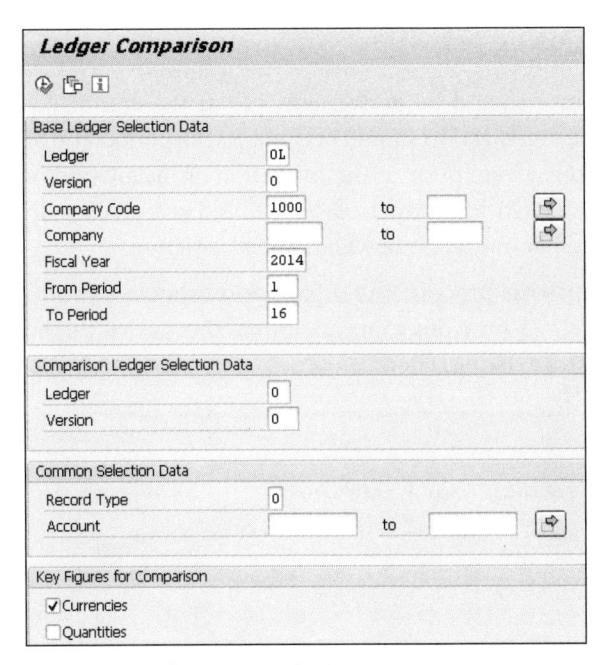

Figure 1.27 Ledger Comparison

Ledger Comparison: Totals

Comparison of Comp. code currency

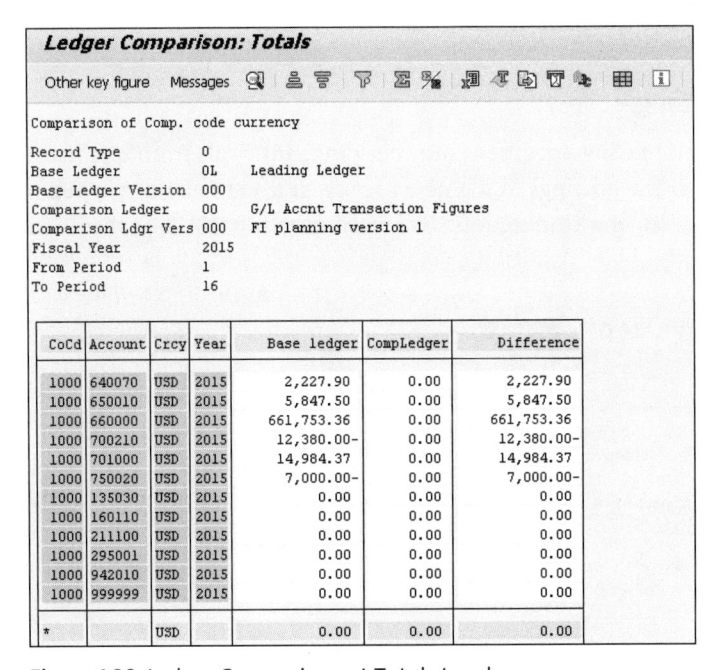

Record Type   0
Base Ledger   0L   Leading Ledger
Base Ledger Version 000
Comparison Ledger   00   G/L Accnt Transaction Figures
Comparison Ldgr Vers 000   FI planning version 1
Fiscal Year   2015
From Period   1
To Period   16

CoCd	Account	Crcy	Year	Base ledger	CompLedger	Difference
1000	640070	USD	2015	2,227.90	0.00	2,227.90
1000	650010	USD	2015	5,847.50	0.00	5,847.50
1000	660000	USD	2015	661,753.36	0.00	661,753.36
1000	700210	USD	2015	12,380.00-	0.00	12,380.00-
1000	701000	USD	2015	14,984.37	0.00	14,984.37
1000	750020	USD	2015	7,000.00-	0.00	7,000.00-
1000	135030	USD	2015	0.00	0.00	0.00
1000	160110	USD	2015	0.00	0.00	0.00
1000	211100	USD	2015	0.00	0.00	0.00
1000	295001	USD	2015	0.00	0.00	0.00
1000	942010	USD	2015	0.00	0.00	0.00
1000	999999	USD	2015	0.00	0.00	0.00
*		USD		0.00	0.00	0.00

Figure 1.28 Ledger Comparison at Totals Level

1.10 Perform Period-End Closing Activities

Migration to SAP S/4HANA Finance should be performed only at the end of the period or fiscal year. Therefore, the organization should perform its full period-end or year-end close in the premigration system prior to the migration or installation of SAP S/4HANA Finance. In addition to closing the period, you should lock all users in the system to whom no installation or migration tasks have been assigned.

Period-end close is a standard business process. The organization should perform this according to its own schedule. SAP provides some additional checks that can be incorporated into the organization's existing schedule.

> **References**
>
> For information on these checks, see the following SAP Notes:
> - SAP Note 1939592: Precheck Report for Migrating to New Asset Accounting
> - SAP Note 2129306: Check Customizing Settings Prior to Upgrade to SAP S/4HANA Finance

The following sections detail the activities you need to perform in your test system and the results you need to document.

1.10.1 Copy Number Ranges

In this activity, you need to copy document number range intervals from one fiscal year into another so that the postings in the new fiscal year don't fail. Do so by executing program RFNRIV20 using Transaction SA38 or Transaction OBH2, as shown in Figure 1.29.

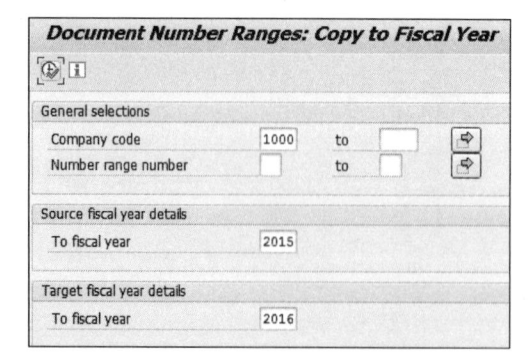

Figure 1.29 Copying Number Ranges from One Fiscal Year to Another

1.10.2 Lock Periods in Materials Management

Certain stocks and valuation data, such as total value, total stock, valuation class, price control indicator, and price unit, are managed by period control. For values and goods movements to be posted to the correct period, the period must be set whenever a new period starts. This is done with period-closing program RMMMPERI using Transaction SA38 so that no MM-related postings can be made, as shown in Figure 1.30. In this scenario, select **Check and Close Period**.

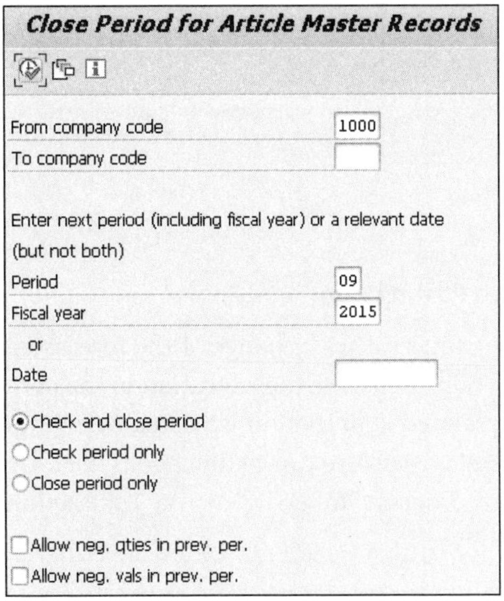

Figure 1.30 Closing Materials Management Period

1.10.3 Perform Closing for Periodic Asset Postings

Executing the asset year-end closing program checks the data for the previous fiscal year and blocks the postings for the current fiscal year from any further changes. It also checks the following:

- Asset value postings in the G/L
- Depreciation postings
- Computation of net book value based on the rules defined for the company code

1   Preparation

In this activity, all previous fiscal years need to be closed for FI-AA except the current fiscal year. Do so by executing program RAJABS00 using Transaction SA38, specifying the company code and fiscal year as shown in Figure 1.31.

Year-end closing Asset Accounting			
Fiscal year to be closed for company code(s)			
Company code	1000	to	
Asset classes asset u. const.		to	
Fiscal year to be closed	2014		
Options			
☑ Test run			

Figure 1.31 Year-End Closing for Asset Accounting

1.10.4   Execute the Periodic Depreciation Posting Run

Any change to asset-related transaction postings causes a change of the forecasted depreciation. However, the asset value isn't updated until the execution of the periodic depreciation posting run when the planned depreciation is posted as a lump sum amount directly to FI. This is a required step before closing the books in FI-AA. You can execute depreciation posting run program RAPOST2000 via Transaction SA38.

1.10.5   Verify Held Documents Status

You need to ensure that all documents in held status have either been posted or deleted before the migration to SAP S/4HANA Finance by following these steps:

1. Use Transaction FB50 to post held documents. In the transaction screen menu bar, choose **Edit • Select Held Document**.
2. Execute program RFTMPBLD using Transaction SA38 to delete held documents.
3. You can also delete individual held documents using Transaction FB50. In the transaction screen menu bar, select **Edit • Delete Held Document**, as shown in Figure 1.32.

1.10 Perform Period-End Closing Activities

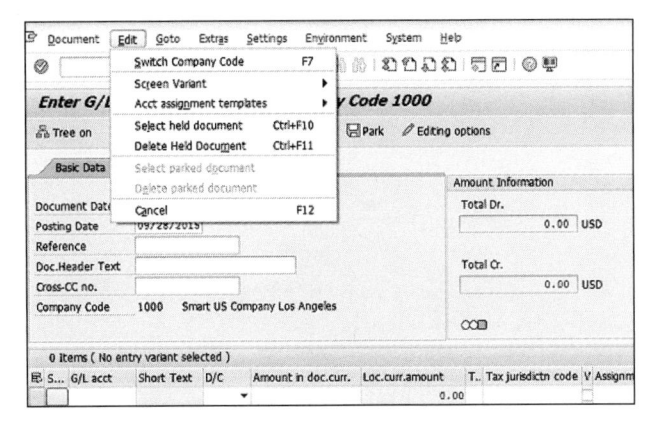

Figure 1.32 Deleting Held Documents

1.10.6 Carry Balances Forward to the Current Fiscal Year

You need to ensure that all ledger balances, including balances in subledgers, have been carried forward to the current fiscal year. You can use Transaction FAGLGVTR to carry forward the balances for all currencies and ledgers from the previous to the new fiscal year for a specific ledger in General Ledger Accounting. The selection screen appears as shown in Figure 1.33.

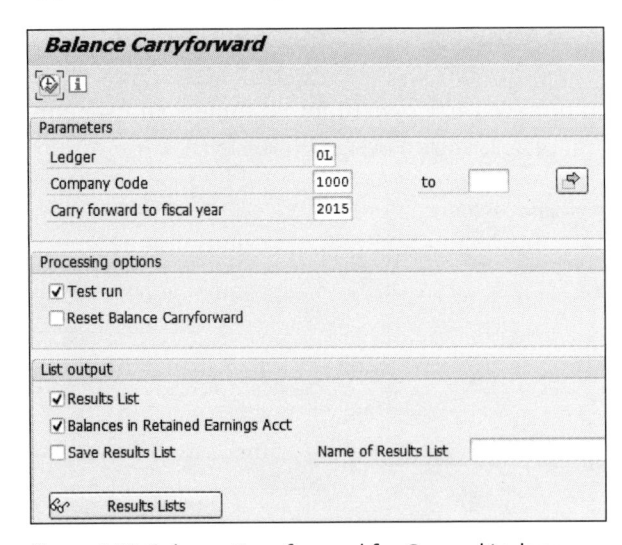

Figure 1.33 Balance Carryforward for General Ledger

The result of the execution appears as shown in Figure 1.34.

1   Preparation

Balance carryforwardLedger 0L for the year 2015 Update run

Balance sheet accounts   Retained earnings accounts   Technical Information   Help

Ty	Message Text
☐	Log for Balance Carryforward
☐	Processing type Update run
☐	Fiscal Year 2015
☐	Ledger 0L
☐	RecType 0
☐	Version 001
☐	Company Code 1000
☐	Balance carry forward successfully completed
☐	List display of records carried forward possible using the "balance sheet" or "retained ear...

Figure 1.34 Balance Carryforward for G/L Successfully Completed

Use Transaction AJRW to carry forward the accumulated asset values from the previous fiscal year to the new fiscal year, as shown in Figure 1.35.

Asset fiscal year change

Company code(s)	1000	to	
New fiscal year	2016		
✓ Test run			
Server group			

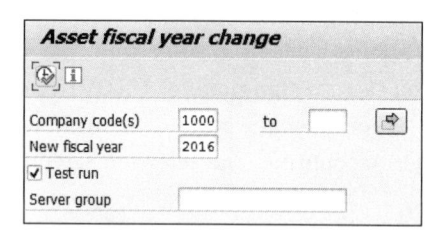

Figure 1.35 Fiscal Year Change for Asset Accounting

Use Transaction F.07 to perform balance carryforward for customers and vendors from the previous to the new fiscal year, as shown in Figure 1.36.

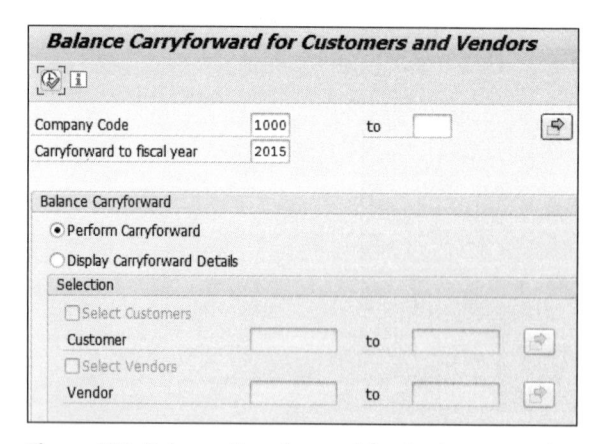

Balance Carryforward for Customers and Vendors

Company Code	1000	to	
Carryforward to fiscal year	2015		

Balance Carryforward
- ● Perform Carryforward
- ○ Display Carryforward Details

Selection
- ☐ Select Customers
- Customer   to
- ☐ Select Vendors
- Vendor   to

Figure 1.36 Balance Carryforward for Customers and Vendors

1.10.7 Reset Valuations for Periods in the Current Fiscal Year

To create your financial statements before migration to SAP S/4HANA Finance, you must run the foreign currency valuation using program FAGL_FCV in Transaction SA38, as shown in Figure 1.37. This valuation will include the following accounts and items:

- **Foreign currency balance sheet accounts**

  The G/L accounts that are valuated in foreign currency have the account type of **Balance Sheet Account**; account currency is maintained as foreign currency, which isn't the company code currency; and **Open Item Management** isn't checked, which means that it's not managed on an open item basis.

- **Open items that were posted in foreign currency**

  Open items that are valuated in foreign currency remain open as on the key date and are posted in a currency other than the company code currency.

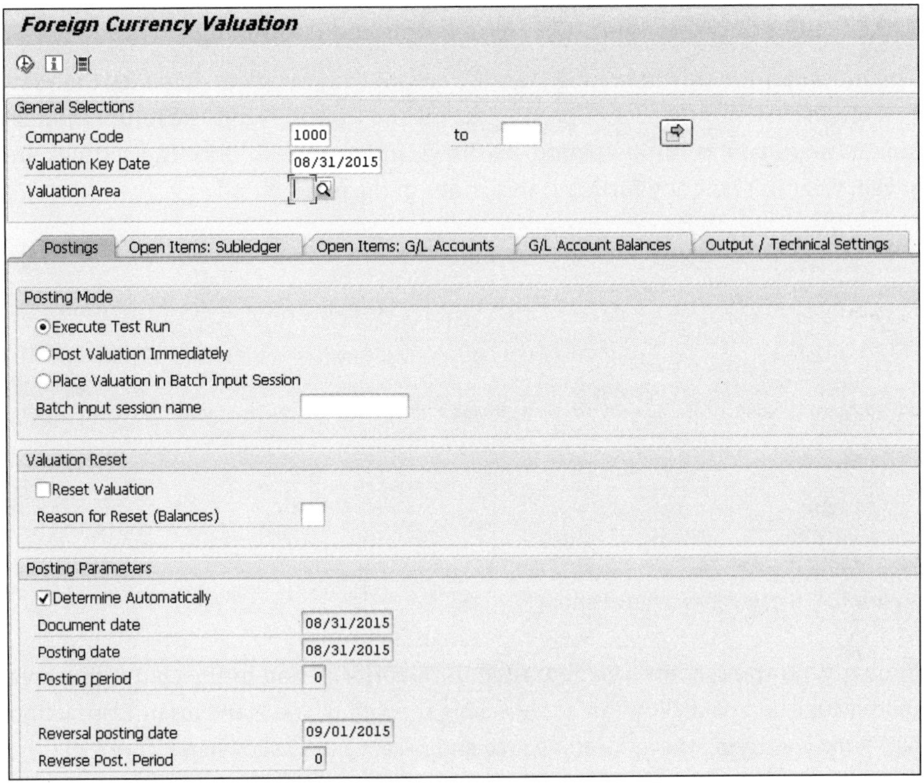

Figure 1.37 Foreign Currency Valuation

In foreign currency valuation, you have the following options:

- You can perform the valuation in either the local currency, which is your company code currency, or in the parallel currency, which is maintained as the group currency in the configuration.
- You can choose from various valuation methods, such as the lowest value principle, per the organization's policy.
- You can translate additional currencies from the local company code currency; a foreign currency valuation automatically performs a currency translation in accordance with GAAP principles.

The best practice is to run the program in test mode, and then analyze the log and any errors that appear in the log. After all the errors have been resolved, you may run the program in production mode to post the valuation to FI.

1.10.8 Lock Prior Periods in SAP ERP Financials and Controlling

You must perform this task using Transaction OB52 after you've completed the year-end closing activities. It locks a posting period and thus prevents the future submission of any updates in that period, as shown in Figure 1.38. Once the settings are saved, you can't post any further transactions in the prior period.

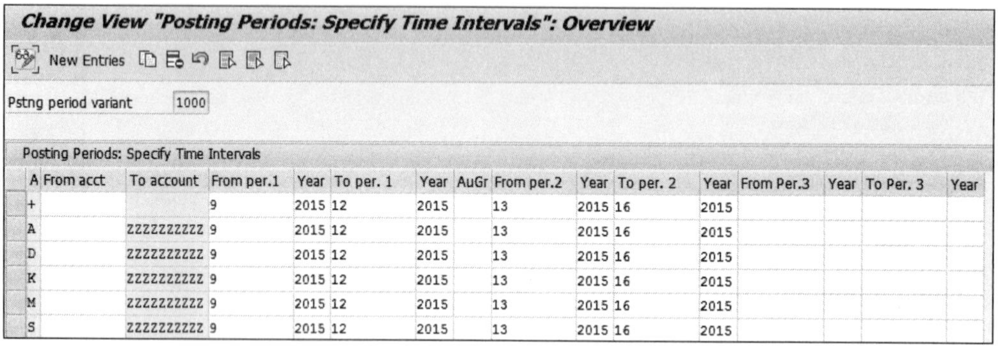

A	From acct	To account	From per.1	Year	To per. 1	Year	AuGr	From per.2	Year	To per. 2	Year	From Per.3	Year	To Per. 3	Year
+			9	2015	12	2015		13	2015	16	2015				
A		ZZZZZZZZZZ	9	2015	12	2015		13	2015	16	2015				
D		ZZZZZZZZZZ	9	2015	12	2015		13	2015	16	2015				
K		ZZZZZZZZZZ	9	2015	12	2015		13	2015	16	2015				
M		ZZZZZZZZZZ	9	2015	12	2015		13	2015	16	2015				
S		ZZZZZZZZZZ	9	2015	12	2015		13	2015	16	2015				

Figure 1.38 Close Prior Posting Period: FI

Similarly, no transactions can be posted in the prior period in the controlling area (both actual and plan). You can do this using the **Actual** and **Plan** tabs in Transaction OKP1 and specifying the controlling area and fiscal year, as shown in Figure 1.39.

1.10 Perform Period-End Closing Activities

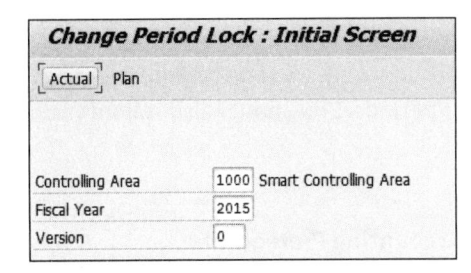

Figure 1.39 Close Prior Posting Period: CO

Subsequently, you can select the period that you want to lock, as shown in Figure 1.40.

Figure 1.40 Closing All Prior CO Periods for Fiscal Year

93

1.10.9 Batch Jobs

You need to check if all the existing batch jobs have been executed and delete any batch jobs that have been scheduled for later periods. You should also refrain from scheduling any new batch jobs.

1.10.10 Execute Report to Confirm Asset Accounting Prerequisites

Using Transaction SA38, execute program RASFIN_MIGR_PRECHECK once again to check whether all the prerequisites related to FI-AA have been complied with after all the period-end and year-end closing activities have been run (see Figure 1.41).

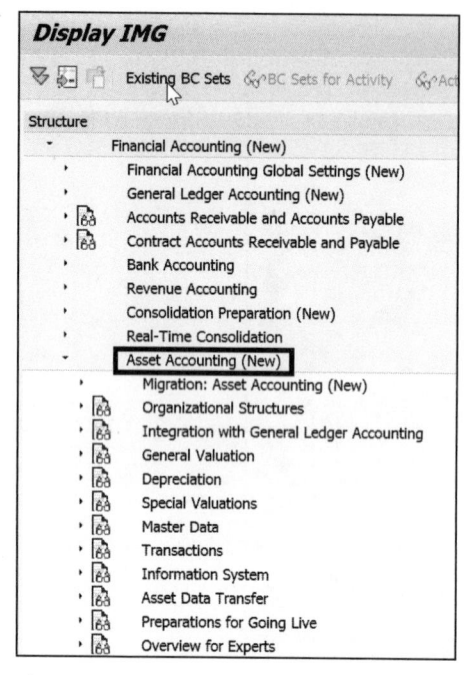

Figure 1.41 Prerequisite Check before FI-AA Migration

1.10.11 Lock Users

All the users in the system who don't have any assigned tasks related to the migration or installation of SAP S/4HANA Finance must be locked from posting any transactions or making any configuration changes.

1.11 Consistency Check before Activation of SAP S/4HANA Finance

Program FINS_MIG_PRECHCK_CUST_SETTNGS via Transaction SA38 must be executed to check the consistency of your ledger, company code, and controlling area settings to determine if a migration to SAP S/4HANA Finance is feasible. The program checks whether the currency settings of the company codes and ledgers are consistent and compatible with the new table architecture.

If you get an error during the execution of this program, you need to resolve it first so that the precheck can be passed. For example, you may get an error related to an SAP organization unit, as shown in Figure 1.42.

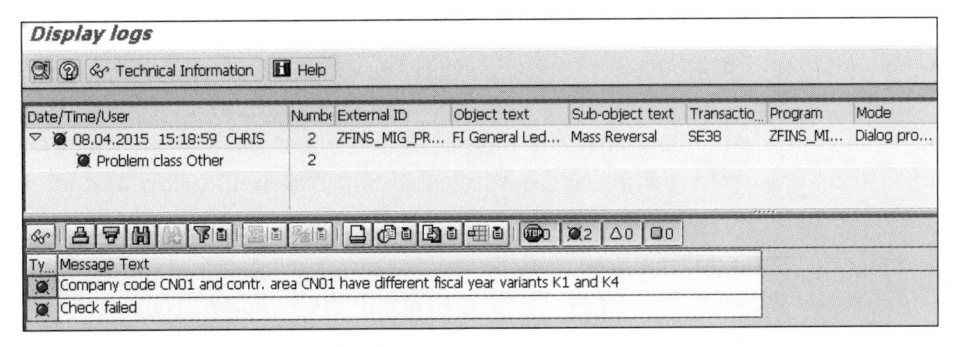

Figure 1.42 Display Log for Precheck Error

To correct this error, you need to change the fiscal year variant to K4 for controlling area CNO1 so that both the company code and controlling area can have the same fiscal year variant.

After the correction of the error, the report log no longer shows any errors (see Figure 1.43).

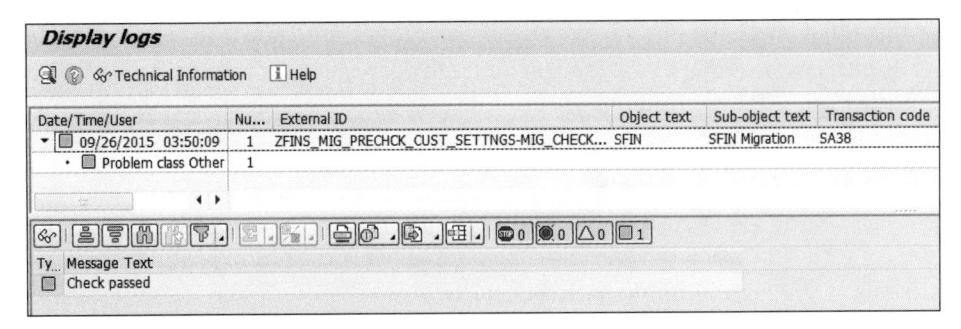

Figure 1.43 Display Log for Precheck Passed

1   Preparation

You may also get the error if, for some company codes, currencies were assigned to a nonleading ledger but not to the leading ledger. In this case, it's necessary to correct the currency assignment for all company codes, even if they aren't actively used.

> **References**
>
> For more information, see SAP Note 2129306: Check Customizing Settings Prior to Upgrade to SAP S/4HANA Finance.

1.12   Execute Business Reconciliation

Before migration, it's prudent that you execute the following programs and transactions and create the documentation for the financial reports and results so that you can compare the data after the migration to check if there is any financial imbalance. This reconciliation will ensure consistent data both before and after migration.

- **Program RFBILA00 (Financial Statements)**
  The report shown in Figure 1.44 creates the balance sheet and P&L statements for a specified reporting period within a fiscal year for the purpose of absolute and relative comparisons for a given time period. Alternatively, planned values can also be used for comparison with the actuals. To do this, specify the planned version number in the **Plan Version** field.

- **Program RKKBSELL (Sales Order Selection)**
  This report is used to analyze sales order items that carry costs and revenues. You can select and analyze these sales order items according to the selection criteria as relevant to your organization. The sales order items with actual costs and revenues that meet the specific criteria set as a filter are shown in user-definable results lists (see Figure 1.45). From an order in the results list, you can navigate and drill down to the detailed reports.

1.12 Execute Business Reconciliation

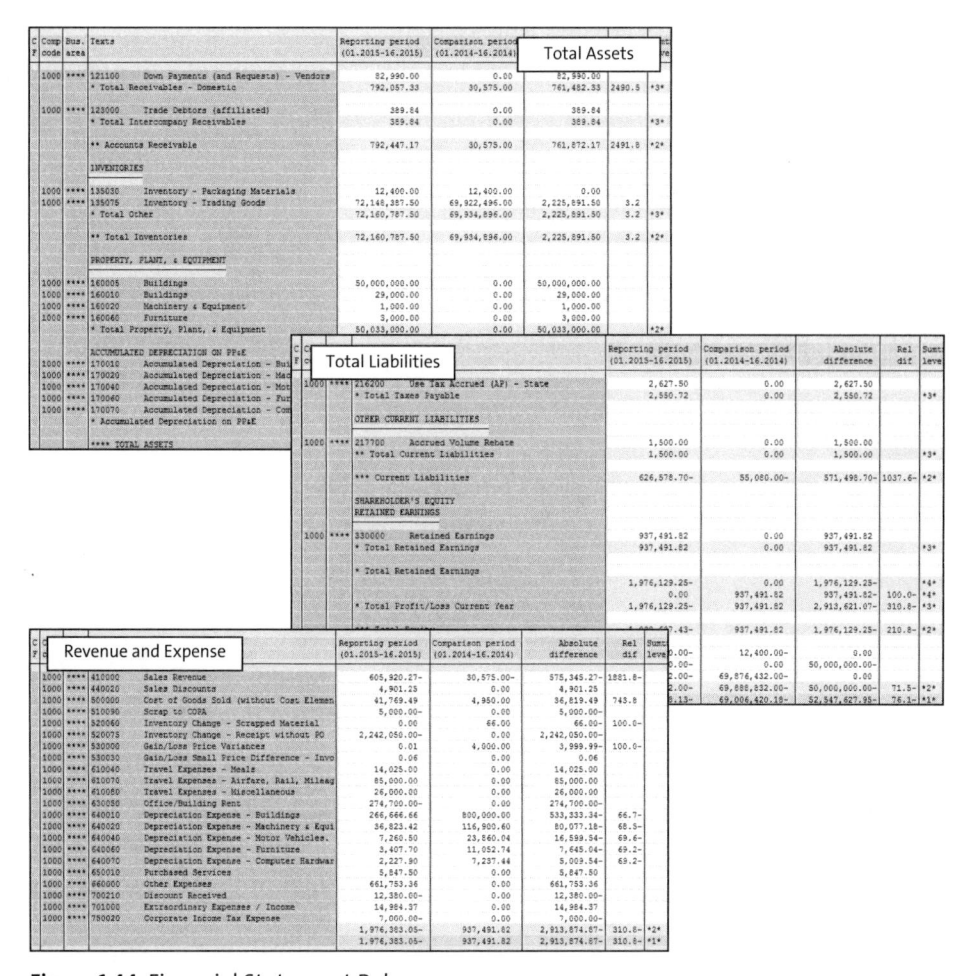

Figure 1.44 Financial Statement Balances

Figure 1.45 Sales Order Selection List

- **Program RFSSLD00 (G/L Account Balance List)**
  The G/L account balance list (see Figure 1.46) shows the following monthly figures:
  - Balance carried forward at the beginning of the fiscal year
  - Total of the period or periods carried forward
  - Debit and credit total of the reporting period
  - End balance of the reporting period
  - Debit balances or credit balances at the close of the reporting period
- **Program RFSOPO00 (G/L Line Items List)**
  This program lists open or cleared items that you can select for specific time intervals. The list shown in Figure 1.47 includes G/L account items that are open at the key date you specify in the selection screen. It also includes the cleared items for which clearing dates are within the range specified in the selection screen. You may choose all accounts or those managed on an open item basis only.

G/L Account Balances

Smart US Company   G/L Account Balances   Time 13:27:28   Date 09/27/201
Los Angeles   Ledger 0L   RFSSLD00/AMAHESHWARI Page
Carryforward Periods 00-00 2015 Reporting Periods 01-16 2015

CoCd	G/L acct	Short Text	Crcy	BusA	Balance Carryforward	Balance,prev.periods	Debit rept.period	Credit report per.	Accumulated balance
1000	640040	Depr Exp - Vehicles	USD		0.00	0.00	7,260.50	0.00	7,260.50
1000	640060	Depr Exp - Furniture	USD		0.00	0.00	3,407.70	0.00	3,407.70
1000	640070	Depr Exp - Hardware	USD		0.00	0.00	2,227.90	0.00	2,227.90
1000	650010	Purchased Services	USD		0.00	0.00	9,247.50	3,400.00	5,847.50
1000	660000	Other Expenses	USD		0.00	0.00	750,763.36	89,010.00	661,753.36
1000	700210	Discount Received	USD		0.00	0.00	600.00	12,980.00	12,380.00-
1000	701000	Extraord Exp/Inc	USD		0.00	0.00	14,994.79	10.42	14,984.37
1000	750020	Corp Inc Tax Exp	USD		0.00	0.00	0.00	7,000.00	7,000.00-
1000	942010	Build&Maint	USD		0.00	0.00	88,110.00	88,110.00	0.00
1000	999999	Legacy Asset transfe	USD		0.00	0.00	50,300,000.00	50,300,000.00	0.00
*1000			USD		0.00	0.00	158,704,363.16	158,704,363.16	0.00

Smart US Company   G/L Account Balances   Time 13:27:28   Date 09/27/2015
Los Angeles   Ledger 0L   RFSSLD00/AMAHESHWARI Page   2
Carryforward Periods 00-00 2015 Reporting Periods 01-16 2015
T O T A L S F R O M A L L C O M P A N Y C O D E S

CoCd	Crcy	BusA	Balance Carryforward	Balance,prev.periods	Debit rept.period	Credieport per.	Accumulated balance
1000	USD		0.00	0.00	158,704,363.16	1504,363.16	0.00
*	USD		0.00	0.00	158,704,363.16	1504,363.16	0.00

Figure 1.46 G/L Account Balances

1.12 Execute Business Reconciliation

G/L line items

Smart US Company
Los Angeles
G/L line items

Pstng Date	Type	DocumentNo	Doc. Date	PK	NP	Assignment	Clearing	Clrng doc.	Crcy	Amount in FC	Amount in local cur.
CoCode 1000		G/L acct 111000				Long Text Petty Cash					
05/27/2015	SA	100000000	05/27/2015	50		20150527			USD		1,000.00-
06/10/2015	DZ	1400000000	06/10/2015	40		20150610			USD		550.00
06/25/2015	SA	100000002	06/25/2015	50		20150625			USD		25,000.00-
06/25/2015	SA	100000003	06/24/2015	50		20150625			USD		12,000.00-
07/16/2015	SA	100000016	07/16/2015	50		20150716			USD		1,000.00-
07/20/2015	SA	100000025	07/20/2015	50		20150720			USD		700.00-
07/25/2015	SA	100000030	07/25/2015	50		20150725			USD		800.00-
07/30/2015	SA	100000029	07/29/2015	50		20150730			USD		1,000.00-
08/04/2015	SA	100000031	08/04/2015	50		20150804			USD		55.00-
08/04/2015	SA	100000032	08/04/2015	50		20150804			USD		60.00-
08/06/2015	SA	100000036	07/17/2015	40		20150806			USD		5,000.00
08/06/2015	SA	100000036	07/17/2015	50		20150806			USD		5,000.00-
* Business Area									USD		41,065.00-
** G/L Account 111000									USD		41,065.00-

Smart US Company
Los Angeles
G/L line items

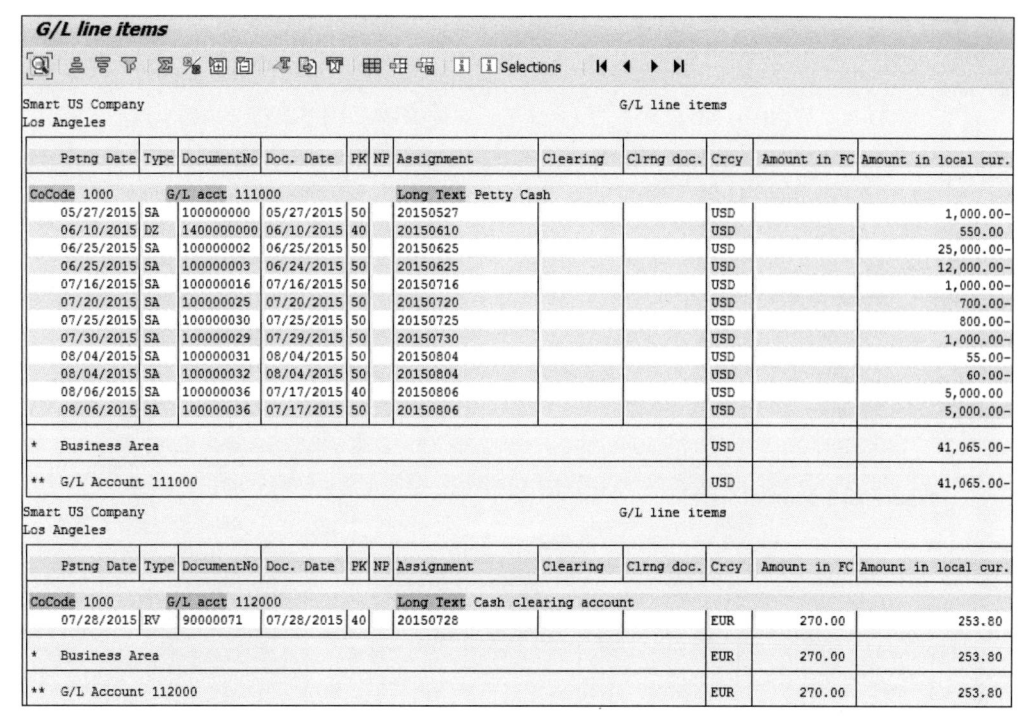

Pstng Date	Type	DocumentNo	Doc. Date	PK	NP	Assignment	Clearing	Clrng doc.	Crcy	Amount in FC	Amount in local cur.
CoCode 1000		G/L acct 112000				Long Text Cash clearing account					
07/28/2015	RV	90000071	07/28/2015	40		20150728			EUR	270.00	253.80
* Business Area									EUR	270.00	253.80
** G/L Account 112000									EUR	270.00	253.80

Figure 1.47 G/L Line Items

- **Program RFBELJ00 (Compact Document Journal)**
  The compact document journal program shows the most important data from document headers and line items for the selected documents. The tabular list shown in Figure 1.48 can be used for a compact journal and for reconciliation with balance lists (accounting reconciliation).

  The summarized version of the journal by period is shown in Figure 1.49 for a quick glance at the balances.

1 Preparation

CoCd	DocumentNo	Year	Type	Pstng Date	Document Status					Reference	Rev. with	Year Crcy	Doc.No.
AccTy	Account		PstKy	(Sub Amount in LC (FC)		Tax Line I Amount (Tax Line)		Tx PK	G/L		LC Amount		GL Itm
1000	90000010	2015	RV	01/01/2015						0090000010		USD	90000010
D	M001		01		69.43	01		3.93-	01 50	410000	36.00-		
									01 50	410000	25.00-		
									01 50	410000	4.50-		
1000	90000011	2015	RV	04/23/2015						PCS-C301		USD	90000011
D	PCS-C301		01		650.00				00 50	410000	325.00-		
									00 50	410000	325.00-		
1000	90000019	2015	RV	06/09/2015						22		USD	90000019
D	PCS-C301		01		550.00				00 50	410000	550.00-		
1000	90000022	2015	RV	06/10/2015						0090000022		USD	90000022
D	PCS-C301		01		419.00				00 50	410000	9.00-		
									00 50	410000	280.00-		
									00 50	410000	130.00-		
1000	90000023	2015	RV	06/10/2015						25		USD	90000023
D	PCS-C301		01		145.80				00 50	410000	130.00-		
									00 50	410000	8.80-		
									00 50	410000	2.00-		
									00 50	410000	5.00-		

Figure 1.48 Journal Details

CoCd	Crcy	Period	LC Debit	LC Credit	SG	Debit (Customer)	Credit (Cust.)	SG	Debit (Vendor)	Credit (Vendor)
1000	USD	01/2015	151,319,360.97	151,319,360.97		40,069.43	0.00		0.00	0.00
1000	USD	02/2015	2,358,596.56	2,358,596.56		60,000.00	0.00		0.00	0.00
1000	USD	03/2015	208,654.54	208,654.54		60,000.00	60,000.00		0.00	0.00
1000	USD	04/2015	170,451.54	170,451.54		90,650.00	0.00		0.00	0.00
1000	USD	05/2015	285,779.00	285,779.00		161,254.00	0.00		0.00	120,000.00
1000	USD	06/2015	1,457,414.30	1,457,414.30		227,714.83	41,361.30		346,500.00	705,867.42
					A				48,990.00	0.00
1000	USD	07/2015	2,526,406.73	2,526,406.73		468,569.19	332,913.24		38,200.00	94,462.00
					A	330,000.00	330,000.00	A	43,000.00	8,000.00
1000	USD	08/2015	182,311.27	182,311.27		5,000.00	100.74		0.00	26,000.00
					A	0.00	5,000.00			
1000	USD	09/2015	300.00	300.00		0.00	0.00		0.00	0.00
1000	USD	2015	158,509,274.91	158,509,274.91		1,113,257.45	434,375.28		384,700.00	946,329.42
					A	330,000.00	335,000.00	A	91,990.00	8,000.00

Figure 1.49 Journal Summary by Period

- **Program RAGITT_ALV01 (Asset History Sheet)**
  An asset history sheet with details of the asset transactions can be created using Report RAGITT01, which can meet country-specific legal requirements. Report RAGITT01 is one of the most detailed period-end closing reports.

  The asset history sheet version helps determine the form and content of the report. You should create the list as shown in Figure 1.50, with totals and individual asset information for better reconciliation after the migration in case of any imbalance.

1.12 Execute Business Reconciliation

```
Asset History Sheet
|◀ ◀ ▶ ▶|  🔍 ≜ ▽ ▼  Σ ⅝  🗐 ⤴ 🗐 ▽ ▥  ⊞ ⊞ ⊞ ⓘ  ≣ 🏛Assets  📄WL  Add to worklist

   Report date: 12/31/2015   Asset History Sheet - 01 Book deprec.
   Created on: 09/27/2015    In compl. w/EC directive 4 (13 col.,wide version) (incomplete)

CompanyCode        BusinessArea         Bal.sheetitem          Bal.sh.acctAPC         AssetClass
1000                                    13                     160020                 2000

     Asset      SNo. Cap.date   Asset description                                Crcy
     APC FY start     Acquisition        Retirement          Transfer       Post-capital.   Invest.support       Current APC
     Dep. FY start   Dep. for year      Dep.retir.           Dep.transfer   Dep.post-cap.   Write-ups            Accumul. dep.
     Bk.val.FY strt                                                                                              Curr.bk.val.

     20002         0   11/01/1996 Machinery 1                                      USD
        800,000.00          0.00              0.00                 0.00            0.00           0.00            800,000.00
        364,036.70-    41,739.13-             0.00                 0.00            0.00           0.00            405,775.83-
        435,963.30                                                                                                394,224.17
     20003         0   04/30/2000 Machinery 2                                      USD
        212,000.00          0.00              0.00                 0.00            0.00           0.00            212,000.00
         65,293.60-    13,496.02-             0.00                 0.00            0.00           0.00             78,789.62-
        146,706.40                                                                                                133,210.38
     20005         0   07/17/2015 Test Asset for Integrated Postings - 1           USD
              0.00      1,000.00              0.00                 0.00            0.00           0.00              1,000.00
              0.00         38.19-             0.00                 0.00            0.00           0.00                 38.19-
              0.00                                                                                                    961.81

  *  Asset Class     2000               Machinery                                  USD
     2,024,000.00      1,000.00              0.00                 0.00            0.00           0.00          2,025,000.00
       858,660.60-   110,508.49-             0.00                 0.00            0.00           0.00            969,169.09-
     1,165,339.40                                                                                              1,055,830.91
```

Figure 1.50 Asset History Sheet

- **Program RAHAFA_ALV01 (Depreciation Run for Planned Depreciation)**
  Execute this report (see Figure 1.51) to identify planned depreciation values for a given period.

- **Program RFKUML00 (Vendor Purchases)**
  The vendor purchase list shown in Figure 1.52 displays purchases in local currency or in one of the output currencies that you specify in the selection screen.

  The following data are displayed at the end of the list for each local currency:
  - Totals per company code
  - Final total for all company codes (per currency)

- **Program RFKEPL00 (Vendor Open Item List)**
  This report (see Figure 1.53) creates a list of line items that can be accrued in time. The list contains vendor items that were posted in the selected period and not yet cleared or paid.

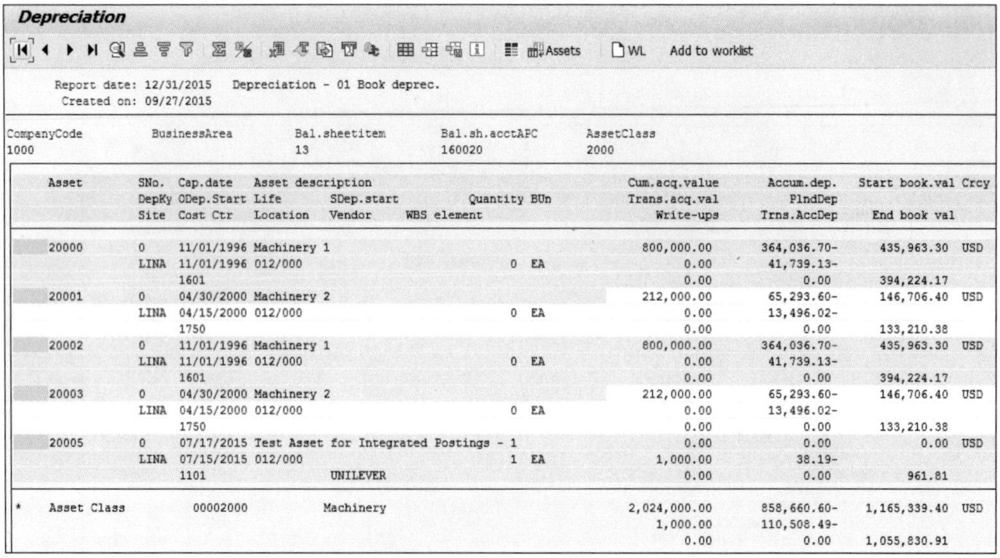

1 Preparation

```
Depreciation
[icons]  Assets   WL   Add to worklist

    Report date: 12/31/2015   Depreciation - 01 Book deprec.
    Created on: 09/27/2015

CompanyCode     BusinessArea       Bal.sheetitem      Bal.sh.acctAPC     AssetClass
1000                               13                 160020             2000

     Asset        SNo.  Cap.date   Asset description                       Cum.acq.value   Accum.dep.    Start book.val  Crcy
                  DepKy ODep.Start Life          SDep.start   Quantity BUn Trans.acq.val   PlndDep
                  Site  Cost Ctr   Location      Vendor       WBS element  Write-ups       Trns.AccDep   End book val

     20000        0     11/01/1996 Machinery 1                             800,000.00      364,036.70-   435,963.30      USD
                  LINA  11/01/1996 012/000                                 0.00            41,739.13-
                        1601                                  0 EA         0.00            0.00          394,224.17
     20001        0     04/30/2000 Machinery 2                             212,000.00      65,293.60-    146,706.40      USD
                  LINA  04/15/2000 012/000                                 0.00            13,496.02-
                        1750                                  0 EA         0.00            0.00          133,210.38
     20002        0     11/01/1996 Machinery 1                             800,000.00      364,036.70-   435,963.30      USD
                  LINA  11/01/1996 012/000                                 0.00            41,739.13-
                        1601                                  0 EA         0.00            0.00          394,224.17
     20003        0     04/30/2000 Machinery 2                             212,000.00      65,293.60-    146,706.40      USD
                  LINA  04/15/2000 012/000                                 0.00            13,496.02-
                        1750                                  0 EA         0.00            0.00          133,210.38
     20005        0     07/17/2015 Test Asset for Integrated Postings - 1  0.00            0.00          0.00            USD
                  LINA  07/15/2015 012/000                                 1,000.00        38.19-
                        1101                  UNILEVER                     0.00            0.00          961.81

*    Asset Class         00002000             Machinery                    2,024,000.00    858,660.60-   1,165,339.40    USD
                                                                           1,000.00        110,508.49-
                                                                           0.00            0.00          1,055,830.91
```

Figure 1.51 Planned Depreciation Details

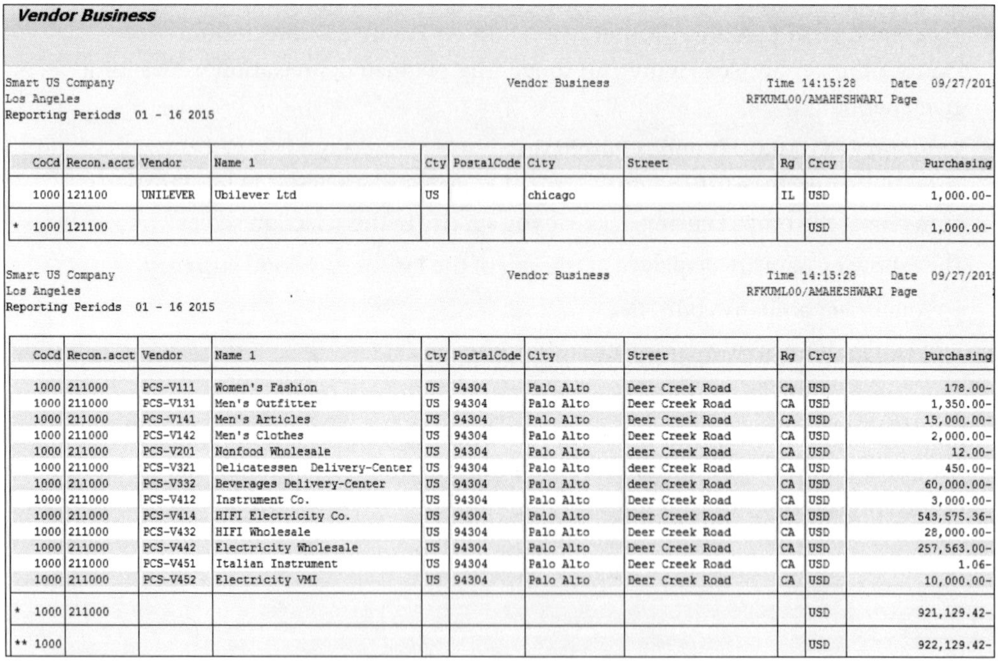

```
Vendor Business

Smart US Company                                 Vendor Business              Time 14:15:28     Date 09/27/201
Los Angeles                                                                   RFKUML00/AMAHESHWARI Page
Reporting Periods 01 - 16 2015

 CoCd  Recon.acct  Vendor    Name 1            Cty  PostalCode  City      Street              Rg   Crcy       Purchasing

 1000  121100      UNILEVER  Ubilever Ltd      US               chicago                       IL   USD        1,000.00-

*1000  121100                                                                                      USD        1,000.00-


Smart US Company                                 Vendor Business              Time 14:15:28     Date 09/27/201
Los Angeles                                                                   RFKUML00/AMAHESHWARI Page
Reporting Periods 01 - 16 2015

 CoCd  Recon.acct  Vendor    Name 1                       Cty  PostalCode  City       Street              Rg   Crcy    Purchasing

 1000  211000      PCS-V111  Women's Fashion              US   94304       Palo Alto  Deer Creek Road     CA   USD        178.00-
 1000  211000      PCS-V131  Men's Outfitter              US   94304       Palo Alto  Deer Creek Road     CA   USD      1,350.00-
 1000  211000      PCS-V141  Men's Articles               US   94304       Palo Alto  Deer Creek Road     CA   USD     15,000.00-
 1000  211000      PCS-V142  Men's Clothes                US   94304       Palo Alto  Deer Creek Road     CA   USD      2,000.00-
 1000  211000      PCS-V201  Nonfood Wholesale            US   94304       Palo Alto  deer Creek Road     CA   USD         12.00-
 1000  211000      PCS-V321  Delicatessen Delivery-Center US   94304       Palo Alto  deer Creek Road     CA   USD        450.00-
 1000  211000      PCS-V332  Beverages Delivery-Center    US   94304       Palo Alto  deer Creek Road     CA   USD     60,000.00-
 1000  211000      PCS-V412  Instrument Co.               US   94304       Palo Alto  Deer Creek Road     CA   USD      3,000.00-
 1000  211000      PCS-V414  HIFI Electricity Co.         US   94304       Palo Alto  Deer Creek Road     CA   USD    543,575.36-
 1000  211000      PCS-V432  HIFI Wholesale               US   94304       Palo Alto  Deer Creek Road     CA   USD     28,000.00-
 1000  211000      PCS-V442  Electricity Wholesale        US   94304       Palo Alto  Deer Creek Road     CA   USD    257,563.00-
 1000  211000      PCS-V451  Italian Instrument           US   94304       Palo Alto  Deer Creek Road     CA   USD          1.06-
 1000  211000      PCS-V452  Electricity VMI              US   94304       Palo Alto  Deer Creek Road     CA   USD     10,000.00-

*  1000 211000                                                                                                 USD    921,129.42-
** 1000                                                                                                        USD    922,129.42-
```

Figure 1.52 Details of Business Conducted with All Vendors

1.12 Execute Business Reconciliation

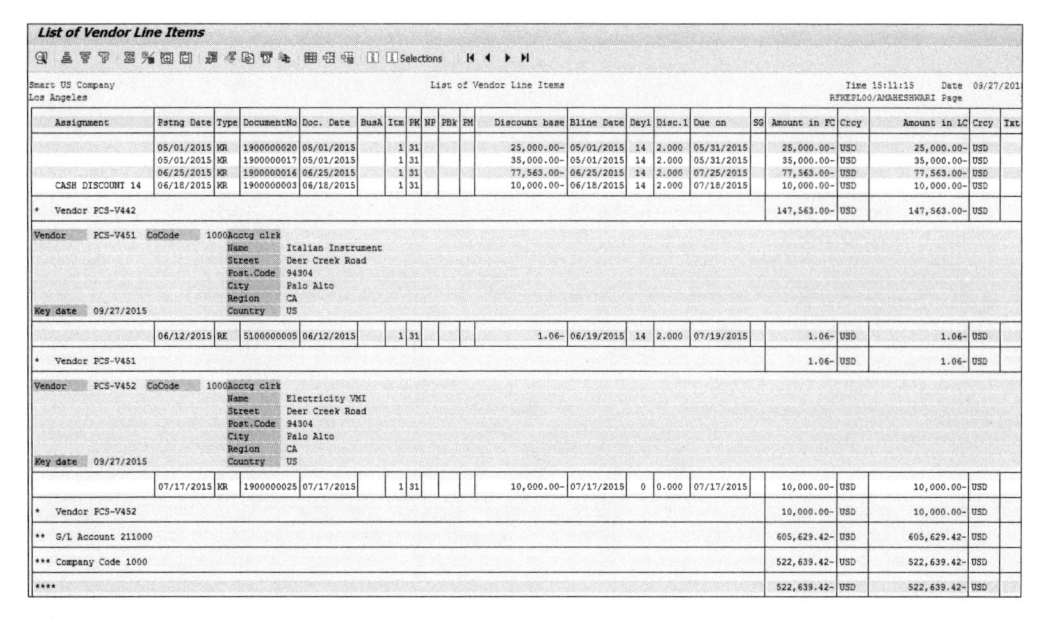

Figure 1.53 Vendor Open Item List

- **Program RFDUML00 (Customer Sales)**
  The customer sales list shown in Figure 1.54 displays the sales in local currency or in any other currency that you specify in the selection screen, along with the exchange rate type. You can configure the layout of the report for the fields that you want to display as the output. The following data is displayed at the end of the list for each local currency:
  - Totals per company code
  - Final total for all company codes (per currency)
- **Program RFDEPL00 (Customer Open Item List)**
  This report (see Figure 1.55) creates a list of the line items that can be accrued. The list contains customer items that were posted to the selected period specified in the selection screen.

Customer Sales

Smart US Company — Customer Sales — Time 15:13:21 Date 09/27/201
Los Angeles — RFDUML00/AMAHESHWARI Page
Reporting Periods 01 - 16 2015

CoCd	Recon.acct	Customer	Name 1	Cty	PostalCode	City	Street	Rg	Crcy	Sales
1000	121000	PCS-C101	Customer with Creditcard	US	94304	Palo Alto	1 Deer Creek Road	CA	USD	713,563.00
1000	121000	PCS-C301	Wholesale Customer	US	94304	Palo Alto	1 Deer Creek Road	CA	USD	10,933.30
1000	121000	PCS-C302	Customer2 for sales order	US	94304	Palo Alto	1 Deer Creek Road	CA	USD	90,004.95
1000	121000	PCS-C303	Customer3 for sales order	US	94304	Palo Alto	1 Deer Creek Road	CA	USD	56,066.50
1000	121000	PCS-C309	Customer for bonus buy	US	94304	Palo Alto	1 Deer Creek Road	CA	USD	27,773.75
1000	121000	PCS-C315	Customer for credit limit	US	94304	Palo Alto	1 Deer Creek Road	CA	USD	840.00
1000	121000	PCS-CPD	CPD Customer	US		CPD		CA	USD	787.48
1000	121000	PCS-R301	Retail Customer	US				TX	USD	281.70
* 1000	121000								USD	900,250.68

Smart US Company — Customer Sales — Time 15:13:21 Date 09/27/201
Los Angeles — RFDUML00/AMAHESHWARI Page
Reporting Periods 01 - 16 2015

CoCd	Recon.acct	Customer	Name 1	Cty	PostalCode	City	Street	Rg	Crcy	Sales
1000	123000	M001	Smart Store 1	US	75001	Los Angeles	101 Smart Retail	CA	USD	60,337.99
1000	123000	M004	Smart Store 4	US	75001	Los Angeles	104 Smart Retail	CA	USD	253.33
* 1000	123000								USD	60,591.32
** 1000									USD	960,842.00

Figure 1.54 Details of Business Conducted with All Customers

List of Customer Line Items

Selections

Smart US Company — List of Customer Line Items — Time 15:17:16 Date 09/27/201
Los Angeles — RFDEPL00/AMAHESHWARI Page

Assignment	Pstng Date	Type	DocumentNo	Doc. Date	BusA	Itm	PK	NP	Dun	PM	Discount base	Bline Date	Day1	Disc.1	Due on	SG	Amount in doc. curr.	Crcy	Amount in local cur.	Crcy	Txt
Customer M004 CoCode 1000 Acctg clrk Name Smart Store 4 Street 104 Smart Retail Post.Code 75001 City Los Angeles Region CA Key date 09/27/2015 Country US																					
	07/23/2015	RV	90000067	07/23/2015		1	01				0.00	07/23/2015	0	0.000	07/23/2015		11.96	USD	11.96	USD	
	07/23/2015	RV	90000069	07/23/2015		1	01				0.00	07/23/2015	0	0.000	07/23/2015		4.61	USD	4.61	USD	
	07/23/2015	RV	90000070	07/23/2015		1	01				0.00	07/23/2015	0	0.000	07/23/2015		136.02	USD	136.02	USD	
* Customer M004																	152.59	USD	152.59	USD	
** G/L Account 123000																	16.20 374.61	EUR USD	389.84	USD	
Customer PCS-C101 CoCode 1000 Acctg clrk Name Customer with Creditcard Street 1 Deer Creek Road Post.Code 94304 City Palo Alto Region CA Key date 09/27/2015 Country US																					
	08/04/2015	DZ	1400000014	08/04/2015		2	19				5,000.00-	08/04/2015	0	0.000	08/04/2015	A	5,000.00-	USD	5,000.00-	USD	
* Customer PCS-C101																	5,000.00-	USD	5,000.00-	USD	
** G/L Account 214010																	5,000.00-	USD	5,000.00-	USD	
*** Company Code 1000																	200,016.20 516,441.94	EUR USD	704,457.17	USD	
****																	200,016.20 516,441.94	EUR USD	704,457.17	USD	

Figure 1.55 Customer Open Item List

- **Program RFDAUB00 (Recurring Entry Documents)**
  This program provides an overview of recurring entry original documents, as shown in Figure 1.56. You can use the program to determine the following:
    - Which documents are carried out in a particular period
    - Which documents aren't carried out
    - Which documents will be carried out during the next run of the recurring entry program

Figure 1.56 Recurring Entry Documents

- **Transaction S_ALR_87013611 (Cost Centers Actual/Plan Report)**
  This report (see Figure 1.57) lists the actual and plan values for a cost center or a cost center group.

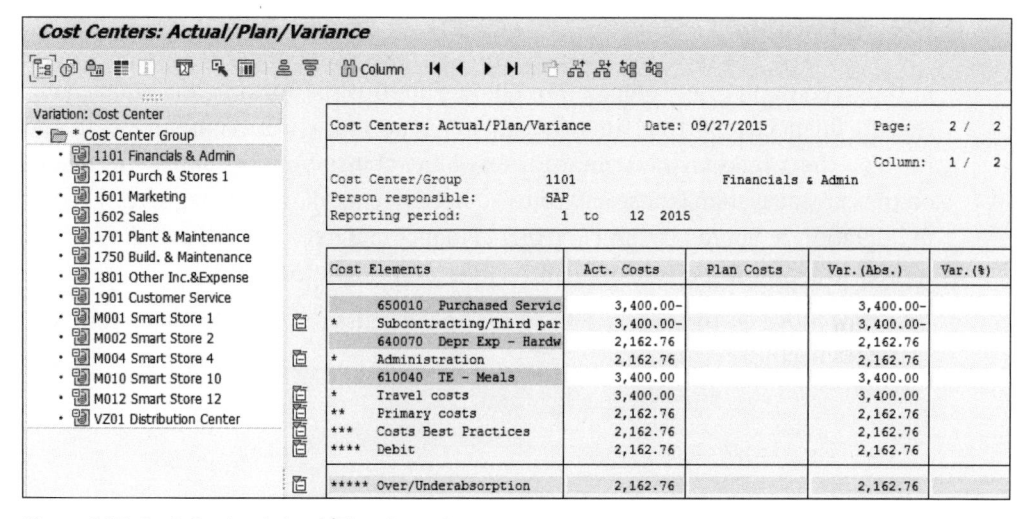

Figure 1.57 Cost Center Actual/Plan Report

1   Preparation

- **Transaction S_ALR_87012993 (Internal Order Actual/Plan Report)**
  This report (see Figure 1.58) provides an overview of the actual and plan data related to internal orders for a specific period for the following units:
  – Cost element
  – Cost element group
  – Statistical key figure

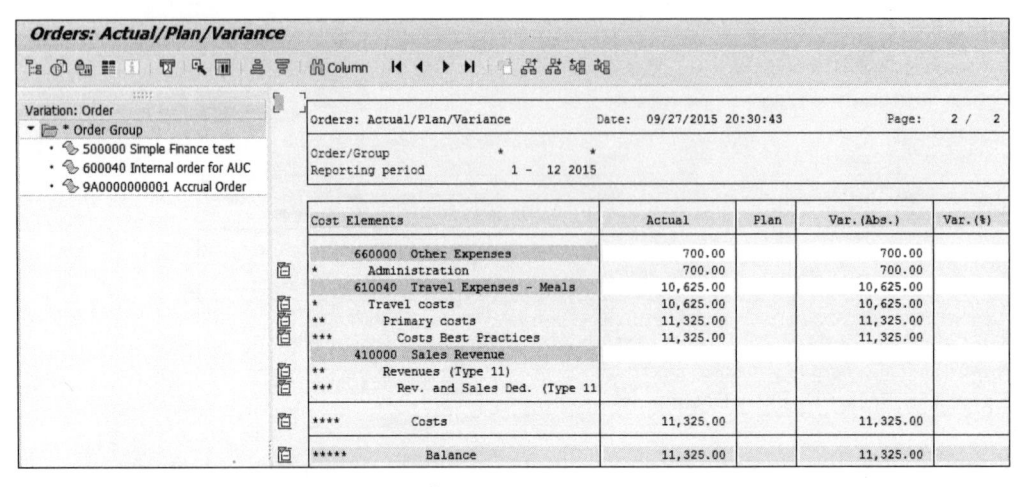

Figure 1.58 Internal Order Actual/Plan Report

1.13   Summary

In the migration project preparation phase, you must perform period-end closing, execute financial reporting, run reconciliation reports to ensure consistent data, and run a precheck report to determine the feasibility of installing SAP S/4HANA Finance on the current system landscape. You also need to check Customizing settings prior to migration or upgrade to SAP S/4HANA Finance and execute and save all financial reports to allow comparison of financial KPIs after migration.

Let's now move on to Chapter 2, in which we'll discuss the installation of your SAP S/4HANA Finance system.

Chapter 2
Installation and Upgrade

This chapter provides the technical steps and activities required to install SAP S/4HANA Finance, including the backup of old tables and creation of SAP HANA compatibility views.

The technical system administrator performs most of the steps and activities to install SAP S/4HANA Finance. The major activities performed in this phase include creating backup tables for totals and index tables and creating SAP HANA views with the same name as the data definition language (DDL) SQL views, also known as *compatibility views*. New programs replace old programs, and the old transaction code points to the new ones, which are updated as required. During this step, you must also install the necessary software components for both the backend and frontend servers.

The system automatically executes the following steps during the installation of SAP S/4HANA Finance:

- Create backup tables for the totals and index tables in the Data Dictionary (DDIC) that are deleted in the new data structures with the extension _BCK and _BAK for SAP ERP Financials (FI) and Controlling (CO) tables, respectively.
- Save the totals and index tables in backup tables.
- Delete the original totals and index tables.
- Create SAP HANA compatibility views with the same names as the totals and index tables with the creation of new Universal Journal table ACDOCA.

After SAP S/4HANA Finance is installed, no postings can be made until the end of the migration.

In this chapter, we'll provide you with an overview of the tasks to perform and items to check prior to your upgrade before walking you through using the Maintenance Planner and installing the necessary software components. We'll then discuss the relevant SAP Notes, the process of HANA-tization, and some opportunities for optimization after installation.

2 Installation and Upgrade

2.1 Installation and Upgrade Checklist

SAP Note 2157996 includes an Excel-based installation/upgrade checklist that will help you verify whether important topics of preparing the installation of and upgrade to SAP S/4HANA Finance have been properly considered.

The checklist focuses on specific aspects and condition prerequisites for the SAP S/4HANA Finance backend installation; the installation/upgrade of the frontend server, such as SAP Fiori, is covered in Chapter 12. The checklist relates to the technical installation/upgrade only. Migration topics and the technical configuration of the system aren't covered.

> **Expert Insight**
>
> You should also check alternative deployment scenarios to see if they are right for your organization. An organization that has complex and large distributed system landscapes involving multiple SAP ERP and non-SAP ERP systems can also benefit from the functionality of SAP S/4HANA Finance without migrating the entire system landscape to SAP S/4HANA Finance all at once.
>
> Central Finance is one of the deployment scenarios for installing SAP S/4HANA Finance; in this scenario, various source systems are connected to the SAP S/4HANA Finance system, which acts as a central system. SAP Landscape Transformation replication server is required to connect these multiple distributed systems to the SAP S/4HANA Finance system. It can be installed as a separate standalone system or on top of any of the source systems or the Central Finance system.
>
> Consult Appendix A for more information about Central Finance.

In the following sections, we'll briefly detail the items you should check before beginning your installation. Before you begin, however, ensure that you're using the latest version of the checklist (see SAP Note 2157996).

2.1.1 SAP HANA and Minimum Versions

First, you must check whether SAP HANA is already in use or the migration to SAP HANA is forthcoming. The implementation team should have sufficient experience or support to install, configure, and run SAP HANA.

References

Some of the resources related to the installation and upgrade are listed here:

- SAP Note 2333141: SAP S/4HANA 1610—Restriction Note
- SAP Note 2346431: SAP S/4HANA 1610—Release Information Note
- http://help.sap.com/hana_platform

1709 Preview

You can consult SAP Note 2524661 (SAP S/4HANA 1709—SAP HANA Database Requirements) for information about the database.

- SAP Note 2482453: SAP S/4HANA 1709 Release Information Note
- SAP Note 2491467: SAP S/4HANA 1709 Restriction Note
- SAP Note 2313884: Simplification List for SAP S/4HANA 1709

Customers already using SAP HANA should update their SAP HANA databases to SAP ERP 6.0 EHP 7 or above and SAP HANA SPS 7 (or above) to allow for migration to SAP S/4HANA Finance. If the required minimum SAP HANA update is planned, check that it's reflected in the project execution plan. Similarly, verify whether the implementation team has sufficient experience or equivalent support to install, configure, and run an SAP ERP EHP upgrade and installation.

The installation of SAP S/4HANA Finance requires SAP ERP 6.0 systems to be updated to EHP 7 or above. The stack calculation (using the Maintenance Optimizer) for the installation of SAP S/4HANA Finance automatically takes this into consideration. The minimum required versions are included in the Applications for FIN 700 instance and are listed in Table 11 of the Administrator's Guide. (Remember that you'll find this at *http://help.sap.com/s4hana_op_1610_002*.)

On the **Systems** tab in the Maintenance Optimizer transaction, the **Target Constellation** always lists the minimum product version such as SAP NetWeaver 7.40 as required by the related SAP ERP enhancement pack. However, the earliest SAP NetWeaver 7.40 version required for SAP S/4HANA Finance is automatically added later to the list of selected files (e.g., SPS 10 for SAP S/4HANA Finance SPS 00).

References

For more information, see SAP Note 2117481, which contains information and references for applying the correct SPS for the SAP S/4HANA Finance installation.

2.1.2 Software Update Manager

Among its many functions, the Software Update Manager (SUM) helps you perform release upgrades, install enhancement packages, apply service packages, and update single components on SAP NetWeaver. SUM checks the current version of the system, analyzes the required components, imports the necessary programs and add-ons, and finally installs all the components that are divided into multiple roadmap steps—which, in turn, are further subdivided into a sequence of phases for monitoring purposes.

SUM is the main tool used to convert your system to SAP S/4HANA Finance. If your source system isn't yet running on an SAP HANA database, use the database migration option (DMO) of SUM to migrate your database to SAP HANA during the conversion.

SAP S/4HANA Finance must be installed using SUM in combination with the Maintenance Optimizer. The Maintenance Optimizer leads you through the planning, downloading, and implementing of new software versions in existing systems. The SAP Add-On Installation Tool (SAINT) isn't supported. Check whether the implementation team has experience using SUM.

With SUM and DMO, you can run the upgrade to SAP ERP 6.0 EHP 7 or above, the database migration to SAP HANA, and the installation of SAP S/4HANA Finance in a single step.

If SAP S/4HANA Finance is installed using SUM with DMO, and the source database isn't SAP HANA, a specific uncritical error message will occur in phase MAIN_SHDRUN/ACT_UPG. Check whether the project team is aware of the error and is prepared for the procedure to resolve it and proceed.

> **References**
>
> For more information, see SAP Note 2019282: View Activation Errors during S/4HANA Finance Installation Using SUM with DMO.

During the SAP S/4HANA Finance installation process, aggregate (e.g., table GLT0) and application index (e.g., table BSIS) tables are deleted and replaced with identically named compatibility view tables that only have read access. These views ensure that database SELECT statements will retrieve the same information without breaking the code in the existing programs and routines. The content from the old tables is saved into backup tables that will be used for the application data migration.

Before you begin, check whether the latest version of SUM is available and downloaded to install/update SAP S/4HANA Finance.

> **References**
>
> See the following for more information:
> - SAP Note 2117481: Release Information Notes Related to SAP S/4HANA Finance
> - SAP Note 1813548: Database Migration Option (DMO) of SUM 1.0 up to SP 13
> - *http://service.sap.com/sltoolset*, under **Software Logistics Toolset 1.0 • SUM**

2.1.3 SAP HANA Live

SAP S/4HANA Finance requires certain SAP HANA Live packages. Check whether the implementation team has experience using SAP HANA lifecycle manager and SAP HANA application lifecycle management for SAP HANA 1.0 SPS 9 onward.

You should also check whether the team is clear regarding the set of SAP HANA Live packages and the required SP levels that will be installed.

For SAP S/4HANA Finance, the mandatory packages are SAP HANA CONTENT HBA SAP ERP 100 (HCO_HBA_ECC 100) and SAP HANA CONTENT HBA SAP S/4HANA Finance 200 (HCO_HBA_Simple Finance700 200). All other packages are optional and depend on your planned usage of SAP Fiori/SAP Smart Business.

> **References**
>
> For more information, see SAP Note 1967187: Activation Errors for SAP HANA Content Package SAP.HBA.ECC in SAP S/4HANA Finance.

2.1.4 Administrator's Guide, Release Information Note, and Browser Support

Make sure the team assigned to install SAP S/4HANA Finance and the related SAP HANA Live packages has done the following:

- Fully read and understood the latest version of the SAP S/4HANA Finance Administrator's Guide, especially Chapter 3 and Chapter 4 (see *http://help.sap.com/sfin300*)
- Fully read and understood the latest version of the SAP S/4HANA Finance Release Information Note (RIN)
- Studied the browser prerequisites (SAP Note 1971111) for SAP S/4HANA Finance in regard to SAP Business Client and/or SAP Fiori (as applicable)

2.1.5 SAP Cash Management, Cost Objects, and Cost Object Hierarchies

If SAP Cash Management is used, you need to switch to the new SAP Cash Management within SAP S/4HANA Finance. A separate license is required for installing this component.

> **References**
>
> See the following for more information:
>
> - SAP Note 2149337: Released Scope of SAP Cash Management Powered by SAP HANA, as Part of SAP S/4HANA Finance
> - SAP Note 2044295: SAP Cash Management Powered by SAP HANA: License and Usage Information

You should also check if the general cost object and/or cost object hierarchies (from Product Cost Controlling [CO-PC]) are currently in use. Check for usage of Transactions KKBC_KTR, KKC1, KKC2, KKC3, KKCS, KK88, KKAV, KKH1, KKH2, or KKH3. This functionality from FI isn't offered with SAP S/4HANA Finance.

2.1.6 Industry Solutions and Add-Ons

Check SAP Note 2119188 for the comprehensive list of industry solutions that are released for use with SAP S/4HANA Finance and related release restrictions. You should also check SAP Note 2103558 and SAP Note 2392527 for the list of industry and compatibility add-on software components that haven't yet been released for use with SAP S/4HANA Finance or have restrictions in usage.

Ensure that this list of industry solutions is checked against the currently used software components (compare with content in table CVERS) or planned-to-be-used software components. Industry/add-on software packages are attributed in such a way that incompatible packages can't be combined during the installation/upgrade. Maintenance Optimizer and SUM will raise related errors, which shouldn't be ignored.

> **References**
>
> For more information, see the following:
>
> - SAP Note 2035994: Installation with Components/Products Not Yet Released for the SAP S/4HANA Finance Add-On
> - SAP Note 2214213: Restrictions That Exist for SAP S/4HANA Finance

2.1.7 Maintenance Optimizer

The Maintenance Optimizer is a part of SAP Solution Manager and is intended to help with and keep track of EHP installations, upgrades, and SPS updates. It calculates and downloads the files needed and then generates XML with the package queue for Enhancement Package Installer (EHPI) or Support Package Manager (SPAM).

Ensure that the Maintenance Optimizer can be used: SUM requires a stack XML file created via Maintenance Optimizer to install SAP S/4HANA Finance.

To check whether the SAP Solution Manager instance with the Maintenance Optimizer is available and connected to the system to be upgraded to SAP S/4HANA Finance, follow these steps in SAP Solution Manager:

1. Use Transaction LMDB, and select the system that you want to connect to and install SAP S/4HANA Finance on (see Figure 2.1).

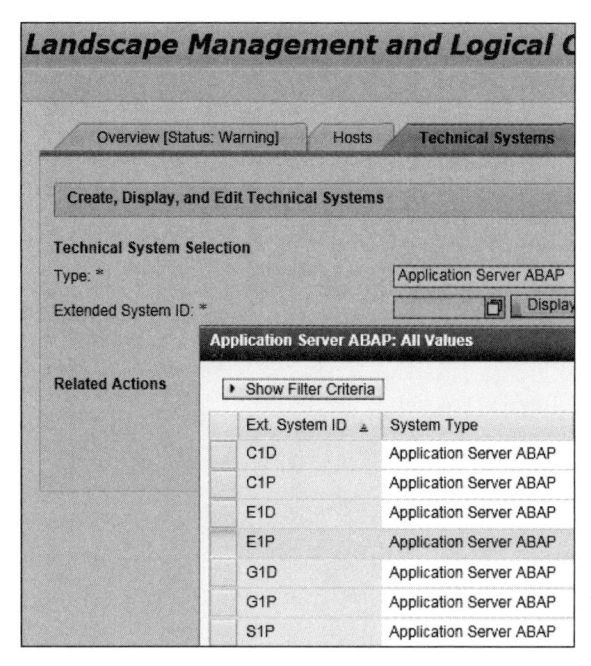

Figure 2.1 Landscape Management and Logical Components

2. In the **Related Product Systems and Technical Systems** tab, check whether the **Product Version** is assigned to the **Product Instance**. As an example, this might look as depicted in Table 2.1.

2　Installation and Upgrade

Product Version	Product Instance
SAP ERP 6.0	SAP ERP Server
SAP ERP 6.0 EHP 7	ABAP Technology for SAP ERP 6.0 EHP 7
	Applications for FIN 700
	Central Applications
	Financial Services
	Human Capital Management
	Master Data Governance
	Strategic Enterprise Mgmt.
SAP Fiori Approve Requests X1 1.0	Approve Requests INT NW740
	Approve Requests UI NW740
SAP Fiori ERP Applications X1 1.0	Central App INT NW740
	Central App UI NW740
	HCM INT NW740
	HCM UI NW740
	Travel INT NW740
	Travel UI NW740
KPI Modeler 1.0	Frontend Serv. Cont KPI Model.
SAP Analytic Apps for ERP 1.0	Frontend Serv. Cont ERP Analy.
SAP Analytics Foundation 1.0	Frontend Analy. FND NW 7.4
SAP EWM 9.3	EWM on SAP ERP
	EWM UI Features

Table 2.1 Related Product Systems

2.1 Installation and Upgrade Checklist

Product Version	Product Instance
SAP Fin. Closing Cockpit 2.0	SAP FCC NW 740
SAP Fiori for SAP FM 1.0	UI for FM on NW740
SAP Fiori for SAP SFIN 1503	UI for FIN NW740
SAP Gateway 2.0	Gateway GIL NW 740
	Gateway PGW NW 740
	Gateway SCS
	Gateway Server CBS NW 740
	Gateway Server CNT NW 740
	Gateway Server Core NW 740
	Gateway SPI NW740
SAP NetWeaver 7.4	Application Server ABAP
SAP Screen Personas 3.0	Screen Personas 2.0
	Screen Personas for NW
SAP SFinancials 1503	Central Applications (FIN)
SAP Smart Business for ERP 1.0	Frontend Serv. Cont ERP NW 7.4
SAP Smart Business for FM 1.0	Frontend Serv. Cont FM NW 7.40
SAP Smart Business for RTL 1.0	Frontend Serv. Cont RTL NW 7.4
SAP Smart Business SFIN 1503	Frontend Serv. Cont sFIN NW7.40
SAP UI Fiori Config V1.0	SAP UI Fiori Config

Table 2.1 Related Product Systems (Cont.)

3. Use Transaction SMSY, and make sure all the systems and logical components that are required have been selected and are active, as shown in Figure 2.2.

2   Installation and Upgrade

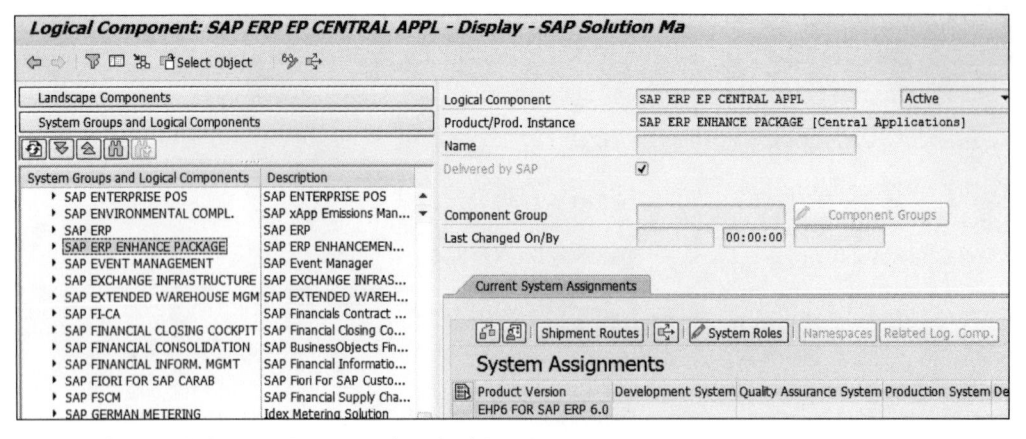

Figure 2.2 System Groups and Logical Components

SAP S/4HANA Finance software packages will be visible in Maintenance Optimizer/ SAP Mobile Platform only if you've licensed the product.

Check if you have the correct SAP S/4HANA Finance license and that SAP S/4HANA Finance is visible to the related S-user in Maintenance Optimizer/SAP Mobile Platform after registration with the General Availability Care program.

> **1709 Preview**
>
> As we'll discuss shortly, you should use Maintenance Planner. Beginning with SAP S/4HANA 1709, Maintenance Optimizer cannot be used and is replaced with Maintenance Planner.

2.1.8   Target Stack XML and SAP NetWeaver Kernel

Check whether a target stack XML can be created and related software packages can be downloaded via Maintenance Optimizer. Make sure you didn't overrule any error messages regarding the required SP levels or compatibility of component versions.

For the update to the target SAP NetWeaver SPS, the SAP NetWeaver kernel version may need to be updated. Check whether the required minimal SAP NetWeaver kernel version update is already planned and reflected in the project execution plan.

2.1.9 Customer Code

Check whether the team understands that SAP S/4HANA Finance replaces FI. Check whether the activities for Transactions SPDD/SPAU are properly planned for all FI application components.

Plan for Transactions SPDD/SPAU if you modified any SAP standard code either in software components SAP_FIN, EA-FIN, and FSCM_CCD (for release 617), or in SAP_APPL, EA-APPL, and FINBASIS (for all lower releases).

Note that SAP S/4HANA Finance isn't following the business function/switch concept and has a significantly changed FI-CO data model. Any outbound/inbound interfaces to FI are downward-compatible with the classic FI, whereas custom-owned code that integrates with SAP code on a more granular level may have to be adapted to the new data model.

SAP S/4HANA Finance doesn't support the same transactions and reports as classic FI. Consequently, customer roles (menus and authorizations) and customer code may need to be adapted.

Determine whether you've assessed the scope and effort for related adaptations. There are special steps to be performed to adapt custom-defined fields and interfaces to the new accounting data model.

2.1.10 Data Definition Language Statement Corrections

SAP S/4HANA Finance makes heavy use of data definition language statement (DDLS) views (also known as Core Data Services [CDS] views).

Based on the DDL description, these views generate representations in the DDIC and in the SAP HANA database. The ABAP Development Tools (ADT) are required for manual corrections or enhancements of these views, so check whether the project team knows how to use ADT. Although we recommend preparing your technical team to use ADT, not doing so shouldn't keep you from the installation of and migration to SAP S/4HANA Finance.

2.2 Review Data Model Changes

Upon the installation of SAP S/4HANA, the totals and application index tables in the current SAP ERP environment would be removed and replaced by identically named DDL SQL views, also known as *compatibility views*. These views are generated from

DDL sources and ensure database SELECTs work as before. However, the write access to these tables (including INSERT, UPDATE, DELETE and MODIFY) would be removed from both SAP S/4HANA *as well as* from any custom code that calls these tables. For example, the original table BSID would have a compatibility view BSID in the DDL source BSID_DDL where the backup for the original table would be stored in BSID_BCK.

In some later releases, SAP changed the strategy where some of the tables were replaced the Universal Journal table ACDOCA. In this case, the compatibility views do not have the same name as the original tables. Here, the database interface (DBI) redirects all related database table SELECTs to a compatibility view, which retrieves the same data based on the new data model from table ACDOCA. For example, the original table ANLP would have a compatibility view FAAV_ANLP in the DDL source FAA_DDL, where the view to read the content of the database table would be from FAAV_ANLP_ORI.

> **References**
>
> For more information, see the following SAP Notes:
> - SAP Note 2270333: Data Model Changes in SAP S/4HANA
> - SAP Note 1976487: Information about Adjusting Customer-Specific Programs to the Simplified Data Model in SAP S/4HANA Finance

With the installation of the SAP S/4HANA, certain transaction codes and programs in the finance and controlling application areas have been replaced with newer transactions, programs, or Web Dynpro applications. Use Transaction STO3N to check which transaction codes and programs have been used by your organization in the past to create a change management plan and communicate these changes to the end users.

> **References**
>
> For more information, refer to SAP Note 1946054: List of Reports and Transactions Replaced in Comparison to SAP ERP 6.0 EHP 7.

2.3 Use the Maintenance Planner

The Maintenance Planner is an SAP solution that helps you plan and maintain systems in your landscape. You can plan complex activities such as installing a new system or updating existing systems. You can schedule all changes to be deployed at a convenient time to minimize downtime. This essential administrative tool will help you complete a major part of your application lifecycle management. With the Maintenance Planner, you can do the following:

- Explore all the systems and system tracks in your landscape.
- Plan a new system installation.
- Plan update or upgrade activities for an existing system.
- Group systems into tracks and perform collective maintenance.
- Analyze dependent systems impacted by your change.
- Identify and evaluate changes to the landscape.

As noted earlier in this chapter, the use of the Maintenance Planner is mandatory for conversion to SAP S/4HANA. This step creates the download files (add-ons, packages, database drivers, stack files) that SUM uses to install SAP S/4HANA Finance. Specifically, the Maintenance Planner checks (a) whether the add-ons in the system are accepted for the conversion and (b) whether business functions active in the system are accepted for conversion.

The Maintenance Planner then creates the stack configuration file, which is used by SUM to update the existing system and convert to SAP S/4HANA.

In addition, the Maintenance Planner needs to perform its activities before the prechecks because the precheck report also requires the stack.xml file as an input.

Your technical team should thoroughly study the details as listed in the Maintenance Planning Guide for SAP Solution Manager 7.1 SP 05, where the Maintenance Planner has been listed to allow changes to planning in the current landscape per the data provided by SAP Solution Manager Landscape Management Database (LMDB). The Maintenance Planner is the successor to the Maintenance Optimizer, Landscape Planner, and Product System Editor in the LMDB. The Maintenance Planner consolidates and simplifies some critical tasks, such as defining the dependencies for product maintenance, creating the stack configuration files, and selecting archives.

> **References**
>
> For more information, see SAP Note 2174410: Maintenance Planner: Known Limitations.

2.4 Install the Related Software Component Version

SAP Note 2171868 provides the details of the new names and numbering for product versions in SAP S/4HANA Finance and its add-on components. You'll need to install both backend- and frontend-related software component versions before migrating to SAP S/4HANA Finance, as follows:

- **Backend**

    The new software components for SAP S/4HANA Finance were introduced for SAP ERP 6.0 with EHP 7. SAP S/4HANA Finance can only be deployed after you install or upgrade your SAP ERP prior versions to SAP ERP 6.0 and then install EHP 7 or above. FIN development packages were reassigned to new software components SAP_FIN, EA-FIN, FSCM_CCD, and so on.

    SAP_FIN 720 is the main software component for installing SAP S/4HANA Finance. The content of software components EA-FIN and FSCM_CCD was retrofitted into SAP_FIN 720. For technical reasons, EA-FIN and FSCM_CCD are kept temporarily as empty containers.

> **References**
>
> For more information, see SAP Note 2117481: SAP S/4HANA Finance Support Pack Stack (SPS) Dependencies—Backend.

- **Frontend**

    As of the release of SAP S/4HANA Finance, all SAP Fiori and SAP Smart Business apps are provided with UIAPFI70 200, which needs to be installed. SAP Smart Business requires six SAP HANA content packages to be deployed to the backend of the SAP HANA database.

    SAP S/4HANA Finance also requires installation of SAP Gateway 2.0 and SAP Business Client 7.40 with SPS 10.

> **References**
>
> For more information, see SAP Note 2122588/2117719: SAP S/4HANA Finance Support Pack Stack (SPS) Dependencies—Frontend.

The installation of SAP S/4HANA Finance is comprised of four basic software products. The following list provides you with the minimum required product versions. The first two relate to the backend component, and the last two relate to the frontend:

1. SAP S/4HANA Finance based on EHP 7 or above for SAP ERP 6.0, SAP NetWeaver 7.4, and SAP HANA 1.0
2. SAP HANA Live for SAP S/4HANA Finance based on SAP HANA Live 1.0 for SAP ERP and SAP HANA 1.0
3. SAP Fiori for SAP S/4HANA Finance based on SAP Gateway 2.0 or SAP NetWeaver 7.4
4. SAP Smart Business for SAP S/4HANA Finance based on the SAP Smart Business foundation component 1.0

SAP S/4HANA Finance can be installed in one step with the update of underlying software layers using SUM and the database migration using SUM with DMO. For greenfield system installations, SAP offers a one-step installation package combining SAP ERP 6.0 with EHP 7 and SAP S/4HANA Finance, which can be deployed by the Software Provisioning Manager (SWPM). Installing SAP S/4HANA Finance as a second step after the installation of SAP ERP 6.0 EHP 7 or above is no longer required. This reduces the implementation time and the effort required for the installation.

Some organizations that are already on SAP ERP 6.0 with EHP 7 or above and are risk-averse may still want to achieve their target goal in a sequence of steps. It's possible to implement SAP Business Suite on SAP HANA, which just changes the database to SAP HANA, and then implement the latest version of SAP S/4HANA Finance.

2.5 Apply SAP Notes

Table 2.2 lists the SAP Notes that must be applied to avoid issues during the installation and upgrade of the SAP S/4HANA Finance system. You'll apply these SAP Notes at various stages of the installation process, as noted in the table.

SAP Note	Description
Before Installation of SAP S/4HANA Finance	
1925679	DB Views FMKK_BKPF_BSIK and FMKK_BKPF_BSAK Were Deleted
1941711	Dump: INSERT_PROGRAM_NAME_BLANK during After-Import Processing of SXCI/SXSD
1936455	Error in RS_TYPE_EXISTENCE_CHECK/Program RUTPRERN2VIEW Hangs Endlessly

Table 2.2 SAP Notes to Be Applied

2 Installation and Upgrade

SAP Note	Description
1845848	Removing Generated Fields ("_COUNTER", "_FISCPER",...)
1845847	SAP HANA View Generation w/o Fields _COUNTER, _FISCPER, _BUZEI3
2172805	SAP Simple Finance Upgrade: "COPC_V_PAYRQ_H" Not Activated, SAPK-70005INSAPFIN Included in the Target stack-xml
2202445	Virtual Hierarchies Not Transported to Target System
2207750	SQL-Fehler "Cannot Use Duplicate Index Name" in MAIN_SHDCRE/SUBMOD_SHDDBCLONE/DBCLONE
During Installation of SAP S/4HANA Finance	
2146844	Conversion Program: Pool/Cluster to Transparent Terminates with Return Code 8 Because Views Could Not Be Created
2096457	Errors in ACT_UPG during SPDD: Customer Version of Table Cannot Be Accessed
2139357	SAP Simple Finance OP: Activation Errors during Installation of Support Packages
2086899	Upgrade Phase MAIN_SHDRUN/ACT_UPG Returns Error Messages
After Installation, before Data Migration	
2259159	sFIN Migration: Wrong Values in Field ACDOCA-PREC_AWITEM
2265477	sFIN Migration: Duplicate ACDOCA Records for Classic G/L
2266209	sFIN Migration: ACDOCA-RKCUR Not Filled for All Items in Nonleading Ledgers
2269775	sFIN Migration: Wrong BLART & AWITGRP for ACDOCA Items Created from COEP Items of Business Transaction COIE or INV*
2250671	Migration: Step "Enrichment" Fails
2265261	Syntax Error in CL_FINS_CO_MIG_UTIL: Invalid Statement for "COBK"
2262531	CL_FINS_CO_MIG_COB: Syntax Error "Invalid Statement for COSP_BAK"
2276510	sFIN Migration: Empty ACDOCA-KSL for COEP and Classic G/L
2276979	sFIN migration: Missing CO Amounts Not Displayed in Reconciliation of Line Items

Table 2.2 SAP Notes to Be Applied (Cont.)

Applying these SAP Notes during the appropriate installation phase will ensure consistency with minimal errors as some of these notes mitigate the common errors encountered during the installation process.

2.6 Content Deployment with SAP HANA Application Lifecycle Management

SAP HANA application lifecycle manager can be used to deploy SAP HANA content packages for SAP HANA Live and SAP Smart Business apps. SAP HANA content package installation is performed as an additional step using SAP HANA application lifecycle manager after the installation of SAP S/4HANA Finance using SUM.

SAP HANA Live virtual data model (VDM) packages need to be installed in the following sequence:

1. HANA CONTENT HBA SAP ERP 100
2. HANA CONTENT HBA SAP SFIN 200

2.7 Perform HANA-tization

HANA-tization is the first step after migration to the SAP HANA database. It enables your code to run properly on the new SAP HANA database by adopting the paradigm shift in underlying architecture from a traditional relational database to an in-memory SAP HANA database. This is one of the most important steps for any SAP HANA migration project.

HANA-tization includes checks and actions to be taken after the SAP HANA migration—specifically in custom developments to check if they can run without any disruption. This ensures functional correctness of the organization's existing business processes.

During the migration to SAP HANA, most pool and cluster database tables are transformed to transparent database tables (depooling/declustering) so that the tables can be used in analytic scenarios because applying logical operations on pool and cluster tables at the database level is restrictive.

2   Installation and Upgrade

> **References**
>
> For more information on this topic, see the following SAP Notes:
>
> - SAP Note 1785057: Recommendations for Migrating Suite Systems to SAP HANA
> - SAP Note 1892354: Optimization and Handling for Cluster and Pool Tables in HANA Database

This section covers the checks and tools involved in this HANA-tization process.

2.7.1   HANA-tization Checks

Table 2.3 illustrates the key activities and the actions required to check and find all issues and mitigation plans related to HANA-tization.

Key Elements	Actions Required
Programs using a physical cluster/pool	Use a list of known cluster/pool tables and a where-used list to identify custom programs that could have sorting problems.
Programs using default sorting behavior	Use a new code inspector to identify the default sorting behavior of the transparent tables that can't be checked before the upgrade.
Known migration problems as listed in SAP Notes	Identify and research postmigration problems in the SAP Service Marketplace to avoid any further errors.
Database-specific features (native SQL)	Scan all the Y and Z packages using Transaction CODE_SCANNER, and identify all such instances.
Database-specific features (database hints)	Scan all the Y and Z packages using Transaction CODE_SCANNER, and identify all such instances.

Table 2.3 Checks for HANA-tization

This table is only valid for custom ABAP code; SAP provides the updated programs for standard ABAP as a part of the migration.

2.7.2 HANA-tization Tools

With the migration to the SAP HANA database, many technical changes take place. Table 2.4 provides the recommended list of tools and approaches that you can use to identify the change and take corrective action thereafter.

Technical Change	Tools for Identification	Activities after Identification	Phase
DB migration—native SQL, DB hints, ABAP Database Connectivity (ADBC)	Transaction CODE_SCANNER	Analyze each database-specific feature, and replace them per the SAP HANA database feature.	Before migration
Depooling/declustering—sorting behavior	Enhanced Static Code Inspector	Add the ORDER BY PRIMARY KEY clause or the explicit SORT statement.	After upgrade, before migration
Depooling/declustering—use of physical cluster/pool	None	Usage of this is very rare. Manual analysis and testing are required.	After upgrade, before migration
SQL on transparent table Sorting behavior	Enhanced Static Code Inspector	Add the ORDER BY PRIMARY KEY clause or the explicit SORT statement.	After migration
Direct access/analysis of technical index information (e.g., using the DB_EXISTS_INDEX function module)	Transaction CODE_SCANNER	Direct access/analysis may fail as many of the secondary indexes won't exist after migration. Use an alternative approach.	After migration

Table 2.4 Tools for HANA-tization

The ABAP Test Cockpit (ATC) tool can be used for static ABAP code checks with SAP NetWeaver 7.02 SP 12/SAP NetWeaver 7.31 SP 5 onward.

2.8 Optimization

Traditionally, application logic is executed in the ABAP application server, and data is copied between the data and application server. This is an expensive and data-intensive process. With AS ABAP 7.4 for SAP HANA, it's possible to "push down" calculation-intensive logic on the data set from the application server to the database server. The SAP HANA database then performs the calculation and sends the resulting data set.

Optimization is an optional phase in any SAP HANA migration engagements, through which you can implement code pushdown and improve the performance of ABAP applications, as illustrated in Figure 2.3.

The optimization approach that you need to follow and some of the related key tools and best practices are discussed in the following sections.

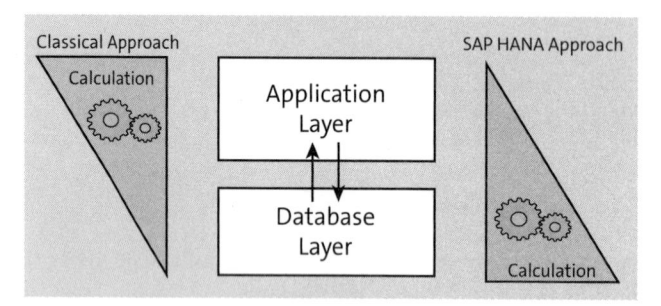

Figure 2.3 Code Pushdown Approach

2.8.1 Optimization Approach

You need to accomplish the following key optimization tasks:

- Identify the list of potential programs based on input from business users and SAP-provided tools—for example, performance statistics.
- Execute different SAP-provided new or existing tools to identify different hot spots in which optimization can be performed. These tools include the Code Inspector, SQL Monitor (Transaction SQLM), Performance Tuning Worklist (Transaction SWLT), Runtime Analysis (Transaction SAT), and so on.
- Manually review the identified hot spots to check whether they can be combined in fewer SAP HANA artifacts. For example, multiple SQL queries and ABAP processing can be combined in a single SAP HANA calculation view and/or procedure.

- Copy the ABAP programs to the new name <original program name>_H.
- Develop SAP HANA artifacts (views, procedures, etc.) using SAP HANA Studio, and use these artifacts in ABAP programs via ADT.
- Test the new program *_H in multiple systems (DEV, QA, etc.) with varying sets of data and high volumes.
- Transport SAP HANA artifacts and ABAP changes together to production using the SAP HANA transport container.
- After realizing performance benefits for a defined period, old programs (without "_H") can be logically deleted—for example, renaming a package to "z*obsolete*" and so on—as a part of obsolete custom developments. You can use the SAP tool Custom Development Management Cockpit (CDMC) for clearing analysis to execute this activity.

2.8.2 Optimization Tools

You can use the optimization tools listed in Table 2.5 for analysis and development purposes.

Tool Name (Transaction, etc.)	Purpose
Transaction SAT/SE30	Finds out which part of the program is taking more time via Runtime Analysis
SQL Monitor (SQLM)	Captures aggregated SQL runtime data over a longer period in the production system and determines the SQL profile of an application
ABAP Test Cockpit (ATC, Code Inspector)	Enhances quality assurance, identifies potential performance issues
SQL Performance Tuning Worklist (Transaction SWLT)	Combines the result of a code analysis with relevant runtime data from a production system
SAP HANA Studio	Performs modeling and development for SAP HANA
ABAP Development Tools (ADT)	Integrates SAP HANA artifacts with ABAP and is used for regular ABAP development

Table 2.5 Tools for Optimization

2.8.3 Optimization Best Practice

You can use the SAP List Viewer (ALV) optimized for SAP HANA to display large tabular data. Some SAP HANA-specific code patterns can be identified in custom ABAP programs that can be used for optimization. We recommend the best practices listed in Table 2.6.

ABAP Pattern	Suggested Action
Joins on transactional tables	Define the external view (attribute/analytic). Read from the external view instead.
SQL on SAP index tables (i.e., table VAPMA)	Define the external view (attribute/analytic). Read from the external view instead.
Locate all "for all entries SQL"	Define the external view (attribute/analytic). Read from the external view instead.
Clusters of related SQL tables (i.e., tables VBAK, VBUK, VBAP)	Define the external view (attribute/analytic). Read from the external view instead.
Access to clustered tables	Modify data manipulation language (DML) for implicit access to the clustered table. Modify SELECT without the ORDER clause.
Sort internal tables sourced from SQL	Define the external view (attribute/analytic), or push the logic to the DB layer (SQL script).
Condense internal tables sourced from SQL	Define the external view (attribute/analytic), or push the logic to the DB layer (SQL script).

Table 2.6 Best Practices for Optimization

2.8.4 SAP HANA Modeling

You need to choose the right type of SAP HANA views for modeling, such as implementing code pushdown, based on the following conditions:

- For simple joins and calculated expressions in a SQL query, use the attribute view.
- If any aggregation is required during a read from a table, use the analytic view.
- If the logic to fetch data is slightly complex, use the graphical calculation view.
- If the logic is more complex, you can use calculation engine (CE) functions.

- If the logic is more complex, and more features are required, use the scripted calculation view or procedures.

2.9 Summary

Installing SAP S/4HANA Finance replaces classical SAP ERP Financials. After the installation of SAP S/4HANA Finance, no additional postings are possible until the end of the migration. All the clients are unusable until the migration is complete.

In the installation phase, some of the steps that are executed include creating backup tables for the totals tables and index tables in the DDIC that are deleted (tables *_BCK in FI and tables *_BAK in CO), saving the totals tables and index tables in backup tables, and deleting the original totals tables and index tables. SAP HANA compatibility views with the same original names for the totals tables and index tables and the new line item table ACDOCA (Universal Journal table) are also created.

SAP S/4HANA Finance can be installed in one step by updating the underlying software layers using SUM and the database migration using SUM with DMO. (The Central Finance deployment scenario acts as an alternative option for organizations that can realize the benefit of SAP S/4HANA Finance capabilities without migrating the existing large and complex distributed system landscapes; we'll talk more about that in Appendix A).

Let's now move on to Chapter 3, in which we'll discuss the Customizing for the General Ledger that you need to perform as part of your SAP S/4HANA Finance migration.

Chapter 3
Preparation and Migration for General Ledger

This chapter highlights the Customizing for the General Ledger and currencies, the integration of postings from Controlling, and the creation of ledger groups required for the migration to SAP S/4HANA Finance. It discusses the architecture, configuration, and functionality impact that SAP S/4HANA Finance has on General Ledger Accounting.

The following are some of the key Customizing steps that you need to perform for migration to the new General Ledger (new G/L) as part of the overall SAP S/4HANA migration:

- Checking and adopting fiscal year variants
- Defining the currency settings
- Migrating G/L settings
- Defining settings for the journal entry ledger
- Reviewing the assignment of ledger and company code to accounting principles
- Defining the ledger for the Controlling (CO) version
- Defining document types for postings in CO
- Defining offsetting account determination
- Defining the source ledger for migration of balances
- Defining settings of the controlling area
- Executing a consistency check of G/L settings
- Activating the required business functions

This configuration is completed under **SAP Customizing Implementation Guide** • **Migration to SAP S/4HANA Finance** • **Preparations and Migration of Customizing** • **Preparations and Migration of Customizing for General Ledger**, as shown in Figure 3.1.

3   Preparation and Migration for General Ledger

```
Display IMG

  ≽  ⊟  ⓘ      Existing BC Sets      ⓘⓘ BC Sets for Activity      ⓘⓘ Activated BC Set
Structure
 ⌄ ▣   SAP Customizing Implementation Guide
   ›       SAP Commercial Project Management
   ›       OpenText Archiving and Document Access for SAP Solutions
   ›       OpenText Business Suite for SAP Solutions
   • ▣ ⊕  Activate Business Functions
   ⌄      Migration to SAP S/4HANA Finance
     • ▣     Info: Migration and Migration Paths to SAP S/4HANA Finance
     ⌄       Preparations and Migration of Customizing
       • ▣ ⊕ Check Customizing Settings Prior to Migration
       • ▣ ⊕ Define Message Types for Posting Before and During Migration
       • ▣ ⊕ Set Number of Jobs for Activities in Mass Data Framework
       ⌄     Preparations and Migration of Customizing for General Ledger
         • ▣    Activate SAP Reference IMG for Financial Accounting (New)
         • ▣ ⊕ Check and Adopt Fiscal Year Variants
         • ▣ ⊕ Define Currency Settings for Migration
         • ▣ ⊕ Migrate General Ledger Customizing
         • ▣ ⊕ Define Settings for Ledgers and Currency Types
         • ▣ ⊕ Review the Assignment of Ledger and Company Code to Acc.-Principles
         • ▣ ⊕ Define Ledger for CO Version
         • ▣ ⊕ Define Document Types for Postings in Controlling
         • ▣ ⊕ Define Document Type Mapping for CO Business Transactions
         • ▣ ⊕ Check and Define Default Values for Postings in Controlling
         • ▣ ⊕ Define Offsetting Account Determination Type
         • ▣ ⊕ Define Source Ledger for Migration of Balances
         • ▣ ⊕ Check and Define Settings for Substitution for Cost-of-Sales Accounting
         • ▣ ⊕ Check and Define Settings of Controlling Area
         • ▣ ⊕ Execute Consistency Check of General Ledger Settings
         • ▣    Activate Business Functions
       ›     Preparations and Migration of Customizing for Asset Accounting
       ›     Preparations and Migration of Customizing for Controlling
       ›     Preparations and Migration of Customizing for Material Ledger
       ›     Preparations for Migration of House Bank Accounts
       ›     Preparatory Activities and Migration of Customizing for Credit Management
     ›       Data Migration
     ›       Activites after Migration
```

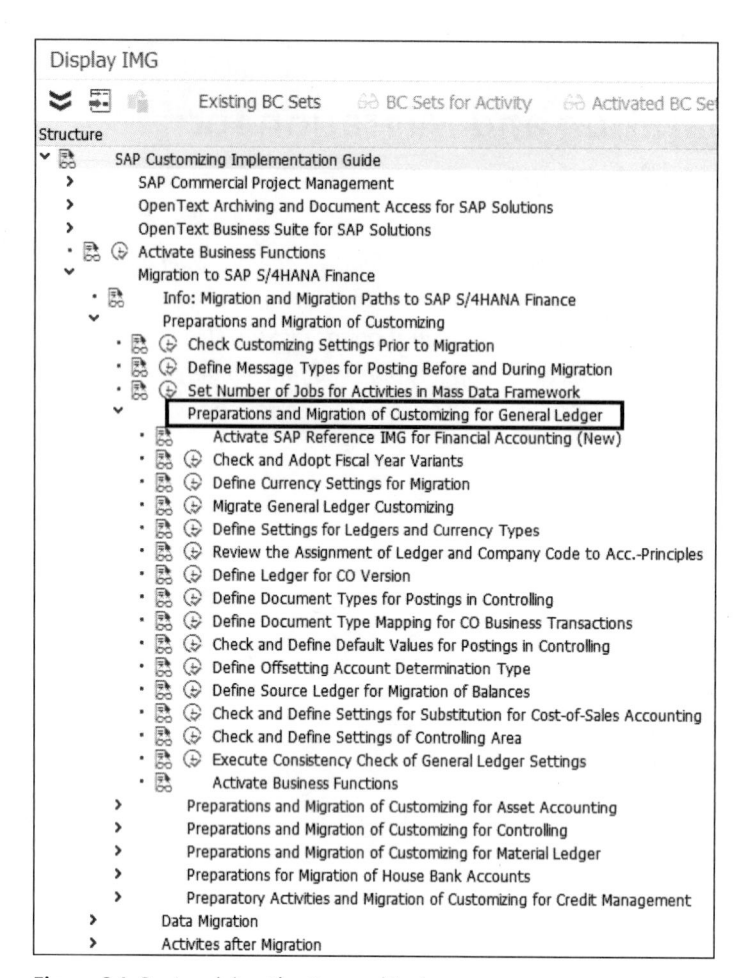

Figure 3.1 Customizing the General Ledger

Let's begin by activating the SAP reference IMG structure for SAP ERP Financials.

3.1   Activate SAP Reference Implementation Guide for Financial Accounting (New)

In this activity, you activate the SAP reference IMG structure for FI and the menu path that is associated with it by following these steps:

1. Select Transaction SA38.
2. Enter the program RFAGL_SWAP_IMG_NEW.
3. Select **Execute**.
4. Under **Activate/Deactivate New Implementation Guide**, choose **Activate New IMG**, and then select **Execute** (see Figure 3.2).

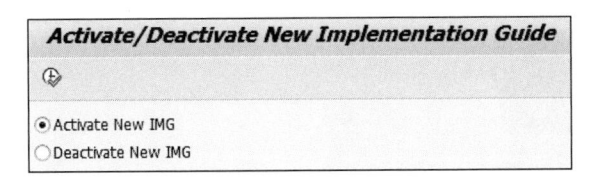

Figure 3.2 Activating the New Implementation Guide

5. In another SAP session, enter the program RFAGL_SWAP_MENU_NEW.
6. Select **Execute**.
7. Under **Activate/Deactivate New Menu**, choose **Activate New Menu**, and then select **Execute** so that the relevant structure is visible (see Figure 3.3).

Figure 3.3 Activating the New Menu

3.2 Check and Adopt Fiscal Year Variants

The migration to the Universal Journal requires the same fiscal year variant to be used in both FI and CO.

In this activity, you compare the fiscal year variants between controlling areas and their assigned company codes. If an inconsistency exists in the fiscal year variant configuration, a report is created with a proposal for the required configuration change. You need to execute the report as part of the migration process. The fiscal year variants of CO and FI must be aligned before the migration of the transaction data can be started. The report lists all CO areas and company codes that need to be changed, as well as the number of the posting periods and special periods.

3   Preparation and Migration for General Ledger

The **Det. FYV for CoAr** (determined fiscal year variant for controlling area) and **Det. FYV for CoCd** (determined fiscal year variant for company code) columns provide the proposal for the configuration change. The report must be executed using Transaction FINS_MIG_FYV for all relevant controlling areas.

If no changes are required, the information window shown in Figure 3.4 appears.

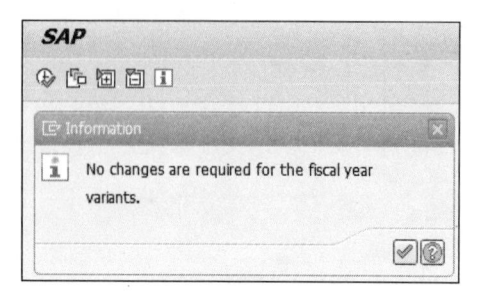

Figure 3.4 Aligning Fiscal Year Variants between CO and FI

3.3   Define Currency Settings for Migration

In this activity, the currency settings are established so that the Universal Journal entry provides amount information for all currency types, including the one that was only used in the CO module prior to the migration to SAP S/4HANA Finance.

In classical SAP, statistical postings in CO did not require a mandatory local currency posting, but in SAP S/4HANA Finance, the Universal Journal always requires a posting in a local currency. Thus, the exchange rate type needs to be defined so that these CO-related transactions can be migrated along with a local currency amount using the exchange rate type and the posting date. If the exchange rate type setting is not defined, then the affected transactions are migrated with zero as the amount.

The settings also need to be defined for amounts that used currency types only in CO, determining whether to use FI currency Customizing or the CO approach in the SAP S/4HANA instance going forward.

> **Expert Insight**
>
> You might encounter an error titled **Currency Types 10/20/70 in Document Header Inconsistent**, which might be the result of the CO area currency being changed from currency type 10 to 30 in the past, resulting in the migration error (shown in Figure 3.5).

3.4 Migrate General Ledger Customizing

In this situation, you should ignore the inconsistency as it pertains to the past closed fiscal years. Moreover, the pre- and post-migration reports should reconcile.

Figure 3.5 Error in Currency Type

3.4 Migrate General Ledger Customizing

In this activity, you migrate all the ledgers to the new configuration using Transaction FINS_MIG_LEDGER_CUST, as shown in Figure 3.6.

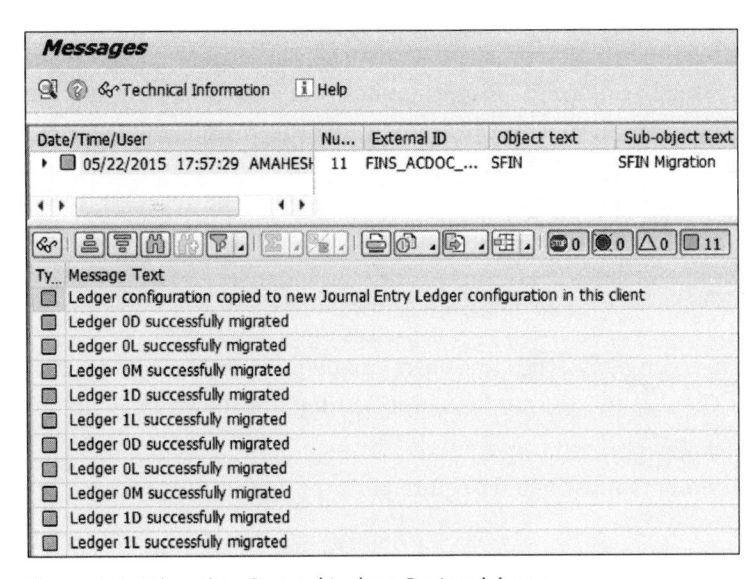

Figure 3.6 Migrating General Ledger Customizing

The following settings are migrated:

- Company code assignments
- Currency settings

135

3   Preparation and Migration for General Ledger

- Fiscal year variant
- Open period variant
- Settings for real-time integration of CO and FI

After all these items are migrated successfully, you can proceed to the next step.

3.5   Define Settings for Ledgers and Currency Types

In this activity, you define ledgers, which you use in accounting. Only one ledger can be defined as the leading ledger (the standard leading ledger is 0L). There are two types of ledgers:

1. **Standard ledger**

   The *standard ledger* consists of all journal entries related to any business transactions.

2. **Extension ledger**

   Introduced in SAP S/4HANA Finance, an *extension ledger* is assigned to a standard ledger, from which it inherits all journal entry postings. The ledger type *extension ledger* has been named as *appendix ledger,* as shown in Figure 3.7. Any specific adjustments required to be posted only to the appendix ledger aren't duplicated in the standard ledger. Thus, the appendix ledger takes the base values from the standard ledger and then combines the specific appendix ledger postings. This prevents multiple data footprints and significantly reduces data redundancy because the journal entries don't need to be posted to both the appendix and the standard ledger.

You also need to assign company codes to ledgers and define currency settings and fiscal year variants. The step-by-step configuration settings are shown in Figure 3.7 through Figure 3.10.

The following requirements must be met before performing this Customizing activity:

- Company codes are configured with currency, fiscal year variants, and open period variants.
- Controlling areas are configured with currency types and fiscal year variants.
- Company codes are assigned to controlling areas.

3.5 Define Settings for Ledgers and Currency Types

- Migration and Customizing of the ledger is completed.
- Ledger 0L is configured as the leading ledger.
- The leading ledger is assigned to all company codes.

In this Customizing setting, **Ledger 0L** needs to be assigned as the **Leading** ledger (see Figure 3.7). Here, you also need to create all the other standard (nonleading) ledgers and appendix ledgers required for parallel accounting for the organization.

Change View "Ledger for the unified Journal Entry": Overview

Ledger	Leading	Ledger Type	Ledger Name	Underl. Ldgr.
0D	☐	Standard Ledger		
0L	✓	Standard Ledger	Leading Ledger	
0M	☐	Standard Ledger		
1D	☐	Standard Ledger		
1L	☐	Standard Ledger	Leading Ledger	
L1	☐	Standard Ledger	Parallel Ledger	
Z1	☐	Extension Ledger	Appendix Ledger	0L

Figure 3.7 Standard Ledger Customizing

In this Customizing setting, all company codes need to be assigned to the leading ledger 0L. Here, you also need to configure company code assignments to other ledgers, along with currency settings, fiscal year variants, and open period variants for nonleading ledgers. If you want to perform parallel accounting using G/L accounts instead of various ledgers, you need to select the **Parallel GL Accts** checkbox (see Figure 3.8).

Change View "Company Code Settings for the Ledger": Overview

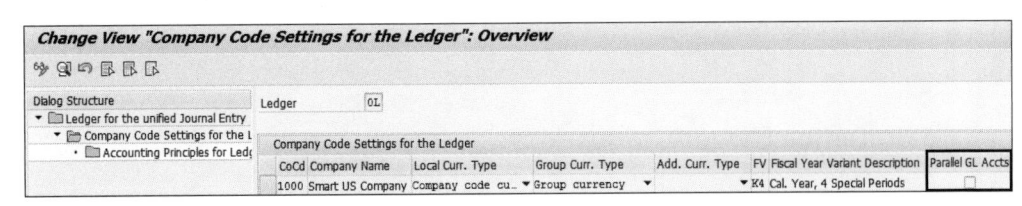

CoCd	Company Name	Local Curr. Type	Group Curr. Type	Add. Curr. Type	FV Fiscal Year Variant Description	Parallel GL Accts
1000	Smart US Company	Company code cu...	Group currency		K4 Cal. Year, 4 Special Periods	☐

Figure 3.8 Ledger Assignment to Company Code

In this Customizing setting, you need to assign accounting principles to the ledger. This assignment ensures that documents posted for a particular accounting principle are posted to the assigned ledger, whereas documents for which the

137

accounting principle hasn't been assigned are posted to all ledgers (see Figure 3.9 and Figure 3.10).

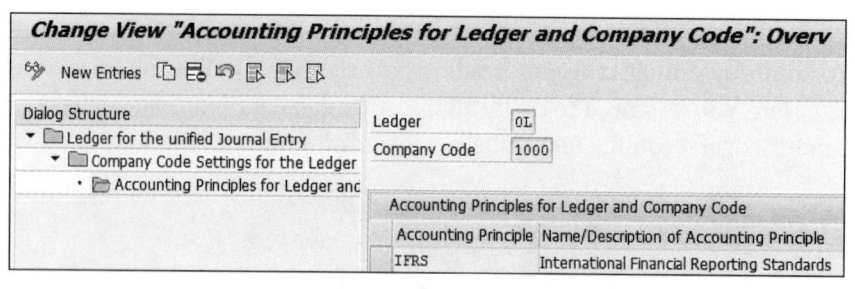

Figure 3.9 Accounting Principle Assignment to Ledger 0L and Company Code

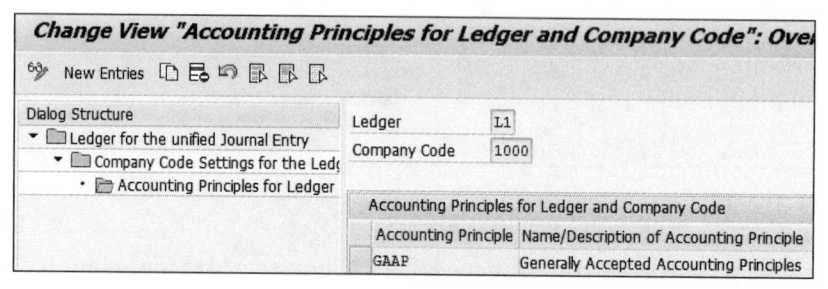

Figure 3.10 Accounting Principle Assignment to Ledger L1 and Company Code

> **References**
>
> For more information, see SAP Note 1951069: Different Fiscal Year Variants in General Ledger Accounting (New).

3.6 Define Ledger Groups

In this activity, you define ledger groups, as shown in Figure 3.11. The creation of ledger groups simplifies the individual functions and processes of General Ledger Accounting. You can create as many ledger groups as needed and can assign any number of ledgers in a ledger group as needed to meet your business goals.

3.6 Define Ledger Groups

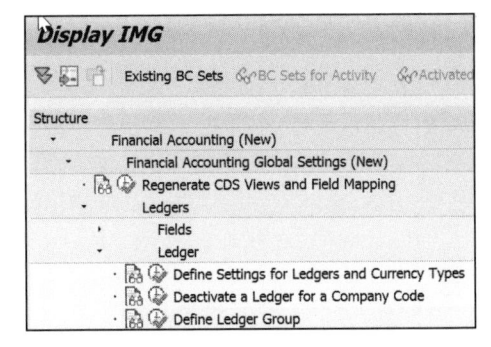

Figure 3.11 Customizing the Ledger Group

When a ledger is created in the system, a ledger group with the same name is automatically created, whereby data for an individual ledger can be posted and accessed merely by entering the ledger group. Some properties of ledger groups include the following:

- You can rename the ledger group that was created automatically when creating the ledger.
- You can create ledger groups that enable you to bring several ledgers together for joint processing in a function.
- If a ledger group isn't specified while posting an entry, the system posts to all the ledgers by default. Thus, creating ledger groups for all ledgers isn't required.

Within the ledger group, you need to assign one ledger as the representative ledger by selecting the **Rep. Ledger** checkbox, as shown in Figure 3.12. The best practice is to have the leading ledger 0L as your representative ledger. Posting to all the ledgers is determined by the posting period of the representative ledger. If the posting period of the representative ledger is open while the posting period of the nonrepresentative ledger is closed, the system still posts to all the ledgers. The criteria for a representative ledger are as follows:

- Any ledger can be assigned as a representative ledger if all the ledgers in the group have a fiscal year variant that is different from the one assigned to the company code.
- If a ledger in the group has the same fiscal year variant as assigned to the company code, then that ledger must be assigned as the representative ledger within the ledger group.

139

3   Preparation and Migration for General Ledger

Thus, you may not be able to use the same ledger group for all the active company codes within the organization.

Change View "Ledger Assignment": Overview

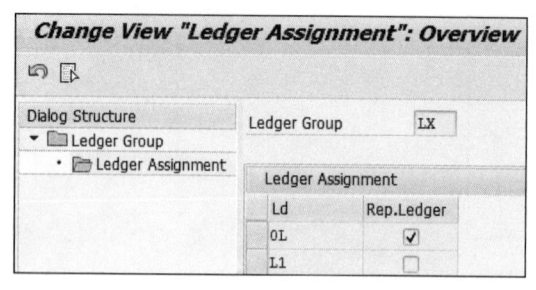

Dialog Structure	Ledger Group	LX
▼ Ledger Group		
• Ledger Assignment	Ledger Assignment	
	Ld	Rep.Ledger
	0L	✓
	L1	☐

Figure 3.12 Defining the Ledger Group and Representative Ledger

3.7   Assign the Accounting Principle to the Ledger Group

After the ledger groups are created, you need to assign the ledger group to the accounting principle for the organizational legal and statutory reporting requirements. You can do so by choosing **SAP Customizing Implementation Guide • Financial Accounting (New) • Financial Accounting Global Settings (New) • Ledgers • Parallel Accounting • Assign Accounting Principle to Ledger Groups**, as shown in Figure 3.13.

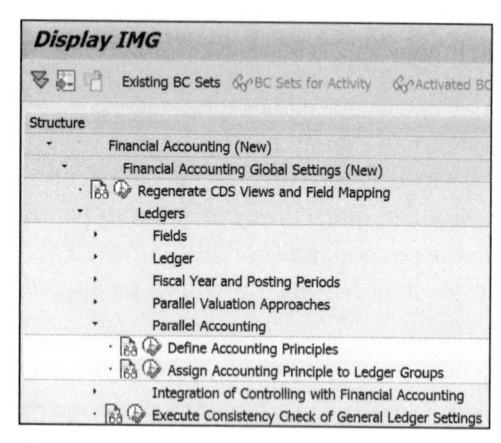

Display IMG

Structure
- Financial Accounting (New)
  - Financial Accounting Global Settings (New)
    - Regenerate CDS Views and Field Mapping
    - Ledgers
      - Fields
      - Ledger
      - Fiscal Year and Posting Periods
      - Parallel Valuation Approaches
      - Parallel Accounting
        - Define Accounting Principles
        - Assign Accounting Principle to Ledger Groups
      - Integration of Controlling with Financial Accounting
      - Execute Consistency Check of General Ledger Settings

Figure 3.13 Assign Accounting Principle to Ledger Groups

Upon execution of this Customizing transaction, you then assign the accounting principle to the ledger group, as shown in Figure 3.14.

3.9 Define the Ledger for the Controlling Version

Assignment of Accounting Principle to Target Ledger Group		
Accounting Principle	Target Ledger Group	Description
	0L	
60	0L	
GAAP	L1	Non-Leading Ledger
HGB	0L	
IAS	0L	
IFRS	0L	

Figure 3.14 Ledger Groups Assigned to Accounting Principles

3.8 Review the Assignment of Ledger and Company Code to Accounting Principles

In this activity, you need to evaluate the accounting principle as assigned to the combination of ledger and company code. When a journal entry is posted with an accounting principle in the universal journal, the settings here drive posting to all the ledgers that are assigned the accounting principle as selected in the journal entry, as shown in Figure 3.15.

Ledger	Company Code	Acc.Princ.	Name/Description of Accounting Principle	Company Name	Ledger Name
0L	1001	IFRS	Internation Financial Reporting Standards	US Legal Entity 1	Leading Ledger
A1	E101	UGAP	US GAAP	US Legal Entity 1 - EHT	Appendix Ledger
N1	1002	LGAP	Local GAAP	CA Legal Entity 1	Non Leading Ledger

Figure 3.15 Assignment of Ledger and Company Code to Accounting Principle

3.9 Define the Ledger for the Controlling Version

In this activity, you define a ledger in which all actual data relevant to CO is posted by assigning **Version 0** to a ledger. The version is assigned at the company code level, and the same ledger needs to be used for all company codes.

Currently, **Version 0** needs to be assigned to the leading ledger for all company codes that are assigned to a CO area, as shown in Figure 3.16.

141

3   Preparation and Migration for General Ledger

The fiscal year variant of the company code must be identical to that of the controlling area.

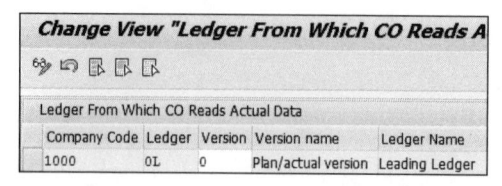

Figure 3.16 Assigning the Ledger to the CO Version

3.10   Define Document Types for Postings in Controlling

In this activity, you create and define new document types for CO-related postings. For example, you can create a separate document type that can be used for the reposting or allocation of primary costs. For document types used in CO, you must select the **G/L Account** indicator under the **Account Types Allowed** section.

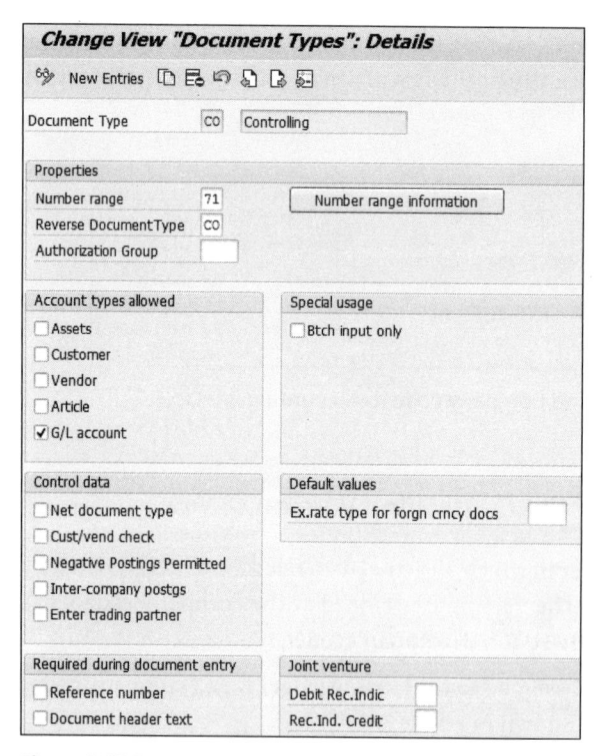

Figure 3.17 Document Type Properties for CO

142

In the example shown in Figure 3.17, **Document Type CO** is defined with account type **G/L Account** checked.

3.11 Define Document Type Mapping for Controlling Business Transactions

In this activity, you define a variant for mapping CO business transactions to document types. You must conduct and define this mapping exercise for all CO actual posting business transactions.

A default mapping variant is generated during the Customizing activity for the migration of the ledger in which all CO business transactions are mapped to the document type associated with the CO-FI real-time integration, as shown in Figure 3.18.

Variant for Mapping CO Transact. to Doc. Types		
DocType Mapping Var.	Text	Default Variant
1000	CO-FI Real time Integration	✓

Figure 3.18 Variant for Mapping the CO Transaction to Document Types

Figure 3.19 shows how the CO business transactions are assigned to the document type.

DocType Mapping Var. 1000

Mapping of CO Bus. Transactions to Document Types

CO Business Transaction	Text	Document Type	Cross-Company Document Type
RKIU	Actual Overhead Assessment	SA	SA
RKIV	Actual Overhead Distribution	SA	SA

Figure 3.19 Mapping of CO Transactions to Document Types

3.12 Check and Define Default Values for Postings in Controlling

In this activity, you define default values for posting CO business transactions in which the user interfaces don't allow any document type or ledger group as an input while posting. If a default ledger group isn't specified in this Customizing activity, all CO-related transactions are posted to all the ledgers, as shown in Figure 3.20.

Figure 3.20 Default Values for Postings in CO

To define the ledger group and assign the ledgers (see Figure 3.21), use the Customizing menu path **Financial Accounting (New)** • **Financial Accounting Global Settings (New)** • **Ledgers** • **Ledger** • **Define Ledger Group**.

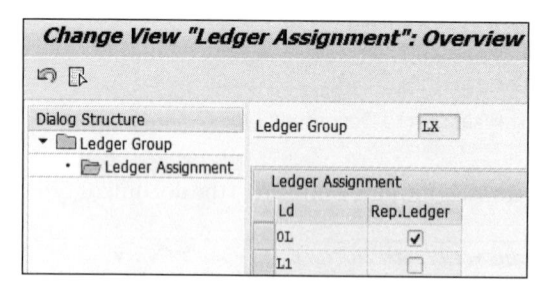

Figure 3.21 Ledger Group Assignment

Here, you first create ledger groups as required, provide a description for each of the groups, and then assign ledgers as applicable to each of the ledger groups. When posting a document, you can specify a ledger group so that all the documents are posted only to those ledgers that are in that group.

The system assigns a representative ledger within a group that has more than one ledger. The representative ledger is used to determine the posting period and to check if the period is open for posting. If the representative ledger is open, the system still posts to all the ledgers in the group, even though the posting period for the other ledgers in the group might be closed.

3.13 Define the Offsetting Account Determination Type

In this activity, you define the offsetting account determination for all applications. This activity needs to be executed before the migration to SAP S/4HANA Finance.

You should choose the **As Case 2, but Including Line Items Generated Automatically** option, as shown in Figure 3.22, because this option always displays the offsetting account with the highest amount, along with the line items that are generated automatically.

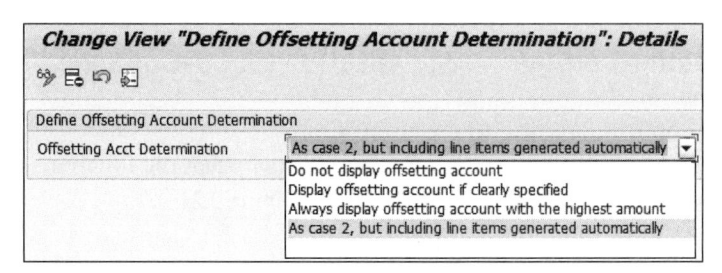

Figure 3.22 Define Offsetting Account Determination

3.14 Define the Source Ledger for Migration of Balances

In this activity, you define the source ledger and the source database table of the balances for General Ledger Accounting from which you want to transfer the opening balances. To do so, you use the following information:

- Target ledger
- Company code (you can specify "*" to apply the settings to all company codes)
- Starting fiscal year (by specifying the year as "0001", you apply the settings for all fiscal years)

Organizations using the new G/L can specify one entry per ledger, where the source and target ledger are equal. In the example in Figure 3.23, **0L** is defined as both the source and target ledger for **CoCd 1000** for the purpose of migration of balances.

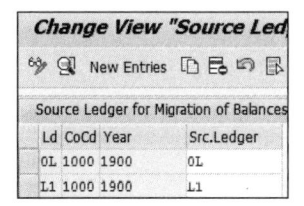

Figure 3.23 Source Ledger for Migration of Balances

> **Expert Insight**
>
> If your organization was on classic G/L before and migrated to new G/L, then you have to specify a minimum of two line items. The first line item states the year from which the classic G/L ledger 00 was the source, and the second line item states the year from which the new G/L ledger 0L was the source. In both the cases, the target ledger remains 0L only.

3.15 Check and Define Settings for Substitution for Cost-of-Sales Accounting

In this activity, you define substitution rules; it's relevant only when the functional area is being used for cost-of-sales accounting, as shown in Figure 3.24.

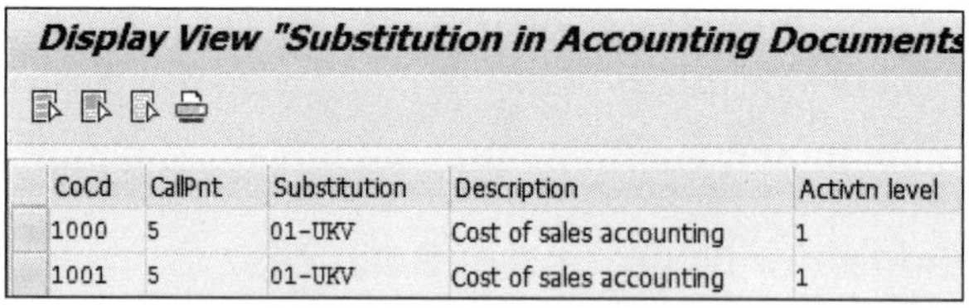

CoCd	CallPnt	Substitution	Description	Activtn level
1000	5	01-UKV	Cost of sales accounting	1
1001	5	01-UKV	Cost of sales accounting	1

Figure 3.24 Define Substitution Settings

3.16 Check and Define Settings of Controlling Area

In this activity, you need to define and validate the setting for the controlling area because SAP S/4HANA Finance behaves a bit differently compared to classic SAP ERP.

In SAP S/4HANA Finance, posting to an account assignment object such as a cost center is only possible from the company code defined in the master data of the account assignment object. This limitation is only applicable for external accounting; cross-company cost allocation will continue to work using intercompany clearing accounts. Thus, the **CoCd Validation** indicator should be checked for the current fiscal year and all future fiscal years at a minimum, as shown in Figure 3.25.

3.18 Activate Business Functions

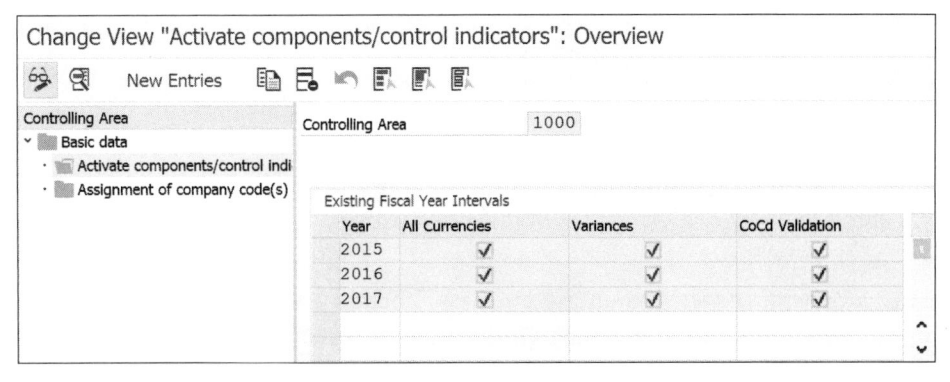

Figure 3.25 Activate Control Indicators for Controlling Area

Because the transaction currency is always recorded in a single Universal Journal in SAP S/4HANA Finance, you should activate and check the **All Currencies** boxes in the controlling area, as shown in Figure 3.25. In classic SAP ERP, it was possible to post only in CO, but with the integration of CO with FI in SAP S/4HANA Finance, the postings within CO are also posted to the G/L using the Universal Journal. Therefore, you should check the **All Currencies** indicator and record all amounts in the transaction currency as well; otherwise, you might get an error message stating **Activate Control Indicator "All Currencies" (CO Area XXXX/FiscYr XXXX)**.

3.17 Execute Consistency Check of General Ledger Settings

In this activity, the Customizing settings for the ledgers are checked using Transaction FINS_CUST_CONS_CHK. This check must be executed before migration of transaction data with no error messages. You should receive the **Check Passed** message, as shown in Figure 3.26, upon execution of this consistency check.

Figure 3.26 Consistency Check of General Ledger Settings

3.18 Activate Business Functions

In this activity, you need to activate the business functions that are necessary for migrating to SAP S/4HANA Finance. You must activate the following business functions in the Customizing system using Transaction SFW5 and then import them into the production system:

- FIN_GL_CI_1

    This General Ledger Accounting business function helps to optimize the processes related to parallel accounting, as well as planning and reporting based on profit centers.

- FIN_GL_CI_2

    This General Ledger Accounting business function enhances the processes for parallel accounting by enabling its integration with CO.

- FIN_GL_CI_3

    This business function helps to improve the processes related to periodic tasks and optimize the usage of archive functionality. Analysis of actual/actual comparison between the ledgers can be done while conducting the financial statement analysis. This business function also plays an important role in managing the assigned numbers when assets are transferred.

All three business functions activate functionality in G/L, which is mandatory for the implementation of SAP S/4HANA Finance (see Figure 3.27).

E1D - Switch Framework: Change Business Function Status		
Check Discard Changes Activate Changes Switch Framework Browser Display L		
Business Function Set	SAP Retail	
Name	Description	Planned Status
• FIN_GL_CI_1	New General Ledger Accounting	Business func. will remain activated
• FIN_GL_CI_2	New General Ledger Accounting 2	Business func. will remain activated
• FIN_GL_CI_3	New General Ledger Accounting 3	Business func. will remain activated

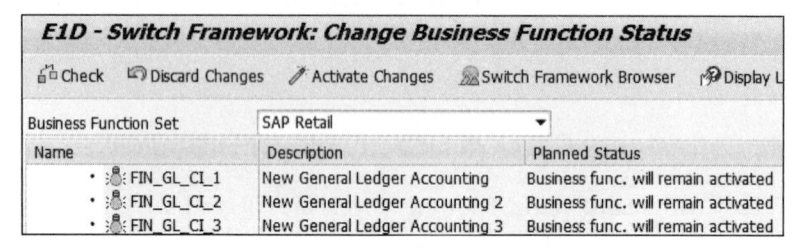

Figure 3.27 New General Ledger Business Functions Activated

Now that you've set up and customized the G/L, let's take a look at what impact this has on your architecture, functionality, and configuration.

3.19 Key Changes to the General Ledger

With the emergence of SAP S/4HANA Finance, SAP eliminated redundant data, such as aggregates and indexes, and continued the reduction of the memory footprint and table design. This section analyzes the major impact that SAP S/4HANA Finance's

3.19 Key Changes to the General Ledger

table architecture design, business process transactions, and configuration changes have had on General Ledger Accounting, as well as the impact on some related areas.

Traditionally, SAP stored SAP General Ledger (G/L), customer, and vendor balances and open item statuses in various database tables to support reporting. With the introduction of SAP S/4HANA Finance, the same reporting can be achieved directly from table ACDOCA without storing balances or open item statuses separately. All the fields from submodules such as Controlling (CO), Asset Accounting (FI-AA), SAP Material Ledger (ML), and Profitability Analysis (CO-PA) are available in table ACDOCA. The roadmap for SAP is to use table ACDOCP for planning data and table ACDOCC for consolidation data.

In an earlier version of SAP ERP Financials (FI), the secondary cost elements couldn't be displayed in the financial statement. In SAP S/4HANA Finance, the secondary cost elements are created as G/L accounts, which allows secondary cost elements to be included and viewed in the financial statement version as well.

> **1709 Preview**
>
> With the release of SAP S/4HANA 1709, the Universal Journal can be implemented or migrated from various scenarios, as follows:
>
> - The organization is using new G/L, with parallel ledgers and document splitting activated.
> - The organization is using classic G/L. An important point to note here is that after moving from classic G/L to the Universal Journal, you can subsequently introduce parallel ledgers and document splitting as two separate projects in any sequence. Although parallel ledgers functionality was introduced with the 1605 release of the SAP S/4HANA Finance add-on, document splitting was introduced with version 1709. Both options require a fiscal year change in SAP S/4HANA as a prerequisite step.
> - The organization is using classic G/L and undertook the migration to a new G/L project.

3.19.1 Architectural Impact

The biggest change to the architecture of General Ledger Accounting is the new journal entry, which consists of a header record (table BKPF) and the respective line items record (table ACDOCA), as shown in Figure 3.28. The attributes of these tables are as follows:

- With SAP S/4HANA Finance, when you post a journal entry, the header record is posted in table BKPF, and the line item record is posted in table ACDOCA. There are rare exceptions in which only line item records in table ACDOCA are written, without a corresponding document header record. This includes transactions related to carryforward, corrections in migration, and so on.
- The corresponding line items have artificial document numbers beginning with a letter (e.g., *A*).
- Table ACDOCA contains all fields (350+) required for G/L, CO, FI-AA, ML, and CO-PA.
- Tables ACDOCA and BSEG don't store completely identical dimensions.
- Table ACDOCA has fields from CO, ML, and FI-AA that aren't in table BSEG; similarly, table BSEG has dedicated fields for open item management/payment that aren't in table ACDOCA.
- Due to the 999-document line item posting limitation, table BSEG is usually aggregated. This limitation doesn't exist in table ACDOCA.
- Table ACDOCA stores all CO internal postings; these aren't posted to table BSEG.
- Table ACDOCA stores carryforward transaction postings and correction line items from migration; these lines aren't stored in table BSEG.
- Table ACDOCA is a line item table with full integration with all applications, as shown in Figure 3.29.
- Fast multidimensional reporting is possible from table ACDOCA without replicating data to SAP Business Warehouse (SAP BW).
- The Universal Journal can be extended easily with custom fields such as the derivation tools from CO-PA and standard coding block extensibility. The respective custom fields as required are added to the Universal Journal table (Transaction OXK3).

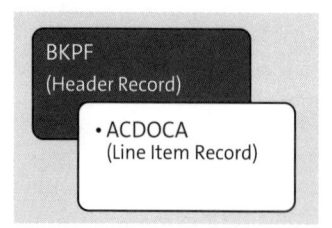

Figure 3.28 Journal Entry Architecture

3.19 Key Changes to the General Ledger

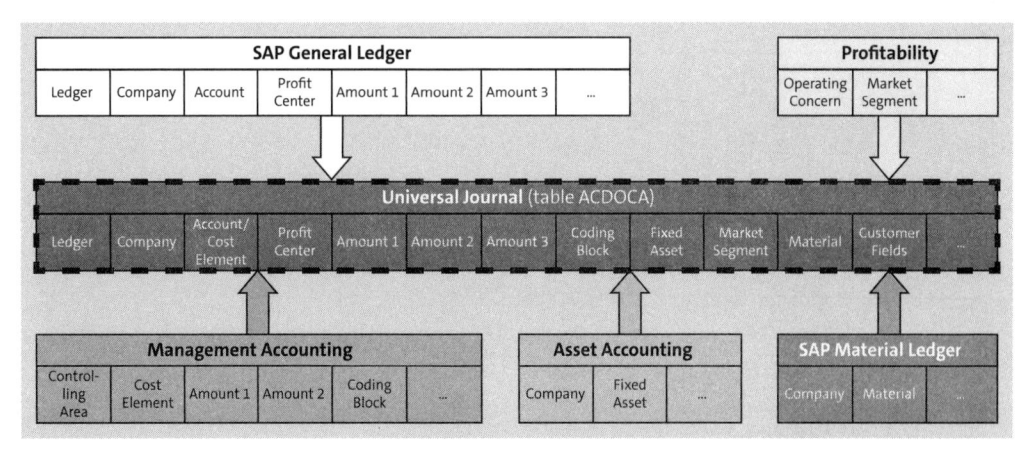

Figure 3.29 Universal Journal Entry

There are also several technical changes in General Ledger Accounting:

- Table ACDOCA stores the data previously stored in table FAGLFLEXA and table FAGLFLEXT.
- Table ACDOCA also stores the data of new G/L public sector industry tables and joint venture accounting.
- Customer-specific new G/L fields ZZ<CUST>T and ZZ<CUST>A are stored in table ACDOCA, as shown in Figure 3.30.
- A compatibility view exists for table FAGLFLEXA and table FAGLFLEXT.
- A compatibility view is provided for the new G/L industry tables and customer-specific new G/L tables. The views are numbered consecutively, such as ZFGLV_GLTT_Cx and ZFGLV_GLSI_Cx, where x is a number.
- Access to old data in tables is still possible via the V_<TABLENAME>_ORI view (e.g., V_FAGLFLEXA_ORI).
- The old data of table FAGLFLEXT is stored in table FAGLFLEXT_BCK.
- Customers can access the old data in customer-defined new G/L tables that are created as views in the Data Dictionary (DDIC). The V_FAGLFLEXA_ORI view can be used as a template.

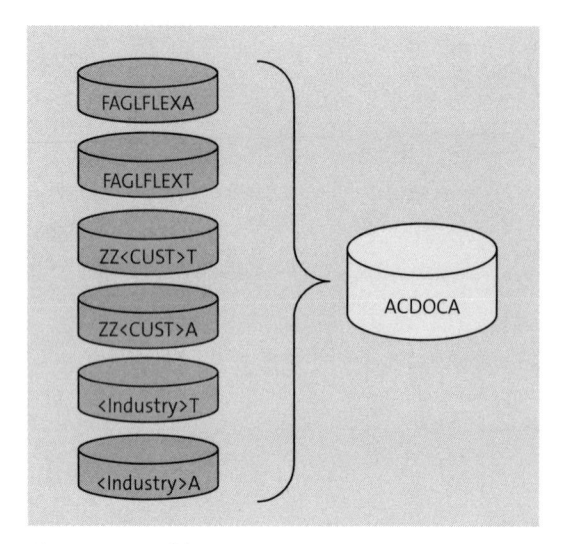

Figure 3.30 Table ACDOCA Structure

SAP S/4HANA Finance also provides for the unification of master data maintenance for G/L accounts and cost elements with the introduction of account type and cost element attributes in Transaction FS00.

The following are some of the features related to ledgers, document postings, and deployment that have been impacted with the introduction of SAP S/4HANA Finance:

- **Document number in CO**
    - Transactions posted in CO use a CO document number—for example, repostings (Transactions KB11 and KB41).
    - Original documents (prima nota) are used for the Universal Journal entry.
    - The existing Customizing for CO document numbers is still valid.
    - The field name in the Universal Journal entry is CO_BELNR.
- **Journal entries triggered from other applications (FI, Logistics, etc.)**
    - A cryptic document number is generated into field CO_BELNR; this number is needed for CO compatibility views.
    - The Universal Journal entries from CO can be grouped by the CO document number generated (e.g., cross-company postings).

- **Document summarization**
  - Document summarization is still possible for other tables because table ACDOCA stores the complete detail needed for all components based on table ACDOCA (G/L, FI-AA, ML, CO, CO-PA).
  - Table BSEG's three-digit (999) line item posting limitation still exists in SAP S/4HANA Finance, but because table ACDOCA stores the full detail and has a six-digit field for line item numbering and posting, extensive summarization is still possible.
- **FI postings with SAP S/4HANA Finance**
  - Table ACDOCA posted via the accounting interface is similar to table FAGLFLEXA (new G/L) in the past.
  - Entries previously stored in tables COEP, FAGLFLEXA, ANEP, MLIT, and so on are stored in table ACDOCA.
  - Table BSEG entries aren't changed.
  - Costing-based CO-PA, Profit Center Accounting, Special Purpose Ledger (FI-SL), and Enterprise Controlling Consolidation System (EC-CS) work as before.
- **Document numbers with SAP S/4HANA Finance**
  - With the Universal Journal, any journal entry created can write to components such as G/L, CO, ML, and FI-AA. A single legal document number is generated and populated in tables BKPF and ACDOCA in field BELNR. This document number is year-dependent and company code-specific.
  - The system generates a transaction number for CO. This number is captured in the CO_BELNR field for CO, and it generates a new number for every 999 lines. In short, one FI (legal) document can have many corresponding CO document numbers, but they are all linked.
- **Cost element plan and category**
  - G/L and cost element planning don't work in SAP S/4HANA Finance as a stand-alone function. SAP BPC for SAP S/4HANA Finance needs to be activated for planning to work.
  - The statistical account assignment setting is made for fixed assets and material account objects to flow in accounting documents. It eliminates the feature of traditional FI to create cost element category 90 for fixed assets accounts.

- **Parallel delta versions for actuals in CO**
  With FI and CO now merged into the Universal Journal, parallel valuation in all areas is provided based on parallel ledgers. Therefore, the existing solution based on parallel delta versions for actuals in CO must be adapted.
- **Concept of prima nota**
  - The prima nota, which acts as the source document, triggers the creation of journal entries. The prima nota also allows the complete reversal process of the journal entries.
  - For every manual FI posting (Transactions FB01, FB50, FB60, FB70, etc.), the prima nota is stored in table BSEG.
  - For classic manual CO postings and posting via BAPIs, the prima nota is stored in table COEP.
  - No prima nota is required for allocation postings such as assessment, settlement, and so on because the data are written to table ACDOCA only.
  - For material price changes (Transaction MR21) or material debit/credit (Transaction MR22), the prima nota is created in the ML (tables MLHD, MLIT, etc.).
- **Ledger: leading, nonleading, and extension (appendix)**
  - The leading ledger concept remains the same; that is, it contains a full set of line items in table ACDOCA and is the source for actual CO data (assigned to actual version 0).
  - Nonleading standard ledgers, as in the earlier version, can still be assigned to selected company codes. A nonleading ledger contains a full set of line items in table ACDOCA. It inherits the currency configuration of the leading ledger and can have a different fiscal year variant and open period variant.
  - The appendix ledger contains only adjustment postings. In reporting, the appendix ledger inherits postings of the base ledger, as shown in Figure 3.31.
  - The appendix ledger is assigned to the base ledger and only accepts ledger-specific manual adjustment postings. It inherits currency settings and the fiscal year variant of the base ledger but can have a separate open period variant and company code assignment. Thus, the appendix ledger takes the base from the standard ledger. This prevents multiple data footprints and significantly reduces data redundancy because the journal entries don't need to be posted to both the appendix and the standard ledger.

3.19 Key Changes to the General Ledger

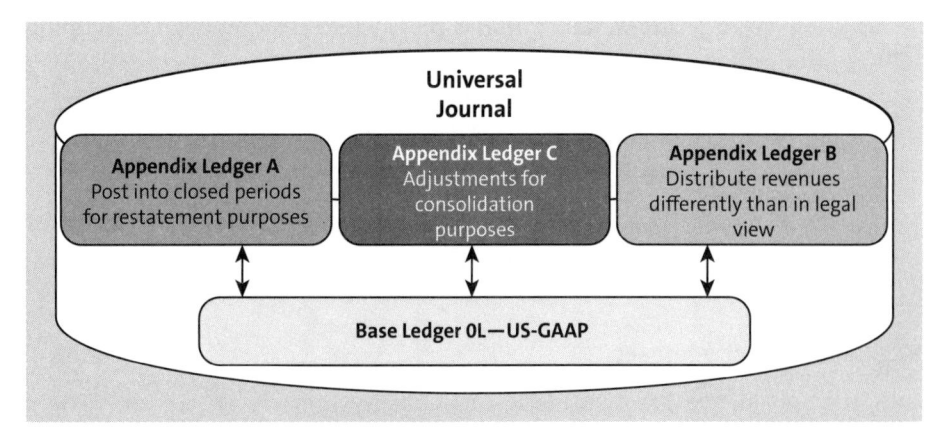

Figure 3.31 Introduction of Appendix Ledger

- The appendix ledger can report on all the transaction data of the base ledger, so it allows you to create views without affecting the base ledger. This is reflected in the ledger architecture illustrated in Figure 3.32.

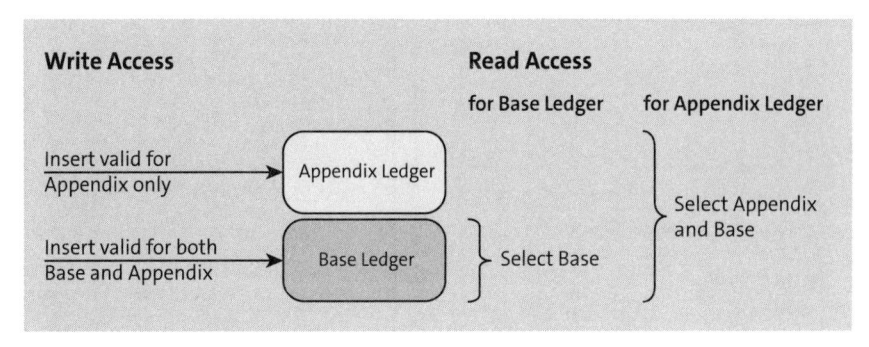

Figure 3.32 Ledger Architecture

- **Usage of Central Finance**
  - Remember that Central Finance is one of the deployment methods to migrate to SAP S/4HANA Finance. It isn't a product by itself. (See Appendix A for more information!)
  - Central Finance breaks out the FI/CO applications from the other applications via Application Link Enabling (ALE).

155

3 Preparation and Migration for General Ledger

- By using ALE, a technical foundation is provided to customers for integrating business processes in a discrete environment.
- This deployment fits the scenarios of a multi-ERP (both SAP and non-SAP) system landscape, a highly customized SAP system, and various legacy systems.
- This deployment model needs a separate license for Central Finance and an installation of the SAP Landscape Transformation replication server.

3.19.2 Functionality Impact

SAP S/4HANA Finance has two major functionality impacts on General Ledger Accounting. First, the open item reports shown in Figure 3.33 have been removed from SAP S/4HANA Finance due to the introduction of the Universal Journal.

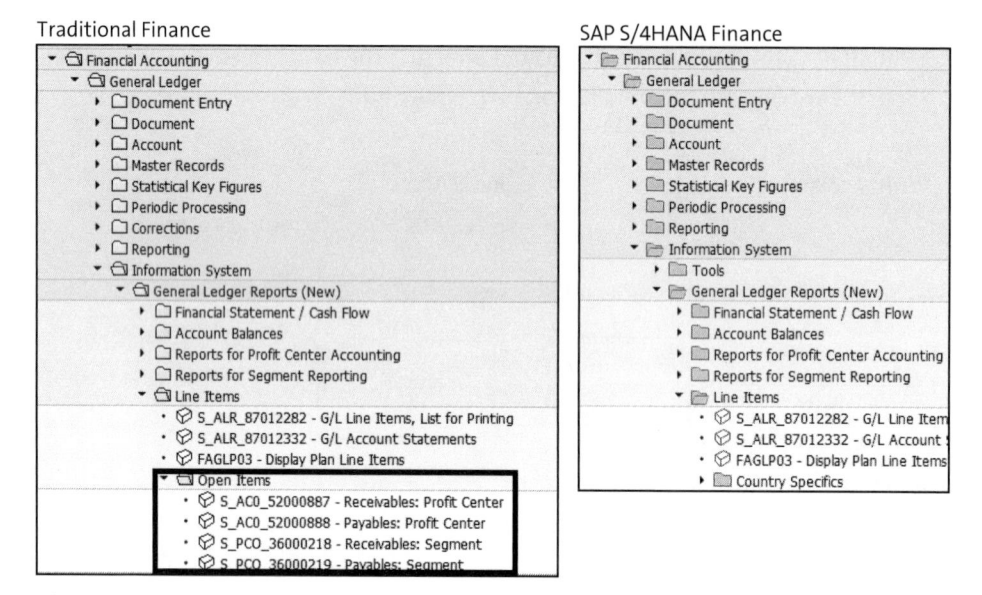

Figure 3.33 Open Item Reports

Second, processing of Transaction FAGLGVTR for balance carryforward has now been simplified with SAP S/4HANA Finance, as shown in Figure 3.34.

3.19 Key Changes to the General Ledger

Traditional Finance / SAP S/4HANA Finance

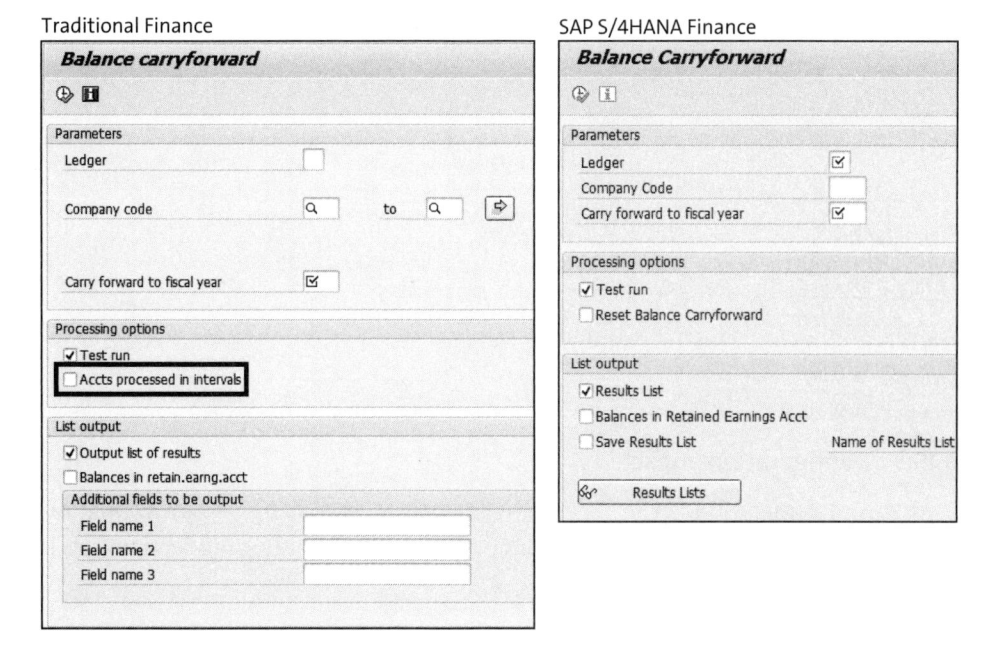

Figure 3.34 Balance Carryforward

In addition, the transactions listed in Table 3.1 have been replaced in SAP S/4HANA Finance.

Old Transaction	New Transaction
FAGL_FC_VAL	FAGL_FCV
FS01/FS02/FS03	FS00

Table 3.1 Changes in Transaction Codes Related to General Ledger Accounting

This list illustrates the changes to the G/L underlying tables that have occurred with the introduction of SAP S/4HANA Finance:

- New table introduced in SAP S/4HANA Finance:
  - ACDOCA
- Obsolete tables removed in SAP S/4HANA Finance, along with index tables:
  - BSIS
  - BSAS

3   Preparation and Migration for General Ledger

- GLT0/GLT1/GLT3
- BSID
- BSAD
- KNC1/KNC3
- BSIK
- BSAK
- LFC1/LFC3
- FAGLFLEXT
- FAGLFLEXA

3.19.3 Configuration Impact

With the implementation of SAP S/4HANA Finance, several changes to the configuration of General Ledger Accounting have taken place. In the following sections, we'll take a closer look at the biggest changes.

Copy Company Code

You can now assign a controlling area at the initial stage while setting up new company codes. The company codes copy functionality has been expanded in SAP S/4HANA Finance and now includes the controlling area assignment, as shown in Figure 3.35.

If you copy the company code with controlling area assignment, then the currency settings are consistent. Otherwise, you need to check and adjust the setting of the currency after it's assigned to a controlling area.

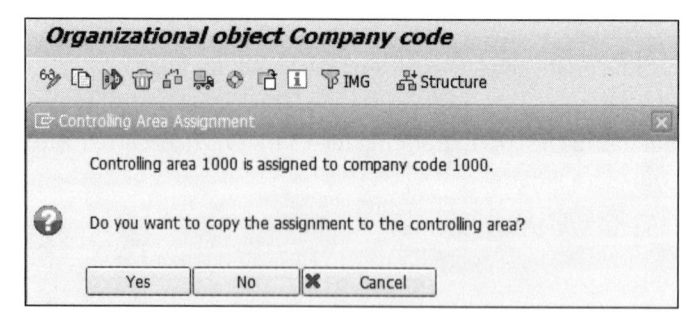

Figure 3.35 Edit, Copy, Delete, and Check Company Code

3.19 Key Changes to the General Ledger

If the controlling area isn't included when copying a company code, the currency setting needs to be validated after the controlling area assignment is made for the company code.

Consistency Check

You can now use Transaction FINS_CUST_CONS_CHK to check the consistency of the currency conversion settings for ledger/company assignments, as shown in Figure 3.36.

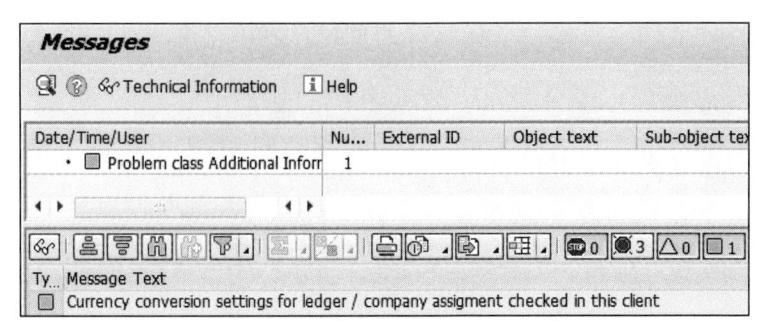

Figure 3.36 Currency Conversion Settings Check

You'll have to clean up all inconsistencies and make sure all errors are addressed. The check is performed during posting for all the company codes in scope during implementation.

Document Summarization

You can configure the maximum document summarization for table BSEG while table ACDOCA still contains the full line item detailed data. For compatibility reasons, the document line item number in table BSEG (BUZEI) is still limited to 999 lines, but the document line item number in table ACDOCA (DOCLN) has 6 digits. You can mitigate the BUZEI limitation with high document summarization in table BSEG.

Universal Journal Entry Organization

A ledger assigned to a company code represents an accounting principle. SAP S/4HANA Finance has a new configuration table for ledgers of the Universal Journal entry. New G/L ledgers are migrated to the new Universal Journal entry ledgers and are no longer assigned to total or line item tables because line items are always persistent in table ACDOCA.

3   Preparation and Migration for General Ledger

Ledger Configuration

The ledger definition has undergone a change, as depicted in Figure 3.37.

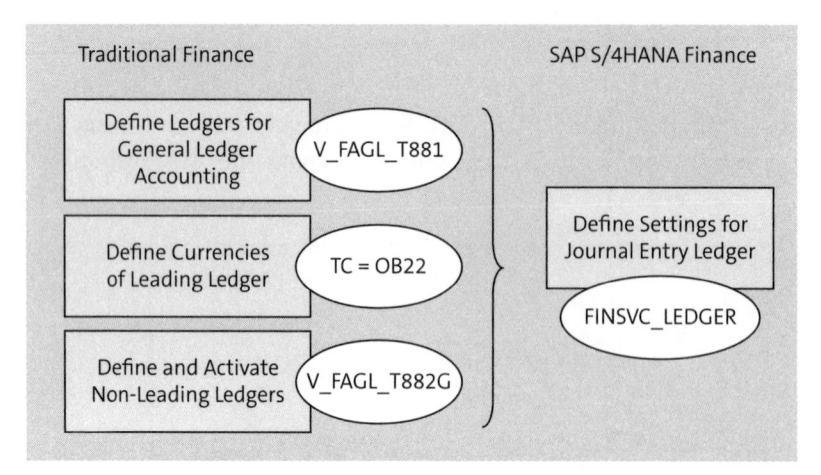

Figure 3.37 Comparison of Ledgers in Traditional Finance and SAP S/4HANA Finance

The new ledger architecture in SAP S/4HANA Finance has the following components:

- **Leading ledger**
  - There must be exactly one leading ledger, which is assigned to all company codes.
  - The leading ledger defines the document number (field BELNR) for all ledgers.
  - Ledger 0L is delivered as the leading ledger (default setting).
  - The leading ledger is in sync with financial operations processes such as Accounts Receivable/Accounts Payable (AR/AP) open item management.
  - The leading ledger is the basis for actual CO data (assigned to actual version 0).
  - The leading ledger contains a full set of line items in table ACDOCA.
- **Additional nonleading standard ledgers**
  - Nonleading ledgers can be assigned to selected company codes.
  - These ledgers contain a full set of line items in table ACDOCA.
  - These ledgers inherit the currency configuration of the leading ledger.
  - In these ledgers, deviating fiscal year variants/open period variants are possible.

3.19 Key Changes to the General Ledger

- **Appendix ledger**
  - The ledger type extension ledger, which is named *appendix ledger* in Figure 3.38, is defined on top of a base ledger. This base ledger is a standard ledger.
  - The appendix ledger inherits all transaction data of the underlying base ledger while reporting.
  - This ledger contains line items posted to the appendix ledger only.
  - This ledger inherits currency settings and the fiscal year variant of the base ledger.
  - This ledger allows for a separate company code assignment (a subset of the base ledger).
  - This ledger allows for a separate open period variant.
  - The appendix ledger can be used to create management views without duplicating the data from the base ledger.
  - The appendix ledger can't be part of ledger groups, except a generated group containing the ledger itself.
  - The appendix ledger only accepts manual postings (Transactions FB01L, FBB1, KB11, and KB41).
  - Many appendix ledgers can be assigned to the same base ledgers, but an appendix ledger can't be stacked on top of another appendix ledger.

You define the ledgers and their types per your organization's requirements, mainly driven by legal and management reporting (see Figure 3.38).

Ledger	Leading	Ledger Type	Ledger Name	Underl. Ldgr.
0D	☐	Standard Ledger		
0L	☑	Standard Ledger	Leading Ledger	
0M	☐	Standard Ledger		
1D	☐	Standard Ledger		
1L	☐	Standard Ledger	Leading Ledger	
L1	☐	Standard Ledger	Parallel Ledger	
Z1	☐	Extension Ledger	Appendix Ledger	0L

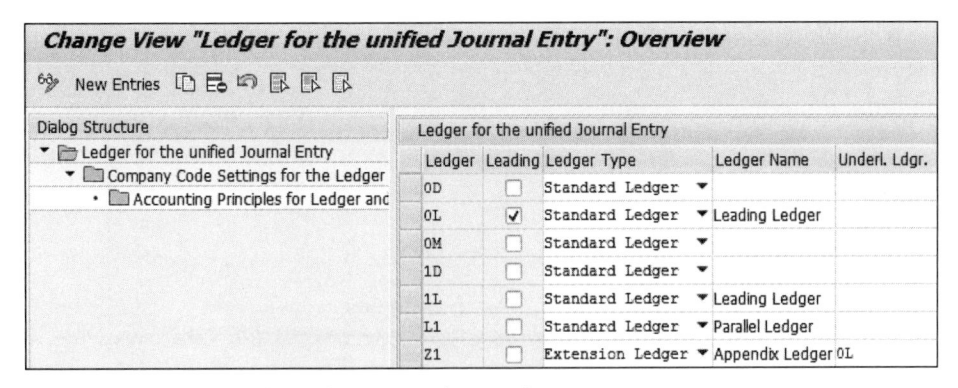

Figure 3.38 Defining Ledgers for Universal Journal Entry

3   Preparation and Migration for General Ledger

The **Fiscal Year Variant** entry must match the controlling area setting for the leading ledger. The nonleading ledger may have different fiscal year variants.

The assignment of the ledger to the company code and its currency settings is shown in Figure 3.39.

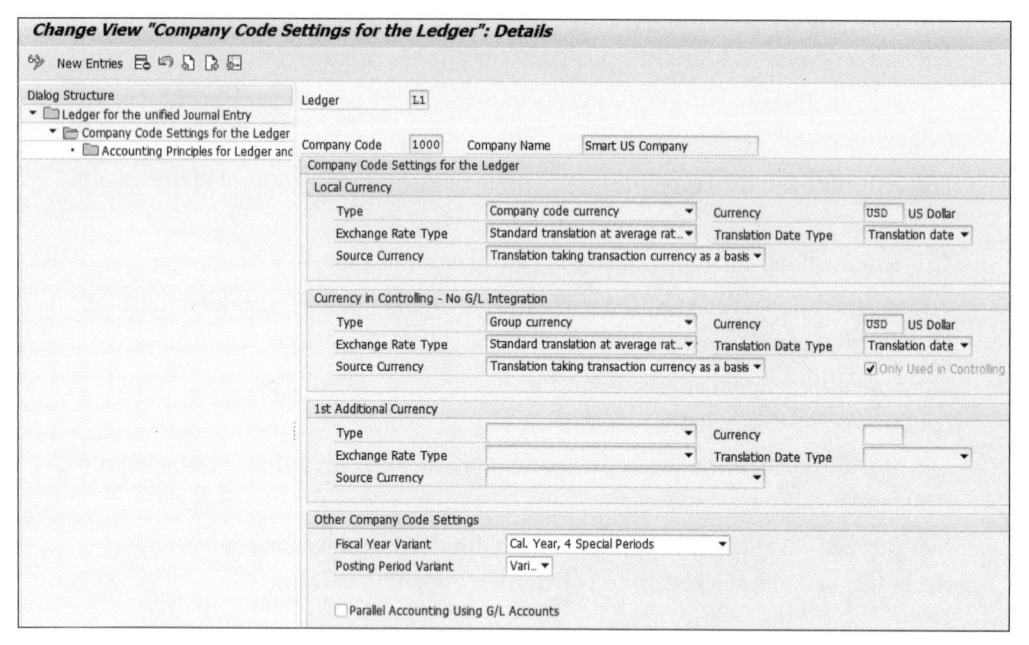

Figure 3.39 Company Code Assignment to Ledger

Each ledger, standard or appendix, is assigned to an **Accounting Principle** as shown in Figure 3.40.

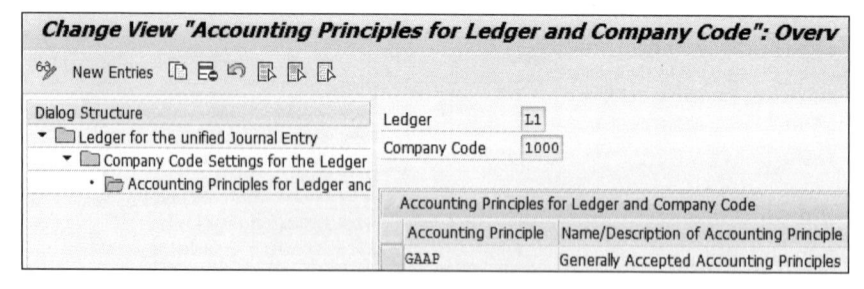

Figure 3.40 Ledger Assignment to Accounting Principle

3.19 Key Changes to the General Ledger

Document Types and Numbering

Going forward in SAP S/4HANA Finance, accounting entries in SAP will have a common document number. As such, the existing use of document type/number combinations in the **General Ledger View** per ledger is now obsolete.

The standard document type and number of the entry view are used for all ledgers except when otherwise required, as shown in Figure 3.41.

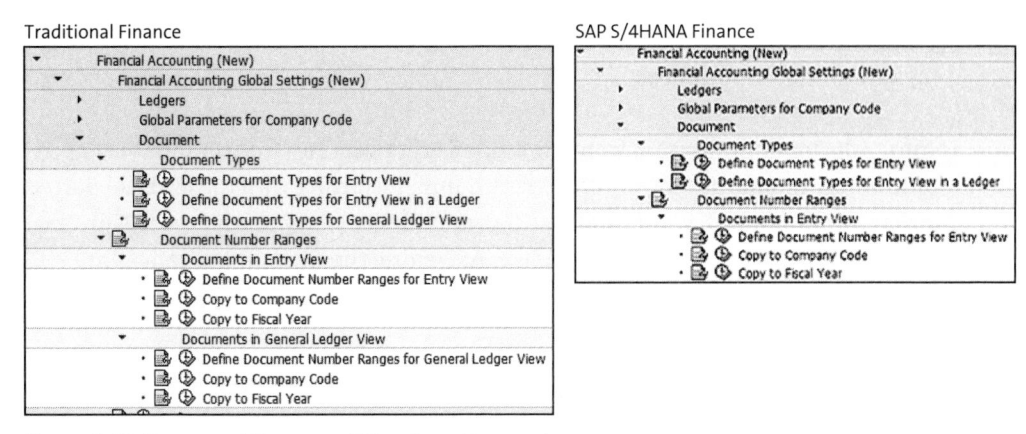

Figure 3.41 Document Types and Numbers Comparison

Document Posting

The FI document for G/L accounts still generates CO documents, as illustrated in Figure 3.42 and Figure 3.43.

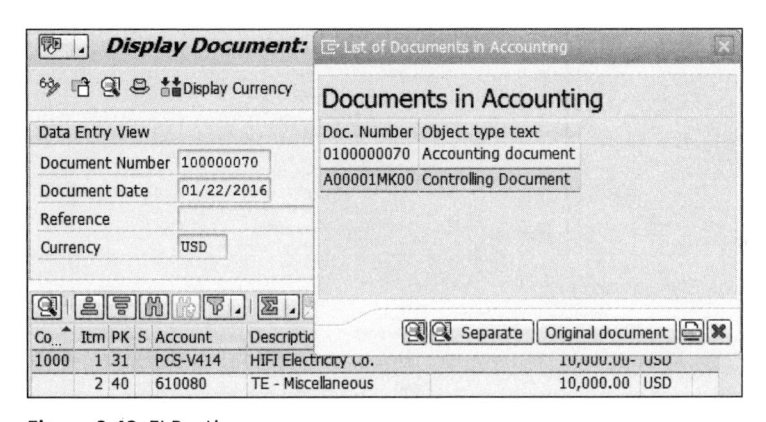

Figure 3.42 FI Posting

3   Preparation and Migration for General Ledger

```
Display Actual Cost Documents
Document    Master Record

Layout              1SAP     Primary cost posting
COarea currency     USD      USD
Valuation View/Group 0       Legal Valuation

DocumentNo Doc. Date Document Header Text           RT RefDocNo
PRw QTy Object              CO object name   Cost Elem. Cost element na

A00001MK00 01/22/2016                                R  100000070
   1 CTR 1801            Other Inc.&Expense  610080  TE - Miscellane
```

Figure 3.43 CO Document Posting

The CO document generated from the journal entry postings from FI and other applications has an internal cryptic document number (starting with the letter *A*) posted into the CO_BELNR field. It's needed for CO compatibility views, and it groups Universal Journal entries from the CO perspective. As before, the CO number ranges are still needed for internal CO postings.

Integration of SAP ERP Financials and Controlling

In SAP S/4HANA Finance, CO is integrated in real time into the new G/L. Both primary and secondary cost elements are created as G/L accounts and are now part of the chart of accounts. Only account determination for intercompany accounts remains, as shown in Figure 3.44.

Traditional Finance
- Financial Accounting (New)
  - Financial Accounting Global Settings (New)
    - Ledgers
      - Fields
      - Ledger
      - Fiscal Year and Posting Periods
      - Parallel Accounting
      - Real-Time Integration of Controlling with Financial Accounting
        - Define Variants for Real-Time Integration
        - Assign Variants for Real-Time Integration to Company Codes
        - Define Rules for Selecting CO Line Items
        - Define Field Transfers for Real-Time Integration
      - Define Account Determination for Real-Time Integration
        - Define Intercompany Clearing Accounts
        - Define Account Determination for Real-Time Integration
      - Transfer CO Documents Retrospectively

SAP S/4HANA Finance
- Financial Accounting (New)
  - Financial Accounting Global Settings (New)
    - Regenerate CDS Views and Field Mapping
    - Ledgers
      - Fields
      - Ledger
      - Fiscal Year and Posting Periods
      - Parallel Accounting
      - Integration of Controlling with Financial Accounting
        - Define Document Types for Postings in Controlling
        - Define Document Type Mapping Variants for CO Business Transactions
        - Check and Define Default Values for Postings in Controlling
        - Define Ledger for CO Version
      - Define Account Determination
        - Define Intercompany Clearing Accounts

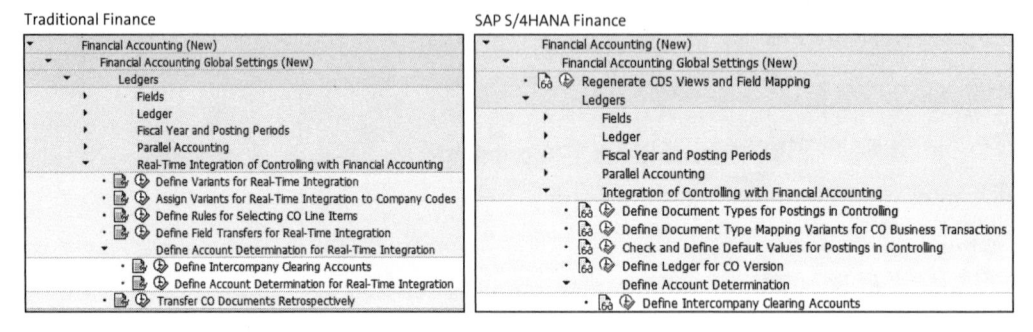

Figure 3.44 Integration of CO with FI

With the introduction of SAP S/4HANA Finance, the concept of the reconciliation ledger has been eliminated, as shown in Figure 3.45. The need doesn't arise now because CO and FI have been integrated via architectural changes in the G/L and cost element master data.

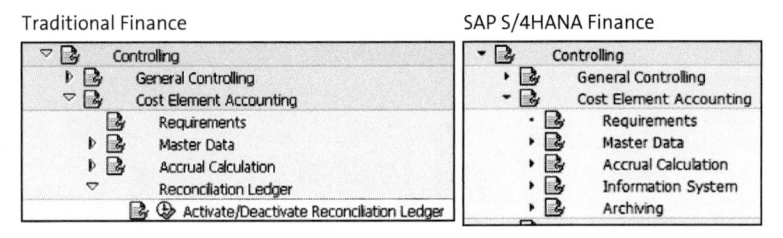

Figure 3.45 Elimination of the Reconciliation Ledger

Similarly, the transaction for posting CO documents to FI is no longer available in SAP S/4HANA Finance, as shown in Figure 3.46. Due to the real-time integration of FI and CO, the data is populated to CO at the same time that it's posted to FI. Unlike earlier versions of SAP, you don't have to run a reconciliation program between FI and CO, so the probability of getting an error or entries not posted is now significantly reduced.

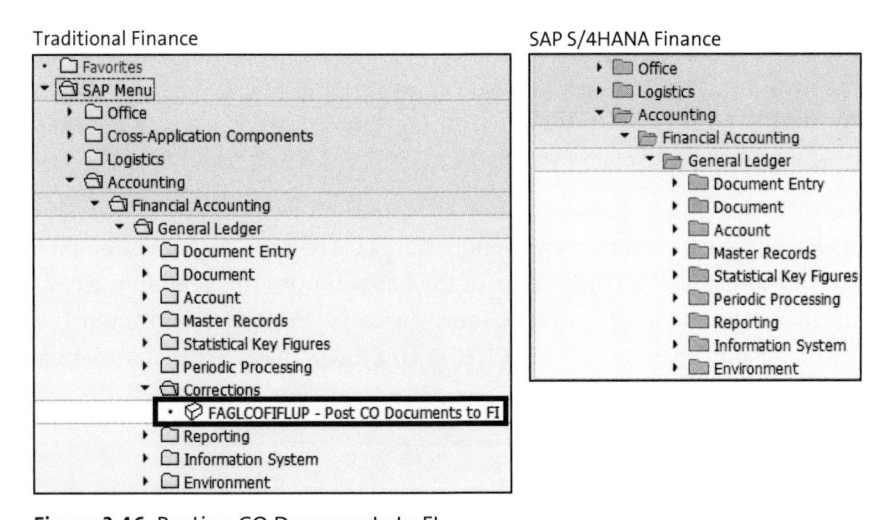

Figure 3.46 Posting CO Documents to FI

Define Ledger for the Controlling Version

In SAP S/4HANA Finance, **Version 0** must be assigned to the leading **Ledger 0L** for all company codes, as shown in Figure 3.47. CO transactions can write to several ledgers, but they only read data from one ledger.

3 Preparation and Migration for General Ledger

Change View "Ledger From Which CO Reads Act				
Ledger From Which CO Reads Actual Data				
Company Code	Ledger	Version	Version name	Ledger Name
1000	0L	0	Plan/actual version	Leading Ledger

Figure 3.47 Defining the Ledger for CO Version

3.19.4 Customer and Vendor Master Data

In SAP S/4HANA 1511, customer and vendor master data were changed to business partner master data. Business partner records are now the central source and single point of entry to create, edit, manage, and display master data for business partners, customers, and vendors. Transaction BP is now used to create both the customer and vendor master data.

The following transactions became unavailable in SAP S/4HANA 1511 and later versions: FD01, FD02, FD03, FD05, FD06, FD0, FK01, FK02, FK03, FK05, FK06, FK08, MAP1, MAP2, MAP3, MK01, MK02, MK03, MK05, MK06, MK12, MK18, MK19, V-03, V-04, V-05, V-06, V-07, V-08, V-09, V-11, V-21, V-22, V-23, VAP1, VAP2, VAP3, VD01, VD02, VD03, VD05, VD06, XD01, XD02, XD03, XD05, XD06, XD07, XK01, XK02, XK03, XK05, XK06, and XK07.

You must clean up your customer and vendor data before it can be converted into an SAP S/4HANA business partner. Some of the key activities involved in the conversion include (a) activating business function CA_BP_SOA and (b) running the business partner precheck Report PRECHECK_UPGRADATION_REPORT to verify the results.

> **References**
>
> For information on the business partner conversion process, see the following SAP Notes:
>
> - SAP Notes 2211312, 2210486, and 2216176: Conversion Prechecks
> - SAP Note 1623677: Report for Checking the Customizing for Customer Vendor Integration
> - SAP Note 954816: Transactions for Creating or Linking Business Partners from/to Customers/Vendors

3.19.5 Credit Management Impact

SAP S/4HANA doesn't support SAP ERP Financials Accounts Receivable Credit Management. The corresponding function in SAP S/4HANA Finance is SAP Credit Management.

You need to perform the migration from the old Credit Management (FI-AR-CR) to the new SAP Credit Management, which is comprised of the following elements:

- Master data
- Configuration data
- Credit exposure data
- Credit decision data

The business processes related to credit management remain the same, but you'll need to use new transactions for some of the processes, such as the following:

- Transaction UKM_BP is used for maintaining the credit account master data; the old Transaction FD32 is no longer supported.
- Transaction UKM_MY_DCDS is used to release credit-blocked sales orders; the old Transaction VKM1is no longer supported.
- Credit limit check for sales document types can only be specified as type D in SAP Credit Management or left empty (no credit limit check) because credit limit check types A, B, and C aren't supported anymore.
- Credit checks when changing critical fields and payment guarantee-related letters of credit have been removed from the Sales and Distribution (SD) side of SAP Credit Management.
- SAP S/4HANA supports credit checks based on the maximum document value, which wasn't supported in the previous version.
- The following transactions aren't available in SAP S/4HANA Finance:
  - F.28: Customers: Reset Credit Limit
  - F.31: Credit Management—Overview
  - F.32: Credit Management—Missing Data
  - F.33: Credit Management—Brief Overview
  - F.34: Credit Management—Mass Change
  - FCV1: Create A/R Summary
  - FCV2: Delete A/R Summary
  - FCV3: Early Warning List
  - FD24: Credit Limit Changes

- FD32: Change Customer Credit Management
- FDK43: Credit Management—Master Data List
- S_ALR_87012215: Display Changes to Credit Management
- S_ALR_87012218: Credit Master Sheet
- VKM2: Released SD Documents
- VKM3: Sales Documents
- VKM5: Deliveries

- The following reports aren't available in SAP S/4HANA Finance:
  - RFARIO20: FI-ARI: Extract from Credit Master Data
  - RFARIO30: FI-ARI: Import Credit Master Data
  - RFDFILZE: Credit Management: Branch/Head Office Reconciliation Program
  - RFDKLI*: Credit Management Control Area Data Reports

In SAP S/4HANA Finance, CO is integrated in real time with the new G/L. Both primary and secondary cost elements are created as G/L accounts using Transaction FS00 and are now part of the chart of accounts.

In traditional FI, the leading ledger posts in real time, and the nonleading ledger posts periodically. In SAP S/4HANA Finance, now both leading and nonleading ledgers are created as the standard ledger. The newly introduced appendix ledger can report on all transaction data of the base ledger, and it allows you to create views without affecting the base ledger.

3.20 Key Changes to Period-End Closing

The Universal Journal provides a single source of truth: journal entries across multiple applications are posted in a single table, reducing data redundancy and the system footprint. This provides real-time access to data across all dimensions, easier extensibility of custom fields, and process optimization for an accelerated close. SAP S/4HANA Finance not only helps eliminate some of the closing tasks, such as SAP ERP Financials and Controlling reconciliation, but also accelerates some of the month-end tasks (e.g., providing a faster depreciation run because depreciation is now calculated in real time on individual assets during any asset transaction rather than during the period-end depreciation run). So let's analyze the major changes SAP S/4HANA Finance has made in the architecture design, the business process transactions, and the configuration of the period-end closing process.

3.20.1 Architectural Impact

The architectural impacts that SAP S/4HANA Finance has on period-end closing include the following:

- CO-relevant postings not only check the CO period close but also check the G/L open and close periods. At month end, you must assign the posting to the secondary costs account type in the G/L period close.
- In the CO period lock, you must specify which transaction you need to lock for specific periods.
- No separate balance carryforward is needed in new Asset Accounting (FI-AA). The general balance carryforward of FI also transfers the new Asset Accounting balance by default.
- Current planned depreciation values are calculated automatically for the new year after performing the balance carryforward.
- Period-end closing tasks for deriving market segment information have been eliminated, resulting in (a) no more settlement of sales order items and (b) no cost center allocations to profitability.
- The bottlenecks for intercompany reconciliation are removed because it can be run anytime with immediate results.
- The SAP Financial Closing cockpit integrates with SAP Fiori and facilitates users running/scheduling tasks from the apps.

Overall, the architecture of SAP S/4HANA Finance allows for a significant performance improvement and acceleration of processes that will reduce the month-end processing time to create a soft close.

3.20.2 Functionality Impact

Table 3.2 lists the transactions that have been replaced or have become obsolete in period-end closing with SAP S/4HANA Finance.

Old Transaction	New Transaction
FAGL_FC_VAL	FAGL_FCV
KKAK	KKAKH
KKAO	KKAOH

Table 3.2 Changes in Transaction Codes Related to Period-End Closing

3   Preparation and Migration for General Ledger

Old Transaction	New Transaction
KKS1	KKS1H
CO88	CO88H
VA88	VA88H
KO8G	KO8GH
CJ8G	CJ8GH

Table 3.2 Changes in Transaction Codes Related to Period-End Closing (Cont.)

In addition, some functionality has been removed entirely, including the SAP Financial Closing Cockpit activity to roll up values (**Rollup**), as shown in Figure 3.48.

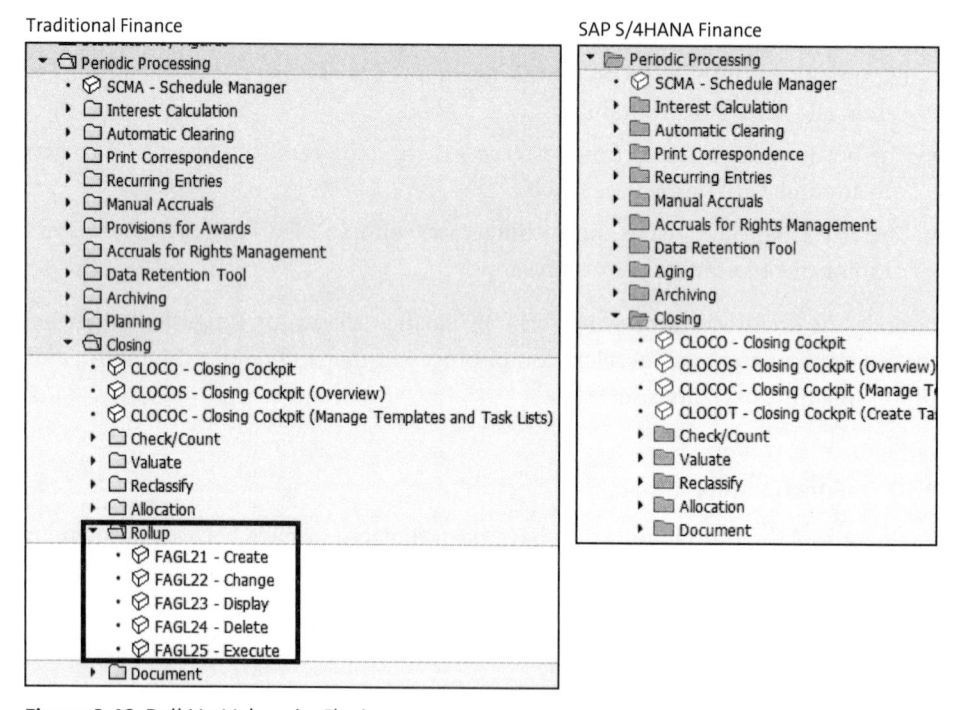

Figure 3.48 Roll Up Values in Closing

The **Profit and Loss Adjustment** activity and the **Balance Sheet Adjustment** activity transaction codes also are no longer available, as shown in Figure 3.49. Prior to SAP

S/4HANA Finance, there were three options under **Reclassify**: **F.19—GR/IR Clearing**, **F.50—Profit and Loss Adjustment**, and **Balance Sheet Adjustment**. Now, **F.19—GR/IR Clearing** is the only option that remains in SAP S/4HANA Finance.

SAP S/4HANA Finance
- Periodic Processing
  - SCMA - Schedule Manager
  - Interest Calculation
  - Automatic Clearing
  - Print Correspondence
  - Recurring Entries
  - Manual Accruals
  - Accruals for Rights Management
  - Data Retention Tool
  - Aging
  - Archiving
  - Closing
    - CLOCO - Closing Cockpit
    - CLOCOS - Closing Cockpit (Ov
    - CLOCOC - Closing Cockpit (Ma
    - CLOCOT - Closing Cockpit (Cr
    - Check/Count
    - Valuate
    - Reclassify
      - F.19 - GR/IR Clearing
    - Allocation

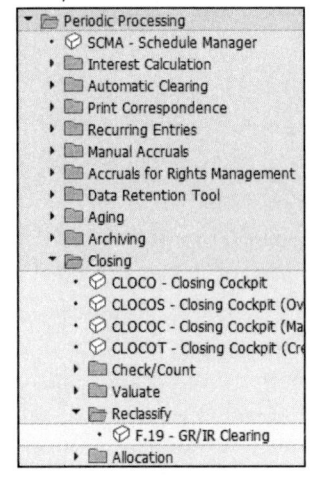

Figure 3.49 Closing Adjustment Postings

SAP S/4HANA Finance introduced one relevant new table in this area (table ACDOCA) and removed two obsolete tables (FAGLFLEXT and FAGLFLEXA), along with the index tables.

FI and CO are closed simultaneously with the implementation of SAP S/4HANA Finance. You can use the new SAP Financial Closing cockpit, which is available via Transaction FCLOCOC and Transaction FCLOCO.

SAP S/4HANA Finance provides better insight during the period, leverages the soft-closing process, and accelerates the month-end financial close by providing the following advantages:

- Real-time profitability is provided by instant derivation of market segment information from various CO-PA characteristics. All these fields are now part of the Universal Journal line item. Complex derivation rules for getting this data are no longer required.

- Real-time and correct asset acquisition values are provided without the wait for the periodic posting run during the closing process.

More than 35 new predefined SAP HANA Live views have also been added in SAP S/4HANA Finance. These views can help generate finance reports from multiple reporting tools, such as SAP BusinessObjects, SAP Lumira, SAP Fiori, and so on, which facilitate the month-end closing process.

> **1709 Preview**
>
> With the release of SAP S/4HANA 1709, SAP has relaunched the new SAP Financial Closing cockpit with the end goal of achieving faster close, complying with all governance issues, and providing transparency for all activities and tasks. It will now be part of the core SAP S/4HANA solution rather than an add-on feature.
>
> The SAP Financial Closing cockpit enables automated tasks along with a user-friendly dashboard reflecting all the manual activities assigned to a particular user. It provides all notifications to users via workflows so that any lags can be avoided while maintaining the entire audit trail and documentation of all the tasks performed. It also provides the real-time status of the closing tasks and both the corporation and its subsidiaries can analyze the pending tasks with an action-oriented approach.

3.20.3 Security Impact

With SAP S/4HANA Finance, SAP delivered new end-user roles that can be used as templates for creating company-specific roles in the following areas:

- General Ledger (G/L)
    - SAP_SFIN_ACC_ACTUALPOSTING
    - SAP_SFIN_ACC_CLOSING
    - SAP_SFIN_ACC_MASTERDATA
    - SAP_SFIN_ACC_REPORTING
- Accounts Payable/Accounts Receivable (AP/AR)
    - SAP_SFIN_AP
    - SAP_SFIN_AR
- Cost center planning
    - SAP_SFIN_COST_CENTER_MD
- Controlling (CO)
    For CO functions, the new role names are shown in Figure 3.50.

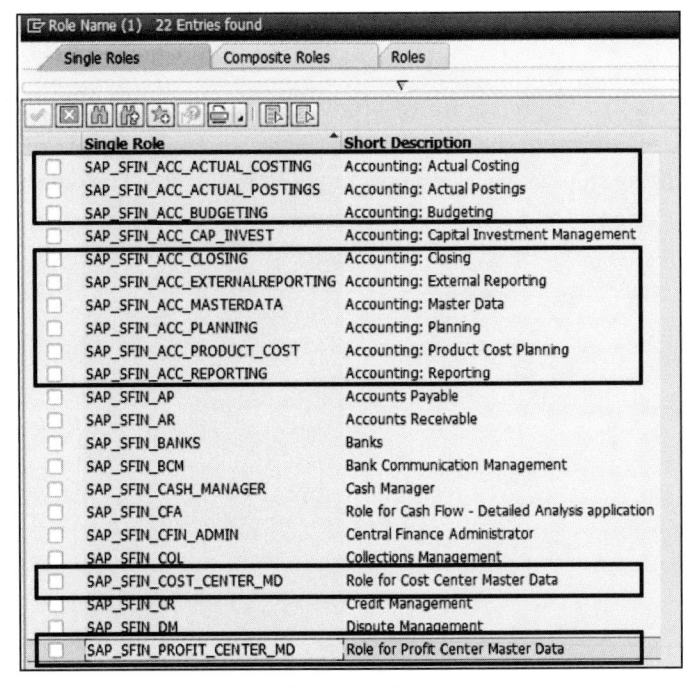

Figure 3.50 Security Roles for Controlling

You should now understand the essential changes to the period-end closing process, from the elimination of the need to reconcile FI and CO, to the numerous reports and SAP HANA views available to you. The ultimate result should be a smoother and quicker period-end process, with fewer pain points to overcome.

3.21 Summary

You'll need to execute the Customizing steps for the G/L before migration to SAP S/4HANA Finance to accommodate the required changes. This requires checking the consistency of the fiscal year variants between company code and controlling area, defining the ledgers and their assignment to the accounting principle, setting up the postings in CO, and activating any missing business functions.

In traditional FI, the leading ledger posts in real time and the nonleading ledger posts periodically. In SAP S/4HANA Finance, now both leading and nonleading ledgers are created as the standard ledger. The newly introduced appendix ledger can report on all transaction data of the base ledger, and it allows you to create views without affecting the base ledger.

You should now understand the prerequisites, preparations, migration requirements, and change impacts related to the new General Ledger Accounting, and you can perform the Customizing steps as well. Let's now move on to Chapter 4, in which we'll discuss the Customizing for the new Asset Accounting.

Chapter 4
Preparation and Migration for Asset Accounting

With the installation of SAP S/4HANA Finance, new Asset Accounting replaces classic Asset Accounting. This chapter focuses on the Customizing and activation steps related to new Asset Accounting, including performing the prechecks, migrating and defining the chart of depreciation, and specifying the posting rules.

Before you can migrate to SAP S/4HANA Finance, you need to customize the new Asset Accounting in the system, which replaces the classic Asset Accounting (classic FI-AA) in the new system. We cover the key customization steps that you need to perform for migration to the new Asset Accounting in this chapter.

The SAP S/4HANA Finance migration includes performing prechecks for using the new Asset Accounting, checking accounting principle and ledger group settings, assigning the accounting principle to the ledger group, making any additional manual settings in Customizing for new Asset Accounting, and checking the prerequisites for activating the new Asset Accounting. Other tasks you must perform include determining and migrating active charts of depreciation, changing definitions of depreciation areas, defining transfer rules for the posting values and depreciation terms of a depreciation area, checking the currency type of depreciation areas, and, finally, activating the Customizing switch for new Asset Accounting. All the major steps, along with any additional details, are shown in Figure 4.1.

When you install SAP S/4HANA Finance, the system shows the Customizing structure for new Asset Accounting in the SAP Reference IMG, as shown in Figure 4.1. By default, it hides the Customizing structure for classic FI-AA.

4   Preparation and Migration for Asset Accounting

```
Display IMG
    Existing BC Sets    BC Sets for Activity    Activated BC Sets for A
Structure
  ▼  Conversion of Accounting to SAP S/4HANA
    •  Info: SAP S/4HANA Customizing and Data Migration
    ▼  Preparations and Migration of Customizing
      •  Check Customizing Settings Prior to Migration
      •  Define Message Types for Posting Before and During Migration
      •  Set Number of Jobs for Activities in Mass Data Framework
      ▸  Preparations and Migration of Customizing for General Ledger
      ▼  Preparations and Migration of Customizing for Asset Accounting
        ▼  ┌──────────────────────────────────────────────┐
           │  Migration from Classic to New Asset Accounting │
           └──────────────────────────────────────────────┘
          •  Prepare New Asset Accounting
          ▼  Migration for New Asset Accounting
            •  Migrate Charts of Depreciation
            •  Display Migration Log
            •  Perform Additional Manual Activities
            •  Check Prerequisites for Activating Asset Accounting (New)
          •  Activate Asset Accounting (New)
        ▼  Adjustments in New Asset Accounting
          •  Info: Adjustments in New Asset Accounting
          •  Adjust Parameters in Chart of Depreciation
          •  Display Migration Log
```

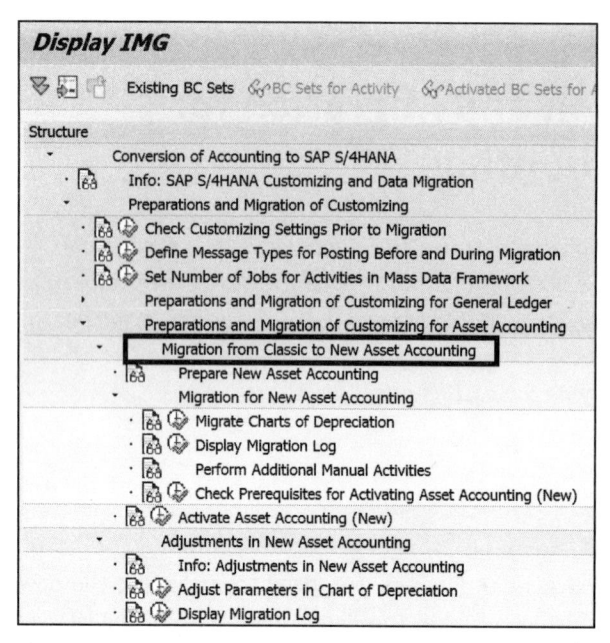

Figure 4.1 Customizing New Asset Accounting

No postings to FI-AA are allowed until the migration of Customizing and transaction data is complete. After the migration activities are complete, and the new Asset Accounting has been activated, you can't revert to classic FI-AA. New Asset Accounting needs to be configured in preparation for migrating to SAP S/4HANA Finance. Some of the tasks will include setting the new Asset Accounting activation status to **In Preparation**, creating a new ledger group for local valuation, assigning the ledger group to the local generally accepted accounting principles (GAAP), and assigning all the active company codes to the chart of depreciation. You'll also be responsible for configuring and assigning the accounting principle to the depreciation areas, setting up accounts assigned to the local accounting principle as asset reconciliation accounts, creating and assigning the technical clearing account, specifying alternative document types for accounting principle-specific document postings, and defining the depreciation area for quantity updates.

4.1 Prerequisites

Before you install SAP S/4HANA Finance, you must ensure that the prerequisites are met by using program RASFIN_MIGR_PRECHECK for preliminary checks. You must import this program to your system via SAP Note 1939592 before you install SAP S/4HANA Finance. Perform this check in all your SAP clients: the development client, the test client, and the production client.

You must activate the SAP ERP Financials (FI) Extension (EA-FIN) because it provides the depreciation calculation program (DCP), which is used for the new depreciation calculation.

As a prerequisite, you also need to migrate the assigned chart of depreciation.

You must ensure that the parallel currencies in the leading ledger of General Ledger Accounting and the depreciation areas of the leading valuation in FI-AA are the same.

The company codes that are assigned to the same chart of depreciation should have the same number and type of parallel currencies used in General Ledger Accounting.

Make sure that the period-end closing has been performed along with the reconciliation of the asset subsidiary ledger with the General Ledger (G/L). If you happen to install SAP S/4HANA Finance at the close of the fiscal year, you should also perform year-end closing before the migration.

4.2 Install SAP S/4HANA Finance with New Asset Accounting

After you start the installation of SAP S/4HANA Finance, it's no longer possible to post any transactions in FI-AA. If you were already using classic FI-AA, then you only need to migrate your charts of depreciation and check and possibly add to delta Customizing. If you weren't already using FI-AA and now want to use it in the future, you must configure your system completely for FI-AA.

You'll also need to complete the relevant steps for migrating to the new General Ledger Accounting before you can customize the new Asset Accounting.

4.3 Migrate Charts of Depreciation

You either need to migrate the charts of depreciation automatically using the migration program or do it manually. You should run the migration program FAA_CHECK_MIG2SFIN as a test run first, as shown in Figure 4.2, so that you can correct any errors before processing the update run. If you run the program as an update run, the system updates the tables for the depreciation areas.

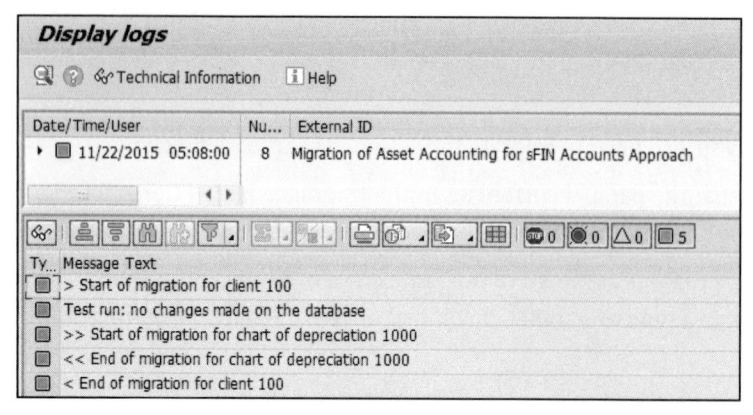

Figure 4.2 Migrating Chart of Depreciation

You'll have to manually migrate the charts of depreciation in the following cases:

- Your charts of depreciation couldn't be migrated during the automatic migration because the migration program doesn't recognize the starting situation defined in your system.

- Your charts of depreciation are assigned to a deactivated company code, and because the deactivated company code's data hasn't been archived yet, the company code must be migrated with the document migration. This chart of depreciation should therefore be migrated manually.

The migration is possible at any time by making the following settings in Customizing for new Asset Accounting:

- Assignment of accounting principles and ledger groups to depreciation areas: **Asset Accounting (New)** • **Valuation** • **Depreciation Areas** • **Define Depreciation Areas**

- Settings for posting to the G/L (for each depreciation area): **Asset Accounting (New)** • **Valuation** • **Depreciation Areas** • **Define Depreciation Areas**

- Value transfer for acquisition and production costs (APC): **Asset Accounting (New) • Valuation • Depreciation Areas • Specify Transfer of APC Values**
- Transfer of depreciation terms: **Asset Accounting (New) • Valuation • Depreciation Areas • Specify Transfer of Depreciation Terms**
- Use of parallel currencies: **Asset Accounting (New) • Valuation • Currencies • Specify the Use of Parallel Currencies**

You can also use these activities if you want to check the Customizing settings after charts of depreciation have been migrated automatically.

4.4 Customization Prior to Activation

After migrating the charts of depreciation, you have to make additional Customizing settings, as described in the following subsections, before you can check and activate new Asset Accounting.

4.4.1 Define Asset Balance Sheet Accounts of Parallel Valuation

This step is required if you're using the accounts approach for parallel valuation. It isn't relevant if you're using the ledger approach. In this activity, you can define G/L accounts as reconciliation accounts for depreciation areas of a parallel valuation of FI-AA, or you can define them again as accounts for normal posting.

In the accounts approach, one or more additional valuations are represented by separate depreciation areas in which the posting is made to separate accounts in the G/L. Before the migration, these asset balance sheet accounts were posted directly in FI.

In the future, the asset values for both the leading and parallel valuation will be posted directly in FI-AA. Thus, these asset balance sheet accounts must be defined as asset reconciliation accounts because they will only be allowed to be posted in FI-AA.

You can change the existing balance sheet accounts of the parallel valuation that were posted directly as asset reconciliation accounts for the future in Customizing under **Asset Accounting (New) • Preparations for Going Live • Production Startup • Accounts Approach**. You can reset the reconciliation accounts for parallel valuations, as shown in Figure 4.3.

4 Preparation and Migration for Asset Accounting

G/L Account	G/L Acct Long Text	Recon. account for acct type
160000	Land & Land Improvements	Assets
160010	Buildings	Assets
160020	Machinery & Equipment	Assets
160030	Leasehold Improvements	Assets
160040	Motor Vehicles	Assets
160050	Office Equipment	Assets
160060	Furniture	Assets
160070	Computer Hardware	Assets
160080	Computer Software	Assets
160090	Assets under Construction	Assets
160095	Down Payment - Acquisition	Assets
160200	Low Value Assets	Assets
170000	Accumulated Depreciation - Land Improvements	Assets
170010	Accumulated Depreciation - Buildings	Assets
170020	Accumulated Depreciation - Machinery & Equipment	Assets

Figure 4.3 Defining Reconciliation Accounts for New Asset Accounting

Before the migration to SAP S/4HANA Finance, you need to check and reconcile the balance sheet values of both FI-AA and General Ledger Accounting for parallel valuations as part of closing operations.

4.4.2 Define the Depreciation Area for a Quantity Update

In this activity, you specify which depreciation area you want to use for updating quantities in your chart of depreciation. This setting is relevant if you're using collective low-value assets in your organization. When there is a posting made to this depreciation area, the quantities are updated in the asset master record. The Customizing is done under **Asset Accounting (New) • General Valuation • Depreciation Areas • Define Depreciation Area for Quantity Update**.

4.4.3 Define the Technical Clearing Account for Integrated Asset Acquisition

This is a necessary process to post an integrated asset acquisition in SAP S/4HANA Finance. When you post an asset acquisition through a vendor using Transaction F-90, and input all the necessary parameters (including a debit to the fixed asset and a credit to the vendor account), new Asset Accounting breaks the posting into the following two components:

1. The first document is created with document type **AA**, which is posted for the specified ledger/ledger group with a debit to the asset and a credit to the technical clearing account, as specified in Customizing. In Figure 4.4, the document is posted for **Accounting Principle IFRS**, whereas in Figure 4.5, the document is posted for **Accounting Principle US GAAP**.

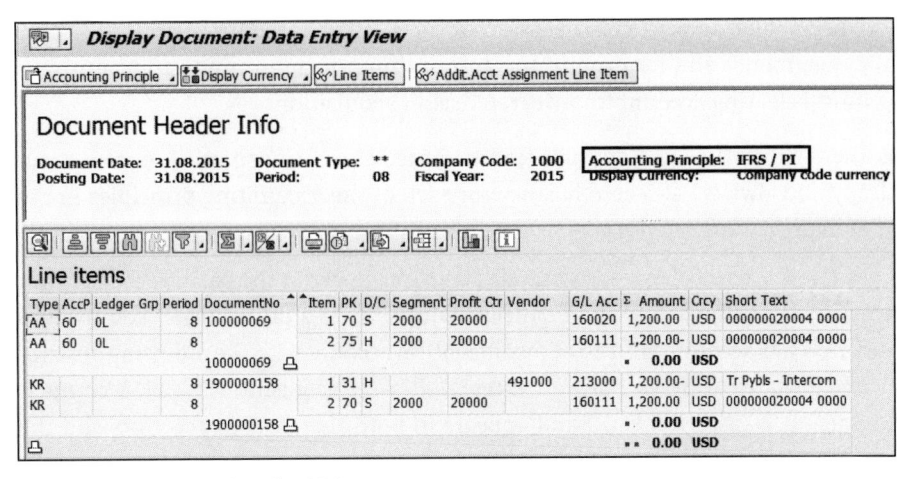

Figure 4.4 FI-AA Posting for IFRS

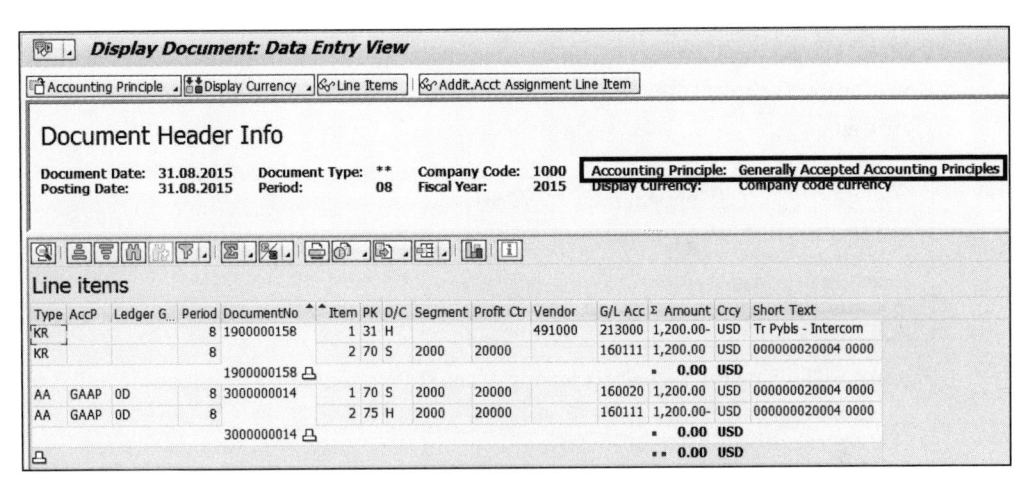

Figure 4.5 FI-AA Posting for US GAAP

2. The second document is created with document **Type** KR, which is not posted to any specific ledger/ledger group.

4 Preparation and Migration for Asset Accounting

The business transaction is thus divided into an operational part and a valuating part during the integrated asset acquisition posting:

- For the operational part (vendor invoice), a ledger-group-independent document valid for all accounting principles is posted against the technical clearing account for integrated asset acquisitions.
- For each valuating part (capitalization of the asset), a separate ledger-group-specific document valid for each of the accounting principles is posted against the technical clearing account for integrated asset acquisitions.

Thus, the technical clearing account for integrated asset acquisitions is posted automatically and always has a zero balance for each of the accounting principles in the chart of depreciation.

Because it has a zero balance, this account doesn't appear in the balance sheet, but it appears in notes attached to the financial statement. As a prerequisite, you need to create a new G/L account as an asset reconciliation account with the following description: "technical clearing account for integrated asset acquisitions." This account is created using Transaction FS00 and appears in both the chart of accounts and the company code section.

You need to assign this G/L account in the FI-AA account determination for your chart of accounts in Customizing under **Asset Accounting (New)** • **Integration with General Ledger Accounting** • **Technical Clearing Account for Integrated Asset Acquisition** • **Define Technical Clearing Account for Integrated Asset Acquisition**, as shown in Figure 4.6.

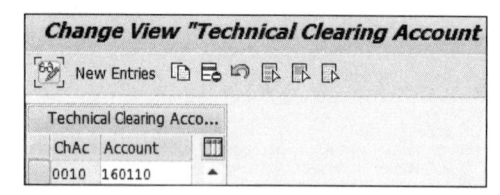

Figure 4.6 Defining the Technical Clearing Account for Integrated Acquisition

4.4.4 Specify an Alternative Document Type for Accounting Principle-Specific Documents

If your organization is using the new G/L with document splitting activated, and you want the document splitting rules for the valuating document (asset acquisition) and the operative document (Accounts Payable) to be different, you'll need to specify separate document types for the valuating document that are valid for each of the accounting principles. Alternatively, if your organization policy is to have separate document types for both valuating and operative documents, this Customizing activity needs to be executed.

You need to check if the existing document types can be used for this activity, or if you need to create a new one to assign to the valuating documents.

You assign the alternative document type for the posting of your accounting-principle-specific valuating documents in Customizing under **Asset Accounting (New) • Integration with General Ledger Accounting • Integrated Transactions: Alternative Doc. Type for Accounting-Principle-Specific Documents • Specify Alternative Document Type for Accounting Principle-Specific Documents**.

4.4.5 Specify Revenue Distribution for Asset Retirement

You can distribute revenues generated from the retirement of assets for a company code either on the net book value or on an acquisition and production cost (APC) basis. In this Customizing step, you need to specify the method for distribution of revenue for asset retirement under **Asset Accounting (New) • Transactions • Retirements • Gain/Loss Posting • Define Revenue Distribution for Fixed Asset Retirement**, as shown in Figure 4.7.

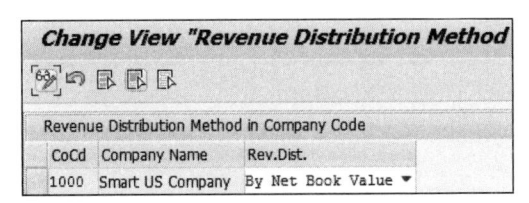

Figure 4.7 Revenue Distribution Method for Asset Retirement

4.4.6 Post Net Book Value Instead of Gain/Loss

In this step, for each company code level, you need to specify the posting method for the retirement of an asset due to the sale or scrapping of that asset. By default, the standard process is to post a gain or a loss during the asset retirement; however, based on your legal and organizational requirements, you can configure the process to post the net book value of the assets for a depreciation area. In that case, the net book value is posted to the account for clearing of revenue from asset sales to either vendors or affiliated companies.

In some countries (e.g., France), you're legally required to post the net book value. Therefore, you need to check if it's a legal requirement to post the net book value for individual depreciation areas and then configure accordingly in Customizing under **Asset Accounting (New) • Transactions • Retirements • Gain/Loss Posting • Post Net Book Value Instead of Gain/Loss • Specify Depreciation Areas for Net Book Value Posting**.

First, you must identify the company codes for which you require the use of this posting option. Next, you need to identify the depreciation areas within the company codes for posting the net book value to a revenue clearing account during the asset retirement process.

4.4.7 Check Transaction Types

In the existing SAP ERP environment, if some of the transaction types that you had been using were restricted to certain depreciation areas, those transaction types can't be used after the migration. You need to ensure that the current, nonrestricted transaction types are adequate to meet your requirements. If not, then you must create new transaction types that aren't restricted to depreciation areas to bridge the gap.

4.5 Check Prerequisites for Activating New Asset Accounting

After you've migrated the charts of depreciation, made the assignments to the company codes, and performed the additional manual Customizing settings, you can then determine whether the prerequisites for activating the new Asset Accounting have been met.

In this activity, you check the prerequisites for parallel valuation in the new Asset Accounting. The prerequisite for changing the leading valuation in the new General Ledger Accounting is met by setting up and activating the business function FIN_AA_PARALLEL_VAL using Transaction SFW5, as shown in Figure 4.8.

E1D - Switch Framework: Change Business Function Status			
🔍 Check ↩ Discard Changes ✏ Activate Changes 🔍 Switch Framework Browser 📄 Display Leg			
Business Function Set	SAP Retail		
Name		Description	Planned Status
• FIN_AA_PARALLEL_VAL		FI-AA, Parallel Valuation	Business func. will remain activated

Figure 4.8 Business Function FIN_AA_PARALLEL_VAL Activated

You then need to execute Transaction FAA_CHECK_ACTIVATION to check if all prerequisites are met for activating the business function PARALLEL_VAL Customizing switch and if all periodic postings have been successfully completed.

You can activate new Asset Accounting using the business function PARALLEL_VAL Customizing switch. This program checks whether all the prerequisites for activating new Asset Accounting have been met. You also need to ensure that no postings are made between the execution of Transaction FAA_CHECK_ACTIVATION and the import of the PARALLEL_VAL Customizing switch, as shown in Figure 4.9.

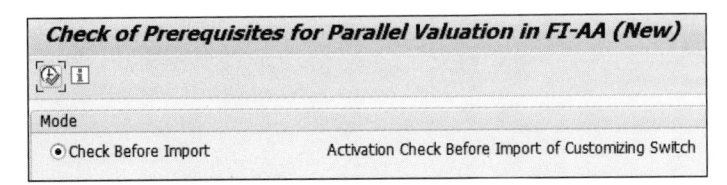

Figure 4.9 Check Prerequisites for Parallel Valuation in FI-AA

The report must show a green light under the **Type** column, as shown in Figure 4.10. Otherwise, activation of new Asset Accounting isn't possible.

Figure 4.10 Checking Data before Activating the PARALLEL_VAL Customizing Switch

4.6 Determine Active Charts of Depreciation

In this Customizing step, you need to check if all the active charts of depreciation have been migrated and assigned to the company code before any documents can be migrated, as shown in Figure 4.11.

You need to perform the following activities:

1. Check if all active and relevant company codes are assigned the correct chart of depreciation.
2. Delete the assignments for charts of depreciation that aren't relevant or are unused.

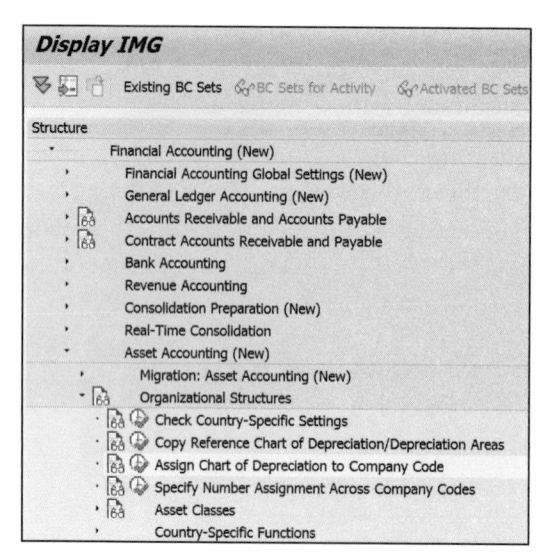

4 Preparation and Migration for Asset Accounting

Figure 4.11 Determining Active Charts of Depreciation

All links between "sample" charts of depreciation and company codes must be deleted because they will trigger an error during new Asset Accounting activation (see Figure 4.12).

Figure 4.12 Assigning Charts of Depreciation to Company Codes

4.7 Change Definitions of Depreciation Areas

The migration of the chart of depreciation is done in such a way that the Customizing settings (as depicted in Figure 4.13) allow all depreciation areas to post immediately to the G/L instead of periodically. This also applies for reserves for special depreciation areas, as shown in Figure 4.14.

4.7 Change Definitions of Depreciation Areas

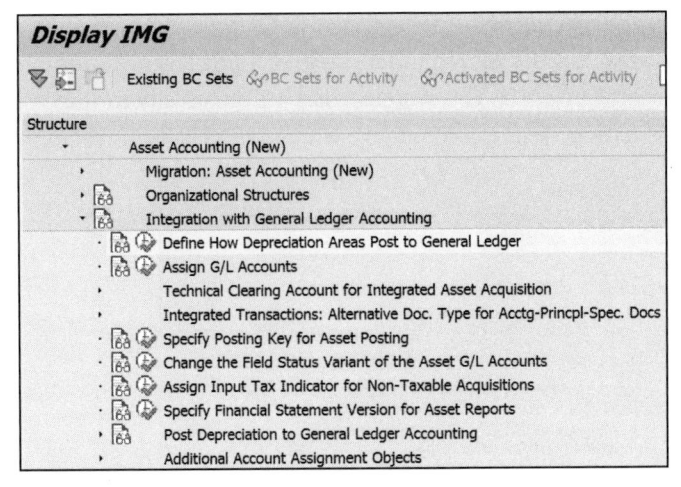

Figure 4.13 Depreciation Area Definition

For your depreciation areas, you may select one of following four options in the **G/L** column shown in Figure 4.14 to specify if and how they should post automatically to the G/L:

1. **Area Does Not Post**
2. **Area Posts Depreciation Only**
3. **Area Posts in Real Time**
4. **Area Posts APC Immediately and Depreciation**

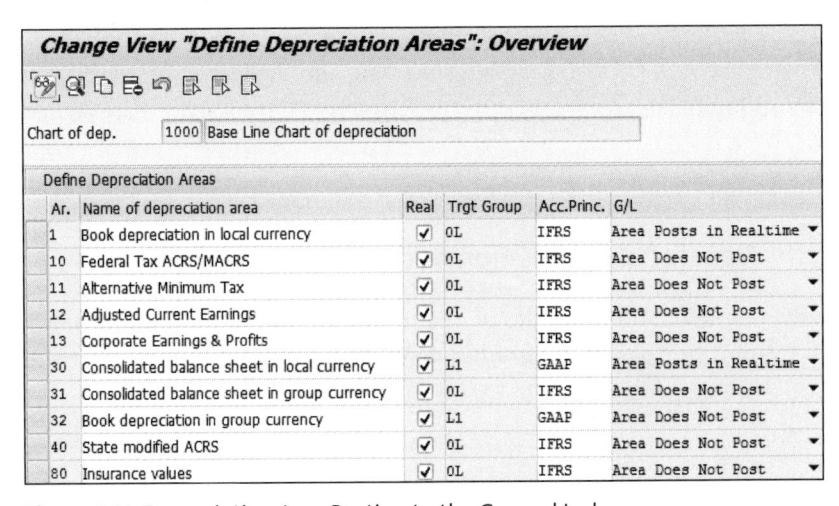

Figure 4.14 Depreciation Area Posting to the General Ledger

The standard depreciation areas in the SAP reference chart of depreciation are set up so that book depreciation area 01 posts APC transactions and depreciation automatically to the G/L, as shown in Figure 4.15. The system posts automatically to the G/L from other standard depreciation areas in accordance with country-specific requirements.

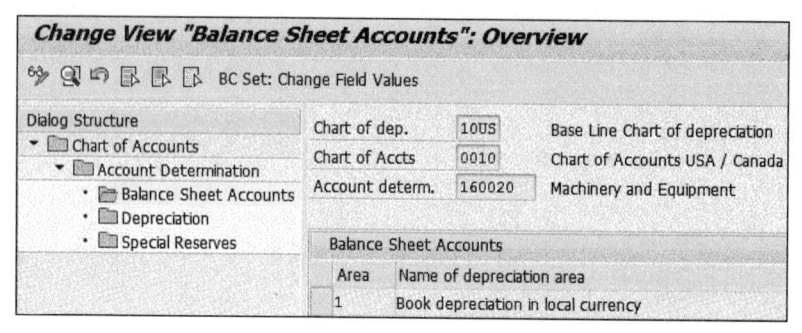

Figure 4.15 Account Determination Assignment to Chart of Depreciation

It's normally sufficient to post APC transactions and depreciation from one area automatically to the G/L. You might need additional areas that post automatically to the G/L for the following reasons:

- For cost-accounting purposes, you want to post depreciation that differs from book depreciation to expense accounts or cost elements.
- You need special valuations for the balance sheet (e.g., special reserves).
- You have special requirements for legal consolidation of your corporate group.
- If you're using the new General Ledger Accounting and the ledger approach, you can specify additional depreciation areas from which APC transactions are posted automatically to the G/L.

4.8 Specify Transfer of Acquisition and Production Cost Values

In this activity, you define transfer rules of APC posting values of depreciation areas, as shown in Figure 4.16. These transfer rules define the depreciation areas that will have identical asset values, as shown in Figure 4.17.

4.8 Specify Transfer of Acquisition and Production Cost Values

```
▼    Asset Accounting (New)
  ▶    Migration: Asset Accounting (New)
  ▶ 🗒  Organizational Structures
  ▶ 🗒  Integration with General Ledger Accounting
  ▼ 🗒  General Valuation
     • 🗒 ⊕ Set Chart of Depreciation
     ▼ 🗒   Depreciation Areas
        • 🗒 ⊕ Define Depreciation Areas
        • 🗒 ⊕ Define Depreciation Area for Quantity Update
        • 🗒 ⊕ Specify Transfer of APC Values
        • 🗒 ⊕ Specify Transfer of Depreciation Terms
     ▶        Länderspezifische Einstellungen
```

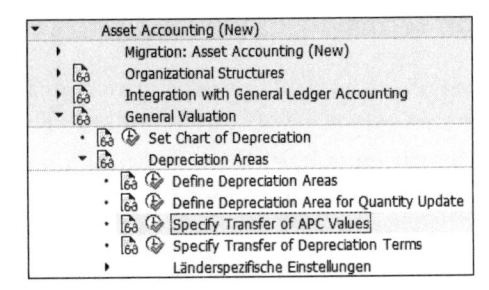

Figure 4.16 Specify Transfer of APC Values

In the **ValAd** column in Figure 4.17, you specify the reference depreciation area from which the values can be adopted to another depreciation area. The system transfers the posting amounts of any transactions that affect APC from this area to the dependent area.

Change View "Depreciation areas: Rules fo

Chart of dep. 1000 Base Line Chart of depreciation

Ar.	Name of depreciation area	ValAd	Ident.
01	Book depreciation in local currency	00	☐
10	Federal Tax ACRS/MACRS	01	✓
11	Alternative Minimum Tax	01	✓
12	Adjusted Current Earnings	01	✓
13	Corporate Earnings & Profits	01	✓
30	Consolidated balance sheet in local currency	00	☐
31	Consolidated balance sheet in group currency	01	✓
32	Book depreciation in group currency	30	✓
40	State modified ACRS	01	✓
80	Insurance values	01	✓

Figure 4.17 Depreciation Area Rules

You must adhere to the following rules when transferring APC values:

- A transfer of APC values is only possible from depreciation areas that have been assigned the same accounting principle.
- For those depreciation areas that post their APC in real time to General Ledger Accounting, the depreciation area must never use values from another depreciation area.
- When transferring values from one depreciation area to another, it doesn't make any difference if the depreciation area adopts values from an area that has a key either greater or smaller than its own key.

189

4.9 Specify Transfer of Depreciation Terms

In this activity, you specify how the depreciation terms from one depreciation area are adopted in another depreciation area, as shown in Figure 4.18. The terms can be transferred between depreciation areas that have been assigned the same accounting principle. A depreciation area can also adopt depreciation terms from a depreciation area that has a larger key than it does.

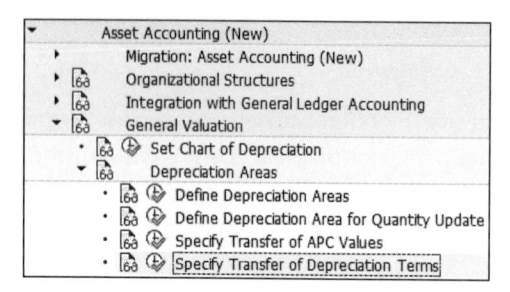

```
▼    Asset Accounting (New)
  ▶      Migration: Asset Accounting (New)
  ▶ 🗁   Organizational Structures
  ▶ 🗁   Integration with General Ledger Accounting
  ▼ 🗁   General Valuation
      • 🗎 ⊕ Set Chart of Depreciation
      ▼ 🗁   Depreciation Areas
          • 🗎 ⊕ Define Depreciation Areas
          • 🗎 ⊕ Define Depreciation Area for Quantity Update
          • 🗎 ⊕ Specify Transfer of APC Values
          • 🗎 ⊕ Specify Transfer of Depreciation Terms
```

Figure 4.18 Specify Transfer of Depreciation Terms

It's only possible to adopt depreciation terms from depreciation areas that have the same ledger group. For those depreciation areas that post their APC to General Ledger Accounting in real time, the following applies:

- Depreciation areas that manage APC are never allowed to adopt depreciation terms from another depreciation area. In that case, enter "00" as the key for the depreciation area.

- The other depreciation areas that post in real time (e.g., areas for investment support or revaluation) can adopt depreciation terms from another area, so long as both areas have the same ledger group.

Within the Customizing activity shown in Figure 4.19 using Transaction OABD, you specify the depreciation area from which the depreciation terms are adopted by the current depreciation area in the **TTr** (transfer of depreciation terms from depreciation area) column. The terms can be transferred only from a depreciation area to which the same accounting principle is assigned. A depreciation area can also adopt depreciation terms from a depreciation area that has a larger key than it does, as shown in Figure 4.19.

In the standard system, changes to control parameters in the reference depreciation area aren't automatically transferred to dependent depreciation areas that adopt depreciation terms. Instead, you can change the depreciation terms in dependent depreciation areas in the asset master record. However, when you set the **Identical** checkbox shown in Figure 4.19, the system transfers all changes in the reference depreciation area to the dependent depreciation areas, where it's then not possible to change them.

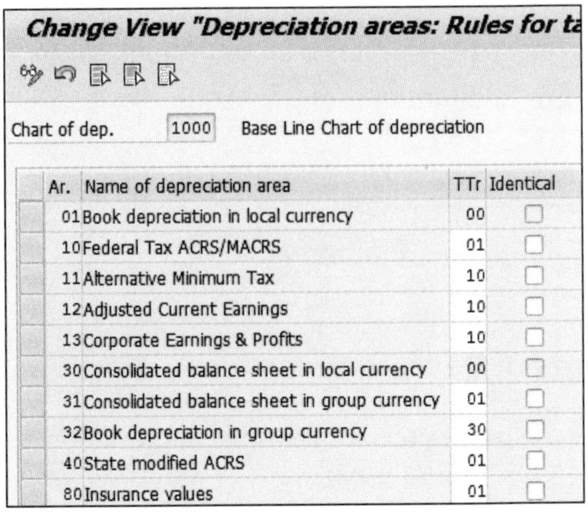

Figure 4.19 Rules for Takeover of Depreciation Terms

4.10 Activate New Asset Accounting

In this activity, the new Asset Accounting functionality is activated, as shown in Figure 4.20. When you execute this Customizing transaction, the system performs various checks and then saves this setting if no errors are encountered. After the checks have been passed successfully and the settings have been saved, new Asset Accounting becomes activated. From this point onward, you can post using the new posting logic.

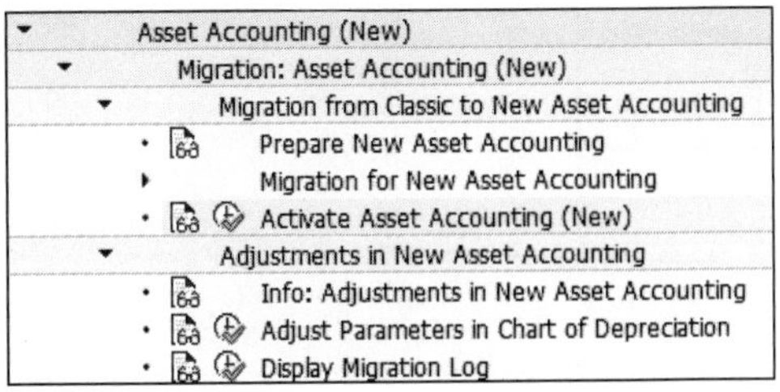

Figure 4.20 Activate New Asset Accounting

4 Preparation and Migration for Asset Accounting

After executing the Customizing setting in Figure 4.20, you'll be taken to the new Asset Accounting activation screen, where you can select the **Actv.** (active) option shown in Figure 4.21, and then save.

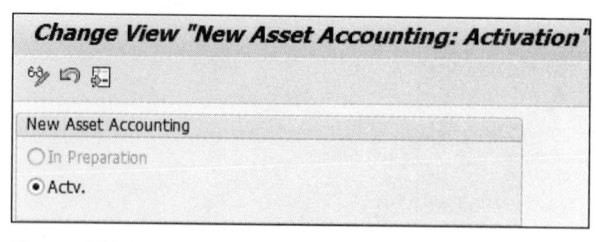

Figure 4.21 New Asset Accounting Active

4.11 Adjust Parameters in Charts of Depreciation

This activity supports you in adjusting the parameters for charts of depreciation, as shown in Figure 4.22.

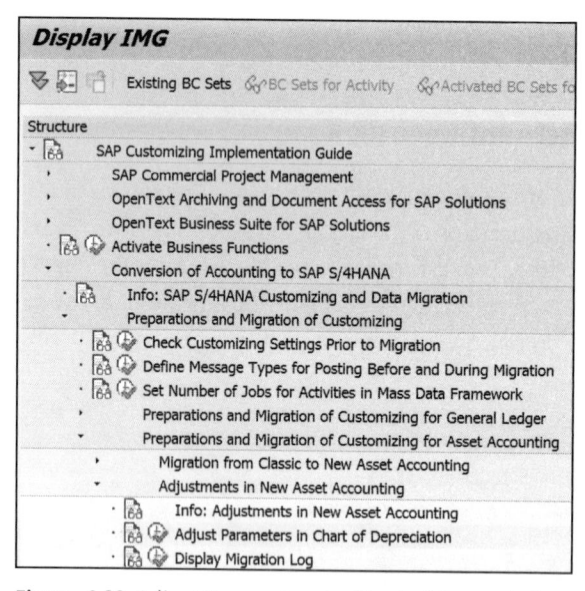

Figure 4.22 Adjust Parameters in Chart of Depreciation

You can use this activity, if necessary, to make the following adjustments:

- **Assign the accounting principle**
  An accounting principle is assigned to each depreciation area, including the non-posting depreciation areas. The system derives the accounting principle from the relevant ledger group already assigned to the depreciation area.

  For each set of depreciation areas that are assigned to the same accounting principle, only one depreciation area is allowed to manage APC and have the option **Area Posts in Real Time** or **Area Posts APC Immediately, Depreciation Periodically**.

- **Change posting indicator for depreciation areas**
  The system changes the settings for posting in the G/L, whereby the depreciation areas that represent reserves for special depreciation—for example, in the future—post immediately to the G/L. The execution of the program highlighted in Figure 4.22 changes the depreciation areas for the specified chart of depreciation to **Depreciation Area Posts Balance Sheet Value Immediately, Depreciation Periodically**.

The charts of depreciation are adjusted manually in the following cases:

- The parameters of the charts of depreciation couldn't be adjusted automatically because the program doesn't recognize the starting situation defined in your system.
- Adjusting the charts of depreciation manually is standard procedure, regardless of circumstances.
- The charts of depreciation in FI-AA are assigned to a deactivated company code. The data of this deactivated company code aren't archived; therefore, this data must be migrated with the document migration.

4.12 Display Migration Log

You can use this activity to display the migration log of the charts of depreciation during either the test run or the update run, as shown in Figure 4.23. Any error messages must be resolved before you can mark the migration to new Asset Accounting as complete.

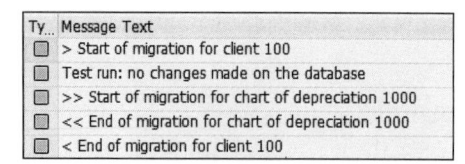

4 Preparation and Migration for Asset Accounting

Ty...	Message Text
☐	> Start of migration for client 100
☐	Test run: no changes made on the database
☐	>> Start of migration for chart of depreciation 1000
☐	<< End of migration for chart of depreciation 1000
☐	< End of migration for client 100

Figure 4.23 Job Log for Adjusting Parameters in a Chart of Depreciation

4.13 Key Changes to Asset Accounting

With the emergence of SAP S/4HANA Finance, SAP has eliminated the reconciliation steps between asset accounting and the general ledger. In this section, we analyze the impact SAP S/4HANA Finance has had on the table architecture design, the business process transactions, the functionality, and the configuration of Asset Accounting.

With the introduction of SAP S/4HANA Finance, classic FI-AA is no longer available. You can use both the ledger approach and account approach with the new Asset Accounting. The usage of the new depreciation calculation program is mandatory and comes with the activation of the business function EA-FIN.

4.13.1 Architectural Impact

With SAP S/4HANA Finance, there is a change to the architecture and underlying table structure in new Asset Accounting, as shown in Figure 4.24. All actual FI-AA line item postings are stored in table ACDOCA, and the header information is stored in table BKPF. All statistical line item information related to FI-AA is stored in table FAAT_DOC_IT.

Plan data that used to be stored in table ANLP and table ANLC is now stored in table FAAT_PLAN_VALUES, whereas year-dependent depreciation attributes are stored in table FAAT_YDDA in SAP S/4HANA Finance. Thus, FI-AA tables ANEK, ANEP, ANEA, ANLP, and ANLC won't be updated going forward.

Upon the creation of the asset, planned depreciation values are calculated on a real-time basis and are stored in table FAAT_PLAN_VALUES. If there are any errors (e.g., inconsistent depreciation key) while calculating planned depreciation, that asset's planned depreciation value will be empty and won't be updated.

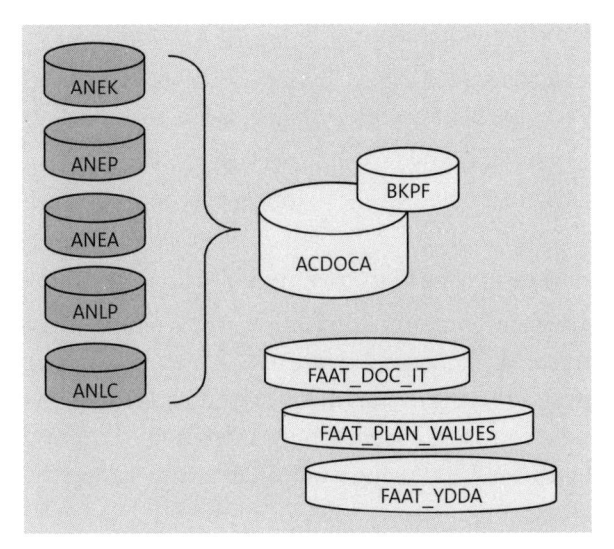

Figure 4.24 New Asset Accounting Architecture

During the month-end depreciation run, actual postings will use the planned depreciation values from table `FAAT_PLAN_VALUES`. Assets with errors won't stop the full depreciation run. An asset with issues/errors won't have an actual depreciation posting and will be reflected in the depreciation run log.

4.13.2 Functionality Impact

SAP S/4HANA Finance has had a significant impact on the functionality, transaction codes, and tables within FI-AA, which we'll discuss in the following sections.

General Functionality Changes

The following functional changes have been made to FI-AA with the introduction of SAP S/4HANA Finance:

- Reporting is based on line items and the virtualization of totals has been removed.
- All non-statistical line items in FI-AA are stored as Universal Journal entries.
- Reconciliation isn't required with G/L or within FI-AA itself. General Ledger Accounting and new Asset Accounting are reconciled due to the Universal Journal entry.

4   Preparation and Migration for Asset Accounting

- Depreciation is now posted for the individual asset.
- Reporting is done for any Controlling (CO) object by individual asset, such as depreciation for the cost center (e.g., CC1) by asset (e.g., Mac1).
- The asset depreciation run takes significantly less time because the depreciation values are computed and posted in real time and are no longer part of the depreciation run itself.
- Periodic posting runs are no longer valid due to the real-time update.
- For each accounting principle, a corresponding depreciation area is required. For each currency in a G/L, a corresponding derived depreciation area is required. Fiscal year variants for fixed assets differing in start date or end date as compared to the fiscal year variants for the company code are only supported by a workaround (discussed in SAP Note 1951069) and require thorough testing before the upgrade.
- Accurate values are now posted from the start using multiple parallel documents.
- If a period is skipped, a depreciation run can be re-executed for an asset for the skipped period.
- If some assets have errors during the depreciation run due to missing accounts in the account assignment, when you re-execute the deprecation run after fixing those errors, it picks up only the assets to which corrections were made.
- The posting logic in new Asset Accounting has changed as follows:
  - The operational entry document posts a debit to the technical clearing account and a credit to the vendor account. This document doesn't update the asset values, and the asset data are only used to perform checks.
  - The accounting principle-specific documents are posted with a debit to the asset reconciliation account and a credit to the technical clearing account. This document updates the asset line items. This is applicable for both the ledger approach and the account approach, when multiple postings occur for each of the ledger groups assigned to the accounting principles for each depreciation area.

As an illustrative example, an asset acquisition from a vendor is made using Transaction F-90 in a one-step process (see Table 4.1).

4.13 Key Changes to Asset Accounting

Account	Amount
Asset (G/L) account	Debit $10,000 USD
Vendor account	Credit $10,000 USD

Table 4.1 Debits and Credits in SAP ERP 6.0

Whereas in SAP S/4HANA Finance, the technical clearing account for integrated asset acquisition has been introduced and is posted using a three-step process, as shown in Table 4.2.

Account	Amount
Technical clearing account	Debit $10,000 USD
Vendor account	Credit $10,000 USD
Asset (G/L) account	Debit $10,000 USD
Technical clearing account	Credit $10,000 USD

Table 4.2 Debits and Credits in SAP S/4HANA Finance

The first step, during which the technical clearing account is debited, is shown in Figure 4.25.

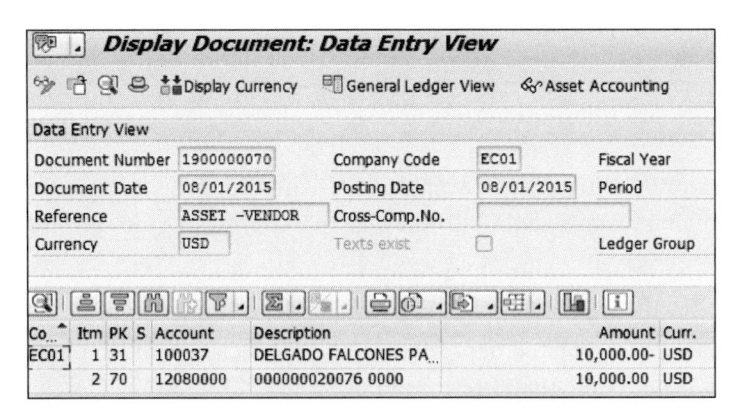

Figure 4.25 Asset Accounting Posting to Vendor

4 Preparation and Migration for Asset Accounting

In the same document, there are other corresponding accounting documents that post the other leg of the accounting entry, debiting the asset reconciliation account, and crediting the technical clearing account. Separate documents are posted to each of the ledgers within the ledger group that are assigned to the accounting principle associated with the depreciation area, as shown in Figure 4.26.

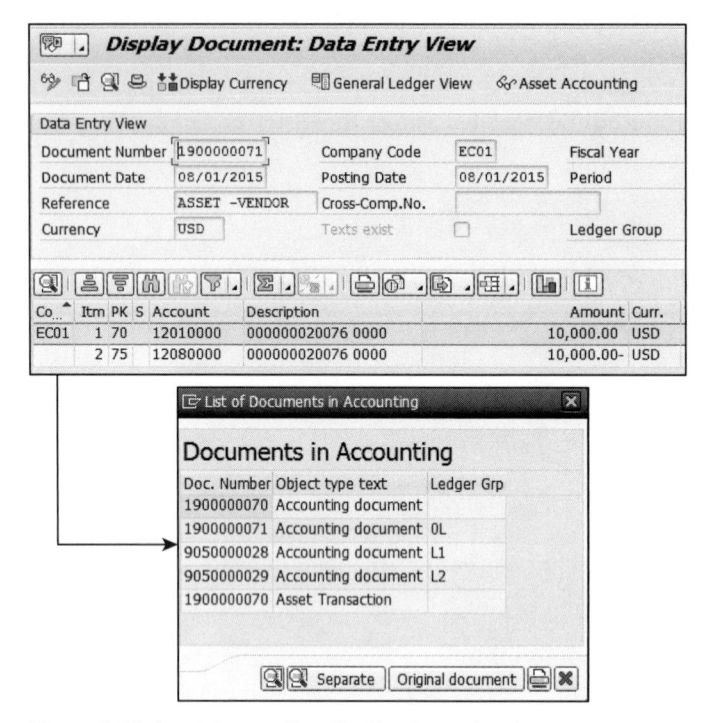

Figure 4.26 Asset Accounting Posting to an Asset

In a nutshell, Transaction AS91 used to be a single transaction to load asset master data and values for previous years and the current year. In SAP S/4HANA Finance, it's a three-step process:

1. Master data are loaded through Transaction AS91.
2. Asset historical values, accumulated depreciation, and depreciation for the year are loaded through Transaction ABLDT.
3. The current year acquisitions are managed through Transaction AB01.

4.13　Key Changes to Asset Accounting

Asset migration through Transaction AS91 doesn't upload values in SAP S/4HANA Finance.

In addition, in SAP S/4HANA Finance, the **Depreciation Run** selection screen has been simplified with a new screen that has the following attributes:

- You can now run depreciation posting for an accounting principle that can be entered on the selection screen.
- You need to enter the server group entered in SAP S/4HANA Finance.
- The **Reason for Posting Run** section, which includes **Planned Posting Run**, **Repeat**, **Restart**, and **Unplanned Posting Run** radio buttons, has now been eliminated in SAP S/4HANA Finance, as shown in Figure 4.27.
- The **Depreciation Posting Run** detailed log option reports depreciation at the individual asset level with corresponding cost center information, as shown in Figure 4.28.

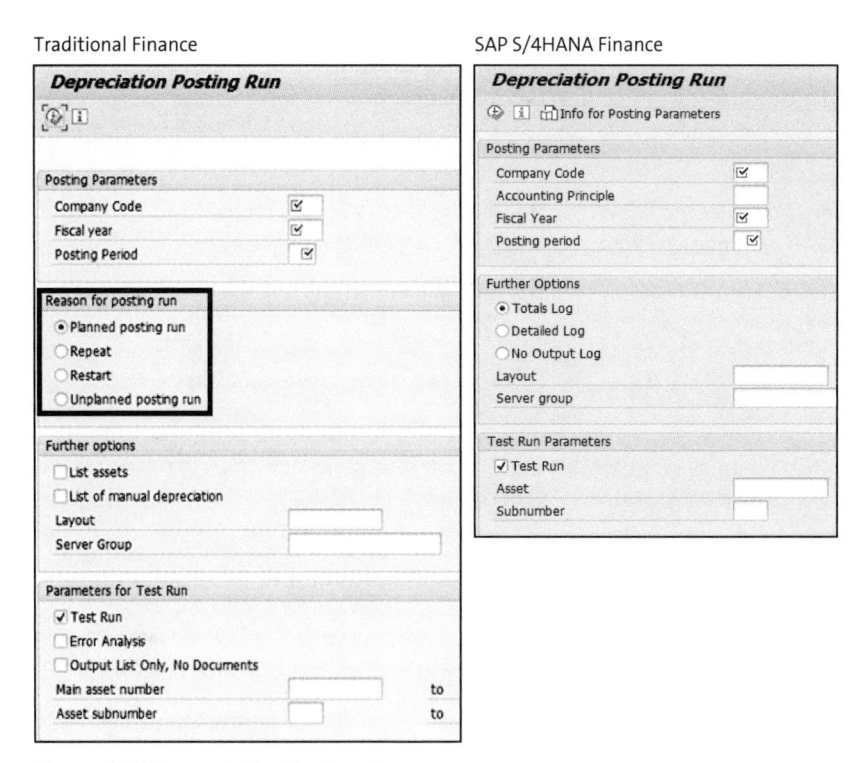

Figure 4.27　Depreciation Posting Run

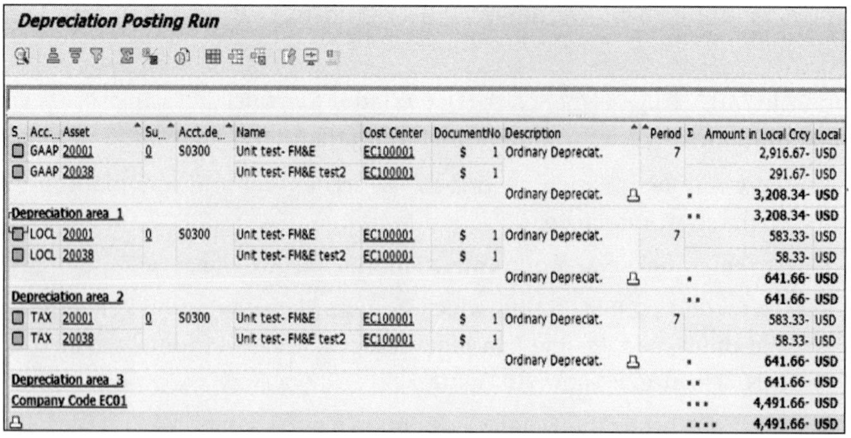

4   Preparation and Migration for Asset Accounting

Figure 4.28 Depreciation Posting Run Log

Changes in Transaction Codes

Table 4.3 details those transactions that have been replaced or that became obsolete in new Asset Accounting in SAP S/4HANA Finance.

Old Transaction	New Transaction
Transaction ABST2 (Reconciliation Analysis FI-AA; no longer required)	Transaction FAGLGVTR used for the G/L close process
Transaction AB01 (Create Asset Postings)	Transaction AB01L
Transaction ASKB <RAPERB200> (Periodic APC Run)	Obsolete; posting now performed directly to G/L
Transaction ABST(L) < RABST01 > (Reconciliation Program G/L-AA)	Obsolete; no FI-AA tables any longer to reconcile with G/L, just table ACDOCA
Transaction ABST2 < RABST02> (Reconciliation Program G/L-AA)	Obsolete; no FI-AA tables any longer to reconcile with G/L, just table ACDOCA
Transaction AB02 (Change Asset Document)	Changes in asset documents made via Transaction FB02
Transaction AW01_AFAR (Asset Explorer; old depreciation)	Not available anymore (replaced by Transaction AW01N)

Table 4.3 Changes in Transaction Codes Related to New Asset Accounting

4.13 Key Changes to Asset Accounting

Old Transaction	New Transaction
Transaction ABF1/ABF1L (Post Differences in Asset Accounting)	Not required because the ledger can be entered directly in the transaction
Transaction OASV (Transfer Balances)	Not required; now a real-time functionality
Transaction FAA_GL_RECON (Consistency Check for FI-AA [New] and FI-G/L [New])	Not required; now a real-time functionality
Transaction RAGITT01 (Asset History Sheet)	New Program S_ALR_87011990

Table 4.3 Changes in Transaction Codes Related to New Asset Accounting (Cont.)

Table Changes

The following changes were made to the underlying tables in FI-AA with the introduction of SAP S/4HANA Finance:

- **New tables introduced**
    - ACDOCA
    - FAAT_DOC_IT
    - FAAT_YDDA
    - FAAT_PLAN_VALUES
- **Obsolete tables removed**
    - Tables ANEP, ANEA, ANLP, and ANLC were replaced by table ACDOCA but are still supported by means of compatibility views.
    - Statistical items from tables ANEP, ANEA, ANLP, and ANLC were moved to table FAAT_DOC_IT but are still supported through compatibility views.
    - Planned values from tables ANLP and ANLC were moved to table FAAT_PLAN_VALUES but are still supported through compatibility views.
- **Actual items**
    - Actual data of tables ANEK, ANEP, ANEA, ANLP, and ANLC are now stored in table ACDOCA. Table ANEK data are also stored in table BKPF.
    - Compatibility FAAV_<TABLENAME> views (e.g., FAAV_ANEK) are provided to reproduce the old structures.

4 Preparation and Migration for Asset Accounting

- Old data can still be accessed in tables via the FAAV_<TABLENAME>_ORI views (e.g., FAAV_ANEA_ORI).
- **Statistical items**
  - Statistical data stored previously in tables ANEP, ANEA, ANLP, and ANLC are now stored in table FAAT_DOC_IT.
  - Planned data stored previously in tables ANLP and ANLC are now stored in table FAAT_PLAN_VALUES.

4.13.3 Configuration Impact

With the implementation of SAP S/4HANA Finance, the configuration changes discussed in the following subsections have occurred.

Define How Depreciation Areas Post to the General Ledger

The chart of depreciation is migrated in such a way that no areas post periodically; all areas post immediately to the G/L, as shown in Figure 4.29. This also applies to reserves for special depreciation areas. The delta depreciation area is no longer required.

Ar.	Name of depreciation area	Real	Trgt Group	Acc.Princ.	G/L
1	Book depreciation in local currency	✓	0L	IFRS	Area Posts in Realtime
10	Federal Tax ACRS/MACRS	✓	0L	IFRS	Area Does Not Post
11	Alternative Minimum Tax	✓	0L	IFRS	Area Does Not Post
12	Adjusted Current Earnings	✓	0L	IFRS	Area Does Not Post
13	Corporate Earnings & Profits	✓	0L	IFRS	Area Does Not Post
30	Consolidated balance sheet in local currency	✓	L1	GAAP	Area Posts in Realtime
31	Consolidated balance sheet in group currency	✓	0L	IFRS	Area Does Not Post
32	Book depreciation in group currency	✓	L1	GAAP	Area Does Not Post
40	State modified ACRS	✓	0L	IFRS	Area Does Not Post
80	Insurance values	✓	0L	IFRS	Area Does Not Post

Figure 4.29 Defining Depreciation Areas

Specify Transfer of Acquisition and Production Cost Values

In this activity, you define transfer rules pertaining to the posting of APC values for depreciation areas, as shown in Figure 4.30. These transfer rules ensure that certain depreciation areas have similar asset values.

4.13 Key Changes to Asset Accounting

Change View "Depreciation areas: Rules for

Chart of dep. 1000 Base Line Chart of depreciation

Ar.	Name of depreciation area	ValAd	Ident.
01	Book depreciation in local currency	00	☐
10	Federal Tax ACRS/MACRS	01	✓
11	Alternative Minimum Tax	01	✓
12	Adjusted Current Earnings	01	✓
13	Corporate Earnings & Profits	01	✓
30	Consolidated balance sheet in local currency	00	☐
31	Consolidated balance sheet in group currency	01	✓
32	Book depreciation in group currency	30	✓
40	State modified ACRS	01	✓
80	Insurance values	01	✓

Figure 4.30 Specifying Transfer of Acquisition and Production Cost Values

Specify Transfer of Depreciation Terms

In this activity, you specify how the depreciation terms for a depreciation area are adopted from another depreciation area, as shown in Figure 4.31. You can specify whether the adoption of values is optional or mandatory. If you specify an optional transfer, you can change the proposed depreciation terms in the dependent areas in the asset master record.

Change View "Depreciation areas: Rules for

Chart of dep. 1000 Base Line Chart of depreciation

Ar.	Name of depreciation area	TTr	Identical
01	Book depreciation in local currency	00	☐
10	Federal Tax ACRS/MACRS	01	☐
11	Alternative Minimum Tax	10	☐
12	Adjusted Current Earnings	10	☐
13	Corporate Earnings & Profits	10	☐
30	Consolidated balance sheet in local currency	00	☐
31	Consolidated balance sheet in group currency	01	☐
32	Book depreciation in group currency	30	☐
40	State modified ACRS	01	☐
80	Insurance values	01	☐

Figure 4.31 Specifying the Transfer of Depreciation Terms

For a mandatory transfer, you can't maintain any depreciation terms in the asset master record. In this way, you can ensure that depreciation is uniform in certain depreciation areas.

Activate New Asset Accounting

In this Customizing activity, you activate the new functions for new Asset Accounting by selecting the **Actv.** (active) option in the **New Asset Accounting** area, as shown in Figure 4.32.

The system performs various checks before saving this setting. If the checks are successfully executed and subsequently saved, new Asset Accounting is activated, and you can then start posting using the new posting logic.

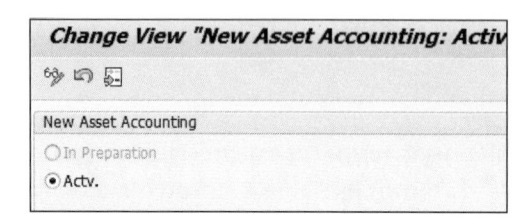

Figure 4.32 Activating New Asset Accounting

Technical Clearing Account for Integrated Asset Acquisition

The business transaction pertaining to FI-AA is allocated into an operational part and a valuating part during the integrated asset acquisition posting:

- For the operational part (vendor invoice), a ledger-group-independent document valid for all accounting principles is posted against the technical clearing account for integrated asset acquisitions.
- For each valuating part (asset posting with capitalization of the asset), a separate ledger-group-specific document valid for each of the accounting principles is posted against the technical clearing account for integrated asset acquisition, as shown in Figure 4.33.

Thus, the technical clearing account for integrated asset acquisitions is posted automatically and always has a zero balance for each of the accounting principles in the chart of depreciation.

4.13 Key Changes to Asset Accounting

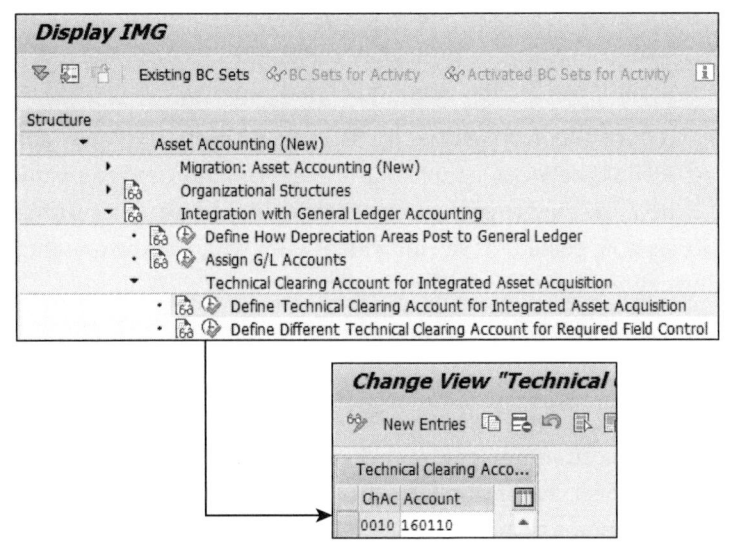

Figure 4.33 Defining the Technical Clearing Account for Asset Acquisition

4.13.4 Closing Process Impact

The closing process is impacted by new Asset Accounting with SAP S/4HANA Finance in the following ways:

- Real-time integration of the asset with the G/L occurs, eliminating reconciliation steps.
- The APC posting run isn't required with SAP S/4HANA Finance.
- The planned depreciation value of the asset is reflected in real time and is updated with every master data change and every asset transaction posting.
- No separate program is executed for balance carryforward in FI-AA. The general balance carryforward transaction of FI transfers AA balances by default.
- Planned depreciation is automatically calculated for the new year after the balance carryforward (year-end close) is performed.
- The depreciation posting run is executed faster due to simple processing logic, new data structures, and parallel processing.

You now understand the biggest changes that SAP S/4HANA introduced to FI-AA. In classic FI-AA, Transaction AS91 was a single transaction that loaded asset master data and values for previous years and the current year. In SAP S/4HANA Finance, it's a three-step process.

You've also seen that a valuation difference now exists between the leading and non-leading ledgers due to separate accounting principles. Ledger-specific separate number ranges must also be maintained for document types that generate asset postings.

The technical clearing account generates entries for asset acquisition from a vendor using Transaction F-90. All links between sample charts of depreciation and company codes must be deleted because they trigger an error during new Asset Accounting activation. Depreciation is now posted for the individual asset with a corresponding depreciation area being defined for each accounting principle.

4.14 Summary

SAP S/4HANA Finance introduced some significant changes in the FI-AA module. You need to execute the special check Report RASFIN_MIGR_PRECHECK for FI-AA installation and check whether the new asset depreciation is active. You also need to set up a parallel area for each additional currency used in the corresponding G/L. You need to ensure that all inconsistencies and errors are fixed during the migration, and it's prudent to involve all the stakeholders to evaluate relevant data for acceptance of migration.

After reading this chapter, you should now understand the Customizing and migration steps for the new Asset Accounting. Let's now move on to Chapter 5, in which we'll discuss the steps you need to take to customize Controlling for your SAP S/4HANA Finance migration.

Chapter 5
Preparation and Migration for Controlling

This chapter covers the Customizing steps required for Controlling in an SAP S/4HANA Finance migration. It outlines the configuration, setup, and activation of the operating concern for account-based Profitability Analysis.

With the introduction of SAP S/4HANA Finance, the Controlling (CO) and Financial Accounting (FI) components have now been merged. Cost and revenue information is now stored in the single Universal Journal entry table ACDOCA, which is reconciled in real time with the income statement. The entries in the new simplified Profitability Analysis (CO-PA) are posted to the same Universal Journal entry table. Therefore, account-based CO-PA is recommended for usage with SAP S/4HANA Finance.

Costing-based CO-PA is still available, and you can use both types of CO-PA in parallel. However, account-based CO-PA is the default solution because line items in the new table ACDOCA are account-driven. With account-based CO-PA, the relevant accounts are updated for any revenue posting or cost of goods sold (COGS) posting, and they are assigned to the correct market segment characteristics.

Some of the key activities that you need to perform to customize CO as part of the overall SAP S/4HANA Finance migration include executing SAP Business Warehouse (SAP BW) delta extraction for account-based CO-PA, adapting the settings for profitability segment characteristics, maintaining the operating concern and its banking add-on, activating account-based CO-PA, and, finally, transporting the operating concern.

This configuration is completed under **SAP Customizing Implementation Guide • Conversion of Accounting to SAP S/4HANA • Preparations and Migration of Customizing • Preparations and Migration of Customizing for Controlling**, as shown in Figure 5.1.

5   Preparation and Migration for Controlling

```
Structure
  ▸ SAP Customizing Implementation Guide
       ▸ SAP Commercial Project Management
       ▸ OpenText Archiving and Document Access for SAP Solutions
       ▸ OpenText Business Suite for SAP Solutions
       ▸ Activate Business Functions
       ▾ Conversion of Accounting to SAP S/4HANA
            ▸ Info: SAP S/4HANA Customizing and Data Migration
            ▾ Preparations and Migration of Customizing
                 ▸ Check Customizing Settings Prior to Migration
                 ▸ Define Message Types for Posting Before and During Migration
                 ▸ Set Number of Jobs for Activities in Mass Data Framework
                 ▸ Preparations and Migration of Customizing for General Ledger
                 ▸ Preparations and Migration of Customizing for Asset Accounting
                 ▾ Preparations and Migration of Customizing for Controlling
                      ▸ Execute BW-Delta Extraction for Account-Based CO-PA
                      ▸ Adapt Settings for Profitability Segment Characteristics
                      ▸ Maintain Operating Concern
                      ▸ Activate Account-Based Profitability Analysis
                      ▸ Transport Operating Concern
                 ▾ Preparations and Migration of Customizing for Material Ledger
                      ▸ Migrate Material Ledger Customizing
                 ▸ Preparations for Migration of House Bank Accounts
                 ▸ Preparatory Activities and Migration of Customizing for Credit Management
```

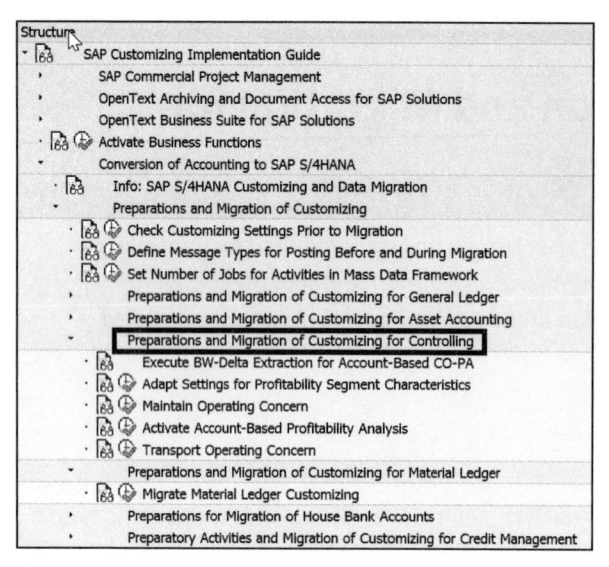

Figure 5.1 Customizing Migration for Controlling

When you activate account-based CO-PA, you might need to add or enhance additional fields in the Universal Journal table ACDOCA.

5.1   Execute SAP Business Warehouse Delta Extraction for Account-Based Profitability Analysis

You need to execute a delta extraction in SAP BW for those account-based CO-PA data sources for which you use the delta procedure. This is necessary because account-based CO-PA line items not extracted before the migration may be ignored after the migration when the next delta is loaded. The volume of data that resides in CO-PA and needs to be transferred to SAP BW can be quite large. Thus, delta extraction is recommended to transfer data from CO-PA to SAP BW.

5.2   Adapt Settings for Profitability Segment Characteristics

In this activity, settings for profitability segment characteristics (segment level) are deleted (as shown in Figure 5.2) because in SAP S/4HANA Finance, each profitability segment contains all available characteristics. A summarization of specific characteristics is no longer possible or needed. This includes the settings for distributed CO-PA characteristics (segment level).

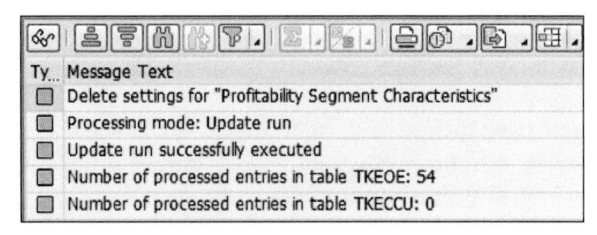

Figure 5.2 Delete Settings for Profitability Segment Characteristics Using Report FCO_MIGRATION_COPA

5.3 Maintain the Operating Concern

In this activity, the operating concern is activated for account-based CO-PA. If this setting isn't made, the new profitability reporting won't be available.

You can also include custom-defined fields from the CI_COBL structure in your operating concern using this activity.

On the **Maintain Operating Concern** screen, fill in the **Operating Concern** field, and then press [Enter]. The green stoplight box next to **Status** at the bottom of Figure 5.3 indicates whether you can now work with the operating concern.

Figure 5.3 Maintain Operating Concern

For your operating concerns, set the **Account-based** indicator on the **Data Structure** tab. If the status is either amber or red, you need to investigate by clicking the **Actions** button and then selecting the status to display the error log during activation.

> **Expert Insight**
>
> You might come across an error indicating that at least one or more new characteristics were added to your operating concern but weren't included in database table ACDOCA (Universal Journal line item). To resolve this error, execute program FCO_ADD_COPA_FIELD_TO_ACDOCA for your operating concern in the background using Transaction SA38. This program adds the new characteristics to the relevant field in database table ACDOCA.

After all errors from the action log have been resolved, the operating concern status as shown in Figure 5.4 will become green, meaning that the operating concern is active. Data can now be posted to the operating concern, and the reports can be executed.

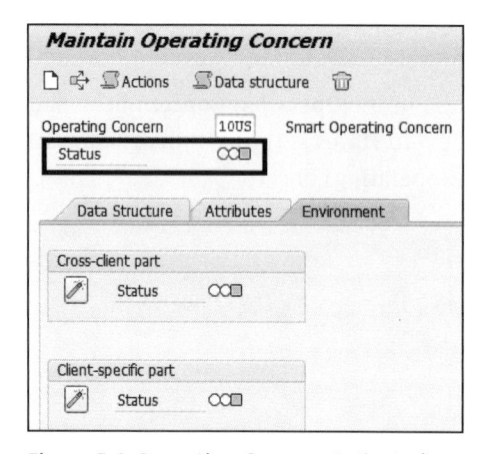

Figure 5.4 Operating Concern Activated

5.4 Activate Account-Based Profitability Analysis

In this activity, you activate account-based CO-PA for your operating concerns by selecting **3** in the **Active Status** column, as shown in Figure 5.5. If this setting isn't made, the new profitability reporting won't be available. Error messages may also appear—for example, when posting to profitability segments.

5.6 Preparations and Migration for Material Ledger

Figure 5.5 Activating CO-PA

If your organization is using costing-based CO-PA, you must activate account-based CO-PA and either continue to use both or deselect costing-based CO-PA and use just the account-based CO-PA going forward. Only the account-based CO-PA entries are posted in the Universal Journal.

5.5 Transport Operating Concern

In this activity using Transaction **KE3I**, you transport the definition of your operating concerns by selecting **Operating Concern** and clicking **Execute** in the screen shown in Figure 5.6.

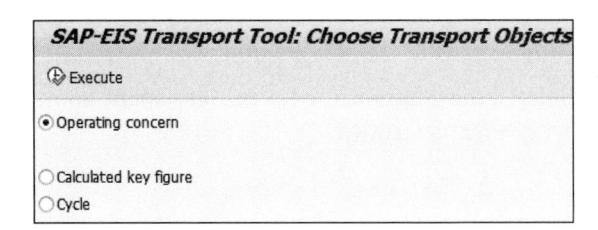

Figure 5.6 Transporting Operating Concern

5.6 Preparations and Migration for Material Ledger

With SAP S/4HANA Finance, you need to migrate to and use the Material Ledger (ML) if it was already in use in the prior version of SAP or if you're also using logistics functionality in SAP S/4HANA.

211

Migration to the ML has its own step in the IMG, but since the preparation and migration process is so short, we have bundled it in this book with the rest of the Controlling topics here in Chapter 5.

The configuration shown in Figure 5.7 is completed under **SAP Customizing Implementation Guide** • **Conversion of Accounting to SAP S/4HANA** • **Preparations and Migration of Customizing** • **Preparations and Migration of Customizing for Material Ledger**.

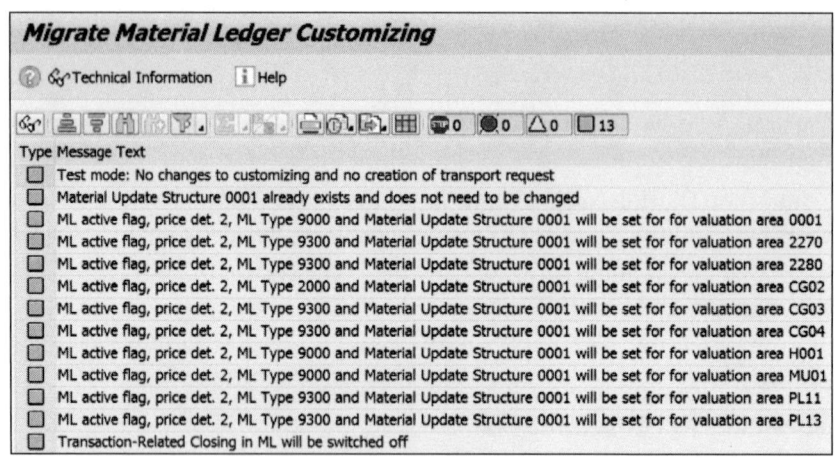

Figure 5.7 Customizing for Material Ledger Migration

You need to first execute the migration in test mode and check that no errors are encountered before executing this transaction in update mode. If the transaction is successfully executed, the Customizing settings for the ML are migrated.

Now that you've migrated and completed the Customizing for CO, let's spend some time reviewing what's changed with CO in SAP S/4HANA.

5.7 Key Changes to Controlling

CO contains internal accounting data and the account assignment objects needed to produce management-oriented reports and analysis. Unlike SAP ERP Financials, this component isn't governed by any legal requirements and provides management with the flexibility to obtain reports in various dimensions for better analysis and decision-making.

5.7 Key Changes to Controlling

With the emergence of SAP S/4HANA Finance, primary and secondary cost elements are now an integral part of General Ledger (G/L) accounts, and SAP ERP Financial Accounting-Controlling reconciliation is done by design. This section provides the architecture, configuration, and functionality impact that SAP S/4HANA Finance has on CO.

5.7.1 Functionality Impact

In SAP S/4HANA Finance, accounting documents are posted using a common document number. The FI documents for profit and loss (P&L) accounts still generate CO documents. To maintain consistency and CO compatibility views, the document type and document number Customizing settings are maintained for the internal CO postings and to assign the actual version of CO to the ledger. With the integration of FI and CO, there is no requirement for a reconciliation ledger going forward.

In the past, any CO-related postings were updated in both the line item table (COEP) and totals table (COSP for primary, COSS for secondary). With SAP S/4HANA Finance, the totals tables are no longer required because data can be aggregated from the line item table, which is also used for reporting. This avoids data redundancy. All actuals data continues to be stored in the line item table COEP. Two new tables—COSP_BAK and COSS_BAK—have been created to store planned data related to primary and secondary costs, respectively.

The Universal Journal has its own currency fields in FI, and CO has its own currency settings. The currency concepts used separately in FI and CO have now been combined. You can enhance the journal entry by adding the coding block and Profitability Analysis (CO-PA) characteristics. Access to old data in tables is still possible via the V_<table name>_ORI compatibility views.

In the following sections, we'll analyze how the merge of cost elements to G/L accounts has impacted the CO postings and how allocations have eliminated the need for FI-CO reconciliation. We'll also evaluate how multiple currencies are maintained and kept compatible between FI and CO, discuss the changes to the posting logic for CO documents, and explore the enhancements to the ML.

Cost Elements

Cost elements are no longer required in SAP S/4HANA Finance because they are created as G/L accounts using Transaction FS00 and are part of the chart of accounts. A new field for the cost element category has been introduced in the G/L master record. The default account assignment is maintained using Transaction OKB9, not in the traditional cost element master data.

5 Preparation and Migration for Controlling

Customizing settings that require cost elements such as costing sheets or settlement profiles and the business transactions in which cost elements are used will continue to be defined by the cost element category settings from the G/L master records.

Cost element groups continue to be available in SAP S/4HANA Finance for grouping the accounts and for reporting purposes.

Allocations

With the introduction of the new Universal Journal in SAP S/4HANA Finance, all CO postings are posted directly as Universal Journal entries, as shown in Figure 5.8. Secondary cost elements are now part of G/L accounts in FI and don't require separate assignment in CO.

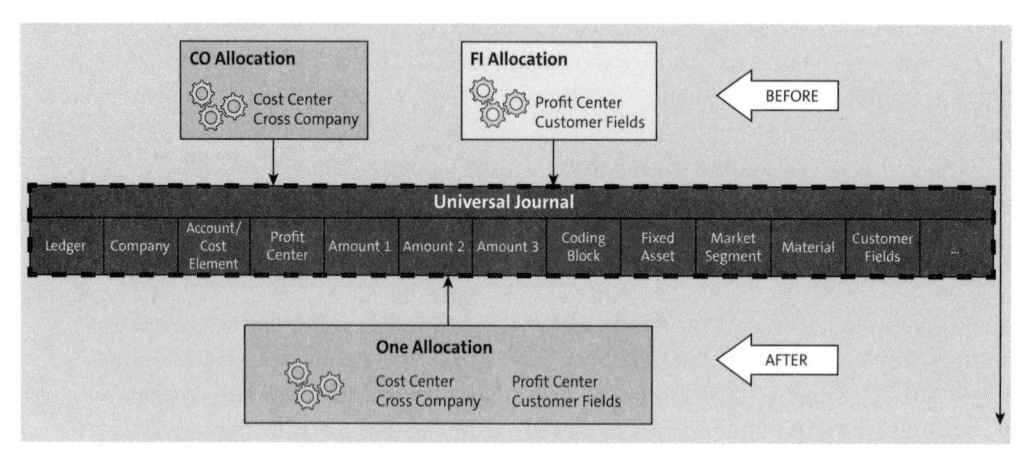

Figure 5.8 New Allocation in SAP S/4HANA Finance

Currencies

The old settings for currency in FI and CO and the new currency settings for SAP S/4HANA Finance are shown in Table 5.1 and Table 5.2.

Currency Types in FI	
First local/legal currency	10
Second local currency	30/40/50/60
Third local currency	30/40/50/60

Table 5.1 Currency Settings in SAP ERP FI and CO

Currency Types in FI	
Currency Types in CO	
Controlling area currency	20
Company code currency	10

Table 5.1 Currency Settings in SAP ERP FI and CO (Cont.)

Currency Types in the Universal Journal			
Local/legal currency	10	First additional currency	30/40/50/60
Global CO/FI currency	20	Second additional currency	N/A

Table 5.2 Currency Settings in SAP S/4HANA Finance

The following are some important details regarding the new features introduced to CO with SAP S/4HANA Finance:

- Currency settings for Universal Journal entries need to be compatible with both CO and FI currency settings.
- FI supports a maximum of three currencies.
- CO supports a maximum of two currencies.
- Currency settings for the leading ledger define the settings for nonleading ledgers.
  Exception: In the new G/L, the leading ledger currency that is supported for migrating the new G/L configurations can be deselected.
- Currency fields are created in table ACDOCA to map different currencies.
- The following amount fields are used in database table ACDOCA:
  - WSL: original transaction currency (document currency)
  - TSL: line item currency
  - HSL: local currency
  - KSL: global currency for FI and CO (currency in CO)
  - OSL: first additional currency
  - VSL: second additional currency in FI
  - CO_OSL: object currency of CO

5   Preparation and Migration for Controlling

Integration of SAP ERP Financials and Controlling

G/L account mapping of CO real-time integration with the new G/L is now obsolete. Secondary cost elements are now created as G/L accounts and are part of the chart of accounts.

On the configuration side, document types that you want to use for posting in CO need to be defined and require the **G/L** indicator to be set. These document types need to be linked to the CO business transaction via a variant.

The fiscal year variants of all controlling areas used by an organization and their assigned company codes must be the same.

Document Numbers in Controlling

Transactions posted in CO are assigned a CO document number in the following situations:

- Reposting is performed (Transactions KB11 and KB41).
- The original document (prima nota) is posted to the Universal Journal.
- The existing customization for the CO document number is still valid.
- Journal entries triggered from other applications (FI, Logistics, etc.) generate a cryptic document number into the CO_BELNR field, in which the CO documents are posted in the Universal Journal entry. This document number is needed for CO compatibility views.

The Universal Journal entries from CO can be grouped by the CO document number that is generated (e.g., cross-company postings). Regarding migrated CO documents, the migration tool writes the CO document number in the CO_BELNR field for journal entries that are migrated, as shown in Figure 5.9.

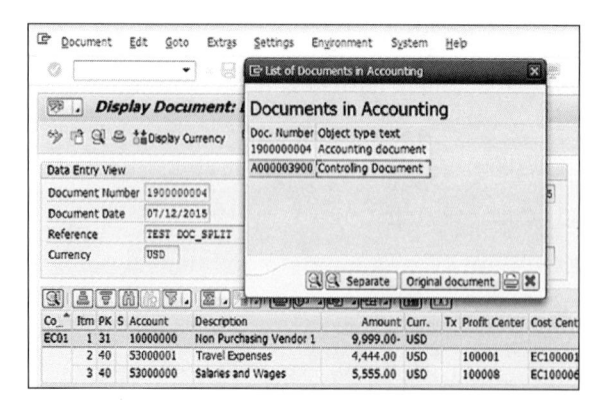

Figure 5.9 CO Document Postings

5.7 Key Changes to Controlling

Material Ledger

The following changes have been made to the ML in SAP S/4HANA Finance:

- ML data migrates to the new Universal Journal entry table ACDOCA (line item).
- ML data is updated to table ACDOCA automatically when executing and carrying out the **Migrate Balance Activity** in Customizing.
- Only period total records are migrated. The migration of ML documents, index table CKMI1, and summarization records doesn't take place.
- The contents of the following ML tables are now stored in table ACDOCA: MLHD, MLIT, MLCD, BSIM, MLPP, MLPPF, MLCR, MLCRF, and MLPRF.
- Prima nota information remains in tables MLHD, MLIT, MLPP, and MLCR for any manual price change or material debit/credit.
- Contents of all the ML tables, as listed in Figure 5.10, are stored in table ACDOCA, and data contents of table MLHD are stored in table BKPF.

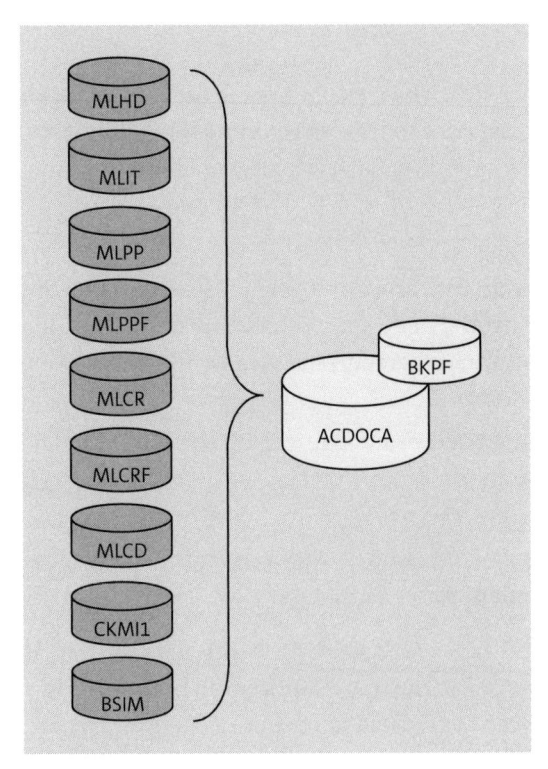

Figure 5.10 Material Ledger Table Structure

- The `V_<TABLENAME>` compatible views are available for all the ML tables listed in Figure 5.10.
- The `V_<Table name>_ORI` extension is used to access old tables.
- Prices and values in the material master are taken directly from the Universal Journal for multiple valuations (price determination 2).
- There has been no change for multilevel actual costing (price determination 3) because the costing run is still needed to update inventory values at period-end close.
- Separate currency Customizing of the ML is obsolete as of SAP S/4HANA Finance 1511. The ML now acts on the currencies defined for the leading ledger in FI.

Migrating General Ledger Accounting to SAP S/4HANA Finance requires changes to the current application configuration and migration of master data and transaction data. This is required because ML and CO are combined in a common data structure.

Transfer Pricing

As of on-premise SAP S/4HANA Finance 1605, the transfer pricing functionality can be used for valuating the transfer of goods or services based on legal requirements, groups, or profit centers. Transfer prices provide parallel valuation methods for three types of valuation:

1. **Legal valuation**
   Provides the business transactions from the company's point of view, in which the pricing is driven from legal requirements and tax-optimization strategies. This valuation emphasizes intercompany pricing agreements.
2. **Group valuation**
   Considers the group as a whole: the processes are valuated by eliminating intercompany and inter-profit-center profits/markups.
3. **Profit center**
   Considers the profit centers as independent entities within the group. This valuation emphasizes agreed-on management prices.

A new approach for parallel valuations has been implemented with the merge of FI and CO into the Universal Journal table ACDOCA. The transfer prices can be updated in a ledger with all valuation views, or they can be updated in separate ledgers for an individual valuation view. In the multiple valuation, no specific valuation view is assigned to the ledger, while the currency type of all valuations is assigned to this ledger. In the single valuation ledger, a separate ledger is assigned for each specific valuation view, and each ledger bears the currency of the valuation view.

To perform this customization, go to the **Preparations and Migration of Customizing for General Ledger** area and set the **Transfer Prices** option as **Active**.

General Cost Objects and Cost Object Hierarchies

General cost objects were removed from SAP S/4HANA Finance in SAP S/4HANA 1511 FPS 02. The associated functions were previously found in the **Controlling • Product Cost Controlling • Cost Object Controlling • Intangible Goods and Services** menu path. You may want to consider using internal orders instead.

Cost object hierarchies are also no longer available within SAP S/4HANA Finance. The associated functions were previously found in the **Controlling • Product Cost Controlling • Cost Object Controlling • Product Cost by Period** menu path. You may consider using summarization hierarchies for aggregation of costs on manufacturing orders instead.

Changes in Transaction Codes

The following transactions are no longer available in SAP S/4HANA, beginning with version 1610:

- KA01, KA02, KA03: Create/Change/Display Primary Cost Elements
- KA06: Create Secondary Cost Elements
- KKC1, KKC2, KKC3: Create/Change/Display General Cost Object
- KKPH: General Cost Objects, Collective Entry
- KKH1, KKH2, KKH3: Create/Change/Display Cost Object Groups
- KK16, KK17: Cost Object Planning by Cost Element/Activity
- KK46, KK47: Cost Object Planning by Statistical Key Figure
- KKC4, KKC5, KKC6: Create/Change/Display Cumulative Cost Object Planning
- KKBC_KTR: Analyze Cost Object
- KKC5: Display Cost Object Line Items
- CPTG, CPTH: Template Allocation for Cost Objects
- KKN1, KKN2: Revaluation of Actual Prices for Cost Objects
- KKPZ, KKPJ: Overhead Allocation for Cost Objects
- KK88, KK89: Settlement of Cost Objects
- KKPHIE: Cost Object Hierarchy

5 Preparation and Migration for Controlling

> **Expert Insight**
>
> For Transaction KKPHIE, consider using an order hierarchy KKBC_HOE_H instead and building the hierarchy nodes using Transaction KKR0.

- KKP2: Change Hierarchy Master Record
- KKP4: Display Cost Object Hierarchy
- KKP6: Cost Object Analysis
- KKPX, KKPY: Actual Cost Distribution: Cost Objects
- KKAO, KKAV: WIP Calculation for Cost Object Hierarchies
- KKP5, KKPT: Variance calculation for Cost Object Hierarchies
- OMX2: Assign Currency Types to Material Ledger Type
- OMX3: Assign Material Ledger Types to Valuation Area

5.7.2 Configuration Impact

In addition to the changes to functionality, SAP S/4HANA Finance has also introduced several changes to the configuration of the CO component. In the following sections, we'll briefly discuss some of the most relevant differences.

Integration of Controlling with SAP ERP Financials

With the implementation of SAP S/4HANA Finance and its new architecture, separate reconciliation of FI and CO is no longer required. Real-time integration of CO with the new G/L also is no longer required, as shown in Figure 5.11.

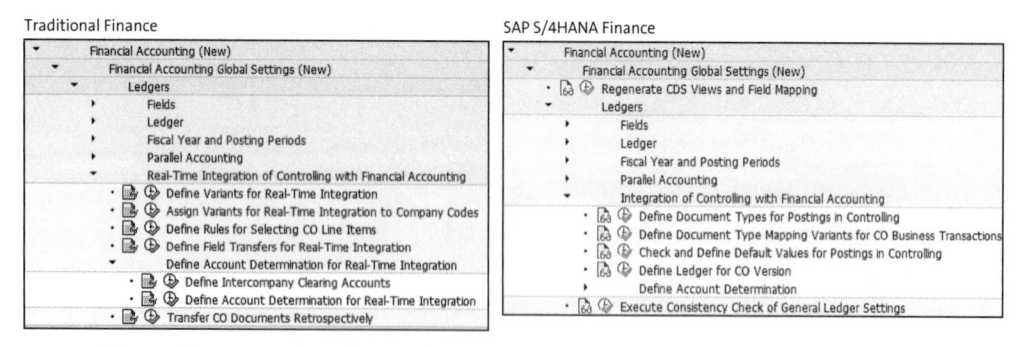

Figure 5.11 Integration of CO with FI

5.7 Key Changes to Controlling

Cost Element as a General Ledger Account

In the creation of a G/L account using Transaction FS00, a new **Account Type** field has been added that allows primary and secondary cost elements to be created on the same screen (see Figure 5.12).

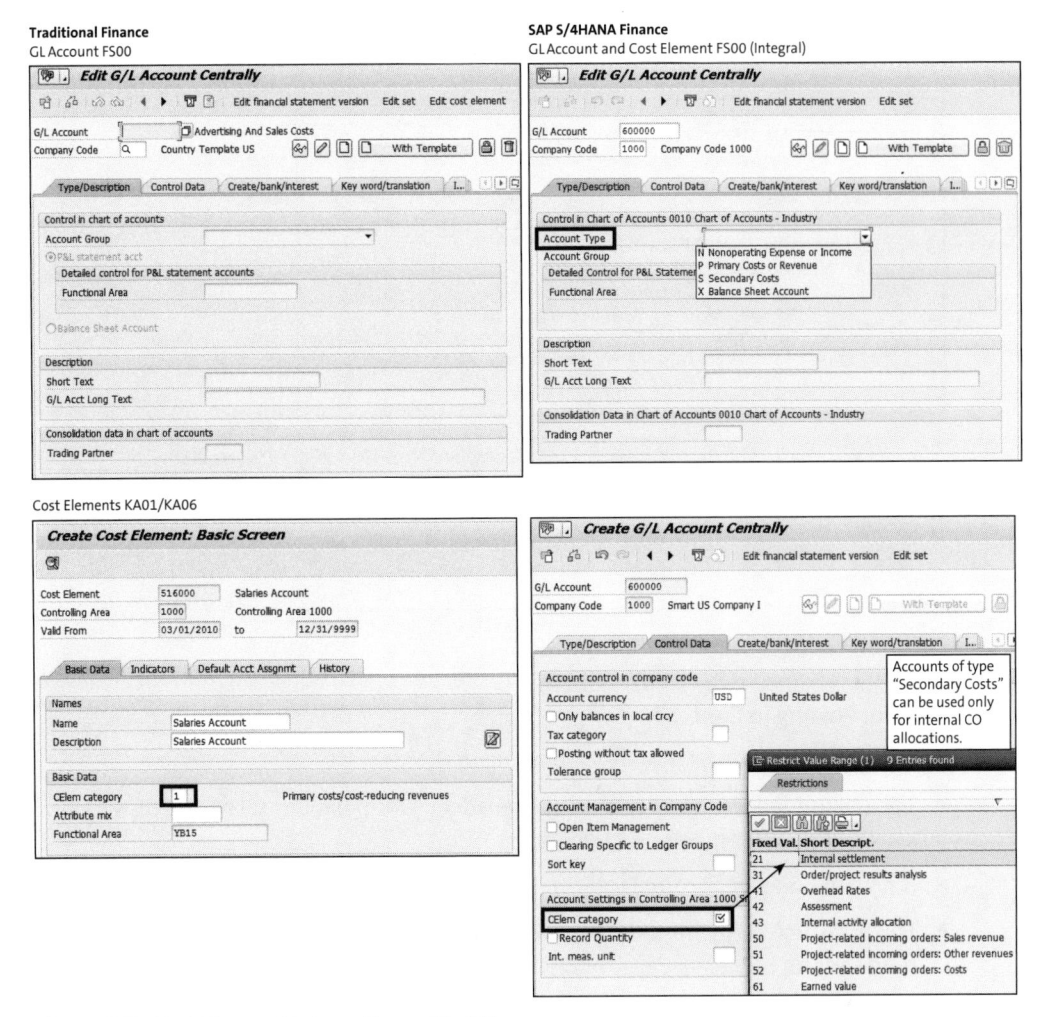

Figure 5.12 Cost Element Integration with G/L

Transaction KA01 (Create Cost Element) and Transaction KA06 (Create Secondary Cost Element) are no longer in use in SAP S/4HANA Finance.

221

Ledger for Controlling

In SAP S/4HANA Finance, you need to define a ledger that represents CO by assigning **Version** 0 to a ledger. This is done at the company code level, but it needs to be the same for all company codes. In SAP S/4HANA Finance, the leading ledger is assigned version 0 for all company codes, which are assigned to a controlling area, as shown in Figure 5.13.

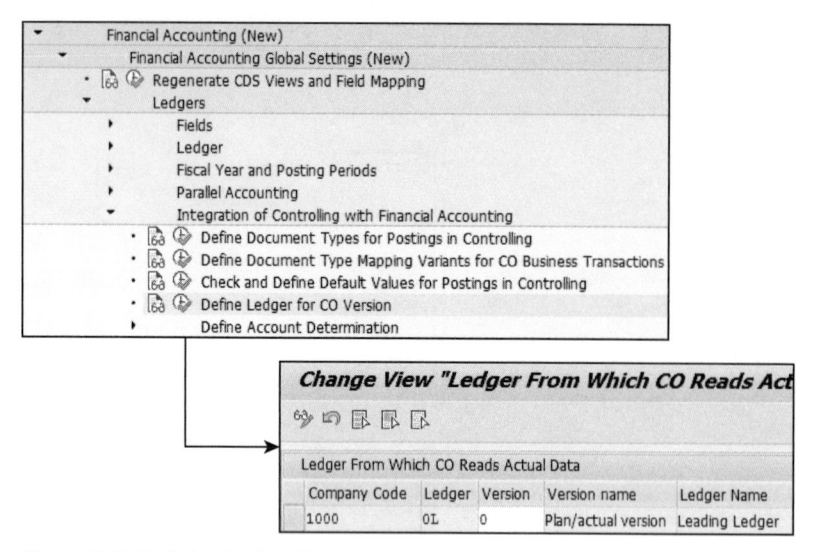

Figure 5.13 Defining Ledger for CO Version

Rule for Posting in Controlling

The following are the new rules for posting in CO:

- The default ledger group is used if the ledger group isn't entered in Transactions KB11 and KB41, as shown in Figure 5.14.
- If no default ledger group is configured, then all ledgers are updated.
- The document type for CO transactions is derived from the document type mapping variant.

5.7 Key Changes to Controlling

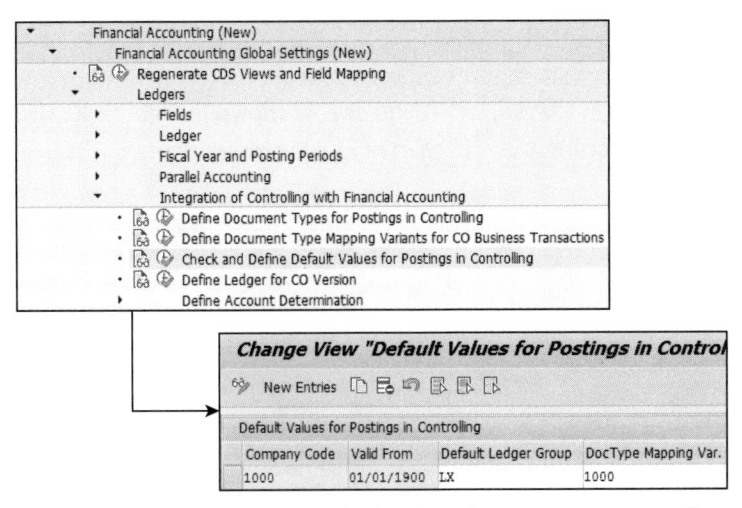

Figure 5.14 Check and Define Default Values for Postings in Controlling

Ledger View in Customizing

Many components and customization settings from the **Ledger** tab of the **SAP Customizing Implementation Guide** menu are no longer available in SAP S/4HANA Finance because they are no longer required (see Figure 5.15).

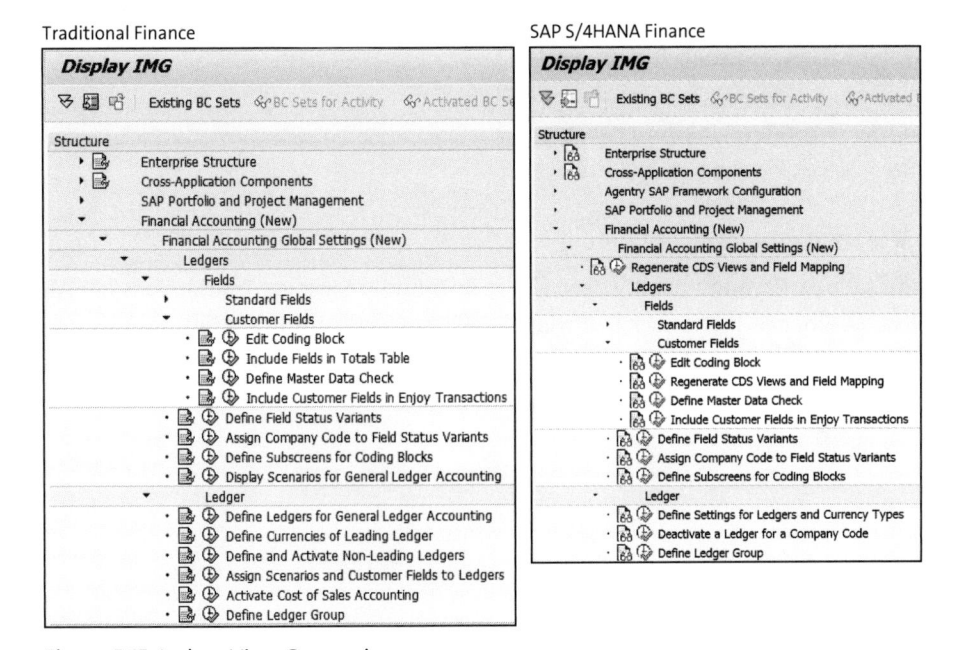

Figure 5.15 Ledger View Comparison

223

5   Preparation and Migration for Controlling

General Ledger Accounting Planning

The **Planning** tab in General Ledger Accounting has been removed due to the new settings and sequencing of tabs in SAP S/4HANA Finance. As shown in Figure 5.16, G/L planning and cost element planning are now part of SAP Business Client.

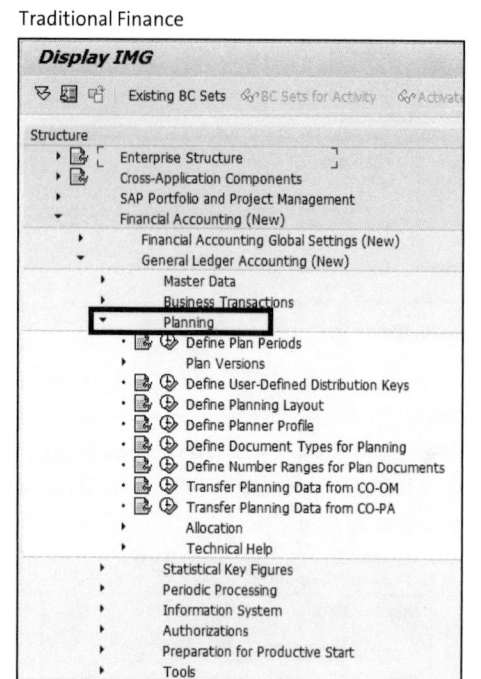

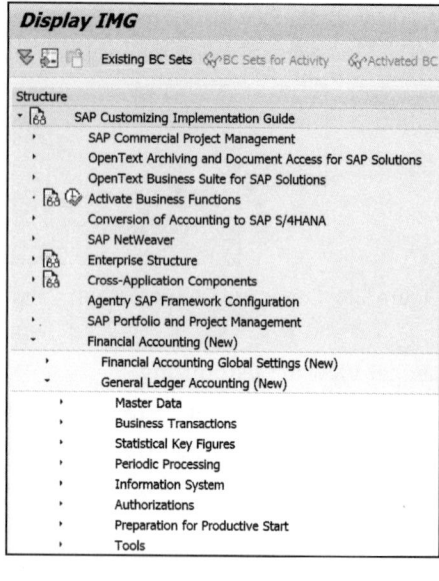

Figure 5.16 G/L Planning

Cash Journal View

There's a new **Cash Journal** link (see Figure 5.17) under **Business Transactions** in SAP S/4HANA Finance. If you click it, it will take you to the Customizing settings for **Cash Journal** under **Bank Accounting**, as shown in Figure 5.18. The Cash Journal is used to manage and display cash transactions and balances.

5.7 Key Changes to Controlling

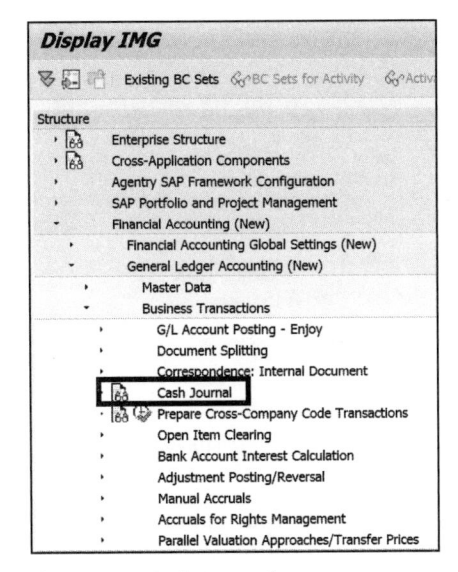

Figure 5.17 Cash Journal

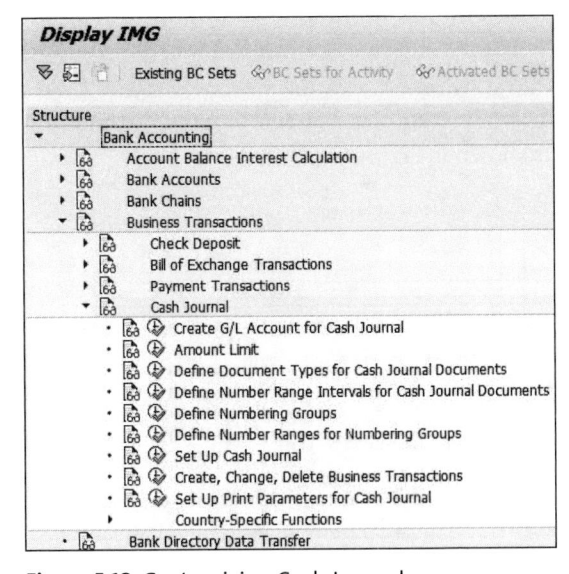

Figure 5.18 Customizing Cash Journal

Report Hierarchies Added

A new section that includes **Set Report Relevancy for Hierarchies** and **Replicate Runtime Hierarchies** has been introduced in SAP S/4HANA Finance, as shown in Figure 5.19.

5   Preparation and Migration for Controlling

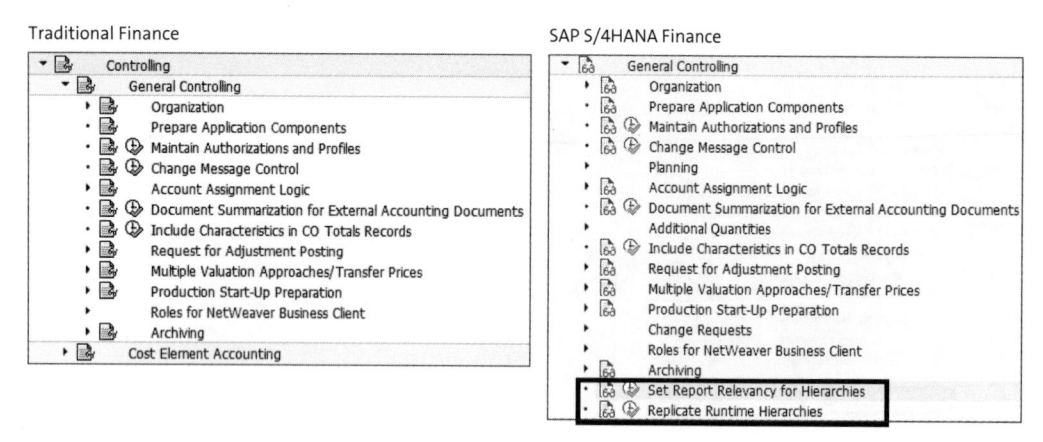

Traditional Finance
- Controlling
  - General Controlling
    - Organization
    - Prepare Application Components
    - Maintain Authorizations and Profiles
    - Change Message Control
    - Account Assignment Logic
    - Document Summarization for External Accounting Documents
    - Include Characteristics in CO Totals Records
    - Request for Adjustment Posting
    - Multiple Valuation Approaches/Transfer Prices
    - Production Start-Up Preparation
    - Roles for NetWeaver Business Client
    - Archiving
  - Cost Element Accounting

SAP S/4HANA Finance
- General Controlling
  - Organization
  - Prepare Application Components
  - Maintain Authorizations and Profiles
  - Change Message Control
  - Planning
  - Account Assignment Logic
  - Document Summarization for External Accounting Documents
  - Additional Quantities
  - Include Characteristics in CO Totals Records
  - Request for Adjustment Posting
  - Multiple Valuation Approaches/Transfer Prices
  - Production Start-Up Preparation
  - Change Requests
  - Roles for NetWeaver Business Client
  - Archiving
  - **Set Report Relevancy for Hierarchies**
  - **Replicate Runtime Hierarchies**

Figure 5.19 Set Report Relevancy for Hierarchies and Replicate Runtime Hierarchies

In the **Replicate Runtime Hierarchies** Customizing activity, you replicate set-based hierarchies and financial statement hierarchies manually to backend database tables `HRRP_NODE` and `HRRP_DIRECTORY`. Replicating the hierarchies helps you perform analytics and improves the system runtime.

Reference and Simulation Costing View

In the **Product Cost Planning** section, the **Reference and Simulation Costing** tab isn't available in SAP S/4HANA Finance, as shown in Figure 5.20.

Traditional Finance
- Controlling
  - General Controlling
  - Cost Element Accounting
  - Cost Center Accounting
  - Internal Orders
  - Activity-Based Costing
  - Product Cost Controlling
    - Product Cost Planning
      - Basic Settings for Material Costing
      - Material Cost Estimate with Quantity Structure
      - Material Cost Estimate Without Quantity Structure
      - Price Update
      - Selected Functions in Material Costing
      - **Reference and Simulation Costing**
      - Ad Hoc Cost Estimate
    - Cost Object Controlling
    - Actual Costing/Material Ledger
    - Information System

SAP S/4HANA Finance
- Controlling
  - General Controlling
  - Cost Element Accounting
  - Cost Center Accounting
  - Internal Orders
  - Activity-Based Costing
  - Product Cost Controlling
    - Product Cost Planning
      - Basic Settings for Material Costing
      - Material Cost Estimate with Quantity Structure
      - Material Cost Estimate Without Quantity Structure
      - Price Update
      - Selected Functions in Material Costing
      - Ad Hoc Cost Estimate

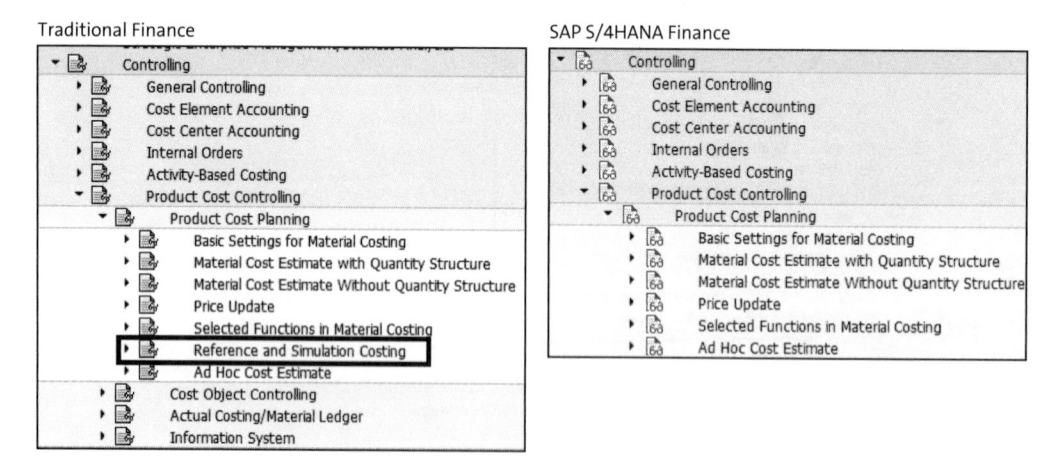

Figure 5.20 Reference and Simulation Costing

SAP S/4HANA no longer supports the creation of cost estimates with reference to the base planning objects. You should use Transaction CKECP to prepare ad-hoc cost estimates and Transaction CKUC to prepare multilevel material cost estimates when BOMs and routings are not available for the relevant material. You may also refer to SAP Note 2349294 for further details.

Assign Currencies to Material Ledger

In the **Actual Costing/Material Ledger** section, the **Assign Currency Types to Material Ledger Type** tab isn't available in SAP S/4HANA Finance, as shown in Figure 5.21.

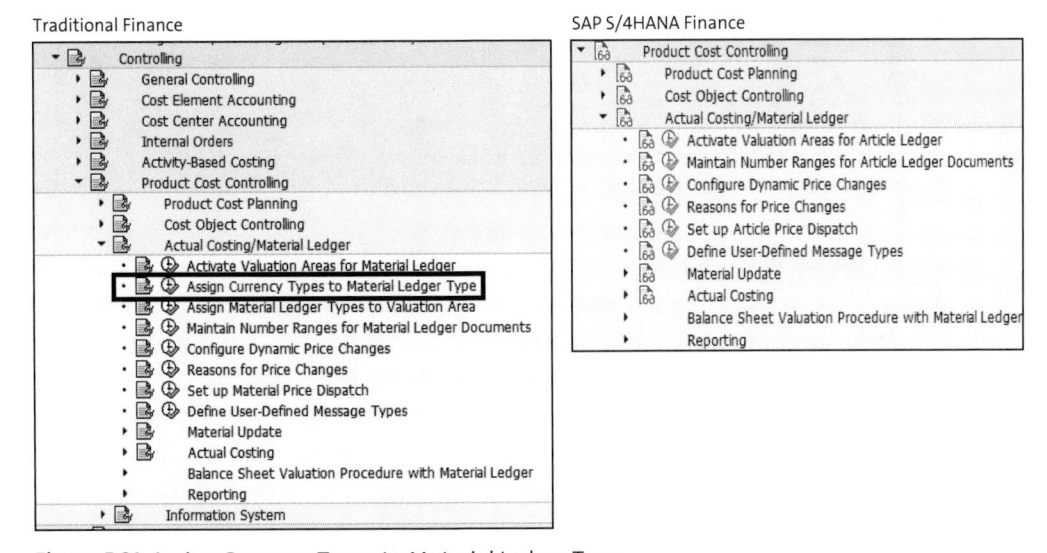

Figure 5.21 Assign Currency Types to Material Ledger Type

Assign Material Ledger Type to Valuation Area

In the **Actual Costing/Material Ledger** section, the **Assign Material Ledger Types to Valuation Area** tab isn't available in SAP S/4HANA Finance, as shown in Figure 5.22.

With SAP S/4HANA, you can no longer use a material ledger type that references currency settings defined in FI or CO. Now, you must explicitly define the currency and valuation types that are relevant for Material Ledger.

5 Preparation and Migration for Controlling

Traditional Finance

- Controlling
  - General Controlling
  - Cost Element Accounting
  - Cost Center Accounting
  - Internal Orders
  - Activity-Based Costing
  - Product Cost Controlling
    - Product Cost Planning
    - Cost Object Controlling
    - Actual Costing/Material Ledger
      - Activate Valuation Areas for Material Ledger
      - Assign Currency Types to Material Ledger Type
      - **Assign Material Ledger Types to Valuation Area**
      - Maintain Number Ranges for Material Ledger Documents
      - Configure Dynamic Price Changes
      - Reasons for Price Changes
      - Set up Material Price Dispatch
      - Define User-Defined Message Types
    - Material Update
    - Actual Costing
    - Balance Sheet Valuation Procedure with Material Ledger
    - Reporting
  - Information System

SAP S/4HANA Finance

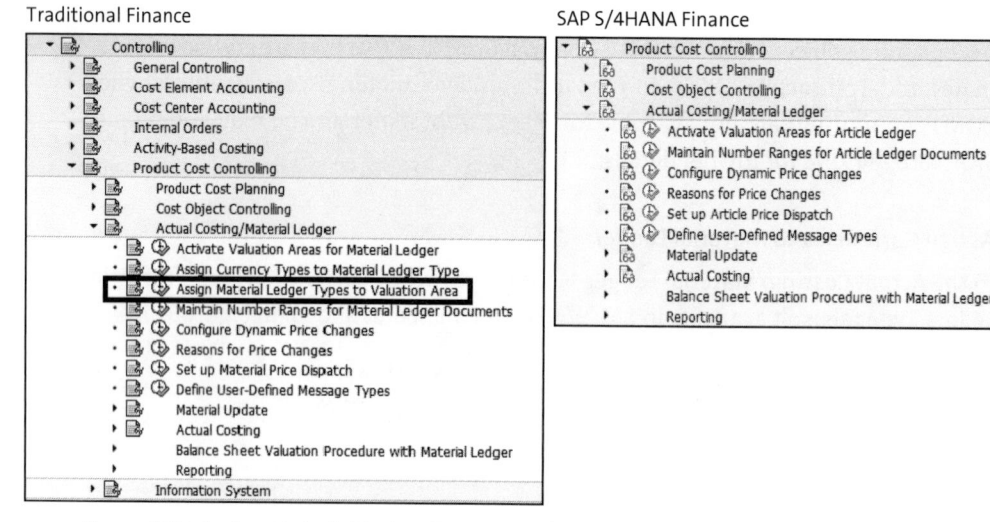

- Product Cost Controlling
  - Product Cost Planning
  - Cost Object Controlling
  - Actual Costing/Material Ledger
    - Activate Valuation Areas for Article Ledger
    - Maintain Number Ranges for Article Ledger Documents
    - Configure Dynamic Price Changes
    - Reasons for Price Changes
    - Set up Article Price Dispatch
    - Define User-Defined Message Types
  - Material Update
  - Actual Costing
  - Balance Sheet Valuation Procedure with Material Ledger
  - Reporting

Figure 5.22 Assign Material Ledger Types to Valuation Area

Cost of Goods Sold Posting

An optional Customizing activity is also provided to refine the COGS posting in the G/L and account-based CO-PA. The COGS amount is refined according to the cost component split. The fixed value of the COGS amount is stored in the corresponding value field in the CO line item table. This assignment of the Customizing activity is time-dependent.

With SAP S/4HANA Finance, both G/L accounts in FI and cost elements in CO are created and processed together in one chart of accounts. The CO component is now fully integrated with FI and is executed based on accounts. There is only one master data maintenance for G/L accounts and cost elements.

The transaction for posting CO documents to FI is no longer available in SAP S/4HANA Finance. Due to the real-time integration of FI and CO, the data gets populated to CO at the same time that it's posted to FI. Unlike earlier versions of SAP, a reconciliation program between FI and CO is no longer required, which significantly reduces the probability of entries not getting posted.

5.8 Key Changes to Profitability Analysis

Recall that in SAP S/4HANA Finance, all Profitability Analysis characteristics are part of the Universal Journal table ACDOCA line item fields. This section describes the architecture, configuration, and functionality impact that SAP S/4HANA Finance has on Profitability Analysis (commonly shortened to CO-PA).

CO-PA allows you to assess your organization's profitability, contribution margin, and cost variances. You can evaluate this information by market segments or business units (e.g., sales organization, business area, or profit center) and use it to support corporate planning and decision-making. The market segments can be classified into various categories based on your organization's requirements such as products, customers, orders, and so on. Two forms of CO-PA are available:

1. **Account-based CO-PA**
   The costs and revenues in account-based CO-PA are stored in accounts and use cost and revenue elements. Account-based CO-PA provides a profitability report that is permanently reconciled with FI.

2. **Costing-based CO-PA**
   The costs and revenues in costing-based CO-PA are grouped by value fields and costing-based valuation approaches. Costing-based CO-PA provides access to a complete, short-term profitability report.

You can use both forms of CO-PA in parallel, as stated earlier. However, account-based CO-PA is the recommended solution to use with SAP S/4HANA Finance. With account-based CO-PA, any revenue posting or COGS posting is updated to the appropriate accounts and assigned to the correct market segment characteristics.

Now, let's analyze the impact of SAP S/4HANA Finance on the architecture design, the business process transactions, and the configuration of CO-PA.

5.8.1 Architectural Impact

As stated, SAP recommends using account-based CO-PA in SAP S/4HANA Finance. Several enhancements have been made to make account-based CO-PA more powerful, enabling you to do the following:

- Split the COGS posting among multiple accounts.
- Split the production variance posting among multiple accounts.
- Define up to three additional quantity fields for the controlling area along with their dimensions and units of measure.

Profitability characteristics are also immediately derived at the point in time of each primary document, so settlement runs are no longer required.

The following architectural changes in CO and G/L will impact account-based CO-PA as well:

- In SAP S/4HANA Finance, you can have the same characteristics in account-based CO-PA and costing-based CO-PA.
- There's no need for the operating concern setting, so settings for the controlling area will apply.
- Characteristics are defined in the operating concern, and there are no value fields. Instead, the secondary cost elements used in the assessment cycles, indirect allocation cycles, settlement rules, and so on determine the level of detail that will be visible in account-based CO-PA.
- All the fields that used to be stored in table CE4* become part of the Universal Journal entry.
- Derivation rules determine market segments from cost objects on a real-time basis during posting.
- Profitability characteristics are derived immediately when the primary document is posted.
- The Universal Journal stores all real and statistical account assignments; subsequent processing only can be performed on real account assignments.
- A new posting mechanism separates the price difference posting into accounts, thus providing more details in the income statement (FI) and in account-based CO-PA.
- A new posting mechanism enables the standard cost component to be split on the G/L account and to distinguish fixed and variable values.
- Custom-specific CO-PA fields are updated in the Universal Journal and leveraged by derivation rules. You may also modify the coding block.

5.8.2 Functionality Impact

Table 5.3 lists the transactions that have been replaced or have become obsolete in CO-PA with the introduction of SAP S/4HANA Finance.

Old Transaction	New Transaction
KEQ4	Not applicable
KE21	KE21N

Table 5.3 Changes in Transaction Codes Related to CO-PA

Old Transaction	New Transaction
KE23	KE24
K088	KO88J

Table 5.3 Changes in Transaction Codes Related to CO-PA (Cont.)

The following new tables were introduced with SAP S/4HANA Finance:

- ACDOCA
- CE4SFIN

In addition, for account-based CO-PA, actual data is stored in table ACDOCA. Table COEP is no longer used for this purpose.

> **References**
> For more information on transactions and programs that have been removed or partially replaced in SAP S/4HANA Finance, check SAP Note 1946054: Transaction Codes and Programs—Comparison.

Account-based CO-PA is activated using program FCO_ADD_COPA_FIELD_TO_ACDOCA in Transaction SA38. Account-based CO-PA is permanently reconciled with FI because the data is posted in the same Universal Journal table ACDOCA structure.

If you used costing-based CO-PA before the implementation of SAP S/4HANA Finance, and account-based CO-PA is activated during the migration, both approaches will exist simultaneously and work correctly in the baseline landscape. However, this isn't recommended.

The following additional functionalities are new:

- Each of the three possible additional quantity fields are associated with a base dimension and can have a standard unit of measure specified so that the total quantity can be computed and can be used as a driver for allocation to CO-PA.
- The line item postings are updated with the quantity and unit of measure as specified in Customizing.
- The additional quantity fields can be used for top-down distribution in account-based CO-PA.

- The additional quantity fields can be used in assessment cycles for allocating overhead costs to account-based CO-PA.
- Business Add-In (BAdI) `FCO_COEP_QUANTITY` is implemented using Transaction SE18 to add the logic for additional quantity fields for a controlling area.

5.8.3 Configuration Impact

The implementation of SAP S/4HANA Finance has changed how we define profitability segment characteristics, eliminated the need to integrate with SAP HANA as a separate activity, and removed the ability to define segment-level characteristics for distributed Profitability Analysis. Let's look closer.

Define Profitability Segment Characteristics

In the **Profitability Analysis • Structures** section, the **Define Profitability Segment Characteristics** option is no longer a separate task in SAP S/4HANA Finance (as it was in SAP ERP), as shown in Figure 5.23.

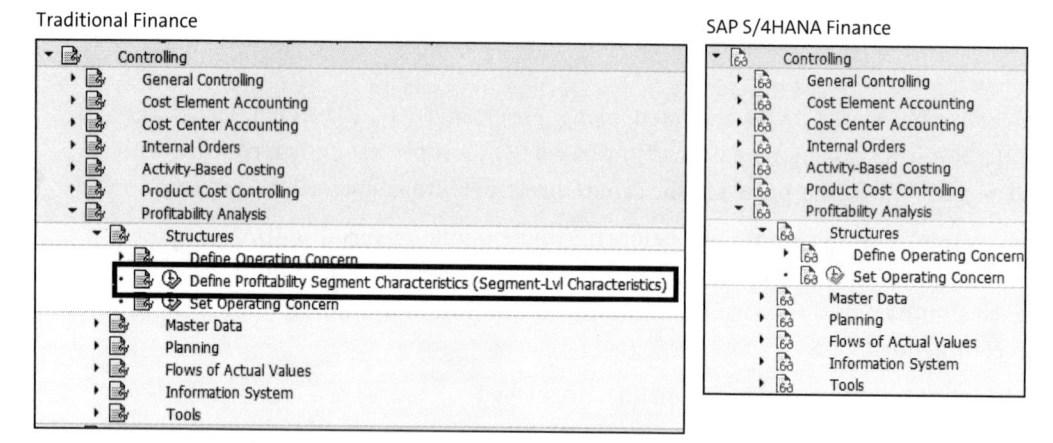

Figure 5.23 Define Profitability Segment Characteristics

SAP HANA Integration

In the **Profitability Analysis • Tools** section, the **SAP HANA Integration** option is no longer available in SAP S/4HANA Finance, as shown in Figure 5.24.

With SAP S/4HANA Finance, CO-PA data is integrated with SAP HANA in real time, so a separate task to integrate with SAP HANA is no longer required.

5.8 Key Changes to Profitability Analysis

Traditional Finance
- Controlling
  - General Controlling
  - Cost Element Accounting
  - Cost Center Accounting
  - Internal Orders
  - Activity-Based Costing
  - Product Cost Controlling
  - Profitability Analysis
    - Structures
    - Master Data
    - Planning
    - Flows of Actual Values
    - Information System
    - Tools
      - Summarization Levels
      - **SAP HANA Integration**
      - Analysis
      - Production Startup
      - Data Transfers Between CO-PA and Other Systems
      - Authorization Management
      - Utilities
      - SAP Enhancements

SAP S/4HANA Finance
- Profitability Analysis
  - Structures
  - Master Data
  - Planning
  - Flows of Actual Values
  - Information System
  - Tools
    - Summarization Levels
    - Analysis
    - Production Startup
    - Data Transfers Between CO-PA
    - Authorization Management
    - Utilities
    - SAP Enhancements

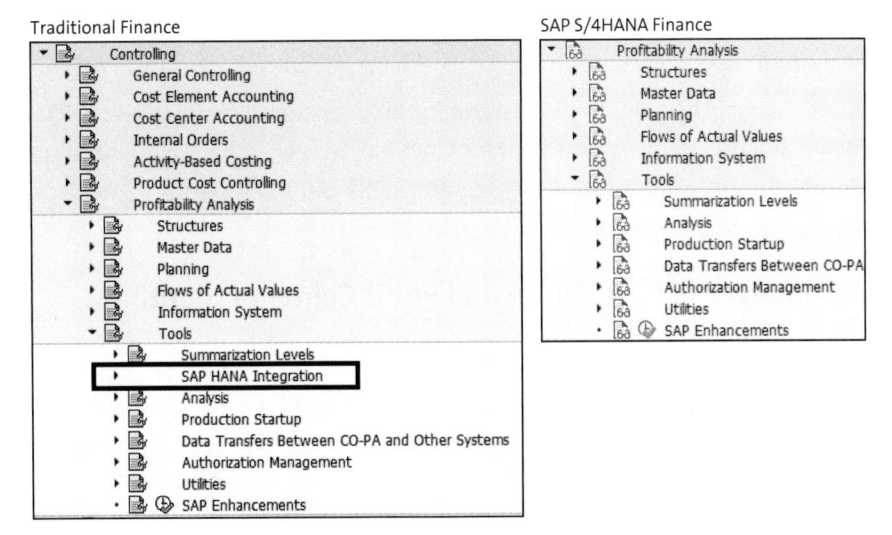

Figure 5.24 SAP HANA Integration

Segment-Level Characteristics for Distributed Profitability Analysis

In the **Profitability Analysis • Tools • Data Transfers Between CO-PA and Other Systems • Distributed Profitability Analysis** section, the **Define Segment Level Characteristics for Distributed CO-PA** option is no longer available in SAP S/4HANA Finance, as shown in Figure 5.25.

Traditional Finance
- Profitability Analysis
  - Structures
  - Master Data
  - Planning
  - Flows of Actual Values
  - Information System
  - Tools
    - Summarization Levels
    - SAP HANA Integration
    - Analysis
    - Production Startup
    - Data Transfers Between CO-PA and Other Systems
      - Initial Steps
      - CO-PA External Data Transfer
      - Data Transfer from SAP BW
      - Data Transfer via FI/CO Document
      - Distributed Profitability Analysis
        - Generate/Update Message Type
        - Activate Distributed Profitability Analysis
        - **Define Segment-Level Characteristics for Distributed CO-PA**
        - Run Initial Supply for Distributed Profitability Analysis
        - Subsequent Posting of CRM Billing Documents
        - Data Transfer to SAP Business Information Warehouse
    - Authorization Management
    - Utilities
    - SAP Enhancements

SAP S/4HANA Finance
- Data Transfers Between CO-PA and Other Systems
  - Initial Steps
  - CO-PA External Data Transfer
  - Data Transfer from SAP BW
  - Data Transfer via FI/CO Document
  - Distributed Profitability Analysis
    - Generate/Update Message Type
    - Activate Distributed Profitability Analysis
    - Run Initial Supply for Distributed Profitability Analysis
    - Subsequent Posting of CRM Billing Documents
    - Data Transfer to SAP Business Information Warehouse
  - Authorization Management
  - Utilities
  - SAP Enhancements

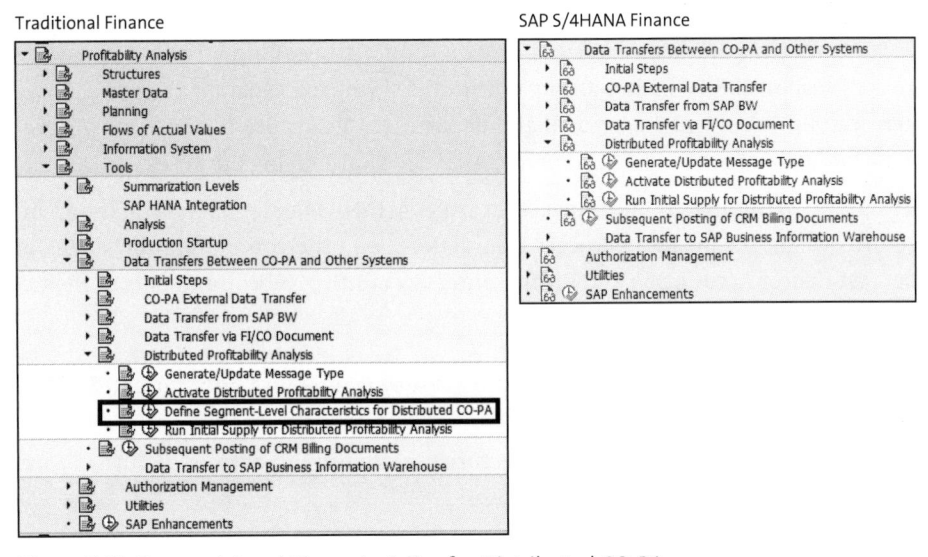

Figure 5.25 Segment-Level Characteristics for Distributed CO-PA

You should now understand the essential changes SAP S/4HANA introduces to CO-PA, with the intent of supporting account-based CO-PA in the future.

Three additional quantity fields for the controlling area can now be defined along with its dimension and unit of measure, which provides business benefits in the allocation and distribution of costs to account-based CO-PA using the quantity as the driver.

5.9 Key Changes to Cost Center and Profit Center Accounting

Let's look specifically at cost center and profit center accounting.

In SAP S/4HANA Finance, separate steps to reconcile SAP ERP Financials and Controlling are no longer required. This section describes the architecture, configuration, and functionality impact that SAP S/4HANA Finance has on cost center accounting and profit center accounting.

Cost center accounting is used for controlling purposes to analyze costs for management decisions within your organization. The costs incurred by the organization are captured using cost centers as cost objects. In an ideal scenario, all costs should be allocated to the source from which it was incurred, but the challenge lies in allocating overhead-related costs. Cost center accounting helps analyze the overhead costs based on where they were incurred within the organization.

Profit center accounting, on the other hand, is used to determine profit and loss for specific profit centers using either period accounting or the cost-of-sales approach. *Profit centers* are the organizational units within a controlling area that represent areas of responsibility within an organization for which a separate operating statement can be calculated. Functional and department heads use this operating statement for internal controlling and managerial decision-making purposes.

In this section, we analyze the impact that SAP S/4HANA Finance has had on the architecture design, the business process transactions, and the configuration changes of the Cost Center Accounting and Profit Center Accounting subcomponents of the CO module.

5.9.1 Architectural Impact

A change has been made to the architecture and underlying table structure in Cost Center Accounting, as shown in Figure 5.26.

5.9 Key Changes to Cost Center and Profit Center Accounting

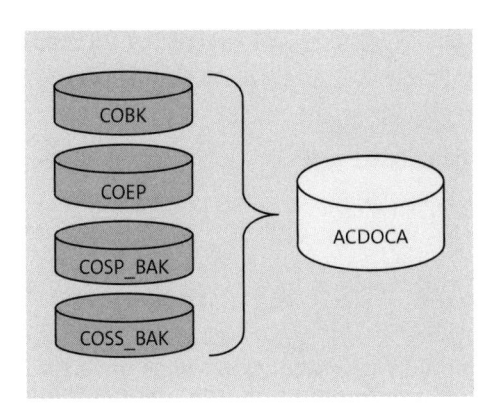

Figure 5.26 Cost Center Accounting Architecture

Architecture changes in SAP S/4HANA have impacted the Cost Center Accounting processes in the following ways:

- **Actual items**
  - Actual data of table COEP (WRTTP = 04 and 11) are now stored in table ACDOCA (04 = actual data, and 11 = statistical actual). All other values are still stored in table COEP.
  - Actual data for orders or projects continuing for long periods of time and stored in table COSP_BAK and COSS_BAK are now stored in table ACDOCA, as shown in Figure 5.26.
  - The V_<TABLENAME> compatibility views (e.g., V_COEP) are provided to reproduce the old structures. For example, ABAP programs that require access to table COEP are now redirected to the new Universal Journal table ACDOCA via the V_COEP compatibility view.
  - Access to old data in tables is still possible via the V_<TABLENAME>_ORI views (e.g., V_COEP_ORI).
  - Table COBK is used as before. The target is to replace the content from table COBK to table BKPF.
  - Table BSEG postings remain unchanged in SAP S/4HANA Finance.
  - Table COSP_BAK stores primary cost data.
  - Table COSS_BAK stores secondary cost data.

5   Preparation and Migration for Controlling

- Two new Core Data Services (CDS) views (COSP and COSS) are created for read-only access. The COSP view is a union of table COEP and table COSP_BAK; the COSS view is a union of table COEP and table COSS_BAK.
- All secondary cost elements need to be created as P&L accounts (type S). Secondary cost elements will appear in G/L reporting.

- **Nonactual items**
    - Value types other than 04 and 11 are still stored in tables COEP, COSP_BAK, and COSS_BAK.
    - Cost elements have been moved into the G/L account logic, which means no time dependency for cost elements and no default account assignments in the cost element master.
    - P&L accounts can be classified as cost elements, which means cost elements became G/L accounts with the G/L account type primary costs or revenue.
    - The use of the **Cost Element Type** field remains unchanged, so secondary cost elements can still be posted only from CO allocations.
    - Default account assignments maintained in the cost element master are migrated to Transaction OKB9.
    - Secondary cost elements appear in G/L reporting.
    - The CO document number still exists but is replaced by a technical document number. This is updated in table ACDOCA in the field CO_BELNR. This field is needed to support the compatibility views.

There are no specific changes to Profit Center Accounting in SAP S/4HANA Finance, though there has been a change in the G/L structure and cost element/cost center architecture.

5.9.2   Functionality Impact

SAP S/4HANA Finance has changed the table structure but hasn't greatly impacted the business process functionality as far as cost centers and profit centers are concerned. The biggest impact is that neither cost center planning nor profit center planning works in SAP S/4HANA Finance as a standalone function. SAP BPC for SAP S/4HANA Finance also needs to be activated for the planning functionality to work.

5.9 Key Changes to Cost Center and Profit Center Accounting

All allocation, reposting, and settlement functionality will continue to run as before. Activities such as price calculation, variance calculation, work in process (WIP) calculation, and results analysis will also continue similarly in SAP S/4HANA Finance.

Table 5.4 lists the changes to transaction codes for Cost Center Accounting and Profit Center Accounting. Note that the only Profit Center Accounting change is from Transaction FBL3 to Transaction FBL3H.

Old Transaction	New Transaction
Primary cost element transactions: KA01/KA02/KA03	FS00
Secondary cost element transactions: KA06	FS00
KB11	KB11N
KB21	KB21N
KB31	KB31N
KB33	KB33N
KB34	KB34N
KB51	KB51N
KB41	KB41N
KB15	KB15N
KSS1	KSS1H
KP06, KP07, KP65, KP66, KP67, KPF6, KPF7, KO14, KPG7	New Web Dynpro: FCOM_IP_CC_COSTELEM01
FBL3	FBL3H

Table 5.4 Changes in Transaction Codes Related to Cost Center Accounting and Profit Center Accounting

The process for cost center planning using Transaction KP06 is now replaced with the SAP Business Client view shown in Figure 5.27.

5   Preparation and Migration for Controlling

Traditional Finance

Change Cost Element/Activity Input Planning: Initial Screen

Layout	1-101	Cost Elements Acty-Indep./Acty-Dependent

Variables

Version	0	Plan/actual version
From period	4	April
To period	4	April
Fiscal year	2016	

Cost Center
  to
  or group

Activity Type
  to
  or group

Cost Element
  to
  or group

Entry
● Free   ○ Form-Based

SAP S/4HANA Finance—SAP Business Client

Cost Centers: Primary Cost Planning (Basic)

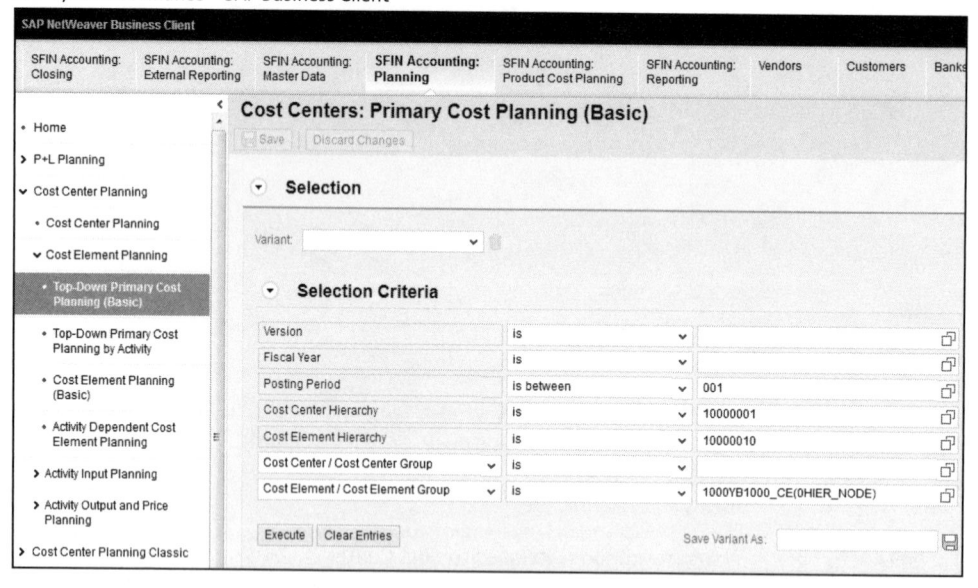

Selection

Variant:

Selection Criteria

Version	is		
Fiscal Year	is		
Posting Period	is between	001	
Cost Center Hierarchy	is	10000001	
Cost Element Hierarchy	is	10000010	
Cost Center / Cost Center Group	is		
Cost Element / Cost Element Group	is	1000YB1000_CE(0HIER_NODE)	

Figure 5.27 Cost Center Planning Using SAP Business Client

The changes to tables are as follows:

- New table introduced in SAP S/4HANA Finance:
  – Table ACDOCA

5.9 Key Changes to Cost Center and Profit Center Accounting

- Obsolete tables removed in SAP S/4HANA Finance:
  - Table COSS: cost table for internal posting
  - Table COSP: cost table for external posting

> **1709 Preview**
> With SAP S/4HANA 1709, you can now create flexible profit center and cost center hierarchies based on master data attributes and tags.

The new Web Dynpro drilldown reports for cost centers can be obtained by activating the Web Dynpro applications listed in Table 5.5.

Report Description	Web Dynpro Application
Cost Centers—Plan/Actual	FIS_FPM_OVP_IPCC1
Cost Centers—Plan/Actual YTD	FIS_FPM_OVP_IPCC2
Cost Centers—Plan/Actual with Currency Translation	FIS_FPM_OVP_IPCC3
Cost Centers—Actuals	FIS_FPM_OVP_IPCC4
Internal Orders—Plan/Actual	FIS_FPM_OVP_IPIO1
Internal Orders—Plan/Actual YTD	FIS_FPM_OVP_IPIO2
Internal Orders—Plan/Actual with Currency Translation	FIS_FPM_OVP_IPIO3
Internal Orders—Actuals	FIS_FPM_OVP_IPIO4

Table 5.5 Web Dynpro Cost Center and Internal Order Drilldown Reports

The new Web Dynpro drilldown reports for profit centers can be obtained by activating the Web Dynpro applications listed in Table 5.6.

Report Description	Web Dynpro Application
Profit Centers—Plan/Actual	FIS_FPM_OVP_IPPC1
Profit Centers—Plan/Actual YTD	FIS_FPM_OVP_IPPC2
Profit Centers—Plan/Actual with Currency Translation	FIS_FPM_OVP_IPPC3

Table 5.6 Web Dynpro Profit Center Drilldown Reports

5 Preparation and Migration for Controlling

Report Description	Web Dynpro Application
Profit Centers—Actuals	FIS_FPM_OVP_IPPC4
P&L—Plan/Actual	FIS_FPM_OVP_IPPL1
P&L—Plan/Actual YTD	FIS_FPM_OVP_IPPL2
P&L—Plan/Actual with Currency Translation	FIS_FPM_OVP_IPPL3
P&L—Actuals	FIS_FPM_OVP_IPPL4

Table 5.6 Web Dynpro Profit Center Drilldown Reports (Cont.)

With the introduction of SAP S/4HANA Finance, the old Cost Center Accounting and Profit Center Accounting transaction codes and table structure have been replaced by new transaction codes and compatibility views for the old tables. Remember that neither cost center planning nor profit center planning works in SAP S/4HANA Finance as a standalone function. New SAP HANA views and Web Dynpro reports will aid you in your use of Cost Center Accounting and Profit Center Accounting.

5.10 Summary

Activation of account-based CO-PA during migration is recommended to access all the new profitability reporting available in SAP S/4HANA Finance. Although costing-based CO-PA is still available, and both approaches can be used in parallel, we recommend using the account-based approach while using the SAP S/4HANA Finance solution.

After reading this chapter, you should now understand and be able to perform the Customizing for CO. Let's now move on to Chapter 6, in which we'll discuss the migration process for house bank accounts.

Chapter 6
Preparation and Migration for House Bank Accounts

This chapter highlights the steps required for customizing the migration of house bank accounts as part of the overall SAP S/4HANA Finance migration. This activity is important if you plan to use SAP Cash Management.

In this chapter, you'll learn how to perform all the necessary Customizing activities related to the migration of house bank accounts. Before you work with bank account master data, make sure you've properly configured the Customizing settings under **SAP Customizing Implementation Guide • Conversion of Accounting to SAP S/4HANA • Preparations and Migration of Customizing • Preparations for Migration of House Bank Accounts**, as shown in Figure 6.1.

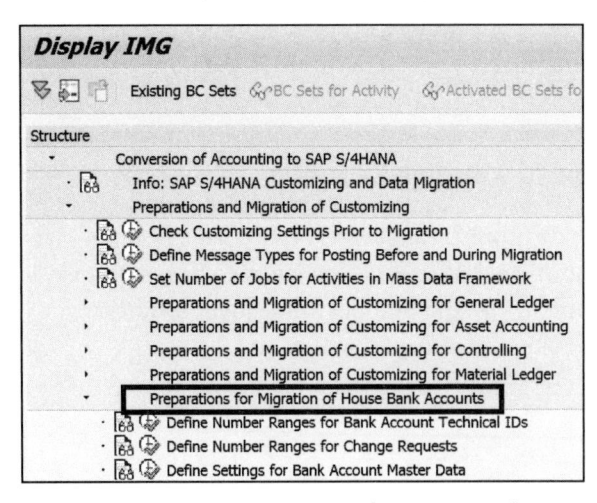

Figure 6.1 Customizing Migration for House Bank Accounts

6 Preparation and Migration for House Bank Accounts

Let's now jump into defining number ranges for bank account technical IDs and change requests, as well as defining the major settings for bank account master data.

6.1 Define Number Ranges for Bank Account Technical IDs

In this activity, you define and create number range intervals (internal or external number ranges) for bank account technical IDs, as shown in Figure 6.2. When you create bank account master data, a technical ID is automatically assigned. This setting facilitates the migration of house bank accounts.

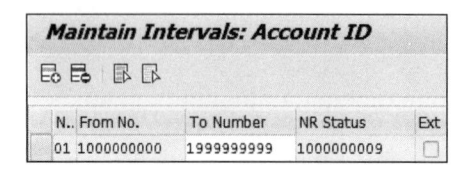

Maintain Intervals: Account ID

N..	From No.	To Number	NR Status	Ext
01	1000000000	1999999999	1000000009	☐

Figure 6.2 Defining Number Ranges for Bank Account IDs

To create a new number range interval, enter a two-digit number for the interval in the first column, and specify a number range in the **From No.** and **To Number** fields. To decide from which number interval the bank account technical IDs should be taken, specify the interval number in the **Define Number Ranges for Bank Account Technical IDs** Customizing activity. If you want to use an external number range instead of the system-generated number, you need to check the **Ext** box.

6.2 Define Number Ranges for Change Requests

In this activity, you define and create number range intervals for Bank Account Management change requests, as shown in Figure 6.3. Whenever a change request is created in Bank Account Management, the next number in a sequential order is automatically assigned from the number range you specified.

Maintain Intervals: FC_CREQID

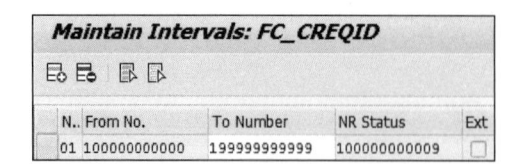

N..	From No.	To Number	NR Status	Ext
01	100000000000	199999999999	100000000009	☐

Figure 6.3 Defining Number Range for Change Requests

To create a new number range interval, you follow *almost* the same steps as you just did to create a new number range interval. You enter a two-digit number for the interval in the first column and specify a number range, as shown in Figure 6.3. To decide from which number interval the change request IDs should be taken, specify the interval number in the **Define Number Ranges for Change Requests** Customizing activity. If you want to use an external number range for the change requests instead of the system-generated number, you need to check the **Ext** box.

6.3 Define Settings for Bank Account Master Data

In this activity, you define the basic settings for the bank account master data. In the following subsections, you'll find the details of each structure shown in the left panel in Figure 6.4.

Before you begin, you must define and assign the number range created earlier, to the bank account master data, shown in the right panel in Figure 6.4.

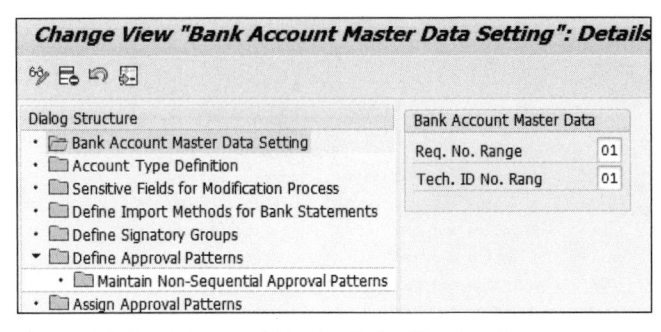

Figure 6.4 Bank Account Master Data: Number Range

6.3.1 Bank Account Types

One of the attributes in the bank account master data setting is **Account Type Definition**, as shown in Figure 6.5. You can define different types of accounts based on various business requirements. Account types are used for analyzing various reporting and planning dimensions. Using bank account types, you can also define different approval patterns for bank accounts of different types.

As part of the migration of house bank accounts, you define the bank account type and direction, provide a brief description, and designate it as an operating or functional account. To add a new bank account type in this Customizing screen, select **New Entries**, and then specify the following (see Figure 6.5):

- **Type**
  Enter a unique type ID of 10 characters or less.

- **Description**
  Enter a brief description of the account type, such as "current account".

- **Direction**
  Specify whether the direction of the cash flow used for this bank account is incoming, outgoing, or both.

- **Attribute**
  Specify if the created bank account type is an **Operating Account** or a **Functional Account**. *Operating accounts* reflect daily business transactions, such as receiving incoming payments from customers and issuing outgoing payments to vendors, whereas *functional accounts* reflect other financial activities, such as loans, investments, and fund-raising activities.

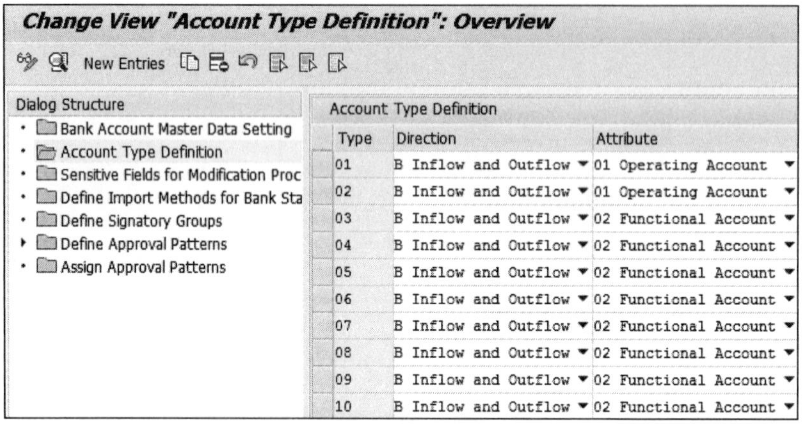

Figure 6.5 Bank Account Master Data: Account Type

6.3.2 Define Sensitive Fields to Be Protected from Changes

You can make changes to sensitive fields, as shown in Figure 6.6. For any changes to the existing sensitive fields or to add new entries in the sensitive fields list as defined in this section, a workflow change request is triggered if SAP Business Workflow is enabled.

6.3 Define Settings for Bank Account Master Data

Change View "Sensitive Fields for Modification Process": Overview		
Object	Field name	Field Description
BAM Bank Account	ACC_NUM	Bank Account Master Data: Account
BAM Bank Account	IBAN	IBAN (International Bank Account Nu
CURR Currency	WAERS	Currency Key
OVD Overdraft Limit	AMOUNT	Overdraft Limit Amount
OVD Overdraft Limit	WAERS	Currency Key
SIGN Signature	BATCH_AMOUNT	Maximum Amount for Payment Batch
SIGN Signature	BNAME	Bank Account Master Data: Signatory
SIGN Signature	PAY_AMOUNT	Maximum Amount for Payment
SIGN Signature	VALID_TO	Valid To (Signatory)

Dialog Structure:
- Bank Account Master Data Setting
- Account Type Definition
- Sensitive Fields for Modification Process
- Define Import Methods for Bank Statem
- Define Signatory Groups
- Define Approval Patterns
- Assign Approval Patterns

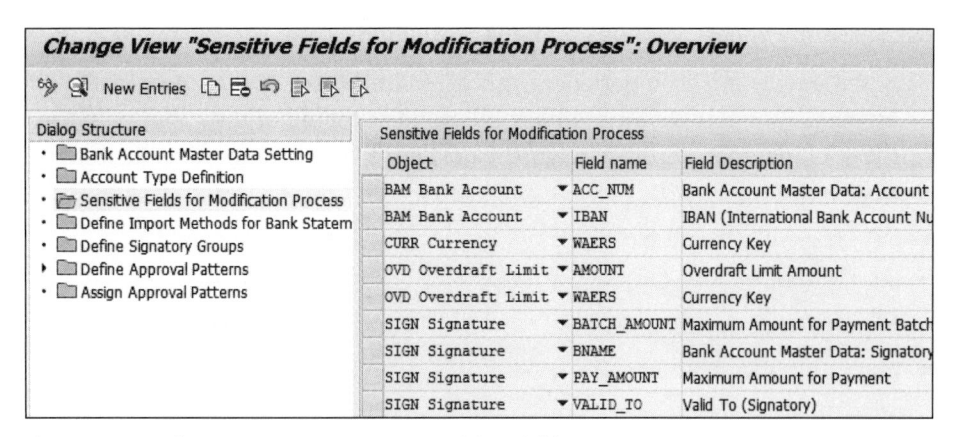

Figure 6.6 Bank Account Master Data: Sensitive Fields

You can specify a sensitive field from the following possible objects:

- **Bank Account**
  On the **General Data** tab, you can select fields such as **Bank**, **Country**, **Company Code**, and so on.

- **Currency**
  On the **General Data** tab, you can select fields such as **Account Currency**, **IBAN**, and so on.

- **Overdraft Limit**
  On the **Overdraft Limit** tab, you can select fields such as **Overdraft Limit Amount**, **Currency**, **Valid From**, **Valid To**, and so on.

- **Signature**
  On the **Signatories** tab, you can select fields such as **Signatory Group ID**, **Maximum Amount for Payment**, and so on.

- **House Bank**
  On the **Connectivity Path** tab, you can select fields such as **Bank Account Number**, **House Bank Account ID**, **G/L Account**, and so on.

Thus, based on your organization's requirements, you can select the appropriate object and the corresponding fields within that object to define the sensitive fields. This will then trigger a workflow and approval process for any modification to these fields.

6.3.3 Define Import Methods for Bank Statements

Bank statements can be imported using different methods—for example, via SWIFT or by manual import. As an example, following are some of the commonly used import methods that you can configure in the **Define Import Methods for Bank Statements** tab (see Figure 6.7):

- Import directly from a bank
- Import manually
- Import end-of-day statements
- Import intraday statements

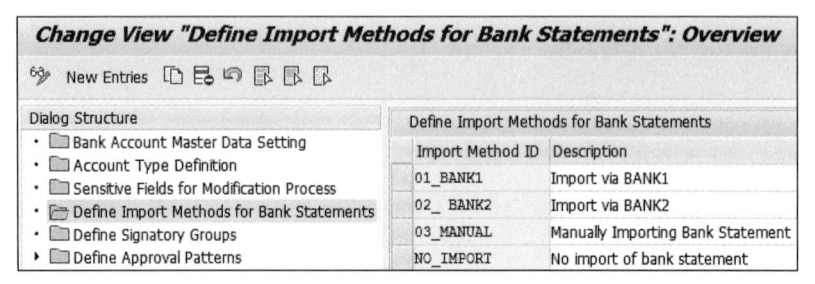

Import Method ID	Description
01_BANK1	Import via BANK1
02_ BANK2	Import via BANK2
03_MANUAL	Manually Importing Bank Statement
NO_IMPORT	No import of bank statement

Figure 6.7 Bank Account Master Data: Import Methods

After the Customizing is done with all the possible entries as shown in Figure 6.7, then in the bank account master record, users can define the import methods for bank statements on the **General Data • Bank Statement Data** tab; all these entries will be available in a dropdown menu in the bank master record.

6.3.4 Define Signatory Groups for Payment Approvals

Various groups of authorized signatories must be defined to suit the organization's business purposes. The signatory function is enabled in the Customizing activity under **Financial Supply Chain Management • Cash and Liquidity Management • Bank Account Management • Enable Signatory Control**.

When signatory control is enabled, the system checks the signatory information in the bank account master data and enables the users who are assigned the role of a signatory in Bank Account Management to approve or reject payment documents.

Different signatories can be grouped and organized into business groups based on the business unit/function and organizational hierarchy, as shown in Figure 6.8.

6.3 Define Settings for Bank Account Master Data

A common example occurs when both the HR and Finance departments need to sign off on salary payment, so you create two signatory groups, one for each department.

Change View "Define Signatory Groups": Overview

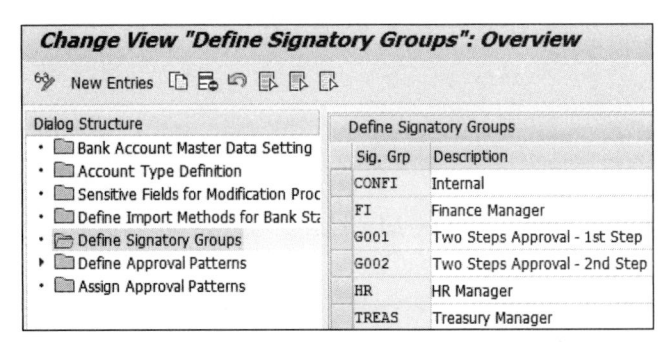

Sig. Grp	Description
CONFI	Internal
FI	Finance Manager
G001	Two Steps Approval - 1st Step
G002	Two Steps Approval - 2nd Step
HR	HR Manager
TREAS	Treasury Manager

Figure 6.8 Bank Account Master Data: Define Signatory Groups

You can define multiple signatory groups for any given bank account in the bank account master data. The system automatically sends any approval requests to eligible signatories in the relevant signatory groups using criteria such as the amount limit the signatory has assigned.

6.3.5 Define the Signatory Groups and Approval Sequence for Approval Patterns

Two types of approval patterns can be defined for payments: sequential and nonsequential (see Figure 6.9). Approval patterns represent different approval processes. To define an approval pattern, you specify the signatory groups involved and their corresponding approval sequences.

You can configure the approval patterns for the following scenarios:

- **Single signature**
  Define a sequential approval pattern with only one step.

- **Joint signature—signatories approve the payment in a certain order**
  Define a sequential approval pattern with two to four signatory groups.

- **Joint signature—signatories approve the payment regardless of the sequential order**
  Define a nonsequential approval pattern with two or more signatory groups.

247

Change View "Define Approval Patterns": Overview						
New Entries						
Dialog Structure	Define Approval Patterns					
• Bank Account Master Data Setting	Pattern	Appr. Seq.		Sig. Grp	Crcy	Min. Amount for Payment
• Account Type Definition	P001	1 First Step	▼	G001		
• Sensitive Fields for Modification Proc	P001	2 Second Step	▼	G002		
• Define Import Methods for Bank Sta	P003	0 Non-Sequential	▼		USD	75,000.00
• Define Signatory Groups					
▼ Define Approval Patterns					
• Maintain Non-Sequential Approv					
• Assign Approval Patterns					

Figure 6.9 Bank Account Master Data: Define Approval Patterns

For sequential approval patterns, the signatory groups approve payments in sequential order. You can define up to four steps for a sequential pattern. The second-step signatory group can only receive the approval request after the first-step signatory group has approved the payment; the same is true for the third-step and fourth-step signatory groups. Approval is completed when all the signatory groups under the signatory pattern have approved the payment. For a signatory group under a sequential approval pattern, you can't specify the approval sequence value as **Non-Sequential**.

For nonsequential signatory patterns, the signatory groups approve payments irrespective of the sequential order configured. All the signatory groups receive the approval request at the same time, but any two of the signatory groups can approve the payment and complete the approval process. For signatory groups under a nonsequential approval pattern, you must specify the approval sequence pattern as **Non-Sequential**.

6.3.6 Assign Approval Patterns

In this Customizing activity, you maintain the values and assign approval patterns to the combination of company codes and account types, and maintain the priority, as shown in Figure 6.10. The logic of the approval pattern assignment works as follows:

- If the approval pattern is assigned to a company code, but the account type is left blank, then the pattern is valid for all account types applicable for that company code.
- If the approval pattern is assigned to an account type, but the company code is left blank, then the pattern is valid for all company codes applicable for that account type.

6.3 Define Settings for Bank Account Master Data

- If multiple approval patterns are assigned to the same account type or company code, then the sequence of approval pattern is determined by the priority of the approval pattern assigned to the combination of account type and/or company code. The **Priority** value **0** has the highest priority, and the higher number has the lower priority.

Change View "Assign Approval Patterns": Overvie

Dialog Structure	Assign Approval Patterns

CoCd	Type	Pattern	Priority
1000	01	P001	1
1000	02	P001	1
1000	03	P001	1
1000	04	P001	1
1000	05	P001	1
1000	06	P001	1

Dialog Structure:
- Bank Account Master Data Setting
- Account Type Definition
- Sensitive Fields for Modification Proc
- Define Import Methods for Bank Sta
- Define Signatory Groups
- Define Approval Patterns
  - Maintain Non-Sequential Approv
- Assign Approval Patterns

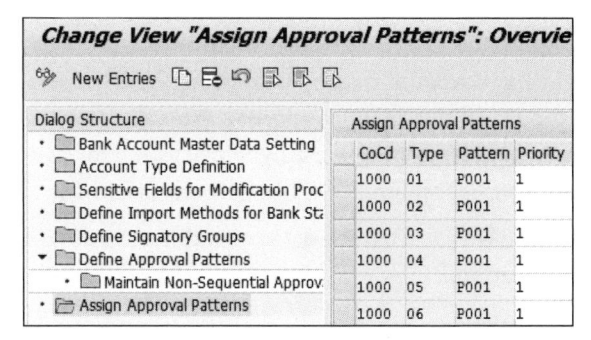

Figure 6.10 Bank Account Master Data: Assign Approval Patterns

The approval pattern defines a payment approval workflow by specifying the signatory groups involved and their corresponding approval sequences. The approval pattern priority determines the priority of approval patterns when multiple signatory patterns are assigned to the same company code or account type.

1709 Preview

SAP S/4HANA 1709 is bringing new changes to house bank accounts:

- Bank fee analysis has been introduced as part of bank relationship management. This means that organizations can now analyze the bank fees being charged to them and decide whether they want to optimize or harmonize their number of banks or perhaps negotiate with their banks to reduce bank fees.
- The workflow functionality for Bank Account Management has been simplified.
- New functionality allows organizations to integrate with Bank Communication Management and automate the process of clearing the postings from the incoming electronic bank statements via machine learning.

6.4 Summary

The Customizing steps for migrating house bank accounts are key and are a prerequisite if you're planning to use the new SAP Cash Management functionality. You need to define various types of bank accounts per the requirements of your organization and its business activities. These account types can be used in reporting and planning analysis.

In this chapter, you learned about the bank account master data settings and the sensitive fields for which making any modifications requires approval. You also learned how to define and assign the approval patterns, integrate a signatory group for payment approval, and customize and prepare for migration of house bank accounts.

Let's now move on to Chapter 7, in which we'll discuss the data migration activities of your SAP S/4HANA Finance implementation.

Chapter 7
Data Migration

This chapter introduces the data migration process, which involves regenerating compatibility views for the old table structure, merging cost elements and General Ledger accounts, performing various checks on the data, enriching the data, and a few other activities.

In the data migration project phase, you need to execute multiple steps, including migrating cost elements, enriching data, migrating line items and balances, reconciling and comparing migrated data, and finally completing the migration. For each of the steps, you need to verify the technical checks and logs and correct any errors encountered during the process.

The following are some of the key customization steps that you need to perform for the migration of data as part of the overall SAP S/4HANA Finance migration:

- Creating compatibility views for the line items
- Creating totals tables and index tables
- Partitioning the new Universal Journal table ACDOCA based on the volume of records for better performance
- Migrating the cost elements to General Ledger (G/L) accounts
- Enriching, checking, and reconciling the transaction data
- Migrating the line items and balances to the new data structure
- Reconciling the migrated data with the premigrated balances

You can adopt the *near-zero downtime* (NZDT) technique for the migration to minimize disruption to the normal business operations related to the migration. Let's begin by partitioning the Universal Journal entry.

7 Data Migration

7.1 Partitioning of the Universal Journal Entry Line Items Table

In this activity, you can partition table ACDOCA (Universal Journal line item), either because of an existing high data volume on the line item postings that you're migrating from SAP ERP or because you anticipate your postings will exceed two billion records in the near future (see Figure 7.1).

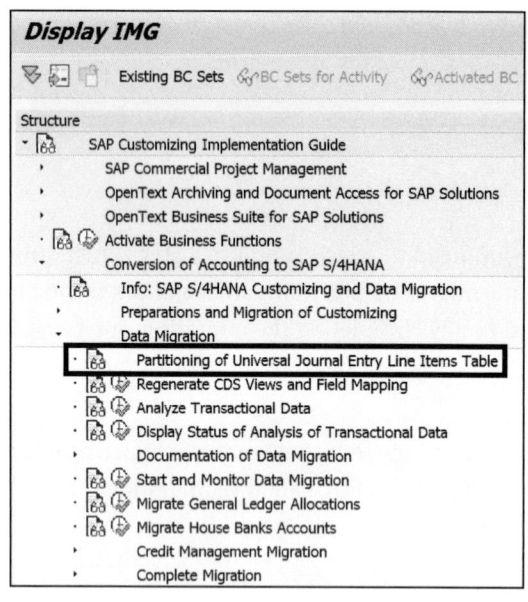

Figure 7.1 Configuring Partitioning of Universal Journal Entry Table

Note that table ACDOCA is a simple repository of journal entries across multiple applications without redundancy. During the migration to SAP S/4HANA Finance, table ACDOCA is filled from the G/L, Controlling (CO), SAP Material Ledger (ML), and Asset Accounting (FI-AA) areas, as shown in Figure 7.2.

Based on the number of transactions and data volume in the respective applications, table ACDOCA can contain a high number of records, which can have a negative effect on the performance of select and merge operations.

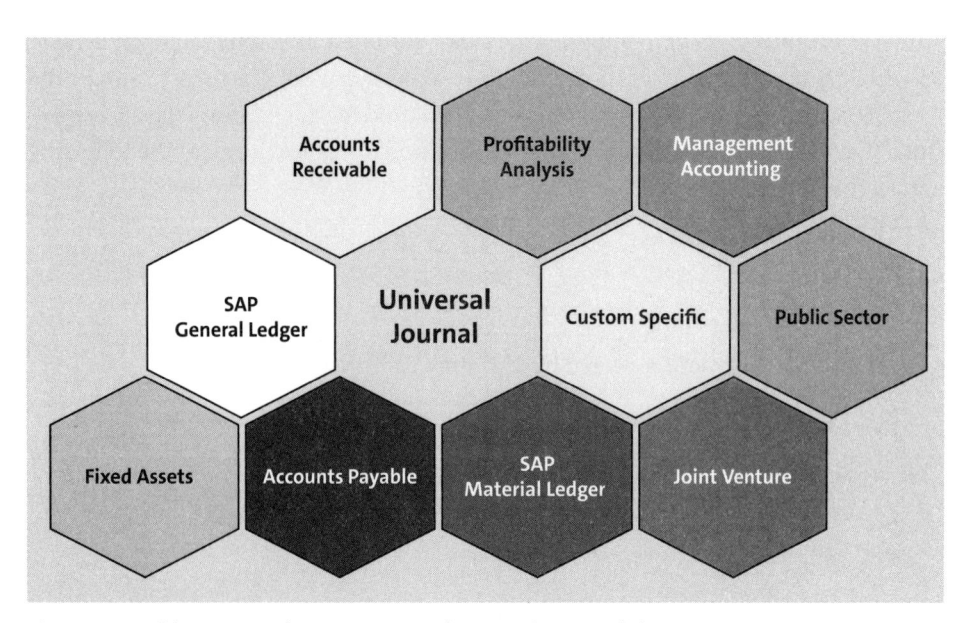

Figure 7.2 Table ACDOCA's Components from Various Modules

Partitioning table ACDOCA can mitigate this effect. SAP recommends 300 to 500 million records as an optimum partition size. Partitioning splits tables horizontally into disjunctive subtables or partitions. In this way, large tables are broken down into smaller, more manageable parts. Consider the following additional advice about partitioning table ACDOCA:

- Run a test migration on a copy of the production system to determine the resulting number of records in table ACDOCA.
- Partition table ACDOCA only if you expect more than 500 million records.
- You must partition the table if you expect to reach two billion records.
- Use the BELNR field (document number) as a partitioning criterion.

7.2 Regenerate CDS Views and Field Mapping

The Customizing activity using Transaction FINS_MIG_REGENERATE, as shown in Figure 7.3, checks whether the data definition language (DDL) source to be used is up-to-date and then regenerates different kinds of Core Data Services (CDS) views.

These views include both compatibility views for line items and totals tables and views being used in the migration procedure. To prevent data inconsistences in the Data Dictionary (DDIC), CDS views are also generated for any custom-specific extensions that have been used along with the SAP standard tables in any of the following applications:

- SAP General Ledger (G/L)
- Controlling (CO)
- SAP Material Ledger (ML)
- SAP Cash Management powered by SAP HANA
- Asset Accounting (FI-AA)

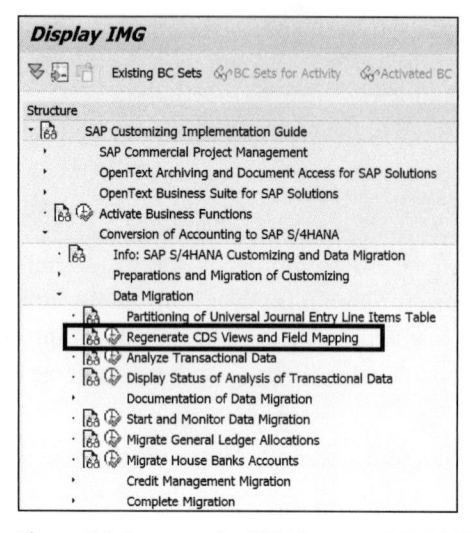

Figure 7.3 Regenerate CDS Views and Field Mapping

Before you can start using CDS to define the objects that comprise your persistence model, you need to ensure that certain prerequisites are met. Execute the activities in Customizing under **Conversion of Accounting to SAP S/4HANA** • **Data Migration** • **Regenerate CDS Views and Field Mapping** to do the following:

- Regenerate the compatibility and data migration views to adapt them to the configuration of custom-specific entities.
- Generate the redirection of SELECT statements from the concerned database tables to the corresponding compatibility views.
- Regenerate the mapping of custom-specific fields in the data migration procedure.

7.2 Regenerate CDS Views and Field Mapping

The SAP Basis team should complete this activity because it requires S_DEVELOP authorization to activate the DDIC objects. During this activity, the SAP Basis team might face the errors shown in Figure 7.4.

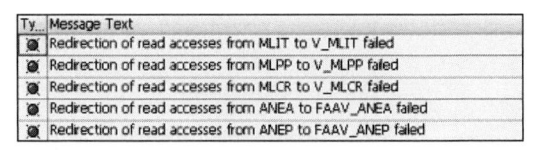

Ty...	Message Text
⊘	Redirection of read accesses from MLIT to V_MLIT failed
⊘	Redirection of read accesses from MLPP to V_MLPP failed
⊘	Redirection of read accesses from MLCR to V_MLCR failed
⊘	Redirection of read accesses from ANEA to FAAV_ANEA failed
⊘	Redirection of read accesses from ANEP to FAAV_ANEP failed

Figure 7.4 Error Messages during Regeneration of CDS Views

These errors need to be resolved by resetting the CDS views using SAP Note 1987083. This note suggests that you execute Report FINS_MIGRATION_STATUS using Transaction SA38 (see Figure 7.5).

SFin Migration Status

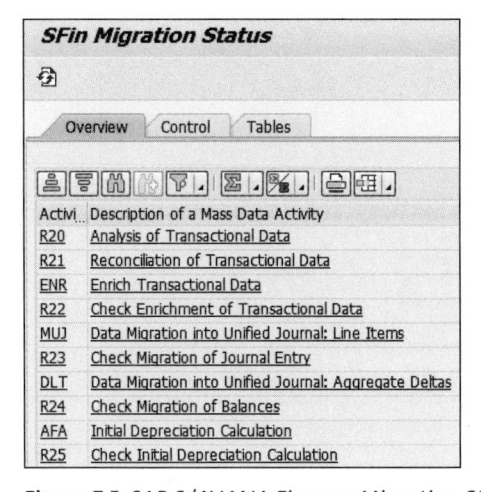

Activi...	Description of a Mass Data Activity
R20	Analysis of Transactional Data
R21	Reconciliation of Transactional Data
ENR	Enrich Transactional Data
R22	Check Enrichment of Transactional Data
MUJ	Data Migration into Unified Journal: Line Items
R23	Check Migration of Journal Entry
DLT	Data Migration into Unified Journal: Aggregate Deltas
R24	Check Migration of Balances
AFA	Initial Depreciation Calculation
R25	Check Initial Depreciation Calculation

Figure 7.5 SAP S/4HANA Finance Migration Status Report

The report provides the status of activities that have been finished (the green square icon ⬛), those that are still running (the yellow triangle icon ▲), and those waiting to be completed (the red circle icon ●).

Read access from custom ABAP programs or reports to select data from prior tables will work as before. The read access is automatically redirected to the compatibility views of the prior tables and is read from the Universal Journal as the new single source of truth. The advantage of this new architecture is that reconciliation is no longer required, and the memory footprint is reduced significantly.

7 Data Migration

> **References**
>
> For more information, see SAP Note 1987083: Regeneration of CDS Views.

7.3 Analyze Transactional Data

In this Customizing activity, you analyze whether all the transactional data is complete and correct. Be sure to execute this check in your test system first so that any inconsistency can be corrected before moving to the production environment, as shown in Figure 7.6, even if no transactional data exists.

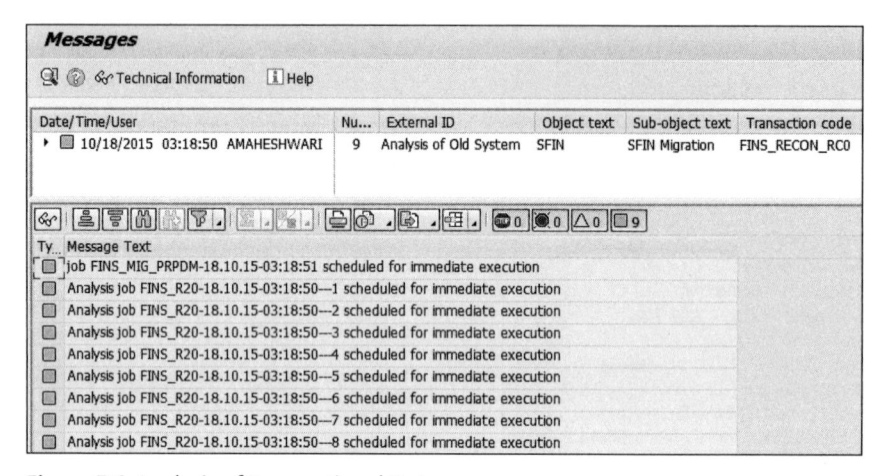

Figure 7.6 Analysis of Transactional Data

The following checks are performed in the background:

- Zero-balance check
- Document line items have a document
- Line items are missing
- Clearing information is missing
- Clearing specific to ledger groups field is valid in line item table
- Entries are missing in backup-index tables or duplicate entries exist in backup index tables
- Information about archiving or partially archived documents is missing in backup tables of indices

- All currency information of the documents matches the Customizing currency
- Open item management flags of master and transactional data are identical
- Document date of the document header is a valid date

> **Expert Insight**
> We recommend that you execute this step in all clients, even if no transactional data exists in a client, so that the migration status can be set as complete.

7.4 Display Status of Analysis of Transactional Data

After you've analyzed the transactional data, you need to make sure no errors are encountered during the execution. If there is an error, the migration process must be stopped and the error corrected before you execute further migration steps. An application log is provided, which can be displayed and analyzed later using Transaction SLG1.

You may also come across a situation during the analysis of transaction data in which the system displays a list of error messages, as shown in Figure 7.7.

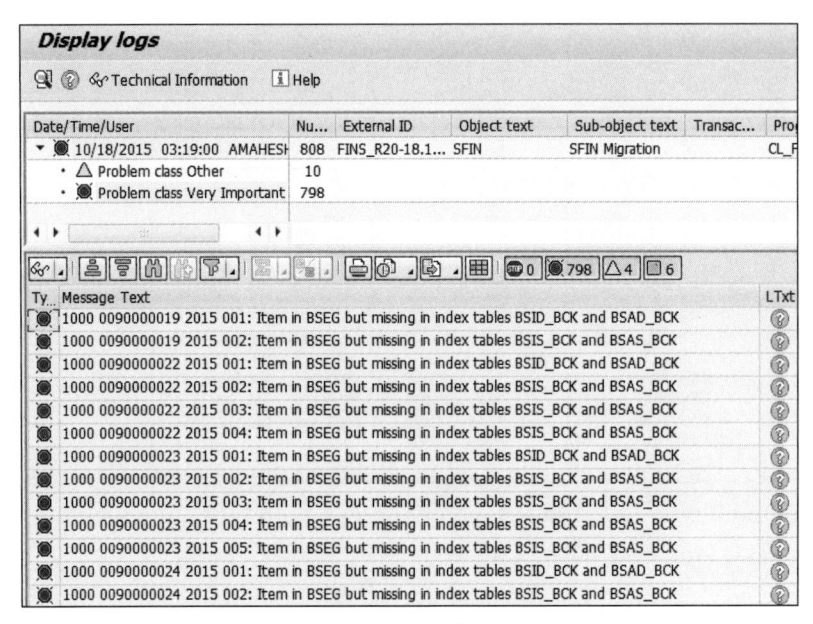

Ty	Message Text	LTxt
	1000 0090000019 2015 001: Item in BSEG but missing in index tables BSID_BCK and BSAD_BCK	
	1000 0090000019 2015 002: Item in BSEG but missing in index tables BSIS_BCK and BSAS_BCK	
	1000 0090000022 2015 001: Item in BSEG but missing in index tables BSID_BCK and BSAD_BCK	
	1000 0090000022 2015 002: Item in BSEG but missing in index tables BSIS_BCK and BSAS_BCK	
	1000 0090000022 2015 003: Item in BSEG but missing in index tables BSIS_BCK and BSAS_BCK	
	1000 0090000022 2015 004: Item in BSEG but missing in index tables BSIS_BCK and BSAS_BCK	
	1000 0090000023 2015 001: Item in BSEG but missing in index tables BSID_BCK and BSAD_BCK	
	1000 0090000023 2015 002: Item in BSEG but missing in index tables BSIS_BCK and BSAS_BCK	
	1000 0090000023 2015 003: Item in BSEG but missing in index tables BSIS_BCK and BSAS_BCK	
	1000 0090000023 2015 004: Item in BSEG but missing in index tables BSIS_BCK and BSAS_BCK	
	1000 0090000023 2015 005: Item in BSEG but missing in index tables BSIS_BCK and BSAS_BCK	
	1000 0090000024 2015 001: Item in BSEG but missing in index tables BSID_BCK and BSAD_BCK	
	1000 0090000024 2015 002: Item in BSEG but missing in index tables BSIS_BCK and BSAS_BCK	

Figure 7.7 Error Messages during Analysis of Transaction Data

7 Data Migration

Analyze and resolve the issues before you move ahead with the next activity, which involves checking why the documents are in table BSEG and not in the index tables, as follows:

1. Checking the document numbers in table BSEG, you may discover that the document numbers exist, as shown in Figure 7.8.

Client	Company Code	Document Number	Fiscal Year	Line item
100	1000	0090000019	2015	001
100	1000	0090000019	2015	002
100	1000	0090000022	2015	001
100	1000	0090000022	2015	002
100	1000	0090000022	2015	003
100	1000	0090000022	2015	004
100	1000	0090000023	2015	001
100	1000	0090000023	2015	002
100	1000	0090000023	2015	003
100	1000	0090000023	2015	004
100	1000	0090000023	2015	005
100	1000	0090000024	2015	001
100	1000	0090000024	2015	002

Figure 7.8 Entries in Table BSEG

2. Checking the document numbers in table BSID_BCK, you may find that the document number such as 90000019 doesn't exist, as shown in Figure 7.9.

Client	Company Code	Customer	Fiscal Year	Document Number	Line item	Posting Date
100	1000	M001	2015	0090000010	001	01/01/2015
100	1000	PCS-C301	2014	0090000000	001	11/09/2014
100	1000	PCS-C301	2014	0090000002	001	11/10/2014
100	1000	PCS-C301	2014	0090000004	001	11/10/2014
100	1000	PCS-C301	2014	0090000006	001	11/10/2014
100	1000	PCS-C301	2014	0090000008	001	11/10/2014
100	1000	PCS-C301	2015	0090000011	001	04/23/2015

Figure 7.9 Entries in Table BSID_BCK

7.4 Display Status of Analysis of Transactional Data

3. Checking the document numbers in table BSIS_BCK, you may find that the same document numbers shown in table BSEG don't exist (in our example, the document numbers start at 4900000437), as shown in Figure 7.10.
4. Checking the document numbers in table BSAD_BCK, you may find that those document numbers don't exist in this table either, as shown in Figure 7.11, where the table is empty.
5. Checking the document numbers in table BSAS_BCK, you may find that the document numbers as shown in table BSEG are missing, as shown in Figure 7.12 where the table is also empty.

Cl.	CoCd	G/L	Clearing	Clrng doc.	Assignment	Year	DocumentNo	Itm	Pstng Date
100	1000	0000135075			20150202	2015	4900000437	1	02/02/2015
100	1000	0000520075			20150202	2015	4900000437	2	02/02/2015
100	1000	0000135075			20150202	2015	4900000438	1	02/02/2015
100	1000	0000135075			20150202	2015	4900000438	3	02/02/2015
100	1000	0000135075			20150202	2015	4900000438	5	02/02/2015
100	1000	0000135075			20150202	2015	4900000438	7	02/02/2015
100	1000	0000135075			20150202	2015	4900000438	9	02/02/2015

Figure 7.10 Entries in Table BSIS_BCK

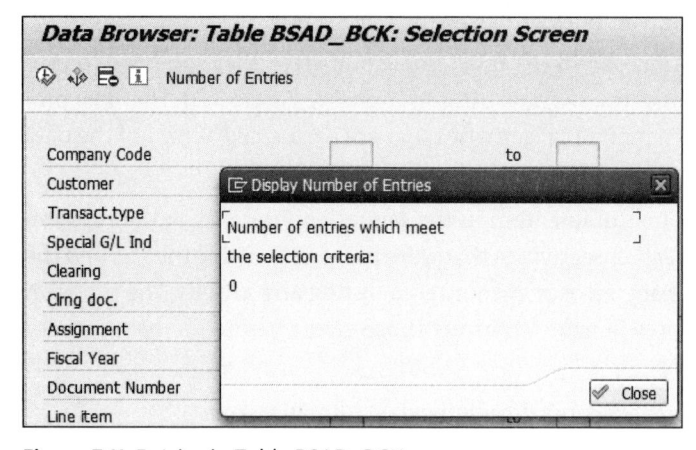

Figure 7.11 Entries in Table BSAD_BCK

7 Data Migration

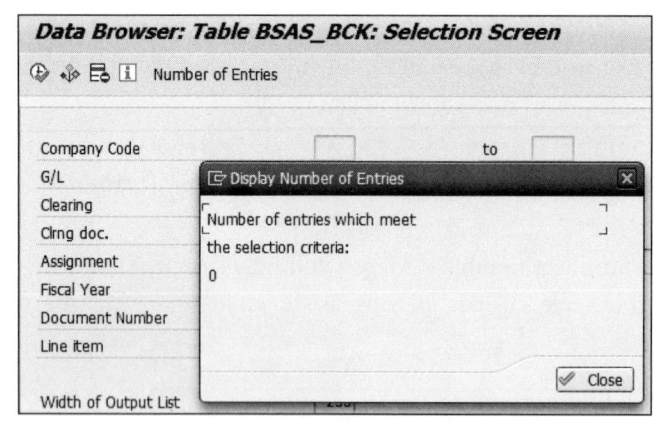

![Data Browser: Table BSAS_BCK: Selection Screen showing a Display Number of Entries dialog indicating 0 entries meet the selection criteria]

Figure 7.12 Entries in Table BSAS_BCK

The origin of this error might be that postings were made in the middle of the migration process—after SAP S/4HANA Finance was installed but before the migration process was fully executed—resulting in table inconsistencies. It's prudent to complete the migration by following the Customizing activities in sequence while holding off on any transaction postings until the migration is complete.

7.5 Start and Monitor Data Migration

This Customizing activity is one of the most important steps that you need to execute after the installation of the SAP S/4HANA system (see Figure 7.13). This step provides a snapshot of all the individual activities that are performed as part of the data migration run.

When you double-click the run line item in the **Migration Runs** box at the top, you can analyze the details of all the activities that were processed during the run and the status of each activity. If any error is encountered during any activity, the program execution is stopped. You will have to correct those errors before the next activity can be executed.

The following activities are executed during the data migration run:

- Migration of cost elements
- Technical check of transactional data
- Material ledger migration

7.6 Migration of Cost Elements

- Enrichment of data
- Migration of line items
- Migration of balances
- Calculation of depreciation and totals values

```
Display IMG
   Existing BC Sets    BC Sets for Activity    Activated BC
Structure
    Conversion of Accounting to SAP S/4HANA
        Info: SAP S/4HANA Customizing and Data Migration
        Preparations and Migration of Customizing
        Data Migration
            Partitioning of Universal Journal Entry Line Items Table
            Regenerate CDS Views and Field Mapping
            Analyze Transactional Data
            Display Status of Analysis of Transactional Data
            Documentation of Data Migration
                Migration of Cost Elements
                Technical Check of Transactional Data
                Material Ledger Migration
                Enrichment of Data
                Migration of Line Items
                Migration of Balances
                Calculation of Depreciation and Totals Values
                [Start and Monitor Data Migration]
                Migrate General Ledger Allocations
                Migrate House Banks Accounts
                Credit Management Migration
                Complete Migration
```

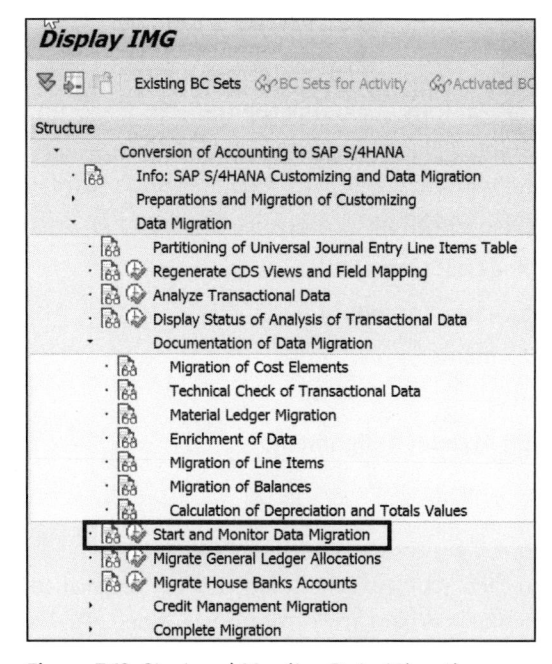

Figure 7.13 Start and Monitor Data Migration

Although the **Start and Monitor Data Migration** Customizing activity executes and provides the status of all the key activities and steps listed in the upcoming two sections, you can alternatively execute specific programs and transactions to check these individual activities. Let's look at these individual transactions now.

7.6 Migration of Cost Elements

In the **Start and Monitor Data Migration** Customizing activity, the migration of cost elements activity is executed for the new Universal Journal architecture with the merged master data model for G/L accounts (FI) and cost elements (CO). With the introduction of SAP S/4HANA Finance, both primary and secondary cost elements are created as G/L accounts using Transaction FS00.

261

7 Data Migration

With the migration of SAP S/4HANA Finance, the CO and FI components have now been merged into one line item in table ACDOCA. All business transactions, both external and internal, are recorded on G/L accounts in the Universal Journal entry. Cost elements are now created and managed as G/L accounts and are no longer maintained separately in CO. The secondary cost elements, as used in classic CO, are also created as G/L accounts.

With this new approach, several activities are performed that categorize the secondary cost elements as part of the chart of accounts, including the transfer of account assignments and authorizations, which are replaced by G/L account authorizations. The **Start and Monitor Data Migration** Customizing activity executes and provides the status of all the following key activities and steps:

- Check Consistency of G/L Accounts and Cost Elements
- Migrate Secondary Cost Elements to Chart of Accounts
- Display Status of Migration of Cost Elements
- Migrate Default Account Assignments
- Display Status of Migration of Default Account Assignments
- Adopt Authorizations
- Define Authorizations and Profiles

However, if you prefer to walk through each activity rather than execute them all at once, you can. This section explains each one. Where any error occurs, it needs to be resolved before moving to the next step.

7.6.1 Check Consistency of G/L Accounts and Cost Elements

You can execute program FINS_MIG_PRECHECK_CUST_SETTNGS using Transaction SA38 to check the consistency between the G/L accounts and cost elements. An inconsistency might be, for example, that no G/L account exists for a primary cost element. You need to correct all the inconsistencies that are found so that the G/L account master records will have the correct account types after migration.

When you execute this report, you might encounter the errors shown in Figure 7.14. To resolve these errors, you need to confirm whether the accounts listed are actually primary cost elements. If they are, you then need to create the missing cost element as a G/L account with the primary cost element account type. You need to correct the indicated inconsistencies or the G/L account master records will have the incorrect account types after the migration.

7.6 Migration of Cost Elements

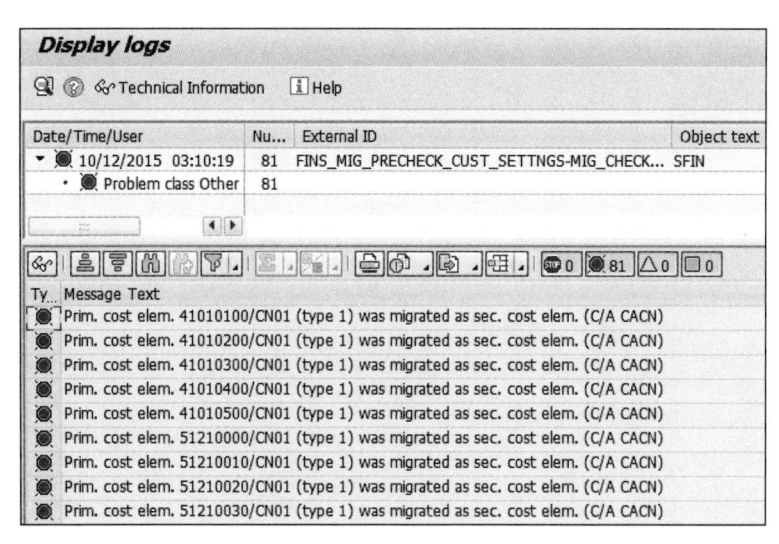

Figure 7.14 Errors from Checking Consistency of G/L Accounts and Cost Elements

In Transaction FS00, you input the G/L account (see Figure 7.15) related to the inconsistency displayed in the report. Here, you check and display the **Account Type** (highlighted in Figure 7.15), and then go to **G/L Account • Change** from the top menu bar to change the **Account Type** value to **Primary Costs or Revenue** and the **Account Group** value to **P&L Statement Accounts**, as shown in Figure 7.16.

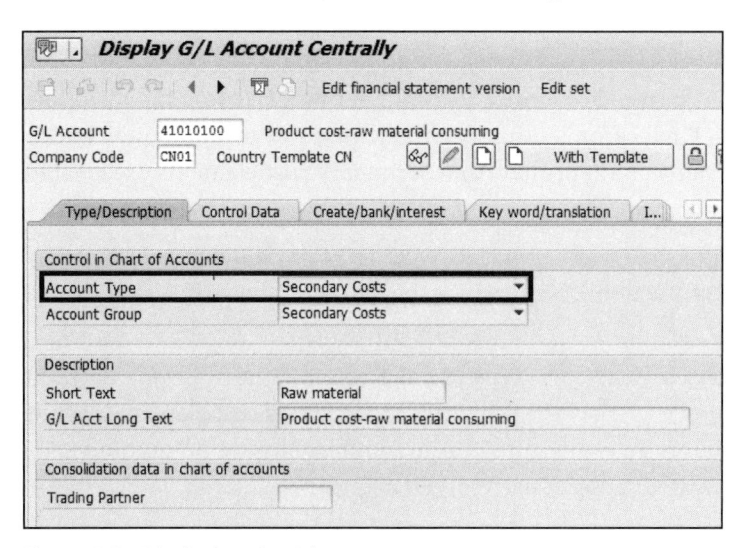

Figure 7.15 Displaying the G/L Account

263

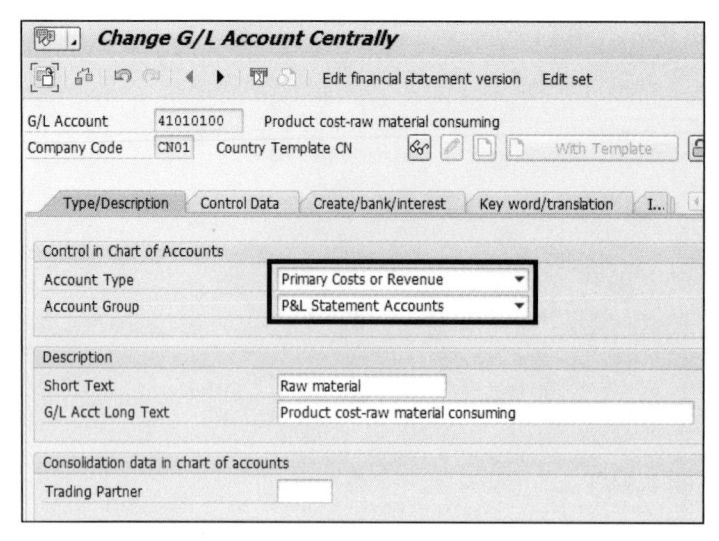

Figure 7.16 Changing the G/L Account

7.6.2 Migrate Secondary Cost Elements to the Chart of Accounts

In SAP S/4HANA Finance, the master data of G/L accounts and cost elements have been merged. In the merged master data model, both primary and secondary cost elements are created and represented as G/L accounts and must be maintained in the same transaction used for maintaining G/L accounts: Transaction FS00 (Edit G/L Account Centrally).

G/L accounts share a chart of accounts and a number range. Before the introduction of SAP S/4HANA Finance, only primary cost elements were represented as G/L accounts. After the merge, both primary and secondary cost elements are created as G/L accounts.

This activity is executed via Transaction FINS_MIG_GCM or via program FINS_MIG_CHECK_GCM using Transaction SA38, in which the messages shown in Figure 7.17 are displayed.

A new database field, GLACCOUNT_TYPE (type of a G/L account), must be populated in table SKA1, in which you can select the primary and secondary cost element account types for the G/L accounts (refer to Figure 7.16). In addition, missing G/L account master records must be created for secondary cost elements.

7.6 Migration of Cost Elements

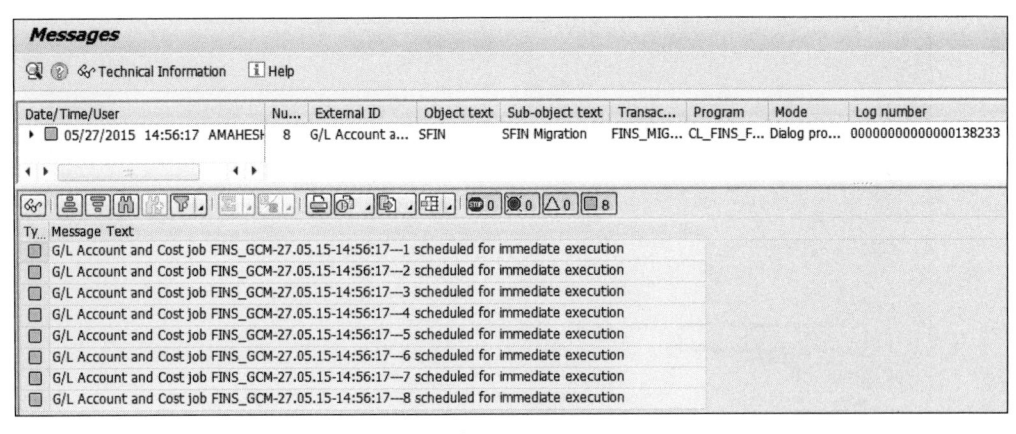

Figure 7.17 Migration of Cost Elements to G/L Accounts

The merge creates the following objects:

- Entries for G/L accounts of the G/L secondary costs account type in tables SKA1, SKB1, and SKAT
- A new field for the type of a G/L account (GLACCOUNT_TYPE) added to table SKA1 and filled with the correct entries

For the GLACCOUNT_TYPE field, you can choose from the following values:

- **X**: balance sheet account
- **N**: non-operating expense or income
- **P**: primary costs or revenue
- **S**: secondary costs

This step fills the GLACCOUNT_TYPE field in table SKA1 and creates the missing records for secondary cost elements in the G/L account tables SKA1 and SKB1.

7.6.3 Display Status of Migration of Cost Elements

In this activity, you use Transaction FINS_MIG_MONITOR_GCM to check the status of the migration of secondary cost elements to the G/L account master to verify if all the secondary cost elements have been created as G/L accounts. If there are no errors, it will have a status of **Finished** with a green circle, as highlighted in Figure 7.18. If an error occurs, use Transaction FS00 to analyze the error for the specific cost element that hasn't yet been created as a G/L account.

7 Data Migration

Figure 7.18 Status of G/L Accounts and Cost Elements Merge

7.6.4 Migrate Default Account Assignments

When cost elements are migrated to the chart of accounts, all the required fields from cost elements are also migrated to the chart of accounts, except the account assignment, which is moved from master data table CSKB to customization table TKA3A. You can access the default assignment setting through Transaction OKB9.

You can migrate default account assignments using Transaction FINS_MIG_DAA, as shown in Figure 7.19.

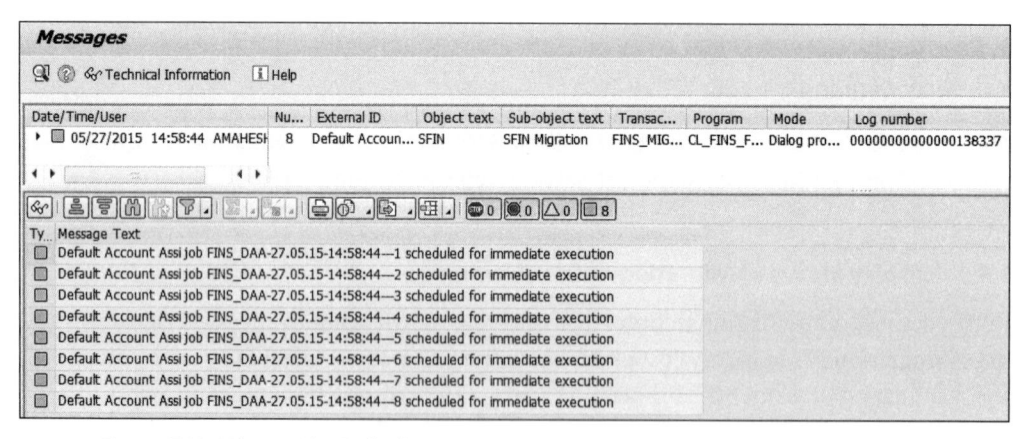

Figure 7.19 Migrate the Default Account Assignment

7.6 Migration of Cost Elements

In particular, the fields for default assignment based on cost center or internal order need to be completed from the joint master data record, as shown in Figure 7.20.

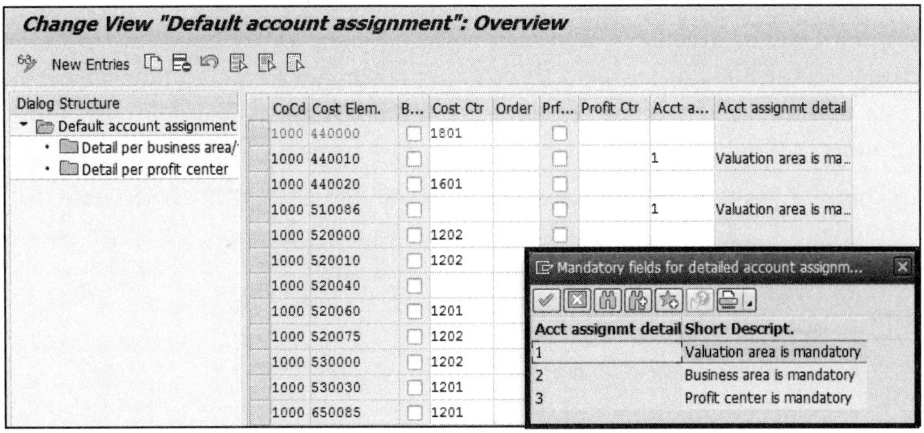

Figure 7.20 Changing the Default Account Assignment

7.6.5 Display the Status of the Default Account Assignments Migration

In this activity, you use Transaction FINS_MIG_MONITOR_DAA to check the status of the settings transfer for default assignments for cost centers or internal orders from the cost element master to Customizing table TKA3A (see Figure 7.21).

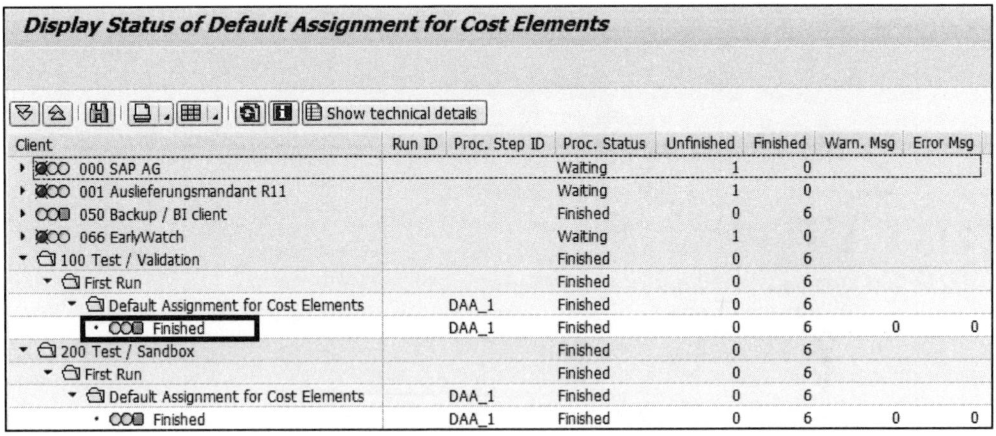

Figure 7.21 Display Status of Default Assignment for Cost Elements

267

7 Data Migration

7.6.6 Adopt Authorizations

The integration of cost elements and G/L accounts requires adjustments to authorizations for creating cost elements. If you want to maintain accounts of the primary costs or revenue account type, you need to have the authorization to create or change cost element master data. If you want to maintain accounts of the secondary costs account type, you need to have the authorization to create or change G/L accounts.

To check or change the authorizations for the FUCN_GL_ACCOUNTANT role (**G/L Accountant**), use Transaction PFCG, as shown in Figure 7.22.

The following relevant required authorizations are defined here:

- CO: cost element master (K_CSKB)
- FI: change authorization for certain fields (F_SKA1_AEN)
- FI: account authorization (F_SKA1_BES)
- FI: authorization for company codes (F_SKA1_BUK)
- FI: authorization for charts of accounts (F_SKA1_KTP)

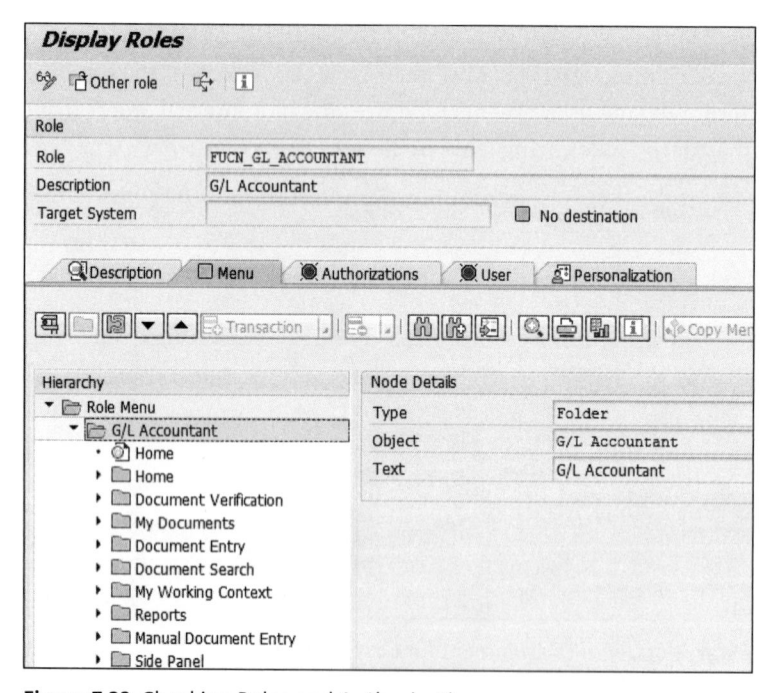

Figure 7.22 Checking Roles and Authorizations

7.6.7 Define Authorizations and Profiles

In this activity, the SAP Basis team needs to create and change the appropriate roles for the users who have been involved with creating and maintaining G/L accounts, primary cost elements, and secondary cost elements. These three master data activities have now been merged into Transaction FS00 (Edit G/L Account Centrally) with new entries under the **Account Type** and **Account Group** dropdown lists, as shown in Figure 7.23.

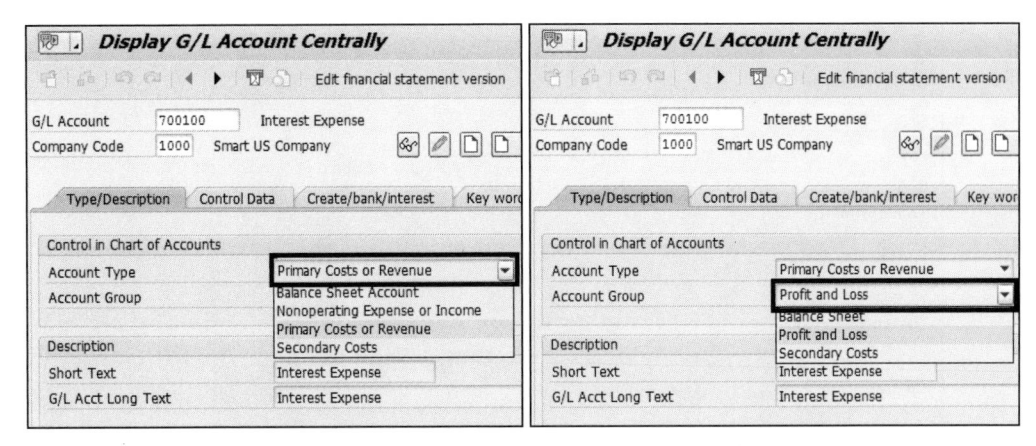

Figure 7.23 Primary and Secondary Cost Elements Settings in Transaction FS00

The following sequence of steps and instructions describes the procedure for creating a simple role in SAP by creating the user profile and providing the correct authorization:

1. Provide a name for the role, and select the **Single Role** button (see Figure 7.24).

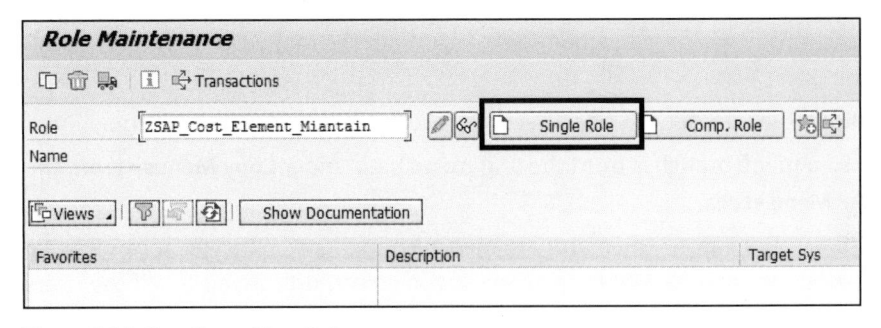

Figure 7.24 Creating a New Role

7 Data Migration

Note that the default roles provided by SAP begin with the prefix "SAP_". If you're creating your own user roles, don't use the SAP namespace; it's recommended to start your custom roles with "Z" to distinguish them from the standard roles provided by SAP.

2. On the **Create Roles** screen, provide a description of the role in the **Description** field, and describe the detailed functionality for this role in the **Long Text** box (see Figure 7.25).

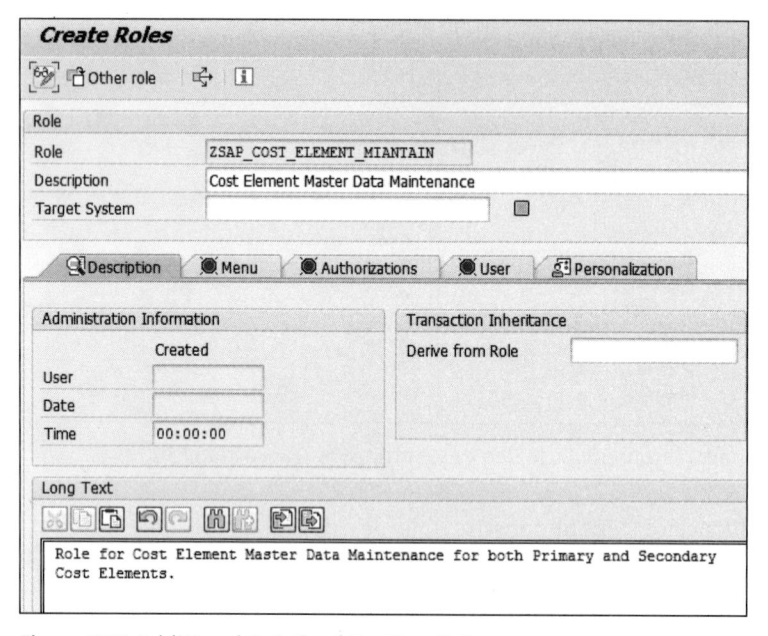

Figure 7.25 Additional Details of the New Role

3. Transactions need to be assigned to the role from the **Menu** tab in one of the following ways:
   - Specify the transaction code directly by clicking the **Transaction** button.
   - Assign menu branches from the SAP menu path under **Copy Menus • From the SAP Menu • Local**.

The transactions from the menu are displayed in Figure 7.26, which can also be navigated through the **SAP Easy Access** logon screen user menu by all the users who are assigned to this role.

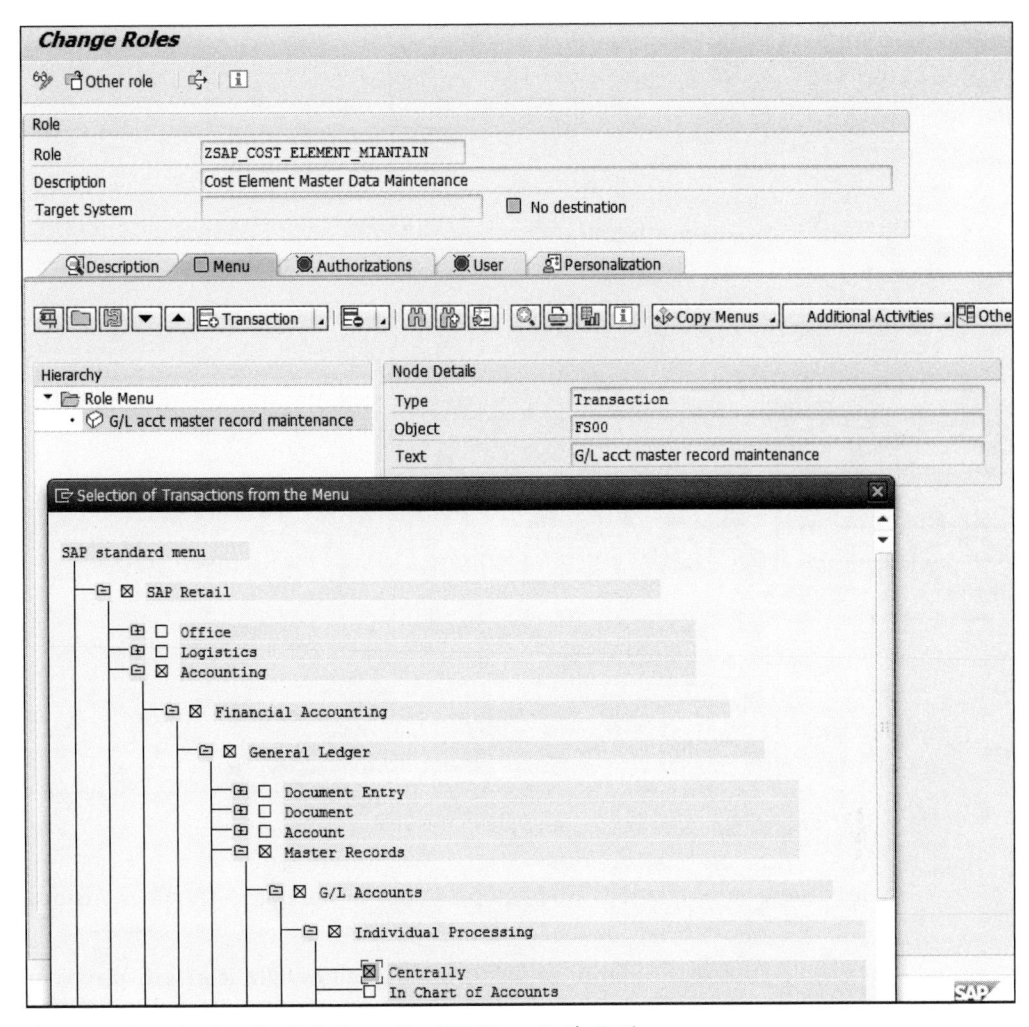

Figure 7.26 Assigning the Role from the SAP Menu Path Option

4. On the **Authorizations** tab, select the **Change Authorization Data** button, as shown in Figure 7.27. Based on the selected role, a dialog box is displayed in which the organizational levels need to be maintained. These authorization fields can be maintained together for various objects and levels of authorization, such as company codes that occur in several authorization objects. When a value is assigned to the organizational level, the authorization field is maintained for all levels of authorization in the hierarchy tree. Thus, all authorizations for that object are displayed in a tree-like structure that is proposed by SAP for the chosen transaction.

7   Data Migration

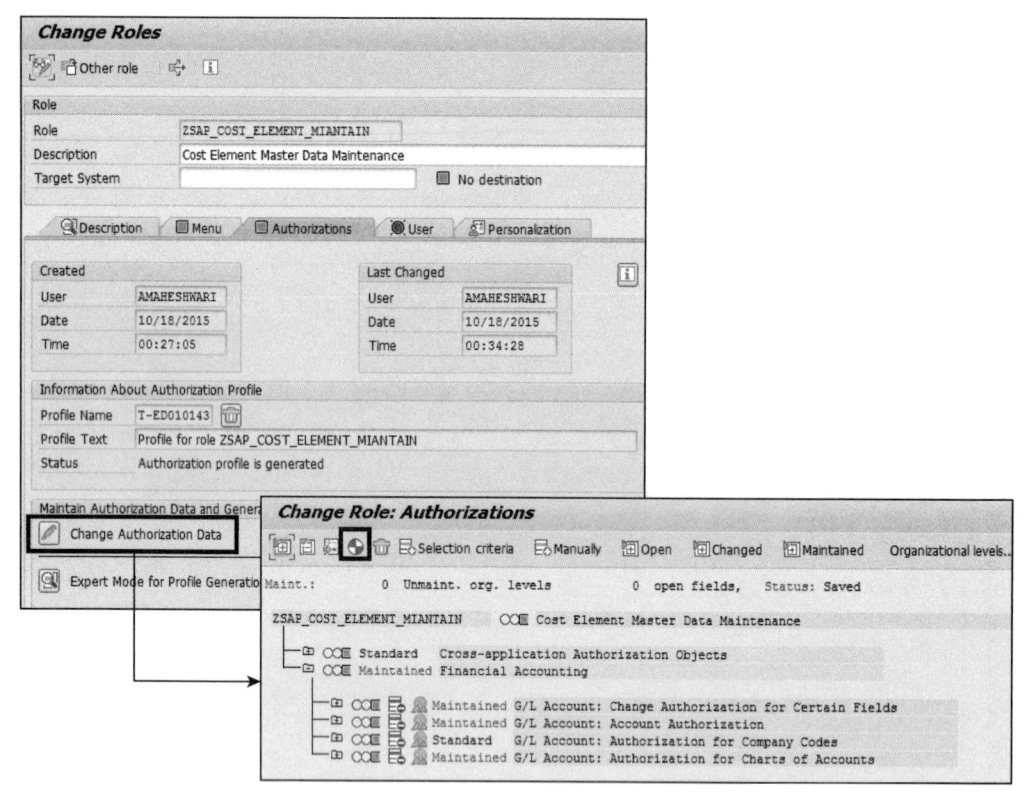

Figure 7.27 Changing the Authorization Data in the Role

Some of these authorizations are prepopulated with standard SAP values. Actions to take on this screen include the following:

- Manually process the authorization values if a yellow light icon is displayed in the tree structure. The values need to be entered by clicking a white line next to the name of the authorization field. After the values have been maintained, the authorizations are treated as manually changed.

- Add values to organizational levels if red light icons are displayed to indicate the missing levels. You can enter new values or change the existing ones by choosing **Organizational Levels**.

- Create an authorization profile by executing **Generate**. Provide a name for the authorization profile in the subsequent dialog box, or use the valid name in the

7.6 Migration of Cost Elements

customer namespace that is proposed. After the profile is created, you may exit the tree display.
- Delete an authorization by first deactivating it and then marking it for deletion, if necessary.

5. On the **User** tab, you can now assign the users to this new role as shown in Figure 7.28. The users you include in this list will be authorized to execute the transactions included in this role. These users can also navigate and display the transactions in their **SAP Easy Access** menu, as well as create a **Favorites** folder and include their most commonly used transactions in this folder. You can include user IDs in the list as follows:
   - Add a single entry or make a selection from the possible dropdown entry list.
   - Add several users at the same time by including multiple selections from the list, such as all users in a particular user group or all users in the SAP system. To do this, first choose **Selection** on the **User** tab, and then select additional value pushbuttons.
   - Use the roles as applicable within the organization.

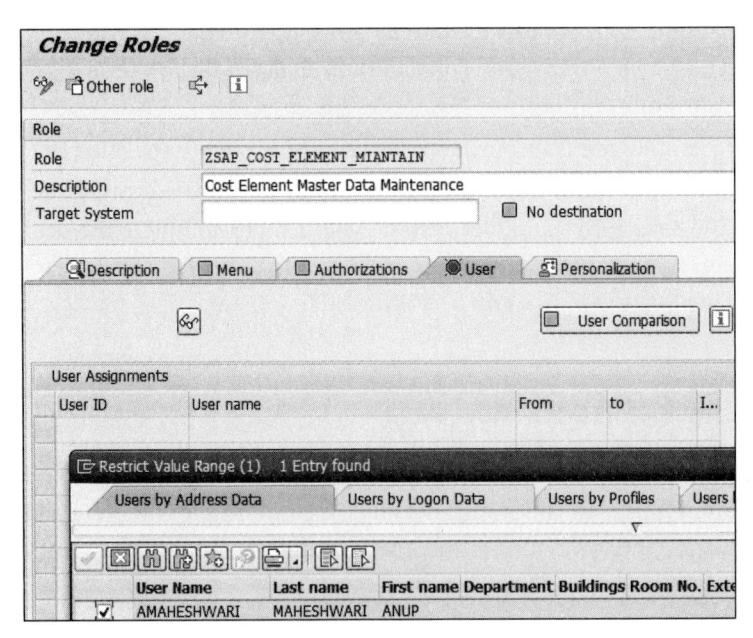

Figure 7.28 Assigning User IDs to the Role

273

The generated authorization profiles are entered in the user master records automatically when the user master record comparison is performed. To do this, you need to go to the **User** tab in Transaction PFCG and then click the **User Comparison** tab.

If you make changes to the users assigned to the role or generate an authorization profile for them, you must then compare the authorization profiles with user master records. Profiles that are no longer current are removed from the user master records, and the current profiles are inserted into them.

In addition to general information about the date and time of the last user master comparison, the system displays status information about the user master comparison in this window.

If you don't have any requirement to provide the authorization to the user for a particular period and want to use the default period (current date until 12.31.9999), no further action is necessary. If you want to include period restrictions, you need to schedule and run Report PFCG_TIME_DEPENDENCY daily. This report updates the user master records automatically and must be scheduled if you're using SAP ERP HCM Organizational Management.

6. You can transport the role to another system by entering the role in a transport request and selecting **Role • Transport**. You can then indicate if the user assignment should be transported.

   The authorization profiles are transported unless you've explicitly specified that you don't want to transport the profiles.

7. After importing the roles into the target system, you need to complete the user master comparison again for the imported roles. You can start this comparison manually or execute Report PFCG_TIME_DEPENDENCY.

7.7 Technical Check of Transaction Data

After the installation of SAP S/4HANA Finance, the Customizing activity **Start and Monitor Data Migration** is used to check whether all FI documents are complete and correct, as well as to identify and correct inconsistent documents in the system

7.7 Technical Check of Transaction Data

before starting the data migration process. Although this Customizing activity executes and provides the status of all the following key activities and steps, you can alternatively execute specific programs and transactions to check or correct the two activities:

- **Reconcile Transactional Data**
- **Display Status of Technical Reconciliation of Transactional Data**

Let's walk through each activity.

7.7.1 Reconcile Transactional Data

In this activity, you need to check that the FI documents are consistent and ready to be migrated by executing Transaction FINS_RECON_RC1, as shown in Figure 7.29.

The program reconciles the existing transactional data to ensure that the data migration is executed correctly. It checks necessary prerequisites for the programs (e.g., having a document header for each line item, which is needed for the corresponding joint statement to work properly), and it checks that both parts of a set of redundant data (e.g., documents and application indices) are consistent. You must resolve every inconsistency before you start the data migration.

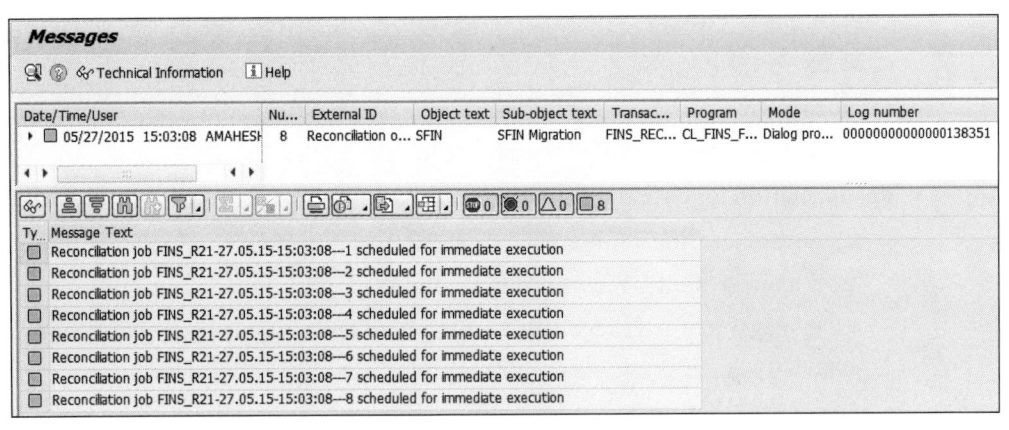

Figure 7.29 Transaction Data Fully Reconciled before Data Migration

275

You need to check for the following:

- **G/L document**
  - The WAERS field of the document header is filled.
  - Line items exist for each header (depending on document type) and vice versa.
  - Every document has a zero balance.
- **New G/L document (only applied if already active)**
  - New G/L line items exist for table BSEG and vice versa.
  - The existing transactional data is used if aggregated to the table BSEG level (BUZEI field).
  - Every document has a zero balance based on the new G/L line items.
  - The same values are used for certain attributes: BUDAT, RACCT, and RWCUR.
- **G/L, Accounts Payable (AP), Accounts Receivable (AR) application indices**
  - An index entry exists for each document line and vice versa, if required.
  - The most important fields (BUKRS, BELNR, GJAHR, BUZEI, BUDAT, BLDAT, DMBTR, SAKNR, HKONT, LIFNR, KUNNR) are equal.
  - The flag stating whether the corresponding document of an application index entry is already archived (XARCH) is set correctly.
  - The original content of the application indices is saved in tables with _BCK as the suffix.
- **CO document**
  - A document header exists for each line item.
- **Reconciliation for data consistency**
  - Aggregates and line items are reconciled in separate reports.
  - Asset management is reconciled in separate reports.
  - ML management isn't reconciled on the item level because only balances are migrated.

7.7.2 Display Status of Technical Reconciliation of Transactional Data

In this Customizing activity using Transaction FINS_MIG_MONITOR_RC1, you display the status of the overall technical reconciliation of transactional data pertaining to FI-AA, CO, G/L, and ML, as shown in Figure 7.30.

7.7 Technical Check of Transaction Data

▼ 📁 First Run		Finished
▼ 📁 AA - Reconciliation	REC_1_AA	Finished
• ⬚ Finished	REC_1_AA	Finished
▼ 📁 CO - Reconciliation	REC_1_CO	Finished
• ⬚ Finished	REC_1_CO	Finished
▼ 📁 GL - Reconciliation	REC_1_GL	Finished
• ⬚ Finished	REC_1_GL	Finished
▼ 📁 ML - Reconciliation	REC_1_ML	Finished
• ⬚ Finished	REC_1_ML	Finished
▼ 📁 Delta Run 1	1	Finished
▼ 📁 AA - Reconciliation	1 REC_1_AA	Finished
• ⬚ Finished	1 REC_1_AA	Finished
▼ 📁 CO - Reconciliation	1 REC_1_CO	Finished
• ⬚ Finished	1 REC_1_CO	Finished
▼ 📁 GL - Reconciliation	1 REC_1_GL	Finished
• ⬚ Finished	1 REC_1_GL	Finished
▼ 📁 ML - Reconciliation	1 REC_1_ML	Finished
• ⬚ Finished	1 REC_1_ML	Finished

Figure 7.30 Status of Technical Reconciliation of Transaction Data

Figure 7.31 shows the log for the reconciled G/L transactional data.

Display logs

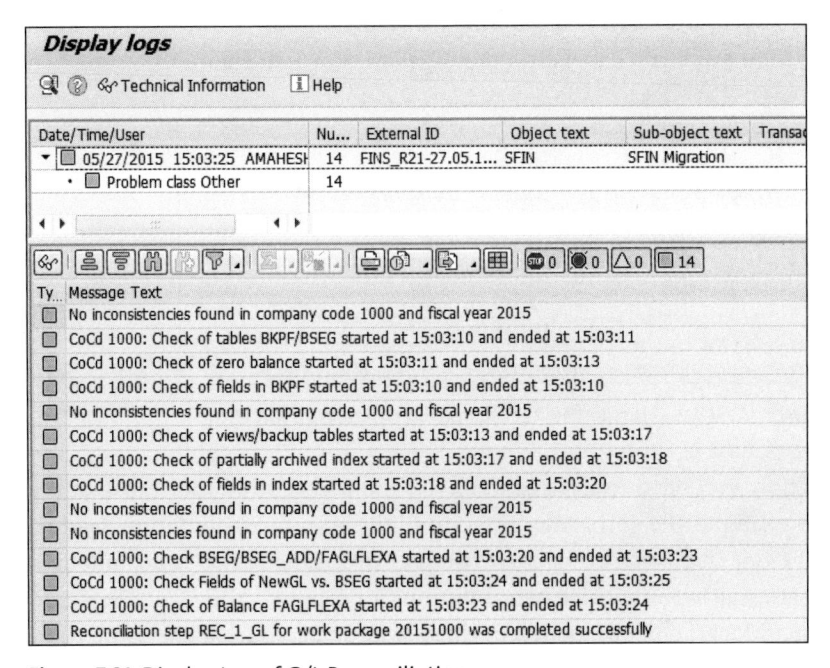

Date/Time/User	Nu...	External ID	Object text	Sub-object text	Transa
▼ 05/27/2015 15:03:25 AMAHESH	14	FINS_R21-27.05.1...	SFIN	SFIN Migration	
• Problem class Other	14				

Ty	Message Text
	No inconsistencies found in company code 1000 and fiscal year 2015
	CoCd 1000: Check of tables BKPF/BSEG started at 15:03:10 and ended at 15:03:11
	CoCd 1000: Check of zero balance started at 15:03:11 and ended at 15:03:13
	CoCd 1000: Check of fields in BKPF started at 15:03:10 and ended at 15:03:10
	No inconsistencies found in company code 1000 and fiscal year 2015
	CoCd 1000: Check of views/backup tables started at 15:03:13 and ended at 15:03:17
	CoCd 1000: Check of partially archived index started at 15:03:17 and ended at 15:03:18
	CoCd 1000: Check of fields in index started at 15:03:18 and ended at 15:03:20
	No inconsistencies found in company code 1000 and fiscal year 2015
	No inconsistencies found in company code 1000 and fiscal year 2015
	CoCd 1000: Check BSEG/BSEG_ADD/FAGLFLEXA started at 15:03:20 and ended at 15:03:23
	CoCd 1000: Check Fields of NewGL vs. BSEG started at 15:03:24 and ended at 15:03:25
	CoCd 1000: Check of Balance FAGLFLEXA started at 15:03:23 and ended at 15:03:24
	Reconciliation step REC_1_GL for work package 20151000 was completed successfully

Figure 7.31 Display Log of G/L Reconciliation

Figure 7.32 shows the log for the reconciled CO transactional data.

277

7   Data Migration

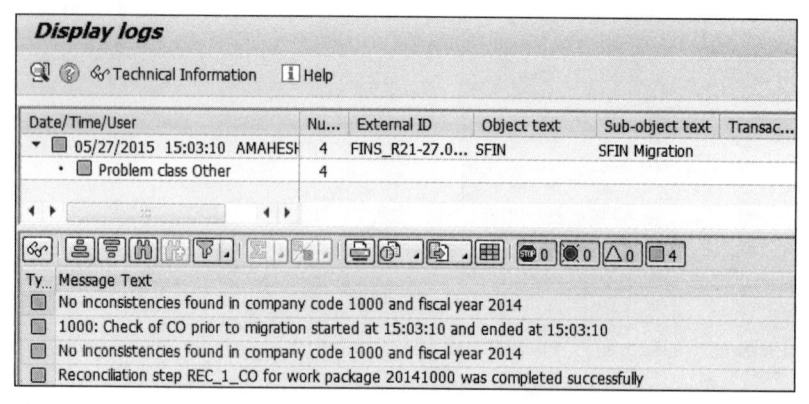

Display logs					
🔍 ⓘ 🔧 Technical Information ℹ Help					
Date/Time/User	Nu...	External ID	Object text	Sub-object text	Transac...
▼ ☐ 05/27/2015 15:03:10 AMAHESH	4	FINS_R21-27.0... SFIN		SFIN Migration	
• ☐ Problem class Other	4				

Ty...	Message Text
☐	No inconsistencies found in company code 1000 and fiscal year 2014
☐	1000: Check of CO prior to migration started at 15:03:10 and ended at 15:03:10
☐	No inconsistencies found in company code 1000 and fiscal year 2014
☐	Reconciliation step REC_1_CO for work package 20141000 was completed successfully

Figure 7.32 Display Log of CO Reconciliation

If there are any errors, the migration process must be stopped, and the error should be corrected before further migration steps are executed.

You may also come across a situation during the reconciliation of transaction data in which the system displays a list of error messages, as shown in Figure 7.33.

```
L1 1010 2012 0090000233 001: No entry in FAGLFLEXA for this line item of BSEG (Ledger L1)
L1 1010 2012 0090000233 002: No entry in FAGLFLEXA for this line item of BSEG (Ledger L1)
L1 1010 2012 0090000233 003: No entry in FAGLFLEXA for this line item of BSEG (Ledger L1)
L1 1010 2012 0100000000 001: No entry in FAGLFLEXA for this line item of BSEG (Ledger L1)
L1 1010 2012 0100000000 002: No entry in FAGLFLEXA for this line item of BSEG (Ledger L1)
L1 1010 2012 0100000000 003: No entry in FAGLFLEXA for this line item of BSEG (Ledger L1)
L1 1010 2012 0100000001 001: No entry in FAGLFLEXA for this line item of BSEG (Ledger L1)
L1 1010 2012 0100000001 002: No entry in FAGLFLEXA for this line item of BSEG (Ledger L1)
L1 1010 2012 0100000001 003: No entry in FAGLFLEXA for this line item of BSEG (Ledger L1)
L1 1010 2012 0100000002 001: No entry in FAGLFLEXA for this line item of BSEG (Ledger L1)
L1 1010 2012 0100000002 002: No entry in FAGLFLEXA for this line item of BSEG (Ledger L1)
```

Figure 7.33 Error Messages during the Reconciliation of Transaction Data

In this situation, you need to analyze the issue and identify the root cause of the error. In this example, the entry was posted in all the ledgers except for nonleading ledger L1. The document isn't ledger-specific, which means that if a document is posted, it posts to all ledgers, which happened only for company code 1010. However, when a similar document was analyzed, which was posted during the same time, then it was observed that the system posted to all ledgers within the ledger groups, as shown in Figure 7.34.

7.7 Technical Check of Transaction Data

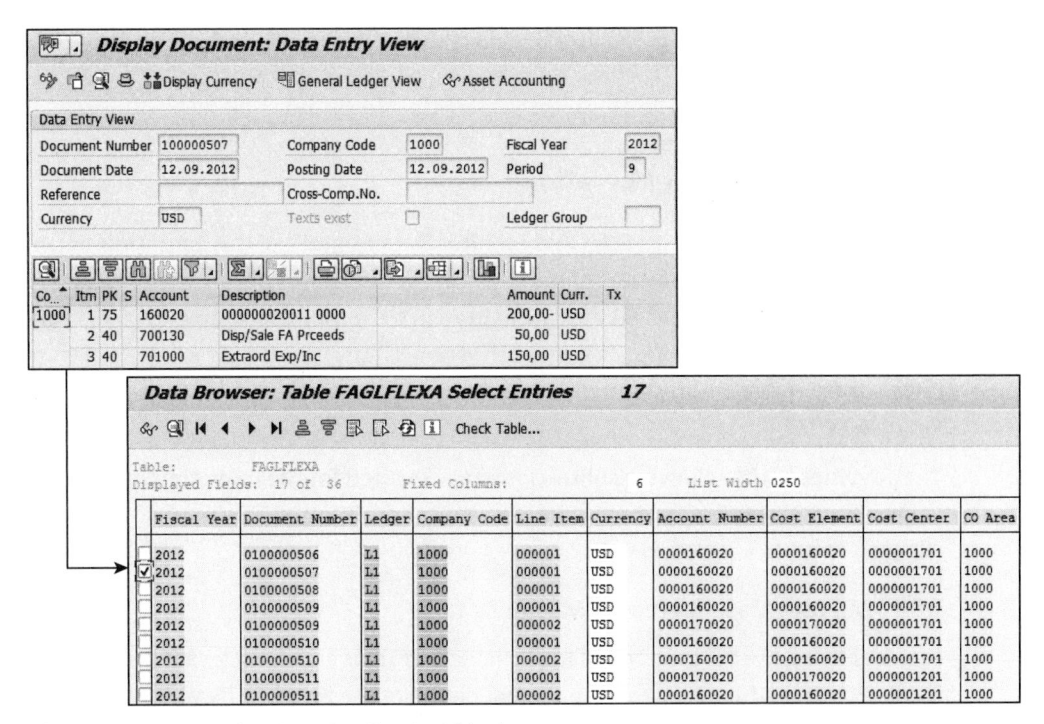

Figure 7.34 Transaction Data Posting to All Ledgers

It's possible that ledger L1 was added to the group later after the transactional data was posted.

You may also encounter an error stating that the open item flag in table BSEG differs from the open item flag in table SKB1, as shown in Figure 7.35.

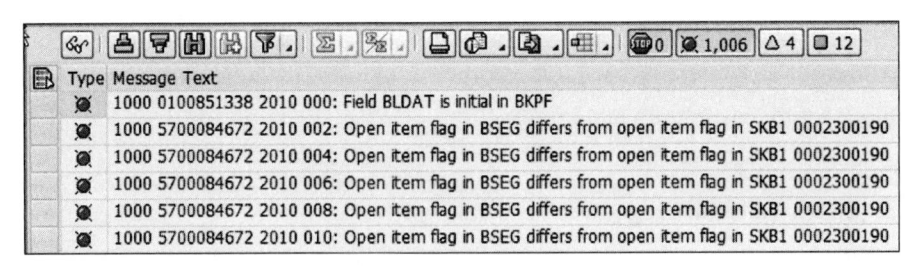

Figure 7.35 Error Message in Open Item Management

279

In this situation, we recommend referring to and implementing SAP Notes 475261, 16172, 57170, and 14285 to resolve the issues.

7.8 Material Ledger Migration

In the Customizing activity **Start and Monitor Data Migration**, the migration of the ML is executed as part of the migration process. ML migration is mandatory for SAP S/4HANA, even if the ML functionality isn't used in the source system. This migration is essential when the source system is any version of SAP ERP 6.0 or lower or when the source system is SAP S/4HANA version 1503 or lower (Simple Finance 1.0/2.0).

The activities in the following subsections are executed for the migration of material ledger.

7.8.1 Migrate Material Ledger Master Data

In this activity, the ML is activated for all valuation areas and the relevant master data is created in all ML currencies from the last period of the previous fiscal year until the period in context for the migration. This migration does not activate actual costing, which is still an optional feature in SAP S/4HANA. If you're using actual costing in the source system, data related to actual costing will be transferred to the new data structures in SAP S/4HANA using the following tables:

- ML document table MLDOC
- ML document cost component split table MLDOCCCS
- Extract of ML document table MLDOC_EXTRACT
- Extract of ML document cost component split table MLDOCCCS_EXTRACT
- Object list for costing run table MLRUNLIST

7.8.2 Check Material Ledger Master Data

Once the ML migration activity is executed, check and verify that the data migrated is correct and the values from the existing inventory and material ledger tables ties up in aggregation with the new table ACDOCA. If you encounter any significant errors that need to be corrected, you'll need to accept those errors, make the corrections, then restart the ML migration execution again.

7.8.3 Migrate Material Ledger Order History

If the ML wasn't active in the source system for any valuation area before migrating to SAP S/4HANA, this activity converts all existing purchase order history table records in tables EKBE, EKBEH, EKBZ, and EKBZH and all existing production order history table records in tables MLAUFCR and MLAUFCRH into the ML currencies.

7.8.4 Check Material Ledger Production Order and Purchase Order History

Once the ML order history records are migrated, this activity performs due diligence: it checks if all purchase order history and production order history records have been converted properly into the ML currencies.

If the data doesn't need to be migrated for the order history records, it should be deleted or archived before the migration so as to minimize the migration downtime.

7.9 Enrichment of Data

In the Customizing activity **Start and Monitor Data Migration**, you enrich and migrate transactional data into SAP S/4HANA. This Customizing activity executes and provides the status of the following key activities and steps listed:

- Enrich Transactional Data
- Display Status of Enrichment of Transactional Data
- Check of Migrated Documents
- Display Status of Check of Migrated Documents

However, if you prefer to walk through each activity rather than execute them all at once, you can. This section explains each activity.

7.9.1 Enrich Transactional Data

In this activity using Transaction FINS_MIGRATION, you enrich transaction data and documents and migrate them to SAP S/4HANA, as shown in Figure 7.36.

7 Data Migration

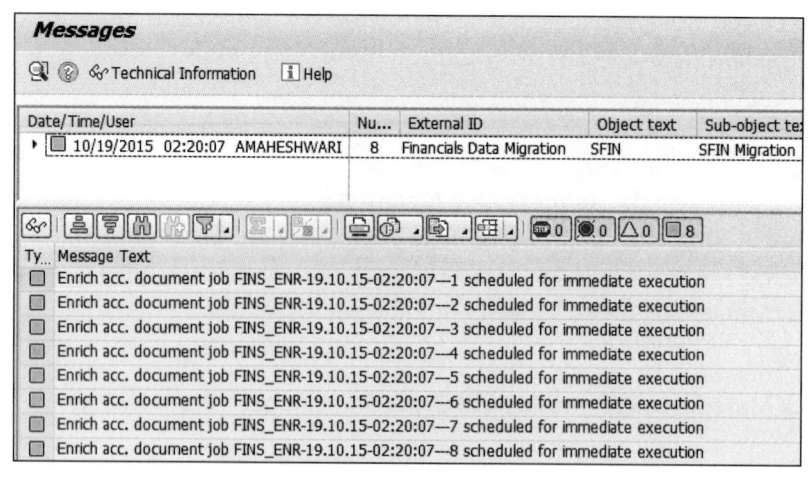

Figure 7.36 Executing Transaction Data Enrichment

This program consists of the following steps:

1. Fill table `BSEG` fields from table `BKPF`.
2. Fill table `COEP` from table `COBK` and table `OBJNR`.
3. Fill profit center fields into CO line items.
4. Fill company code data into old CO line items.
5. Fill company code data into old CO totals.
6. Fill table `BSEG_ADD` from table `FAGLBSIS/AS`.
7. Fill table `COSP_BAK-BUKRS` and table `COSS_BAK-BUKRS`.

7.9.2 Display Status of Transactional Data Enrichment

In this activity using Transaction FINS_MIG_MONITOR, you can display the status of the transactional data enrichment for SAP S/4HANA, as shown in Figure 7.37. If the checks result in errors, then you need to check and correct the error causing the migration failure. When you've completed the corrections, you must start the migration again.

7.9 Enrichment of Data

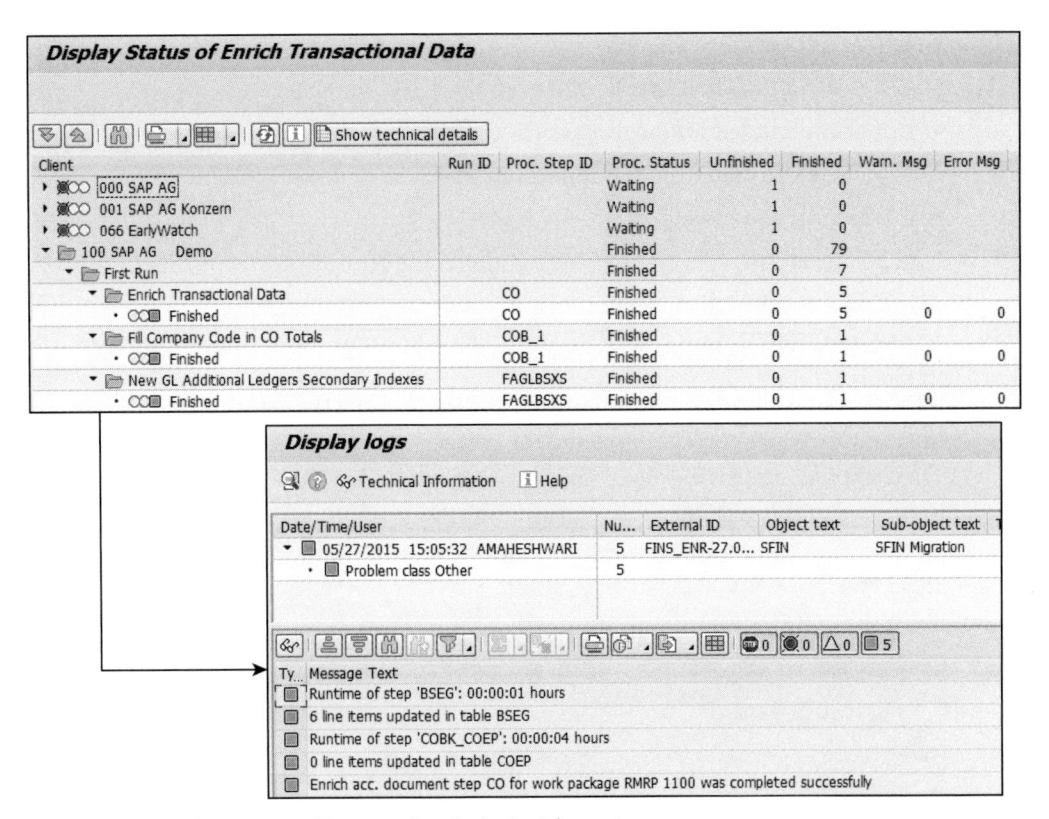

Figure 7.37 Display Status of Transaction Data Enrichment

7.9.3 Check of Migrated Documents

In this step, you need to execute the activity to check the migrated documents. You execute this step after you enrich the transactional data because it checks the result of that step of the migration. This step should be executed before the subsequent steps in Customizing related to migration of line items and migration of balances are executed because it checks fields that are used in the next migration steps.

The following documents are checked for inconsistency related to FI, CO, and any specific ledger-related posting:

283

7 Data Migration

- **G/L document**
  - Cross-check of fields replicated from table BKPF to table BSEG
- **Application index for ledger-specific clearing**
  - Fields replicated from the application index to table BSEG_ADD
- **CO document and balances**
  - All fields derived from the object number (table OBJNR) correctly filled
  - Cross-check of fields replicated from table COBK to table COEP
  - Derived fields: PRCTR, BUKRS

If the check results in errors, you must check and correct the error causing the migration failure. When you've completed the corrections, you must repeat the migration again until all errors have been resolved. The results in Figure 7.38 were found upon execution of this activity using Transaction FINS_RECON_RC2.

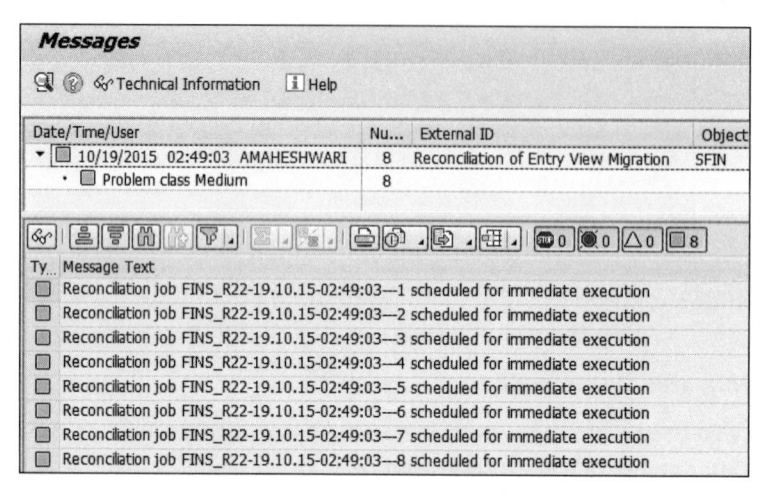

Figure 7.38 Execution of Migrated Documents Check

7.9.4 Display Status of Migrated Documents Check

In this activity, you display the status of the migrated documents using Transaction FINS_MIG_MONITOR_RC2, as shown in Figure 7.39. If there are any errors, they need to be resolved before you move to the next activity.

7.10 Migration of Line Items into New Data Structure

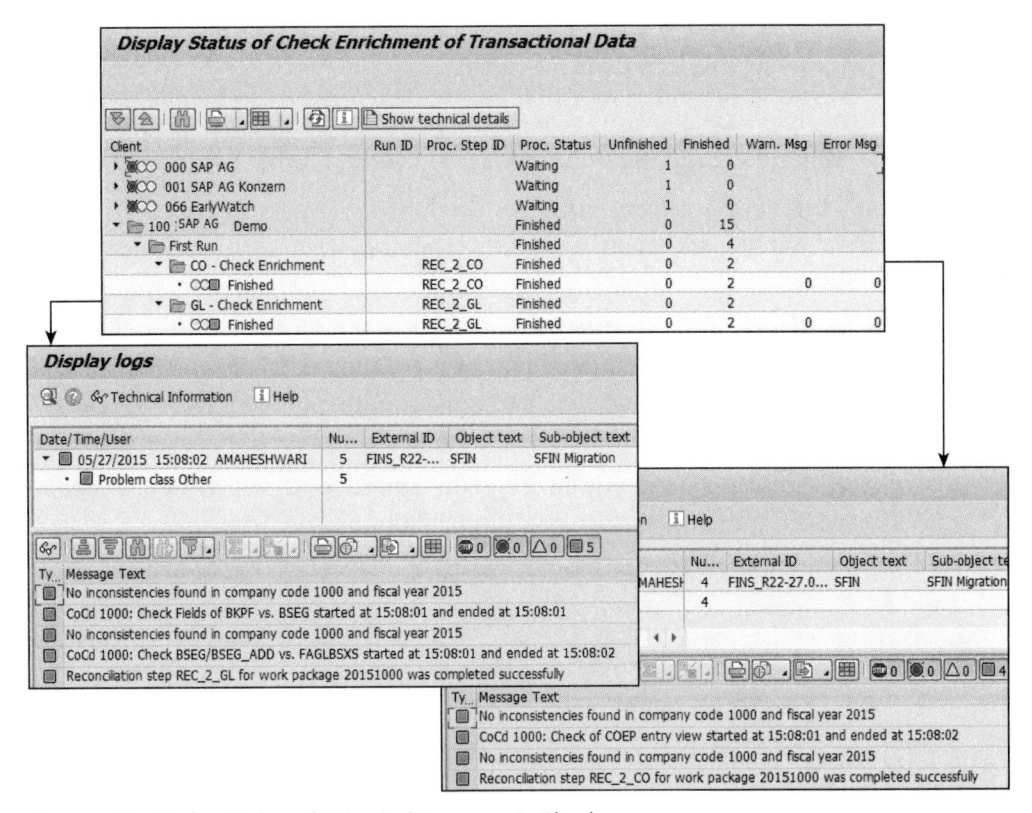

Figure 7.39 Display Status of Migrated Documents Check

7.10 Migration of Line Items into New Data Structure

After all the migration tasks related to the enrichment of data are complete, you need to migrate documents and line items to the new Universal Journal data structure. All the line items from tables BSEG, FAGLFLEXA, and COEP are migrated to table ACDOCA.

The Customizing activity **Start and Monitor Data Migration** executes and provides the status of all the following key activities and steps related to **Migration of Line Items into New Data Structure**:

- Migrate Accounting Documents to Universal Journal Entry Structure
- Display Status of Document Migration to Universal Journal Entry
- Check Migration of Accounting Documents to Universal Journal Entry
- Display Status of Check of Accounting Document Migration

285

However, if you prefer to walk through each activity rather than execute them all at once, you can. Let's walk through each activity.

7.10.1 Migrate Accounting Documents to Universal Journal Entry Structure

In this Customizing activity using Transaction FINS_MASS_DATA_MASTER, you migrate accounting documents to the Universal Journal entry structure, as shown in Figure 7.40.

You must migrate the transactional data to SAP S/4HANA before executing this step. It populates the Universal Journal entries by combining the transactional data of FI, G/L, CO, and FI-AA. In addition, the characteristics of account-based CO-PA are added to items that are assigned to a profitability segment.

If the checks result in errors, you must execute corrective actions. When you've completed and resolved all the errors, start the migration activity again.

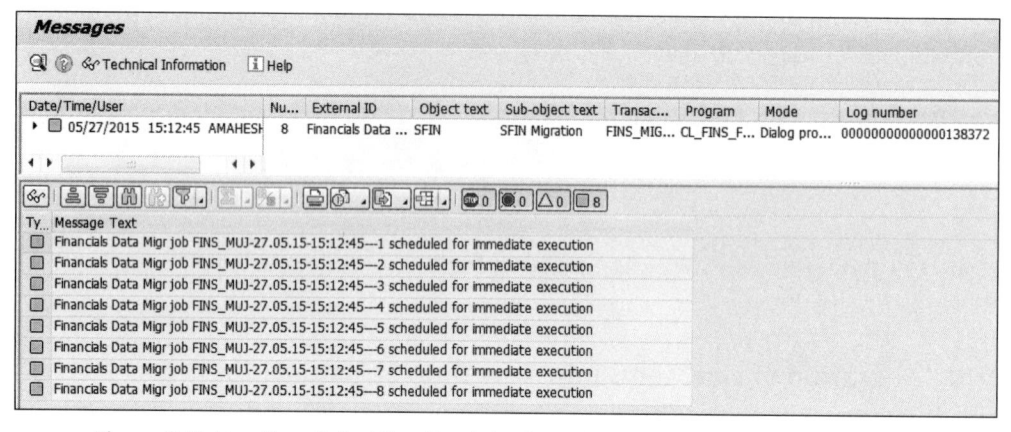

Figure 7.40 Line Item Data Migration into the Universal Journal

7.10.2 Display the Status of Document Migration to Universal Journal Entry

In this activity using Transaction FINS_MASS_DATA_MONITOR, you display the status of the migration of the accounting documents. After the **Migrate Accounting Documents to Universal Journal Entry Structure** activity is complete without any errors, the next **Display Status** step is executed as shown in the sequence of Customizing steps shown earlier. Figure 7.41 shows the error-free status of the previous activity.

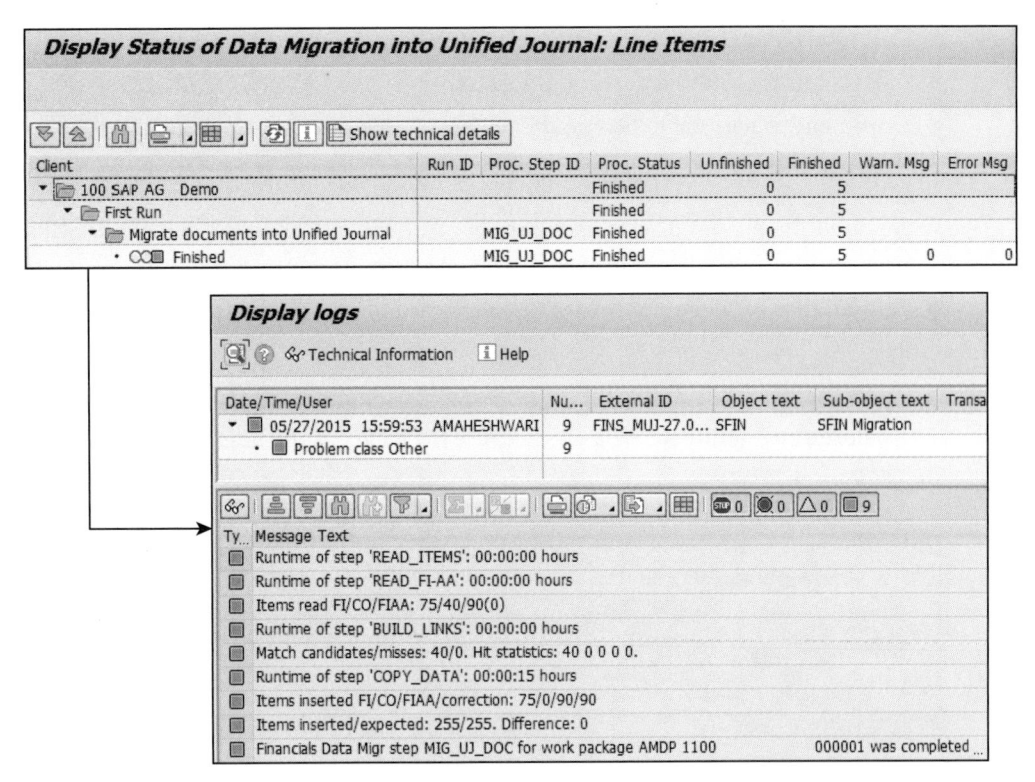

7.10 Migration of Line Items into New Data Structure

Figure 7.41 Display Status and Log for Data Migration into the Universal Journal

7.10.3 Check Migration of Accounting Documents to Universal Journal Entry

If the status of **Migration of Accounting Documents to Universal Journal Entry Structure** shows **Error** or **Warning**, then you need to recheck the accounting documents in the Universal Journal. This activity checks whether all accounting documents have been migrated correctly.

You need to execute this reconciliation step after the migration of line items of the different applications into table ACDOCA. For the new G/L, CO, and FI-AA line items, the compatibility view, which reproduces the original line item table, is compared to the original values. For table BSEG, no compatibility view exists, and the check is executed directly.

You need to consider the following former line item tables for the check:

- New G/L line item tables (e.g., table FAGLFLEXA), including industry and customer tables

287

7 Data Migration

- Cost totals for external postings (table COSP)
- Costs totals for internal postings (table COSS)
- Document header (table ANEK) and line items (table ANEP) for asset management

In addition, the following consistency checks should be performed for table ACDOCA:

- No duplicate entries (this is necessary because table ACDOCA isn't delivered with a primary key so the database ensures this condition is met)
- Zero balance for documents with line items from G/L (CO doesn't guarantee zero balance)

You must execute this step using Transaction FINS_RECON_RC3, as shown in Figure 7.42, before you migrate the balances because the balances will be calculated from the line items in the future.

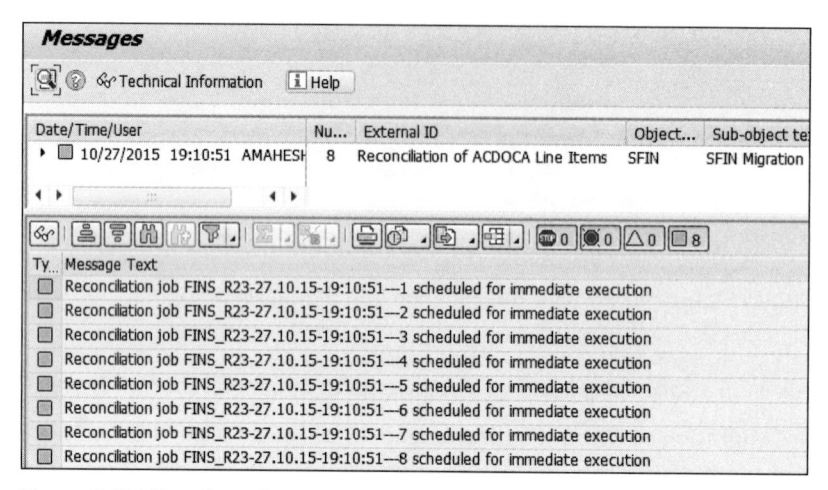

Figure 7.42 Migration of Accounting Documents

> **Expert Insight**
>
> All the previously mentioned checks need to be performed, and all errors need to be resolved before moving to the next activity.

7.10.4 Display Status of Accounting Document Migration Check

In this step, the status of the migration of accounting documents is displayed using Transaction FINS_MIG_MONITOR_RC3, as shown in Figure 7.43.

7.11 Migration of Balances

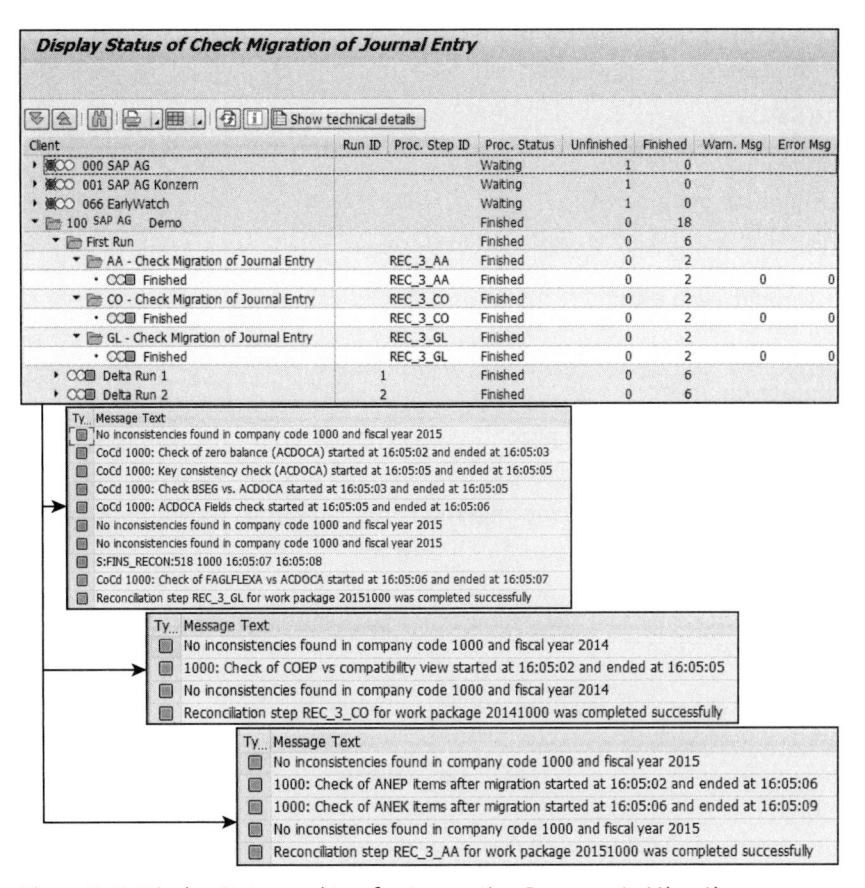

Figure 7.43 Display Status and Log for Accounting Documents Migration

You can't proceed further before resolving any errors encountered during the process.

7.11 Migration of Balances

After the **Migration of Line Items into New Data Structure** step is complete using the Customizing activity **Start and Monitor Data Migration**, you need to migrate the balances. All the delta G/L totals and line item balances and the delta CO totals and line item balances are migrated to table ACDOCA. The entries are made with a special document number starting with a letter, and they don't show up in line item reports.

Although the **Start and Monitor Data Migration** Customizing activity executes and provides the status of all the following key activities and steps related to **Migration of**

289

7   Data Migration

Balances, you can alternatively execute specific programs and transactions to check or correct these individual activities:

- Migrate Balances
- Display Status of Migration of Balances
- Check Migration of Balances
- Display Status of Check of Migration of Balances

Let's walk through each activity.

7.11.1   Migrate Balances

In this activity using Transaction FINS_MASS_DATA_MASTER, you need to migrate the balances as shown in Figure 7.44. You must execute this step even in clients that have no transactional data so that the migration program can set the status of the client to **Finished**.

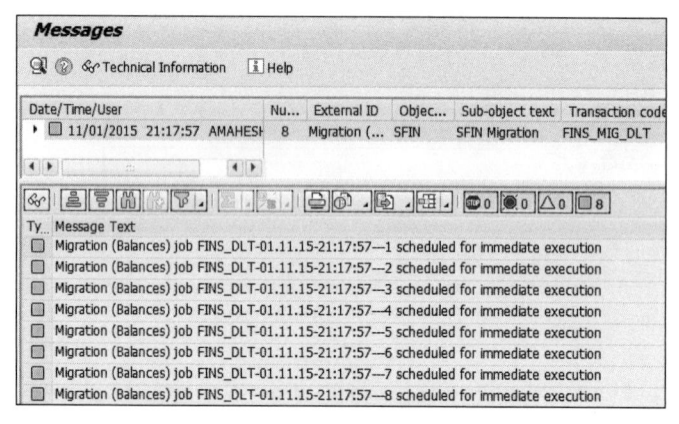

Figure 7.44   Execute Migration of Balances

If the check results in errors, you must check and correct the error causing the migration failure. When you've completed the corrections, you must start the migration again until all the errors are resolved.

7.11.2   Display Status of Migration of Balances

After the migration activity is complete, you'll have to check the status by executing the **Display Status of Balance Migration** activity using Transaction FINS_MASS_DATA_MONITOR.

7.11 Migration of Balances

In our example, four error messages appeared during this execution, as shown in the **Error Message Log** in Figure 7.45. If you encounter any errors, you must first analyze the errors before you move to execute the next steps.

Client	Run ID	Proc. Step ID	Proc. Status	Unfinished	Finished	Warn. Msg	Error Msg
▼ 🗁 100 SAP AG Demo			Finished	0	8		
▼ 🗁 First Run			Finished	0	8		
▼ 🗁 Migration of Balances (all Applications)	DLT		Finished	0	6		
• ☐ Finished	DLT		Finished	0	6	0	4
▼ 🗁 Customer Master (Transaction Figures)	KNCX		Finished	0	1		
• ☐ Finished	KNCX		Finished	0	1	0	0
▼ 🗁 Vendor Master (Transaction Figures)	LFCX		Finished	0	1		
• ☐ Finished	LFCX		Finished	0	1	0	0

Figure 7.45 Display Status of Balance Migration

Figure 7.46 shows the details of some errors that you might encounter while executing the migration of balances.

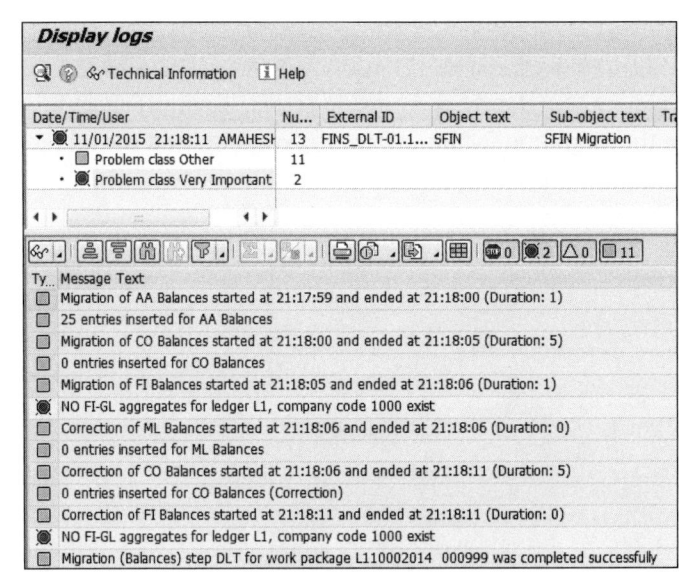

Display logs

Date/Time/User	Nu...	External ID	Object text	Sub-object text	Tr
▼ ● 11/01/2015 21:18:11 AMAHESH	13	FINS_DLT-01.1...	SFIN	SFIN Migration	
• ☐ Problem class Other	11				
• ● Problem class Very Important	2				

Ty... Message Text
- Migration of AA Balances started at 21:17:59 and ended at 21:18:00 (Duration: 1)
- 25 entries inserted for AA Balances
- Migration of CO Balances started at 21:18:00 and ended at 21:18:05 (Duration: 5)
- 0 entries inserted for CO Balances
- Migration of FI Balances started at 21:18:05 and ended at 21:18:06 (Duration: 1)
- NO FI-GL aggregates for ledger L1, company code 1000 exist
- Correction of ML Balances started at 21:18:06 and ended at 21:18:06 (Duration: 0)
- 0 entries inserted for ML Balances
- Correction of CO Balances started at 21:18:06 and ended at 21:18:11 (Duration: 5)
- 0 entries inserted for CO Balances (Correction)
- Correction of FI Balances started at 21:18:11 and ended at 21:18:11 (Duration: 0)
- NO FI-GL aggregates for ledger L1, company code 1000 exist
- Migration (Balances) step DLT for work package L110002014 000999 was completed successfully

Figure 7.46 Error Log for Migration of Balances

Existing aggregates from subledgers won't be corrected to a balance that is consistent with G/L because no such balance exists. This issue needs to be investigated and resolved before moving forward with the next step.

291

7.11.3 Check Migration of Balances

In this activity using Transaction FINS_RECON_RC4, you need to check if all balances have been migrated correctly. Execute this reconciliation step after the balances for applications such as G/L, CO, FI-AA, and ML have been migrated into table ACDOCA and other related tables. For every former table containing aggregated information, there is a compatibility view that reproduces it. This reconciliation step checks and reconciles the balances and values for all fields. As information from different applications is merged, you need to resolve any deviations for the following situations:

- There are inconsistencies between aggregates from different applications, and the system doesn't reconcile in G/L.
- The system takes the cost center from CO and doesn't reconcile this field in FI.
- The system takes the amount from ML and doesn't reconcile this field in FI.
- The system doesn't reconcile the logical system (LOGSYS) in FI.
- If the aggregates from one application are already archived for a given fiscal year, but they aren't archived for a different application for the same fiscal year, these values aren't shown for any of the applications.

Therefore, you need to execute the transaction check migration of balances to find the results as shown in Figure 7.47. If the check results in errors, you must check and correct the error causing the migration failure. When you've completed the corrections, you must start the migration again.

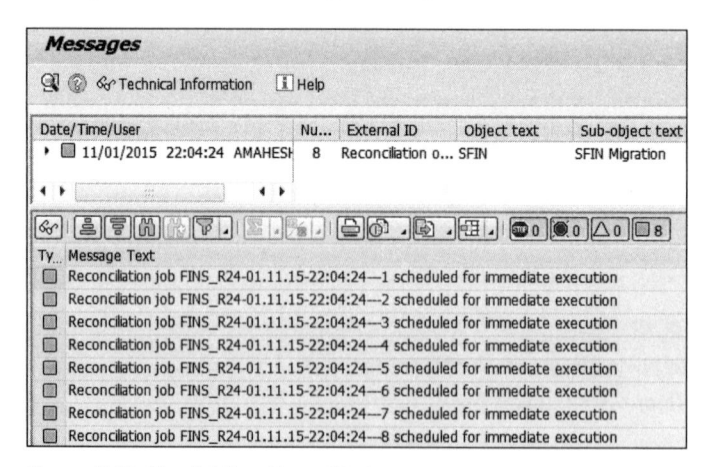

Figure 7.47 Check Migration of Balances

7.11.4 Display Status of Migration of Balances Check

In this activity using Transaction FINS_MIG_MONITOR_RC4, you display the status of the migration of balances, as shown in Figure 7.48.

Figure 7.48 Displaying the Status of the Migration of Balances Check

In your migration, you may see errors like the ones in Figure 7.49.

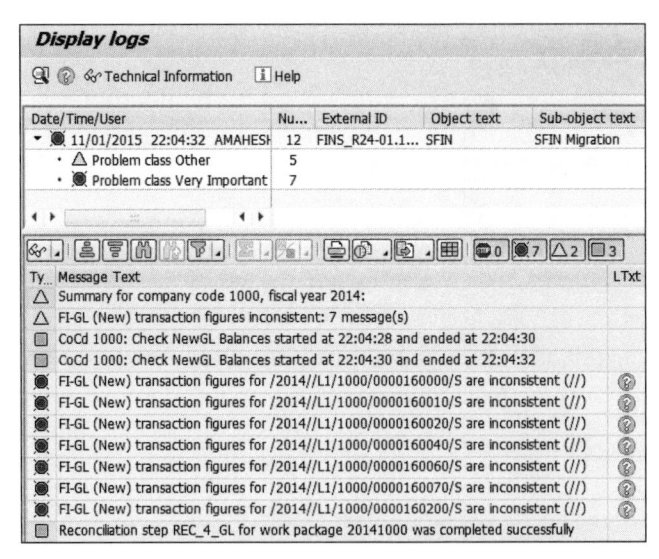

Figure 7.49 Error Log in G/L while Checking Migration of Balances

For existing entries in table FAGLFLEXT_BCK, you can use Transaction SE16 with the FGLV_REC_N_SUM view to analyze inconsistencies between the FAGLFLEXT view and

7　Data Migration

table `FAGLFLEXT_BCK`. If you check table `ACDOCA`, you'll find that items exist with no relation to document numbers, as shown in Figure 7.50.

ACDOCA: Display of Entries Found

Table to be searched		ACDOCA		Universal Journal Entry Line Ite			
Number of hits		25					
Runtime		0		Maximum no. of hits	50		

Ld	CoCode	Year	DocumentNo	LnItm	GLFY	Account	LCurr	LC Amount
L1	1000	2014	DA00000000	000001	2014	160000	USD	231,826.08
L1	1000	2014	DA00000000	000002	2014	160000	USD	51,608.68
L1	1000	2014	DA00000000	000003	2014	160000	USD	231,826.08
L1	1000	2014	DA00000000	000004	2014	160010	USD	16,000,000.00
L1	1000	2014	DA00000000	000005	2014	160010	USD	16,000,000.00
L1	1000	2014	DA00000000	000006	2014	160020	USD	800,000.00
L1	1000	2014	DA00000000	000007	2014	160020	USD	212,000.00
L1	1000	2014	DA00000000	000008	2014	160020	USD	800,000.00
L1	1000	2014	DA00000000	000009	2014	160020	USD	212,000.00
L1	1000	2014	DA00000000	000010	2014	160040	USD	99,563.26

Figure 7.50 Checking Table ACDOCA for Document Numbers

Now, investigating further, you'll find that in ledger L1, the balance for account 160000 was carried forward from the previous year, 2014, as shown in Figure 7.51.

Balance Display: G/L Accounts For the Ledger L1

Account Number	160000	Land & Land Imprvmts
Company Code	1000	Aldo Inc.
Fiscal Year	2014	
All Documents in Currency	*	Display Currency　USD

Period	Debit	Credit	Balance	Cumulative balance
Bal.Carryforward				515,260.84
1				515,260.84
2				515,260.84
3				515,260.84
4				515,260.84
5				515,260.84
6				515,260.84
7				515,260.84
8				515,260.84
9				515,260.84
10				515,260.84
11				515,260.84
12				515,260.84
13				515,260.84
14				515,260.84
15				515,260.84
16				515,260.84
Total				515,260.84

Figure 7.51 G/L Account 160000 Balance in Ledger L1

When checking the same G/L account 160000 balance in the leading ledger OL, you'll find that there was no balance carryforward that happened from the previous fiscal year (in our case, in Figure 7.52, this is 2014).

Balance Display: G/L Accounts For the Ledger OL				
Document Currency	Document Currency	Document Currency		
Account Number		160000	Land & Land Imprvmts	
Company Code		1000	Aldo Inc.	
Fiscal Year		2014		
Display More Chars				
All Documents in Currency		*	Display Currency	USD

Period	Debit	Credit	Balance	Cumulative balance
Bal.Carryforward				
1				
2				
3				
4				
5				
6				
7				
8				
9				
10				
11				
12				
13				
14				
15				
16				
Total				

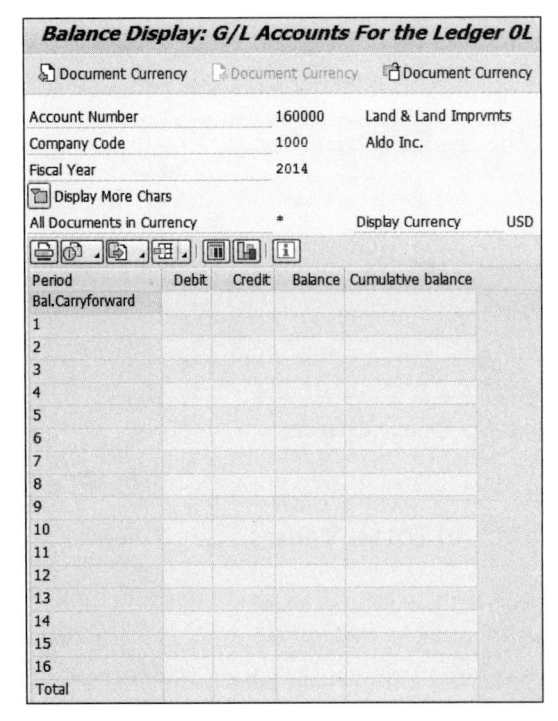

Figure 7.52 G/L Account 160000 Balance in Ledger OL

If you check the balance of account 160000 for ledger L1 in table FAGLFLEXT_BCK, you'll find that no balance exists in this table. This means that there should also be no such entry in table ACDOCA.

On further investigation, the data entry view for account 160000 looked fine, but the G/L view for ledger L1 definitely had an error because there was no credit entry in the document posting. In table ACDOCA, the credit entry has been stored without document reference, which triggered the error. Similarly, Figure 7.53 depicts the error as encountered in the migration of balances in the CO section.

7 Data Migration

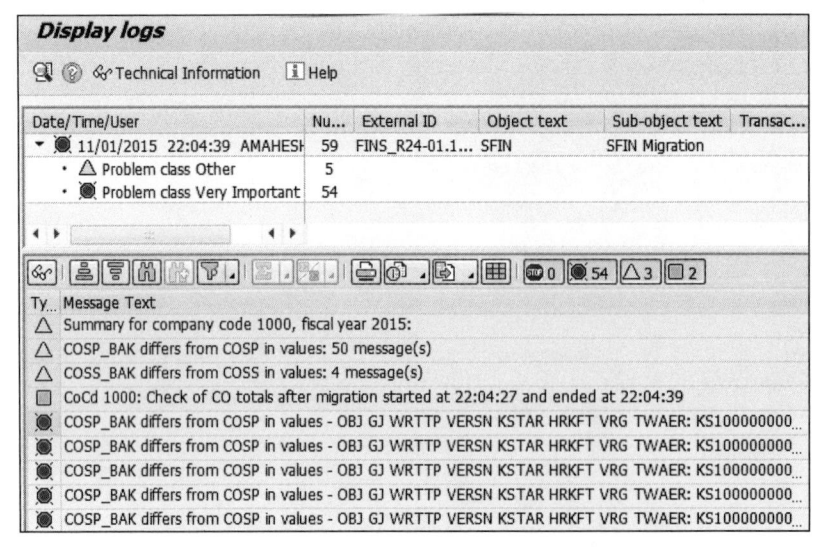

Figure 7.53 Error Log in CO While Checking Migration of Balances

7.12 Calculation of Depreciation and Totals Values

The planned depreciation values for FI-AA need to be built as part of the migration of balances where the following prerequisites must be met:

- The Customizing steps for the new Asset Accounting have been completed.
- New Asset Accounting has been activated.
- General Ledger Accounting and FI-AA's transactional data have been migrated.

Although the Customizing activity **Start and Monitor Data Migration** executes and provides the status of all the following key activities and steps related to **Calculation of Depreciation and Total Values**, as an alternative, you can also execute specific programs and transactions to check or correct these individual activities:

- **Calculate Initial Depreciation Values**
- **Display Status of "Calculate Initial Depreciation Values"**
- **Check Initial Depreciation and Total Values**
- **Display Status of "Check Initial Depreciation and Total Values"**

Let's walk through each activity.

7.12.1 Calculate Initial Depreciation Values

Perform this activity using Transaction FINS_MIG_AFA to build the planned depreciation values for FI-AA, as shown in Figure 7.54. This activity is based on program FAA_DEPRECIATION_CALCULATE, which is related to the calculation of depreciation.

Identifying the cumulative depreciation of an asset and posting the depreciation expense in FI take place in the system at different points in time:

- The planned depreciation is determined either with any change in the asset master record or with any posting on the asset related to acquisition or retirement, and it's updated in the database on a real-time basis.
- The execution of the depreciation run adopts the planned asset values and posts them in FI. The document posting is updated in FI at the individual asset level.

You execute this activity after you've migrated the transaction data. However, if you have difficulty doing this due to time and resource constraints, it's possible to defer the execution of this activity, but you must ensure that the activity is executed at the latest by the time the first run takes place to post depreciation.

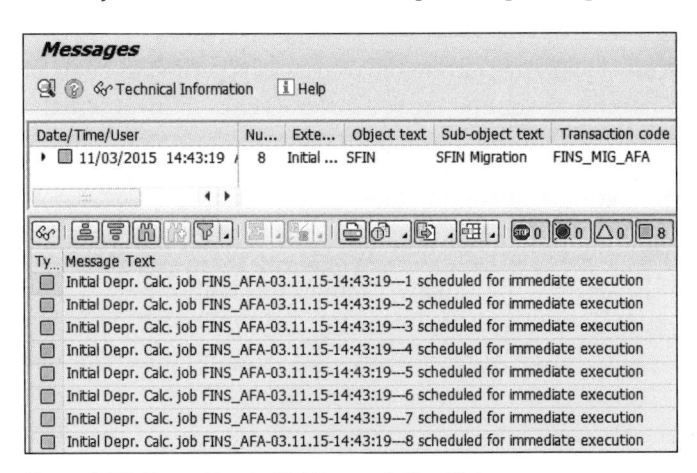

Figure 7.54 Executing Initial Depreciation Values

You need to run the program with the following settings:

- **General Selections**
  Don't specify any restrictions.
- **Further Options**
  Check program FAA_DEPRECIATION_CALCULATE (Calculate Depreciation) for possible system overload.

7   Data Migration

- **Parameters for Test Run**
  Execute the program in an **Update Run**.

7.12.2   Display Status of Calculate Initial Depreciation Values

In this activity using Transaction FINS_MIG_MONITOR_AFA, you display the status for the calculation of initial depreciation values, as shown in Figure 7.55.

Figure 7.55 Display Status of Initial Depreciation Calculation

In our example, we encountered an error during the display that needed to be fixed using Transaction AFAR. This must be done before you can proceed to the next activity.

7.12.3   Check Initial Depreciation and Total Values

In this Customizing activity using Transaction FINS_RECON_RC5, you once again reconcile the total values and the depreciation values, as shown in Figure 7.56.

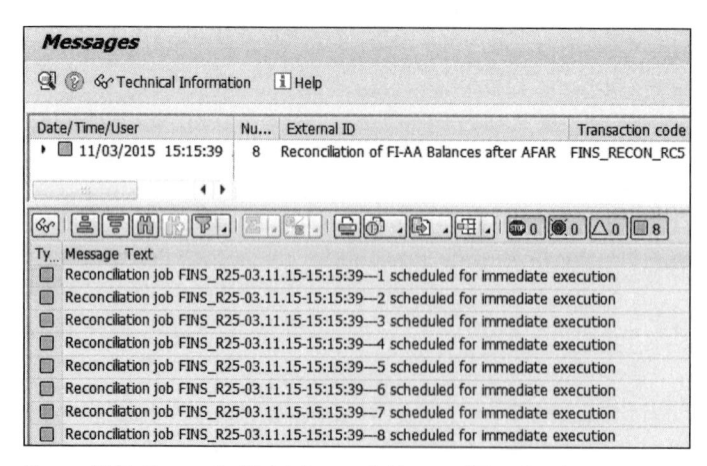

Figure 7.56 Reconcile FI-AA Depreciation and Total Balances

7.12.4 Display Status of Check Initial Depreciation and Total Values

In this activity using Transaction FINS_MIG_MONITOR_RC5, you display the status for the check on the initial depreciation values and total values, as shown in Figure 7.57.

Figure 7.57 Display Status of Check Initial Depreciation Calculation

In this activity, you might encounter some error messages that need to be corrected before you can move to the next activity. If you deep-dive into the error message shown in Figure 7.57, you'll find that, in this case, there is a mismatched balance for table ANLC (see Figure 7.58).

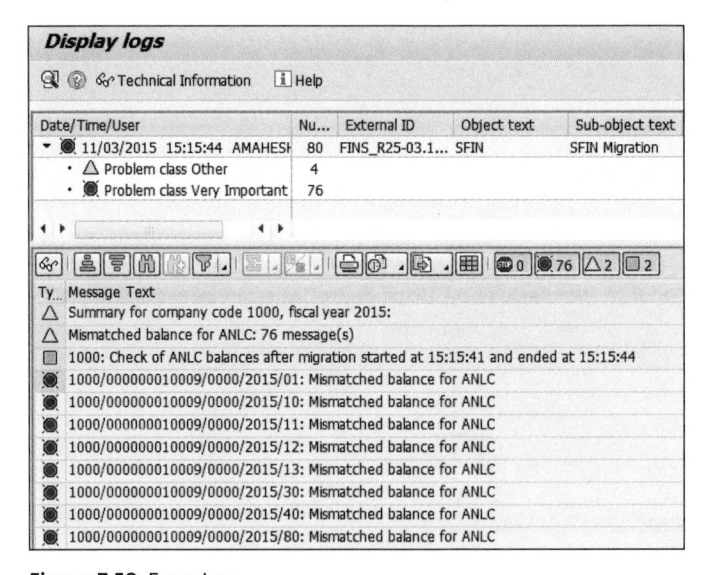

Figure 7.58 Error Log

Upon analyzing the entries for **Asset 10009** in table ANLC for the relevant fiscal year, you'll find that no depreciation is posted for this asset (see Figure 7.59).

7   Data Migration

Table to be searched	ANLC	Asset Value Fields	
Number of hits	8		
Runtime	00:00:02	Maximum no. of hits	500

CoCode	Asset	SNo.	Year	Area	Acq.year	Acq.Code	Per	No.	Error	EUL	/ DSL	/ Asset value	Ord. dep.
1000	10009	0	2015	1								20,000.00	0.00
1000	10009	0	2015	10								20,000.00	0.00
1000	10009	0	2015	11								20,000.00	0.00
1000	10009	0	2015	12								20,000.00	0.00
1000	10009	0	2015	13								20,000.00	0.00
1000	10009	0	2015	30								31,500.00	0.00
1000	10009	0	2015	40								20,000.00	0.00
1000	10009	0	2015	80								20,000.00	0.00

Figure 7.59 Table ANLC Display for Error Resolution

Now, on the other side, if you check the Asset Explorer using Transaction AW01N for the same asset balances, you'll find that depreciation was posted for this asset, as shown in Figure 7.60.

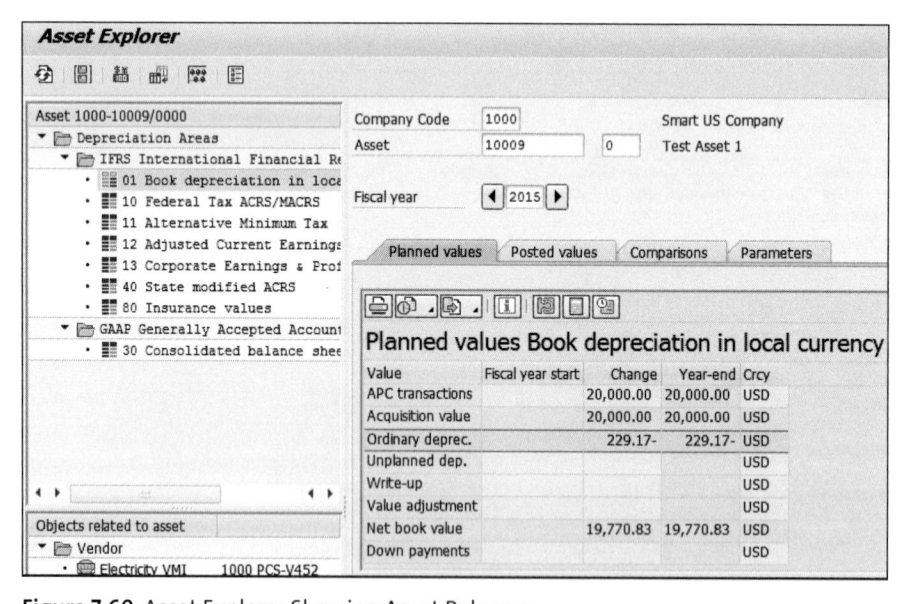

Figure 7.60 Asset Explorer Showing Asset Balances

Thus, you must analyze all these errors on a case-by-case basis and resolve them based on the error messages as displayed in the logs. Finally, when you run the status

300

check for initial depreciation calculation, you should be able to get the log to where the depreciation and total values are reconciled and synced in full (see Figure 7.61).

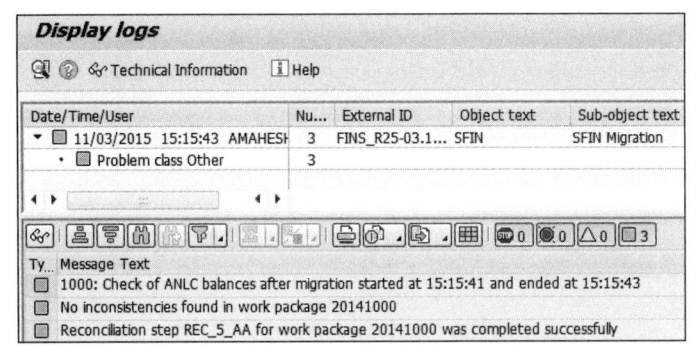

Figure 7.61 Display Log after the Resolution of Errors

You may encounter a **Line Items ANEP/ANEA Differs from Totals ANLC** error, as shown in Figure 7.62.

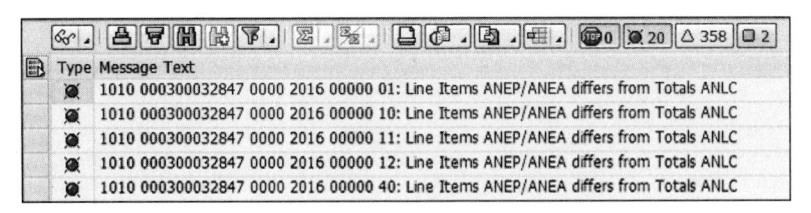

Figure 7.62 Error Log for Reconciliation of Transaction Data

> **Expert Insight**
>
> We recommend running program FINS_MIG_AA_CHECK_RC45 using Transaction SE38. This program identifies differences by analyzing tables ANEA, ANLP, and ANLC and helps in the reconciliation process.

7.13 Migrate General Ledger Allocations

In this Customizing activity using Transaction FINS_MIG_GL_ALLOC, you need to adjust and change the existing G/L allocation cycles for actual values based on assessments and distributions. This is necessary because an allocation cycle references a sum table that might have been replaced by the new Universal Journal entry table.

7   Data Migration

All G/L allocation cycles that refer to the new flexible G/L summary table FAGLFLEXT are changed to the new ACDOCA compatibility view of the new Universal Journal entry in cycle-dependent table entries. In addition, all field usage definitions for fields of table FAGLFLEXT are copied to new entries for the same fields of the ACDOCA compatibility view to ensure that the migrated cycle definitions remain valid.

Perform the following steps for this activity:

1. Run the program with both **Test Run** and **Extended Checks** selected, and select **Display Log**, as shown in Figure 7.63.

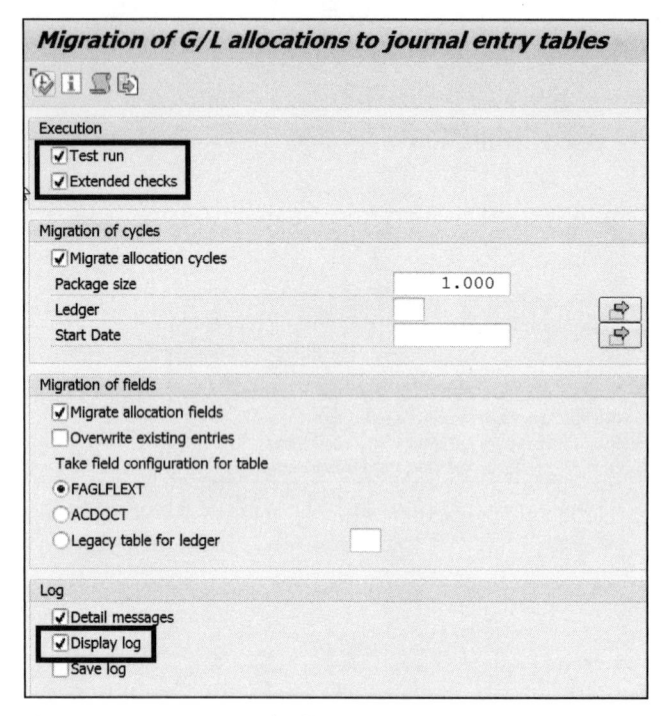

Figure 7.63 Executing G/L Allocation Migration in Test Mode

2. Analyze the messages and resolve any errors.
3. Run the program again in update mode by *unchecking* the **Test Run** checkbox shown in Figure 7.63. If several records are to be migrated, it's advisable to execute the report in the background. You can also restrict the operation to a set of individual ledgers.
4. Check the log to ensure that no problems are reported, as shown in Figure 7.64.

7.13 Migrate General Ledger Allocations

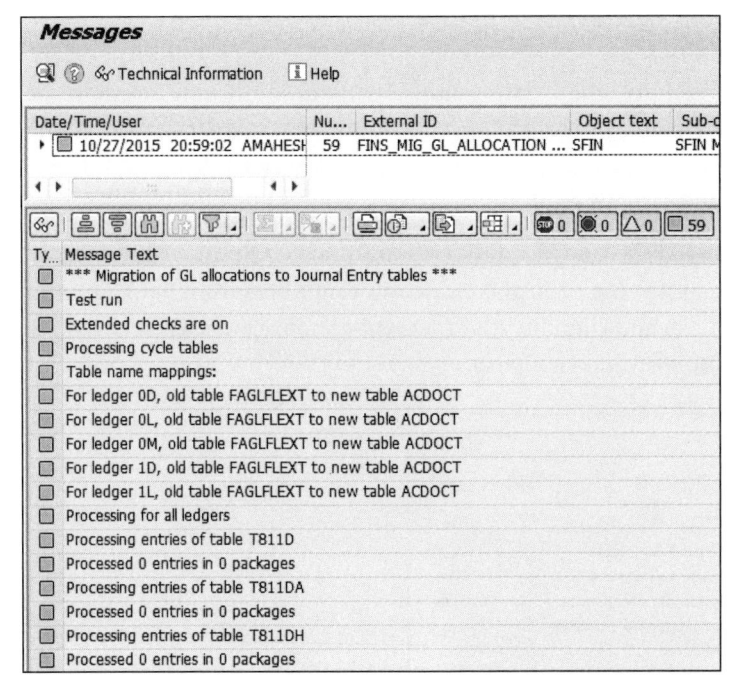

Figure 7.64 Test Run for Migration of G/L Allocation with No Errors

5. Check the allocation settings by running Transaction GCA9 after you've reviewed the log, and resolve any inconsistencies. The execution of Transaction GCA9 should result in the message shown in Figure 7.65.

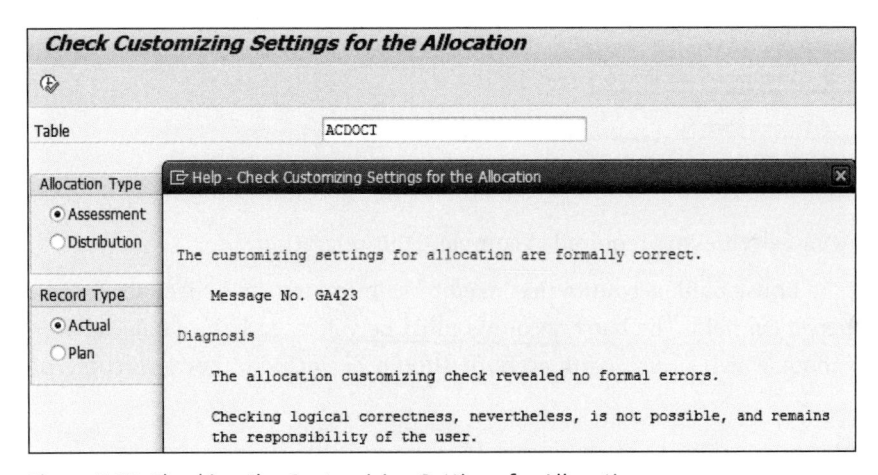

Figure 7.65 Checking the Customizing Settings for Allocation

303

7.14 Migrate House Bank Accounts

In this Customizing activity, the existing house bank account data needs to be migrated to the bank account master data in Bank Account Management (see Figure 7.66). The logic of deriving bank account numbers from house bank account data is defined technically by creating a BAdI.

The BAdI is used in the SAP Cash and Liquidity Management component. You can use this BAdI to define the mapping logic of bank account numbers from Bank Account Management in SAP Cash and Liquidity Management to house bank account data in bank master data (FI-BL-MD) and vice versa.

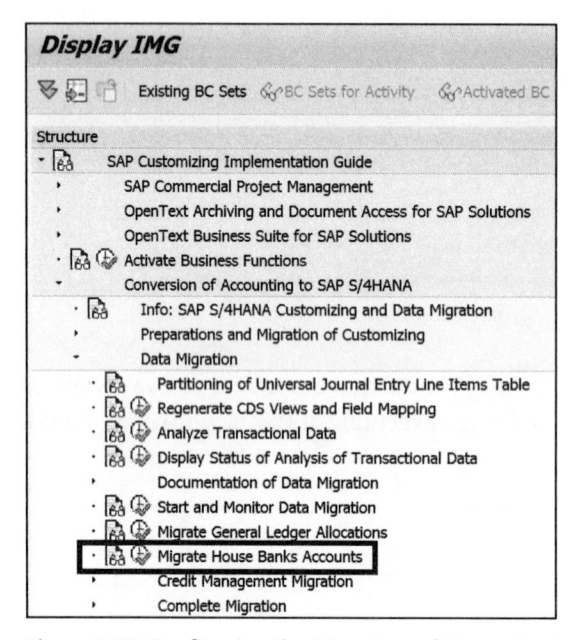

Figure 7.66 Configuring the Migration of House Bank Accounts

The following activities are required to complete this migration step:

1. Select the house bank accounts that need to be migrated, and specify a date in the **Opened On** field. The bank accounts must be validated before a decision is made about which house bank account should be included because some of

the house bank accounts might have been closed or may be no longer active in the system.

2. Set the account types for multiple house bank accounts by selecting the house bank account entries, and then click the **Set Account Type** button.
3. Click the **Execute** button at the top left within Transaction FCLM_BAM_TRANSACTION.
4. Bank accounts are created based on selected house bank accounts. Verify the migration status by checking the **Status** icon displayed at the end of each house bank account entry, as shown in Figure 7.67.
5. Some data isn't stored with house bank accounts and thus can't be created automatically. In such cases, you must maintain the required attributes manually for each bank account in the Web Dynpro application using Transaction NWBC, or you can perform a mass import of data from an XML file by using the Import and Export Bank Accounts tool.

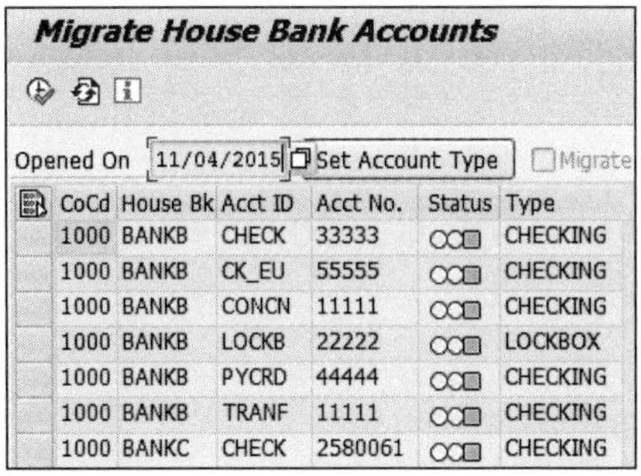

Figure 7.67 Migrate House Bank Accounts

7.15 Credit Management Migration

SAP Credit Management now resides in the Financial Supply Chain Management (FIN-FSCM-CR) component. Transaction UKM_BP is new and is used to edit master data for all credit management activities.

The Customizing activity for migration of credit management data is shown in Figure 7.68.

7   Data Migration

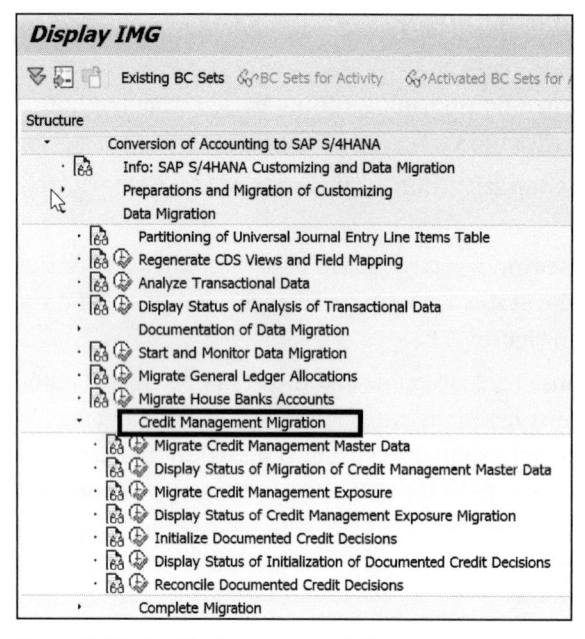

![Display IMG screenshot showing the Structure tree with Conversion of Accounting to SAP S/4HANA expanded, highlighting Credit Management Migration with its sub-activities]

Figure 7.68 Credit Management Migration

The following activities are executed during the credit management migration execution:

- Migrate Credit Management Master Data
- Display Status of Migration of Credit Management Master Data
- Migrate Credit Management Exposure
- Display Status of Credit Management Exposure Migration
- Initialize Documented Credit Decisions
- Display Status of Initialization of Documented Credit Decisions
- Reconcile Documented Credit Decisions

Let's walk through each activity.

7.15.1   Migrate Credit Management Master Data

The customer master record, which is now maintained as a business partner in SAP S/4HANA, is associated with one risk class for all the segments. The credit limit for the customer is computed with the following logic while migrating the risk class data:

- If the credit control area is mapped to the main segment, the credit limit of the customer is migrated from this credit control area.
- If the credit control area is not mapped to the main segment but a centralized customer master data is maintained, the credit limit of the customer will be computed and migrated from this central master data.
- If the credit control area is not mapped to the main segment and a centralized customer master data also is not maintained, the credit limit of the customer will be computed and migrated as the sum of all credit limits from all credit control areas for that customer.

7.15.2 Display Status of Migration of Credit Management Master Data

Check the status of the migration of credit management master data. You need to take corrective action if you encounter any errors during the migration.

7.15.3 Migrate Credit Management Exposure

In this Customizing activity, the credit values of open orders and deliveries are migrated to the credit exposure, and the historical payment pattern data from credit management is recalculated based on the data stored in Account Receivables. The migrated credit exposure data is checked using Transaction UKM_BP.

7.15.4 Display Status of Credit Management Exposure Migration

Check the migration status of credit exposure related to the values of open order and deliveries as committed and the recalculation of historical payment behavior and patterns.

7.15.5 Initialize Documented Credit Decisions

In SAP S/4HANA, all sales and delivery documents that are blocked by SAP Credit Management are managed with documented credit decisions using Transaction UKM_CASE, as shown in Figure 7.69. You use this activity to initialize documented credit decisions in SAP Credit Management, which can then be easily searched to analyze, check, release, or reject the blocked documents.

7   Data Migration

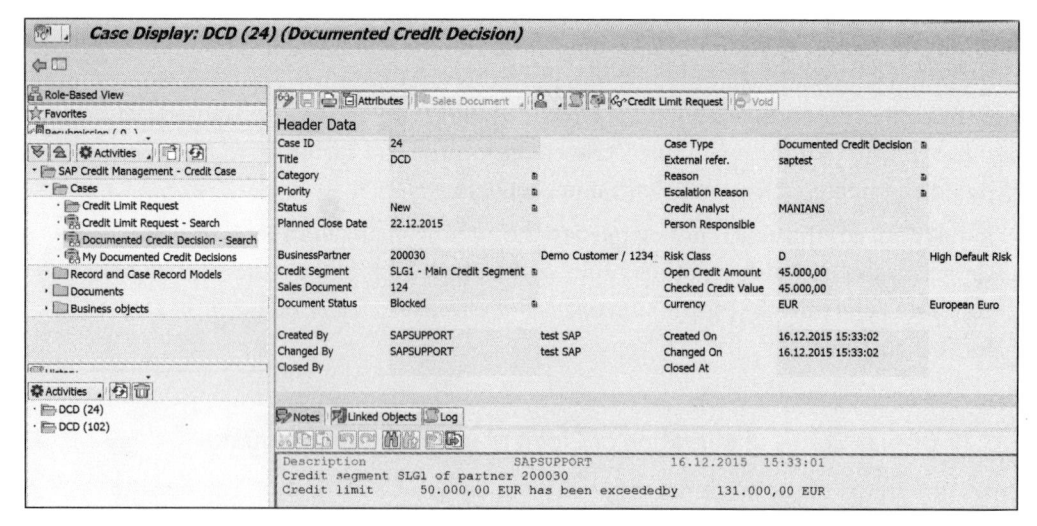

Figure 7.69 Documented Credit Decision

7.15.6 Display Status of Initialization of Documented Credit Decisions

Check the migration status of all the sales and delivery documents that are blocked by SAP Credit Management.

7.15.7 Reconcile Documented Credit Decisions

In this Customizing activity, you can reconcile a documented credit decision created for each of the sales and delivery documents blocked by SAP Credit Management.

7.16 Complete the Migration

In this Customizing activity, you'll extract all the reports and reconcile the reports and data as compiled in Chapter 1, Section 1.12, before the migration (see Figure 7.70). This ensures that the migration to SAP S/4HANA has been carried out successfully.

7.16 Complete the Migration

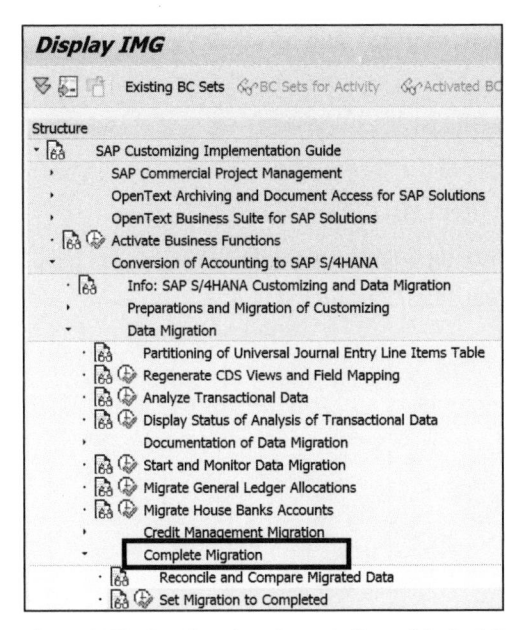

Figure 7.70 Configuring Completion of Data Migration

7.16.1 Reconcile and Compare Migrated Data

Perform the following comparisons and reconciliations for the migrated data and ledgers to ensure that the migration has been performed successfully and correctly:

1. Reconcile source ledger 0 with leading ledger 0L, as shown in Figure 7.71. To perform this activity, use Transaction GCAC (Ledger Comparison).
2. If you've used a currency ledger, reconcile this ledger with the leading ledger 0L using Transaction GCAC.
3. Compare the data and key figures after the migration with the data before the migration by running the following programs and transactions:
   - Program RFBILA00: Financial Statements
   - Program RAGITT_ALV01: Asset History Sheet
   - Program RAHAFA_ALV01: Depreciation Run for the Planned Depreciations
   - Transaction S_ALR_87013611: Totals Report for Cost Centers
   - Program RKKBSELL: Sales Order Selection
   - Program RFSSLD00: G/L Account Balance List
   - Program RFSOP000: G/L Line Items List

309

7 Data Migration

- Program RFBELJ00: Compact Document Journal
- Program RFKUML00: Vendor Sales
- Program RFKEPL00: Vendor Open Item List
- Program RFKUML00: Customer Sales
- Program RFDEPL00: Customer Open Item List
- Program RFDAUB00: Customer Recurring Entry Original Documents
- Transaction GR55: Cost Centers: Actual/Plan/Variance

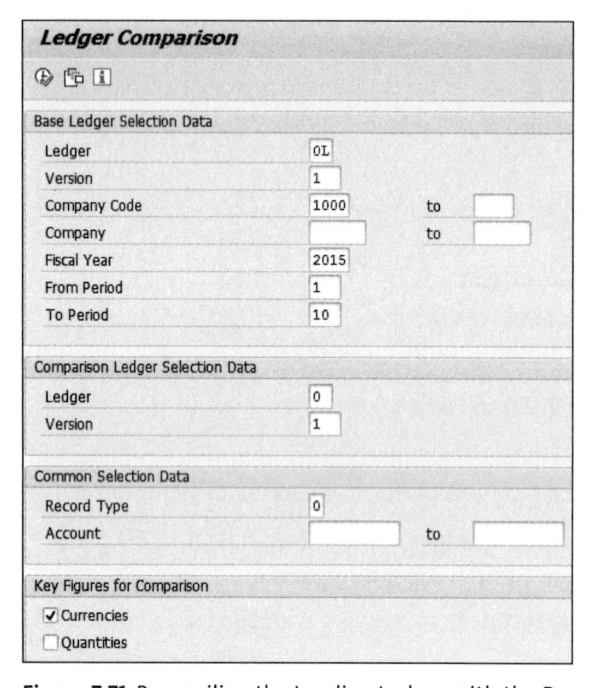

Figure 7.71 Reconciling the Leading Ledger with the Base Ledger

7.16.2 Set Migration to Completed

If the comparison of the data doesn't produce any errors, you've completed the migration successfully. In this activity, you set the migration status to **Complete**. After the settings for migration are completed, users can make postings in the system.

The **Completed** indicator should be set only if you've finished all activities required for a complete migration, your data is complete, and you've corrected all erroneous data during the migration process.

7.17 Migration with Near-Zero Downtime

Reducing the business downtime requires minimizing the technical downtime (optimization of the software update tools) and the time spent on other tasks executed in the downtime—for example, ramp-down, implementation of customer transports, validation procedures, and so on.

The NZDT method has been designed and introduced to minimize the downtime related to SAP software updates. The process is recommended when it's critical for the organization's business to feel minimal effects from the transition and migration to SAP S/4HANA. In the NZDT procedure, the most critical steps are performed on the clone system (discussed ahead) and are completed during uptime. The risk related to these tasks is removed from the downtime. If any unexpected incident occurs, the issue can be resolved on the clone without impacting the business downtime due to unavailability of the system. If critical errors are identified in the downtime and the migration needs to be cancelled, the previous production system will still be available and can be reconnected and provided to end users with minimal effort.

On the other hand, this method requires hardware investment and more resources, time, and effort, which, in turn, leads to a higher cost of migration.

7.17.1 Near-Zero Downtime

The NZDT method includes the following actions:

1. Create a clone of the production system.
2. Perform an upgrade of the existing system to SAP ERP 6.0 EHP 7 or above with SAP HANA as the database.
3. Install SAP S/4HANA Finance on this clone system.
4. Perform SAP S/4HANA Finance data migration and validation.
5. Inform the business users about the downtime required for performing delta migration and final data validation.
6. Resync the migrated clone with the production system; the clone system now becomes the new production system.

The following activities are performed in the production system before creating the clone of the production system:

- Precheck whether SAP S/4HANA Finance can be installed
- Conduct consistency checks

- Close all prior periods
- Take snapshots of all the relevant reports

7.17.2 Restrictions on Business

The following restrictions are imposed on the business in the production system after the clone of the production system has been created:

- General (FI/CO/AA)
  - No archiving
  - No Customizing changes
  - No changes in repository
  - No postings in closed periods
- FI-AA-specific
  - No data transfer for asset data (Transaction AS91)
  - No asset depreciation postings with old depreciation Report RABUCH
  - No asset deactivations via asset transfer posting or full/complete retirement
  - No year-end closing activities in FI-AA (Transactions AJRW, AJAB)
  - No data corrections in FI-AA using any of the reports starting with RACORR*
  - No opening of closed fiscal years
  - No changes in settlement for assets under construction (Transaction AIAB)

7.17.3 Activities on the Clone System

The following activities must be carried out in the clone system:

1. Upgrade to EHP 7 or above and then to SAP S/4HANA Finance.
2. Move all the transports, including SAP S/4HANA Finance Customizing transports.
3. Create CDS views, and redirect custom codes to these new compatible views.
4. Prepare and customize G/L, FI-AA, and CO.
5. Perform migration activities that include migration of cost elements, technical checks of transaction data, enrichment of data, and migration of line items and balances.
6. Perform data validation.

7.17.4 Delta Migration

You start the SAP S/4HANA Finance delta migration by executing program FINS_MIGRATION_START using Transaction SA38 by setting the **Near-Zero-Downtime Mode** parameter (see Figure 7.72). There is no alternative to starting the migration in delta mode.

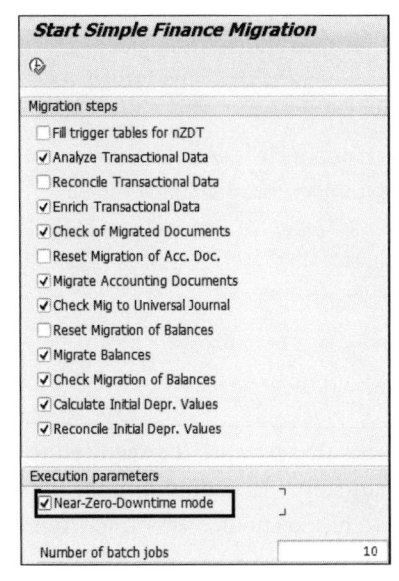

Figure 7.72 Program FINS_MIGRATION_START

Use Transaction FINS_MIG_STATUS to get an overview of all migration activities, whether you're using NZDT or not (see Figure 7.73).

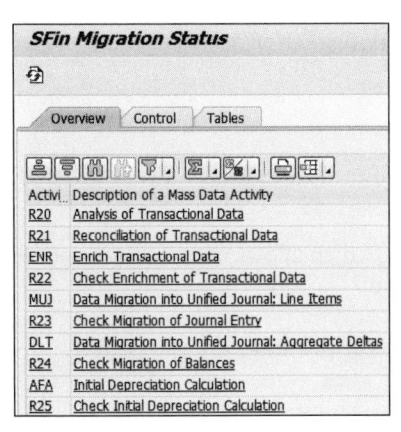

Figure 7.73 Transaction FINS_MIG_STATUS

7 Data Migration

Any errors encountered need to be corrected before moving to the next step, involving data validation and the activities required after the migration.

> **1709 Preview**
>
> With the introduction and usage of the Migration Cockpit starting in SAP S/4HANA 1709, data from the legacy source systems (both SAP and non-SAP systems) can now be migrated and loaded directly to the target SAP S/4HANA system through an RFC connection without first transferring and extracting the data to the intermediate files.
>
> The Migration Cockpit supports standard templates, as well as more fields for the migration of standard objects such as materials, customers, and vendors. Even custom objects can be migrated using the migration object modeler. Transaction LTMC is used to migrate the data via the Migration Cockpit.

7.18 Summary

Ensure that the authorization object FINS_MIG is activated because it's required to execute SAP S/4HANA migration activities. You can start the migration after any period close, but the sequence of steps that needs to be executed is very important here.

In the data migration phase, some of the activities that you'll execute include the following:

- Migrating secondary cost elements into a chart of accounts
- Analyzing and reconciling transaction data prior to migration
- Adding attributes to FI documents and CO line items
- Transferring and merging balances from G/L, FI-AA, CO, and ML applications into Universal Journal table ACDOCA
- Reporting the financial data as consistent when compared with the reports from the premigrated system
- Marking the migration indicator as **Completed**, which allows users to make postings again in the system

Let's now move on to Chapter 8, in which we'll discuss postmigration activities.

Chapter 8
Postmigration Activities

This chapter focuses on postmigration activities, including validating business processes and transactions that used to run before the migration, filling in the due dates and offsetting accounts, and transferring index tables to cold storage to optimize memory consumption and ensure faster data processing.

After the migration and installation of SAP S/4HANA Finance is complete, you need to ensure that the data is reconciled and consistent with the premigration reports. Some of the steps you need to perform in this phase include validating the processes in a test environment, executing postmigration activities such as filling in the offsetting account in SAP ERP Financials documents, ensuring that the house bank accounts have been migrated, and creating cold partitions for the backup tables of the indexes for data aging (see Figure 8.1).

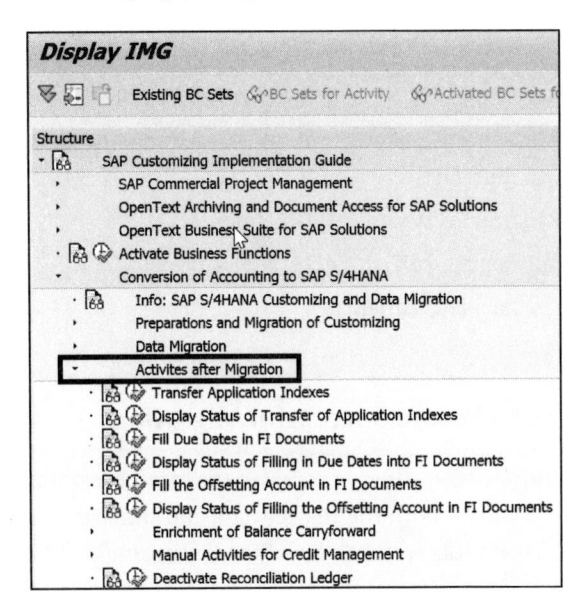

Figure 8.1 Configuring the Activities after Migration

8 Postmigration Activities

This chapter discusses each of these activities in turn. Remember that the postmigration activities can only start after the SAP S/4HANA Finance migration is set to **Complete**. We recommend that they be executed during system downtime, but you may execute them later if you wish.

8.1 Run Reconciliation Reports to Check Data Consistency

You need to execute the following reports and document the results to compare and reconcile the postmigration data with the data extracted before the migration. Any discrepancy found after comparing both data sets needs to be analyzed and resolved to prevent data inconsistency going forward. We recommend that you execute the following programs, reports, and transactions for this purpose:

- Program RFBILA00: Financial Statements
- Report RAGITT_ALV01: Asset History Sheet
- Report RAHAFA_ALV01: Depreciation Run for Planned Depreciation
- Program RKKBSELL: Sales Order Selection
- Report RFSSLD00: SAP General Ledger (G/L) Account Balance List
- Report RFSOPO00: G/L Line Items List
- Program RFBELJ00: Compact Document Journal
- Report RFKUML00: Vendor Sales
- Report RFKOPO00: Vendor Open Item List
- Report RFKUML00: Customer Sales
- Report RFKOPO00: Customer Open Item List
- Report RFDAUB00: Customer Recurring Entry Original Documents
- Transaction S_ALR_87013611: Totals Report for Cost Centers
- Transaction GR55: Cost Centers: Actual/Plan/Variance

8.2 Validate Business Process to Ensure Successful Migration

You need to execute all the transactions and business processes that are necessary for the organization to function and validate both the master data and transaction data to ensure that the migration has been successful. Some of the key business processes to validate include the following:

- Posting journal entries and accruals
- Checking the account determination logic in goods receipt/invoice receipt (GR/IR)
- Making invoice and inventory-related postings
- Executing depreciation runs
- Checking asset-related postings such as asset acquisition and retirement
- Making and receiving payments and clearing open items
- Performing the activities related to period-end close
- Executing and validating the key financial reports and balances related to profit centers, cost centers, Profitability Analysis (CO-PA), and financial statements

8.3 Transfer Application Indexes

If you're using data aging with business function `DAAG_DATA_AGING` active, start moving the indexes into the cold area of the database using Transaction FINS_MIG_INIT_COLD, as shown in Figure 8.2. This step transfers application indexes to the database cold area to reduce main memory consumption and improve system performance.

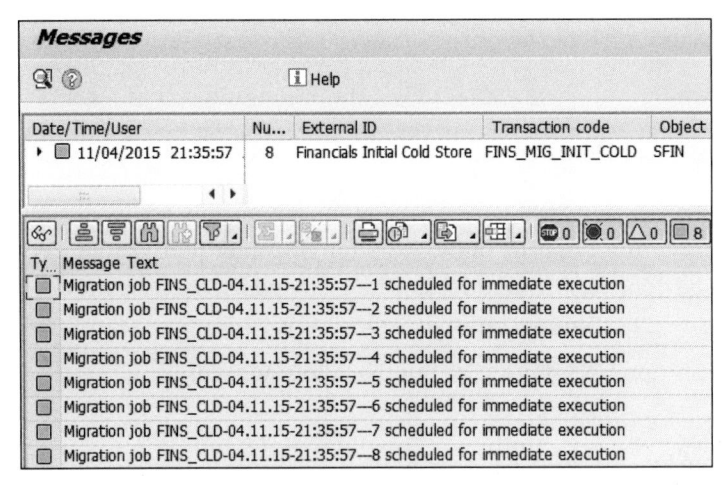

Figure 8.2 Transfer of Application Indexes

Application indices that correspond to already archived documents are stored in tables `BSIS_BCK`, `BSAS_BCK`, `BSID_BCK`, `BSAD_BCK`, `BSIK_BCK`, `BSAK_BCK`, `FAGLBSIS_BCK`, and `FAGLBSAS_BCK`. This program transfers these table entries into the cold area of the database.

8.4 Display Status of Application Indexes Transfer

In this activity, you can display the status of the application indexes transfer to the database cold area using Transaction FINS_MIG_MONITOR_CLD, as shown in Figure 8.3. The authorization objects required for this activity are S_DAAG and S_DAGPTM.

Display Status of Mass Data Process

Client	Run ID	Proc. Step ID	Proc. Status	Unfinished	Finished	Warn. Msg	Error Msg
▸ 000 SAP AG			Waiting	1	0		
▸ 001 SAP AG Konzern			Waiting	1	0		
▸ 066 EarlyWatch			Waiting	1	0		
▾ 100 SAP AG Demo			Finished	0	10		
▾ First Run			Finished	0	5		
▾ GL/AP/AR Secondary Indexes		INDEX	Finished	0	5		
· Finished		INDEX	Finished	0	5	0	0
▸ Delta Run 1	1		Finished	0	5		

Figure 8.3 Display Status of Application Indexes Transfer

If there are no errors, you can move to the next step. All errors need to be thoroughly investigated in the log and corrected before proceeding to the next step.

8.5 Fill Due Dates in FI Documents

You need to execute Transaction FINS_MIG_DUE in the Customizing activity to fill the new due date field in the financial documents for customer and vendor line items. This must also be done for G/L account line items for which the baseline date field is part of the line item posting, as shown in Figure 8.4.

The execution of Transaction FINS_MIG_DUE fills the following fields:

- Field SK1DT (Due Date for Discount 1)
- Field SK2DT (Due Date for Discount 2)
- Field NETDT (Net Due Date)

8.6 Display Status of Filling Due Dates in Financial Documents

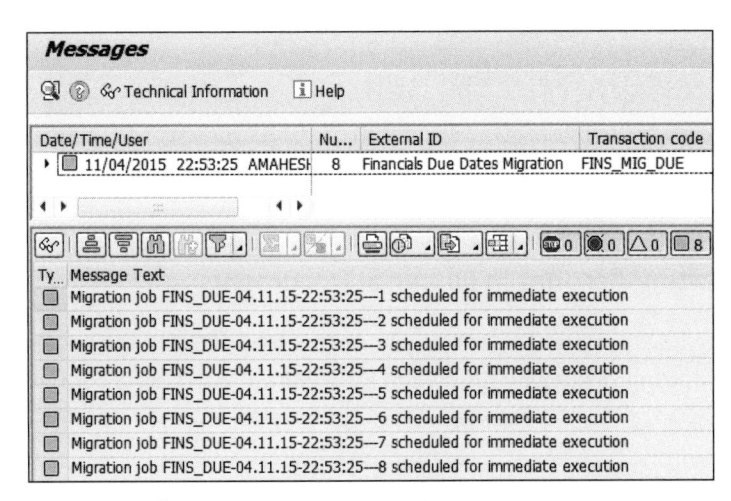

Messages			
Date/Time/User	Nu...	External ID	Transaction code
▶ 11/04/2015 22:53:25 AMAHESH	8	Financials Due Dates Migration	FINS_MIG_DUE

Ty	Message Text
☐	Migration job FINS_DUE-04.11.15-22:53:25—1 scheduled for immediate execution
☐	Migration job FINS_DUE-04.11.15-22:53:25—2 scheduled for immediate execution
☐	Migration job FINS_DUE-04.11.15-22:53:25—3 scheduled for immediate execution
☐	Migration job FINS_DUE-04.11.15-22:53:25—4 scheduled for immediate execution
☐	Migration job FINS_DUE-04.11.15-22:53:25—5 scheduled for immediate execution
☐	Migration job FINS_DUE-04.11.15-22:53:25—6 scheduled for immediate execution
☐	Migration job FINS_DUE-04.11.15-22:53:25—7 scheduled for immediate execution
☐	Migration job FINS_DUE-04.11.15-22:53:25—8 scheduled for immediate execution

Figure 8.4 Fill Due Dates in FI Documents

8.6 Display Status of Filling Due Dates in Financial Documents

In this activity, you display the status of filling the due dates in FI documents using Transaction FINS_MIG_MONITOR_DUE, as shown in Figure 8.5.

Display Status of Fill Due Dates in FI Documents

Client	Run ID	Proc. Step ID	Proc. Status	Unfinished	Finished	Warn. Msg	Error Msg
▶ ◯◯ 000 SAP AG			Waiting	1	0		
▶ ◯◯ 001 SAP AG Konzern			Waiting	1	0		
▶ ◯◯ 066 EarlyWatch			Waiting	1	0		
▼ 🗁 100 SAP AG Demo			Finished	0	2		
▼ 🗁 First Run			Finished	0	1		
▼ 🗁 Net Due Date and Discount Due Dates		DUE_DATES	Finished	0	1		
• ◯◯▦ Finished		DUE_DATES	Finished	0	1	0	0

Figure 8.5 Display Status of Filling in Due Dates

The following processing statuses may be displayed:

- **Waiting**
  Data packages that haven't yet been processed
- **Finished**
  Data packages that have been successfully processed without any errors

8 Postmigration Activities

- **Issues Found**
  Data packages that have error messages in the log

Any error message needs to be investigated and resolved before moving to the next step. You can use Transactions SM37 and SLG1 to complete your investigation.

8.7 Fill the Offsetting Account in Financial Documents

After the due dates are filled without any errors, you can proceed with filling the offsetting account in FI documents using Transaction FINS_MIG_GKONT, as shown in Figure 8.6.

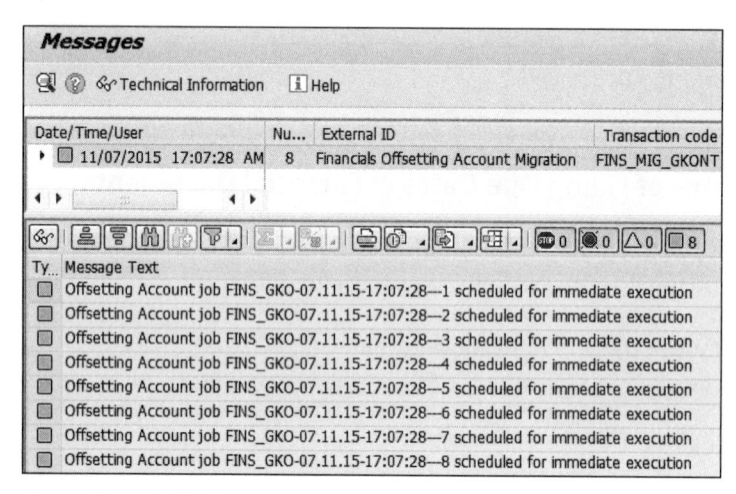

Figure 8.6 FI Offsetting Account Migration

This Customizing activity fills the following fields:

- Field GKONT (Offsetting Account Number)
- Field GKART (Offsetting Account Type)
- Field GHKON (G/L Offsetting Account in General Ledger)

As a prerequisite, you need to define the offsetting account determination type before you fill the offsetting account in FI documents. We recommend choosing the **As Case 2, but Including Line Items Generated Automatically** option when defining the offsetting account determination, as shown in Figure 8.7.

8.8 Display Status of Filling Offsetting Account in Financial Documents

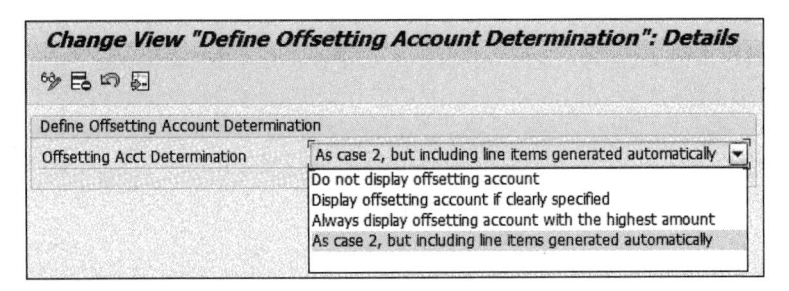

Figure 8.7 Define Offsetting Account Determination

8.8 Display Status of Filling Offsetting Account in Financial Documents

In this activity, you display the status of filling the offsetting account in FI documents using Transaction FINS_MIG_MONITOR_GKO, as shown in Figure 8.8.

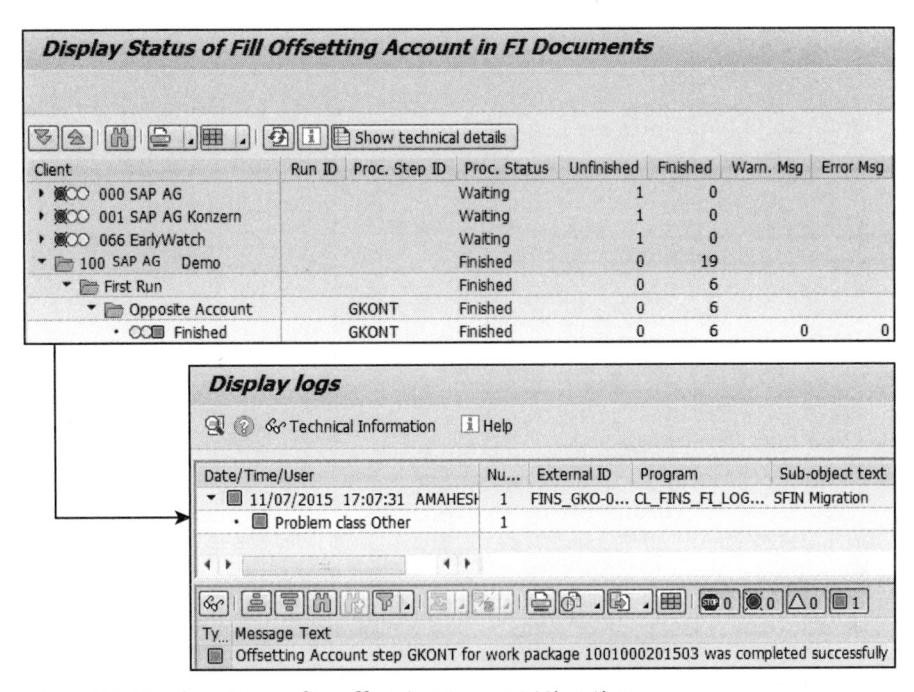

Figure 8.8 Display Status of FI Offsetting Account Migration

321

8 Postmigration Activities

If you don't find any errors, then you can proceed to the data check activity. Any error message needs to be checked, analyzed, and corrected before proceeding further. You can use Transaction SM37 and Transaction SLG1 to complete your investigation.

8.9 Enrichment of Balance Carryforward

During the migration to SAP S/4HANA, this activity involves enriching the balance carryforward, as shown in Figure 8.9. It's also an optional step that can be executed any time after the balances have been migrated. The prerequisite is that all the periods of the previous fiscal year must be closed.

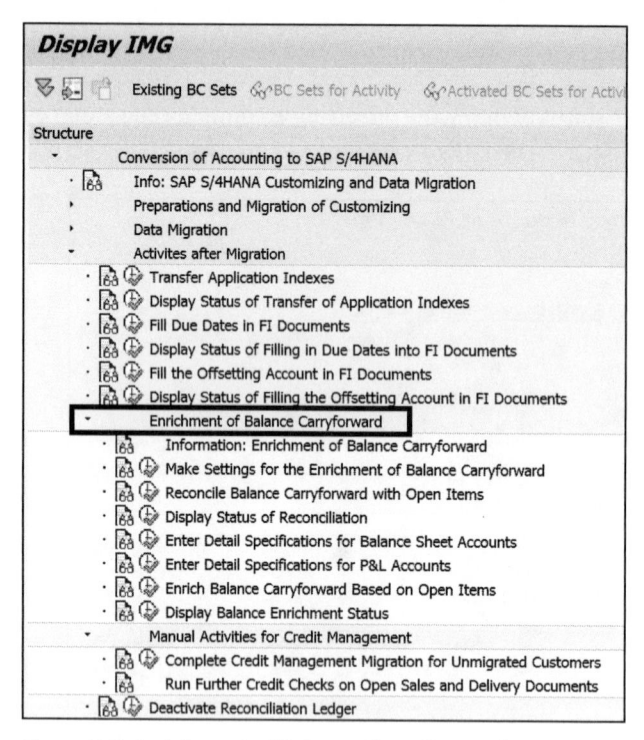

Figure 8.9 Enrichment of Balance Carry Forward

In this activity, you recalculate the balance carryforward for those accounts that are open-item managed. The enriched balance, thus calculated, becomes the opening balance for all future balance carryforward.

322

Perform the following tasks in this activity:

- **Make settings for the enrichment of balance carryforward**
  Define the ledger and the fiscal year for which the balance carryforward needs to be enriched. Make sure that documents exist in the database and haven't been archived for the years that you want the program to execute.
- **Reconcile balance carryforward with open items**
  Reconcile the balance carryforward with the total of all open items for the previous year. This is done for all the ledgers and years that have been selected for the enrichment.
- **Display status of reconciliation**
  Display the status of reconciliation of the balance carryforward with the open items. If the balances do not reconcile, you need to investigate further.
- **Enter detail specifications for balance sheet accounts**
  Carryforward balances on balance sheet accounts with more or fewer account assignments, with attributes such as currency, profit center, and so on.
- **Enter detail specifications for P&L accounts**
  In general, P&L account balances get carried forward to a retained earnings account. In this task, you have the flexibility to execute the balance carryforward program with additional account assignments that can be selected in the Customizing menu.
- **Enrich balance carryforward based on open items**
  Recalculate the balance carryforward from the open items.
- **Display balance enrichment status**
  Monitor and check the status of the reconciliation and display any calculated reports.

8.10 Manual Activities for Credit Management

For customers whose master data was not migrated initially, the following corresponding data also would not be migrated:

- Credit management master data
- Credit exposure data
- Historical payment behavior data
- Initialization of documented credit decisions

8　Postmigration Activities

In this activity, you complete the migration of this missing data.

It's good practice to perform credit checks on your open sales and delivery documents for your customers: their credit status might have been changed under the new credit-monitoring rules. You can execute Report RVKRED09 using Transaction SA38, which checks the credit status of open sales and delivery documents in the background, as shown in Figure 8.10.

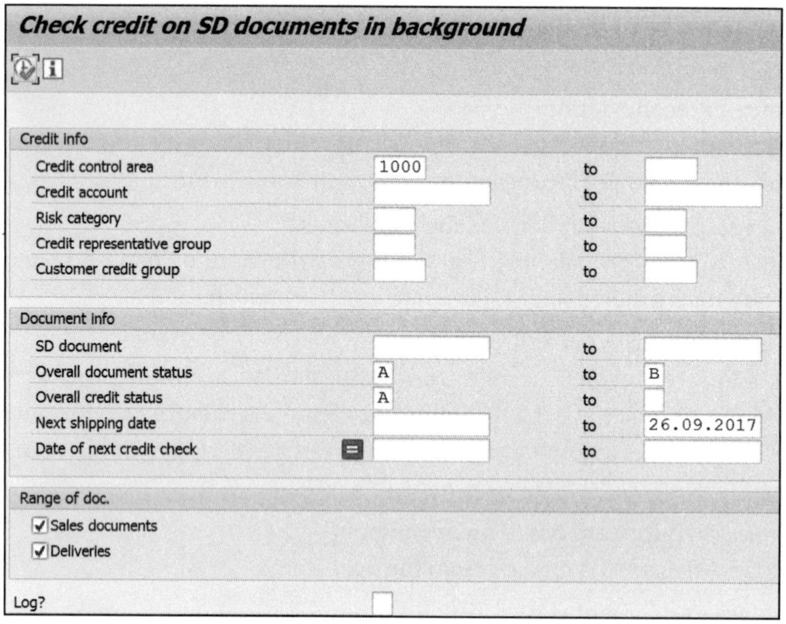

Figure 8.10 Credit Check on SD Documents

8.11　Deactivate Reconciliation Ledger

In this activity, you deactivate the reconciliation ledger for all the controlling areas. With SAP S/4HANA, both the FI and CO modules share a common database table; both have now been merged into the Universal Journal. This means you can deactivate the reconciliation ledger and save the memory resulting from this activity, which is no longer required by design.

8.12 Summary

After reading this chapter, you should be able to finalize the migration to SAP S/4HANA Finance and perform the postmigration activities. These activities include filling due dates, entering the offsetting account, and transferring the application indexes to the cold area of the SAP HANA database.

After the migration, it's prudent to validate all the business processes and transactions to ensure that the system is running at the optimal level without any errors or system dumps, which further reduces the business downtime for end users. The financial reports must also be executed, and the results must reconcile with the figures and data extracted prior to the migration.

Let's now move on to Chapter 9, in which we'll discuss the testing activities for your migration.

Chapter 9
Postmigration Testing

The migration to SAP S/4HANA Finance brings new tables at the backend for the technical ABAP team and new transactions at the frontend for the end users. This chapter focuses on testing the functionality and the organizational change impact that it brings to all the stakeholders during the migration.

After the migration to SAP S/4HANA Finance, you need to check the changed transactions and processes in the system and perform thorough integration testing. Change management and the adaptation to the new system are critical and determine the success of the implementation across the organization.

The project manager or the executive sponsor in charge of the migration effort must provide the required training to end users so that they can support the changes as required for the operations within the organization.

Some of the key activities to measure success include the following:

- Integrating different sources of information such as Profitability Analysis (CO-PA) and other cost objects to generate meaningful business insight and provide strategic input to the CFO's agenda to spot new market opportunities
- Predicting changes in the business environment
- Executing some of the key finance transactional reports to check consistency and validate balances

One of the key elements that drives migration success is to test any customized transactions and reports and check if they run without any errors after the migration. With the SAP HANA in-memory database and the Universal Journal simplified structure, you'll now be able to execute critical reports in much less time. In most cases, the testing results will serve as acceptance criteria from the customers for a successful migration to or implementation of SAP S/4HANA Finance.

9 Postmigration Testing

9.1 Test SAP HANA-Optimized Report Transactions

Once you've installed SAP S/4HANA Finance, you can test the following transactions to check whether they can be executed without any errors:

- Transaction FBL1H: Vendor Line Items
- Transaction FBL5H: Customer Line Items
- Transactions FBL3H, FAGLL03H: G/L Line Items
- Transaction CO88H: Settlement (Plant Selection)
- Transaction VA88H: Settlement (Sales Orders)
- Transaction KO8GH: Settlement (Internal Orders)
- Transaction CJ8GH: Settlement (Projects)
- Transaction KKAKH: Result Analysis
- Transaction KKAOH: WIP Calculation at Actual Cost
- Transaction KKS1H: Variance Calculation with Full Settlement
- Transaction KSS1H: Variance Calculation for Cost Centers

You also need to execute your custom reports to test whether they still run and still produce the same results in the SAP S/4HANA Finance environment as they did in SAP ERP Financials (FI). We also recommend executing the financial statement using Transaction S_ALR_87012284 to test if all the General Ledger (G/L) accounts correctly reflect the balances. Using Transaction SE16N, you can check also if obsolete tables such as tables FAGLFLEXT and GLT0 display the **Generated Table for View** message.

9.2 Test Multidimensional Reporting Capability

With all account-based CO-PA and other fields being part of the same line-item entry table ACDOCA in SAP S/4HANA Finance, you can now use a multidimensional drill-down balance sheet report, which can be organized as **Assets by Fixed Assets**, **Receivables by Customer**, or **Inventory by Material**. The finance team can use such reports to help the business with scenario planning and to react faster to the ever-changing market, location, and product dynamics. The multidimensional CO-PA report should be thoroughly tested, along with the system performance of these reports.

SAP S/4HANA Finance now provides the finance users with new reporting and analytics capabilities with real-time access to data, thus allowing instant insight to action. The historical data can now be used for predictive analysis with reports and dashboards available on mobile devices for more productive usage. It's prudent to test the linkage of the reports using mobile devices to ensure that the functionality works using any mobile device.

Global regulatory compliance capabilities can now be carried out across currencies, languages, and industries with built-in legal compliance and continuous risk assessment along all enterprise processes. Some of the critical statutory reports should be tested and reconciled with the data prior to migration so that the business can continue without any disruption.

9.3 Test Database Footprint Reduction

Replacing the totals and aggregate tables with the compatibility views in SAP S/4HANA Finance reduces the database footprint, memory, and inconsistency by more than 60 percent as a general benchmark. In addition, when data aging is implemented by splitting the actual and historical data, the database usage is further reduced by more than 80 percent, thus bringing a significant reduction of database memory consumption and faster data processing. Decreasing an organization's database size due to the reduction of the aggregation tables helps reduce the cost of storage as well. After the migration, thorough technical and performance testing should be performed and documented on the memory space saved, which can be converted into tangible savings.

End users should realize substantial time-savings benefits for executing some of the critical reports involving large data and calculations during the testing of these reports. Users can now access these reports in real time on the fly rather than having to wait for the batch jobs to finish. Speed and online availability are achieved using the in-memory functionality within SAP HANA and the reduction of the aggregation tables.

9.4 Test Intercompany Reconciliation

You can manually select documents using Transaction FBICS3 and then assign these documents using Transaction FBICA3. Transaction FBICR3 reconciles open items on a real-time basis, thus accelerating the automated matching process and reducing the closing time, as shown in Figure 9.1.

9   Postmigration Testing

The new functionality should be tested, and the benefits should be documented based on feedback from end users about the time it used to take for intercompany reconciliation before the migration and the time it takes now with SAP S/4HANA Finance.

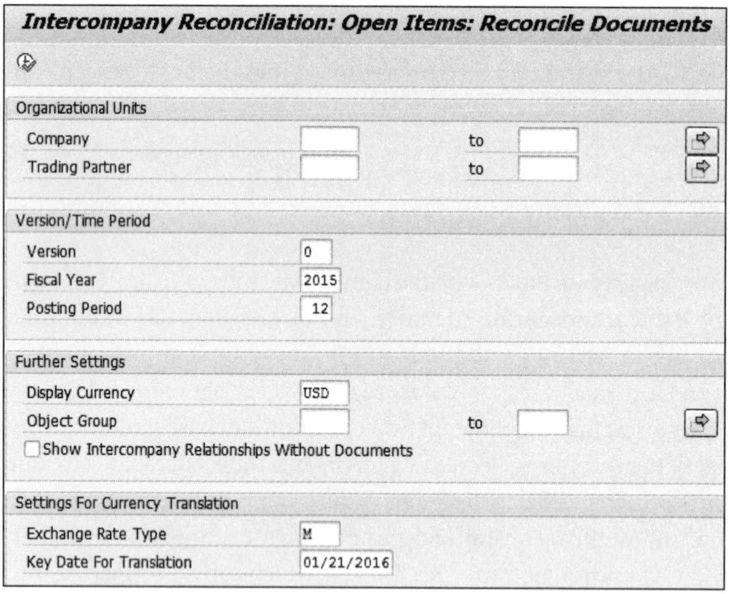

Intercompany Reconciliation: Open Items: Reconcile Documents

Organizational Units		
Company	to	
Trading Partner	to	

Version/Time Period	
Version	0
Fiscal Year	2015
Posting Period	12

Further Settings	
Display Currency	USD
Object Group	to
☐ Show Intercompany Relationships Without Documents	

Settings For Currency Translation	
Exchange Rate Type	M
Key Date For Translation	01/21/2016

Figure 9.1 Intercompany Reconciliation

9.5 Test the New Process Redesign

The posting mechanism for cost of goods sold (COGS) has been refined to reflect the standard cost component split on the G/L account, along with its integration with account-based CO-PA. Work in process (WIP) positions can now be analyzed at a much more granular level for the WIP G/L-account line items, which are linked to the settlement line items via the production order.

All the process redesign and new process mapping must be tested as part of both integration with end-to-end scenario testing and user acceptance testing so that users become aware of the new process that needs to be followed after migration. This will help further reduce business downtime, with users becoming proficient in executing key transactions from the start of the migration to SAP S/4HANA Finance.

9.6 Test Closing Improvement

The closing process in SAP S/4HANA Finance has been improved significantly, with substantial reduction of time, manual tasks, and reconciliation effort to close month-end financials. The data from various sources and legacy systems can now be combined and processed together with real-time updates to the business processes. You now can conduct simulations and run on-the-fly reports for various business scenarios on any device.

After the migration, the first month-end closing process should be tested thoroughly so that users from all functionality areas, including G/L, cost accounting, asset accounting, accounts payable, and accounts receivable can understand and inherit the new closing process without depending on batch jobs. Implementing the SAP Financial Closing cockpit is a good option to streamline the process: the task sequence is assigned to individual users and provides automated notifications after tasks are complete or when there are errors.

9.7 Test the Universal Journal

The Universal Journal in SAP S/4HANA Finance harmonizes internal and external accounting such as FI, FI-AA, Controlling (CO), SAP Material Ledger (ML), account-based CO-PA, and execution of reports from a single set of data at the line-item level, providing a single source of truth for FI. The new concept significantly reduces the data footprint and month-end reconciliation effort and helps to realize the full capabilities of account-based CO-PA where all the CO-PA fields are now part of the Universal Journal table. Note that costing-based CO-PA is still posted to the old CO tables and isn't integrated with the Universal Journal table ACDOCA.

The new Universal Journal needs to be thoroughly tested and verified by posting journal and accrual entries and checking the values posted in all the fields of table ACDOCA. As part of user training, the training and change management teams need to demonstrate SAP S/4HANA Finance's functional and analytical capability across the organization based on individual roles and responsibilities. This also includes demonstrating role-based SAP Fiori apps and their applications: transactional, analytical, or setting key performance indicator (KPI) goals for the business.

As part of the overall testing approach and scope, regression testing needs to be performed for all the existing workflows, reports, interfaces, conversions, enhancements, and forms (WRICEF) objects to ensure that the functionality and data flow across all systems works seamlessly without any breakage.

9.8 Execute Change Management

Change management is a critical component for the organization in the transformational journey to SAP S/4HANA Finance. The following are some of the pragmatic steps that need to be executed to guide the leaders through this change:

- Actively involving the top management and stakeholders from the start of the migration process
- Clearly articulating the change vision and goals across the organization
- Assessing the change impact and formulating the plan to implement and manage the change
- Engaging the employees and end users in all the project phases to adopt the new way of working, either through the new process change or using SAP Fiori apps on mobile devices
- Determining the gaps in the knowledge areas of the employees and executing the knowledge transfer, which should be an ongoing process rather than a one-time training course
- Aligning the organization to enable and emphasize the commitment and desired behaviors to make the migration a success
- Monitoring the acceptance of the change to confirm that desired outcomes are realized and migration benefits are maximized

9.9 Summary

It's prudent for the executive sponsor to test and realize the benefits at the earliest after migration to SAP S/4HANA Finance. This can only happen if all the business processes and changed transactions work seamlessly and the organization is able to adapt to the changes at a faster pace. Most enterprise-level CFOs agree that the global business environment is driving real-time decision-making, and technological innovations such as SAP S/4HANA Finance are now able to provide the necessary insight, in an accessible way, to support this requirement.

Seamless integration between transactions and analytics streamlines and eliminates cycle times and reconciliation of the data, and this needs to be tested, agreed upon, and signed-off on by business owners and subject matter experts, making the migration successful and complete. Testing the functionality will help business users understand the fundamental changes and benefits that the new technology within SAP S/4HANA Finance brings to the business.

The testing scope for the migration to SAP S/4HANA Finance will include unit testing, multiple cycles of integration testing, data-migration testing, regression testing, security testing, performance testing, and user-acceptance testing.

Let's now move on to Part II, in which we'll walk you through the new functionality introduced in SAP S/4HANA Finance: SAP Cash Management, SAP BPC for SAP S/4HANA Finance, and the SAP Fiori apps. Because these new features and functionality are optional and come with SAP S/4HANA, it's important to configure and set them up while implementing or migrating to SAP S/4HANA. We'll begin in Chapter 10 with a discussion of the configuration and functionality of SAP Cash Management.

PART II
Setting Up New Financials Functionality

Chapter 10
SAP Cash Management

This chapter provides insight into the configuration and functionality offered by the new SAP Cash Management. It deals with centralized bank account management, cash operations, and liquidity management processes. SAP Cash Management helps you monitor the liquidity status of your company, mitigate financial risks, and maximize financial benefits.

With SAP S/4HANA, the classic SAP Cash and Liquidity Management has been replaced by the new SAP Cash Management. If you've been using the classic SAP Cash and Liquidity Management, you can migrate the related master data and transaction data to the new SAP Cash Management—but you'll need to configure it from scratch, because it's a replacement rather than an improvement to or upgrade from the existing SAP ERP cash management functionality.

Why make this cash management change? Today's organizations need to improve the accuracy of their cash flow forecasts, optimize internal funding within the subsidiaries across the globe, develop a single source of truth for various bank accounts, improve yield on idle cash, and manage the exposure of foreign exchange and currency risk.

The next-generation SAP Cash Management product provides the solution to these concerns by focusing on the following three components:

1. **Bank Account Management**
   This component deals with the centralized maintenance of bank accounts and the hierarchy, workflow, and approval process for creating, changing, and closing bank accounts, with sequential and non-sequential setups of signatories, and it optimizes the uploading and downloading of bank accounts.

2. **Cash Operations**
   This component deals with the day-to-day management of an organization's working capital, including monitoring the status of incoming bank statements; preparing cash forecast reports comprised of cash receipts, disbursements, and

10 SAP Cash Management

closing balances; managing bank risk and exposure; and approving and monitoring the status of payments for cash pools and concentrations.

> **1709 Preview**
>
> With the onset of version 1709, incoming bank statements and cash clearing can be automated using machine learning models and capabilities.

3. **SAP Liquidity Management**
   This component deals with the complete liquidity planning lifecycle, providing the functionality for hedging foreign currencies and covering the risk exposure, preparing liquidity forecast reports, conducting cash flow analysis, and analyzing plan versus actual reports.

The Customizing settings related to all the components of the new SAP Cash Management are depicted in Figure 10.1.

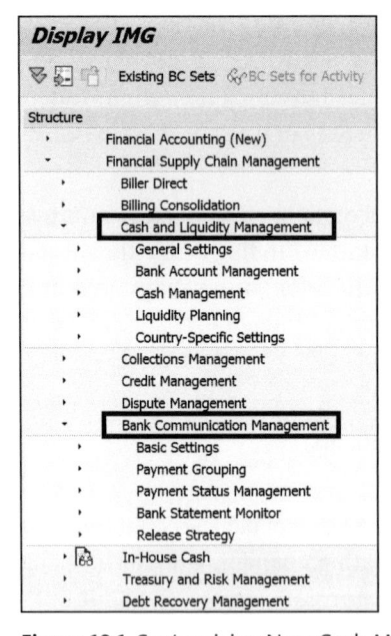

Figure 10.1 Customizing New Cash Management

In this chapter, we'll start by validating the prerequisites for SAP Cash Management before proceeding to set up bank account master data. We'll then walk through the steps for defining the payment-approval process, enabling SAP Business Workflow

338

for Bank Account Management, creating cash pools, and managing cash operations. Finally, we'll explain how to set up transaction data and set up both liquidity management and liquidity planning.

> **References**
>
> For more information on cash management in SAP S/4HANA, we recommend the book *Cash Management with SAP S/4HANA: Functionality and Implementation* by Dirk Neumann and Lawrence Liang (SAP PRESS, 2018, *www.sap-press.com/4479*).

10.1 Validate Prerequisites

You need to ensure that the following prerequisites are fulfilled before you continue with the activities in SAP Cash Management:

- You've installed SAP S/4HANA Finance and activated the business function FIN_FSCM_CLM using Transaction SFW5, as shown in Figure 10.2.

SHT - Switch Framework: Display Business Function Status		
👁 Check 🔎 Switch Framework Browser 💡 Display Legend		
Business Function Set	DIMP Discrete Industries / Mill Prod. ▼	
Name	Description	Planned Status
• 🔹 FIN_FSCM_CLM	SAP Cash Management powered by SAP HANA (Reversible)	Business function (reversible) will remain activated

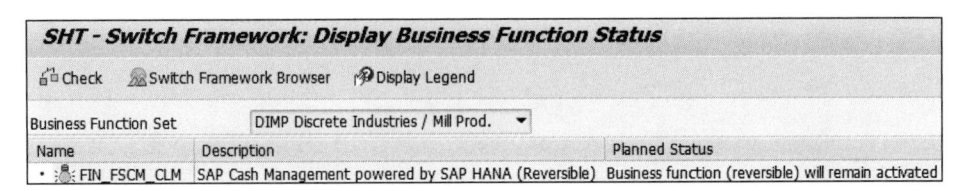

Figure 10.2 Activating Business Function FIN_FSCM_CLM

- You've applied all the SAP Notes listed in SAP Note 2138445 that are relevant to your SAP landscape.
- You've assigned a user the role SAP_SFIN_CASH_MANAGER, which provides the SAP Business Client menu and necessary authorization objects mostly related to Bank Account Management. You also need to assign the role SAP_SFIN_BCR_CASHMANAGER so that the user has proper authorization to group SAP Cash Management-related SAP Fiori tiles. You also need to assign roles to support the backend SAP Fiori transactions related to Bank Account Management, as shown in Figure 10.3.
- You've assigned a user with the SAP Smart Business configuration and SAP HANA authorization roles—for example, /UI2/SAP_KPIFRW5_TCR_S, /UI2/SAP_KPIMOD_TCR_S, and SAP_SMART_BUSINESS_RUNTIME.

339

10   SAP Cash Management

> **References**
>
> For more information, see SAP Note 2138445: SAP Cash Management Powered by SAP HANA.

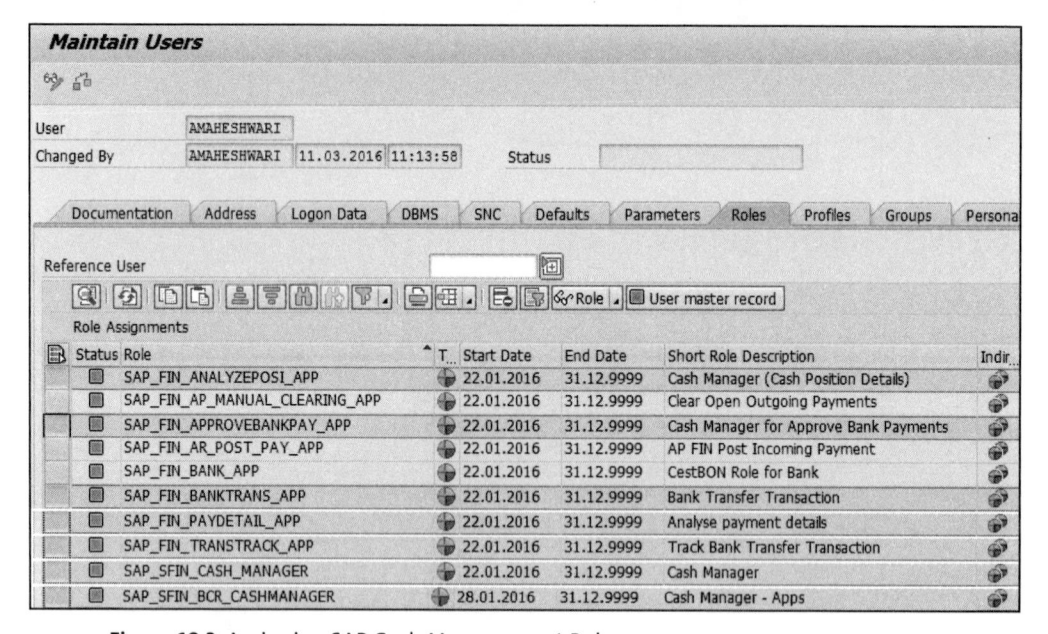

Status	Role	T...	Start Date	End Date	Short Role Description	Indir...
☐	SAP_FIN_ANALYZEPOSI_APP		22.01.2016	31.12.9999	Cash Manager (Cash Position Details)	
☐	SAP_FIN_AP_MANUAL_CLEARING_APP		22.01.2016	31.12.9999	Clear Open Outgoing Payments	
☐	SAP_FIN_APPROVEBANKPAY_APP		22.01.2016	31.12.9999	Cash Manager for Approve Bank Payments	
☐	SAP_FIN_AR_POST_PAY_APP		22.01.2016	31.12.9999	AP FIN Post Incoming Payment	
☐	SAP_FIN_BANK_APP		22.01.2016	31.12.9999	CestBON Role for Bank	
☐	SAP_FIN_BANKTRANS_APP		22.01.2016	31.12.9999	Bank Transfer Transaction	
☐	SAP_FIN_PAYDETAIL_APP		22.01.2016	31.12.9999	Analyse payment details	
☐	SAP_FIN_TRANSTRACK_APP		22.01.2016	31.12.9999	Track Bank Transfer Transaction	
☐	SAP_SFIN_CASH_MANAGER		22.01.2016	31.12.9999	Cash Manager	
☐	SAP_SFIN_BCR_CASHMANAGER		28.01.2016	31.12.9999	Cash Manager - Apps	

Figure 10.3 Assigning SAP Cash Management Roles

10.2   Set Up Bank Account Master Data

Before using SAP Cash Management, you must migrate and set up the bank account master data and configure all the settings as required, as covered in detail in Chapter 6. This section covers the creation of bank accounts either manually or through the upload of a bank directory.

10.2.1   Banks and House Banks

The bank master can be maintained in SAP either by creating it manually through Transaction FI01 (as shown in Figure 10.4) or by using an upload tool through

10.2 Set Up Bank Account Master Data

Transaction BAUP, which is used for transferring a bank directory to the SAP system (table BNKA), to be stored in a country-specific file (as shown in Figure 10.5).

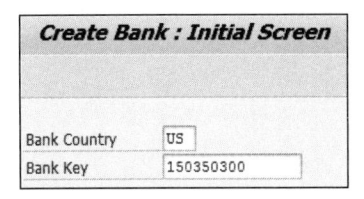

Create Bank : Initial Screen

Bank Country	US
Bank Key	150350300

Figure 10.4 Creating a Bank Using Transaction FI01

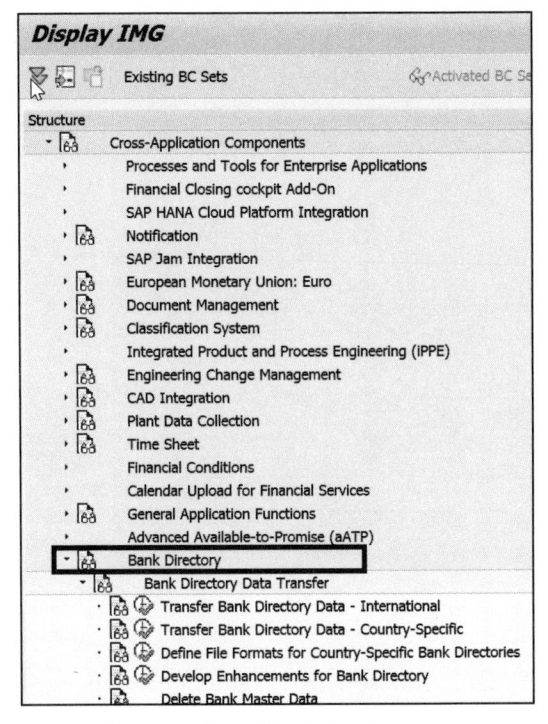

Figure 10.5 Importing a Bank Directory

You can request your house bank to provide you with the bank directory. If this isn't possible, SAP Notes 132012 and 1459715 provide addresses for finding bank directories.

For bank accounts that are being used by the automatic payment program, bank statements, or bank transfers in SAP Cash Management, the house bank and house

10 SAP Cash Management

bank accounts for the bank account must be configured using Transaction FI12_HBANK, as shown in Figure 10.6.

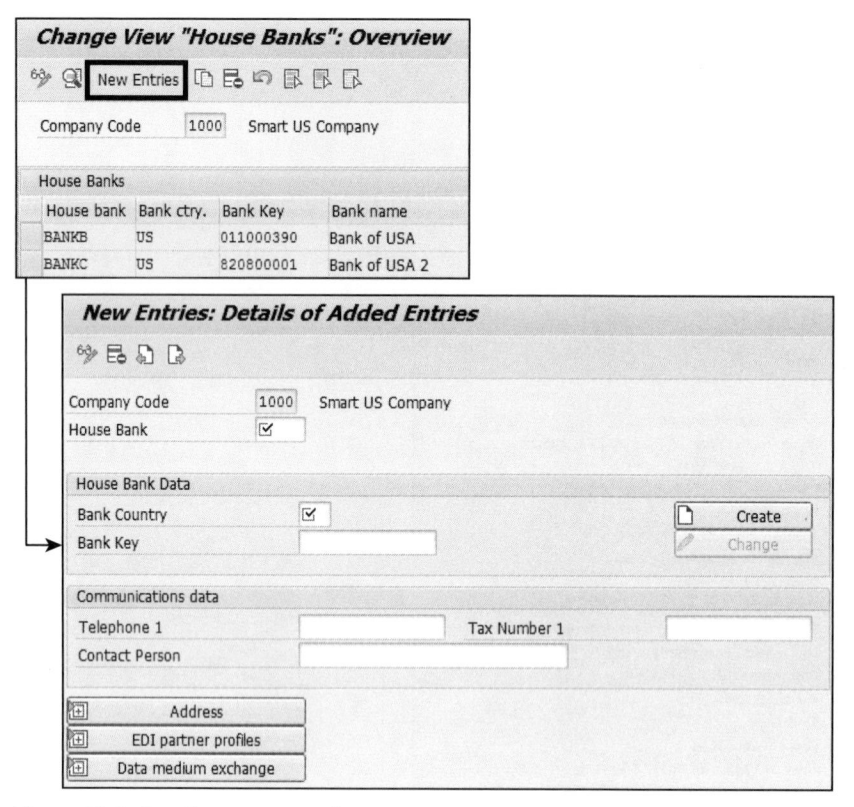

Figure 10.6 Creating House Banks

10.2.2 Migrate House Bank Accounts

With the introduction of SAP S/4HANA Finance, house bank accounts are now merged and incorporated into bank account master data. Because of this change, you need to migrate house bank accounts that were originally stored in database table T012K to table FCLM_BAM_ACLINK2. After the migration, you'll be able to use the house bank accounts as usual.

Migrate your house bank accounts to Bank Account Management by executing Transaction FCLM_BAM_MIGRATION. You might receive the following message:

10.2 Set Up Bank Account Master Data

Connectivity paths of accounts in remote systems have not yet been migrated. Do you want to migrate them? If yes, choose "Yes" and execute the program. Click **Yes** to move forward with the migration process that will generate bank account master data with basic information from house bank accounts, including the following:

- Key information such as house bank, account ID, bank account number, type of account, bank key, bank country, and bank name
- The connectivity path between bank accounts and house bank accounts

The green status light shown in Figure 10.7 indicates that the corresponding new bank account has been created and the linkage has been built. You can also check the migration log using Transaction SLG1.

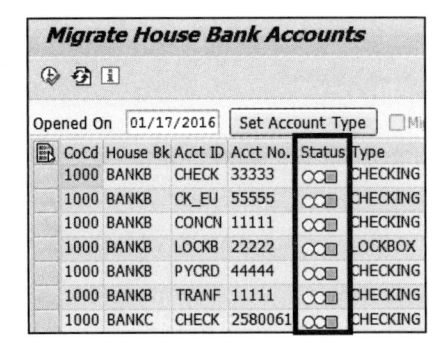

CoCd	House Bk	Acct ID	Acct No.	Status	Type
1000	BANKB	CHECK	33333	⬤	CHECKING
1000	BANKB	CK_EU	55555	⬤	CHECKING
1000	BANKB	CONCN	11111	⬤	CHECKING
1000	BANKB	LOCKB	22222	⬤	LOCKBOX
1000	BANKB	PYCRD	44444	⬤	CHECKING
1000	BANKB	TRANF	11111	⬤	CHECKING
1000	BANKC	CHECK	2580061	⬤	CHECKING

Figure 10.7 Migrate House Banks Accounts

10.2.3 Upload and Download Bank Accounts

You'll find the import and export bank account functionality using Transaction NWBC, as shown in Figure 10.8. Your options here are as follows:

- **Export Bank Accounts to an XML File**
  This option opens the Bank_Accounts.xml file that contains all the active bank account master data.

- **Download XML Spreadsheet Template**
  This option opens the XML_SpreadSheet_Template.xml file in a spreadsheet with a layout that is specifically arranged to resemble the bank account master data user interface.

- **Download XML Schema File for Import Validation**
  This option opens the XML_Schema_Import.xml file that provides the format of

the bank account master data, which can be used to validate the import of the bank account master file.

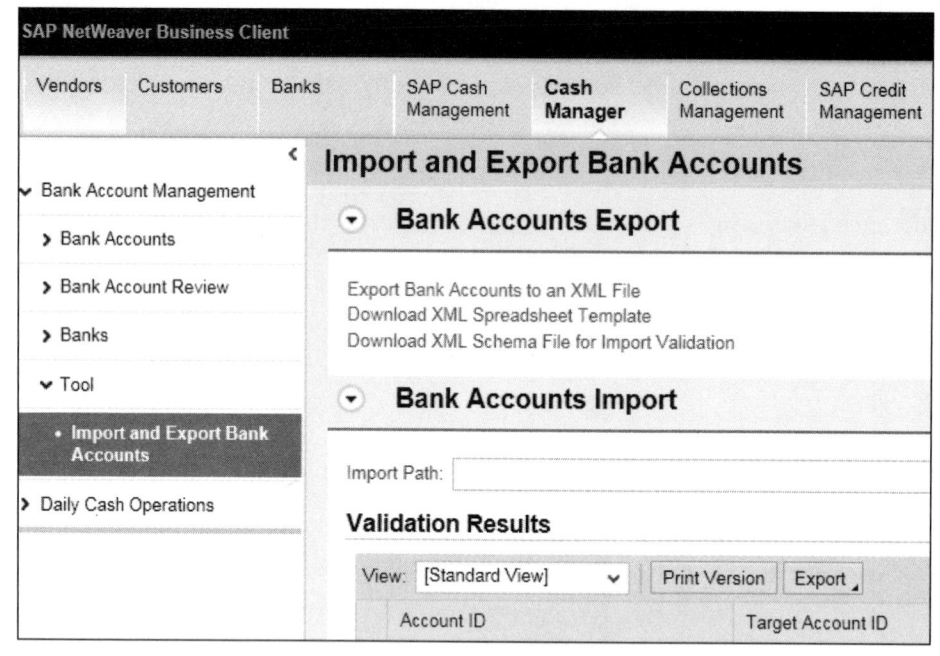

Figure 10.8 Import and Export Bank Accounts Using SAP Business Client

10.3 Define the Payment Approval Process

With Bank Account Management, you can define several approval processes for various bank accounts by configuring signatory groups and approval patterns.

The payment approval process with payment signatories is configured in SAP Bank Communication Management, which is detailed in the following sections. The activities related to the payment approval process are found under **Financial Supply Chain Management • Bank Communication Management**, as shown in Figure 10.9.

10.3 Define the Payment Approval Process

```
Display IMG
    Existing BC Sets    BC Sets for Activity    Activated BC Sets for Activity
Structure
    ▸   Financial Accounting (New)
    ▾   Financial Supply Chain Management
        ▸   Biller Direct
        ▸   Billing Consolidation
        ▸   Cash and Liquidity Management
        ▸   Collections Management
        ▸   Credit Management
        ▸   Dispute Management
        ▾   Bank Communication Management
            ▾   Basic Settings
                ·   Basic Settings for Approval
                ·   BAdI: Additional Fields for BNK_MONI and BNK_APP
                ·   BAdI: Navigation for Customer Fields or Fields not Supported by SAP
                ·   BAdI: Automatic Filter for Batches in BNK_MONI and BNK_APP
            ▾   Payment Grouping
                ·   Rule Maintenance
                ·   Additional Criteria for Payment Grouping
                ·   BAdI for Additional Grouping Criteria
                ·   Payment Medium:Create/Assign Selection Variants
            ▸   Payment Status Management
            ▸   Bank Statement Monitor
            ▸   Release Strategy
```

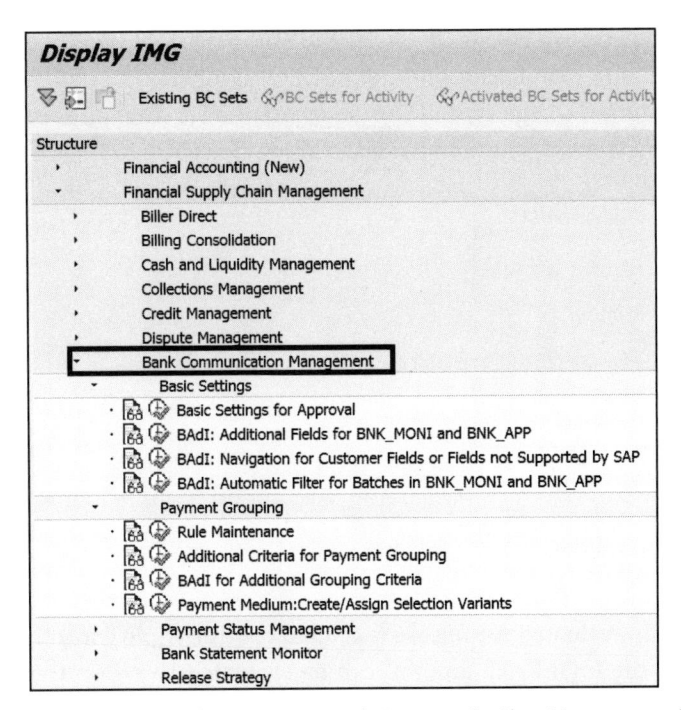

Figure 10.9 Configuring SAP Bank Communication Management

10.3.1 Basic Settings for Approval

When users approve payments and a signature is required, the approval process can be configured in the Customizing activity under **Bank Communication Management • Basic Settings • Basic Settings for Approval**, as shown in Figure 10.10.

```
▾   Financial Supply Chain Management
    ▸   Biller Direct
    ▸   Billing Consolidation
    ▸   Cash and Liquidity Management
    ▸   Collections Management
    ▸   Credit Management
    ▸   Dispute Management
    ▾   Bank Communication Management
        ▾   Basic Settings
            ·   Basic Settings for Approval
            ·   BAdI: Additional Fields for BNK_MONI and BNK_APP
            ·   BAdI: Navigation for Customer Fields or Fields not Supported by SAP
```

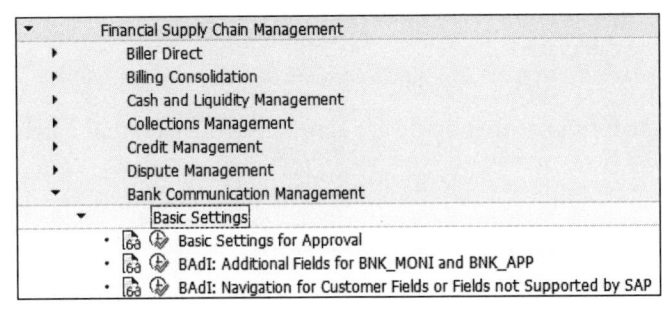

Figure 10.10 Configuring the Basic Settings

345

In this Customizing activity, you can create an entry; select the **Signature Required** checkbox to make the signature mandatory while approving payments; and define the default currency (**Rule Currency**), the type of exchange rate used (**Exchange Rate Type**), and the resubmission date (**Days Resubmission**), as shown in Figure 10.11.

Change View "Basic Settings": Details

Basic Settings	
Rule Currency	USD
Exchange Rate Type	M
Days Resubmission	5
☑ Signature required	

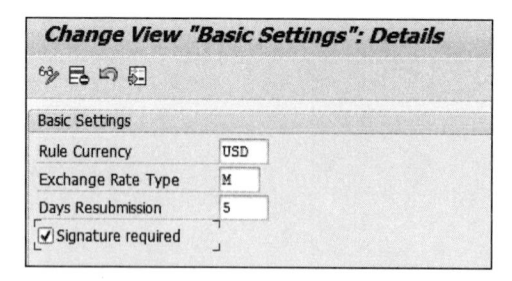

Figure 10.11 Basic Settings for Approval

In detail, these settings are as follows:

- **Rule Currency**
  When a payment batch is evaluated for release (e.g., dual control, triple control, automatic release, etc.), the total batch amount can be evaluated based on the default currency if the payments in the batch consist of different currencies or different company codes (hence, a different local currency).

- **Exchange Rate Type**
  Exchange rate types can be used to define various exchange rates in the system, including an average rate for translation of foreign currency amounts, bank buying, selling rates, and so on.

- **Days Resubmission**
  For resubmission of payments, the number of days from the current date to the resubmission date can be calculated and set.

- **Signature Required**
  If this checkbox is selected, a signature pop-up appears before the payment batch is approved.

10.3.2 Rule Maintenance

In the Customizing activity under **Payment Grouping • Rule Maintenance**, you can create your own rule with a set of parameters for the approval of payments, as shown in Figure 10.12. Each rule within the set should be assigned a priority so that when more than one rule satisfies the criteria for grouping, the batching rule is derived based on the priority assigned to these rules.

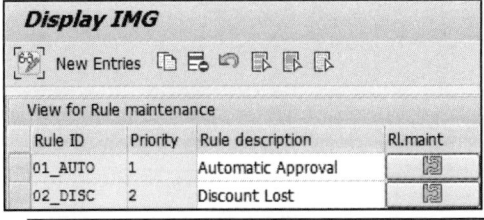

Figure 10.12 Rule Maintenance

You can define **Rule ID 01_AUTO** with **Priority 1** and **Rule ID 02_DISC** with **Priority 2**. If a payment satisfies the criteria for batching, **Rule ID 01_AUTO** is selected due to its higher priority.

10.3.3 Additional Criteria for Payment Grouping

In the Customizing activity under **Payment Grouping • Additional Criteria for Payment Grouping**, you can define grouping criteria for a rule that has already been defined. The additional criteria can group all payments of a batching rule under the same house bank account ID or a certain date as specified in the grouping criteria. Two grouping fields that can be selected for the batching are shown in Figure 10.13.

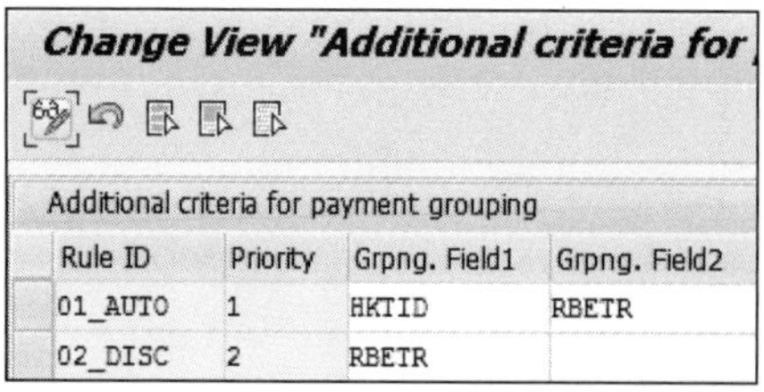

10   SAP Cash Management

Additional criteria for payment grouping			
Rule ID	Priority	Grpng. Field1	Grpng. Field2
01_AUTO	1	HKTID	RBETR
02_DISC	2	RBETR	

Figure 10.13 Additional Criteria for Payment Grouping

For example, say you select the **RBETR** field for batching **Rule ID 02_DISC**. This means that if a batching **Rule ID 02_DISC** is selected, payments are further batched by the amount in local currency, so all payments belonging to **Rule ID 02_DISC** and of the same amount will form a batch.

If the payment batches need to be grouped by house bank account, you must create a **Rule ID** and enter "HKTID" for **Grpng. Field 1**. You can specify another criterion for grouping the payments in **Grpng. Field 2**, if necessary.

10.3.4   Mark Rules for Automatic Payment

If your policy doesn't require approval for payments of small amounts, you can create a rule in the Customizing activity under **Release Strategy • Mark Rules for Automatic Payments (No Approval)**, as shown in Figure 10.14.

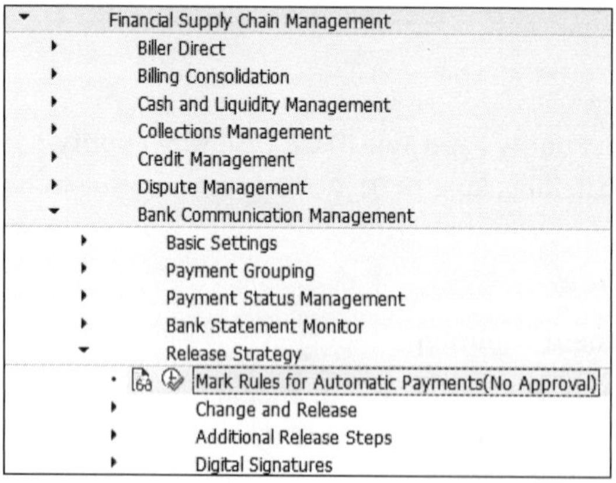

Figure 10.14 Release Strategy

10.3 Define the Payment Approval Process

If the **Rule ID** is marked as **Auto** (automatic), as shown in Figure 10.15, you can skip the approval process workflow in SAP Bank Communication Management and the signatory approval process in Bank Account Management.

If the **Rule ID** isn't set to **Auto**, the approval process workflow in SAP Bank Communication Management and the signatory approval process in Bank Account Management will be triggered.

Figure 10.15 Mark Rules for Automatic Payments (No Approval)

10.3.5 Specify the Signature Method for Approval Using a Simple Signature

To configure the signature method for approving payments, use the Customizing activity under **Release Strategy • Digital Signatures • Specify Signature Method for Approval Using Simple Signature**, as shown in Figure 10.16.

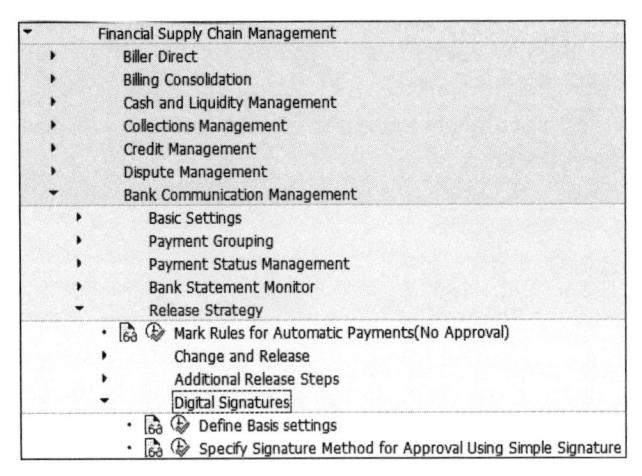

Figure 10.16 Configuring Digital Signatures

In this Customizing activity, you ascertain the settings that are required for approval of payments using a simple signature, which means that only one person needs to sign. The signature process is deemed complete after the authorized person signs the document.

This signature method, along with all the other options, needs to be customized for each signature object, as shown in Figure 10.17. The specified signature method becomes valid for all processors of the application if a signature strategy hasn't been assigned.

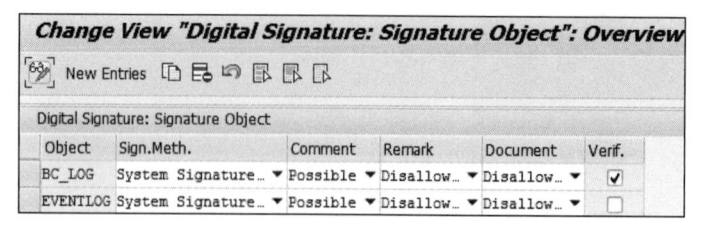

Figure 10.17 Specifying Signature Method for Approval Using Simple Signature

10.3.6 Enable Signatory Control

In this Customizing activity, you enable the payment signatory control for Bank Account Management by assigning function module **FCLM_BAM_BCM_AGT_PRESEL** to process **0BANK002** and function module **FCLM_BAM_BCM_REL_PROC_CTRL** to process **0BANK004**, as shown in Figure 10.18.

If signatory control is enabled, users who are assigned the role of a signatory can approve or reject payment documents in Bank Account Management. If the signatory control isn't enabled, payment documents are approved using the approval process and settings discussed in Section 10.3.5.

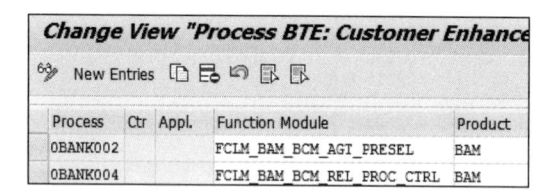

Figure 10.18 Enable Signatory Control

10.3.7 Specify Settings for the Bank Statement Monitor

In this Customizing activity, you specify the settings for the bank statement monitor for all the house bank accounts in your company code that you want to analyze, as shown in Figure 10.19.

10.3 Define the Payment Approval Process

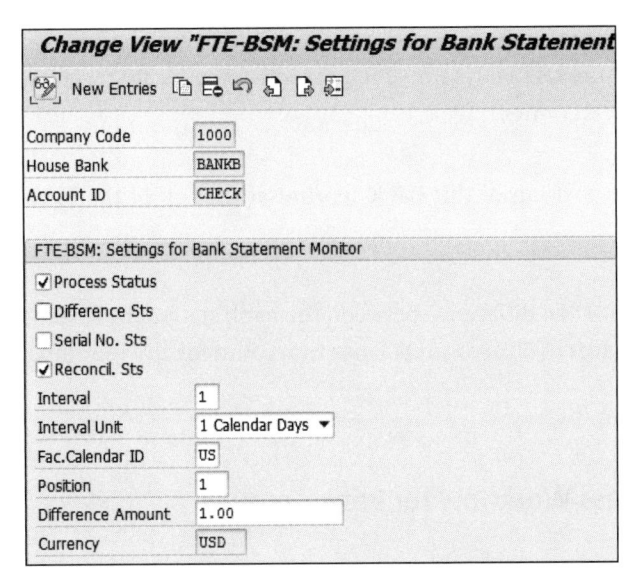

Figure 10.19 Settings for the Bank Statement Monitor

This example shows the **Company Code (1000)**, **House Bank (BANKB)**, and **Account ID (CHECK)** settings for bank statement monitoring, along with the following:

- **Process Status**
  This indicator has been set so that the processing status is displayed on the bank statement monitor. The processing status indicates whether the bank statement has been processed correctly via the following notations:
  - *Red*: no bank statement exists even though Customizing settings have been made.
  - *Yellow*: the bank statement is available; however, not all items are eligible for posting.
  - *Green*: the bank statement was correctly posted in the system.
- **Reconcil. Sts** (reconciliation status)
  By checking this indicator, the status is displayed on the bank statement monitor if there are any open items in the internal account, indicated as follows:
  - *Red*: open items exist.
  - *Yellow*: not all items have been posted yet.
  - *Green*: all items have been successfully posted.

- **Interval**
  This indicator reflects the interval in days for which bank statements are received for the corresponding bank accounts.
- **Position**
  This indicator displays the position of this bank account at the top of the bank statement monitor.
- **Difference Amount**
  This field reflects the permissible difference between the bank statement closing balance and the General Ledger (G/L) account balance to account for any rounding errors.

10.4 Enable SAP Business Workflow for Bank Account Management

SAP provides predefined and standard workflows for opening, changing, closing, and reviewing bank accounts in the bank account master data. You can either use the predefined workflows or create your own workflows according to your business requirements and organizational hierarchy. This section covers the assignment of users in the standard workflows and the configuration required to enable custom workflows if the predefined workflows don't meet your requirements for Bank Account Management.

10.4.1 Maintain Event Type Linkage

To use SAP Business Workflow in Bank Account Management, you need to set up the necessary settings using Transaction SWETYPV, as illustrated next.

The workflow function for Bank Account Management can be enabled by maintaining the event type linkage used in Bank Account Management in the Customizing activity under **Financial Supply Chain Management • Cash and Liquidity Management • Bank Account Management • Maintain the Event Type Linkage for Triggering Workflow Processes** (as shown in Figure 10.20).

10.4 Enable SAP Business Workflow for Bank Account Management

```
▼  Financial Supply Chain Management
   ▶    Biller Direct
   ▶    Billing Consolidation
   ▼    Cash and Liquidity Management
      ▶    General Settings
      ▼    Bank Account Management
         ▶    Basic Settings
         •  Maintain the Event Type Linkage for Triggering Workflow Processes
         •  Define Responsibilities for Rules Used in Workflow Steps
         •  Enable Signatory Control
         ▶    Business Add-Ins (BAdIs)
      ▶    Cash Management
      ▶    Liquidity Planning
```

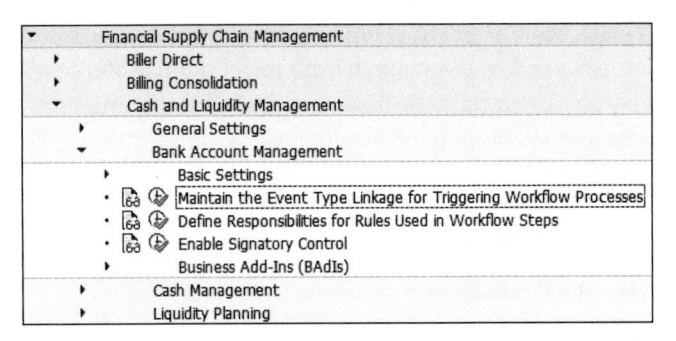

Figure 10.20 Configuring Bank Account Management Workflow

SAP provides a default entry (shown in Figure 10.21) with Business Object Repository (BOR) **Object Type FCLM_CR**, which is the predefined BOR object for Bank Account Management. **Event** is set to **CREATED**, **Receiver Type** to the SAP predefined workflow template **WS74300043**, and **Receiver Function Module** to **SWW_WI_CREATE_VIA_EVENT**.

Change View "Event Type Linkages": Details

Object Category	BOR Object Type
Object Type	FCLM_CR
Event	CREATED
Receiver Type	WS74300043

Linkage Setting (Event Receiver)

Receiver Call	Function Module
Receiver Function Module	SWW_WI_CREATE_VIA_EVENT
Check Function Module	
Receiver Type Function Module	
Destination of Receiver	
Event delivery	Using tRFC (Default)

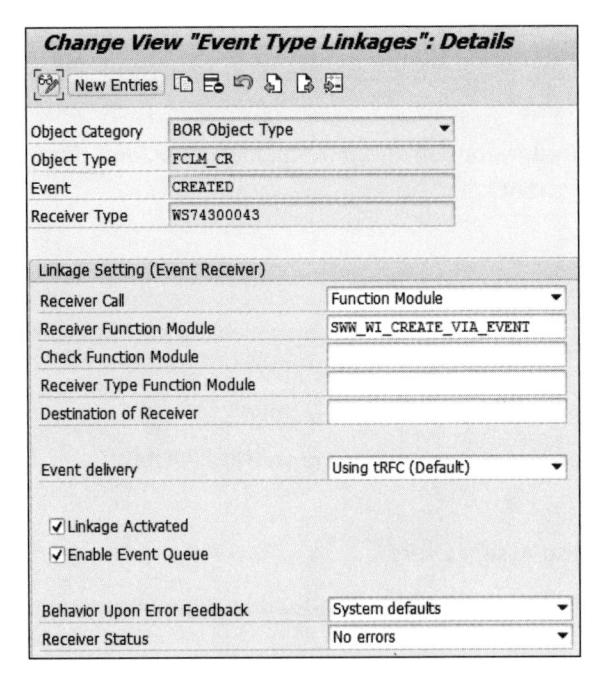

☑ Linkage Activated
☑ Enable Event Queue

Behavior Upon Error Feedback	System defaults
Receiver Status	No errors

Figure 10.21 Maintaining the Event Type Linkage for Triggering Workflow Processes

In this Customizing activity, you need to generate and activate a new entry for the custom workflow if the existing workflow template doesn't fulfill the requirements of your organization. You may also deactivate the linkage in this Customizing activity if you don't want to use the workflow for Bank Account Management. The entry will appear as shown in Figure 10.22.

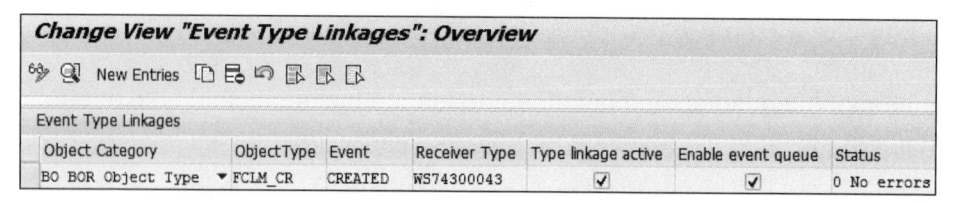

Object Category	ObjectType	Event	Receiver Type	Type linkage active	Enable event queue	Status
BO BOR Object Type	FCLM_CR	CREATED	WS74300043	✓	✓	0 No errors

Figure 10.22 Object FCLM_CR Activated

The following rules apply for activating the event type linkage:

- If you want to use SAP's predefined, out-of-the-box workflow template, the standard linkage in Customizing comes activated by default, and no further customization is necessary.
- If you want to create your own custom workflow template, add and activate a new entry and deactivate the default one.
- If you don't want to use the workflow for Bank Account Management, deactivate the linkage in this Customizing activity.

10.4.2 Define and Maintain Organizational Hierarchy

Define the organization and staffing of your organization by reviewing the following activities:

- To create new organization and staffing, use Transaction PPOCE.
- To change the existing organization and staffing, use Transaction PPOMW.

10.4.3 Define Responsibilities and Assign Users

SAP predefines the following workflow rules for Bank Account Management:

- 74300006: Cash Manager
- 74300007: Bank Accountant
- 74300008: Key User

10.4 Enable SAP Business Workflow for Bank Account Management

To define the responsibilities for rules used in workflow steps, follow these Customizing steps:

1. Complete the Customizing activity under **Financial Supply Chain Management** • **Cash and Liquidity Management** • **Bank Account Management** • **Define Responsibilities for Rules Used in Workflow Steps**, as shown in Figure 10.23.

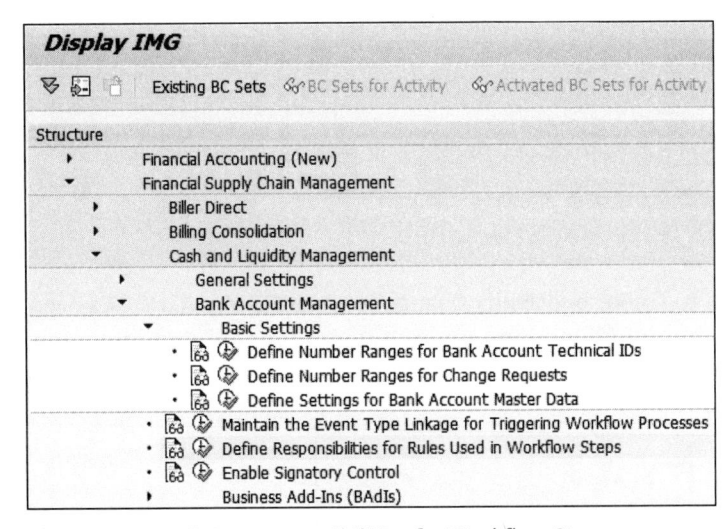

```
Display IMG

  Existing BC Sets   BC Sets for Activity   Activated BC Sets for Activity

Structure
  ▶     Financial Accounting (New)
  ▼     Financial Supply Chain Management
    ▶     Biller Direct
    ▶     Billing Consolidation
    ▼     Cash and Liquidity Management
      ▶     General Settings
      ▼     Bank Account Management
        ▼     Basic Settings
          •   Define Number Ranges for Bank Account Technical IDs
          •   Define Number Ranges for Change Requests
          •   Define Settings for Bank Account Master Data
          •   Maintain the Event Type Linkage for Triggering Workflow Processes
          •   Define Responsibilities for Rules Used in Workflow Steps
          •   Enable Signatory Control
          ▶   Business Add-Ins (BAdIs)
```

Figure 10.23 Defining Responsibilities for Workflow Steps

2. Input "74300007" for **Rule Number**, and click the **Change** icon highlighted in Figure 10.24.

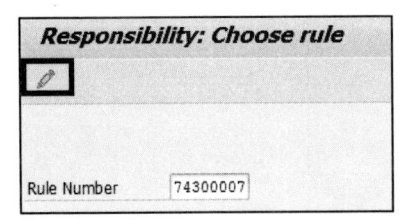

```
Responsibility: Choose rule

Rule Number    74300007
```

Figure 10.24 Assigning the Rule Number for Bank Accountant Role

3. Click the **Create** button at the top of the screen, input the parameters, and click **Execute** (green checkmark), as shown in Figure 10.25.

10 SAP Cash Management

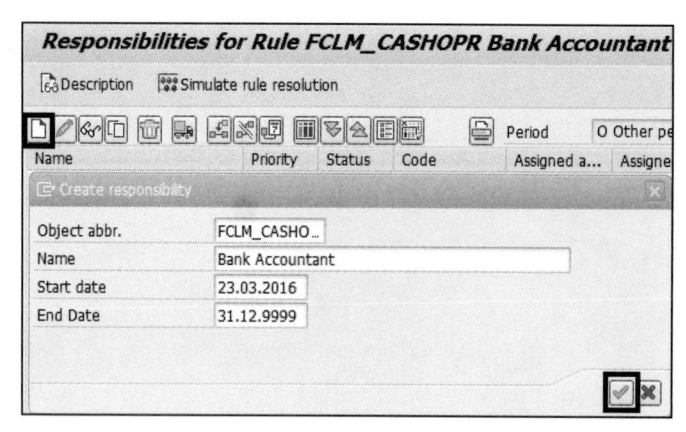

Figure 10.25 Creating a Responsibility for FCLM_CASHOPR

4. You are then taken to the **Responsibility Change for Rule FCLM_CASHOPR** screen shown in Figure 10.26. Input the parameters for **Account Type** and **Company Code**, and then click **Save**.

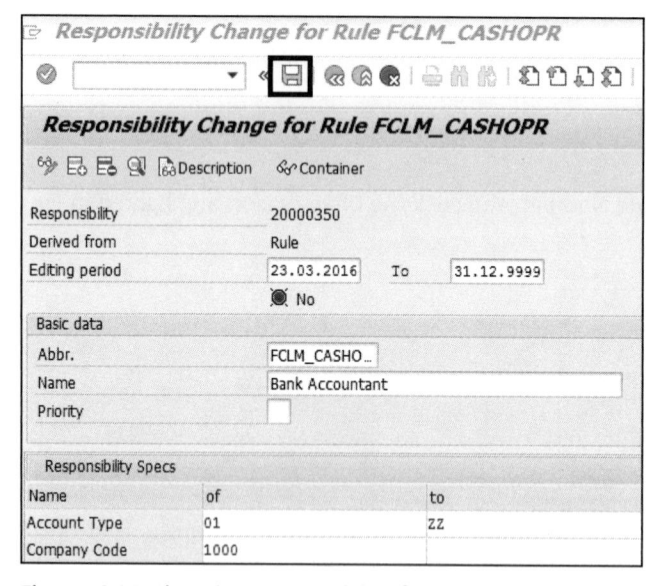

Figure 10.26 Changing Responsibility for FCLM_CASHOPR

5. The status for rule FCLM_CASHOPR has changed from red (no responsibility defined) to green (responsibility complete), as shown in Figure 10.27.

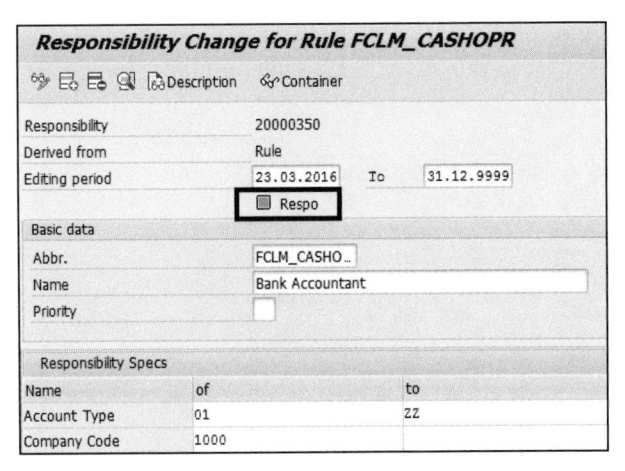

10.4 Enable SAP Business Workflow for Bank Account Management

Figure 10.27 Responsibility Defined for FCLM_CASHOPR

6. After the responsibility has been defined, select the **Bank Accountant** line, and then click the **Insert Agent Assignment** icon highlighted in Figure 10.28. In the pop-up window, select **User**, and then assign the user ID that has been assigned the role of bank accountant, as shown in Figure 10.28.

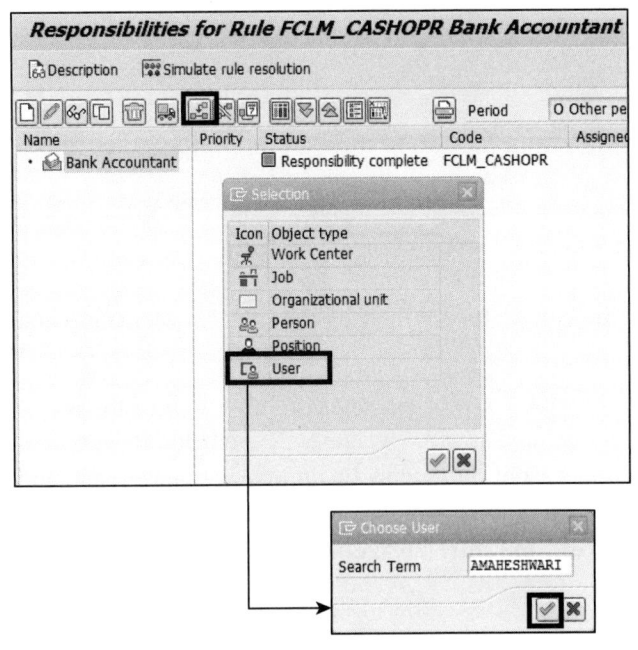

Figure 10.28 Assigning User to Rule FCLM_CASHOPR

357

10 SAP Cash Management

7. After the **User** is assigned to Rule FCLM_CASHOPR, click **Create**. This completes the configuration of assigning the user to rule FCLM_CASHOPR for **Bank Accountant**, as shown in Figure 10.29.

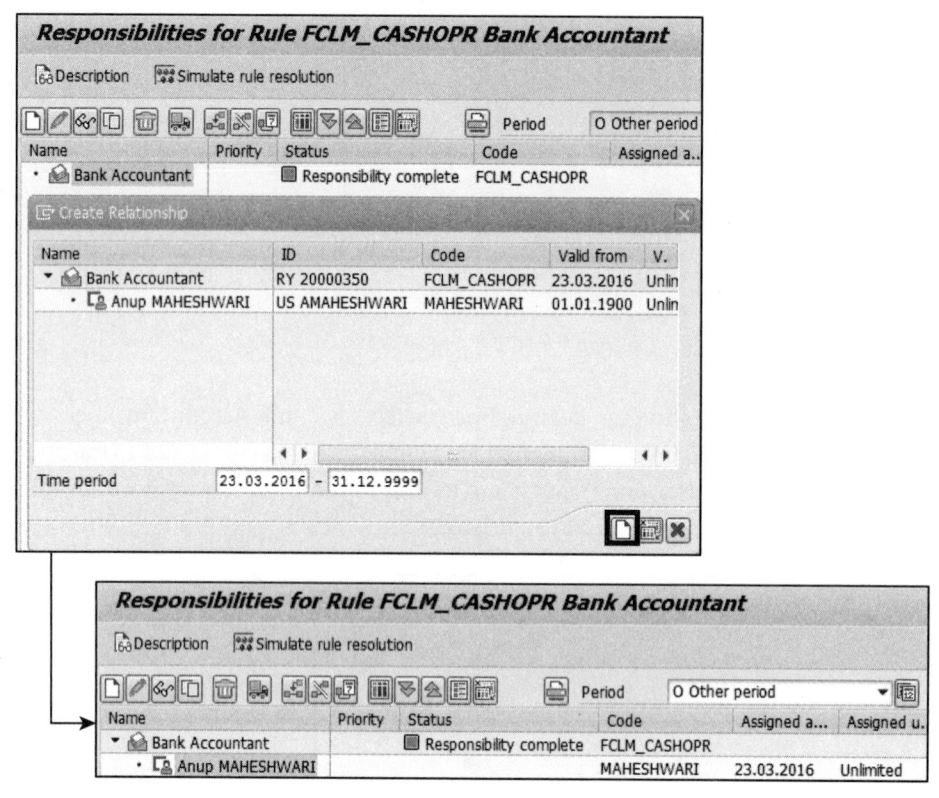

Figure 10.29 User Assigned to the Bank Accountant Rule

You need to follow the same procedure for configuring the rules for 74300006 and 74300008.

When the bank account master data needs to be changed, the workflow process is triggered only by fields that are defined as sensitive fields. These fields are specified in the Customizing activity under **Financial Supply Chain Management • Cash and Liquidity Management • Bank Account Management • Basic Settings • Define Settings for Bank Account Master Data** (refer to Figure 6.6 in Chapter 6, Section 6.3.2).

10.4.4 Create Custom-Defined Workflows

If you want to create your own workflow in Bank Account Management, follow these steps:

1. Define your own rule in Transaction PFAC (Maintain Rule), and complete the parameters for the following elements:
   - **Company Code** (technical name: AGENTDET_BUKRS)
   - **Account Type** (technical name: AGENTDET_ACCTYPE)
2. Assign the rules to the corresponding workflow steps in Workflow Builder using Transaction SWDD.
3. Define the workflow process according to your organization's business requirements by creating workflow templates in Workflow Builder using Transaction SWDD.

10.4.5 Predefined Workflows

SAP S/4HANA Finance comes with predefined workflow templates with embedded rules that can be used to accelerate the process and minimize the cost and time for custom development. This section covers some of the common templates that are used out of the box.

Business Object Repository Object

SAP predefines BOR object FCLM_CR for Bank Account Management, in which the following two events are defined:

1. CREATED
   This method triggers the workflow by generating a change request.
2. PROCESSED
   This method is used as a step in the approval process that was processed.

Rules

The following predefined rules are recommended as defined in SAP S/4HANA Finance for Bank Account Management:

- **74300006 FCLM_CASHMGR**
  This rule is defined for the cash manager role. In Bank Account Management, a cash manager can approve or reject a change request for creating, changing, or closing bank accounts.

- **74300007 FCLM_CASHOPER**
  This rule is defined for the bank accountant role. In Bank Account Management, a bank accountant role is defined to work under the supervision of cash manager and is responsible for negotiating with the bank in opening, changing, and closing bank accounts by maintaining close relationships with the banks.

- **74300008 FCLM_CASHSYSCOLL**
  This rule is defined for the key user. In Bank Account Management, a key user makes necessary configuration changes for bank accounts and house bank accounts to enable them to be used for making payments and processing bank statements.

- **74300013 FCLM_REVWOR**
  This is a fixed rule; you can't define the responsibility and assign it to this rule. The rule retrieves the contact person from the **General Data** tab under the **Internal Contact Persons** section in the **General Contact** field as defined in the bank account master data. Function module `FCLM_BAM_WORKFLOW_REVIEWAGENT` is used with this rule.

Workflow Templates

SAP provides several predefined workflow templates for use in SAP Cash Management. For example, workflow template 74300043 FCLM_AMD can be used for generating the workflow with bank account master data. The standard workflow for the overall process is depicted in Figure 10.30. You can check the actions that trigger the workflow, such as opening, changing, or closing the bank account, and the workflow also includes several subworkflows that can be used to cater to a specific business scenario for your organization.

SAP defines the following subworkflows for the most commonly used business scenarios of opening, changing, and closing bank accounts:

- **74300047 FCLM_AMD_OP (workflow for opening a new bank account)**
  The template comes with the following predefined process:
  - A bank accountant starts the process by creating a bank account master data.
  - This triggers a change request and sends the information to the worklist of the cash manager for approval.

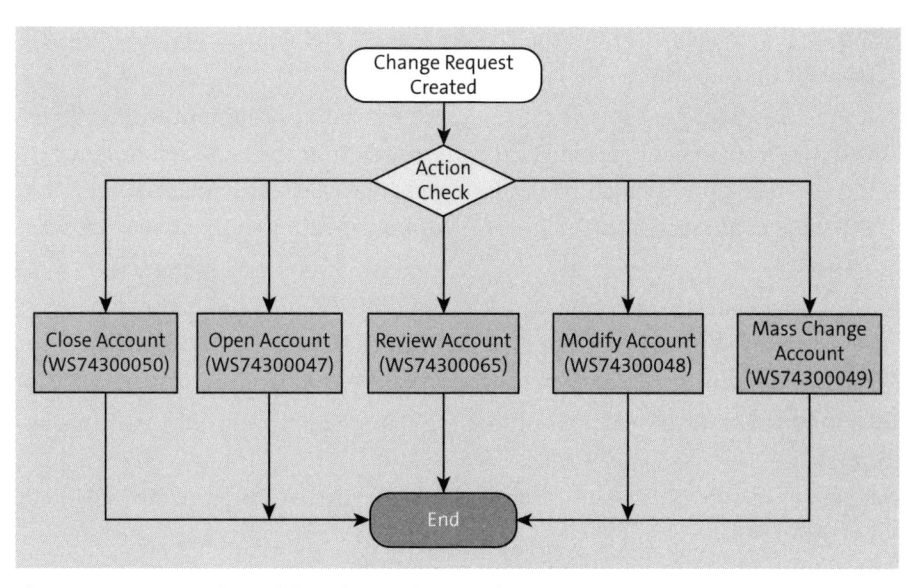

10.4 Enable SAP Business Workflow for Bank Account Management

Figure 10.30 General Workflow for Working with Bank Account Master Data

- The cash manager evaluates the change request and decides to either approve or reject the request.
- If the cash manager approves the request, the bank accountant opens the bank account and maintains necessary information for the bank account master data, such as bank account number, bank country, International Bank Account Number (IBAN), and so on. As a prerequisite, the bank accountant must check if the bank exists before creating the bank account.
- A key user finally completes the necessary configuration, such as creating house bank accounts and assigning these accounts to the appropriate bank account master data. As a prerequisite, the key user should check if the G/L account has been created before the assignment.

- **74300048 FCLM_AMD_MD (workflow for changing a bank account)**
  The template comes with the following predefined process:
  - A bank accountant changes bank account master data by changing any of the fields in the bank master.
  - This triggers a change request and sends the information in the worklist of the cash manager for approval.

- The cash manager evaluates the change request and decides to either approve or reject the request.
- If the cash manager approves the request, the bank accountant works closely with the bank to get the changes incorporated. After the bank accountant gets the confirmation from the bank that the changes have been made at the bank, the changes are then made in SAP S/4HANA by updating the bank account master data.
- A key user updates the configuration as applicable and required. For example, if there has been a change in the overdraft limits, the key user needs to incorporate the new overdraft limits in the house bank account.

- **74300049 FCLM_AMD_MM (workflow for change of signatory in multiple accounts)**
  The process defined in this template is the same as that for template 74300048 FCLM_AMD_MD.

- **74300050 FCLM_AMD_CL (workflow for closing a bank account)**
  The template comes with the following predefined process:
    - A bank accountant initiates the process to close a bank account in the bank account master data.
    - This triggers a change request and sends the information along with business reasons to the worklist of the cash manager for approval.
    - The cash manager evaluates the change request and decides to either approve or reject the request.
    - If the cash manager approves the request, the bank accountant submits the proper documentation and informs the bank to close the bank account.
    - When the bank confirms that the bank account has been closed, the bank accountant closes the account in the **Account Operations** tab.
    - A key user updates the configuration as applicable and required. For example, the key user can change the account description to differentiate it easily from other active house bank accounts before marking the account as closed.

- **74300065 FCLM_AMD_RV (workflow for reviewing bank account master data)**
  The template comes with the following predefined process:
    - A cash manager triggers the bank accounts to be included in a review process.
    - The review request is sent to the worklist of each contact person responsible for the selected bank account for review. The contact person assigned the

responsibility to review bank accounts is defined in the bank account master data on the **General Data** tab under the **Internal Contact Persons** section in the **General Contact** field.

- After the contact person in charge of the bank accounts has reviewed the bank account master data, the account contact person can either note that he or she has reviewed the bank account or make updates to the master data if any incorrect information exists.
- The changes to the bank account master data may activate another workflow, depending on the sensitive fields that are changed and the organizational rules governing those changes.
- The contact person marks the request as complete after reviewing all the bank account entries as requested by the cash manager.
- The cash manager can analyze the review completion rate by using the bank account review status monitor.

> **1709 Preview**
> With SAP S/4HANA release 1709, SAP has simplified bank relationship management with the introduction of bank fee analysis and workflow handling using Bank Account Management.

10.5 Create Cash Pools for Cash Concentration

With Bank Account Management, you can combine all the debit and credit positions that you hold at various accounts and banks into one account by creating cash pools based on the bank account group structure. You can then use the cash concentration functionality to manage your cash centrally. Physical cash concentration enables your organization to optimize the liquidity position across geographic regions to consolidate any surplus liquidity, and the required working capital is financed internally to the maximum extent possible to minimize borrowing and interest costs. To enable the cash concentration function, you need to define the activities discussed in the following subsections, found in Customizing under **Financial Accounting (New)** • **Bank Accounting** • **Business Transactions** • **Payment Transactions**.

The **Payment Request** settings shown in Figure 10.31 are required because cash concentration creates a payment request to process cash transfers.

10 SAP Cash Management

```
Display IMG

   Existing BC Sets   BC Sets for Activity   Activated BC Sets for Activity

Structure
   ▼  Financial Accounting (New)
      ▸  Financial Accounting Global Settings (New)
      ▸  General Ledger Accounting (New)
      ▸  Accounts Receivable and Accounts Payable
      ▸  Contract Accounts Receivable and Payable
      ▼  Bank Accounting
         ▸  Account Balance Interest Calculation
         ▸  Bank Accounts
         ▸  Bank Chains
         ▼  Business Transactions
            ▸  Check Deposit
            ▸  Bill of Exchange Transactions
            ▼  Payment Transactions
               ▼  Payment Request
                     Define Number Ranges for Payment Requests
                     Define Payment Blocking Indicators for Accounting Documents
                     Define Clearing Accts for Receiving Bank for Acct. Transfer
                     Define Clearing Accounts for Cross-Country Bank Account Transfers
               ▼  Payment Handling
                     Define Global Settings
                     Enter Origin Indicators
                     Assign Origin to Combination of Payments
                  Bank Clearing Account Determination
                     Define Account Determination
                     Check Account Determination
```

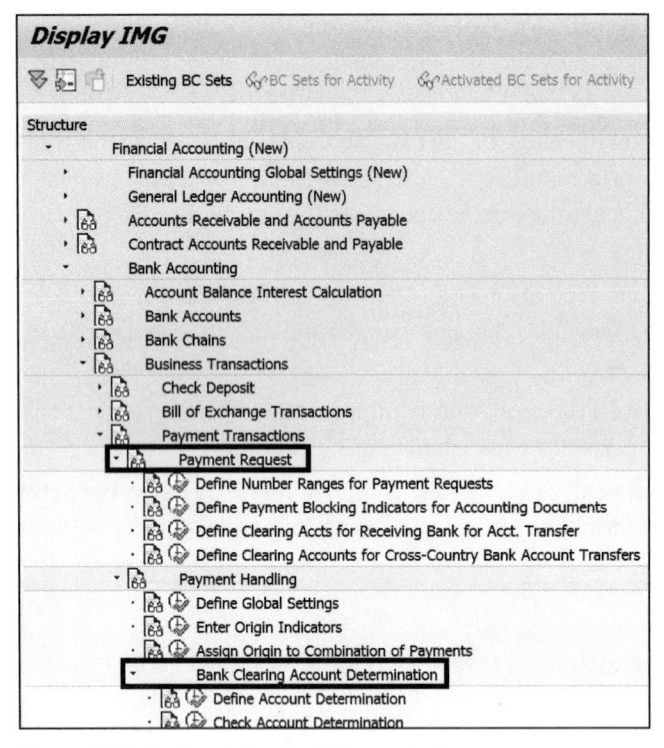

Figure 10.31 Customizing Cash Concentration

10.5.1 Define Clearing Accounts for the Receiving Bank for Account Transfers

In this activity, the offsetting accounts are defined for the receiving bank accounts when there is a transfer from one house bank to another. This amount is posted to this offsetting account when payment is made.

The cash concentration functionality facilitates the creation of payment requests using the payment advice notes, which require you to maintain the clearing account. The offsetting accounts of the paying house bank are determined by the configuration settings in the automatic payment program, which is specified based on the combination of house bank, account ID, payment method, and currency used. If a field is blank, such as **Currency**, then the combination of other values as specified is applicable for all the currencies.

In the example in Figure 10.32, you can transfer cash from house bank **BANKB** and account **ID CONCN** to house bank **BANKB** and account **ID CHECK**.

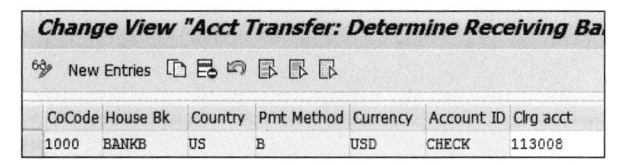

CoCode	House Bk	Country	Pmt Method	Currency	Account ID	Clrg acct
1000	BANKB	US	B	USD	CHECK	113008

Figure 10.32 Defining Clearing Accounts for a Receiving Bank during Account Transfer

10.5.2 Define Clearing Accounts for Cross-Country Bank Account Transfers

In this Customizing activity, a technical clearing account needs to be set up as a G/L master record and assigned to each company code, as shown in Figure 10.33. For processing SAP Treasury and Risk Management payments, payment orders are sent to Bank Accounting (FI-BL). Simultaneously, a document is generated in SAP Treasury and Risk Management containing a line item that needs to be cleared in a technical clearing account from FI-BL. In the payment program using Transaction F111, the payment order is selected and executed. The payment document created during the execution posts to the bank subaccount and simultaneously clears the technical clearing account. In the final execution step, the electronic account statement clears the bank subaccount against the bank account, which will then always reflect the same balance in the balance sheet bank account as the actual bank balance in the bank.

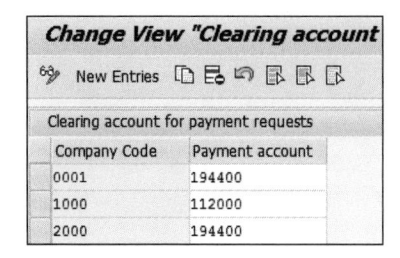

Clearing account for payment requests

Company Code	Payment account
0001	194400
1000	112000
2000	194400

Figure 10.33 Define Clearing Accounts for Cross-Country Bank Account Transfers

10.5.3 Define Account Determination

In this Customizing activity under **Payment Handling • Bank Clearing Account Determination • Define Account Determination**, you can define the bank subaccounts that are posted to in the G/L for payment transactions with bank accounts. The accounts are defined in combination with the house bank account, payment method, currency, and account ID. If a currency isn't specified in the configuration, the bank subaccount is used for posting to all currencies.

The bank subaccounts must be created for the paying company code and be fully maintained, as shown in Figure 10.34.

Change View "Account Determinatio

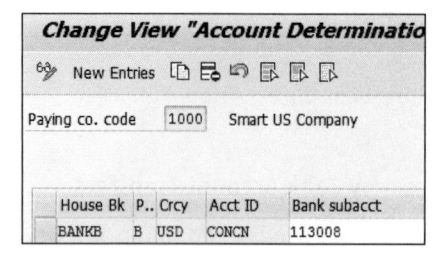

House Bk	P..	Crcy	Acct ID	Bank subacct
BANKB	B	USD	CONCN	113008

Paying co. code 1000 Smart US Company

Figure 10.34 Bank Clearing Account Determination

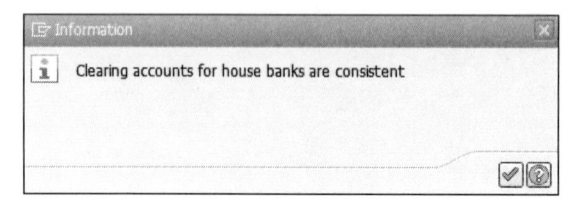

10.5.4 Check Account Determination

This Customizing activity checks for inconsistencies in the bank subaccounts that were defined in the previous section. Inconsistencies might arise due to multiple factors; for example, bank subaccounts assigned in account determination might have been duplicated and defined for payment transactions with customers and vendors. If such inconsistencies persist, you should either change the bank subaccount G/L assignment or check the specifications in the payment program, bank selection, and accounts. When you execute this activity, make sure you see the screen shown in Figure 10.35.

Clearing accounts for house banks are consistent

Figure 10.35 Check Account Determination

If you get an error related to an inconsistency between the table entries T042I and T042Y, you can check and change the configuration using Transactions F110 and F111 in **Environment • Maintain Config**.

10.6 Manage Cash Operations

This section focuses on the key activities of managing cash operations, including monitoring the status of incoming bank statements and preparing a daily cash position forecast with information such as cash receipts, disbursements, and closing balances. A cash manager also needs to oversee and determine the foreign currency exposure and the bank risk by checking the deposits in banks with low ratings, initiating bank transfers and payments, and checking, approving, and monitoring payments.

There are three important settings in SAP Cash Management:

- **Planning Level/Planning Group**
  Indicates the integration with other components
- **Liquidity Item**
  Indicates the origination of cash flow
- **Flow Type**
  Indicates the lifecycle of cash flow

To use SAP Cash Management, you need to make the following configurations in the Customizing activity under **Financial Supply Chain Management • Cash and Liquidity Management • Cash Management** (see Figure 10.36).

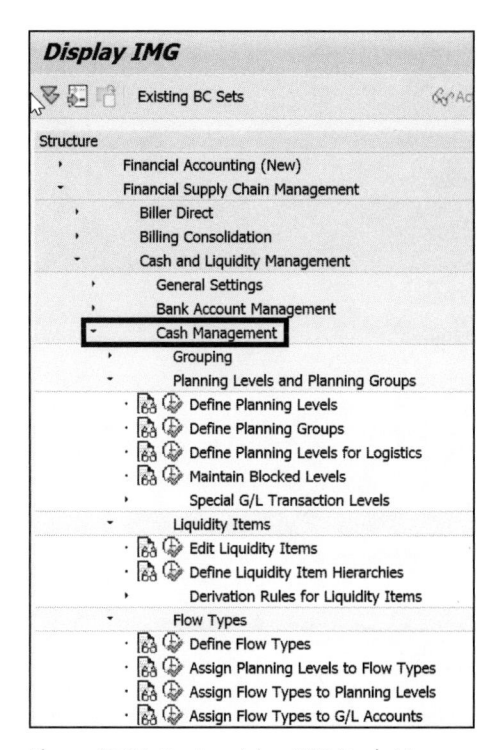

Figure 10.36 Customizing SAP Cash Management

10.6.1 Define and Assign Flow Types

Flow types define and specify the steps in the lifecycle of cash flows, from forecasted cash flows to actual cash flows. Any data consumed by SAP Cash Management applications must have a flow type assignment, such as data records in table BSEG and One Exposure from Operations hub records.

Flow types starting with *90* represent the actual cash flow confirmed by the bank as reflected in the bank statement, whereas flow types starting with numbers from *20* to *80* represent forecasted cash flows for where the payables and receivables will be at a future date.

The flow categories in Table 10.1 come predefined by SAP in database table FQMI_FLOW_CAT.

Flow Category	Flow Level	Flow Category Description
200000	20	Sales Order
200001	20	Purchase Order
200010	20	Fee Receivable
200011	20	Fee Payable
200020	20	MM Interest Receivable
200021	20	MM Interest Payable
200100	20	Money Market Asset
200101	20	Money Market Liability
200200	20	FX Forward Position Buy
200201	20	FX Forward Position Sell
200202	20	FX Forward Position Fixed
201000	20	Fin. Instrument Receivable
201001	20	Fin. Instrument Payable
300000	30	Invoiced Tax Receivable
300001	30	Invoiced Tax Payable

Table 10.1 Flow Types

Flow Category	Flow Level	Flow Category Description
300002	30	Revenue
300003	30	Material Inventory
300004	30	Unclassified P&L
300005	30	Expenses
300010	30	Output Tax Decrease
300011	30	Input Tax Decrease
400000	40	Receivables Inter-Company
400001	40	Payables Inter-Company
500000	50	Receivables from Down Paymt
500001	50	Payables from Down Paymt
600000	60	Regular Receivables Increase
600001	60	Regular Payables Increase
600010	60	Regular Payables Decrease
600011	60	Regular Receivables Decrease
700000	70	Payment Request In
700001	70	Payment Request Out
700002	70	Payment Request Clearing
800000	80	Self-Initiated Cash Transit In
800001	80	Self-Initiated Cash Transit Out
800003	80	Bank-Initiated Cash Transit Out
800004	80	Bank-Initiated Cash Transit In
900000	90	Incoming Bank Cash
900001	90	Outgoing Bank Cash
900050	90	Incoming Bank Cash Forecast

Table 10.1 Flow Types (Cont.)

Flow Category	Flow Level	Flow Category Description
900051	90	Outgoing Bank Cash Forecast
900100	90	Incoming Bank Cash
900101	90	Outgoing Bank Cash
900102	90	Bank Cash Balance Increase
900103	90	Bank Cash Balance Decrease
900104	90	Incoming Bank Cash (CML)
900105	90	Outgoing Bank Cash (CML)
900106	90	Incoming Cash (FI-CA)
900107	90	Outgoing Cash (FI-CA)
900108	90	Cash Balance Increase (IDoc)
900109	90	Cash Balance Decrease (IDoc)
900110	90	Incoming Cash (IDoc)
900111	90	Outgoing Cash (IDoc)
900112	90	Incoming Cash (LP)
900113	90	Outgoing Cash (LP)

Table 10.1 Flow Types (Cont.)

In the steps in the following subsections, you maintain all the account assignment Customizing settings that control the payment program and assign your flow types to the planning level. The flow type differentiates between payables and remitted payments, as well as confirmed deductions and cash in a bank account.

Derive Flow Types for Accounting Documents

Flow types in database table BSEG are derived from G/L account values as posted in the line items of the accounting documents. Define the logic for deriving flow types from the G/L accounts as follows:

1. **Define bank G/L accounts in the bank master data.**
   G/L accounts assigned in the house bank account master data represent the actual

data in the cash flow position that have been confirmed by the bank through the import of electronic or manual bank statements. You define this type of G/L account in the Web Dynpro application under **Bank Account Management • Bank Accounts • Manage Bank Accounts**. Enter the G/L account number in the **House Bank Account Data** section under the **Connectivity Path** tab (see Figure 10.37).

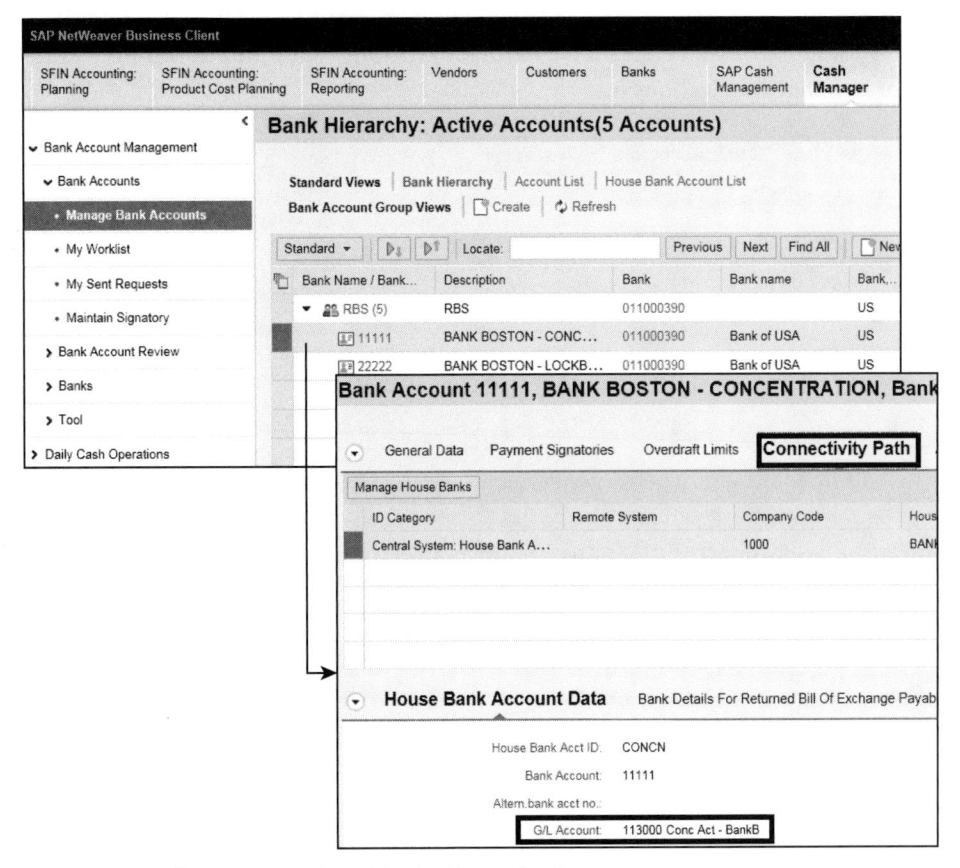

Figure 10.37 G/L Account Assigned to the House Bank

2. **Define the bank clearing accounts for payment transactions.**
   G/L accounts defined as bank clearing accounts represent the forecasted data in the cash flow position. In this case, the payments have been made in the system, but either the outgoing payment file hasn't been remitted to the bank, or the payment received by the bank hasn't yet been confirmed by the receiving bank. In this activity, you make settings that the payment program uses to select the banks or

bank accounts from which payment is to be made. For each house bank, payment method, currency, and account ID combination, you can specify which bank account is to be used for payments.

You define bank clearing accounts determination logic in the Customizing activity under **Financial Accounting (New)** • **Accounts Receivable and Accounts Payable** • **Business Transactions** • **Outgoing Payments** • **Automatic Outgoing Payments** • **Payment Method/Bank Selection for Payment Program** • **Set Up Bank Determination for Payment Transactions** (see Figure 10.38).

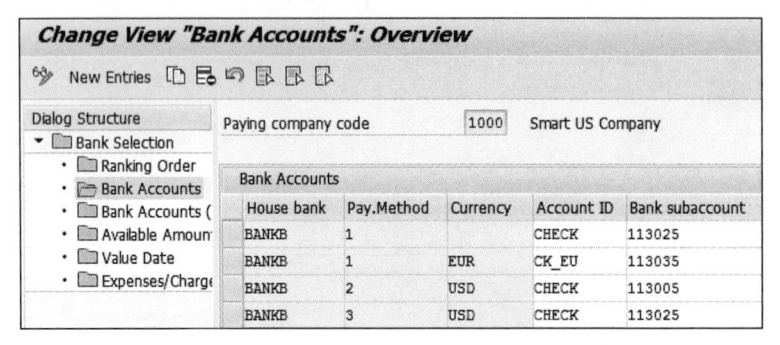

Figure 10.38 Bank Determination for Payment Transactions

3. **Define bank subaccounts for payments between bank accounts.**
   Define the bank subaccounts to be posted to in the G/L for payment transactions with bank accounts in the Customizing activity under **Financial Accounting (New)** • **Bank Accounting** • **Business Transactions** • **Payment Transactions** • **Payment Handling** • **Bank Clearing Account Determination** • **Define Account Determination** (see Figure 10.39).

Figure 10.39 Bank Clearing Account Determination

The G/L account, as specified by the combination of house bank account (**House Bk**), payment method (**PM**), currency (**Crcy**), and account ID (**Acct ID**), represents forecasted data in the cash flow position. If a currency isn't specified in any of the combinations, the bank subaccount applies to all currencies.

If the bank subaccount is specified as an input in the payment request, this entry takes precedence over the account determination settings. This table must be maintained primarily for the use of SAP Cash Management and forecasts related to bank account transfers and cash concentration.

4. **Define clearing accounts for the receiving bank for account transfers.**
   In this activity, the offsetting accounts are defined for the receiving bank accounts when there is a transfer of funds from one house bank to another. This amount is posted to this offsetting account when payment is made.

   The offsetting accounts for the receiving house bank are derived based on the Customizing activity under **Financial Accounting (New)** • **Bank Accounting** • **Business Transactions** • **Payment Transactions** • **Payment Request** • **Define Clearing Accts for Receiving Bank for Acct. Transfer** (see Figure 10.40).

CoCode	House Bk	Country	Pmt Method	Currency	Account ID	Clrg acct
1000	BANKB	US	1			113008
1000	BANKB	US	3			113027
1000	BANKB	US	B	USD	CHECK	113008

   Figure 10.40 Clearing Accounts for Receiving Bank for Account Transfers

5. **Define a clearing account for payment requests.**
   G/L accounts defined as clearing accounts for payment requests represent the forecasted data in the cash flow position for which payment requests are ready for the payment run to be turned into actual payments using Transaction F111. You can use this clearing account for payment requests to group payments, and then post them against bank subaccounts.

   You define payment request clearing accounts in the Customizing activity under **Financial Supply Chain Management** • **Treasury and Risk Management** • **Transaction Manager** • **General Settings** • **Payment Management** • **Payment Requests** • **Define Clearing Account for Payment Requests** (see Figure 10.41).

10   SAP Cash Management

Figure 10.41 Clearing Account for Payment Requests

6. **Define tax G/L accounts.**

    G/L accounts defined as tax accounts represent the forecasted cash flow position related to tax payments. In this activity, you specify the accounts to which the different tax types and categories are to be posted. The system determines these accounts for automatic postings.

    Tax accounts for Account Payable (AP) and Accounts Receivable (AR) are defined in the Customizing activity under **Financial Accounting (New)** • **Financial Accounting Global Settings (New)** • **Tax on Sales/Purchases** • **Posting** • **Define Tax Accounts** (see Figure 10.42).

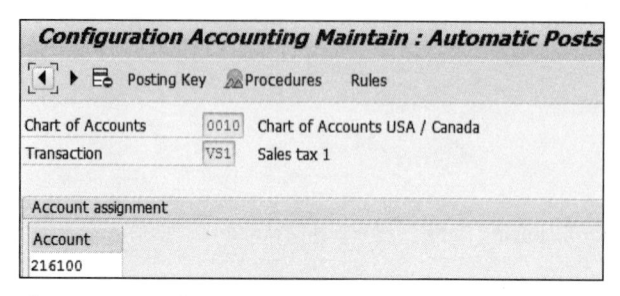

Figure 10.42 Defining Tax Accounts

7. **Define vendor G/L accounts.**

    G/L accounts defined as vendor accounts represent forecasted data in the cash flow position. These accounts are specified as reconciliation accounts in the vendor master data and are identified through the account type K, representing payables data in the corresponding accounting documents.

8. **Define customer G/L accounts.**

    G/L accounts defined as customer accounts represent forecasted data in the cash flow position. These accounts are specified as reconciliation accounts in the customer master data and are identified through the account type D, representing receivables data in the corresponding accounting documents.

Define Custom Flow Types

If the default derivation logic for G/L accounts is sufficient for your organization's cash flow requirements, no additional configuration is required. However, if the default assignment needs to be overruled or flow types to additional G/L accounts need to be assigned, you can do so in the Customizing activity under **Financial Supply Chain Management • Cash and Liquidity Management • Cash Management • Flow Types • Define Flow Types** (see Figure 10.43).

Flow Type	Flow Type Description	Category	Level	Flow Category Description
ZT_01	Incoming Payment	300010	30	Output Tax Decrease
ZT_02	Cash Position	900111	90	Outgoing Cash (IDOC)

Figure 10.43 Defining Flow Types

Assign Planning Levels to Flow Types

In this Customizing activity, you can assign planning levels to flow types. When you upload bank cash balances in Microsoft Excel format to the One Exposure from Operations hub using Transaction FQM21 (Import Bank Cash Balances), the following flow types are assigned to the transactions:

- 900102: Bank cash balance increases BALANCE_AMOUNT > 0
- 900103: Bank cash balance decreases BALANCE_AMOUNT < 0

While evaluating the cash position, if you want to distinguish according to planning level, you must assign the relevant planning levels to the flow types in the Customizing activity under **Financial Supply Chain Management • Cash and Liquidity Management • Cash Management • Flow Types • Assign Planning Levels to Flow Types**, as shown in Figure 10.44.

Flow Type	Flow Type Description	Level	Short text
900103	Bank Cash Balance Decrease	B4	Bank coll.

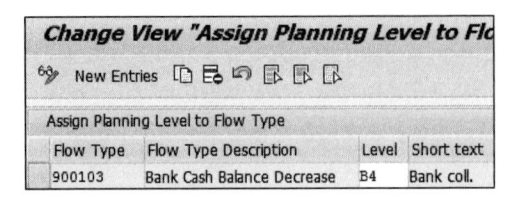

Figure 10.44 Assigning Planning Levels to Flow Types

10 SAP Cash Management

Assign Flow Types to Planning Levels

In this Customizing activity, you can assign flow types to planning levels. When SAP Cash Management is active, the following flow types are assigned to the transactions:

- 900110: Incoming cash (IDoc) when amount > 0
- 900111: Outgoing cash (IDoc) when amount < 0

If you want to analyze the confirmed cash in your cash position, you must assign different flow types depicting both the increase and the decrease to the planning levels that represent elements of confirmed cash. The flow types 900108 (Cash Balance Increase [IDoc]) and 900109 (Cash Balance Decrease [IDoc]) are available in standard SAP to be used for this purpose.

As an illustration, for planning level F0 (Posting to Bank Account), you can assign the flow types 900108 and 900109 for cash balance increase and decrease, respectively. The cash balance mapping to planning level F0 is reflected in the cash position as confirmed cash.

This Customizing is handled under **Financial Supply Chain Management • Cash and Liquidity Management • Cash Management • Flow Types • Assign Flow Types to Planning Levels**, as shown in Figure 10.45.

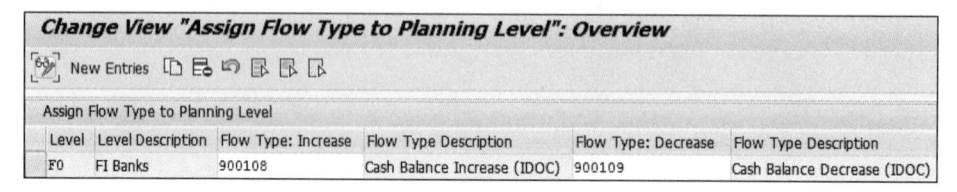

Figure 10.45 Assigning Flow Types to Planning Levels

Assign Flow Types to General Ledger Accounts

The flow types for forecasted cash based on the data from invoices, payments, and bank statements in the One Exposure from Operations hub (database table FQM_FLOW) are derived from the fixed logic as specified in the program. Within this integration, the system classifies accounting document line items into the following categories:

- **Receivables or payables**
  Line item posting on a customer or vendor account
- **Cash in transit**
  Line item posting on a bank clearing account

- **Cash**
  Line item posting on a bank account

The system determines the category in the following ways:

- **Receivable or payable**
  Items with account type K (vendor) or D (customer)
- **Cash in transit**
  Items with a G/L account that has one of the following characteristics:
  - Maintained in account determination of payment program (table T042I), is a balance sheet account (SKA1-XBILK), and isn't a reconciliation account (SKB1-MITKZ)
  - Maintained in account determination of bank-to-bank transfer (table T042Y), is a balance sheet account (SKA1-XBILK), and isn't a reconciliation account (SKB1-MITKZ)
  - Marked as cash-relevant (SKB1-XGKON) and with open-item management (SKB1-XOPVW)
- **Cash**
  Items with a G/L account that has one of the following characteristics:
  - Maintained in-house bank accounts (table T012K)
  - Marked as cash-relevant (SKB1-XGKON) without open-item management (SKB1-XOPVW)

For these accounting document items, the system derives the following flow types:

- **Receivable or payable**
  - 600000: Regular Receivables Increase
  - 600001: Regular Payables Increase
  - 600200: Unallocated Receivables Increase
  - 600201: Unallocated Payables Increase
- **Cash in transit**
  - 800006: Incoming Cash in Transit Increase
  - 800008: Outgoing Cash in Transit Increase
- **Cash**
  - 900006: Incoming Bank Confirmed Cash Increase
  - 900008: Outgoing Bank Confirmed Cash Increase

For items representing payables, receivables, or cash in transit, One Exposure from Operations derives cash forecasts. If the accounting documents contain other items than the ones just described and you want to have them processed by the integration of the financial operations source document into One Exposure from Operations, you have to assign these items to one of the categories mentioned previously. These flow types are delivered as standard, so there's no need to create additional customer-specific flow types for this.

This Customizing activity is handled under **Financial Supply Chain Management • Cash and Liquidity Management • Cash Management • Flow Types • Assign Flow Types to G/L Accounts**, as shown in Figure 10.46.

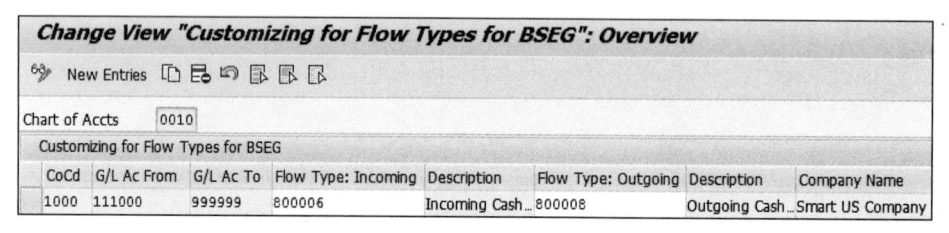

Figure 10.46 Assign Flow Types to G/L Accounts

10.6.2 Define Liquidity Items and Hierarchies

A *liquidity item* specifies the purpose and origination of the cash flow in a business. In the reports generated by SAP Cash Management, you need to classify the cash flows into a structure that has a business relevance for your organization and makes sense for your CFO. You can base the structure on cash flows from operations, cash flows from investments, or cash flows from financing activities, to name a few.

Both SAP ERP Financials (table BSEG) and One Exposure from Operations (table FQM_FLOW) have the **Liquidity Item** field defined in the table. For memo records, end users can enter liquidity-item information when creating memo records.

Liquidity items are configured under **Financial Supply Chain Management • Cash and Liquidity Management • Cash Management • Liquidity Items**, as shown in Figure 10.47.

10.6 Manage Cash Operations

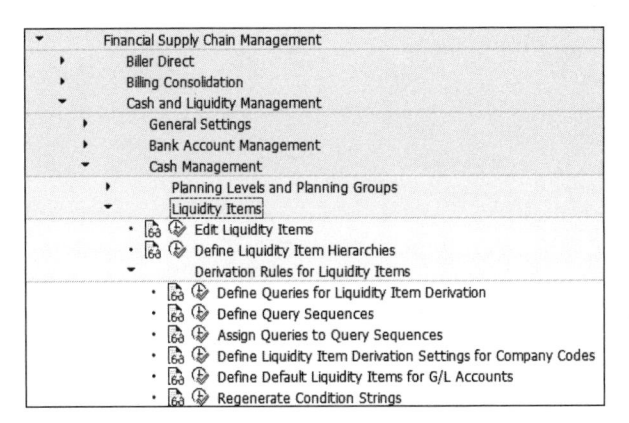

Figure 10.47 Liquidity Items

In the following subsection, you'll create and change liquidity items that impact the inflow and outflow of cash, define and structure the liquidity item hierarchies, and configure the derivation rules of liquidity items for actual and plan data.

Edit Liquidity Items

In this Customizing activity, you can create and change liquidity items. Liquidity items comprise both the source and use of cash flows in your company, so they can be used for financial planning and forecasting in SAP Cash Management. To create a liquidity item, you must define its key, name, and description, along with the cash flow direction.

Cash flow direction denotes whether the cash component assigned in the liquidity item is inflow or outflow. The direction plays a pivotal role in the cash flow calculation for all the reports and planning applications in SAP Cash and Liquidity Management. For example, when you create a liquidity item, such as Customer 01, you should specify the cash flow direction as inflow to present the cash flows related to the incoming payments from your customers.

The liquidity item needs to be defined appropriately, as shown in Figure 10.48. If you want to integrate the outgoing payment to get the correct bank balance data, define a liquidity item by entering "LP_CASHOP" in the **Liquidity Item** column.

If you want to use the currency exchange function, enter the following two liquidity items and their cash flow directions and descriptions:

- **LP_EXF**: "Cash converted from another currency"
- **LP_EXI**: "Cash converted to another currency"

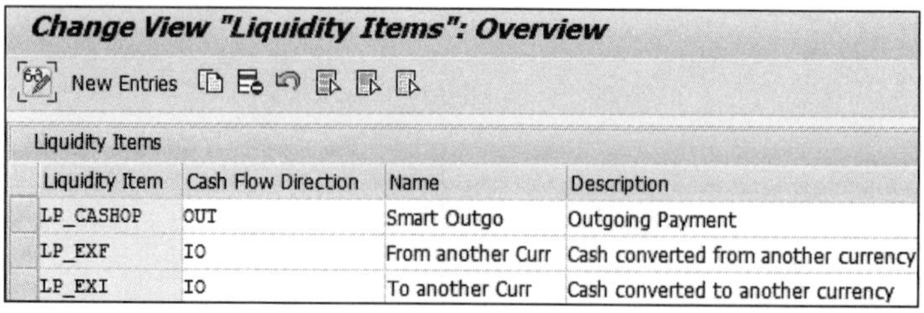
Change View "Liquidity Items": Overview
New Entries
Liquidity Items
Liquidity Item | Cash Flow Direction | Name | Description
LP_CASHOP | OUT | Smart Outgo | Outgoing Payment
LP_EXF | IO | From another Curr | Cash converted from another currency
LP_EXI | IO | To another Curr | Cash converted to another currency

Figure 10.48 Editing Liquidity Items

Define Liquidity Item Hierarchies

Liquidity items also can be structured to represent a liquidity item hierarchy. In this Customizing activity, you can create, modify, transport, and display the hierarchy structures for all liquidity items. The structures are integral parts of reports and functions related to cash and liquidity. You can define different structures for different company codes, intervals, or purposes, according to your business requirements (see Figure 10.49).

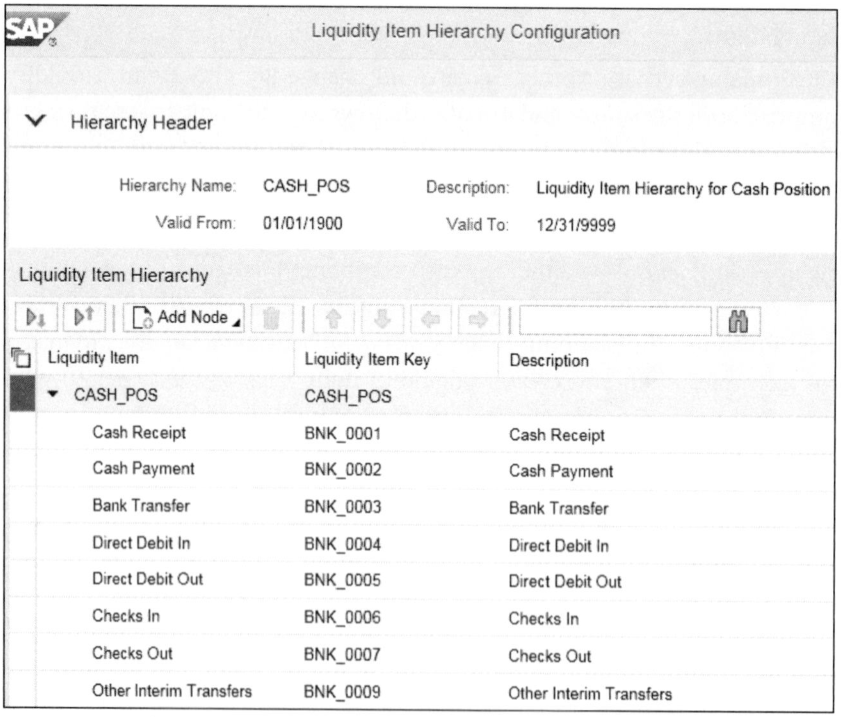
Liquidity Item Hierarchy Configuration
Hierarchy Header
Hierarchy Name: CASH_POS
Description: Liquidity Item Hierarchy for Cash Position
Valid From: 01/01/1900
Valid To: 12/31/9999
Liquidity Item Hierarchy
Add Node
Liquidity Item | Liquidity Item Key | Description
CASH_POS | CASH_POS
Cash Receipt | BNK_0001 | Cash Receipt
Cash Payment | BNK_0002 | Cash Payment
Bank Transfer | BNK_0003 | Bank Transfer
Direct Debit In | BNK_0004 | Direct Debit In
Direct Debit Out | BNK_0005 | Direct Debit Out
Checks In | BNK_0006 | Checks In
Checks Out | BNK_0007 | Checks Out
Other Interim Transfers | BNK_0009 | Other Interim Transfers

Figure 10.49 Liquidity Item Hierarchy Configuration

10.6 Manage Cash Operations

Derivation Rules for Liquidity Items

You need to configure the rules for deriving the liquidity items for both forecasted and actual data using the Customizing activity under **Financial Supply Chain Management • Cash and Liquidity Management • Cash Management • Liquidity Items • Derivation Rules for Liquidity Items**. Complete the following steps:

1. Create a query sequence using Transaction FLQC15.
2. Create queries for linking to the query sequence using Transaction FLQQA1.
3. Assign the queries to the query sequence using Transaction FLQQA5.
4. Define the parameters to derive liquidity items relevant for the company code using Transaction FLQC0.
5. Define the liquidity items for G/L accounts. Liquidity item derivation logic by query and query sequence has higher priority compared to the default value associated with the G/L accounts, as shown in Figure 10.50.
6. Derive liquidity items for source application data in the One Exposure from Operations hub.

Chart...	Co...	Account from	Account to	Incl/excl	F...	Default Value	Name
0010		11001010	11001010	I Inclus...		BNK_0002	Cash Payment
0010		11001020	11001020	I Inclus...		BNK_0003	Bank Transfer
0010		11001030	11001030	I Inclus...		BNK_0009	Other Interim Transf
0010		11001040	11001040	I Inclus...		BNK_0005	Direct Debit Out
0010		11001050	11001050	I Inclus...		BNK_0007	Checks Out
0010		11001060	11001060	I Inclus...		BNK_0006	Checks In
0010		11001070	11001070	I Inclus...		BNK_0006	Checks In
0010		11001080	11001080	I Inclus...		BNK_0001	Cash Receipt
0010		11002010	11002010	I Inclus...		BNK_0002	Cash Payment
0010		11002020	11002020	I Inclus...		BNK_0003	Bank Transfer
0010		11002030	11002030	I Inclus...		BNK_0009	Other Interim Transf
0010		11002040	11002040	I Inclus...		BNK_0005	Direct Debit Out
0010		11002050	11002050	I Inclus...		BNK_0007	Checks Out
0010		11002060	11002060	I Inclus...		BNK_0006	Checks In
0010		11002070	11002070	I Inclus...		BNK_0006	Checks In
0010		11002080	11002080	I Inclus...		BNK_0001	Cash Receipt

Figure 10.50 Defining Default Liquidity Items for G/L Accounts

For data integrated into the One Exposure from Operations hub from source applications such as SAP Treasury and Risk Management, Loans Management, or SAP

Contract Accounts Receivable and Payable (FI-CA) data, default derivation rules don't exist for the liquidity items. You need to create query and query sequences to fill this gap. You should always mark **Origin** as **X**, which specifies that the derivation logic is performed against the structure of the One Exposure from Operations hub.

10.6.3 Define Planning Levels and Planning Groups

The planning level reflects both the actual and forecasted accounting transactions, such as outgoing and incoming checks, sales and purchase orders, receivables and payables, confirmed or unconfirmed payment advices, and so on. A planning group represents a set of characteristics of the customer or vendor group. This enables you to break down incoming and outgoing payments based on the amount and the forecasted cash inflow or outflow based on the terms of payment per the contract terms with customers and vendors. Planning levels are configured under **Financial Supply Chain Management • Cash and Liquidity Management • Cash Management • Planning Levels and Planning Groups**.

In the following section, you define the planning levels and planning groups that help in estimating and displaying the cash position and cash forecast reports.

Define Planning Levels

In this step, you specify a planning level for each business scenario involving movement of funds and allocate this planning level to the appropriate source symbol, as shown in Figure 10.51.

Level	SC	Source	Short text	Planning level long text
F0		BNK	FI Banks	Posting to bank account
F1		PSK	FI C/V	Posting of purchasing & sales

Figure 10.51 Defining Planning Levels

Planning levels are used to display the beginning and ending account balances for all the financial transactions used in SAP Cash Management. In standard SAP, levels starting with prefix *F* or *B* are reserved internally for automatically updating data during posting so that you can readily analyze the cash position without making any updates. Manually created payment advice notes or planned items are allocated to different levels.

The recommended approach is to use the following levels provided by standard SAP:

- Level F0: Bank accounts
- Level F1: Customers and vendors
- Levels B1 to Bn: Bank clearing accounts
- Level CP: Confirmed payment advice notes
- Level UP: Unconfirmed payment advice notes
- Level NI: Noted items

When displaying the cash position, the planning level F0 as assigned in the G/L account master data represents the actual amounts posted to bank accounts. The other levels reflect planned bank account transactions, which include postings to bank clearing accounts or entered payment advice notes. The cash flow position can thus be used to compare planned data with actual data. The assignment of a planning level to a G/L account ensures the calculation of the planning date (field FDTAG) in the accounting documents, as shown in Figure 10.52.

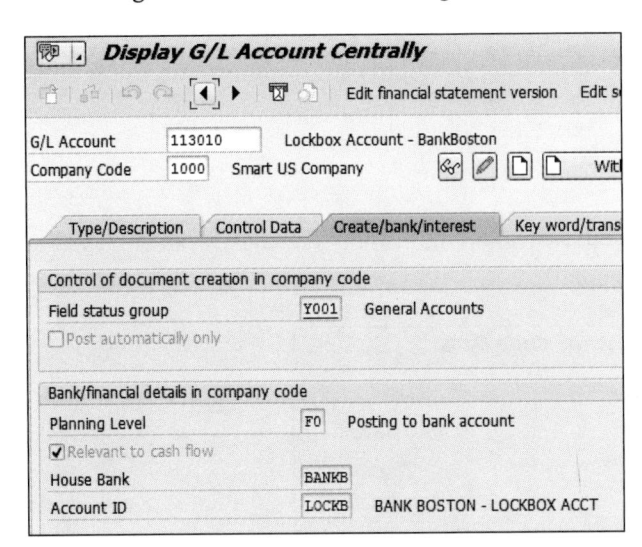

Figure 10.52 Assigning the Planning Level to the G/L Account

Define Planning Groups

In this step, you define the planning groups for different categories of customers and vendors. Remember that the planning group represents characteristics and behavior patterns of the customers or vendors.

10 SAP Cash Management

We recommend that you use the following groups provided by SAP:

- O1: Domestic vendors
- O2: Foreign vendors
- O3: Affiliated companies, vendors
- O4: Major suppliers
- I1: Bank collection for customers
- I2: Domestic customers
- I3: Foreign customers
- I4: Risk customers

You create your planning groups per your requirements, as shown in Figure 10.53. In addition, you allocate your planning groups to a planning level that you've created for your subledger accounts.

Plan. grp	Level	SCn DaCo	Short text	Description
A1	F1	✓	Domestic	Domestic payments (A/P)
A2	F1	☐	Foreign	Foreign payments (A/P)
A3	F1	☐	V-affil	Vendor-affiliated companies
A4	F1	☐	Major ven	Major vendors
A5	F1	☐	HR	Personnel costs
A6	F1	☐	Taxes	Taxes
E1	F1	☐	Receipts	Customer receipts (A/R)
E2	F1	☐	Domestic	Domestic customers

Figure 10.53 Defining Planning Groups

You assign the planning group to customers and vendors by making an entry in the master record, as shown in Figure 10.54.

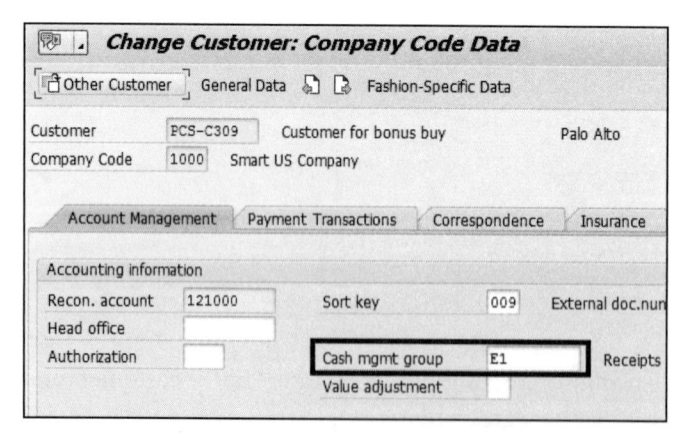

Figure 10.54 Allocating a Planning Group to the Customer Master

10.7 Load Data to One Exposure from Operations

Define Planning Levels for Logistics

In this step, the transactions from the procure-to-pay and order-to-cash processes (from Materials Management [MM] and Sales and Distribution [SD]) are allocated to the appropriate planning levels for updating this data. This allocation is required in this case because the system can't determine the planning level from the master record fields, although it can do the same to access data from FI.

In FI, the planning level for G/L accounts is assigned in the master record from which it derives the level. The planning group is used to specify the subledger accounts that help in determining the level for FI postings. However, in logistics, a business transaction is represented by an internal ID (**Int code** field):

- 1: Purchase Requisition
- 2: Purchase Order
- 3: Scheduling Agreement
- 101: Order

These transactions need to be assigned to a planning level so that you can distinguish them in SAP Cash Management, as shown in Figure 10.55.

Int code	Level	Plan. grp	Planning level long text	Definition of internal ID
1	M1	A1	Purchase requisition	Purchase Requisition
2	M2	A1	Purchase order	Purchase Order
3	M3	A1	Scheduling agreement	Scheduling Agreement
101	S1	E2	Sales Orders	Order

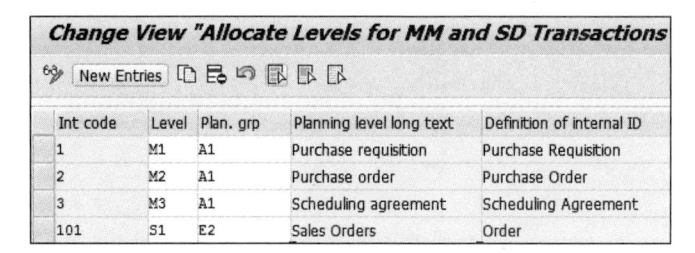

Figure 10.55 Allocating Planning Levels for Logistics

10.7 Load Data to One Exposure from Operations

The *One Exposure from Operations hub* is the central storage location for operational data used to manage an organization's exposures, along with its cash and liquidity position. It acts as the single source of truth for any financial risk. The provision of the data in the One Exposure from Operations hub facilitates working capital planning and computation of risk exposure across the entire organization. Currently, SAP Cash Management uses the One Exposure from Operations hub to acquire data from both the central system and remote systems.

In the following sections, you'll define and integrate the data flows from various applications and remote systems into One Exposure from Operations.

10.7.1 Integration with Source Applications

The following source applications can provide real-time information into the One Exposure from Operations hub, and SAP Cash Management consumes the transaction data from these sources in preparing cash flows and cash position:

- SAP Treasury and Risk Management
- Materials Management (MM)
- Loans Management (FS-CML)
- SAP Contract Accounts Receivable and Payable (FI-CA)

In the Customizing activity, you need to activate the integration for each of the applications in all company codes. Once activated, all new and changed documents of the sending application are stored in One Exposure from Operations.

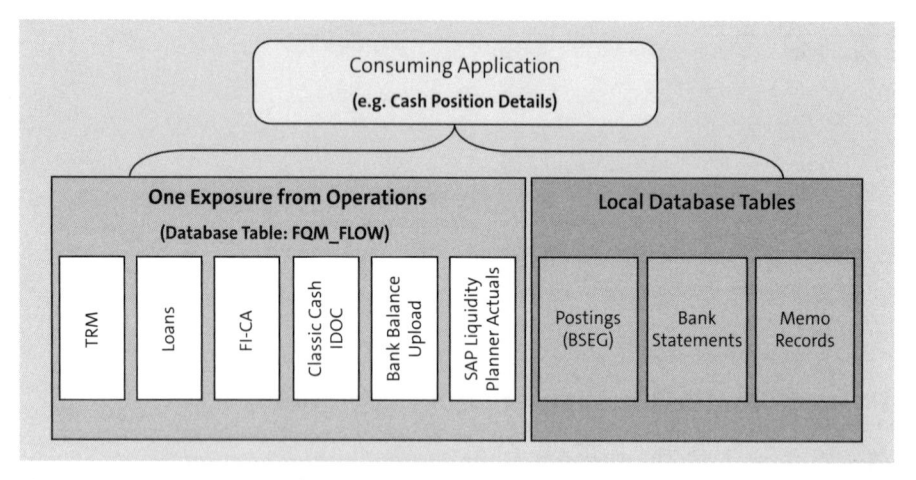

Figure 10.56 illustrates One Exposure from Operations data consumption.

Figure 10.56 One Exposure from Operations Data Consumption

10.7.2 Integration with Remote Systems

With the implementation of SAP S/4HANA Finance, the following cash flow components can be integrated and updated periodically from remote systems into One Exposure from Operations:

- **Bank account balances via Excel upload**
  To upload bank account balances (derived from external sources) in the central system, perform the **Import Bank Cash Balances** activity in the SAP menu under **Accounting • Financial Supply Chain Management • Cash and Liquidity Management • Tools • One Exposure from Operations • FQM21—Import Bank Cash Balances**.

  The import bank cash balances report (FQME_BANK_CASH_BAL_IMPORT) is used to upload bank cash balances into the One Exposure from Operations hub and to update existing balances.

  Connectivity path information and the mapping of planning levels and flow types needs to be maintained in the bank account master data.

- **Expected cash flows from classic SAP Cash Management**
  A request of the central system triggers the transfer of the classic SAP Cash Management data via an IDoc. The activity performed in the central system to retrieve the SAP Cash Management data is carried out by executing the transaction in the SAP menu under **Accounting • Financial Supply Chain Management • Cash and Liquidity Management • Tools • Distribution • FF$4—Retrieve CM Data**.

- **SAP Liquidity Planner actuals via web service**
  The following activities need to be configured for converting company codes and other organizational units from remote systems under the **Financial Supply Chain Management • Cash and Liquidity Management • Cash Management • Data Setup • Inbound Mapping for Integration of Remote Data into One Exposure** Customizing menu path:
  - Convert Company Codes
  - Convert Sender Planning Groups
  - Convert Sender Planning Levels
  - Convert Sender Business Areas

10.8 Set Up Cash Management Transaction Data

This activity sets up transactional data to be used by SAP Cash Management applications. Applications in SAP Cash Management consume data from the following sources:

- Imported bank statements from database tables FEBKO/FEBEP for bank balances as confirmed by the house bank

- Accounting document line items from database tables BSEG and BKPF for cash flows as posted in the system
- Memo records from database table FDES to update information related to cash forecast that isn't posted in G/L
- One Exposure from Operations hub from database table FQM_FLOW for data from other components such as SAP Treasury and Risk Management, Consumer and Mortgage Loans (CML), FI-CA, and integrated data from remote systems

The interim classic SAP Cash Management tables such as FDSB and FDSR aren't used, which saves space by reducing the data footprint in the new SAP Cash Management. You need to perform the Customizing activity for building the SAP Cash Management data posted in accounting under **Financial Supply Chain Management • Cash and Liquidity Management • Cash Management • Data Setup**, as shown in Figure 10.57.

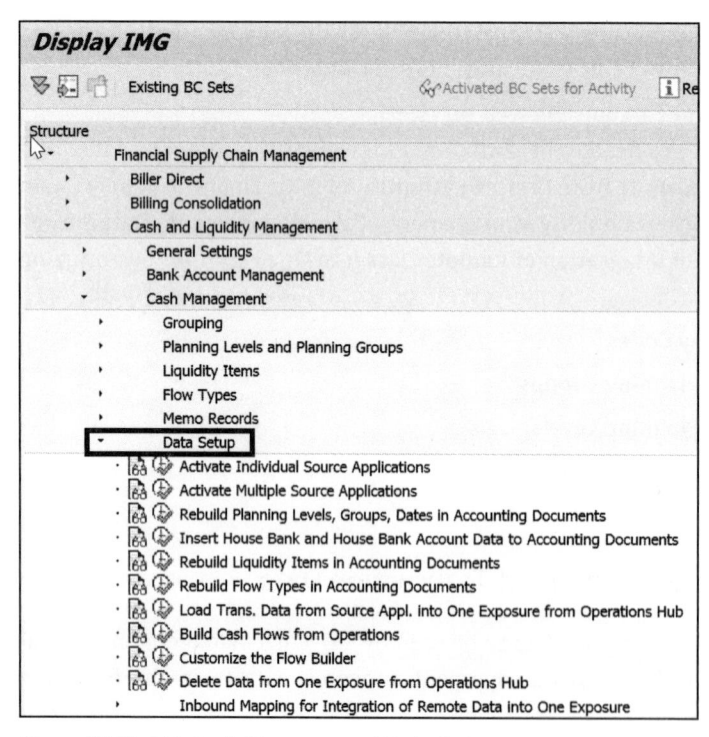

Figure 10.57 SAP Cash Management Data Setup

10.8 Set Up Cash Management Transaction Data

The data setup procedure needs to be executed after the installation of SAP S/4HANA Finance. Data needs to be set up again to reflect any Customizing changes that were made later.

In the following subsections, you'll activate all the source applications so that the data from all these applications flows into the One Exposure from Operations hub, which helps generate the forecasted cash flow reports within SAP Cash Management.

10.8.1 Activate Individual Source Applications

Before activating SAP Cash Management, you first need to determine which sources of information are relevant to SAP Cash Management for each of the company codes. To do so, you need to activate source applications for company codes in the Customizing activity under **Financial Supply Chain Management • Cash and Liquidity Management • Cash Management • Data Setup • Activate Individual Source Applications**. You use this activity to activate or deactivate a single source application for One Exposure from Operations on a company code basis.

After the source application is activated using Transaction FQM_ACTIVATE, the forecasted transactions from this source application are integrated into the One Exposure from Operations hub, which makes the forecasted cash flows available in SAP Cash Management reporting.

The financial transactions in the source application consist of accounting documents such as invoices, payments, and bank statements. In this activity, you enter each combination of source application (**Src. Appl.**) and company code (**CoCd**) individually, as shown in Figure 10.58.

Src. Appl.	CoCd	Company Name
Customer and Mortgage Loans	1000	Smart US Company
One Exposure	1000	Smart US Company
Contract Accounts Receivable and Payable	1000	Smart US Company
Materials Management	1000	Smart US Company
Sales And Distribution Order	1000	Smart US Company
Treasury and Risk Management	1000	Smart US Company

Figure 10.58 Activating Individual Source Applications

10 SAP Cash Management

10.8.2 Activate Multiple Source Applications

To activate or deactivate multiple company codes for several source applications simultaneously, use the **Activate Multiple Source Applications** Customizing activity, as shown in Figure 10.59.

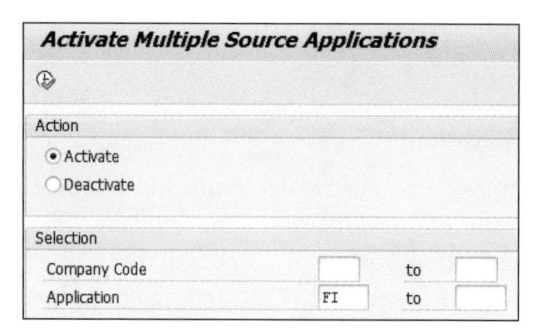

Figure 10.59 Activate Multiple Source Applications Activity

10.8.3 Rebuild Planning Levels, Groups, and Dates in Accounting Documents

You can use this Customizing activity to enter planning groups into customer and vendor master records. Planning groups drive the open items that are updated in SAP Cash Management.

Each row in the table represents selection criteria for the various groups. The logic is as follows:

- Ranking is determined by the priority assigned to the customer or vendor data. When the customer or vendor meets the specified criterion, the master record for that customer or vendor is updated with the group for this record.
- As illustrated in line 1 in Figure 10.60, the customer is assigned to planning **Group US01**, and the **Rec. Pymt Hist.** (record payment history) checkbox is selected in the master record.
- All the other customers in the United States are assigned **Group US02**, while foreign customers are assigned **Group US03**.
- To ensure that all master records are assigned a planning group, always specify at least one simple structure (with the lowest priority) to which the vendor or customer can be matched.
- Use the **Check** button to find out how many master records exist for which the planning group hasn't been assigned yet.

10.8 Set Up Cash Management Transaction Data

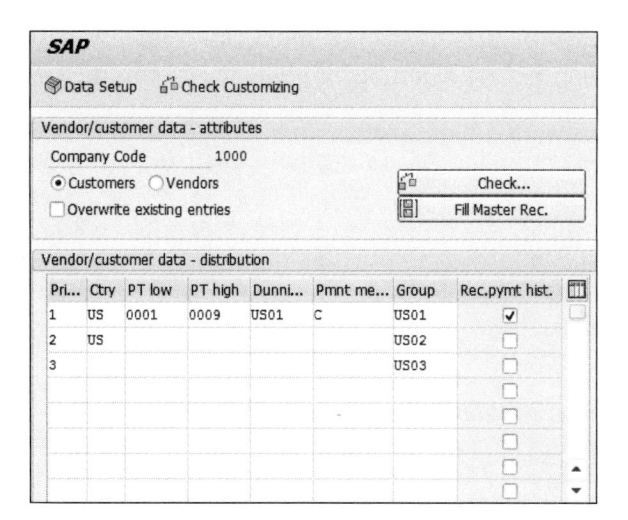

Figure 10.60 Rebuilding Planning Levels, Groups, and Dates in Accounting Documents

- Use this activity to fill data for planning level, planning group, and planning date in table BSEG.
- Use this activity to check if the same planning level has been used in multiple applications or if the same planning group is used in both the customer and vendor master records.

10.8.4 Insert House Bank and House Bank Account Data to Accounting Documents

If you want to use historical SAP Cash Management data in SAP Cash Management applications, you need to execute this program to insert the house bank (field HBKID) and house bank account (field HKTID) data into table BSEG (see Figure 10.61).

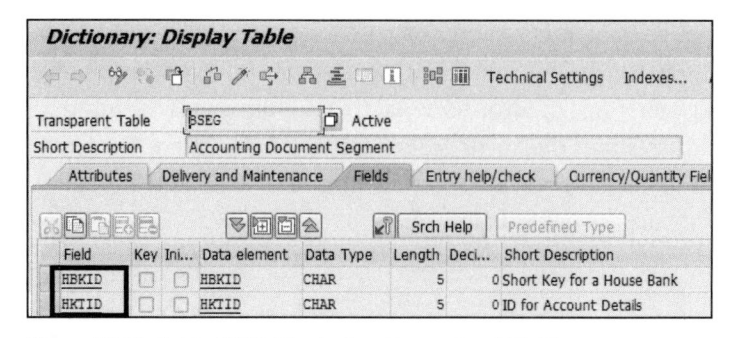

Figure 10.61 Table BSEG Displaying House Bank Fields

391

The program retrieves the house bank and house bank account data from historical transactions and copies it into table BSEG for reporting purposes. It performs the following activities:

- Checks table BSEG and identifies entries that have either one or both of the following fields with null values:
  - HBKID (house bank)
  - HKTID (house bank account)
- Retrieves data from the following sources and updates the entries in table BSEG accordingly:
  - Bank statements: Line items with planning level of F0
  - Payments for open items: Transaction F110
  - Payments for payment requests: Transaction F111

In payments and bank statement transactions, **House Bank** and **House Bank Account** are optional fields. To ensure that the data for these two fields are recorded for relevant transactions and reflected in the reporting, you may set these two fields as mandatory for G/L accounts that have been created as bank clearing accounts and bank accounts. Do so in the Customizing activity under **Financial Accounting (New)** • **Accounts Receivable and Accounts Payable** • **Business Transactions** • **Incoming Payments** • **Incoming Payments Global Settings** • **Make and Check Document Settings** • **Define Field Status Variants**.

10.8.5 Rebuild Liquidity Items in Accounting Documents

In this Customizing activity, liquidity items can be derived for line items that have been posted to ledgers. If the Customizing is set correctly, liquidity items are derived automatically when a financial transaction is posted. However, when you run this Customizing activity to rebuild liquidity items using Transaction FQM_UPD_LITEM, it generates liquidity item data for line items that are posted but don't have liquidity items on them. When generating liquidity items data, the system reads the information from table BSEG, which stores the postings for accounting document line items. The derived liquidity item data is populated back to table BSEG so that other application features can directly use the liquidity information.

10.8 Set Up Cash Management Transaction Data

This Customizing activity provides two modes that are optimized for different scenarios: **Initial Load** is used for first-time runs, and **Rebuild** is used for rebuilding liquidity item data after a first-time run (see Figure 10.62).

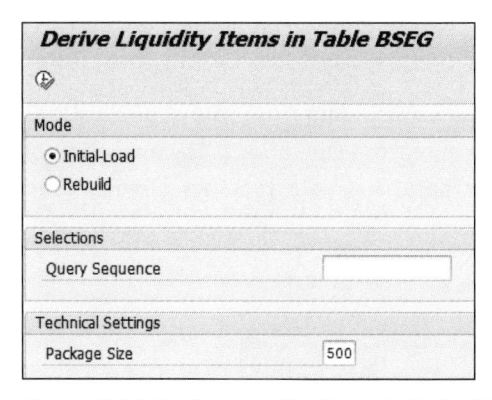

Figure 10.62 Derive Liquidity Items in Table BSEG

10.8.6 Rebuild Flow Types in Accounting Documents

In this Customizing activity, flow types are derived for accounting document line items that have been posted using Transaction FQM_UPD_FLOW_TYPE (Rebuild Flow Types).

In general, flow types are derived automatically when a financial transaction is posted. However, when you run this Customizing activity, it derives flow types for accounting document line items that have been posted but have missing flow types.

In Transaction SE11, the **Accounting Document Segment** table is enhanced with two additional fields—**Flow Type** and **Liquidity Item**—as shown in Figure 10.63.

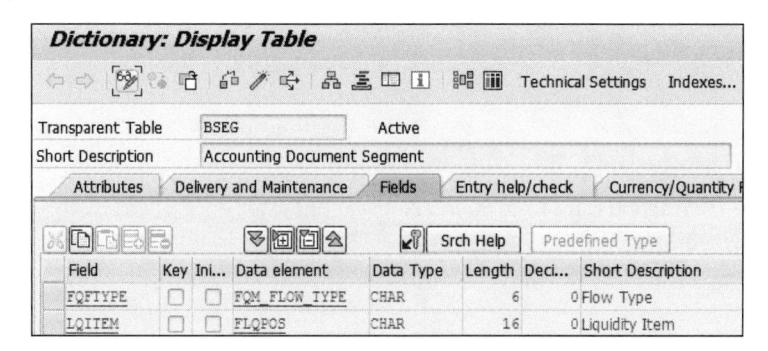

Figure 10.63 Table BSEG Display

393

10.8.7 Load Transaction Data into One Exposure from Operations Hub

You use this Customizing activity to load transaction data from source applications to One Exposure from Operations. You need to load transaction data relevant to SAP Cash Management to One Exposure from Operations using Transaction FQM_INITIALIZE, as shown in Figure 10.64.

After the source application is activated, transaction data from source applications are automatically integrated into One Exposure from Operations. The execution of this Customizing activity integrates the transaction data that has already been posted prior to the activation of the source application. Source applications are activated on a company code basis.

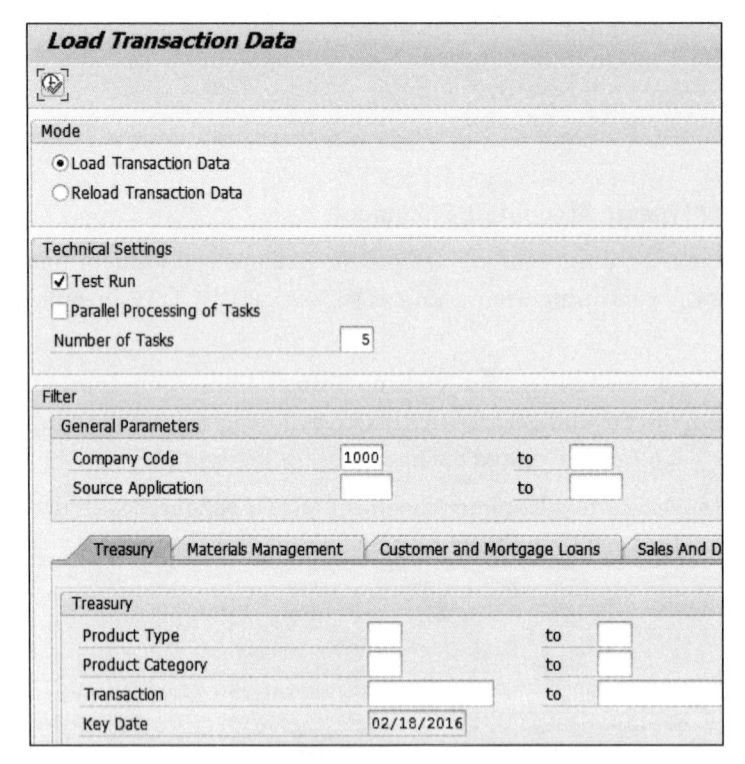

Figure 10.64 Loading Transaction Data from Source Applications into One Exposure from Operations

Select one of the following modes:

- **Load Transaction Data**
  Use this mode initially to load transaction data into One Exposure from Operations, as shown in Figure 10.65.

- **Reload Transaction Data**
  Use this mode to reload transaction data into One Exposure from Operations after an initial load has already been loaded successfully. This corrects the transaction data errors encountered during the initial load in which some configuration settings were set incorrectly, resulting in nonderivation of liquidity items.

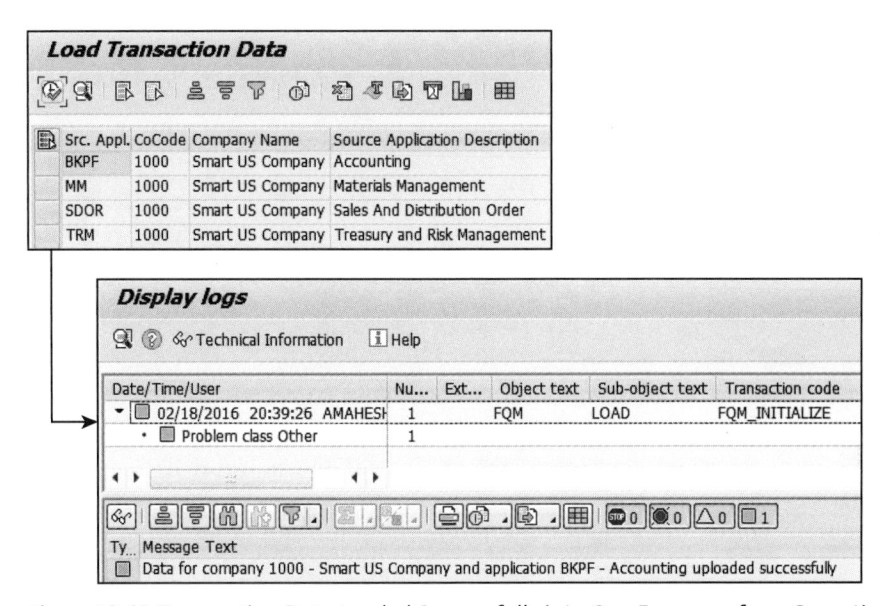

Figure 10.65 Transaction Data Loaded Successfully into One Exposure from Operations

10.9 Set Up SAP Liquidity Management

You need to perform the activities described in this section if you want to use SAP Liquidity Management for SAP S/4HANA Finance. SAP Liquidity Management helps you analyze, monitor, and review the overall liquidity status and health of an organization. It helps the finance team make investment and financing plans and take corrective actions based on the forecasted and actual cash flow position. SAP Liquidity Management can also be used to hedge foreign currency exposure based on the forecast.

10.9.1 Install and Configure SAP BusinessObjects Business Intelligence Content

To use classic InfoSets and operational data providers (ODPs) in SAP BusinessObjects Business Intelligence (BI) tools, you need to complete the basic configuration for SAP Business Warehouse (SAP BW) in your system. Complete the following planning settings in the Customizing activity under **Controlling • General Controlling • Planning • Setup for Planning**:

1. Select the SAP client from the SAP S/4HANA Finance system as the SAP BusinessObjects BI client (see Figure 10.66).

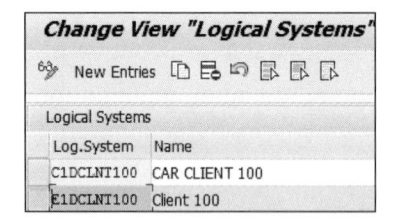

Figure 10.66 Defining Logical Systems

2. Define and assign a logical system to this client, as shown in Figure 10.67.

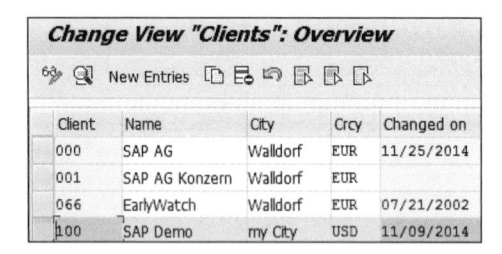

Figure 10.67 Assigning a Logical System to the Client

3. Complete the configuration settings for operational analytics by executing Transaction RSRTS_ACTIVATE_R3IS, as shown in Figure 10.68.

10.9 Set Up SAP Liquidity Management

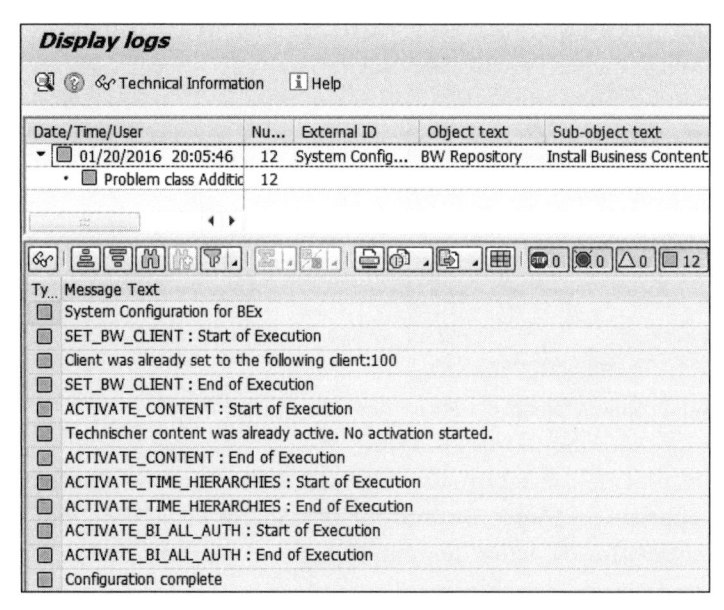

```
Display logs
    Technical Information    Help

Date/Time/User              Nu...  External ID      Object text       Sub-object text
▼ 01/20/2016 20:05:46        12    System Config... BW Repository     Install Business Content
  • Problem class Additic    12

Ty... Message Text
  System Configuration for BEx
  SET_BW_CLIENT : Start of Execution
  Client was already set to the following client:100
  SET_BW_CLIENT : End of Execution
  ACTIVATE_CONTENT : Start of Execution
  Technischer content was already active. No activation started.
  ACTIVATE_CONTENT : End of Execution
  ACTIVATE_TIME_HIERARCHIES : Start of Execution
  ACTIVATE_TIME_HIERARCHIES : End of Execution
  ACTIVATE_BI_ALL_AUTH : Start of Execution
  ACTIVATE_BI_ALL_AUTH : End of Execution
  Configuration complete
```

Figure 10.68 Basic Configuration for Operational Analytics

4. Using the Transport Organizer tools (Transaction SE03), under **Administration • Set System Change Option • Execute**, you can enter the global settings with the prefixes /BIO/ (generation namespace for SAP BusinessObjects BI content) and /BIC/ (business information warehouse: customer namespace) as modifiable for namespaces.

10.9.2 Activate SAP BusinessObjects BI Content

After you've installed the SAP BusinessObjects BI content, you'll need to activate the SAP BusinessObjects BI content bundle required for planning and reporting in the new SAP Cash Management.

You can activate the SAP BusinessObjects BI content bundle FIN_CLM_PLANNING (Liquidity Planning) using the **BI Content Activation Workbench** screen in Transaction BSANLY_BI_ACTIVATION. Follow these steps:

1. Execute Transaction BSANLY_BI_ACTIVATION.
2. On the **BI Content Activation Workbench** screen, choose **Business Category 03**.

10   SAP Cash Management

3. Highlight the **FIN_CLM_PLANNING** row, and click **Activate**, as shown in Figure 10.69. Initially, the status will be shown as **Activation Not Yet Started**.

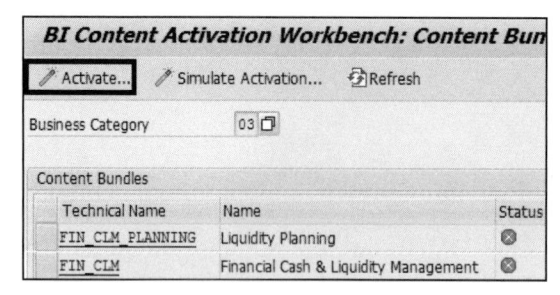

Figure 10.69 Activate SAP BusinessObjects BI Content for Liquidity Planning

4. On the next screen, provide the information for **RFC Destination for Content Objects**, select the appropriate **Source Systems for DataSource Replication** radio button, set **Treatment of Already Active Content Objects** to **Automatic**, and select the **Install All Collected Objects** checkbox (see Figure 10.70).
5. Click **Activate** to start the content activation.
6. Finally, check the activation log to verify there are no errors.

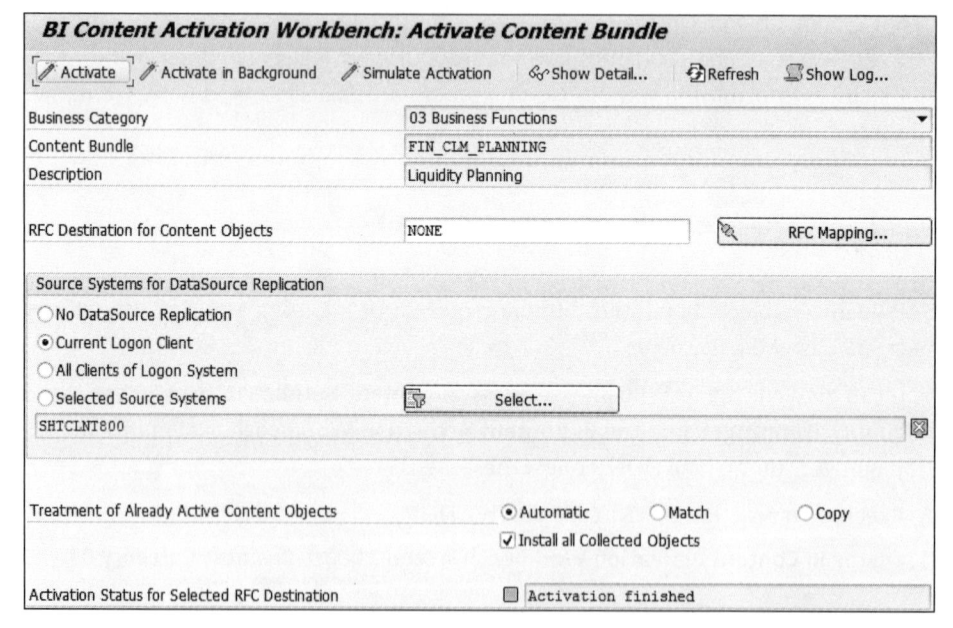

Figure 10.70 Install All Collected Objects Checkbox

If there are no errors during the activation process, you'll see the status for FIN_CLM_PLANNING set to **Activation Finished** with a green box, as shown in Figure 10.71.

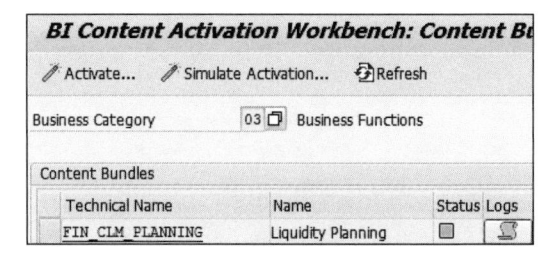

Figure 10.71 Planning Content Bundle Activated

10.9.3 Install Template for Cash Flow Analysis

Follow these steps to install SAP BusinessObjects BI content for cash flow analysis and to access the standard templates:

1. Execute Transaction RSOR, and then click **Object Types** in the left panel under **BI Content**.
2. Expand the middle panel, and search for the object type "Analysis Application".
3. Click **Select Objects** under **More Types** • **Analysis Application** in the middle panel, as shown in Figure 10.72.

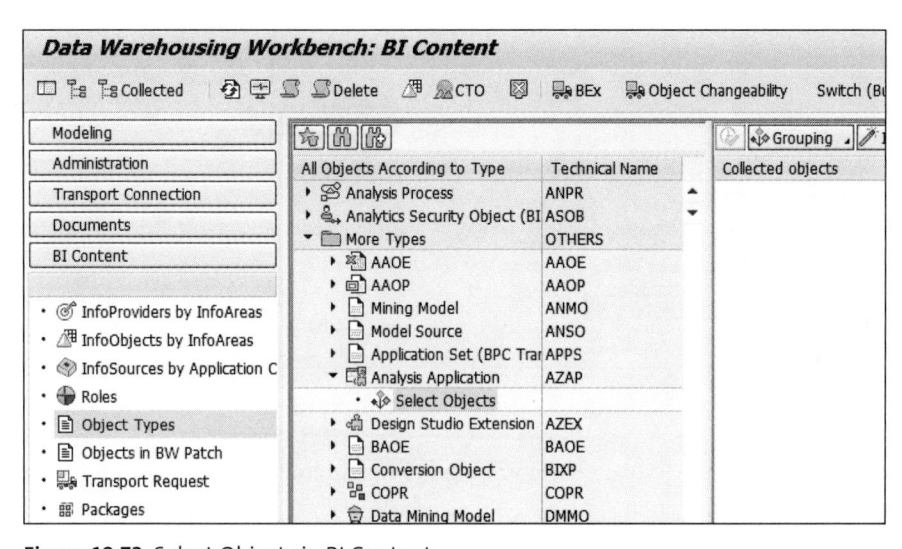

Figure 10.72 Select Objects in BI Content

4. Double-click **Select Objects**, and choose **0ANALYSIS** in the pop-up window (see Figure 10.73).

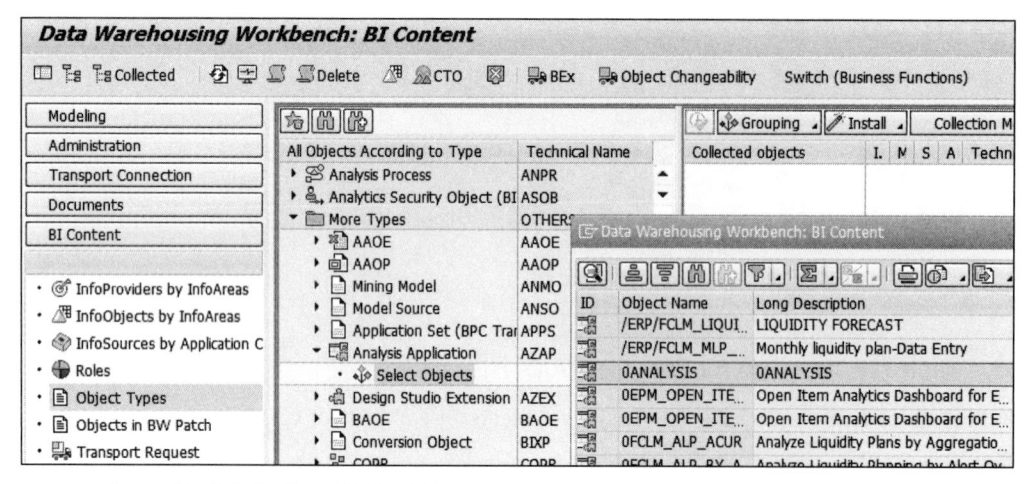

Figure 10.73 Selecting 0ANALYSIS

5. Click the **Install** button at the top to start the content installation, as shown in Figure 10.74.

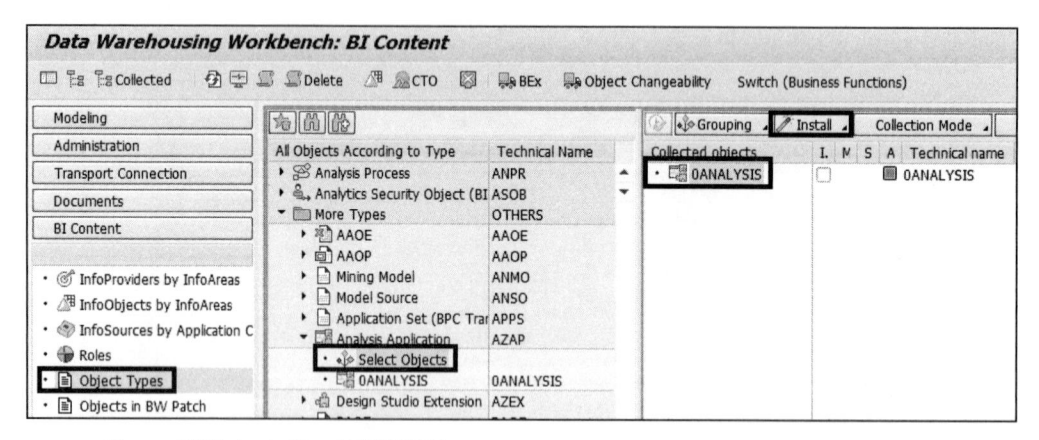

Figure 10.74 Installing 0ANALYSIS

6. Similarly, install and activate the components for **Liquidity Forecast** and **Analyze Liquidity Plan**, as shown in Figure 10.75.

10.9 Set Up SAP Liquidity Management

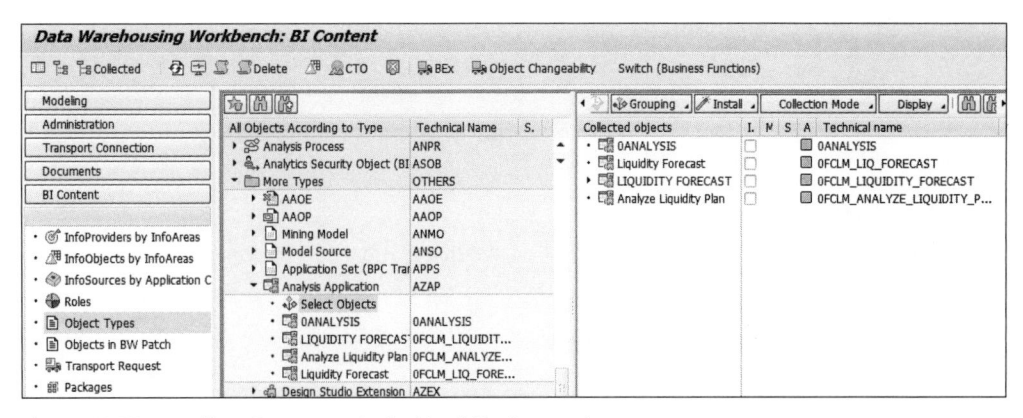

Figure 10.75 Installing Components for Liquidity Forecast

10.9.4 Generate a Planning View

Financial planning data are saved in the SAP BW real-time InfoCube /ERP/SFIN_R01, which can be used by other applications as well. Although the plan data can be accessed by providing an analytic SAP HANA view within the financial planning content, this content is only available after being activated. This means that the external SAP applications can't rely on this SAP HANA view because it will result in errors if the activation is missing.

The following SAP HANA views need to be activated so that the planning data can be integrated:

- SAP HANA FCOM_PLAN_DATA planning data view for InfoCube /ERP/SFIN_R01 is generated in the system-local.sap.erp.sfin.co.pl package.
- The FCO_PLAN_PROXY proxy view is regenerated and provides plan data.

10.9.5 Activate SAP BPC Content

You need to go through the SAP BPC installation guide to make sure that all the SAP BPC-related system settings are configured correctly. You need to activate both **BPC_ACT BPC Embedded Model** and **HANA_ACT Deep HANA Integration Model** in the RSPLS_HDB_ACT maintenance view using Transaction SM30, as shown in Figure 10.76.

401

10 SAP Cash Management

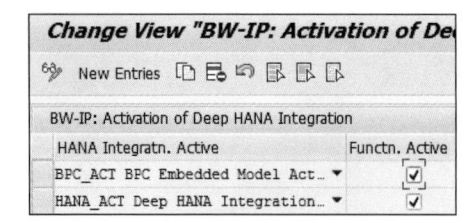

Figure 10.76 Prerequisite for SAP BPC Content Installation

10.9.6 Install SAP BPC Content

Proceed as follows to install SAP BPC-related content:

1. Use Transaction RSOR, and then click **Object Types** in the left panel.
2. Expand the middle panel, and search for the object type "BPC Embedded Environment".
3. Click **Select Objects** under **Planning • BPC Embedded Environment**, as shown in Figure 10.77.

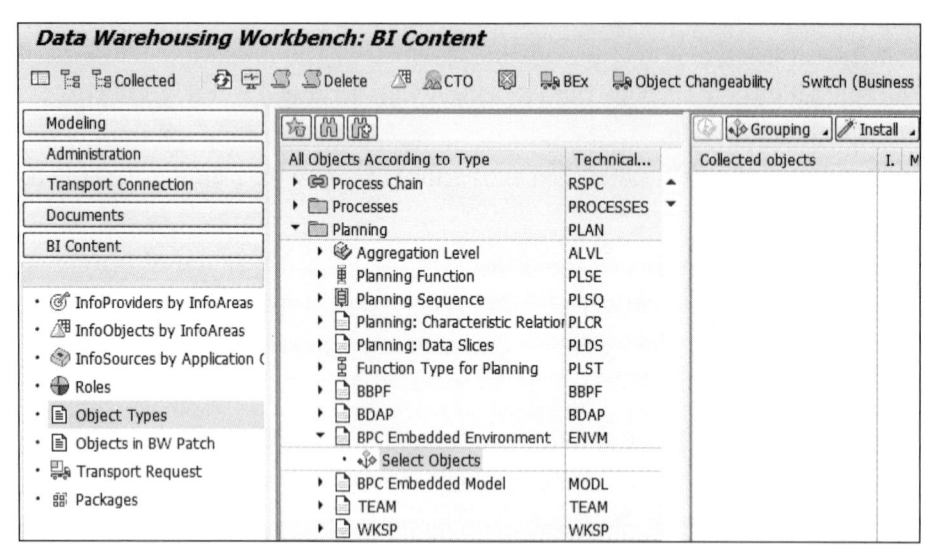

Figure 10.77 Select Objects for BPC Embedded Environment

10.9 Set Up SAP Liquidity Management

4. Select **0FCLM_LP_ENV** in the pop-up window, as shown in Figure 10.78.

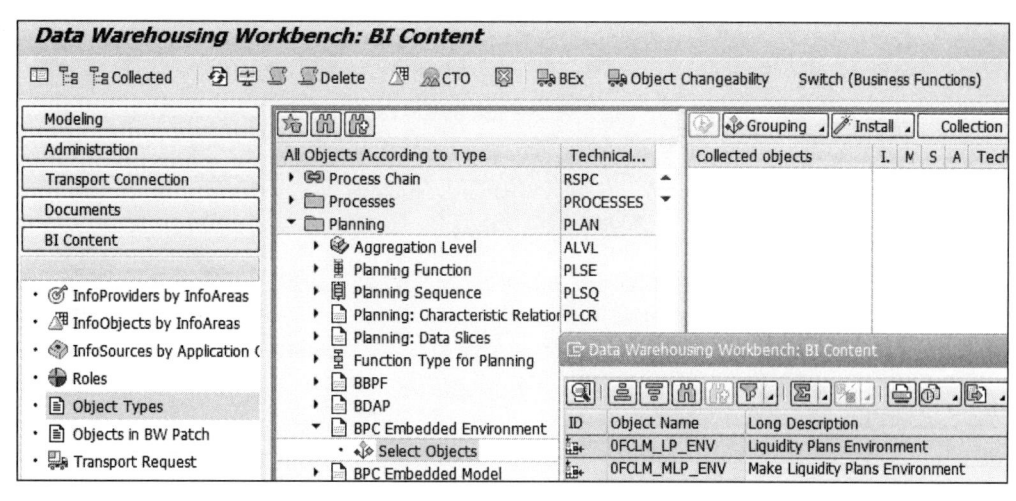

Figure 10.78 Selecting 0FCLM_LP_ENV

5. In the right panel, first click the **Grouping** button at the top, and then choose **Data Flow Afterwards**.

6. Select **0FCLM_LP_ENV**, and then click the **Install** button at the top to start the content installation, as shown in Figure 10.79.

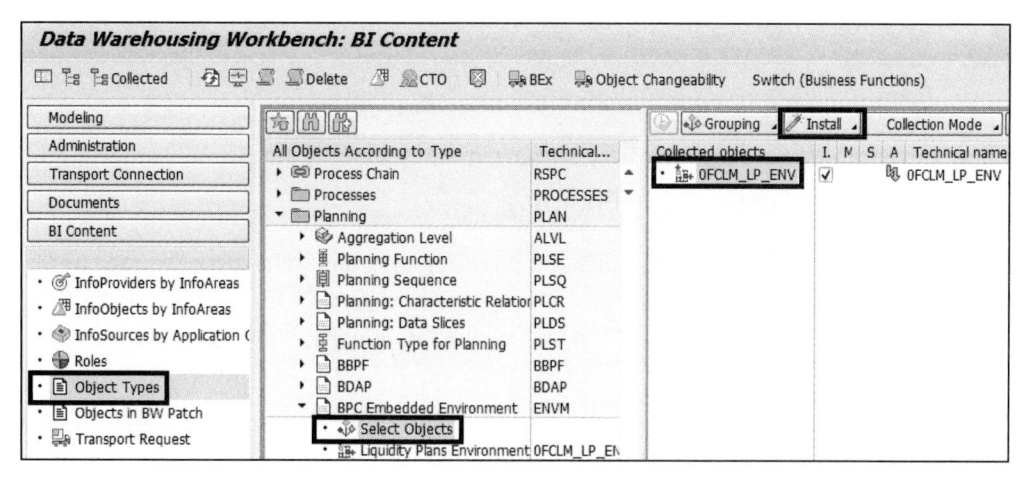

Figure 10.79 Installing 0FCLM_LP_ENV

403

10 SAP Cash Management

After the installation, the screen will look like Figure 10.80.

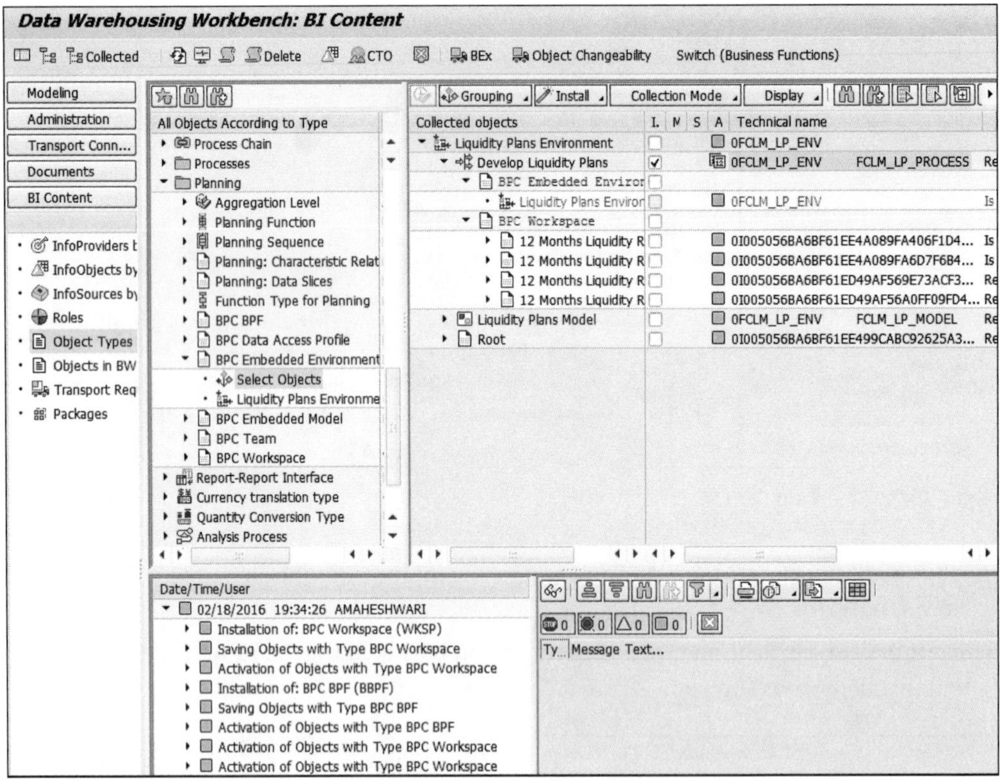

Figure 10.80 SAP BPC Content Installation

10.10 Set Up Liquidity Planning

To configure the planning units and planning unit hierarchy, you need to configure the Customizing activities under **Financial Supply Chain Management • Cash and Liquidity Management • Cash Management • Liquidity Planning**, as shown in Figure 10.81.

10.10 Set Up Liquidity Planning

```
▼   Financial Supply Chain Management
  ▶     Biller Direct
  ▶     Billing Consolidation
  ▼     Cash and Liquidity Management
    ▶     General Settings
    ▶     Bank Account Management
    ▶     Cash Management
    ▼     Liquidity Planning
      •     Specify a BPC Configuration Set
      •     Maintain Planning Unit Settings
      •     Activate Planning Unit Hierarchy
      •     Define Currency Conversion Rules
      •     Define Reference Data Sources
      •     Exclude Liquidity Items Representing Balance Values
      •     Define Liquidity Planning Types
```

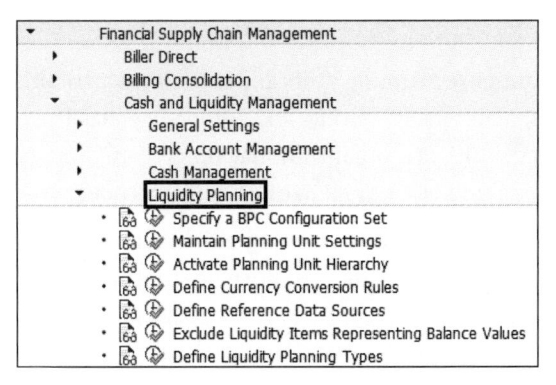

Figure 10.81 Liquidity Planning Customizing

In the following subsections, you'll configure the rules for planning units and their hierarchy.

10.10.1 Specify an SAP BPC Configuration Set

In this Customizing activity, you specify an SAP BPC configuration set that you want to use for liquidity planning, as shown in Figure 10.82. If you want to customize and use your own configuration set, you need to define the following objects in SAP BPC for SAP S/4HANA:

- Environment
- Model
- Process template
- InfoProviders

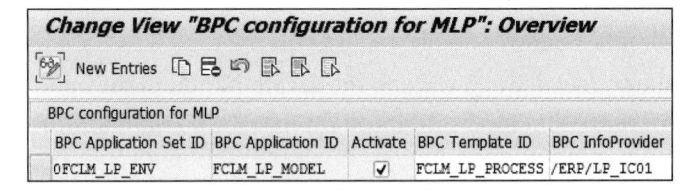

Change View "BPC configuration for MLP": Overview

BPC Application Set ID	BPC Application ID	Activate	BPC Template ID	BPC InfoProvider
0FCLM_LP_ENV	FCLM_LP_MODEL	✓	FCLM_LP_PROCESS	/ERP/LP_IC01

Figure 10.82 Specifying an SAP BPC Configuration Set

405

10.10.2 Create Planning Units

In this Customizing activity, you'll configure planning units and the related attribute descriptions, aggregation currencies, planners, reviewers, and company codes to be used in liquidity planning. Planning units are organizational units that provide liquidity plan data input. Each planning unit is assigned to one company code.

You can define multiple planning currencies for each planning unit. A planning currency must be specified to enter plan amounts into the liquidity plans for the selected planning unit, as shown in Figure 10.83.

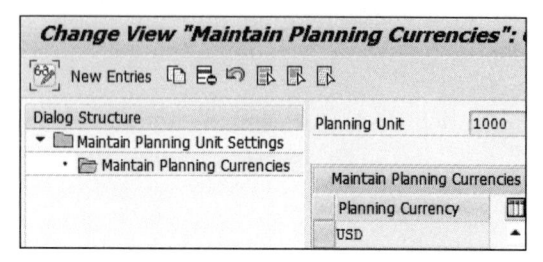

Figure 10.83 Maintaining the Planning Currency

10.10.3 Activate Planning Unit Hierarchy

Use this Customizing activity to activate a planning unit hierarchy (see Figure 10.84) to be used for all liquidity planning activities. Follow these steps:

1. Start SAP BW modeling using Transaction RSA1.
2. Double-click the InfoObject **/ERP/ORG_UNIT**, which can be found under **Modeling • InfoObjects • Financial Management & Controlling • Cash & Liquidity Management • Characteristics**.
3. On the **Hierarchy** tab, choose the **Maintain Hierarchies** button.
4. Create a new planning unit hierarchy by clicking the **Create** button in the **Initial Screen Hierarchy Maintenance**, and specify the hierarchy name and a short description.
5. Add nodes to the hierarchy via the **Planning Unit** button.

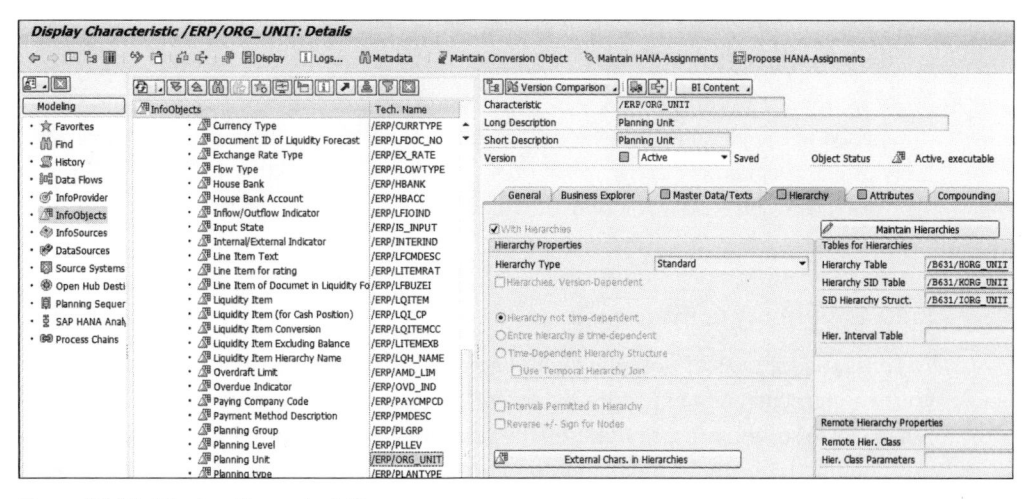

Figure 10.84 Display Characteristics

6. After the planning unit hierarchy has been defined, check the **Planner** and **Reviewer** fields under the **Maintain Planning Unit Settings** Customizing activity, as shown in Figure 10.85. This will make the reviewer of the subsidiary planning unit and the planner of the parent planning unit consistent, which, in turn, will allow you to modify the status of SAP BPC.

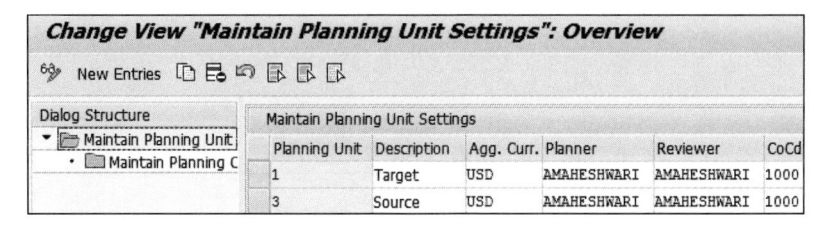

Figure 10.85 Maintain Planning Unit Settings Screen

7. Activate the planning unit hierarchy that will be used for all liquidity planning activities. Once activated, you'll receive the message shown in Figure 10.86.

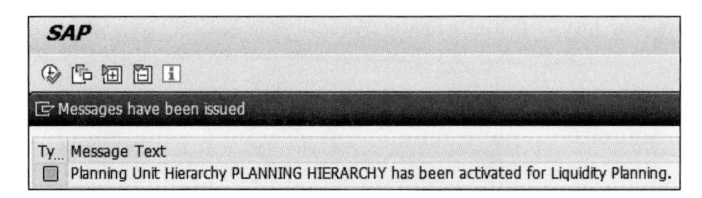

Figure 10.86 Activating Planning Unit Hierarchy

10 SAP Cash Management

> **Expert Insight**
>
> During the activation process, you might find that the planning currency can't be assigned to the planning unit without a company code or that planners and reviewers aren't assigned correctly. To fix these problems, analyze the description of the message and correct the planning unit master data to resolve the issue.

10.10.4 Currency Conversion Rules

To mitigate the risks of possible exchange rate fluctuations, you may want to hedge your foreign currency exposure by converting your cash surplus into another currency. To do so, you must first define the rules for currency conversion using the Customizing activity under **Financial Supply Chain Management • Cash and Liquidity Management • Liquidity Planning • Define Currency Conversion Rules**, as shown in Figure 10.87.

You define a currency conversion rule for each currency that you want to convert. To define a rule, create a new entry and specify the following:

- **Outflow Liquidity Item** (cash outflow liquidity item): **LP_EXI**
- **Inflow Liquidity Item** (cash inflow liquidity item): **LP_EXF**
- **Source Planning Unit**: the planning unit purchasing the currency
- **Target Planning Unit**: the planning unit selling the currency
- **Src. Curr.**: the currency to be sold
- **Tar. Curr.**: the currency to be purchased

Outflow Liquidity I...	Inflow Liquidity Item	Source Planning ...	Target Planning ...	Src. Curr.	Tar. Curr.
BNK_0007	BNK_0006	3	1	EUR	USD
BNK_0007	BNK_0006	3	1	USD	USD
LP_EXI	LP_EXF	3	1	EUR	USD

Figure 10.87 Defining Currency Conversion Rules

10.10.5 Reference Data Sources

There might be business rationale to define reference data sources beyond the standard **Key 001** to **004** sources provided by SAP (see Figure 10.88). This can be addressed by entering new entries in the Customizing activity so that the standard SAP BW modeling provided by SAP can be reused.

Key	Description	Text
001	Actual	Actual Amount
002	Liqudity Forecast	Liqudity Forecast Amount
003	Last Cycle Plan	Plan Amount of Previous Cycle
004	Plan Amount	Plan Amount

Figure 10.88 Defining Reference Data Sources

10.10.6 Exclude Liquidity Items Representing Balance Values

Liquidity items can be represented to reflect both the cash flows and balance values. Liquidity planning computes its calculation from the liquidity items that represent only the cash flows. Thus, the liquidity items that represent balance values need to be removed from the liquidity planning calculation using the Customizing activity so that the plan data are calculated correctly.

10.10.7 Liquidity Planning Types

The planning type is used to classify the different kinds of planning data. SAP provides two predefined planning types, as shown in Figure 10.89:

1. **Monthly rolling plan**
   Liquidity plans of this type are updated every month based on the updated data as posted in the system. The plan is saved as a separate version from each planning cycle.

2. **Nonrolling plan**
   Liquidity plans of this type are constant and not updated on a periodic basis.

Plan Type	Description	Text
M_NOROLL	Non-Rolling Plan	Non-Rolling Plan
M_ROLLING	Monthly Rolling Plan	Monthly Rolling Plan

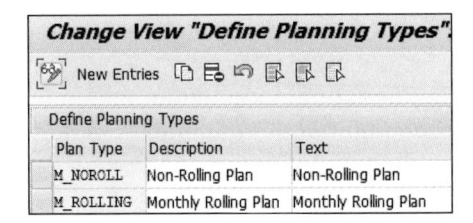

Figure 10.89 Defining Liquidity Planning Types

Now that SAP Cash Management is set up in your SAP S/4HANA system, let's spend a little time thinking through the changes that were made.

10.11 Key System Changes

In this section, we'll analyze the impact SAP S/4HANA Finance has had on the architecture, business process transactions, and configuration of SAP Cash Management and Bank Account Management. We'll start by taking a brief look at SAP Business Client, via which you will perform several configuration activities and execute some transactions. We'll also show how several new SAP Fiori apps fit into your landscape.

10.11.1 SAP Business Client

SAP Business Client is a web-based client with a completely different screen layout from the traditional SAP GUI screen. With the introduction of SAP S/4HANA Finance, some configuration and transaction steps have been moved to SAP Business Client. You'll need SAP Business Client authorization to perform configuration tasks and execute transactions. You can start SAP Business Client by using Transaction NWBC from the SAP GUI client, as shown in Figure 10.90. Launch SAP Business Client by clicking the **SAP** icon next to the relevant role.

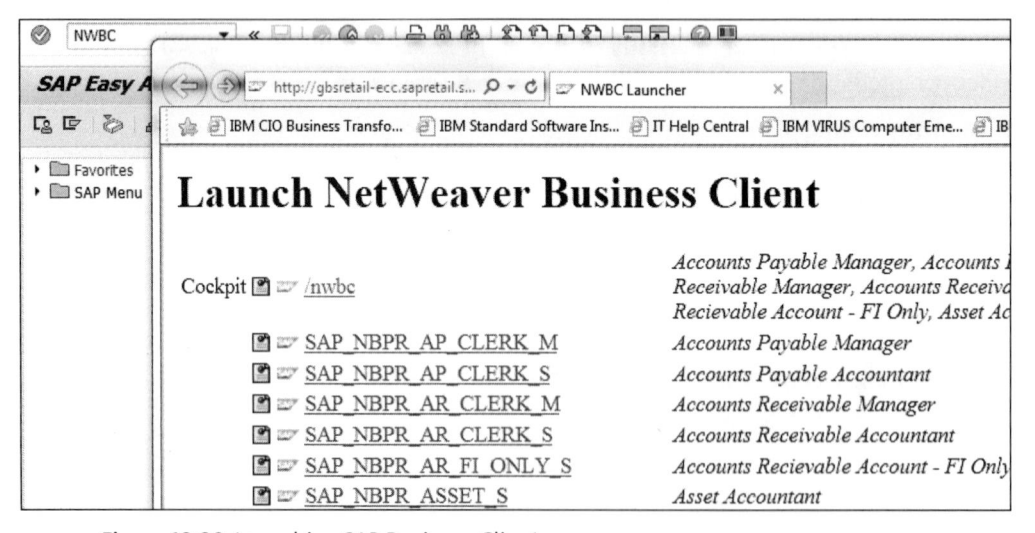

Figure 10.90 Launching SAP Business Client

10.11 Key System Changes

A sample of the options available in SAP Business Client for an individual with the **Cash Manager** role is shown in Figure 10.91.

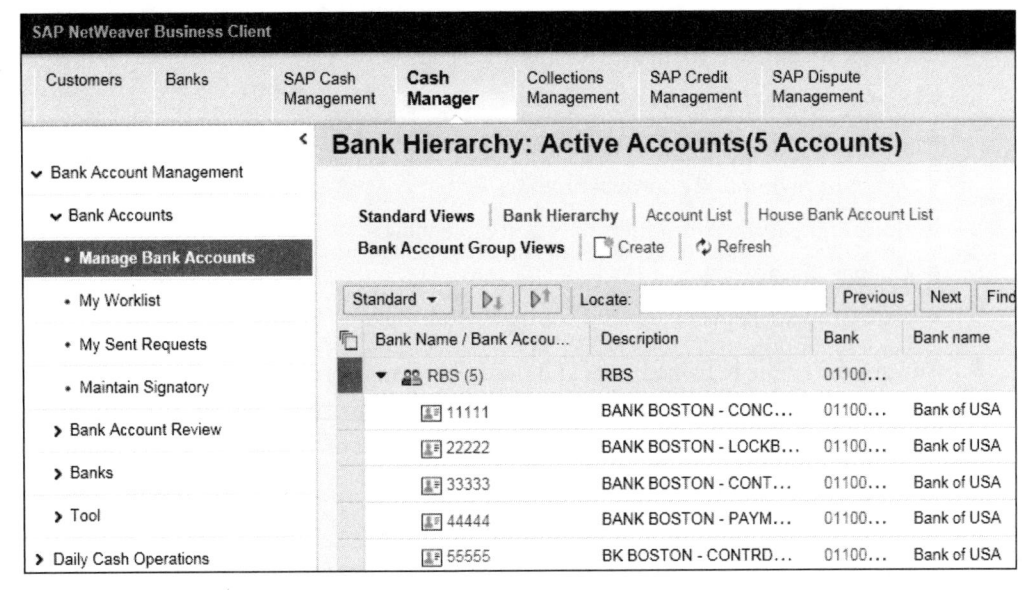

Figure 10.91 Cash Manager Role in SAP Business Client

Click on a header link such as **Bank Hierarchy**, **Account List**, or **House Bank Account List** to browse that specific section and complete its configuration. Bank Account Management configuration and SAP Cash and Liquidity Management configuration have both been moved to SAP Business Client in SAP S/4HANA Finance.

10.11.2 Functionality Impact

Bank Account Management in SAP ERP had the following features:

- Group bank account management
- Overdraft limit
- Bank account maintenance
- Usability
- Multiple currencies

The following additional Bank Account Management functionalities are available in SAP Business Client after migration to SAP S/4HANA Finance:

411

10 SAP Cash Management

- Centralized bank account management
- Account opening with approval process
- Account closing with approval process
- Account-sensitive changes with approval process
- Signatory mass changes with approval process
- Integration with SAP BPC for SAP S/4HANA Finance
- Account review and approval process
- Bank and bank account hierarchy and table view
- Change history
- Side panel to display bank and company code data

You should create bank accounts and house bank masters in the Bank Account Management solution from SAP Business Client. With Bank Account Management, you can create a bank account without linking it with a house bank (i.e., if the bank isn't used for SAP settlements). You can create the bank account first and then later link it to the respective house bank.

Bank account closure should be performed in SAP S/4HANA Finance using the **Bank Closing Date** bank master parameter (by entering the actual closing date instead of the default entry of 12/31/9999).

All the Bank Account Management objects have links to the Electronic Data Interchange (EDI) partner profile and data-exchange medium. This reduces the handover effort if EDI transactions are involved.

The new Cash Operations app in SAP S/4HANA Finance doesn't use the classic SAP Cash Management tables. Most of the information is used from direct tables:

- Accounting from tables BSEG and BKPF
- Memos from table FDES
- Cash and liquidity information from the One Exposure from Operations hub (table FQM_Flow)
- Integrated information from the One Exposure from Operations hub
- Bank statement from tables FEBKO/FEBEP

Additional changes also occurred with the release of SAP S/4HANA 1511 FPS 02, including the following:

- Transactions FI01 (Create Bank), FI02 (Change Bank), FI03 (Display Bank), and FI12 (House Bank/House Bank Account) have been replaced by the SAP Fiori app called Manage Banks.
- The bank hierarchy is now created based on bank business partners.
- House bank accounts can be defined by maintaining the bank account master data on the **Connectivity Path** tab.
- House bank and house bank account are treated as master data instead of configuration data. Database table T012K is redirected to new table FCLM_BAM_ACLINK2.
- Transactions FF7A (Cash Position) and FF7B (Liquidity Forecast) can be executed using the Cash Position Details and Liquidity Forecast SAP Fiori apps.
- Transaction FLQREP (Cash Flow Report) is no longer supported.
- Transaction FF73 (Create Cash Concentration) can be executed using the new Bank Account Management accounts in Web Dynpro or in the Manage Bank Accounts SAP Fiori app.

1709 Preview

With the release of SAP S/4HANA 1709, machine learning tools using SAP Leonardo can be applied in the cash application area, in which the system automatically learns from invoice-clearing history and projects future applications. The New Hedge Management cockpit and hedge accounting functionality have also been introduced as part of the core treasury module to comply with IFRS 9 requirements.

1709 Preview

SAP has introduced the concept of semantic tagging in release 1709. Users can now tag master data and financial statement version components, which can then be used in reports and for analyzing KPIs.

The new cash flow report, which is based on semantic tag infrastructure, now can support multidimensional drilldown reporting based on G/L account, cost center, profit center, fixed asset, and so on. Users can now change the figures by changing the assignment of semantic tags to the financial statement versions.

SAP has introduced new Memo Record and Cash Flow Analyzer SAP Fiori apps that support multiple variants and hierarchies, such as cash flow detail analysis, liquidity forecast detail analysis, actual cash flow, bank account group view, and liquidity item hierarchy view.

> **Expert Insight**
>
> Transaction FF63 (Create Memo Record) and Transaction FF65 (Display Memo Record List) continue to work as normal.

SAP S/4HANA Finance introduced the following new tables:

- V_T012K_BAM
- V_T012T_BAM

SAP S/4HANA Finance removed the following obsolete tables:

- T012K
- T012T

> **Expert Insight**
>
> Interim SAP Cash Management tables are no longer used (tables FDSB/FDSR).

10.11.3 Security Impact

SAP delivers the following authorization objects as part of the SAP_SFIN_CASH_MANAGER SAP cash manager role:

- F_CLM_BAM: Bank Account Management
- F_BNKA_MAN: Bank general maintenance authorization
- F_CLM_BAH: Bank hierarchy
- B_BUPR_BZT: Business partner relationship categories
- F_CLM_LQF: Liquidity Forecast app
- B_BUPA_RLT: Business partner role
- F_CLM_CP: Cash Position app
- S_RS_RO: Analysis office
- F_FEBB_BUK: Company code bank statement

Your SAP Basis team needs to add these roles to the appropriate user as part of the security profile setup and needs to activate all the Bank Account Management objects prior to maintaining the configuration. Otherwise, the logon screen itself won't work, and **Object Missing** error messages will appear. Necessary authorizations in SAP Business Client must be maintained prior to executing the configuration.

10.11.4 Configuration Impact

In SAP ERP, the entire bank master was maintained under one view using Transaction FI12. In comparison, in SAP S/4HANA Finance, the bank master is maintained in a combination of SAP S/4HANA Finance and SAP Business Client using Transaction FI12_HBANK, as shown in Figure 10.92.

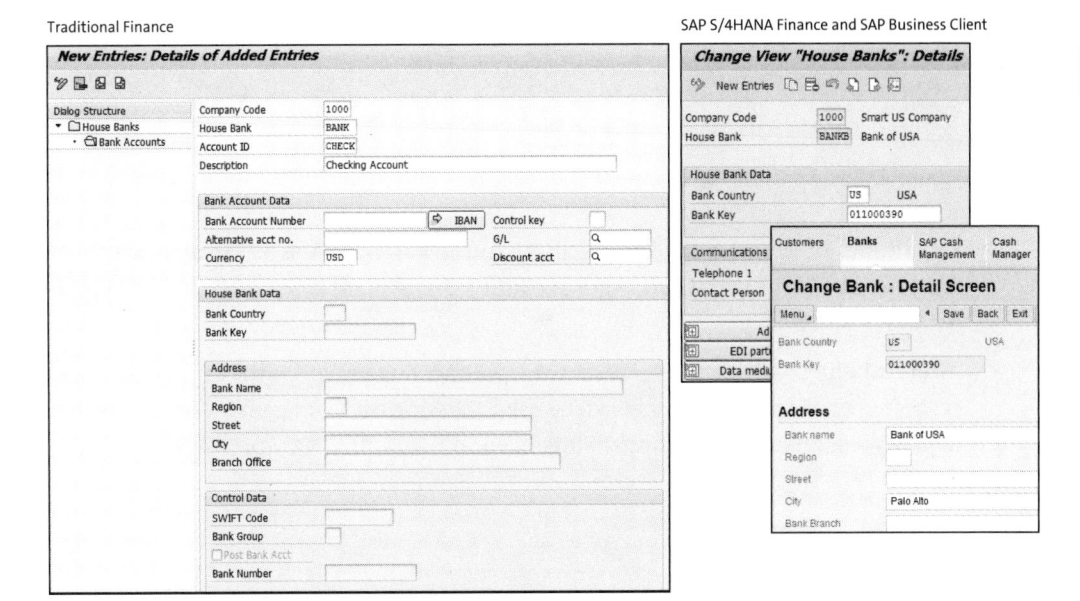

Figure 10.92 Maintaining the Bank Master Data

In SAP ERP, the bank master data structure was rigid, and new fields couldn't be added. However, in SAP S/4HANA Finance, additional fields are available as part of the standard Bank Account Management table `FCLM_BAM_AMD`, and custom fields can easily be added to this table.

In addition, SAP ERP Transaction FF7A for SAP Cash Management has been replaced by the Cash Position SAP Fiori app (see Figure 10.93), and Transaction FF7B has been replaced by the Liquidity Forecast SAP Fiori app.

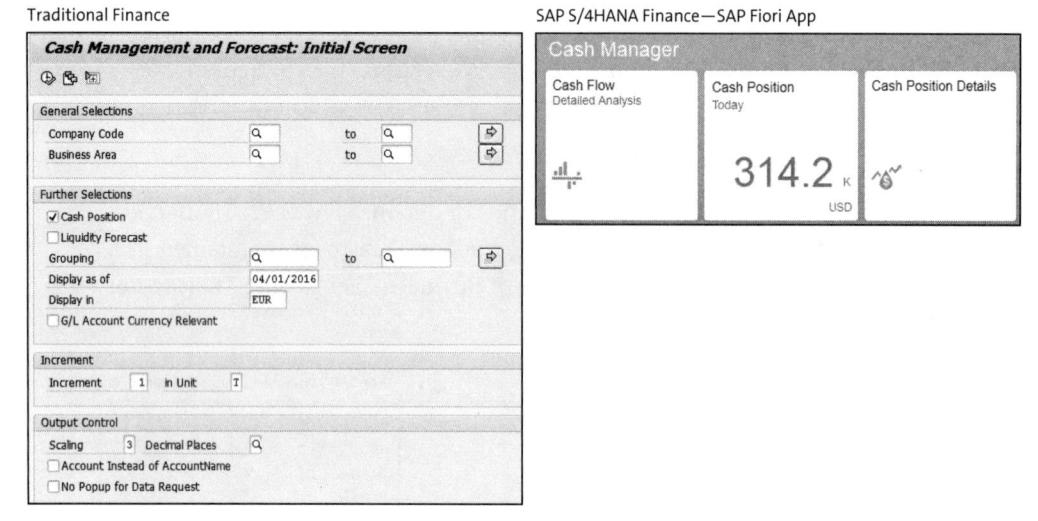

Figure 10.93 SAP Cash Management and Forecast

You should now understand the changes to the basic SAP Cash Management functions such as Cash Operations, Bank Account Management, and SAP Cash and Liquidity Management.

After installing SAP S/4HANA Finance, SAP Cash Management is the only compatible cash-management product that can be used. Classic cash management (including the Liquidity Planner) was no longer supported in SAP S/4HANA from version 1511 onwards.

10.12 Summary

The new SAP Cash Management functionality provides high performance for real-time cash flow analysis and liquidity forecasts. Batch jobs are no longer required in the SAP Cash Management application. The cash manager role now owns and controls bank accounts. SAP Cash Management also enables predictive and planning tasks for cash managers to support daily decision-making and taking appropriate actions.

With this functionality, you can now analyze bank balances and cash positions globally based on data from both SAP systems and non-SAP systems. Liquidity planning and forecasting, along with cash flow analysis, use multidimensional real-time analytics from SAP HANA.

10.12 Summary

This chapter described the customization, workflow, and master data setup related to Bank Account Management, as well as the business purpose, functionality, and required Customizing settings of Cash Operations. You also learned about the customization and functionality of SAP Cash and Liquidity Management and how data are stored in One Exposure from Operations.

Let's now move on to Chapter 11, in which we'll discuss the configuration and functionality of SAP BPC for SAP S/4HANA Finance.

Chapter 11
SAP BPC for SAP S/4HANA Finance

This chapter provides an overview of the prerequisites, system setup, configuration, and functionality offered for financial planning by SAP BPC for SAP S/4HANA Finance. It describes the main components of its architecture, configuration steps for embedded SAP BW, activation of the planning component, and use of SAP BusinessObjects Analysis for Microsoft Office.

SAP Business Planning and Consolidation for SAP S/4HANA (often shortened to SAP BPC for SAP S/4HANA or SAP BPC optimized for SAP S/4HANA Finance, and formerly known as SAP Integrated Business Planning for Finance) is a solution that allows the financial planning from SAP BPC to integrate with SAP S/4HANA Finance and SAP Fiori user interfaces (UIs) and workflows. This effectively replaces the old financial planning capabilities in SAP ERP 6.0 or earlier versions.

With this new functionality, data replication between solutions is no longer required because all components reside in the same server. The plans that are developed in SAP BPC are accessible in SAP S/4HANA Finance for variance analysis. SAP BPC can also access real-time master data and actuals maintained in SAP S/4HANA Finance.

SAP BPC for SAP S/4HANA Finance has been designed to support integrated business planning across the various finance functions so that planning within one area automatically updates corresponding planned values within other areas. It uses SAP BusinessObjects Analysis for Microsoft Office as an add-on tool for conducting analysis of planned data in Excel, which is integrated in real time with the SAP system. This is very convenient from an end-user perspective because users can copy and paste their planned data from the existing spreadsheet to the integrated Excel without creating the planned data from scratch.

SAP BPC for SAP S/4HANA Finance also uses the new Planning Modeler, which acts as the central tool for configuring all planning applications that exist in the SAP Business Warehouse (SAP BW) integrated planning component. In this chapter, we'll discuss the architecture, configuration, authorization, and settings required to activate embedded SAP BW, SAP BusinessObjects BI, planning services and applications, and

11 SAP BPC for SAP S/4HANA Finance

SAP BusinessObjects Analysis for Microsoft Office, which are all the components required collectively to activate SAP BPC for SAP S/4HANA Finance.

The scope of this chapter is to provide a comprehensive view of the implementation of financial planning functionality, which most SAP customers have historically performed in SAP BPC.

> **Expert Insight**
>
> With SAP S/4HANA 1610, SAP released Real-Time Consolidation, a new consolidation solution with a new consolidation table: ACDOCC.
>
> This is an exciting development for SAP customers. However, because implementing Real-Time Consolidation is not part of the core SAP S/4HANA Finance implementation process and instead undertaken as a separate project, we do not cover it this book. Instead, we recommend the 2018 book *Consolidation with SAP S/4HANA* by Thiagu Bala, Ann Cacciottoli, and Eric Ryan (SAP PRESS, 2018). This new book teaches you to manage your financial consolidation with Real-Time Consolidation; set up and perform currency translation, intercompany elimination, and consolidation of investments; and create standard and ad-hoc consolidation reports.

11.1 Planning Overview and Activation

One of the items on any CFO's agenda is to become a strategic partner to the business and engage with team members to drive value based on real-time analysis of financial and operations business scenarios. SAP BPC for SAP S/4HANA Finance is a tool that provides real-time planning across the enterprise and accesses data in real time from SAP S/4HANA Finance without the need for data replication. This integrated data model provides flexibility and a simulated planning process.

Let's first consider the business benefits of and applications used by SAP BPC for SAP S/4HANA Finance.

11.1.1 Business Benefits

Prior to the introduction of SAP S/4HANA Finance, the planning functionality in SAP had the following characteristics:

- Planning done in SAP GUI
- Planning in silos with separate data stores

- Sequential planning process, as shown in Figure 11.1
- Peer-to-peer transfer programs
- Long-running batch jobs
- Cumbersome process of data load and calculation
- Manual steps subject to errors
- Simulation not possible

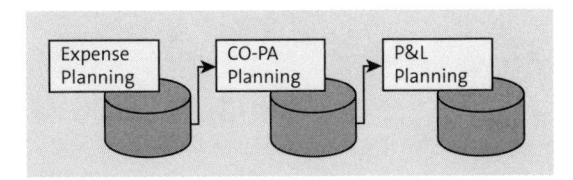

Figure 11.1 Sequential Planning Process in SAP ERP 6.0

With the introduction of SAP BPC for SAP S/4HANA Finance, planning is simplified and enhanced with the following characteristics:

- Common financial planning model
- Parallel planning process
- Real-time access to actual data and master data for modeling and variance analysis, leading to faster decision-making
- Flexible drilldown into various profitability drivers, including customer, product, store, and geographical location
- No data replication because it's deployed directly on the embedded SAP BW of the SAP ERP system
- Identification of trends and forecasts using predictive analysis to help the organization stay ahead of its competitors
- In-memory planning capabilities with SAP HANA-optimized performance
- Faster planning cycles using prebuilt planning models
- Better decisions through end-to-end simulation
- Advanced user experience (UX) with HTML5 and SAP BusinessObjects Analysis for Microsoft Office, using Excel templates

With SAP BPC for SAP S/4HANA Finance, replicating actual master data and actual transaction data is no longer necessary. Instead, while working with the planning workbook, actual data are read in real time from the SAP HANA views for accounting and then aggregated to the required planning level for comparative purposes, as shown in Figure 11.2. Any new transactions or master data that are posted in SAP S/4HANA are immediately reflected in the planning module. The architecture and the capabilities of SAP BPC provide new end-to-end simulation capabilities.

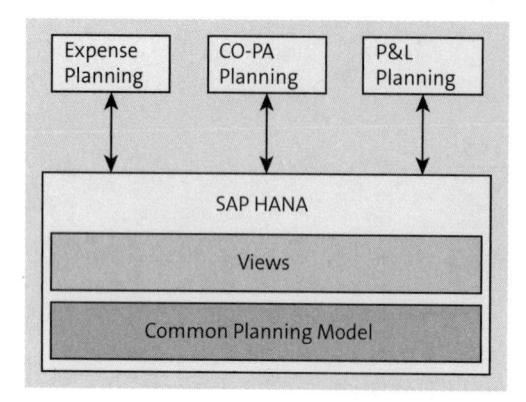

Figure 11.2 Planning in SAP S/4HANA Finance

SAP BPC for SAP S/4HANA Finance includes Overhead Cost Controlling (CO-OM) planning, P&L planning, and profit center planning. If you don't want to install and use SAP BPC for SAP S/4HANA but want to continue with classic FI-G/L and CO-OM planning functions, you need to apply the following SAP Notes:

- SAP Note 2253067: FI-G/L Planning
- SAP Note 2253067: Cost Center Planning by Cost Element
- SAP Note 2148356: Order Planning by Cost Element
- SAP Note 2135362: Project Planning by Cost Element
- SAP Note 2142732: Project Planning Overall

Some of the essential business reasons for implementing SAP BPC for SAP S/4HANA Finance are listed here:

- SAP BPC for SAP S/4HANA Finance comes embedded with SAP S/4HANA. All the planning is done in the same SAP instance and server. No separate SAP BW instance is required for planning.
- SAP BPC for SAP S/4HANA Finance allows organizations using traditional financial planning in SAP ERP 6.0 or lower to rapidly implement the new system while protecting their existing investment, thus minimizing the cost and time to get this new functionality up and running.

- SAP BPC for SAP S/4HANA Finance provides a lot of standard planning templates and calculations covering multiple planning scenarios, which saves time during the planning exercise.
- SAP BPC for SAP S/4HANA Finance takes advantage of SAP HANA views that support real-time access to master data and the SAP ERP Financials and Controlling (FI-CO) transaction tables.
- Organizations that have large volumes of planning data should switch over to SAP BPC for SAP S/4HANA Finance to access truly integrated planning across all finance functions.

11.1.2 Applications Used by Planning

The following applications and components are utilized by SAP BPC for SAP S/4HANA Finance functionality:

- **SAP BusinessObjects Analysis for Microsoft Office**
  Business planning applications for the SAP S/4HANA Finance add-on are integrated into Excel by using SAP BusinessObjects Analysis for Microsoft Office.
- **SAP Business Client**
  SAP S/4HANA Finance offers a set of user roles for using SAP Business Client, a web-based UI. These roles have the prefix *SAP_SFIN_*. SAP Business Client is the integrated environment for all business applications and offers a single point of entry. It can host a wide array of content, including Web Dynpro, SAP GUI applications, and any other web-based content.
- **SAP BPC web client**
  SAP BPC web client is another HTML5 web-based UI used to launch business process flows and perform administrative functions.
- **SAP BPC, version for SAP NetWeaver**
  SAP BPC for SAP S/4HANA Finance is based on the SAP BPC, version for SAP NetWeaver embedded model technology. It delivers content such as templates, queries, planning functions, and so on that aren't available with SAP BPC, version for SAP NetWeaver.
- **Embedded SAP BW**
  SAP BPC for SAP S/4HANA Finance always uses the embedded SAP BW system of the underlying SAP HANA system.
- **SAP Fiori**
  SAP Fiori provides the new SAP UX through the usage of app-based functionality that works seamlessly on desktops, tablets, and smartphones.

11.1.3 Activate Business Functions for Planning

The following business functions are prerequisites that should be activated in SAP BPC for SAP S/4HANA Finance:

- `FIN_CO_CCMGMT`: project planning
- `OPS_PS_CI_1`: technical prerequisite
- `FIN_CO_CCPLAN`: cost center planning
- `FIN_CO_ORPLAN`: internal order planning

Use Transaction SFW5 to activate the needed business functions. After the activation, you'll see the result shown in Figure 11.3.

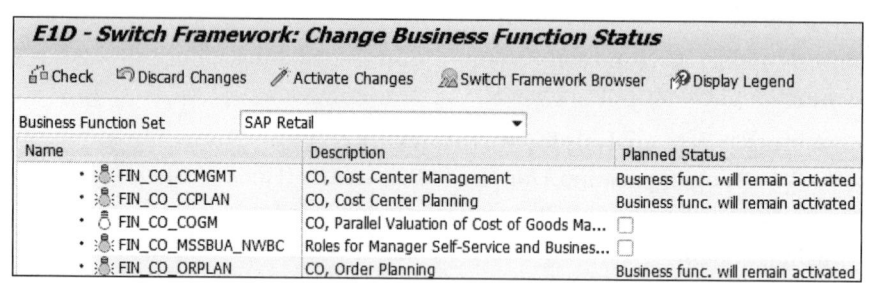

Name	Description	Planned Status
FIN_CO_CCMGMT	CO, Cost Center Management	Business func. will remain activated
FIN_CO_CCPLAN	CO, Cost Center Planning	Business func. will remain activated
FIN_CO_COGM	CO, Parallel Valuation of Cost of Goods Ma...	
FIN_CO_MSSBUA_NWBC	Roles for Manager Self-Service and Busines...	
FIN_CO_ORPLAN	CO, Order Planning	Business func. will remain activated

Figure 11.3 Activating Business Functions

11.2 Architecture

In the traditional SAP ERP system, documents created in the FI module were mirrored/replicated in the CO module, causing duplication and multiple footprints of the same data. With the introduction of new line-item table ACDOCA (Accounting Document Actuals) in which all FI and CO data are posted for the same line item, the reporting is simplified with access to the same single source of data. From SAP S/4HANA 1610 on, the planning data is stored in a new table called ACDOCP (Accounting Document Planning) that has the same structure as the universal journal (ACDOCA).

The new architecture of SAP S/4HANA Finance allows for the following:

- Plan data reporting and plan/actual comparisons are faster.
- With the integration between FI and CO postings, you now can have both bottom-up and top-down planning capabilities by analyzing data from the high-level expense group down to the detailed Profitability Analysis (CO-PA) value field structure. The totals tables and index tables have now been eliminated.

- You can access the planning data without any replication between FI and CO.
- CO historic plan data can be migrated without any impact on the new architecture structure and with all plan data processes remaining the same.
- With cost elements now being represented as General Ledger (G/L) accounts that are reconciled by design, every plan data record is stored at the company code and account level.

The architecture used for SAP BPC for S/4HANA Finance is depicted in the following subsections.

11.2.1 Planning Accelerators

SAP BPC for SAP S/4HANA Finance includes templates that provide support for the following components of your plan:

- Cost center
- Project
- Internal order
- Functional area
- Profit center
- Cost of sales
- Market segment
- Profit and loss items
- Balance sheet items

SAP BPC for SAP S/4HANA Finance also includes queries, planning functions, sequences, InfoObjects, and InfoProviders. All the planning information is reflected in the same InfoCube. SAP delivers a set of sample Excel workbooks for each of the planning components in the preceding list. You can use them as a reference when creating your own planning workbooks.

For balance sheet planning, the accounts are read and copied from the financial statement version, and the planning can be done both at the period level and yearly. The planning can only be carried out if the user is provided access to the SAP_SFIN_ACC_PLANNING role.

For planning purposes, you need to install SAP BusinessObjects Analysis for Microsoft Office to integrate the Excel workbooks with plan data in SAP. When you start planning initially, the planned value in Excel flows into the SAP BusinessObjects Business Intelligence (SAP BusinessObjects BI) plan data cube, which is then copied to SAP ERP so that the existing functionality of allocations and distributions, settlements, depreciation, and so on can be used and integrated with the planned data. After this activity is finished, the data are pushed back to the SAP BusinessObjects BI cube.

> **References**
>
> For more information, see SAP Note 2081400: Compilation of Information for Integrated Business Planning for Finance and SAP Note 2081400: Activating New Business Content for SAP BPC for S/4HANA Finance.

11.2.2 Data Flow Architecture

The data flow architecture for SAP BPC for SAP S/4HANA Finance is depicted in Figure 11.4. It's installed directly on the embedded SAP BW of the SAP S/4HANA system, where no data replication is required. SAP BPC can access both the master data and the actual transactional data in real time from the SAP HANA database. The plans as maintained in SAP BPC access real-time data in SAP S/4HANA Finance and compute the variances.

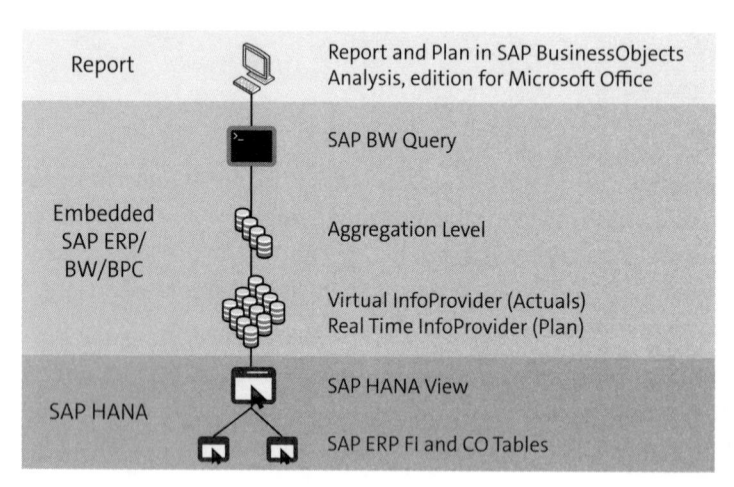

Figure 11.4 Data Flow Architecture for SAP BPC for SAP S/4HANA Finance

11.3 Authorizations

To set up the new UIs for project planning, cost center planning, and internal order planning, you must have at minimum the authorizations listed in Table 11.1 (cross-application authorization objects), Table 11.2 (SAP Basis administration), Table 11.3 (SAP Basis development environment), Table 11.4 (SAP Basis central functions), Table 11.5 (SAP BW service API), and Table 11.6 (SAP BW).

Description	Cross-Application Authorization Objects
Authorization for SAP BusinessObjects BI Content Activation Workbench	BSANL_ACWB, ACTVT: 02, 03, 21, 63
Application Linking and Embedding (ALE)/Electronic Data Interchange (EDI): maintaining logical systems	B_ALE_LSYS, LOGSYS: *
Administration for Internet Communication Framework (ICF)	S_ICF_ADM, ACTVT:07, ICF_HOST: DEFAULT_HOST, Service GUID: *, ICF_TYPE: NODE
Administration for Remote Function Call (RFC) destination	S_RFC_ADM, ACTVT: 01, 02, 36, ICF_VALUE: <Dummy>, RFCDEST: *, RFCTYPE: ' '
Transaction code check at transaction start	Transactions BSANLY_BI_ACTIVATION, RSA1, RSA5, RSD1, RSRT, RSRTS_ACTIVATE_R3IS, RSTCO_ADMIN, SCC4, SE03, SE16, SE37, SE38, SE80, SFW5, SM30, SMX, SPRO, SU01, SU3, SU53

Table 11.1 Cross-Application Authorization Objects

Description	Administration Authorization Objects
System authorizations	S_ADMI_FCD, S_ADMI_FCD: T000, NADM, PADM
Background processing: background administrator	S_BTCH_ADM: BTCADMIN: Y
Background processing: operations on background jobs	S_BTCH_JOB: JOBACTION: DELE; RELE, JOBGROUP: *

Table 11.2 SAP Basis Administration

Description	Administration Authorization Objects
Background processing: background user name	S_BTCH_NAM: BTCUNAME: DDIC
Administration functions in Change and Transport System (CTS)	S_CTS_ADMI: CTS_ADMFCT: EPS1, EPS2, PROJ, SYSC, TABL
System-specific administration (transport)	S_CTS_SADM: CTS_ADMFCT: SYSC, DESTSYS: *, DOMAIN: *
Authorization for file access	S_DATASET: ACTVT: Read, Write; FILENAME: *, PROGRAM: SAPLSTRF S_DATASET: ACTVT: Write, FILENAME: *, PROGRAM: SAPLSLOG
Authorization for GUI activities	S_GUI: ACTVT: 02, 61
Switch settings in Switch Framework	S_SWITCH, ACTVT: 02, OBJNAME: *, OBJTYPE: SFBF S_SWITCH, ACTVT: 02, OBJNAME: Dummy, OBJTYPE: SFBS S_SWITCH, ACTVT: 07, OBJNAME: FIN_CO_CCPLAN, FIN_CO_CCMGMT, OPS_PS_CI_1, OBJTYPE: SFBF
Cross-client table maintenance	S_TABU_CLI: CLIIDMAINT: X
Table maintenance (via standard tools such as Transaction SM30)	S_TABU_DIS: ACTVT: 02, 03; DICBERCLS: SS, SC, ALEO S_TABU_DIS: ACTVT: 03, DICBERCLS: BWC
Table access via generic standard tools	S_TABU_NAM: ACTVT: 03, TABLE: RSADMINA S_TABU_NAM: ACTVT: 02, 03; TABLE: RSADMIN, T000, V_TBDLS
User master maintenance: user groups	S_USER_GRP: ACTVT: 02, CLASS: SUPER
User master maintenance: system-specific assignments	S_USER_SAS: ACTVT: 22, ACT_GROUP: <Dummy>, CLASS: SUPER, PROFILE: <Dummy>, SUBSYSTEM: <Dummy>

Table 11.2 SAP Basis Administration (Cont.)

Description	Development Environment Authorization Objects
ABAP Workbench	S_DEVELOP: ACTVT: 16, DEVCLASS: RS, OBJNAME: RSMANDT, OBJTYPE: FUGR, P_GROUP: <Dummy>
	S_DEVELOP: ACTVT: 16 DEVCLASS: RSO_TLOGO, OBJNAME: RSVERS, OBJTYPE: FUGR, P_GROUP: <Dummy>
	S_DEVELOP: ACTVT: 16, DEVCLASS: <Dummy>, OBJNAME:, SAP_RSADMIN_MAINTAIN, OBJTYPE: PROG, P_GROUP: <Dummy>
	S_DEVELOP: ACTVT: 03, DEVCLASS: RSDRU, SHTTP, OBJNAME: RSICF_SERVICE_ACTIVATION, SAP_RSADMIN_MAINTAIN, OBJTYPE: PROG, AVAS, P_GROUP: BWC
	S_DEVELOP: ACTVT: 42, DEVCLASS: CNVS, CN_PSP_OPR, CO, KAUF, OBJNAME:, AFVC, AUFK, PROJ, PRSP, VSAVC_CN, OBJTYPE: TABL, P_GROUP: <Dummy>
	S_DEVELOP: ACTVT: 03, DEVCLASS: FCOM_PLANNING_CORE, OBJNAME: *, OBJTYPE: WDCA, P_GROUP: <Dummy>
ABAP: program flow checks	S_PROGRAM: P_ACTION: SUBMIT, P_GROUP: BWC, BWA
Transport organizer	S_TRANSPORT: ACTVT: 01, TTYPE: DTRA, TASK
	S_TRANSPORT: ACTVT: 03, TTYPE: *

Table 11.3 SAP Basis: Development Environment

Description	Development Environment Authorization Objects
Applications log	S_APPL_LOG, ACTVT: 03, ALG_OBJECT: RSO_REPOSITORY, ALG_SUBOBJ: BC_INSTALL
	S_APPL_LOG, ACTVT: 03, ALG_OBJECT: RSTCO_UT, ALG_SUBOBJ: ACT_XPRA_MESS
BC-SRV-KPR-BDS: Authorizations for document set	S_BDS_DS, ACTVT: 03, 06, 30, CLASSNAME: BW_META_OBJECTS, CLASSTYPE: OT

Table 11.4 SAP Basis: Central Functions

11 SAP BPC for SAP S/4HANA Finance

Description	Development Environment Authorization Objects
WFEDI: S_IDOCDEFT: Access to IDoc development	S_IDOCDEFT: ACTVT: 03, EDI_CIM: <Dummy>, EDI_DOC: RSSEND, EDI_TCD: WE30 S_IDOCDEFT: ACTVT: 01, 03, 06, EDI_CIM: <Dummy>, EDI_DOC: ZSDAO*, EDI_TCD: WE30

Table 11.4 SAP Basis: Central Functions (Cont.)

Description	SAP BW Service API Authorization Objects
SAP DataSource authorizations	S_RO_OSOA, ACTVT: 23, OLTPSOURCE: *, OSOAAPCO: *, OSOAPART: DEFINITION

Table 11.5 Authorizations: SAP BW Service API

Description	SAP BW Authorization Objects
Data Warehousing Workbench: objects	S_RS_ADMWB, ACTVT: 03, 23, RSADMWBOBJ: INFOOBJECT, INFOAREA, SETTINGS, SOURCESYS S_RS_ADMWB, ACTVT: 66, RSADMWBOBJ: METADATA S_RS_ADMWB, ACTVT: 03, 16, 23, RSADMWBOBJ: BR_SETTING
Planning: aggregation level	S_RS_ALVL, ACTVT: 23, 03, RSALVLOBJ: DEFINITION, RSINFOAREA: /ERP/COOM, RSPLSALVL: *
SAP BusinessObjects BI analysis authorizations in role	S_RS_AUTH, BIAUTH: OBI_ALL
SAP Business Explorer components	S_RS_COMP, ACTVT: 02, 03, 16, RSINFOAREA: /ERP/COOM, RSINFOCUBE:*, RSZCOMPID: *, RSZCOMPTP: REP S_RS_COMP, ACTVT: 03, RSINFOAREA: OBWTCT, RSINFOCUBE: OTCT_*, RSZCOMPID: OTCT_*, RSZCOMPTP: REP
SAP Business Explorer components: enhancements to the owner	S_RS_COMP1, ACTVT: 03, 16, RSZCOMPID: /ERP/COOM*, RSZCOMPTP: REP, RSZOWNER:*

Table 11.6 SAP Business Warehouse

Description	SAP BW Authorization Objects
Data Warehousing Workbench: InfoCube	S_RS_ICUBE, ACTVT: 03,23, RSICUBEOBJ: *, RSINFOAREA: /ERP/COOM, RSINFOCUBE: *
Data Warehousing Workbench: InfoObject catalog	S_RS_IOBC, ACTVT: 23, RSINFOAREA: /ERP/CO, RSIOBJCAT:*
Data Warehousing Workbench: InfoObject	S_RS_IOBJ, ACTVT: 23, RSIOBJ: *, RSIOBJCAT: *, RSIOBJPART: DEFINITION
Data Warehousing Workbench: MultiProvider	S_RS_MPRO, ACTVT: *, RSINFOAREA: /ERP/COOM, RSMPRO: /ERP/COOM_M01, RSMPROOBJ: DEFINITION
Planning function	S_RS_PLSE, ACTVT: *, RSINFOAREA: /ERP/COOM, RSPLF_SRV: *, RSPLSAI VL:*
Planning sequence	S_RS_PLSQ, ACTVT:*, RSPLS_SEQ:*
Planning function type	S_RS_PLST, ACTVT: *, RSPLF_SRVT: /ERP/COOM*, ORSPL*
Authorization object for RS Trace Tool	S_RS_RSTT, ACTVT: 01, RSTTBOBJ: TRACE, USER: *

Table 11.6 SAP Business Warehouse (Cont.)

> **References**
>
> The following SAP Notes should be applied in your system to ensure a smooth planning configuration:
>
> - SAP Note 1904718: BW-IP: DSOs of the Technical Content
> - SAP Note 1901618: Dump When Activating BI Content /ERP/
> - SAP Note 1847922: Termination DBIF_RSQL_INVALID_RSQL When You Activate Content
> - SAP Note 1816332: Object "XYZ ..." (ELEM) Cannot Be Collected
> - SAP Note 1959438: RSRTS_ACTIVATE_R3IS

11.4 Activate Embedded SAP Business Warehouse

Before using SAP BPC for SAP S/4HANA Finance, you need to activate and set up the embedded SAP BW client for the planning functionality to work. You must activate the embedded SAP BW in each system (development, test, production) separately. The following sections walk you through the necessary steps for this activity.

11.4.1 Choose SAP Business Warehouse Client

You must first determine which client should be used as the SAP BW client. Once determined, you can then log on to this client and execute all subsequent steps within this client. In general, the production client is used as the SAP BW client.

11.4.2 Check SAP Business Warehouse Client Setting

There may be a situation in which the setting for the SAP BW client in table RSADMINA exists even if SAP BW isn't used currently. This needs to be checked up front and corrected.

Use Transaction SE16 to display all the data of table RSADMINA. Check to see if there is already an entry reading **BW** in the **CUSTOMIZID** column and an entry in the **BWMANDT** column, as shown in Figure 11.5.

Figure 11.5 Entry in Table RSADMINA

If there are entries in table RSADMINA, use Transaction SE37 to enter function module RS_MANDT_UNIQUE_SET, and then click **Test/Execute** (or press [F8]). Enter the SAP BW client you want to use in the **I_MANDT** field, and click **Execute**. The SAP BW client is now set as shown in Figure 11.6.

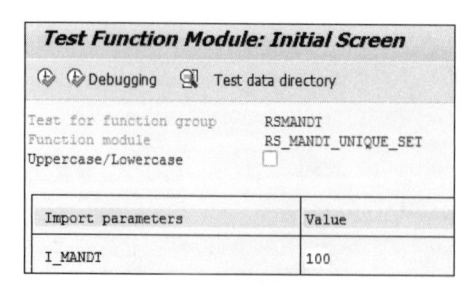

Figure 11.6 Setting Up the SAP BW Client

11.4 Activate Embedded SAP Business Warehouse

If there is no entry in table RSADMINA, or the **BWMANDT** column is blank, then there's no need to run function module RS_MANDT_UNIQUE_SET.

Before you can use operational analytics, you need to complete the basic configuration for SAP BW on your system. This allows you to use operational data providers (ODPs) and classic InfoSets in SAP BusinessObjects BI tools. This Customizing is done using Transaction SPRO under the menu path **SAP NetWeaver • Search and Operational Analytics • Operational Data Provisioning for Operational Analytics • Basic Configuration for Operational Analytics**, as shown in Figure 11.7.

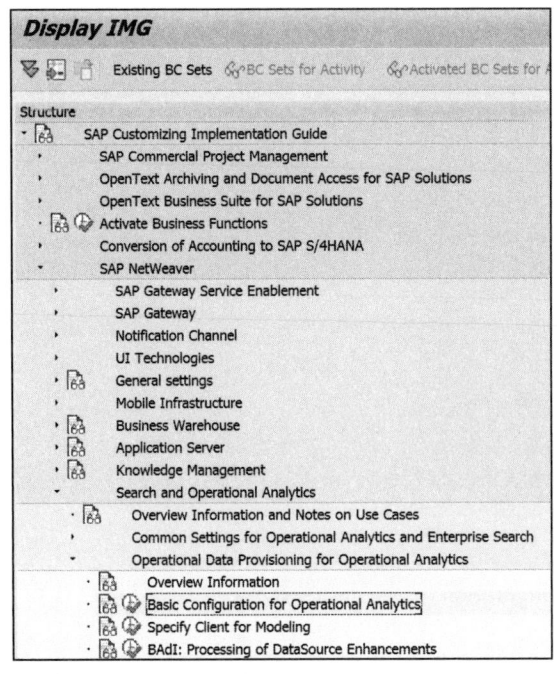

Figure 11.7 Configuration for Operational Analytics

The Customizing steps in the following subsections need to be executed to activate embedded SAP BW.

11.4.3 Set the SAP Business Warehouse Client

First, you need to enter the SAP BW client for which you want to perform the basic configuration, as shown in Figure 11.8. However, if an SAP BW client is already set on the system, you can't change the client.

11 SAP BPC for SAP S/4HANA Finance

Basic Configuration for Operational Analytics

BW Client   100

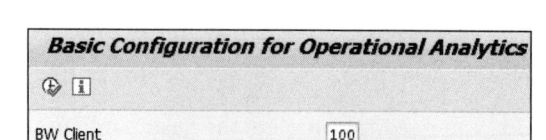

Figure 11.8 Specifying the SAP BW Client for Configuration

After execution, the **Configuration Complete** status should appear, as shown at the bottom of Figure 11.9.

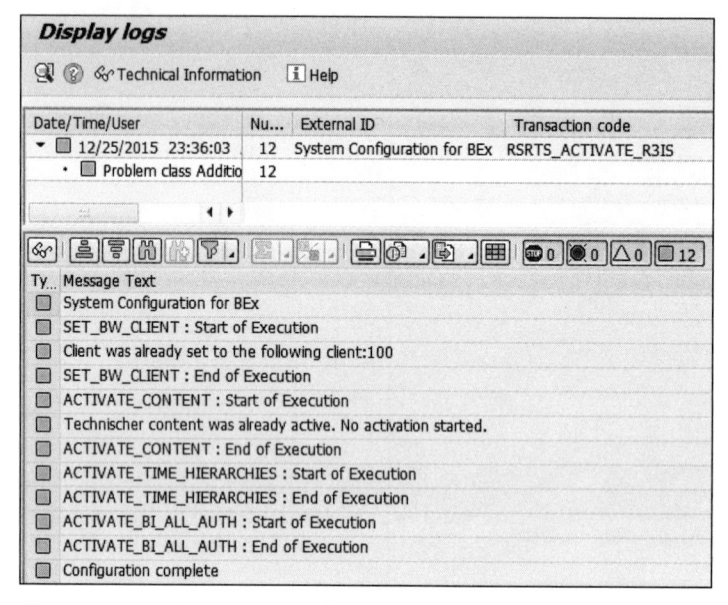

Display logs

Date/Time/User	Nu...	External ID	Transaction code
12/25/2015 23:36:03	12	System Configuration for BEx	RSRTS_ACTIVATE_R3IS
· Problem class Additio	12		

Message Text
- System Configuration for BEx
- SET_BW_CLIENT : Start of Execution
- Client was already set to the following client:100
- SET_BW_CLIENT : End of Execution
- ACTIVATE_CONTENT : Start of Execution
- Technischer content was already active. No activation started.
- ACTIVATE_CONTENT : End of Execution
- ACTIVATE_TIME_HIERARCHIES : Start of Execution
- ACTIVATE_TIME_HIERARCHIES : End of Execution
- ACTIVATE_BI_ALL_AUTH : Start of Execution
- ACTIVATE_BI_ALL_AUTH : End of Execution
- Configuration complete

Figure 11.9 Displaying the Log for Configuration

The technical content is activated and performed by scheduling an activation job using the Data Dictionary (DDIC) user. Messages related to the activation can only be viewed in the job log of activation job BI_TCO_ACTIVATION because these messages can't be displayed by the report. If the activation has been successfully executed, there's no need to schedule the job again.

11.4.4 Assign the Logical System Client

Perform the following steps to define the logical system and then assign it to your SAP BW client:

11.4 Activate Embedded SAP Business Warehouse

1. In the Customizing Transaction SPRO, choose **SAP NetWeaver • Application Server • IDOC Interface/Application Link Enabling (ALE) • Basic Settings • Logical Systems • Define Logical System**, as shown in Figure 11.10.

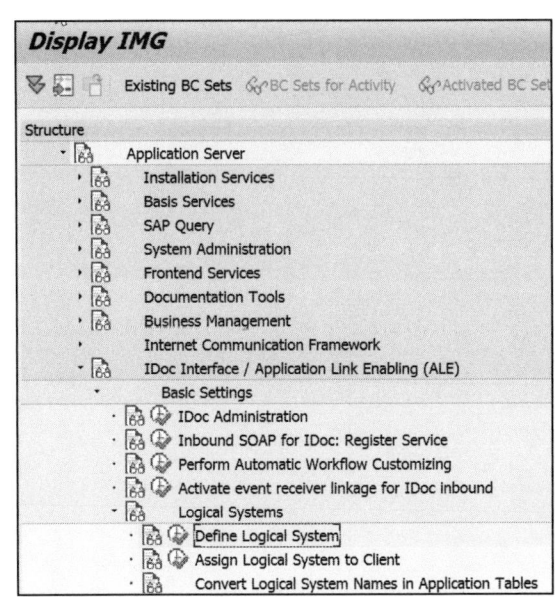

Figure 11.10 Defining the Logical System

2. Create a logical system by executing the Customizing activity **Define Logical System** and then clicking on the **New Entries** button.

3. Enter a name and description of the logical system that you want to create, as shown in Figure 11.11.

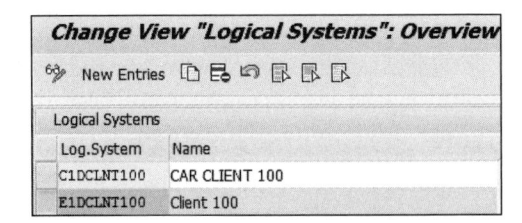

Figure 11.11 Creating an Entry for the Logical System

4. In Customizing Transaction SPRO, choose **SAP NetWeaver • Application Server • IDOC Interface/Application Link Enabling (ALE) • Basic Settings • Logical Systems •**

Assign Logical System to Client. The **Change View "Clients": Details** system screen shown in Figure 11.12 appears.

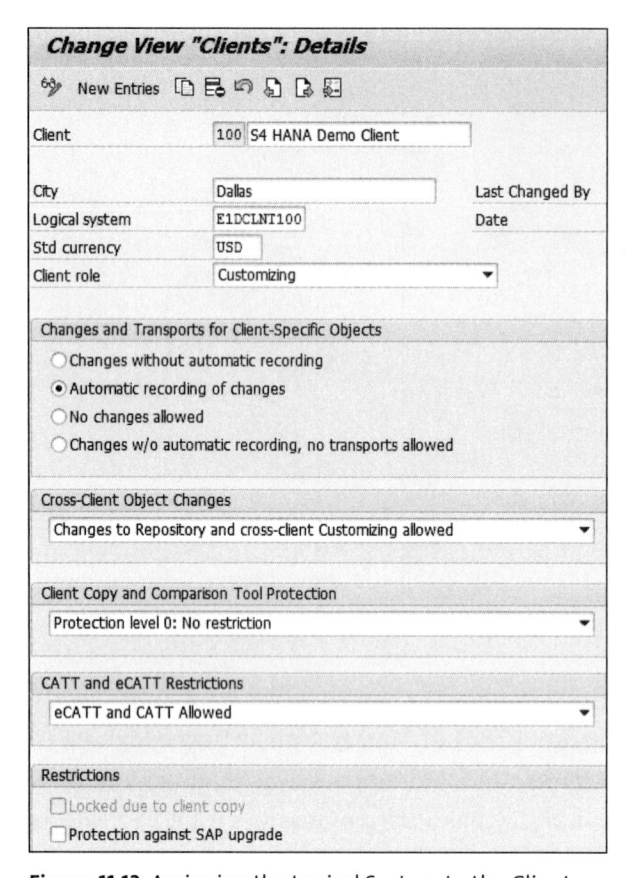

```
Change View "Clients": Details
  New Entries

Client                    100  S4 HANA Demo Client

City                      Dallas                          Last Changed By
Logical system            E1DCLNT100                      Date
Std currency              USD
Client role               Customizing

Changes and Transports for Client-Specific Objects
  ○ Changes without automatic recording
  ● Automatic recording of changes
  ○ No changes allowed
  ○ Changes w/o automatic recording, no transports allowed

Cross-Client Object Changes
  Changes to Repository and cross-client Customizing allowed

Client Copy and Comparison Tool Protection
  Protection level 0: No restriction

CATT and eCATT Restrictions
  eCATT and CATT Allowed

Restrictions
  ☐ Locked due to client copy
  ☐ Protection against SAP upgrade
```

Figure 11.12 Assigning the Logical System to the Client

5. Click the **New Entries** button, and then specify the client and all other parameters in the selection screen. Enter the name of the logical system to which you want to assign the selected client and save your entry.

6. Check the settings per your requirements. Under the **Cross-Client Object Changes** area, choose one of the following settings:
   - **No Changes to Cross-Client Customizing Objects**
   - **Changes to Repository and Cross-Client Customizing Allowed**

7. Set the logical system to the same one created previously in Figure 11.11.

11.4.5 Set SAP Business Warehouse Namespaces to Changeable

You perform this activity when you want to allow or prevent changes to the repository and cross-client Customizing. The global setting can be used to check if the objects in the repository and in cross-client Customizing can be modified.

Every repository object is in a namespace or name range, so to make any changes to these objects, the following settings need to be set to **Modifiable**:

- Global setting
- Namespace or name range
- Software component of the object

In the **Transport Organizer Tools** screen using Transaction SE03, go to the menu path **Administration • Set System Change Option** (as shown in Figure 11.13), and then click **Execute**.

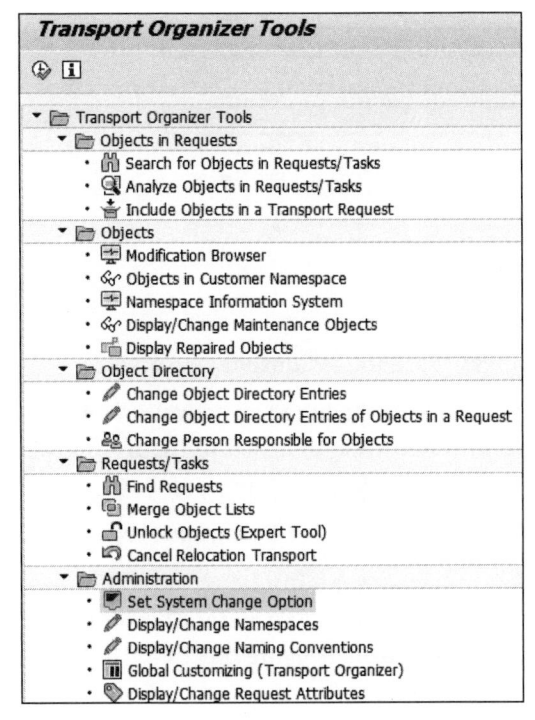

Figure 11.13 Setting the System Change Option

11   SAP BPC for SAP S/4HANA Finance

In the **System Change Option** window, select the namespaces with prefixes **/BIO/** and **/BIC/**, and flag them as **Modifiable** from the dropdown menu (see Figure 11.14).

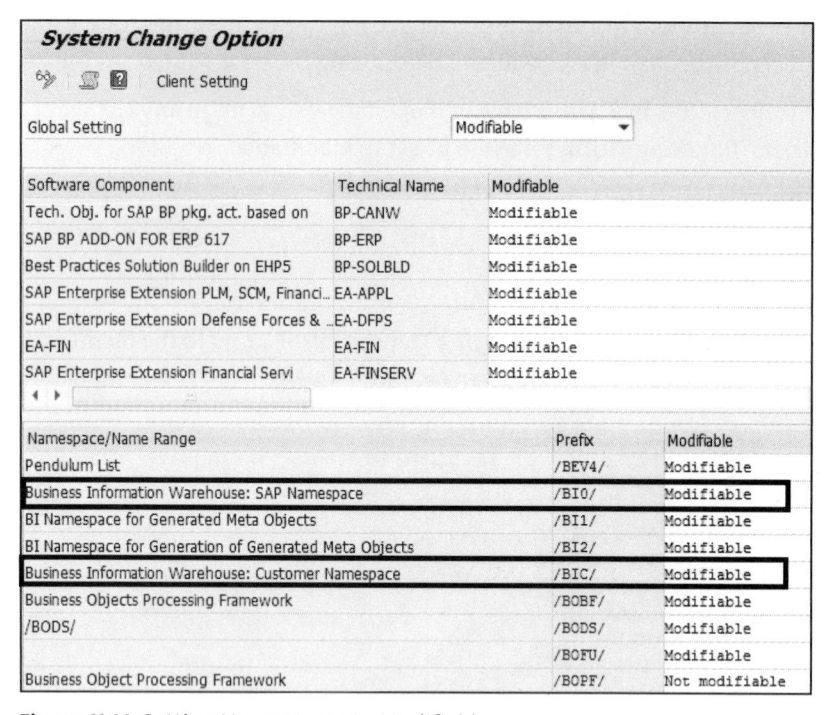

Figure 11.14 Setting Namespaces to Modifiable

11.4.6 Install the Technical SAP Business Warehouse Content

You activate and install the technical content by scheduling an activation job with users who have the profiles SAP_ALL and S_A.SYSTEM assigned to them. To avoid Java error messages when no portal is installed, set the parameters as follows:

1. Start Transaction SU01, enter the DDIC user, and click the **Change** button.
2. Select the **Parameters** tab.
3. Enter parameter "RSWAD_SKIP_JAVA" in the **Set/Get Parameter ID** column, and enter "X" in the **Parameter Value** column, as shown in Figure 11.15.
4. Save all your input parameters.

11.4 Activate Embedded SAP Business Warehouse

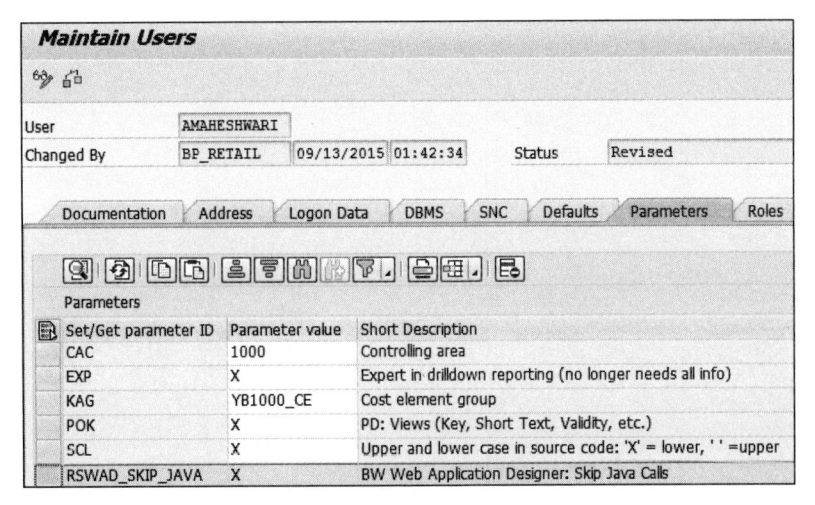

Figure 11.15 Changing User Parameters

5. Go to Transaction RSA1 and click the **Start Installation** button. A message appears, stating that background job BI_TCO_ACTIVATION for activation of the technical BI Content has been scheduled, as shown in Figure 11.16. Call Transaction SMX (Own Jobs), and check that the job has been completed without error messages.

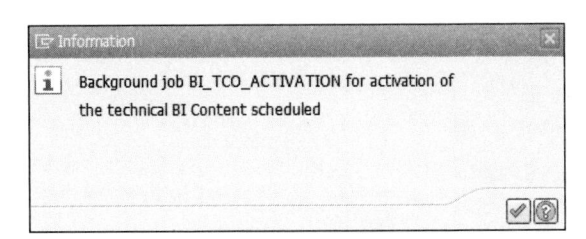

Figure 11.16 Job BI_TCO_ACTIVATION Scheduled

11.4.7 Check Installation Status and Resolve Errors

Check if the **Installation Status** is green and the activation is successful using Transaction RSTCO_ADMIN, as shown in Figure 11.17. If the status is red, it means that errors occurred during installation of the technical content. Start the installation again using Transaction RSTCO_ADMIN. Then, based on the output from the activation log, you need to determine the cause of the errors and define the proper solution.

439

11 SAP BPC for SAP S/4HANA Finance

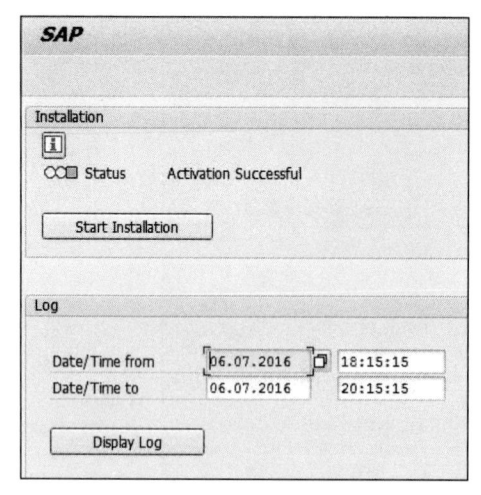

Figure 11.17 Transaction RSTCO_ADMIN Status

Click **Display Log**, and check that it has no red boxes next to error messages, resembling the example in Figure 11.18.

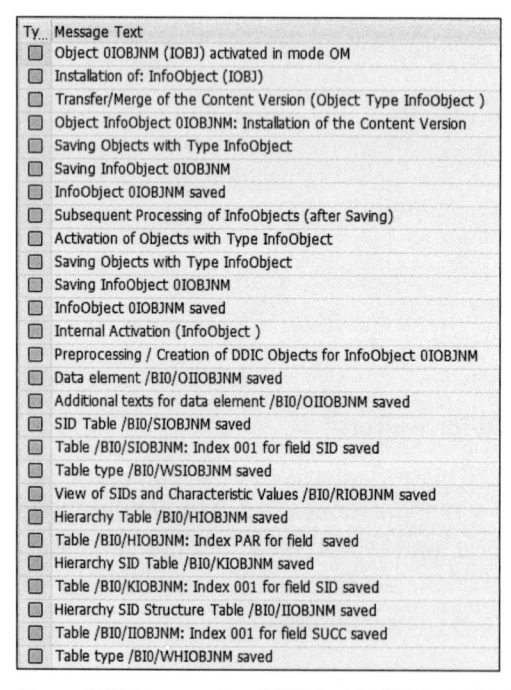

Figure 11.18 Transaction RSTCO_ADMIN Installation Display Log

11.4 Activate Embedded SAP Business Warehouse

> **Expert Insight**
>
> When the activation is executed for a user and there are error messages and authorization problems in the job log, you need to assign the user with the SAP_BW_BI_ADMINISTRATOR role or provide the user with the SAP_ALL authorization to check if this remediates the issue.

If the log instead shows many red lights and error messages, run Transaction RSTCO_ADMIN, and click the **Start Installation** button to run the installation a second time. When the batch job BI_TCO_ACTIVATION has been completed without any errors, recheck the job log again using Transaction RSTCO_ADMIN. In many cases, the second execution of the installation will remediate most of the errors, but if any error still persist, investigate each one on a case-by-case-basis.

11.4.8 Check Planning Content Activation

You can also check if the planning content is already activated by using Transaction RSD1 and checking if InfoObjects ORSPL_* exist in the active version (see Figure 11.19).

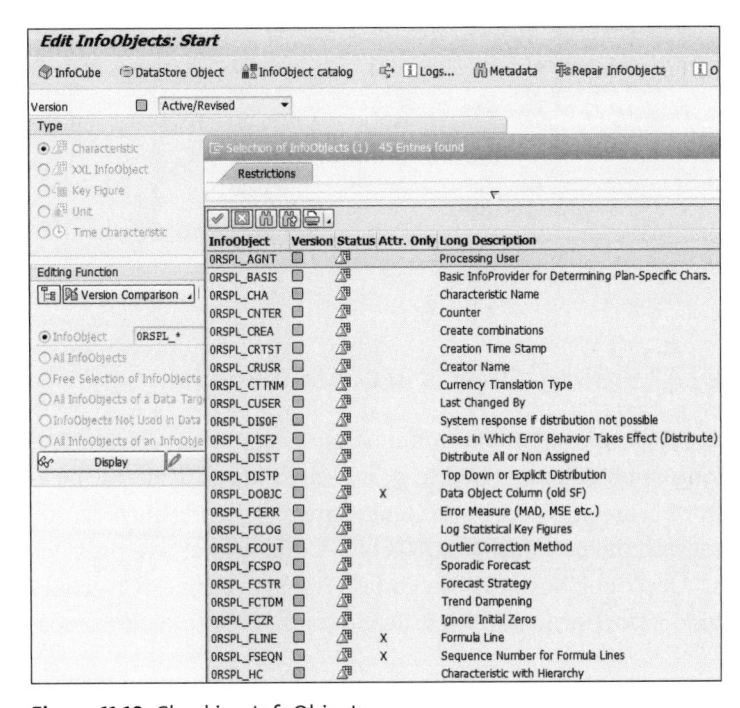

Figure 11.19 Checking InfoObjects

11 SAP BPC for SAP S/4HANA Finance

You should also start Transaction RSA1 to check the objects. When you click on the InfoObjects, you'll find that they all have an active status, as shown in Figure 11.20.

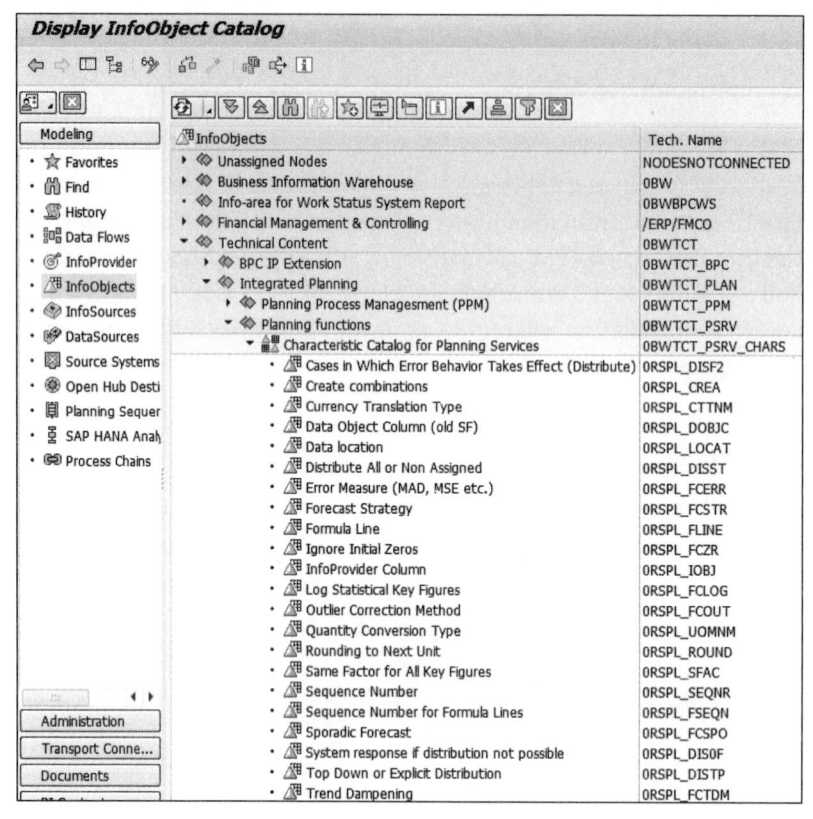

Figure 11.20 Display InfoObject Catalog Screen

11.5 Activate the SAP BusinessObjects BI Content Bundle

An SAP BusinessObjects BI Content bundle contains references to all relevant SAP BusinessObjects BI Content objects that need to be activated to run a specific business scenario. The SAP BusinessObjects BI Content Activation Workbench can be used to activate and search the SAP BusinessObjects BI Content that SAP provides and groups according to various business categories. The SAP BusinessObjects BI Content bundle contains all SAP BusinessObjects BI objects required to analyze a specific business area.

11.5 Activate the SAP BusinessObjects BI Content Bundle

To activate the SAP BusinessObjects BI Content bundle using the SAP BusinessObjects BI Content Activation Workbench, use Transaction BSANLY_BI_ACTIVATION. You'll need to activate the bundles required for the planning function to operate.

11.5.1 Activate the DataSources

Authorization object BSANL_ACWB needs to be assigned to you to display and activate the SAP BusinessObjects BI Content. You also need to check if the required DataSources are active; if not, you need to activate them manually by following these steps:

1. Execute Transaction RSA5, and expand the complete SAP structure, as shown in Figure 11.21.

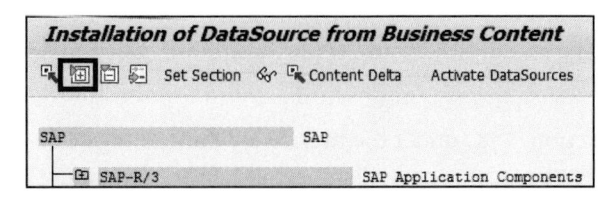

Figure 11.21 Installation of DataSource

2. Use the **Find** functionality to jump to the relevant DataSource, as shown in Figure 11.22.

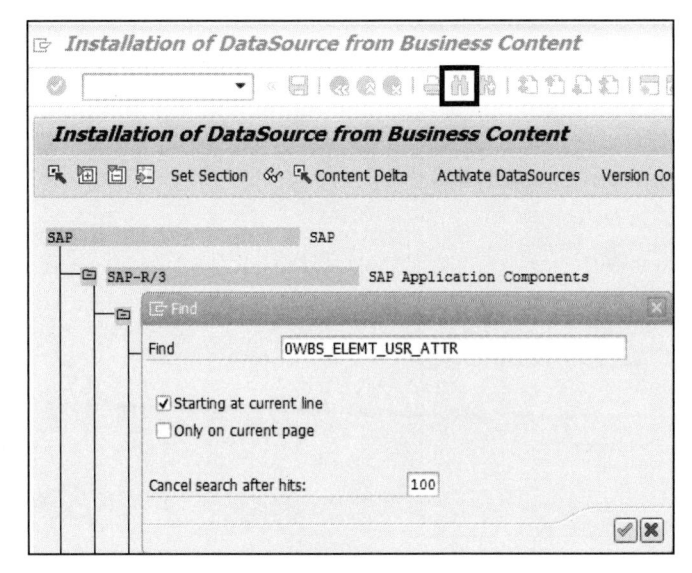

Figure 11.22 Finding the DataSource

443

3. Put your cursor on the DataSource, select the subtree, and click **Activate DataSource**, as shown in Figure 11.23.

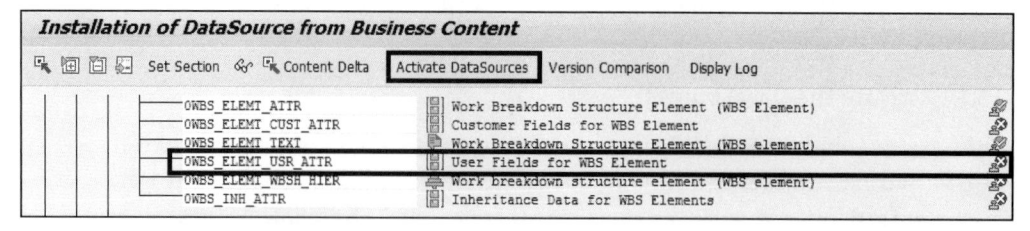

Figure 11.23 Activating the DataSource

11.5.2 Activate the Content Bundle

Follow this sequence to activate the SAP BusinessObjects BI Content bundle for planning:

1. Go to the Customizing Transaction SPRO under the menu path **Controlling • General Controlling • Roles for NetWeaver Business Client • Project Planner and Cost Estimator • Activate BI Content Bundle for Planning**, as shown in Figure 11.24.

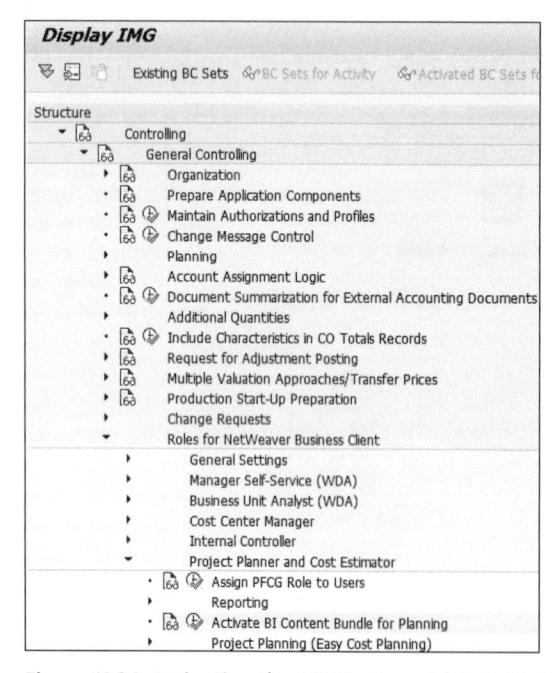

Figure 11.24 Activating the SAP BusinessObjects BI Content Bundle for Planning

11.5 Activate the SAP BusinessObjects BI Content Bundle

2. View and activate predefined SAP BusinessObjects BI Content bundles. This activity launches the SAP BusinessObjects BI Content Activation Workbench, which lists SAP BusinessObjects BI Content bundles according to business categories. You can check the content objects of each bundle and decide whether to activate specific objects while activating the bundle or to exclude them from being activated.

3. Alternatively, if you don't want to use the workbench, the Data Warehousing Workbench in SAP BW can be used to activate SAP BusinessObjects BI Content using Transaction RSOR.

4. To use the cost center manager, internal controller, and project manager roles, you must switch to the business function view and activate the following SAP BusinessObjects BI Content bundles:

   - /ERP/FCOM_PLANNING for the planning applications
   - FIN_REP_SIMPL_3 for the reports included in the report launchpad
   - FIN_REP_SIMPL_4 for the reports included in the report launchpad

5. Upon executing the SAP BusinessObjects BI Content, you'll see the screen shown in Figure 11.25.

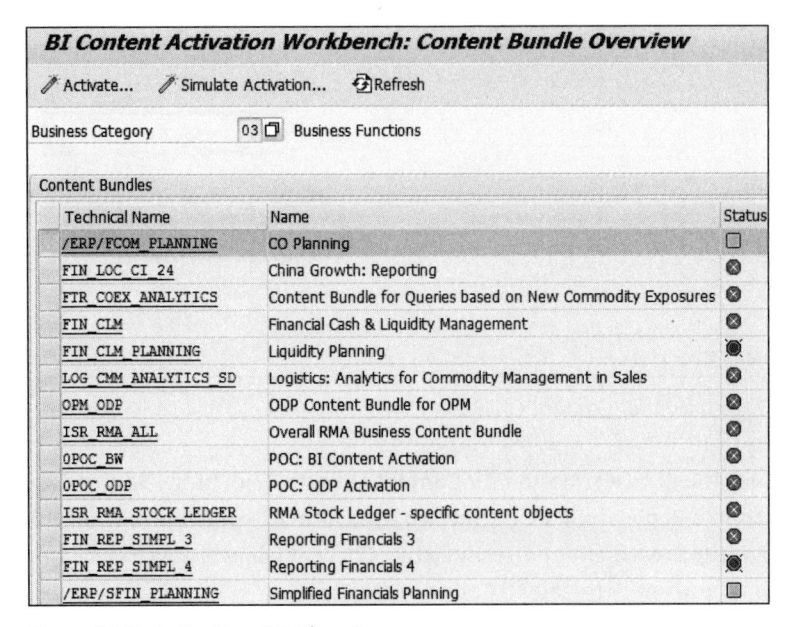

Technical Name	Name	Status
/ERP/FCOM_PLANNING	CO Planning	☐
FIN_LOC_CI_24	China Growth: Reporting	⊗
FTR_COEX_ANALYTICS	Content Bundle for Queries based on New Commodity Exposures	⊗
FIN_CLM	Financial Cash & Liquidity Management	⊗
FIN_CLM_PLANNING	Liquidity Planning	◉
LOG_CMM_ANALYTICS_SD	Logistics: Analytics for Commodity Management in Sales	⊗
OPM_ODP	ODP Content Bundle for OPM	⊗
ISR_RMA_ALL	Overall RMA Business Content Bundle	⊗
OPOC_BW	POC: BI Content Activation	⊗
OPOC_ODP	POC: ODP Activation	⊗
ISR_RMA_STOCK_LEDGER	RMA Stock Ledger - specific content objects	⊗
FIN_REP_SIMPL_3	Reporting Financials 3	⊗
FIN_REP_SIMPL_4	Reporting Financials 4	◉
/ERP/SFIN_PLANNING	Simplified Financials Planning	☐

Figure 11.25 Activating CO Planning

11   SAP BPC for SAP S/4HANA Finance

6. Make sure to select **Business Category 03** for **Business Functions**, select **/ERP/FCOM_PLANNING** under **Technical Name**, and click **Activate**.

   You may select one or several SAP BusinessObjects BI Content bundles in the list that you want to activate. Note that **Business Category 01** is used for selecting **Value Scenarios**, **Business Category 02** for **Processes**, **Business Category 03** for **Business Functions**, and **Business Category 99** for **Others**.

> **References**
>
> For more information, see SAP Note 1972819: Setup Integrated Business Planning for Finance.

7. On the next screen, you'll define an RFC mapping called **NONE** because the RFC mapping functionality isn't required for the local planning content. Make sure to check the **Local** flag as shown in Figure 11.26.

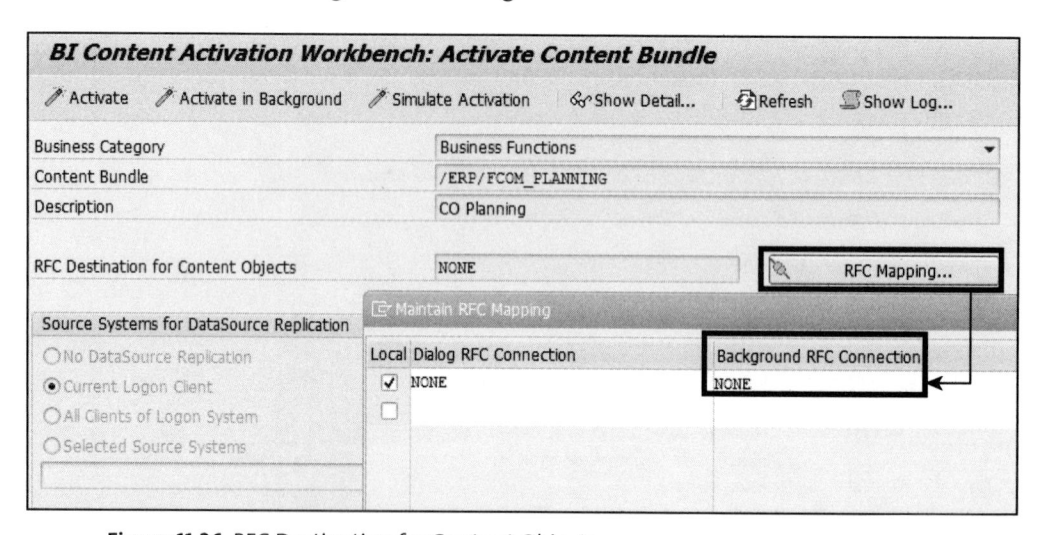

Figure 11.26 RFC Destination for Content Objects

8. Enter "NONE" for the **RFC Destination for Content Objects** field. In the **Source Systems for DataSource Replication** area, select **No DataSource Replication** or **Current Logon Client**. For the **Treatment of Already Active Content Objects** area (see Figure 11.27), select **Copy**, and check **Install All Collected Objects**.

11.5 Activate the SAP BusinessObjects BI Content Bundle

9. The selection in the **Source Systems for DataSource Replication** area determines how the source systems for the SAP BI Content activation are assigned. You can choose the following options to assign the source systems to be used for the SAP BI Content activation:
   - **No DataSource Replication**
     No source system is assigned.
   - **Current Logon Client**
     The currently used logical system is assigned. If you choose this option, the activation run doesn't check whether the system can be used as a source system.
   - **All Clients of Logon System**
     All clients of the current system are assigned.
   - **Selected Source Systems**
     You can manually select and assign the source systems.
10. Click **Activate**, as shown in Figure 11.27.

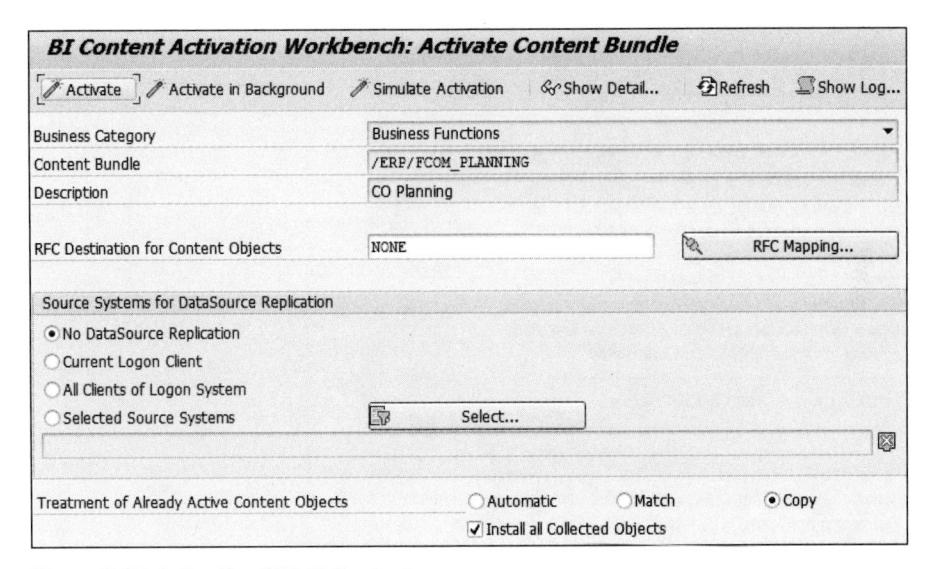

Figure 11.27 Activating SAP BI Content

11. In the **Treatment of Already Active Content Objects** area, the other options might be activated later. Choose **Match** if you've changed the SAP-delivered content. You'll then be asked if the new content version will be merged with the active object. In addition, **Install All Collected Objects** needs to be unchecked when new

447

11 SAP BPC for SAP S/4HANA Finance

SAP-delivered objects are taken into consideration. The system automatically selects between **Match** and **Copy** depending on the object type (see the MERGEFL flag in table RSTLOGOPROP).

12. Click **Activate** to start the activation process, as shown in Figure 11.28.

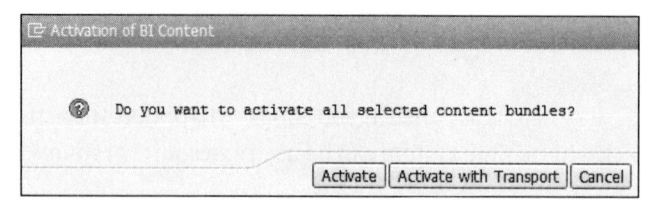

Figure 11.28 Activating Selected Bundles

13. Check the activation log, as shown in Figure 11.29. If there are any errors, they need to be corrected before moving to the next activity.

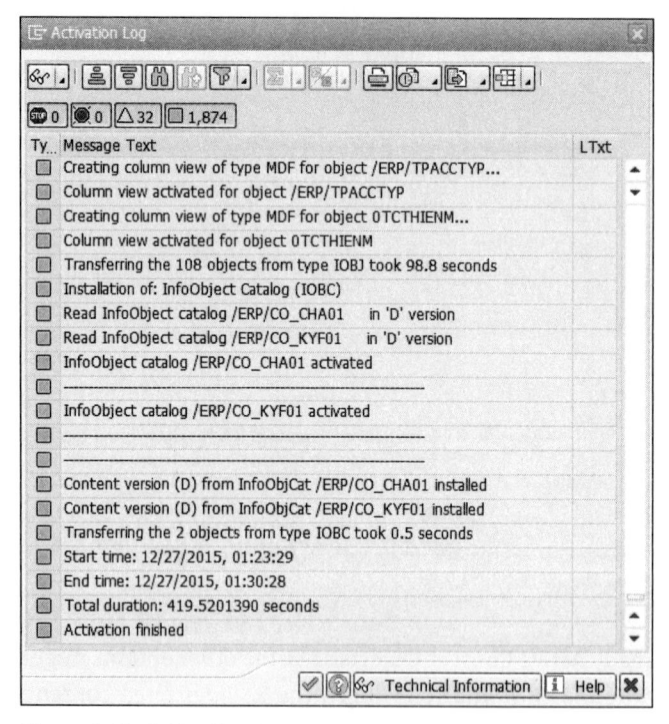

Figure 11.29 Activation Log

11.6 Test the SAP Business Warehouse Installation

After all the required components have been installed and activated, you need to set your user parameter and test whether the planning functionality works and integrates the data in the SAP S/4HANA system, as discussed in the following sections.

11.6.1 Set the User Parameter

Set the user parameter to the relevant controlling area by choosing **System • User Profile • Own Data** (see Figure 11.30).

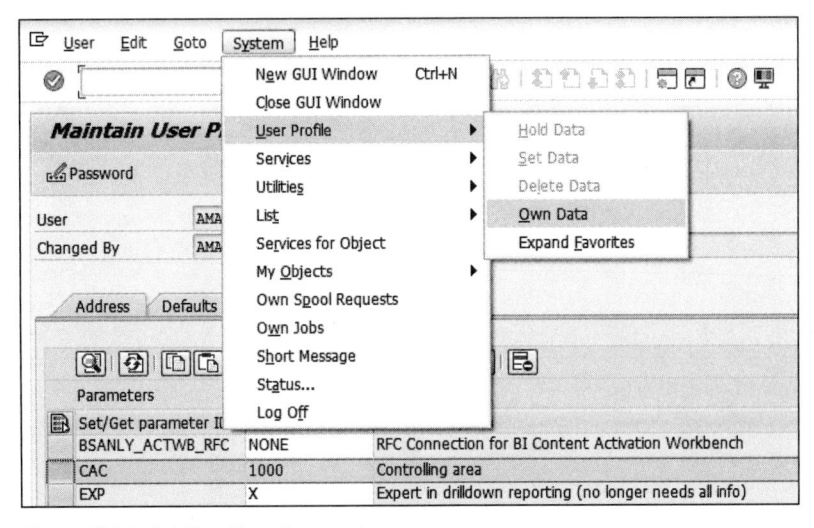

Figure 11.30 Setting User Parameters

In Figure 11.30, for example, the user parameter **CAC** is set to **1000**. User parameter RSPLS_HDB_SUPPORT is used to turn on the SAP HANA calculation engine (CE) for the user.

11.6.2 Test the Planning Query Installation

Using Transaction RSRT, select the dropdown in the **Query** tab and click **InfoAreas**. Here, you can choose any planning area, such as cost center, profit center, project, balance sheet planning, and so on.

Fill in the entries, and choose **Execute** to run the first test, as shown in Figure 11.31. This will bring up the selection screen shown in Figure 11.32.

11 SAP BPC for SAP S/4HANA Finance

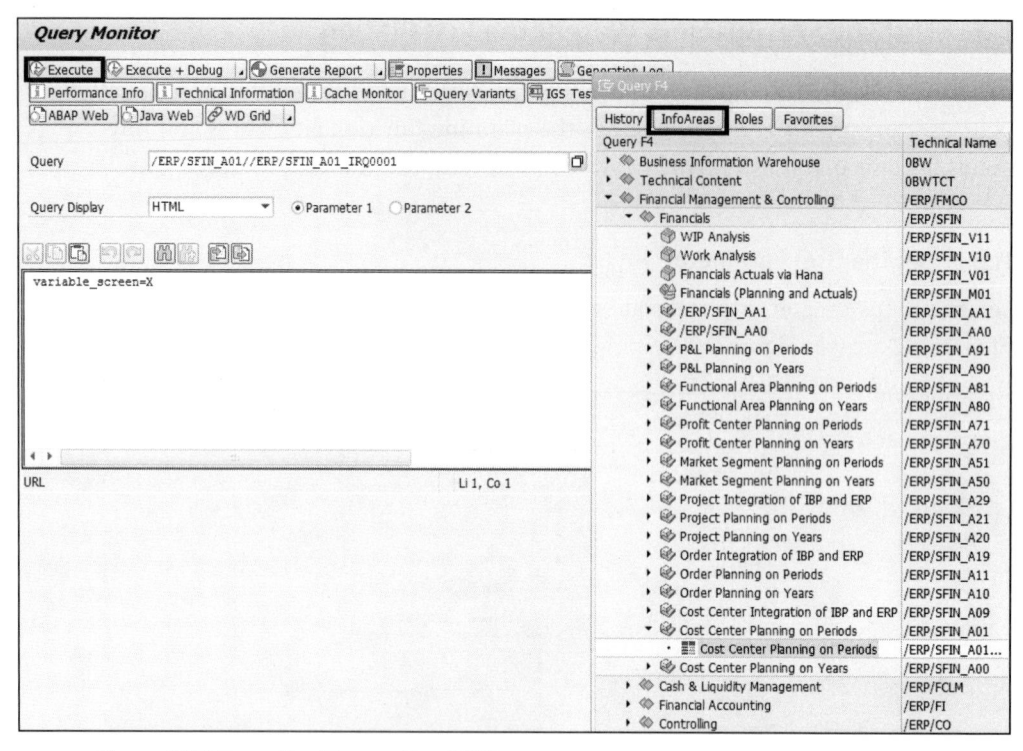

Figure 11.31 Executing Transaction RSRT

Figure 11.32 Executing the Query

11.7 Activate Services and Test Planning Applications

The fields in Figure 11.32 that are marked with an asterisk (*) are mandatory fields that require input. Enter meaningful selection data based on your configuration, and click **Execute** to see the results (see Figure 11.33).

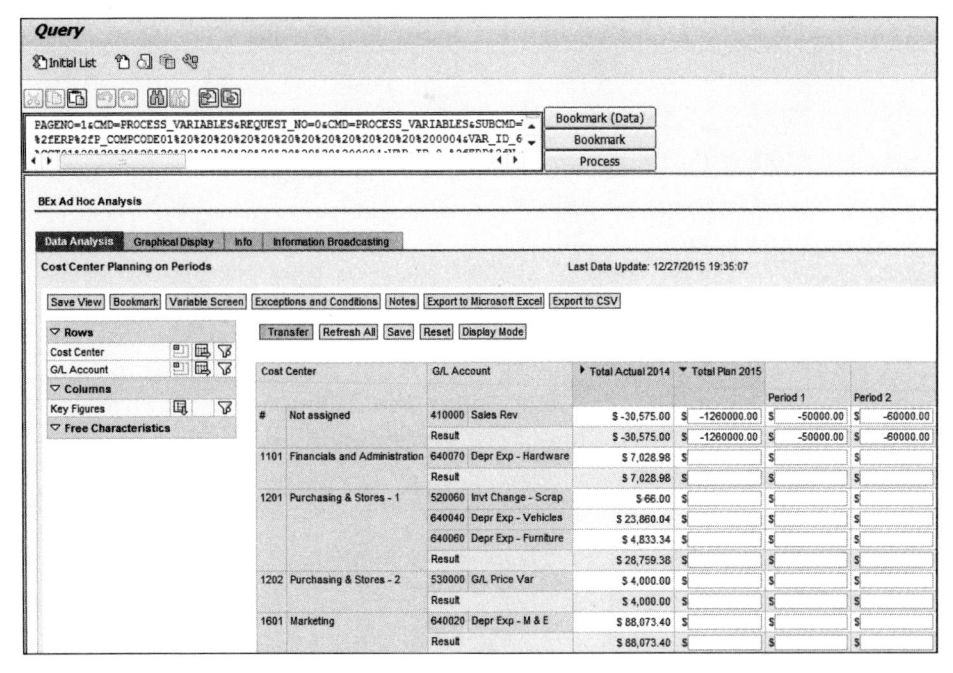

Figure 11.33 Query Execution Results

This test result provides evidence of the correct installation and configuration of the planning functionality. You can type in the planning data in the fields as necessary.

11.7 Activate Services and Test Planning Applications

In this section, you'll set up, validate, and test all the services for your planning applications.

11.7.1 Check General Settings for Web Dynpro

You need to configure the settings for Web Dynpro after the system has been installed and before you start developing Web Dynpro applications, components, and interfaces.

You might have to complete some additional configuration settings for areas related to the Web Dynpro programming model (Internet Communication Manager [ICM], Internet Communication Framework [ICF], and the view designer) and comply with security requirements so that the application operates without any problems.

> **References**
>
> For more information on configuration and activation settings related to Web Dynpro and ICF, refer to the following resources:
>
> - Web Dynpro: *http://bit.ly/2gHkP5M*
> - ICF: *http://bit.ly/2zPB7yb*

11.7.2 Run Report RSICF_SERVICE_ACTIVATION

Run Report RSICF_SERVICE_ACTIVATION using Transaction SE38, as shown in Figure 11.34. This report is used to activate a special service during installation, such as a predefined group of ICF nodes.

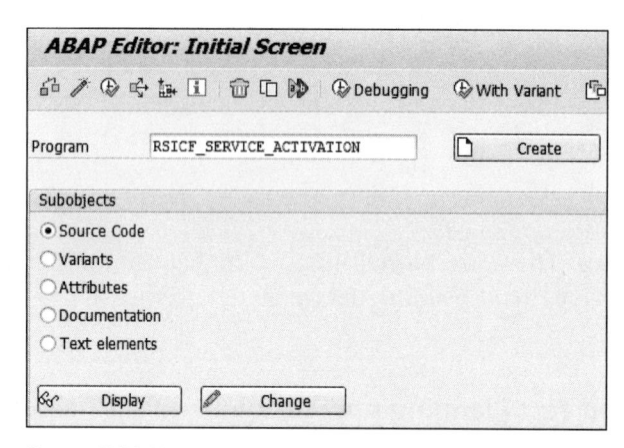

Figure 11.34 Execute Report RSICF_SERVICE_ACTIVATION

Enter "WEB DYNPRO ABAP" in the **Technical Name** field (see Figure 11.35).

11.7 Activate Services and Test Planning Applications

Figure 11.35 Activating ICF

Click **Execute**, and the results should appear without any errors (see Figure 11.36).

Figure 11.36 Report for Activating Special Service

This ensures that all relevant Web Dynpro components and services are installed and active.

11.7.3 Activate Services for the Planning Applications

Use Transaction SICF to activate the required services for the planning applications, such as cost center planning, cost element planning, internal orders planning, or overall project planning.

On the **Maintain Services** screen, first enter "FCOM*IP*" in the **Service Name** field, and then click **Execute** to filter the planning applications, as shown in Figure 11.37. Upon execution, you'll then be able to select the required planning service (see Figure 11.38).

You might see error messages for missing functionality or components if all the required services haven't been activated yet. The missing services must be activated to resolve the errors.

11 SAP BPC for SAP S/4HANA Finance

Figure 11.37 Maintain Services

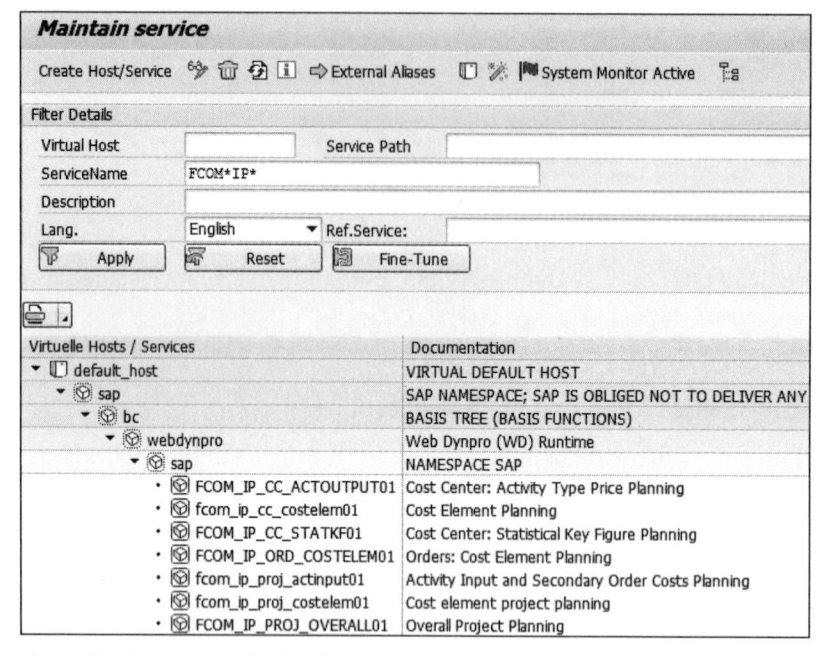

Figure 11.38 Maintain Service Results

11.7.4 Test the New Planning Application

In the new package architecture of SAP S/4HANA Finance, each software component is directly identified with a structure package within the ABAP Development Workbench.

11.7 Activate Services and Test Planning Applications

You need to use Transaction SE80 and select package **FCOM_PLANNING_CORE**, as shown in Figure 11.39.

Object Name	Description
FCOM_IP_ORD_ACTINPUT02	Order Activity Input Planning (Multiple Currencies)
FCOM_IP_ORD_ACTINPUT03	Order Activity Input Planning
FCOM_IP_ORD_ACTINPUT04	Order Activity Input Planning
FCOM_IP_ORD_COSTELEM01	Order Cost Element Planning (Basic)
FCOM_IP_ORD_COSTELEM02	Order Cost Element Planning (Additional Features)
FCOM_IP_ORD_COSTELEM03	Order Top Down Cost Element Group Planning
FCOM_IP_ORD_COSTELEM04	Order Cost Element Planning (Additional Features)
FCOM_IP_PROJ_ACTINPUT01	Project Activity Input Planning
FCOM_IP_PROJ_ACTINPUT02	Project Activity Input Planning (Multiple Currencies)
FCOM_IP_PROJ_ACTINPUT03	Project Secondary Order Costs Planning
FCOM_IP_PROJ_ACTINPUT04	Project Secondary Order Costs Planning (Multiple Curr
FCOM_IP_PROJ_COSTELEM01	Project Cost Element Planning (Basic)
FCOM_IP_PROJ_COSTELEM02	Project Cost Element Planning (Additional Features)
FCOM_IP_PROJ_COSTELEM03	Project Top Down Cost Element Group Planning
FCOM_IP_PROJ_COSTELEM04	Project Cost Element Planning (Multiple Currencies)
FCOM_IP_PROJ_OVERALL01	Project overall planning
FCOM_IP_PROJ_OVERALL02	Project overall planning
FCO_ANLY_INCOME_STATEMEN	Income Statement by Market Segment
FCO_ANLY_WIP_ANALYSIS	WIP Analysis Report
FCO_ANLY_WORK_ANALYSIS	Work Analysis Report

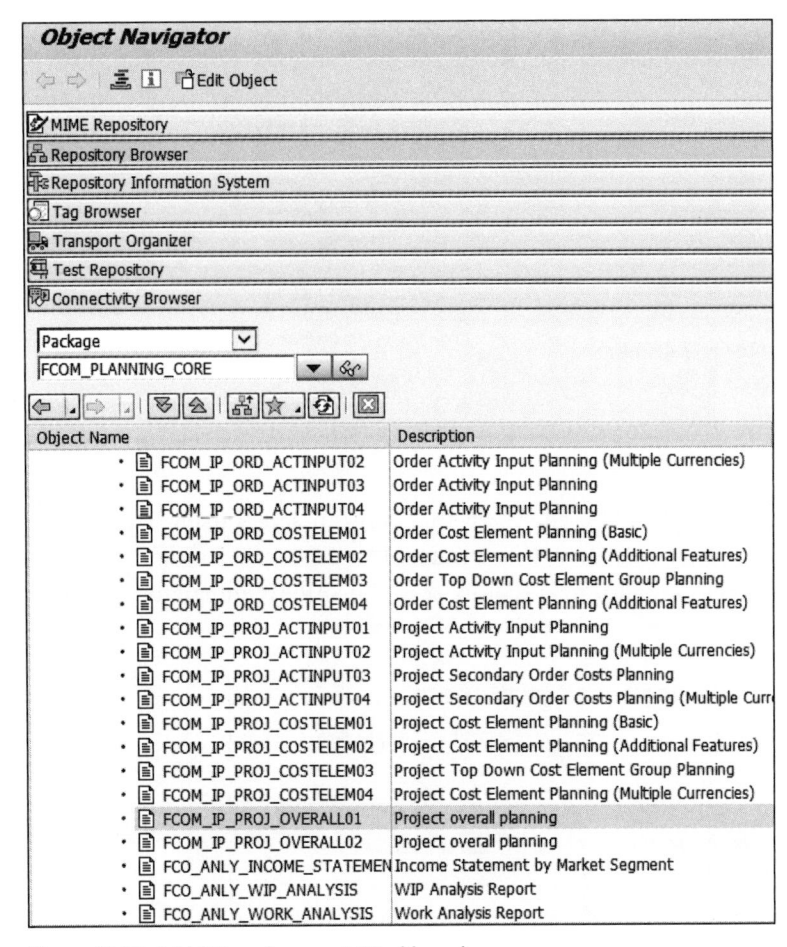

Figure 11.39 ABAP Development Workbench

Right-click **FCOM_IP_PROJ_OVERALL01 (Project Overall Planning)**, and then click **Test**. The **Overall Planning** screen appears, as shown in Figure 11.40.

Enter a **Version** and a **Project**, and then click **Execute**. Now you should see the first results. This test ensures that the planning function is enabled and working in SAP BPC for SAP S/4HANA Finance.

11   SAP BPC for SAP S/4HANA Finance

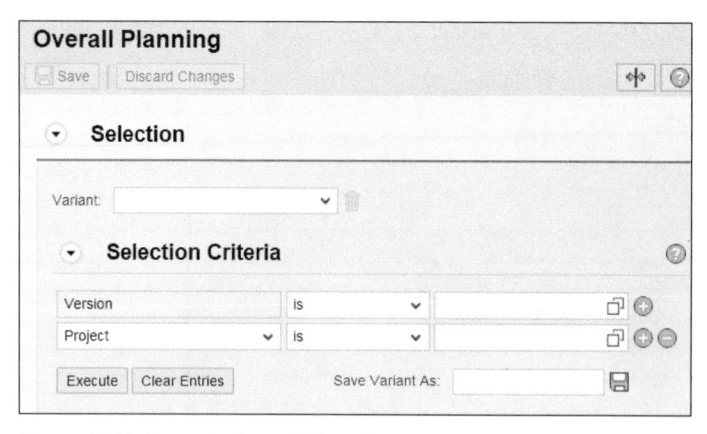

Figure 11.40 Execute Overall Planning

11.8   Planning Modeler

Planning Modeler is an ABAP-based screen that you can access using Transaction RSPLAN, as shown in Figure 11.41. It's the central tool used for modeling and configuring all planning-specific applications that exist in the SAP BW integrated planning component.

Figure 11.41 Planning-Specific InfoProvider Properties

456

11.9 SAP BusinessObjects Analysis for Microsoft Office

The hierarchies and master data for transactional InfoCubes and InfoObjects are maintained in the Data Warehousing Workbench using Transaction RSA1, which forms the basis for any planning customization. All the planning objects are stored within the Data Warehousing Workbench, from which you can navigate into the Planning Modeler.

Characteristic relationships are used to provide valid and smart combinations when planning and to perform derivations, as shown in Figure 11.42. Some of the characteristics are derived based on the values in the master data. For example, the business area and functional area values aren't calculated but are derived based on the values in the cost center master data.

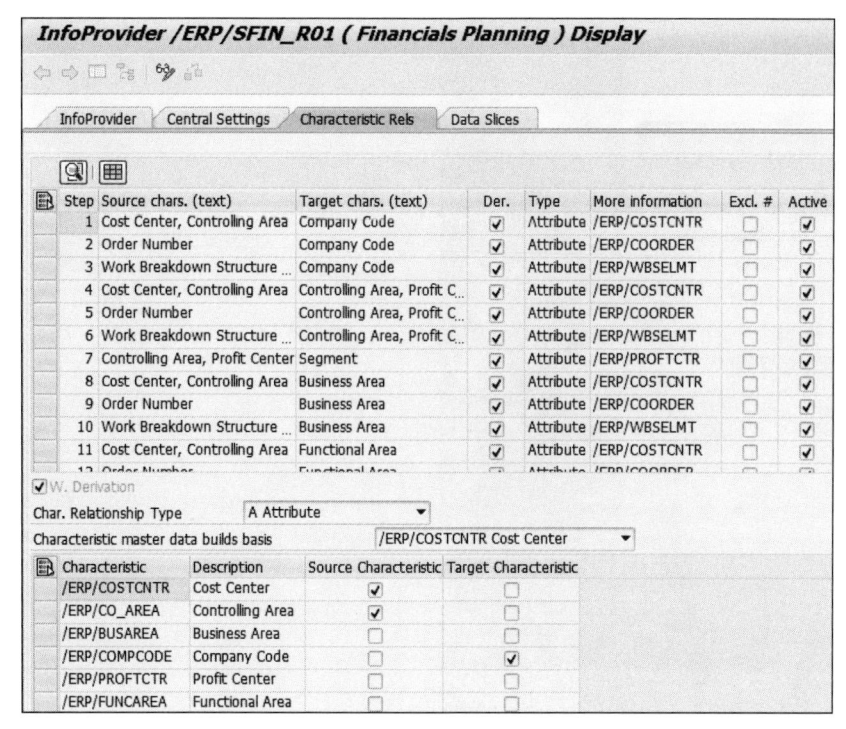

Figure 11.42 Characteristic Relationships in the Planning Modeler

11.9 SAP BusinessObjects Analysis for Microsoft Office

SAP BusinessObjects Analysis for Microsoft Office is used for the centralized creation of analysis content using Excel workbooks and PowerPoint; you can access

11 SAP BPC for SAP S/4HANA Finance

and analyze ad hoc data using Excel and embed SAP BusinessObjects BI data into PowerPoint presentations. This Microsoft Office add-in allows for multidimensional analysis of planning data in Excel and intuitive creation of SAP BusinessObjects BI presentations in PowerPoint, which is very convenient for end users.

To start analysis in Excel, follow these steps:

1. Begin at your desktop. Go to **Start • All Programs • SAP Business Intelligence • SAP BusinessObjects Analysis • Analysis for Microsoft Excel**, as shown in Figure 11.43.

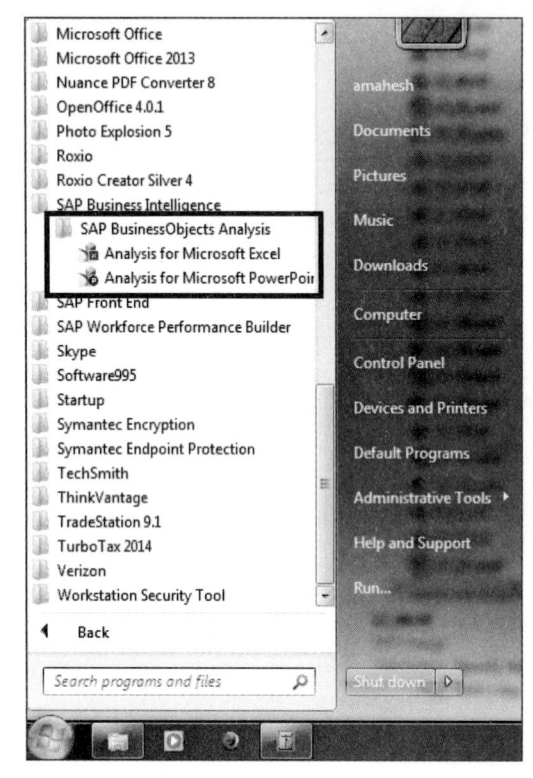

Figure 11.43 Starting Analysis for Microsoft Excel

2. When you open Excel, go to **File • Analysis • Settings**, and check the **Show Planning Group** checkbox (see Figure 11.44) so that the planning function is available by default when you next open SAP BusinessObjects Analysis for Microsoft Office.

11.9 SAP BusinessObjects Analysis for Microsoft Office

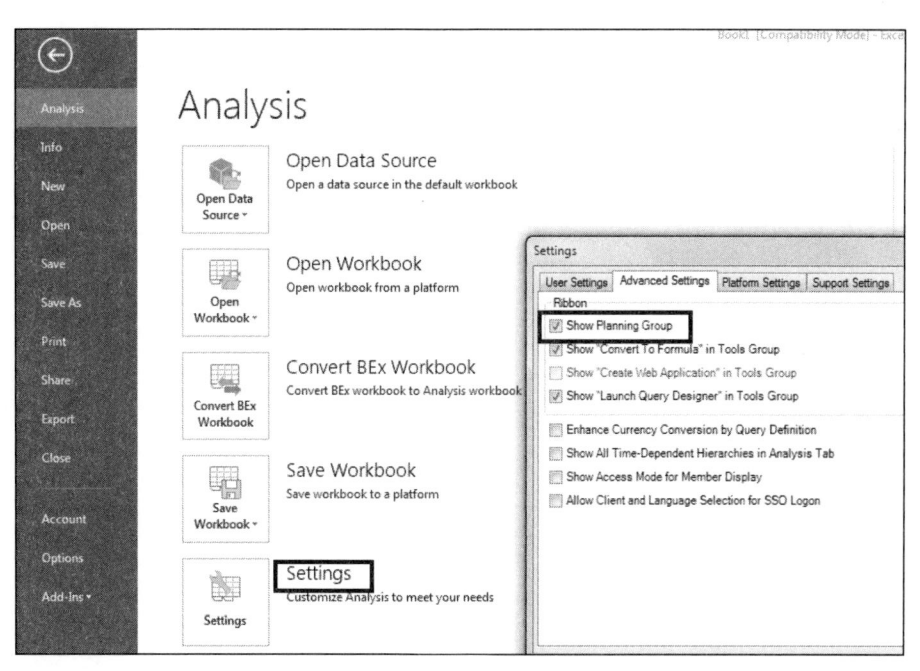

Figure 11.44 Activating the Planning Group

3. Choose **File • Analysis • Open Workbook**, and click the **Open Workbook from the SAP NetWeaver Platform** option, as shown in Figure 11.45.

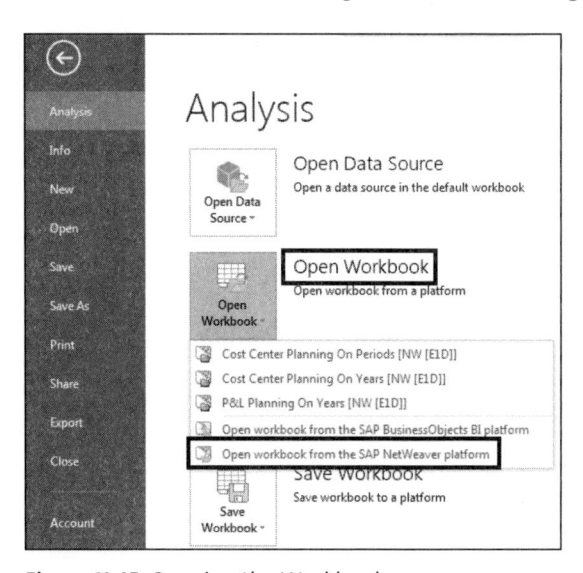

Figure 11.45 Opening the Workbook

459

4. Double-click the workbook that you want to analyze, and enter the planning data. In this example, **Cost Center Planning on Periods** has been selected for analysis in Figure 11.46.

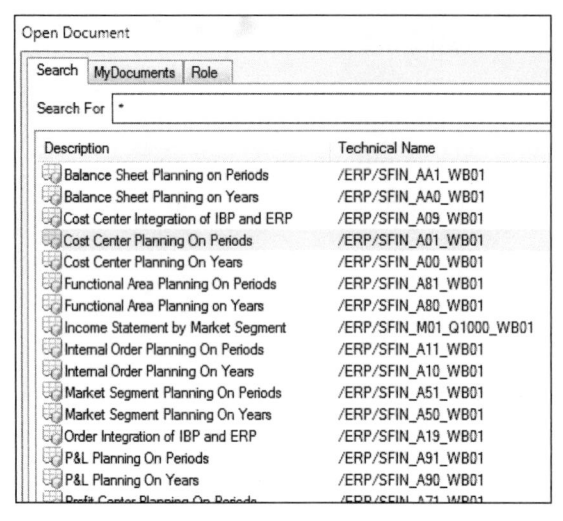

Figure 11.46 Selecting the Workbook for Analysis

5. After you double-click the **Cost Center Planning on Periods** template from the SAP BusinessObjects Analysis for Microsoft Office for Excel add-on, a pop-up screen appears in which you can enter the selection parameters (see Figure 11.47).

Figure 11.47 Selecting the Parameters

6. After providing all the parameters, click **OK**, and you're taken to the **Cost Center Planning on Periods** template. In the template, click the **Copy Actual to Plan** button, and the actual values are allocated to the plan, as shown in Figure 11.48. Alternatively, you can use the **Copy Actual to Plan** values as the base and then modify the plan with manual adjustments, or you can enter all the plan values manually.

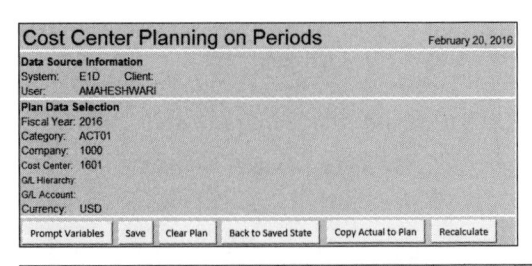

Figure 11.48 Computing the Plan Values

7. When the plan is saved, the data are entered directly and saved in the SAP HANA database. The **Cost Centers—Plan/Actual** report in the SAP Fiori app shows the same plan values (see Figure 11.49).

Figure 11.49 Real-Time Update of Planning Values

You can adapt the analysis workbook to create user-specific or global variants, adapt the layout of the workbook along with the selection parameters, format the layout by modifying the SAP cell styles, remove the buttons that aren't required, add or modify the buttons for planning sequences, add additional queries, and insert charts.

You can check the same data values in SAP BW as well by following these steps:

1. Go to Transaction RSA1 and click **InfoProvider**.
2. Under the menu path **Financial Management & Controlling • Financials**, right-click **Financials Planning**, and then click **Display Data**.
3. In the **Characteristic Selection** screen, select the required characteristics and then press [Enter].
4. When the **/ERP/SFIN_R01** selection screen appears, enter the values of the cost center that you need to check (assuming cost center was one of the selected characteristics in the previous step), and then click the **Field Selection for Output** button.
5. Select the organizational units and key figures that you want to display in your report, and then click **Execute**.
6. When the **/ERP/SFIN_R01** selection screen appears again, click **Execute** on this screen, and the output is displayed as shown in Figure 11.50. Once again, you'll find that the plan values have been integrated into SAP BW on a real-time basis.

...HRTACCT	...DCI	/ERP/GL_ACCT	/ERP/COSTCNTR	Category	Fiscal year	Currency	0UNIT	Amount
0010	S	0000640020	0000001601	ACT01	2016	USD		27,826.08
0010	S	0000440020	0000001601	ACT01	2016	USD		4,901.25

Figure 11.50 SAP BW InfoProvider Output List

11.10 Key System Changes

SAP BPC for SAP S/4HANA Finance is an integral part of SAP S/4HANA; it leverages the BPC features of workflow, work status, and activity logs that allow users to perform operational and tactical planning. The planning experience is enhanced because users can use a single SAP Fiori interface for all their transactional, analytical, and planning needs.

The following are important features or changes with SAP BPC for SAP S/4HANA Finance:

- It can be used to model all possible planning scenarios that an organization might have; the consolidation requirement is addressed by the SAP BPC standard standalone product.

- It allows real-time update of master data and transactional data without duplicating or copying the actual data. It offers the flexibility to integrate with non-ERP instances for the planning data.
- It allows you to customize all planning functions and leverage the KPI modeler and Predictive Analysis Library (PAL) to further extend the planning functions.
- It uses SAP BusinessObjects Analysis for Microsoft Office for reporting purposes and offers standard features of reporting. The cloud version offers a robust dashboard and cockpit compared to the on-premise version, but it can be as scalable as any other planning tool.
- It has the same level of system flexibility as other SAP planning tools. As part of the SAP S/4HANA system, it has the added advantage of following a similar architectural model as the standard SAP BPC tool.

For performing real-time consolidation in SAP S/4HANA, SAP has introduced another SAP HANA table similar to table ACDOCA: table ACDOCC. Table ACDOCC has a similar structure as table ACDOCA, with some extensions designed for the integration with SAP BPC. This table is designed to save the consolidated data from SAP BPC. Several SAP HANA views can be created based on these two SAP HANA tables, and through these SAP HANA views, SAP BPC and SAP BW can read the transaction data directly from SAP S/4HANA without replicating the data to SAP BPC, as was done in the past.

Because the SAP HANA views can only provide read access to the data, a virtual InfoProvider and its writeback class is required to write the data back to SAP S/4HANA. The consolidated data is written back to table ACDOCC through a virtual InfoProvider.

1709 Preview

SAP S/4HANA 1709 enhanced the Product Cost Analysis SAP Fiori app to support new planning functionality to display planned costs for manufacturing orders and a product cost collector. Production order costs can now be reported and analyzed using a multidimensional array.

Setting up the correct profit center and cost center hierarchy plays a vital role in both planning and reporting. The level of effort required to change a hierarchy based on the current organizational environment is very high. With 1709, you can now create flexible hierarchies based on master data attributes and tags.

11.11 Summary

SAP BPC for SAP S/4HANA Finance allows the financial planning from SAP BPC to integrate with SAP S/4HANA Finance. This effectively replaces the old financial planning capabilities in SAP ERP 6.0 or earlier versions.

SAP BPC can access real-time master data and transactional data maintained in SAP ERP for both planned and actual values. Thus, the plans developed in SAP BPC can be used in SAP ERP for variance and other analysis. SAP BPC for SAP S/4HANA Finance provides new end-to-end simulation capabilities.

Let's now move on to Chapter 12, in which we'll discuss the configuration and functionality of the SAP Fiori applications for SAP S/4HANA Finance.

Chapter 12
SAP Fiori Applications

This chapter covers the functionality, architecture, installation, configuration, and application of SAP Fiori apps based on different roles in the finance LOB.

SAP Fiori is a collection of applications with an easy-to-use and customer-friendly end-user experience on desktops, tablets, or smartphones. This is one of the key evolutions and changes with the introduction of SAP Business Suite on SAP HANA and SAP S/4HANA Finance. SAP Fiori has transformed the enterprise user experience (UX) from a complex and feature-rich capability to a simple, intuitive, user-friendly, and mobile experience.

A variety of SAP Fiori apps of various types are available, as illustrated in Figure 12.1. There are three types of apps:

1. **Transactional apps**
   These apps are more oriented toward operational users to post or input transactional data. For example, a user can post a journal entry or an incoming payment.

2. **Fact sheet apps**
   These apps display master data, transactional data, and key facts about central objects and organizational units used in business operations. These apps also help users drill down to the lowest level of information. For example, the Manage Customer Line Items app allows a user to check all the open receivables and drill down further to check invoice postings.

3. **Analytical apps**
   These apps use SAP HANA to provide insight into real-time operations. They help managers track the performance of key performance indicators (KPIs) and make timely decisions. For example, a user can analyze the days sales outstanding (DSO) report or collections progress.

12 SAP Fiori Applications

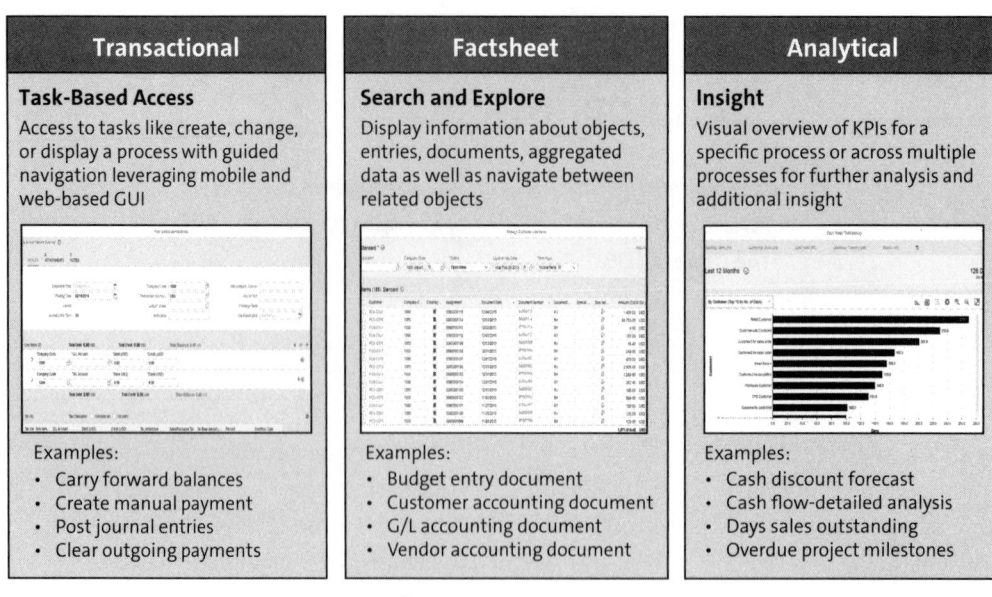

Transactional	Factsheet	Analytical
Task-Based Access Access to tasks like create, change, or display a process with guided navigation leveraging mobile and web-based GUI	**Search and Explore** Display information about objects, entries, documents, aggregated data as well as navigate between related objects	**Insight** Visual overview of KPIs for a specific process or across multiple processes for further analysis and additional insight
Examples: • Carry forward balances • Create manual payment • Post journal entries • Clear outgoing payments	Examples: • Budget entry document • Customer accounting document • G/L accounting document • Vendor accounting document	Examples: • Cash discount forecast • Cash flow-detailed analysis • Days sales outstanding • Overdue project milestones

Figure 12.1 Types of SAP Fiori Apps

In this chapter, you'll explore the architecture, installation, and configuration of SAP Fiori apps. You'll also learn about the functionality of the key apps related to the financial roles in the organization.

12.1 SAP Fiori Project Phases

Before we get too far, let's consider what it means to get SAP Fiori applications up and running. The installation of SAP Fiori is a mini project itself and involves the following project phases to build the platform:

- **SAP backend preparation**
  This phase requires validating prerequisites, verifying the right solution, and deploying the relevant and updated SAP Notes.

- **Infrastructure installation**
  This phase involves installation of SAP Gateway and the SAP UI add-on.

- **Network and security**
  This phase involves the configuration and security of the SAP backend channel proxy.

Installing SAP Fiori also involves multiple steps on the application side:

- Installing and configuring the standard application
- Installing and configuring the workflow application
- Defining roles and user home pages
- Integrating SAP Fiori apps with SAP Mobile Platform
- Branding and marketing the apps

> **References**
>
> Detailed SAP Fiori installation information is outside the scope of this book, but you can find more information on SAP Fiori implementation in the book *SAP Fiori Implementation and Development* by Anil Bavaraju (SAP PRESS, 2017).

12.2 Architecture

Figure 12.2 provides an overview of the architecture required for SAP Fiori apps.

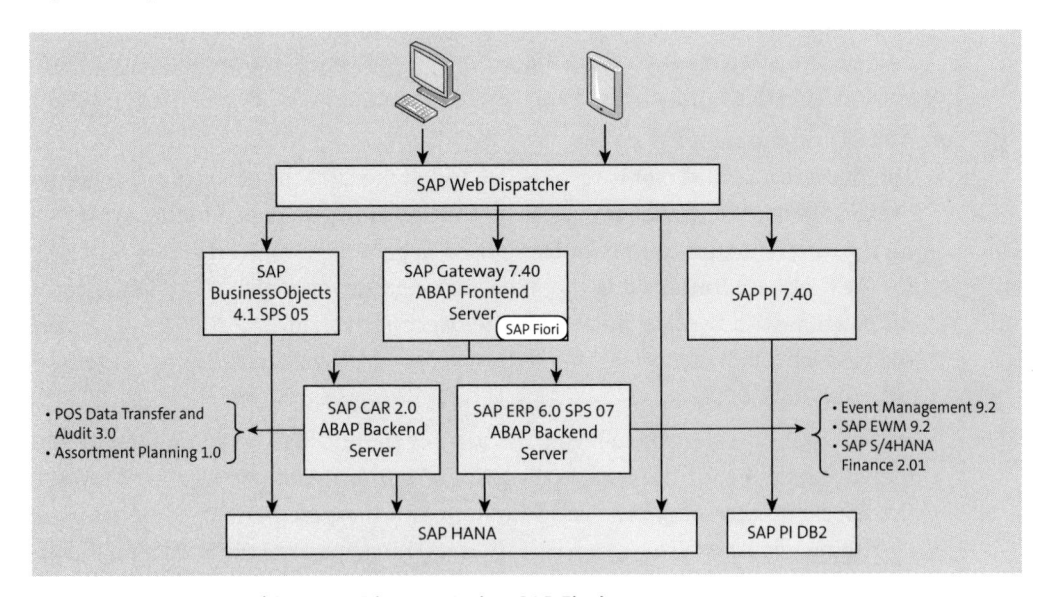

Figure 12.2 System Architecture Diagram Using SAP Fiori

The components of the SAP Fiori landscape are as follows:

- **SAP Web Dispatcher**
  SAP Web Dispatcher works as the reverse proxy for all incoming requests, and it's responsible for routing them securely through the transport layer security to each corresponding system. The SAP Fiori apps send requests to various systems (e.g., SAP BusinessObjects, frontend server, or middleware) based on the application type, the data requested, and the linkage to the connected system landscape. SAP Fiori processing takes place when the user interfaces (UIs) for the SAP Fiori apps are loaded by the clients. During execution, the apps take up the data from the SAP Business Suite backend system. Standard browsers have a similar origin policy of communicating the HTTPS requests for the UI data and the backend data using just one web address.

  A reverse proxy server needs to be installed between the client and the SAP system to act as the sole point of entry for all HTTPS requests. Based on the requests from the apps, the reverse proxy server selects the correct application server, such as ABAP frontend server, SAP HANA XS advanced (SAP HANA XSA), or SAP Gateway server.

- **SAP BusinessObjects Business Intelligence (SAP BusinessObjects BI)**
  SAP BusinessObjects BI acts as the reporting platform and provides many advanced SAP HANA predelivered and custom reports.

- **ABAP frontend server**
  The ABAP frontend server is responsible for all the UI technology. It binds all the backend systems together and presents the SAP Fiori launchpad to the end users. All the infrastructure components required to generate SAP Fiori app-specific UIs for the client are contained in the ABAP frontend server, which also enables communication with the SAP Business Suite backend system. SAP NetWeaver forms the base for the UI components and the gateway deployed on the same server.

  The central UI component acts as a common infrastructure for all SAP Fiori apps, and the SAP Fiori launchpad forms the basis of all the SAP Fiori UIs. All the fundamental functions for the apps, such as login, surface sizing, navigating between the apps, and accessing role-based catalogs and tiles, are performed on the SAP Fiori launchpad. End users can access the SAP Fiori apps from the SAP Fiori launchpad. Some of the specific UIs required for the apps are delivered by SAP Business Suite product-specific add-ons, and they need to be installed on the frontend server also. The central UI component is augmented by the KPI modeling, which provides the added functionality that the SAP HANA XS server requires for the execution of analytical and SAP Smart Business KPI apps. This KPI modeling framework is comprised of reusable elements that enable users to view the KPI tiles and help provide drilldown views.

The interaction between the client and the SAP Business Suite backend is managed by SAP Gateway, which uses OData services to provide backend data and functions and processes the HTTPS requests for OData services. When confronted with an insight-to-action scenario, the transactional apps update data in the SAP Business Suite systems in real time by using this communication channel.

- **SAP Process Integration (SAP PI)**
  SAP PI transfers, maps, and records messages between different systems. It also contains Adobe Document Services for all printing services.

- **ABAP backend server**
  The SAP Business Suite products are installed in the ABAP backend server, which dispenses the business logic and the backend data containing users, roles, and authorizations. SAP continuously releases the add-ons required for the SAP Fiori apps in its support packages. SAP NetWeaver forms the base for the backend server.

- **SAP HANA XSA**
  SAP HANA XSA, which acts as a lightweight application server in SAP HANA, provides the business content (i.e., virtual data models [VDMs]) for analytics.

- **SAP HANA**
  SAP HANA is an in-memory, columnar-based database platform that you can use to process and analyze high volumes of data in real time.

12.3 Configure SAP Fiori

Perform the following configuration steps to set up the system and enable SAP Fiori apps:

1. Use task list SAP_FIORI_LAUNCHPAD_INIT_SETUP in Transaction STC01 to activate the launchpad, OData, and HTTP services on the SAP Gateway system (frontend), as shown in Figure 12.3.

12   SAP Fiori Applications

Display Task List SAP_FIORI_LAUNCHPAD_INIT_SETUP, Build 00002

Autom. Phase	Component	T	Task	Task Description
Prepare	CTS	○	CL_STCT_CREATE_REQ_CUST_FIORI	Create / Select Customizing Request (SE09)
Configuration	GATEWAY	○	CL_STCT_CREATE_SYSALIAS_LOCAL	Create SAP System Alias 'LOCAL'
Configuration	GATEWAY	○	CL_STCT_ACTIVATE_SERVICES_FLP	Activate Gateway OData Services for Launchpad (/IWFND/MAINT_SERVICE)
Configuration	SICF	○	CL_STCT_ACTIVATE_SICF_FLP	Activate HTTP Services for SAP Fiori Launchpad (SICF)
Configuration	SICF	○	CL_STCT_ACTIVATE_SICF_UI5	Activate HTTP Services for UI5 (SICF)
Verification	SECURITY	○	CL_STCT_CHECK_SEC_ICM	Check ICM HTTPS Configuration
Configuration	PROFILE	○	CL_STCT_SET_PROFILE_HTTPS	Set Profile Parameter HTTPS (RZ10)
Configuration	ICM	○	CL_STCT_RESTART_ICM_FOR_HTTPS	Restart ICM for Profile Parameter HTTPS (SMICM)
Configuration	SICF	○	CL_STCT_ACTIVATE_SICF_CACHEBUS	Activate HTTP Service for Cache Buster (SICF)
Configuration	GATEWAY	○	CL_STCT_CUST_FLP_URL_CACHEBUS	Customize Launchpad URL for Cache Buster
Configuration	GATEWAY	○	CL_STCT_SCHED_JOB_CALC_APPIDX	Schedule job for calculation of SAPUI5 Application Index
Configuration	GATEWAY	○	CL_STCT_SET_LAUNCHPAD_URLS	Add Launchpad / Launchpad Designer URLs to Favorites for current user

Figure 12.3 Task List SAP_FIORI_LAUNCHPAD_INIT_SETUP

2. Use task list SAP_SAP2GATEWAY_TRUSTED_CONFIG in Transaction STC01 to create a trusted connection from the SAP system to SAP Gateway, as shown in Figure 12.4.

Display Task List SAP_SAP2GATEWAY_TRUSTED_CONFIG, Build 00000

Phase	Comp.	T	Task	Task Description
Configuration	RFC	○	CL_STCT_CREATE_RFC_SAP2GW	Create / Select ABAP RFC Destination to SAP System (SM59)
Configuration	RFC	○	CL_STCT_CREATE_TRUSTED_SAP2GW	Add SAP System as trusted system (SMT1)
Configuration	SYSTEM	○	CL_STCT_SET_PROFIL_ACCEPT_SSO2	Set Profile Parameter: login/accept_sso2_ticket=1 (RZ10)
Configuration	SYSTEM	○	CL_STCT_SET_PROFIL_CREATE_SSO2	Set Profile Parameter: login/create_sso2_ticket=2 (RZ10)
Configuration	SSO	○	CL_STCT_CONFIG_SSO2_WO_UI	Configure Logon Ticket for Single Sign-On (STRUSTSSO2)

Figure 12.4 Task List SAP_SAP2GATEWAY_TRUSTED_CONFIG

3. Use task list SAP_GATEWAY_ADD_SYSTEM in Transaction STC01 to connect the SAP system (backend) to the SAP Gateway system (frontend), as shown in Figure 12.5.

Display Task List SAP_GATEWAY_ADD_SYSTEM, Build 00000

Phase	Comp.	T	Task	Task Description
Prepare	AUTH	○	CL_STCT_GW_AUTHINFO_MANUAL	Check authorization for current user in SAP System
Prepare	CTS	○	CL_STCT_CREATE_REQUEST_CUST	Create / Select Customizing Request (SE09)
Configuration	RFC	○	CL_STCT_CREATE_RFC_GW2SAP	Create / Select trusted ABAP RFC Destination to SAP System (SM59)
Configuration	SYSTEM	○	CL_STCT_SET_PROFIL_ACCEPT_SSO2	Set Profile Parameter: login/accept_sso2_ticket=1 (RZ10)
Configuration	SYSTEM	○	CL_STCT_SET_PROFIL_CREATE_SSO2	Set Profile Parameter: login/create_sso2_ticket=2 (RZ10)
Configuration	SSO	○	CL_STCT_CONFIG_SSO2_WO_UI	Configure Logon Ticket for Single Sign-On (STRUSTSSO2)
Configuration	GATEWAY	○	CL_STCT_CREATE_SYSALIAS_SAP	Create System Alias for SAP System

Figure 12.5 Task List SAP_GATEWAY_ADD_SYSTEM

12.3 Configure SAP Fiori

4. Use task list SAP_BASIS_SSL_CHECK in Transaction STC01 to perform a basic Secure Sockets Layer (SSL) check, as shown in Figure 12.6.

```
Display Task List SAP_BASIS_SSL_CHECK, Build 00000
    Attributes

Phase          Comp.     T.. Task                         Task Description
Verification   SECURITY  O   CL_STCT_CHECK_SEC_CRYPTO     Check SAP Cryptographic Library
Verification   SECURITY  O   CL_STCT_CHECK_SEC_ICM        Check ICM HTTPS Configuration
Verification   SECURITY  O   CL_STCT_CHECK_SEC_PROFILE    Check SSL Profile Parameter
Verification   SECURITY  O   CL_STCT_CHECK_SEC_SSL_PSE    Check SSL Server and SSL Client Standard PSE
```

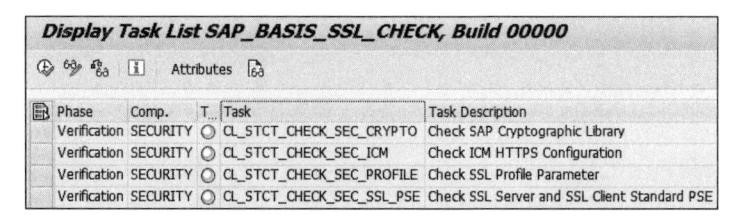

Figure 12.6 Task List SAP_BASIS_SSL_CHECK

5. Create the admin user and end user using Transaction SU01 in the ABAP frontend server, SAP Business Suite on SAP HANA server, and SAP HANA server to provide access to configuration tasks based on the user roles in the organization.

6. Create the user roles using Transaction PFCG to provide users with access to create trusted Remote Function Calls (RFCs) in SAP Gateway (e.g., /UI2/SAP_KPIMOD_TCR_S).

7. Define the trust relationship between the SAP Business Suite system and the SAP Gateway system by configuring the *trusting* system as the SAP Gateway system and the *trusted* system as the SAP Business Suite system (backend system) using Transaction SM59.

8. Activate SAP Gateway using the Customizing menu path **SAP NetWeaver • SAP Gateway • OData Channel • Configuration • Connection Settings • Activate or Deactivate SAP Gateway**, as shown in Figure 12.7.

```
Display IMG
    Existing BC Sets    BC Sets for Activity    Activated BC S
Structure
  SAP Customizing Implementation Guide
    SAP Commercial Project Management
    OpenText Archiving and Document Access for SAP Solutions
    OpenText Business Suite for SAP Solutions
    Activate Business Functions
    Conversion of Accounting to SAP S/4HANA
    SAP NetWeaver
      SAP Gateway Service Enablement
      SAP Gateway
        OData Channel
          Configuration
            User Settings
            Connection Settings
              Connect SAP Gateway to SLD
              SAP Gateway to Consumer
              SAP Gateway to SAP System
              [Activate or Deactivate SAP Gateway]
            Administration
            Composition
```

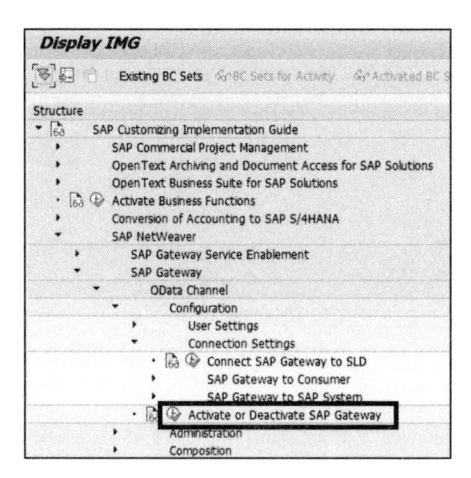

Figure 12.7 Activate or Deactivate SAP Gateway

9. Configure SAP Web Dispatcher, which is a prerequisite to install fact sheets or analytical apps in your system landscape.

10. Activate SAP Fiori launchpad OData services using the Customizing menu path **SAP NetWeaver • SAP Gateway • OData Channel • Administration • General Settings • Activate and Maintain Services**.

11. Configure authorization roles. Multiple users need to be provided with different authorization roles depending on the profiles the users have in the organization. Separate authorization roles need to be configured and assigned to users who need to access and execute the SAP Fiori launchpad (as end users) and the SAP Fiori launchpad designer (as administrators). With the correct roles assigned, users can access the catalogs, groups, and tiles assigned to these roles by a role administrator.

12.4 Install SAP Fiori Apps

Before you start the configuration of SAP Fiori, you must install the complete infrastructure for SAP Fiori apps. After this is complete, there will be configuration activities on both the backend and frontend servers.

In the following subsections, you'll need to configure various infrastructure components to enable the SAP Fiori apps.

12.4.1 Transaction and Fact Sheet Apps

You must carry out the following configuration tasks to enable the transaction and fact sheet SAP Fiori apps:

- **SAP Web Dispatcher**
  - Configure SAP Web Dispatcher.
- **Backend server**
  - Configure SAP NetWeaver Enterprise Search.
  - Activate search and fact sheets in SAP Business Suite foundation.
  - Configure and copy roles, assign users to these roles, and provide authorization on the backend server.

- **Frontend server**
  - Configure SAP Gateway and connect it to SAP Business Suite.
  - Configure and set up SAP Fiori launchpad.
  - Configure product-specific UI add-ons by setting up catalogs, groups, and roles in the SAP Fiori launchpad.

12.4.2 Analytical Apps

You must carry out the following configuration tasks to enable the analytical-based SAP Fiori apps:

- **SAP Web Dispatcher**
  - Specify routing rules to define which URL is forwarded to which system.
- **Specify the user authentication**
  - Enable Single Sign-On (SSO).
- **ABAP frontend server**
  - Configure SAP Gateway.
  - Configure the central SAP UI add-on.
  - Configure SAP Fiori launchpad.
- **KPI data**
  - Enable user access to KPI data.
  - Model KPIs.
  - Configure navigational targets for KPI catalogs.

12.5 SAP Fiori Launchpad

You can install the SAP Fiori launchpad as delivered out of the box by SAP, and then customize it to enhance the UX and meet the organization's requirements by changing the background theme, creating new role-based groups, and adding new tiles from the SAP standard catalog.

In the following sections, you'll configure the SAP Fiori launchpad so that users can access the relevant apps assigned to their roles. Here, you need to set up the navigation screen, create catalogs and tiles, assign the catalogs to the roles, and provide users with the proper access to launch the page.

12.5.1 Frontend User Screen

The standard SAP Fiori screen on the frontend server for a user appears as shown in Figure 12.8.

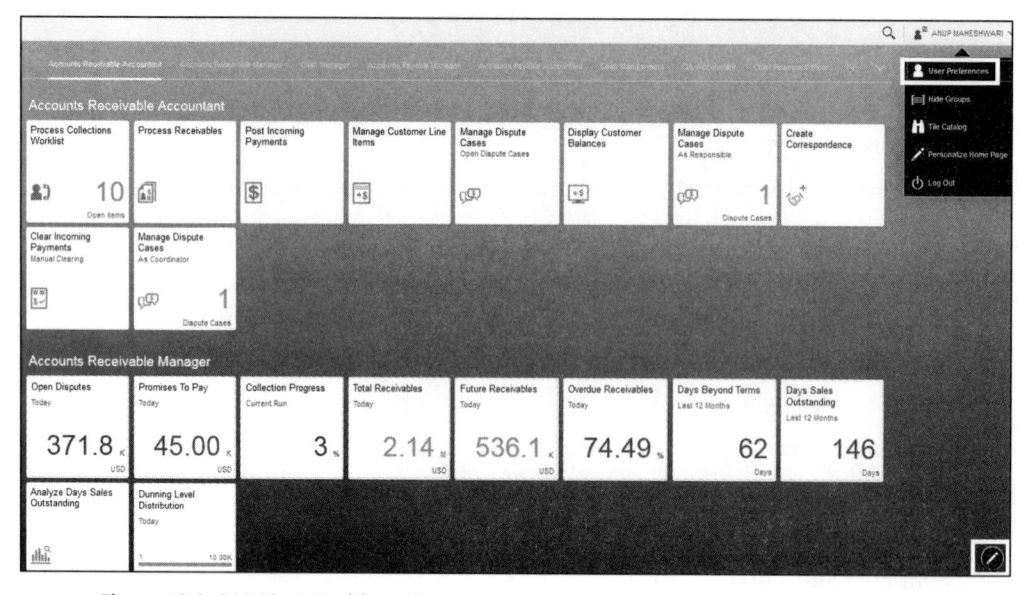

Figure 12.8 SAP Fiori Dashboard

In the **User Preferences** tab at the top-right corner, you can change or update the following attributes:

- **Server Information**
- **Language**
- **Theme** (i.e., background wallpaper)

In the personalized **Home Page** tab at the bottom right, you can add a **Tile** within a **Group** or create a new group (e.g., Cash Manager) by choosing **Add Group**, as shown in Figure 12.9.

The settings made here affect only the specific logged-in user. Global changes for all users must be made on the backend server. If you need to change a parameter for an SAP Fiori app, you can double-click the app and select the correct parameters that you require for analysis. For example, for the **Aging Analysis** tile under the **Accounts Payable Manager Group**, you can select the aging parameters on the report itself, as shown in Figure 12.10.

12.5 SAP Fiori Launchpad

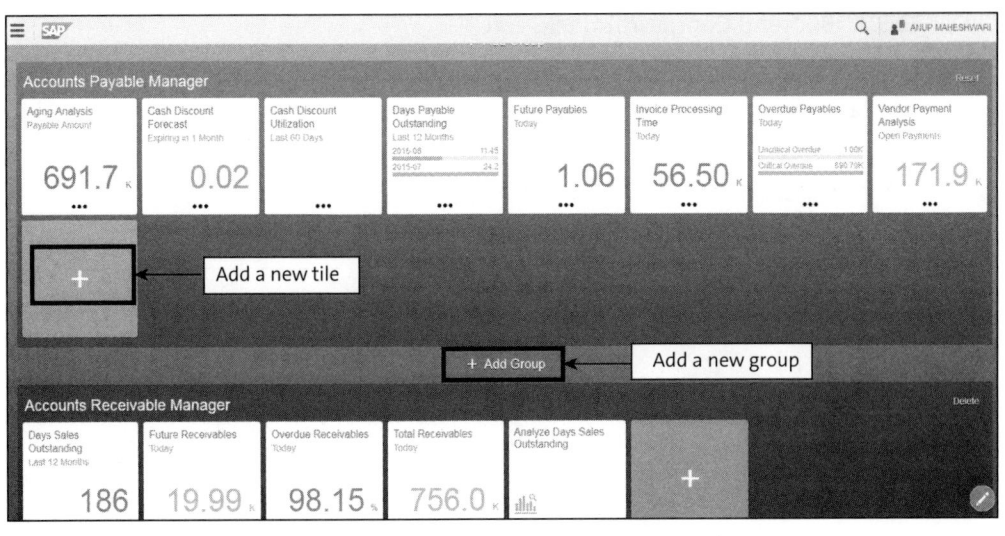

Figure 12.9 Personalizing the SAP Fiori Home Page

Figure 12.10 Selecting the Parameters in SAP Fiori Apps

475

12 SAP Fiori Applications

12.5.2 Backend Configuration Screen

When you go to the backend configuration screen for SAP Fiori, on the left you'll see two tabs, **Catalogs** and **Groups**. In the **Groups** tab, if you go to a group and add or delete a tile, this change is a global change that will be seen by all users. You can also add a tile on this screen. The configuration screen for **Accounts Payable Manager** is shown in Figure 12.11.

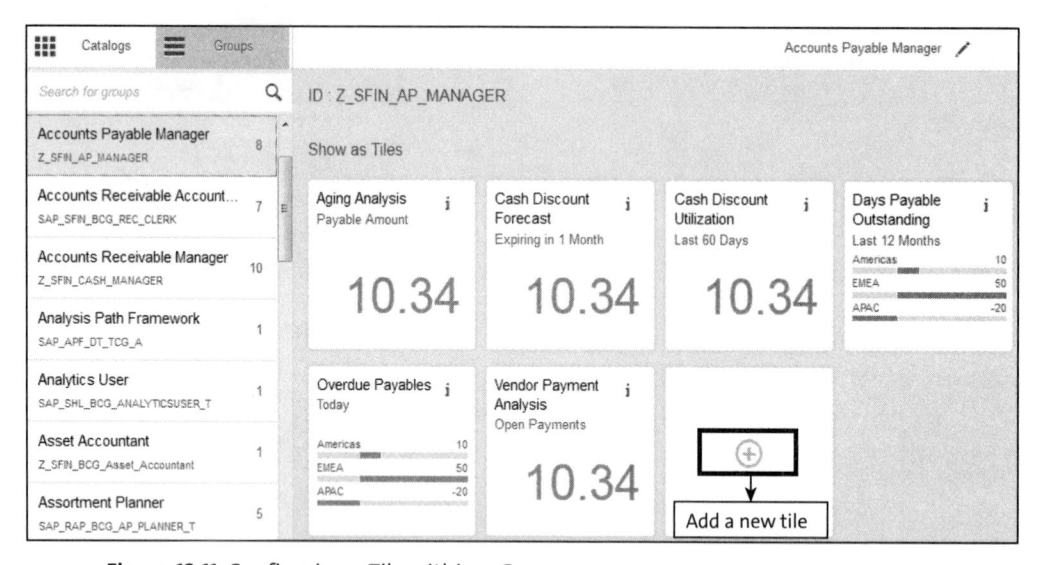

Figure 12.11 Configuring a Tile within a Group

When you go to the **Catalogs** view, the configuration screen will look like Figure 12.12.

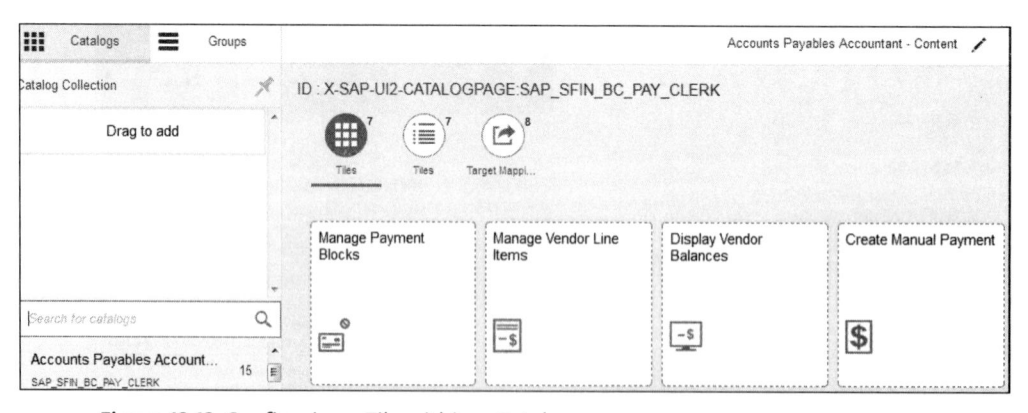

Figure 12.12 Configuring a Tile within a Catalog

476

12.5 SAP Fiori Launchpad

When you double-click the tile, the screen in Figure 12.13 appears; here, you can make all necessary changes, such as the description of the **Title** and how the tile will appear to the end user.

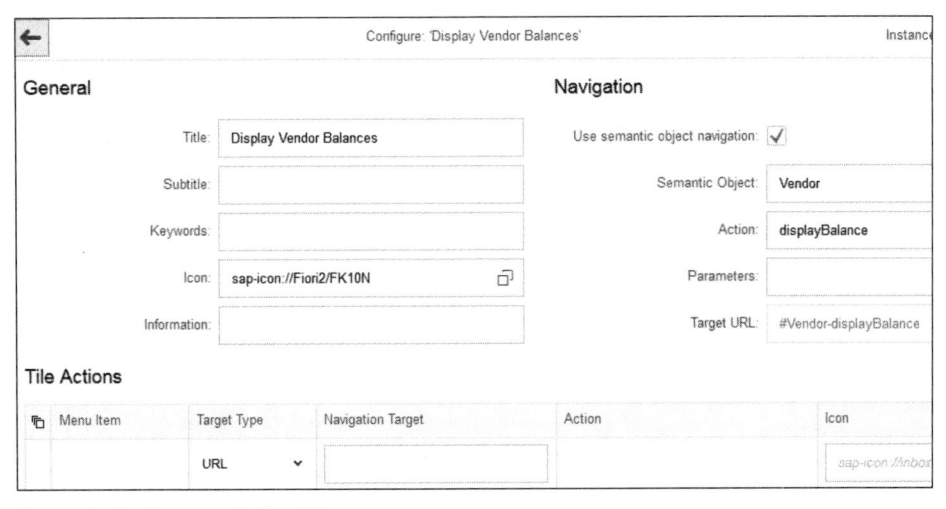

Figure 12.13 Changes to the Tile

Clicking the **Target Mapping** icon within the **Catalog** view allows you to make all the configuration changes to the column, as shown in Figure 12.14.

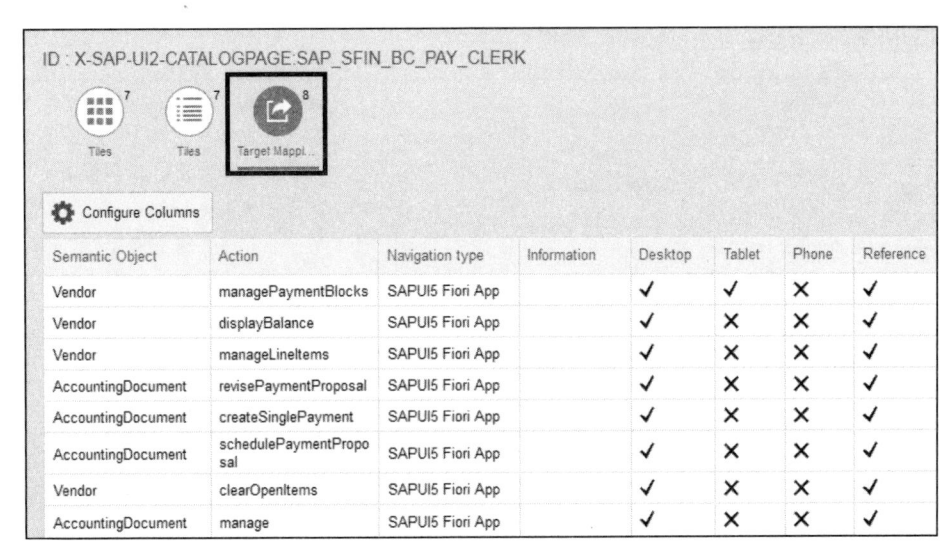

Semantic Object	Action	Navigation type	Information	Desktop	Tablet	Phone	Reference
Vendor	managePaymentBlocks	SAPUI5 Fiori App		✓	✓	✗	✓
Vendor	displayBalance	SAPUI5 Fiori App		✓	✗	✗	✓
Vendor	manageLineItems	SAPUI5 Fiori App		✓	✗	✗	✓
AccountingDocument	revisePaymentProposal	SAPUI5 Fiori App		✓	✗	✗	✓
AccountingDocument	createSinglePayment	SAPUI5 Fiori App		✓	✗	✗	✓
AccountingDocument	schedulePaymentProposal	SAPUI5 Fiori App		✓	✗	✗	✓
Vendor	clearOpenItems	SAPUI5 Fiori App		✓	✗	✗	✓
AccountingDocument	manage	SAPUI5 Fiori App		✓	✗	✗	✓

Figure 12.14 Configuring the Columns and Target Mapping

477

12 SAP Fiori Applications

12.5.3 SAP Smart Business Key Performance Indicators

SAP Smart Business KPIs for SAP S/4HANA Finance is a collection of analytical apps that contains the most important KPIs for people in decision-making roles such as the CFO, accounts receivable and accounts payable managers, cash managers, collections managers, and corporate controllers. The SAP Smart Business KPIs can be configured through the frontend SAP Fiori user screen in the **Configure KPI Tiles** tile under the **KPI Modeler** group, as shown in Figure 12.15.

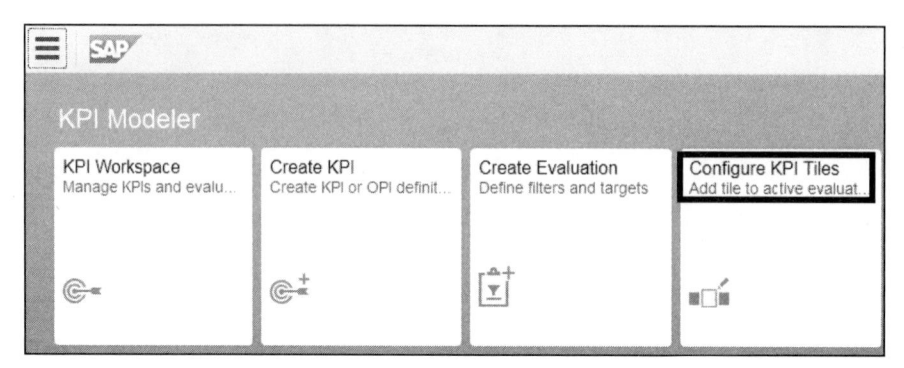

Figure 12.15 Configuring KPIs through KPI Modeler

When you click this tile, you're taken to the KPI tiles configuration. In the example shown in Figure 12.16, the **Aging Analysis** KPI has been chosen for configuration and editing.

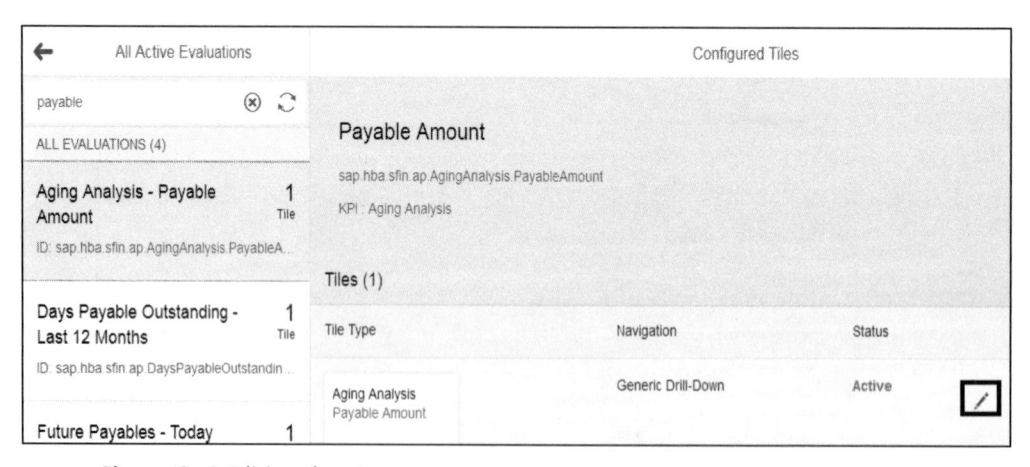

Figure 12.16 Editing the KPI

478

12.5 SAP Fiori Launchpad

Click the **Edit** button to reach the screen shown in Figure 12.17. Here, you have the option to choose the type of tile and description as relevant for a chosen KPI.

Now, click the **Save and Configure Drill-Down** button, as shown in the bottom-right corner of Figure 12.17.

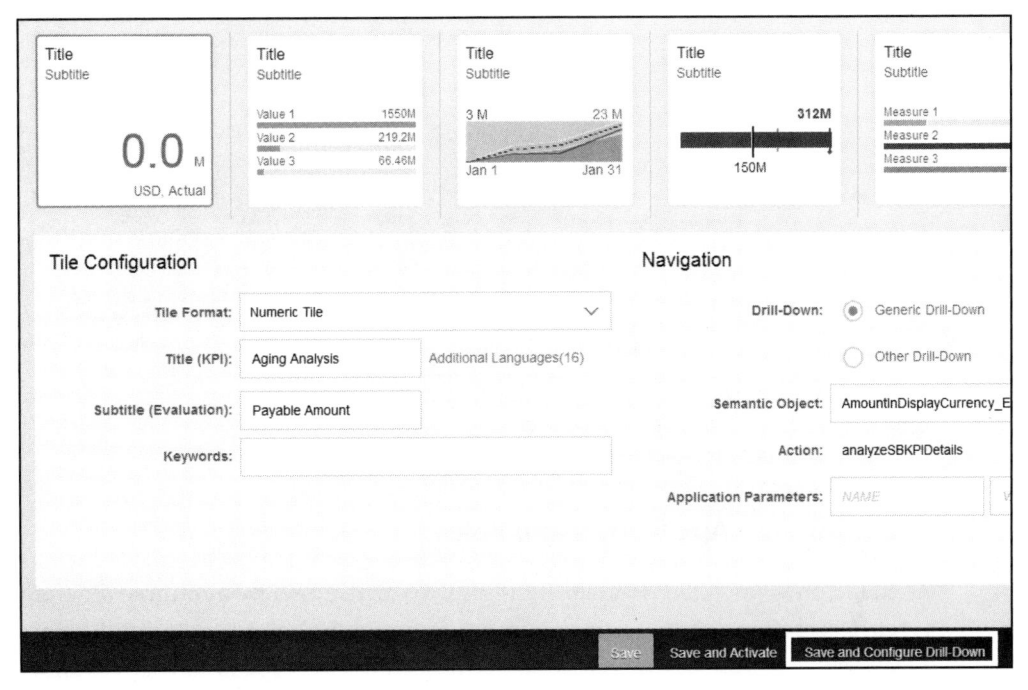

Figure 12.17 Configuring Drilldown for a Tile

Click the **Edit** button once again, and you'll come to the **Drill-Down Chart Configuration** screen (see Figure 12.18), from which you can change and edit the sorting order and the visualization of the chart, including the color, type of chart (column, bar, line, etc.), and the absolute or percentage values, as shown.

479

12 SAP Fiori Applications

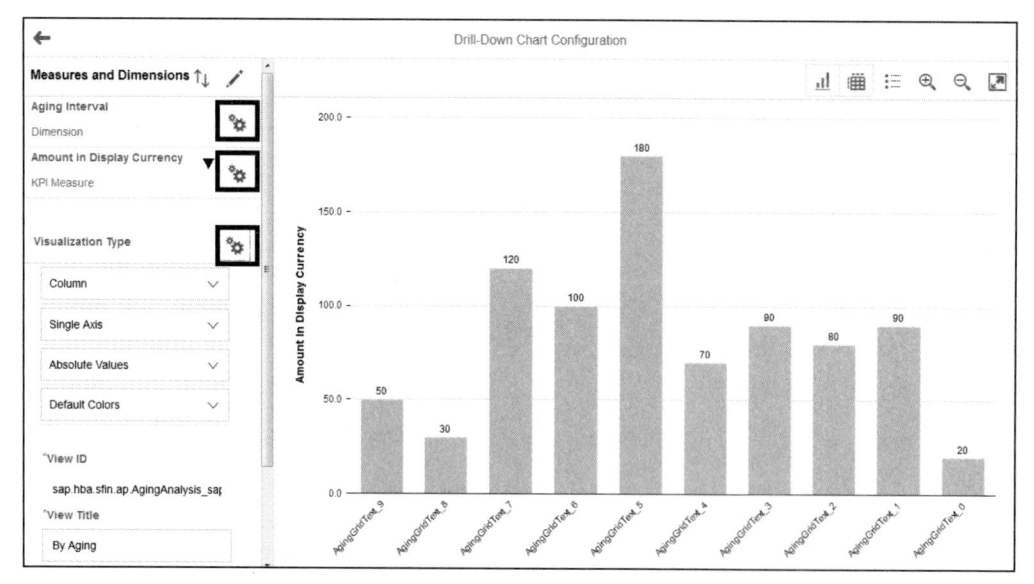

Figure 12.18 Drill-Down Chart Configuration

12.6 SAP Fiori Application and Roles

As stated previously, SAP Fiori apps can be categorized broadly into three different types: transactional, fact sheet, and analytical (which includes SAP Smart Business KPIs). These apps are based on the different functionalities and tasks that fall under (or are often assigned to) a role; consequently, they are considered *role-based*.

Let's discuss some of the SAP ERP Financials roles that are predelivered as part of the standard SAP Fiori package implementation, and highlight a few key apps for them.

12.6.1 General Ledger Accountant

The role of a General Ledger (G/L) accountant is to provide periodic financial statements to comply with regulatory and statutory requirements and thus avoid any penalties for noncompliance. To do this, they ensure that the financial data in terms of journal entries is correctly posted.

12.6 SAP Fiori Application and Roles

Typical activities of this role are as follows:

- Maintain the chart of accounts and organizational unit structure.
- Manage journal entries and financial data reconciliation.
- Manage the postings to all the ledger groups as defined by the accounting principles.
- Manage the period-end closing process for all the financial business processes.
- Resolve any accounting issues within the organization.
- Provide financial statements for statutory and management reporting.
- Maintain account determination and create G/L accounts as required.

These tasks are supported by the apps in Table 12.1.

App Name	App Type	Technology Used
Display G/L Account Balances	Transactional	SAP Fiori (SAP UI5)
Post General Journal Entries	Transactional	SAP Fiori (SAP UI5)
Manage Journal Entries	Transactional	SAP Fiori (SAP UI5)
Display G/L Account Line Items	Transactional	SAP Fiori (SAP UI5)
Display Chart of Accounts	Transactional	SAP Fiori (SAP UI5)
Display Financial Statement	Transactional	SAP Fiori (SAP UI5)
Open Posting Periods	Transactional	SAP Fiori (SAP UI5)
Carry Forward Balances	Transactional	SAP Fiori (SAP UI5)
Post Currency Adjustments	Transactional	SAP Fiori (SAP UI5)
Upload General Journal Entries	Transactional	SAP Fiori (SAP UI5)
Journal Entry Analyzer	Analytical	Web Dynpro (embedded SAP BusinessObjects BI)
Journal Entry History	Analytical	Web Dynpro (embedded SAP BusinessObjects BI)

Table 12.1 SAP Fiori Apps for the G/L Accountant Role

12   SAP Fiori Applications

App Name	App Type	Technology Used
Trial Balance (includes Trial Balance Comparison)	Analytical	Web Dynpro (embedded SAP BusinessObjects BI)
G/L Account	Fact sheet	SAP Fiori (SAP UI5)
Journal Entry	Fact sheet	SAP Fiori (SAP UI5)

Table 12.1 SAP Fiori Apps for the G/L Accountant Role (Cont.)

The SAP Fiori dashboard for the G/L accountant role is shown in Figure 12.19.

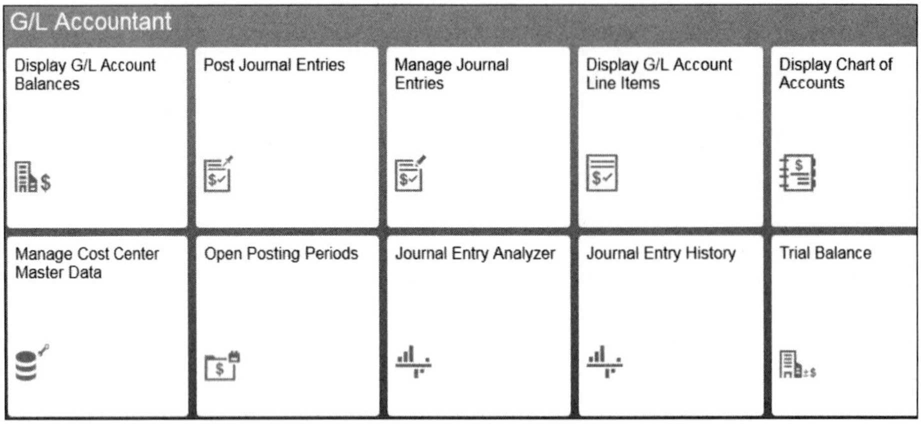

Figure 12.19 G/L Accountant Role: SAP_SFIN_BCR_GLACCOUNTANT

Through the Post General Journal Entries app shown in Figure 12.20, the G/L accountant can post journal entries using his mobile device as well as his desktop, thus increasing productivity. The SAP Fiori screen layout for this app is quite similar to the SAP GUI version so that the learning curve is minimal, and the user has the option to use all the fields that are necessary to post journal entries. Users can also enter notes or add attachments and relevant documents while posting a journal entry.

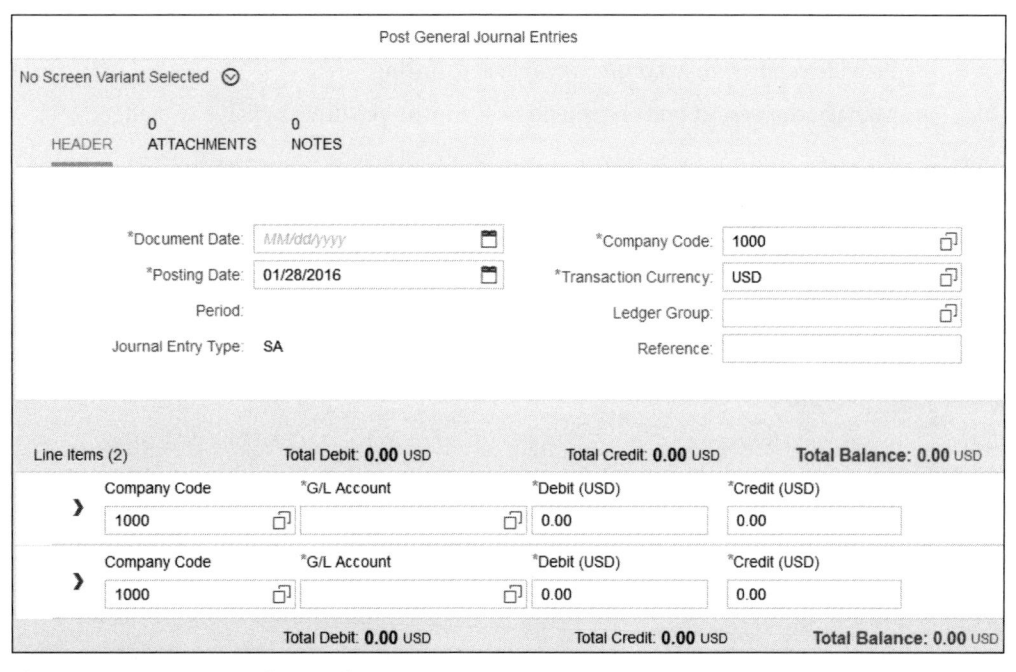

Figure 12.20 Post General Journal Entries

12.6.2 Accounts Payable Accountant

The role of an accounts payable accountant is to maintain a robust and effective invoice management and payment process. Accounts payable accountants make sure that the vendor master data records are maintained accurately with all the data elements required to clear open items and support a timely period-end close. They maintain an optimum balance to maximize the discounts from vendors and keep outstanding payables high to maximize liquidity.

Typical activities of this role are as follows:

- Maintain and create vendor master data.
- Analyze and then release documents during the invoice verification process.
- Process and post vendor invoices and documents.
- Reconcile open items.
- Maintain communication with vendors and other stakeholders.
- Review vendor line items and vendor balances for any errors.

12 SAP Fiori Applications

- Process payments through various payment methods.
- Provide reports for accounts payable accounting.
- Manage the period-end closing process for the accounts payable subledger.

These tasks are supported by the apps in Table 12.2.

App Name	App Type	Technology Used
Vendor Accounting Document	Transactional	SAP Fiori (SAP UI5)
Manage Payment Blocks	Transactional	SAP Fiori (SAP UI5)
Manage Vendor Line Items	Transactional	SAP Fiori (SAP UI5)
Display Vendor Balances	Transactional	SAP Fiori (SAP UI5)
Create Manual Payment	Transactional	SAP Fiori (SAP UI5)
Schedule Payment Proposals	Transactional	SAP Fiori (SAP UI5)
Revise Payment Proposals	Transactional	SAP Fiori (SAP UI5)
Clear Outgoing Payments	Transactional	SAP Fiori (SAP UI5)
Display Process Flow	Transactional	SAP Fiori (SAP UI5)
Monitor Payments	Transactional	SAP Fiori (SAP UI5)
Intercompany Balance Reconciliation	Transactional	SAP Fiori (SAP UI5)

Table 12.2 SAP Fiori Apps for the Accounts Payable Accountant Role

The SAP Fiori dashboard for the accounts payable accountant role is shown in Figure 12.21. You can choose to display only the relevant apps from the preceding list that are applicable for your organization's accounts payable accountant role.

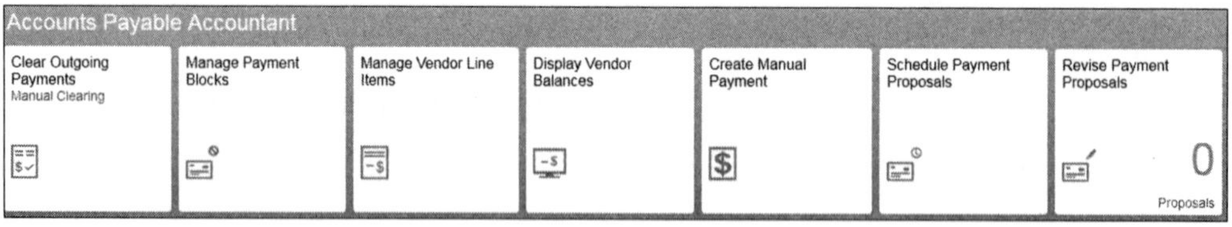

Figure 12.21 Accounts Payable Accountant Role: SAP_SFIN_BCR_PAYABLES_CLERK

The Create Manual Payment app shown in Figure 12.22 allows the user to make a payment to the vendor and clear the open vendor line item. It also allows the user to make a direct payment to the vendor without the open invoice, which is posted as a down payment request. While making a direct payment posting, you must specify the vendor, the bank, and the amount to be paid. This document is then used in the automatic payment run.

On the other hand, you can select multiple open items for a vendor, specify the amount, and then create the payment to be used in the automatic payment run. On successful execution of the payment run, you'll receive a confirmation email with all the details, and the open items are marked as cleared.

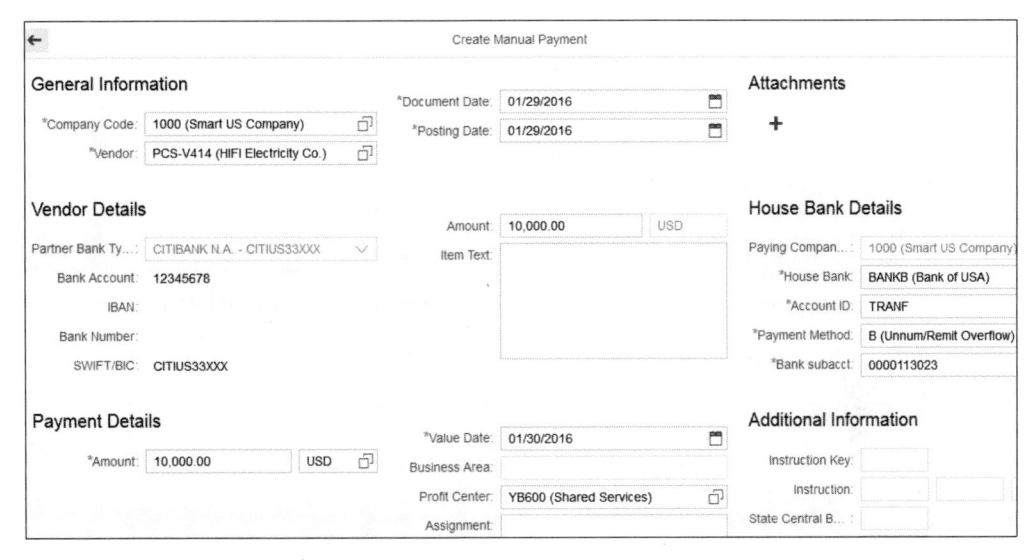

Figure 12.22 Create Manual Payment

12.6.3 Accounts Receivable Accountant

The role of an accounts receivable accountant is to maintain a robust and efficient receivables management process, provide timely collection of payments from customers, and minimize the number of open invoices to keep the overdue receivables at a low level. Accounts receivable accountants make sure that the customer master data records are maintained accurately with all the data elements required to clear open items and support timely period-end close.

12　SAP Fiori Applications

Typical activities of this role are as follows:

- Maintain and create customer master data.
- Process manual incoming payments that didn't clear the open invoices automatically.
- Reconcile open items.
- Maintain communication with customers and other stakeholders for any invoice-, payment-, dispute-, or dunning-related issues.
- Review customer line items and customer balances for any errors.
- Process payments through various payment methods such as lockbox, credit cards, and so on.
- Collect overdue amounts from customers.
- Provide reports for accounts receivable accounting.
- Manage the period-end closing process for the accounts receivable subledger.

These tasks are supported by the apps in Table 12.3.

App Name	App Type	Technology Used
Post Incoming Payments	Transactional	SAP Fiori (SAP UI5)
Process Receivables	Transactional	SAP Fiori (SAP UI5)
Display Customer Balances	Transactional	SAP Fiori (SAP UI5)
Manage Customer Line Items	Transactional	SAP Fiori (SAP UI5)
Create Correspondence	Transactional	SAP Fiori (SAP UI5)
Assign Open Items	Transactional	SAP Fiori (SAP UI5)
Manage Payment Advices	Transactional	SAP Fiori (SAP UI5)
Clear Incoming Payments	Transactional	SAP Fiori (SAP UI5)
Process Collections Worklist	Transactional	SAP Fiori (SAP UI5)
Manage Dispute Cases	Transactional	SAP Fiori (SAP UI5)
Customer Accounting Document	Fact sheet	SAP Fiori (SAP UI5)

Table 12.3 SAP Fiori Apps for the Accounts Receivable Accountant Role

12.6 SAP Fiori Application and Roles

The SAP Fiori dashboard for the accounts receivable accountant role is shown in Figure 12.23.

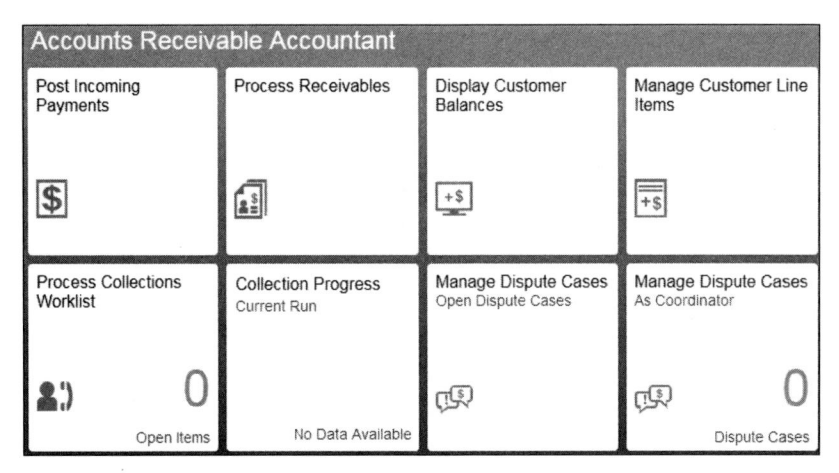

Figure 12.23 Accounts Receivable Accountant Role: SAP_SFIN_BCR_RECEIVABLES_CLERK

Customer balances can be checked with the Display Customer Balances app, as shown in Figure 12.24.

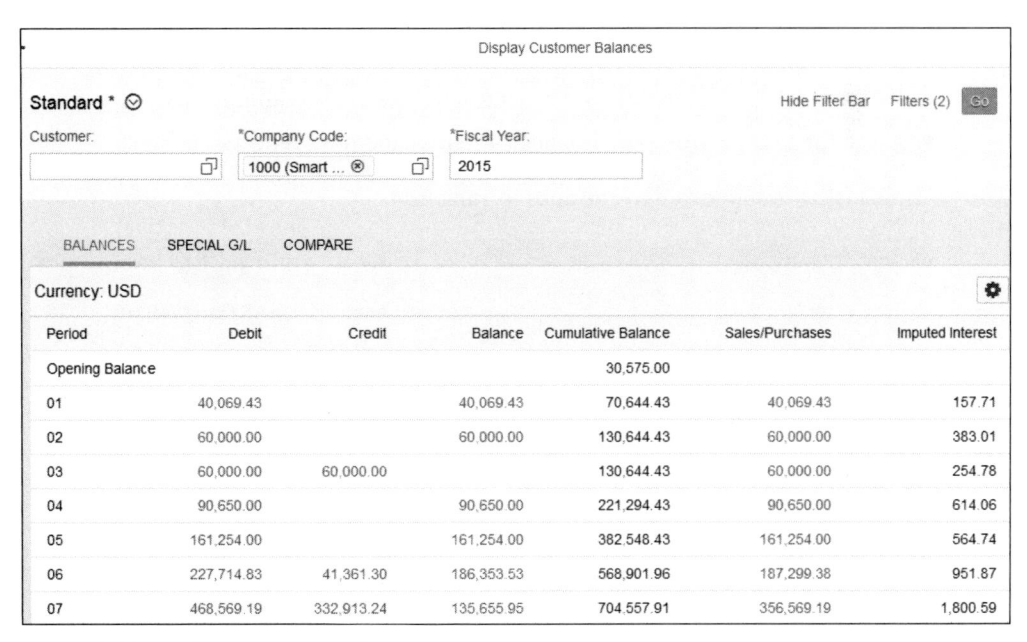

Period	Debit	Credit	Balance	Cumulative Balance	Sales/Purchases	Imputed Interest
Opening Balance				30,575.00		
01	40,069.43		40,069.43	70,644.43	40,069.43	157.71
02	60,000.00		60,000.00	130,644.43	60,000.00	383.01
03	60,000.00	60,000.00		130,644.43	60,000.00	254.78
04	90,650.00		90,650.00	221,294.43	90,650.00	614.06
05	161,254.00		161,254.00	382,548.43	161,254.00	564.74
06	227,714.83	41,361.30	186,353.53	568,901.96	187,299.38	951.87
07	468,569.19	332,913.24	135,655.95	704,557.91	356,569.19	1,800.59

Figure 12.24 Display Customer Balances

487

These balances can be analyzed further by debit, credit, or aggregate balances for a company code and fiscal year or by comparing the revenue between two fiscal years and identifying the increase or decrease by customers. The app allows further drill-down analysis by displaying the amount and details at the line-item level. The app provides the flexibility to hide, unhide, select, and sort the columns per the accounts receivable accountant's requirements, which can be created and saved as a variant so that the report is displayed in the same format every time the app is executed.

12.6.4 Controller

The role of a controller is to maintain the accuracy of accounting and financial reporting, prepare budgets, and perform CO-related month-end closing steps such as cost allocations, work-in-progress calculation, and so on.

Typical activities of this role are as follows:

- Validate financial statements.
- Prepare cost comparison and analysis reports, and provide suggestions for cost reduction.
- Create plan data, and monitor the actual versus planned data.
- Supervise and manage data related to CO cost objects such as cost centers and profit centers.
- Perform CO-specific period-end closing activities such as allocations.
- Assist the CFO by providing financial and management reports.

These tasks are supported by the apps in Table 12.4.

Name of App	Type of App	Technology Used
Cost Center	Fact sheet	SAP Fiori (SAP UI5)
Cost Center Group	Fact sheet	SAP Fiori (SAP UI5)
Cost Centers—Plan/Actual	Analytical	Web Dynpro (embedded SAP BusinessObjects BI)
Cost Centers—Plan/Actual YTD	Analytical	Web Dynpro (embedded SAP BusinessObjects BI)

Table 12.4 SAP Fiori Apps for the Controller Role

12.6 SAP Fiori Application and Roles

Name of App	Type of App	Technology Used
Cost Centers—Plan/Actual with Currency Translation	Analytical	Web Dynpro (embedded SAP BusinessObjects BI)
Cost Centers—Actuals	Analytical	Web Dynpro (embedded SAP BusinessObjects BI)
Cost Center Planning	Transactional	SAP Fiori (SAP UI5)
Manage Cost Center Master Data	Transactional	Web Dynpro
Manage Cost Center Groups	Transactional	Web Dynpro
Import Financial Plan Data	Transactional	SAP Fiori (SAP UI5)
Functional Areas—Plan/Actual	Analytical	Web Dynpro (embedded SAP BusinessObjects BI)
Functional Areas—Plan/Actual YTD	Analytical	Web Dynpro (embedded SAP BusinessObjects BI)
Functional Areas—Plan/Actual with Currency Translation	Analytical	Web Dynpro (embedded SAP BusinessObjects BI)
Functional Areas—Actuals	Analytical	Web Dynpro (embedded SAP BusinessObjects BI)
Internal Order	Fact sheet	SAP Fiori (SAP UI5)
Internal Orders—Plan/Actual	Analytical	Web Dynpro (embedded SAP BusinessObjects BI)
Internal Orders—Plan/Actual YTD	Analytical	Web Dynpro (embedded SAP BusinessObjects BI)
Internal Orders—Plan/Actual with Currency Translation	Analytical	Web Dynpro (embedded SAP BusinessObjects BI)
Internal Orders—Actuals	Analytical	Web Dynpro (embedded SAP BusinessObjects BI)
Manage Internal Order Master Data	Transactional	Web Dynpro
Manage Internal Order Groups	Transactional	Web Dynpro

Table 12.4 SAP Fiori Apps for the Controller Role (Cont.)

12 SAP Fiori Applications

Name of App	Type of App	Technology Used
Market Segments—Plan/Actual	Analytical	Web Dynpro (embedded SAP BusinessObjects BI)
Market Segments—Plan/Actual YTD	Analytical	Web Dynpro (embedded SAP BusinessObjects BI)
Market Segments—Plan/Actual with Currency Translation	Analytical	Web Dynpro (embedded SAP BusinessObjects BI)
Market Segments—Actuals	Analytical	Web Dynpro (embedded SAP BusinessObjects BI)
Profit Center	Fact sheet	SAP Fiori (SAP UI5)
Profit Centers—Plan/Actual	Analytical	Web Dynpro (embedded SAP BusinessObjects BI)
Profit Centers—Plan/Actual YTD	Analytical	Web Dynpro (embedded SAP BusinessObjects BI)
Profit Centers—Plan/Actual with Currency Translation	Analytical	Web Dynpro (embedded SAP BusinessObjects BI)
Profit Centers—Actuals	Analytical	Web Dynpro (embedded SAP BusinessObjects BI)
Manage Profit Center Master Data	Transactional	Web Dynpro
Manage Profit Center Groups	Transactional	Web Dynpro
P&L—Plan/Actual	Analytical	Web Dynpro (embedded SAP BusinessObjects BI)
P&L—Plan/Actual YTD	Analytical	Web Dynpro (embedded SAP BusinessObjects BI)
P&L—Plan/Actual with Currency Translation	Analytical	Web Dynpro (embedded SAP BusinessObjects BI)
P&L—Actuals	Analytical	Web Dynpro (embedded SAP BusinessObjects BI)
Projects—Plan/Actual	Analytical	Web Dynpro (embedded SAP BusinessObjects BI)

Table 12.4 SAP Fiori Apps for the Controller Role (Cont.)

12.6 SAP Fiori Application and Roles

Name of App	Type of App	Technology Used
Projects—Plan/Actual YTD	Analytical	Web Dynpro (embedded SAP BusinessObjects BI)
Projects—Plan/Actual with Currency Translation	Analytical	Web Dynpro (embedded SAP BusinessObjects BI)
Projects—Actuals	Analytical	Web Dynpro (embedded SAP BusinessObjects BI)
Activity Type	Fact sheet	SAP Fiori (SAP UI5)
Manage Activity Type Master Data	Transactional	Web Dynpro
Manage Activity Type Groups	Transactional	Web Dynpro

Table 12.4 SAP Fiori Apps for the Controller Role (Cont.)

The SAP Fiori dashboard for the controller role is shown in Figure 12.25.

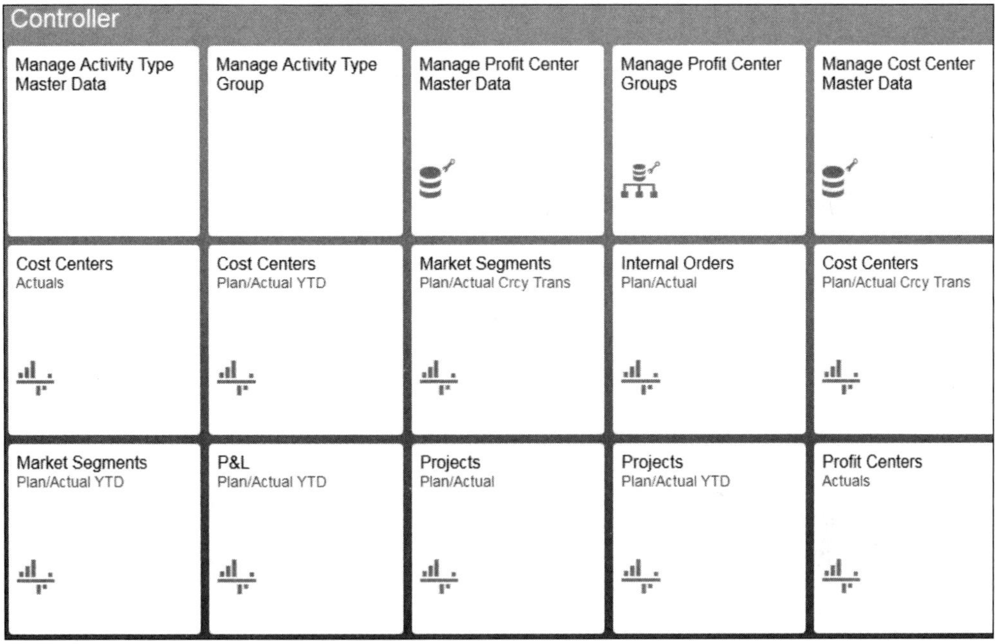

Figure 12.25 Controller Role: SAP_SFIN_BCR_CONTROLLER

12   SAP Fiori Applications

The Profit Centers—Actuals app shown in Figure 12.26 reports the balances for a profit center at a line-item level for each of the G/L accounts for a selected period. It provides the selection screen to input information such as the fiscal year, posting period, segment, profit center, and G/L account. After the selection criteria are confirmed, the system displays a table with columns for the amount in the CO area currency, the amount in transaction currency, and the quantity.

The report can be displayed as data analysis (tabular), graphical display (analytical), or query information (variables and filters). Various fields are available during the selection in the report that can be added to either the column or row axis.

Profit Center		G/L Account		Amt. in CO Area Curr.	Quantity
YB600	Shared Services	Tr Rcvbls - Domestic	121000	$ 0.00	0
		Trade Debtors	123000	$ 0.00	0
		Use Tax AP - State	216200	$ 0.00	0
		Result	Result	$ 177,888.61	0
YB700	Service	Accum Dpr - Bldgs	170010	$ 0.00	0
		Accum Dpr - M & E	170020	$ 0.00	0
		CDA - Checks Out	113025	$ 0.00	0
		Depr Exp - Bldgs	640010	$ 266,666.66	0
		Depr Exp - M & E	640020	$ 8,997.34	0
		Discount Received	700210	$ -180.00	0
		Office/Building Rent	630050	$ -274,700.00	0
		Other Expenses	660000	$ 10,000.00	0
		Retained Earnings	330000	$ 0.00	0
		Sales Commissions	615000	$ -3,000.00	0
		Tr Pybls - Domestic	211000	$ 0.00	0
		Tr Rcvbls - Domestic	121000	$ 0.00	0
		Use Tax AP - State	216200	$ 0.00	0
		Result	Result	$ 7,784.00	0
YB800	Allocation	TE - Meals	610040	$ 10,625.00	0
		Tr Pybls - Domestic	211000	$ 0.00	0
		Use Tax AP - State	216200	$ 0.00	0
		Result	Result	$ 10,625.00	0

Figure 12.26 Profit Centers—Actuals App

12.6.5 Cash Manager

The role of a cash manager is to manage the short-term and long-term liquidity for a legal entity or the entire group. Cash managers maintain bank accounts, provide cash and liquidity forecasts, and manage working capital.

Typical activities of this role are as follows:

- Analyze the daily cash inflow and outflow.
- Optimize funds through cash pooling and concentration to gain maximum returns, manage working capital requirements, and control risk.
- Manage banking relationships, and ensure that payment runs are processed on time without any errors.
- Explore, analyze, and compare variances between actual and cash forecast.
- Promote accurate forecasts in the utilization of cash.

These tasks are supported by the apps in Table 12.5.

App Name	App Type	Technology Used
Manage Bank Accounts	Transactional	Web Dynpro
Make Bank Transfers	Transactional	SAP Fiori (SAP UI5)
Approve Bank Payments	Transactional	SAP Fiori (SAP UI5)
Analyze Payment Details	Transactional	SAP Fiori (SAP UI5)
My Bank Account Worklist	Transactional	Web Dynpro
Cash Position Details	Transactional	SAP Fiori (SAP UI5)
Track Bank Transfers	Transactional	SAP Fiori (SAP UI5)
Maintain Signatory	Transactional	Web Dynpro
Initiate Review Process	Transactional	Web Dynpro
Monitor Review Status	Transactional	Web Dynpro
My Sent Requests	Transactional	Web Dynpro
Manage House Banks	Transactional	SAP Fiori (SAP UI5)

Table 12.5 SAP Fiori Apps for the Cash Manager Role

12   SAP Fiori Applications

App Name	App Type	Technology Used
Cash Flow—Analyzer	Analytical	SAP Fiori (SAP UI5)
Cash Flow—Detailed Analysis	Analytical	SAP Lumira Design Studio
Liquidity Plans	Analytical	SAP Lumira Design Studio
Develop Liquidity Plans	Analytical	SAP Lumira Design Studio
Bank	Fact sheet	SAP Fiori (SAP UI5)
House Bank	Fact sheet	SAP Fiori (SAP UI5)
House Bank Account	Fact sheet	SAP Fiori (SAP UI5)

Table 12.5 SAP Fiori Apps for the Cash Manager Role (Cont.)

The SAP Fiori dashboard for the cash manager role is shown in Figure 12.27.

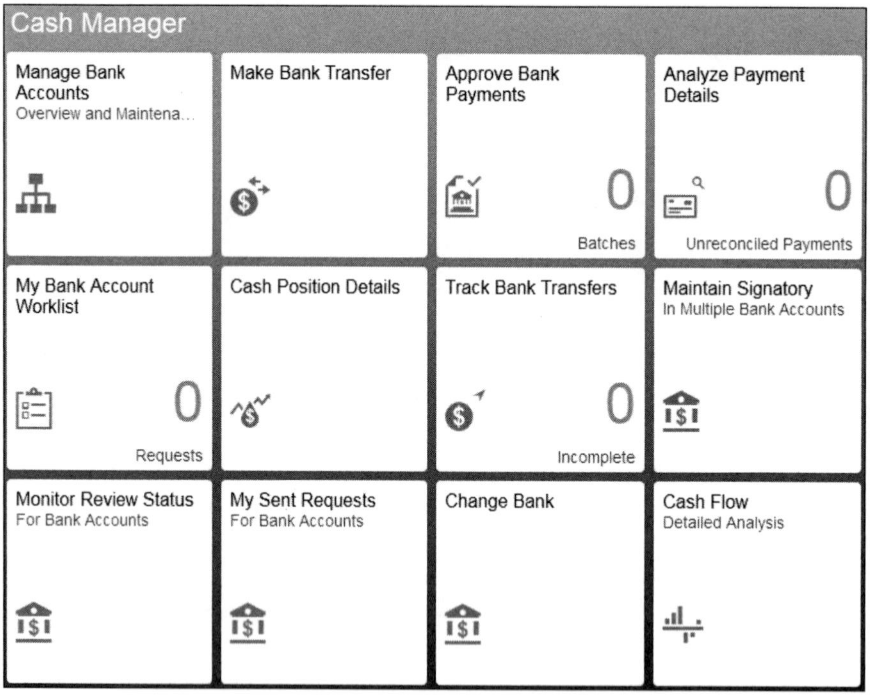

Figure 12.27 Cash Manager Role: SAP_SFIN_BCR_CASHMANAGER

The Manage Bank Accounts transactional app provides an overview of your bank accounts in a hierarchical structure and allows you to maintain bank account master data according to your organization's business requirements, as shown in Figure 12.28.

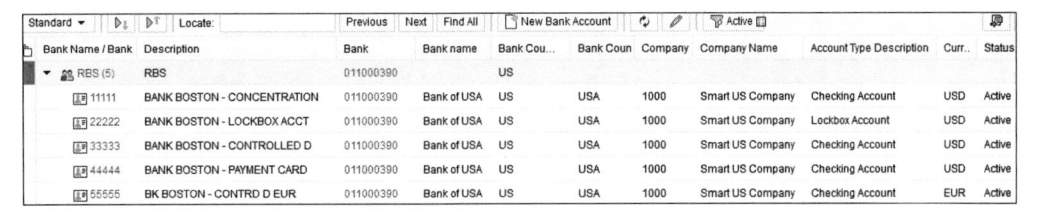

Figure 12.28 Bank Hierarchy: Active Accounts

12.6.6 Cost Manager

The role of a cost manager (also known as a manager of finance info) is to plan and control the budget for variance and comparative analysis and to provide financial reports and analysis to the stakeholders related to expenses, margins, and profitability. In general, the cost manager is responsible for managing the costs for a specific business unit.

Typical activities of this role are as follows:

- Ensure that the cost center and internal order expenses are reported accurately.
- Ensure that costs are allocated correctly based on the rules and logic defined by the business.

These tasks are supported by the apps in Table 12.6.

App Name	App Type	Technology Used
My Unusual Items	Transactional	SAP Fiori (SAP UI5)
My Spend	Transactional	SAP Fiori (SAP UI5)
My Projects	Transactional	SAP Fiori (SAP UI5)
Correction Request	Transactional	SAP Fiori (SAP UI5)
Manage Budget	Transactional	SAP Fiori (SAP UI5)

Table 12.6 SAP Fiori Apps for the Cost Manager Role

12 SAP Fiori Applications

The SAP Fiori dashboard for the cost manager role is shown in Figure 12.29.

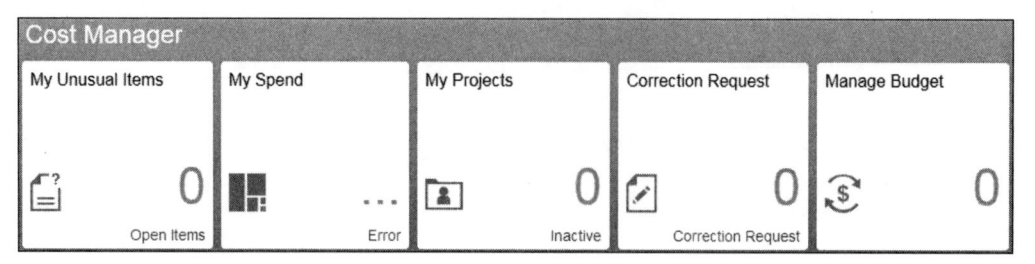

Figure 12.29 Cost Manager Role: SAP_SFIN_BCR_COSTMANAGER

The My Spend transactional app helps you monitor the budget and spending status of your departments and projects, anywhere and anytime (see Figure 12.30). This app consolidates and compares the planned budget and actual spending information and provides user-friendly visualization reports for analysis purposes.

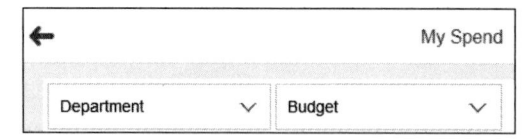

Figure 12.30 My Spend

Nothing is shown in the app in Figure 12.30 because no department is assigned to the user. After a department is assigned, the user can track his or her budget and spending for the assigned department.

12.7 SAP Smart Business Application and Roles

SAP Smart Business for SAP S/4HANA Finance is a collection of analytical apps that contains the most important KPIs for people in decision-making roles such as CFO, accounts receivable and accounts payable managers, collections managers, and corporate controllers. In the following subsections, you'll discover how to enable some of the key SAP Smart Business KPI apps related to various FI managerial roles as applicable for your organization.

12.7.1 For Accounts Payable

SAP Smart Business for accounts payable is the SAP Smart Business cockpit that enables an accounts payable manager to see an overview of key KPIs, monitor progress, and take corrective action as required.

Key features and apps include the following:

- Future Payables
- Overdue Payables
- Cash Discount Forecast
- Cash Discount Utilization
- Aging Analysis
- Invoice Processing Time
- Days Payable Outstanding Analysis
- Vendor Payment Analysis (Manual and Automatic Payments)
- Vendor Payment Analysis (Open Payments)

The SAP Fiori dashboard for the accounts payable manager role is shown in Figure 12.31.

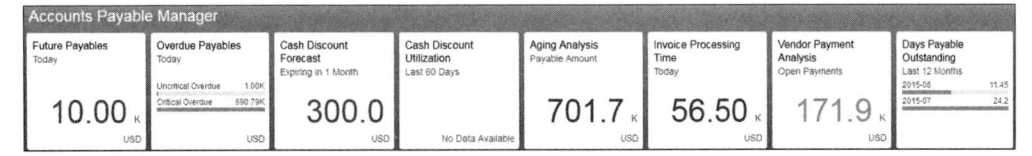

Figure 12.31 Accounts Payable Manager

The Overdue Payables analytical app displays the overdue payables KPI, as shown in Figure 12.32. The amount for overdue payables to the vendors can be analyzed by various parameters such as vendor company code, vendor group, vendor, and reason for payment block. Parameters can be defined for what constitutes critically overdue, and the status can be monitored for critical vendors in your areas of responsibility.

The app provides the potential risk of the critical overdue payments at the company-code level, which can be drilled down into further to specific vendors so that the responsible accounts payable clerk can be notified for further action. This helps resolve any invoice- or product-related issues on time so that the creditworthiness of the organization is maintained by making timely payments.

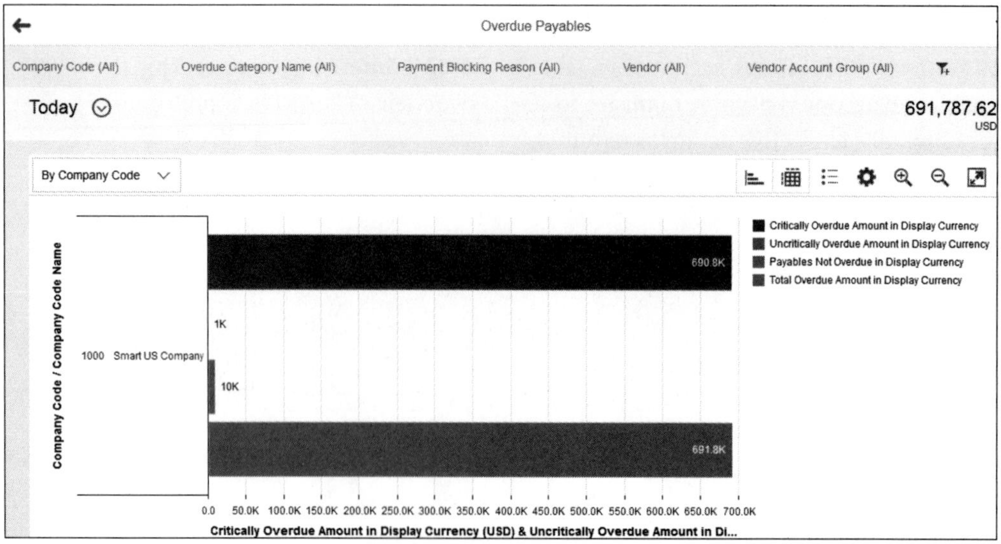

12　SAP Fiori Applications

Figure 12.32 Overdue Payables

12.7.2　For Accounts Receivable

SAP Smart Business for accounts receivable is the SAP Smart Business cockpit that enables an accounts receivable manager to see an overview of key KPIs, monitor progress, and take corrective action as required.

Key features and apps include the following:

- Collection Progress
- Credit Limit Utilization
- Days Beyond Terms
- Days Sales Outstanding
- Dunning Level Distribution
- Future Receivables
- Open Disputes
- Overdue Receivables
- Promises to Pay
- Total Receivables

12.7 SAP Smart Business Application and Roles

The SAP Fiori dashboard for the accounts receivable manager role is shown in Figure 12.33.

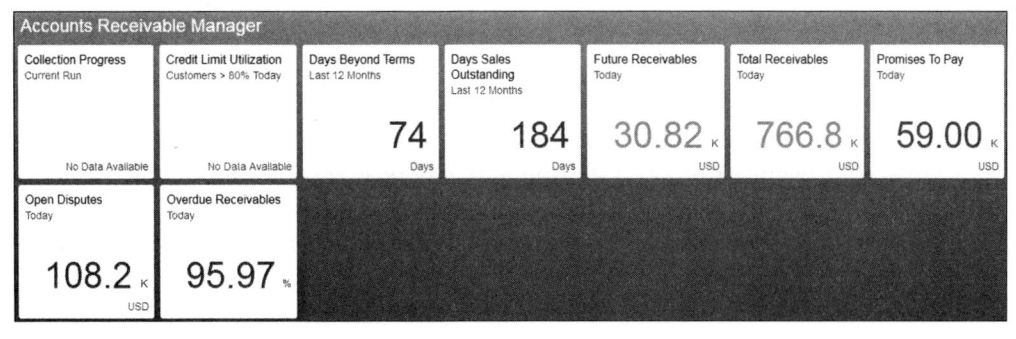

Figure 12.33 Accounts Receivable Manager

The Days Sales Outstanding analytical app displays and measures the KPI for the average number of days taken by the organization to collect receivables. A high DSO figure indicates that the organization is taking too long to convert sales into cash and reflects soft credit terms for customers. The app provides an indication of when the predefined threshold limits are exceeded. You can view the DSO figures in a graphical or tabular format with drilldown to company code, customer, country, accounting clerk, and month, as shown in Figure 12.34.

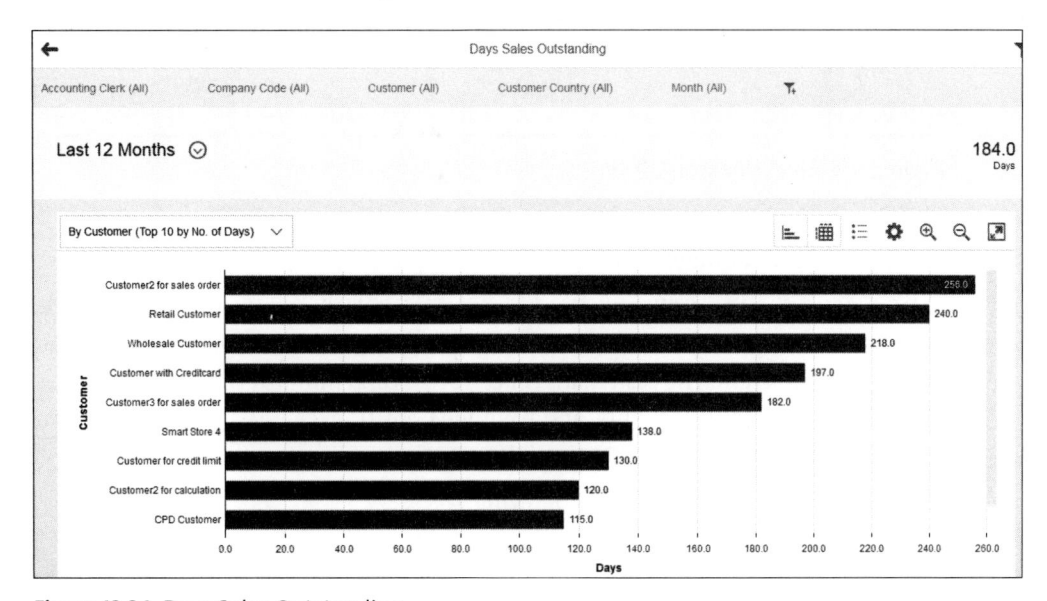

Figure 12.34 Days Sales Outstanding

499

Some of the KPI apps, such as Days Beyond Terms, are more helpful for organizations that have been in business longer and have many years' worth of data for better analysis and decision-making.

12.7.3 For Chief Financial Officers

SAP Smart Business for CFOs is the SAP Smart Business cockpit that enables the CFO to see an overview of key KPIs, monitor progress, and take corrective action as required. The CFO can stay up-to-date on the status of revenue, net sales, gross-to-net sales, gross profit margin, and net profit margin, as shown in Figure 12.35.

Key features and apps include the following:

- Revenue
- Net Sales
- Gross-to-Net Sales
- Gross Margin
- Net Margin

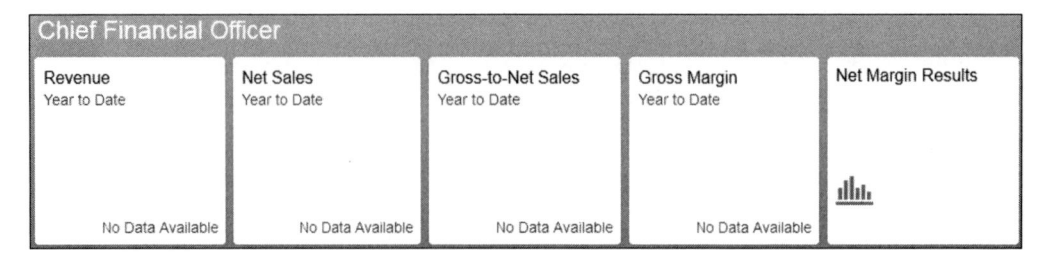

Figure 12.35 Chief Financial Officer

12.7.4 For Cash Management

SAP Smart Business for SAP Cash Management is the SAP Smart Business cockpit that enables the cash manager to see an overview of key KPIs, monitor their progress, and take corrective action. The cash manager can access and monitor the real-time status of cash, liquidity, bank accounts, and payments position; can easily identify certain issues; and can respond quickly as such issues arise.

Key features and apps include the following:

- Bank Risk
- Bank Statement Monitor

- Cash Flow Analysis
- Cash Position
- Deficit Cash Pool
- Liquidity Forecast
- Payment Statistics

A few of these are particularly important. The Cash Flow Analysis analytical app gives insight into any unusual inflow and outflow of cash so that users can promptly remedial action. The Bank Statement Monitor KPI app allows to monitor the status of bank statement imports for all the bank accounts. The Deficit Cash Pool KPI identifies the cash pool deficits so that users can strategically allocate funds to cover the deficit.

12.8 Summary

SAP Fiori offers a simple, easy-to-use, and coherent experience across devices. It also provides role-based, personalized, and flexible deployment options that increase productivity across the organization. With traditional SAP ERP, one transaction is shared across multiple roles, exposing all data and functions to all the users assigned to that transaction. SAP Fiori is a complete transformation in which apps are decomposed for each role, and only the relevant data and functions are shared across users.

Now that you've read this chapter, you should understand the SAP Fiori concept and architecture, including the SAP Fiori project phases. You also learned about the deployment and configuration of landscapes for all three SAP Fiori app types. Finally, you've been given a bird's-eye view of the different roles in SAP Fiori and the tasks assigned to them.

Next, in the appendices, you can walk through the business case of deploying Central Finance to move to SAP S/4HANA. We'll also look at a detailed project plan for migrating to SAP S/4HANA Finance that you can use as a reference/checklist while planning your migration

Appendices

A	Central Finance	505
B	Project Plan for SAP S/4HANA Finance Migration	529
C	The Author	559

Appendix A
Central Finance

This appendix provides insight into the Central Finance deployment option for migrating to SAP S/4HANA. It describes the benefits of and business case for implementing Central Finance, the mapping requirements in SAP Landscape Transformation for transferring data from the source to target system, and a few pro tips for starting the implementation.

This book has provided a guide to migrating to and configuring the financials functionality in SAP S/4HANA. However, many companies may decide that a full-blown data migration is not in their immediate best interests and may inquire about another deployment option that might suit their landscape and data. That deployment option is Central Finance.

In this appendix, we walk through elements of the Central Finance business case, discuss its architecture and new capabilities, and then talk through the setup process.

A.1 The Business Case for Central Finance

The most popular deployment options for SAP S/4HANA Finance include greenfield implementation, and brownfield or migration from SAP ERP to SAP S/4HANA Finance—but both options have pros and cons. The limitation of the greenfield option is that it requires a longer timeframe and more resources, meaning increased implementation costs. The downside of migration is that it can only take place if the organization is already on classic SAP. What happens if an organization has multiple ERP systems (SAP and non-SAP) or legacy systems in the ecosystem and wants to harness the benefit of a single source of truth and real-time data that comes with SAP S/4HANA Finance? Do they need to wait for years for a greenfield implementation, along with all the connected interfaces?

Central Finance provides an alternate deployment option that brings about the following benefits, in a nutshell:

- A single source of truth: Central Finance is an SAP S/4HANA platform in which financial transactions from the source system are replicated in the Central Finance system in real time for centralized processing and reporting. This implementation approach simplifies the organization's ecosystem because it's based on a single source of truth.
- A single platform: Central Finance provides a common finance platform to support an organization's master data and finance processes, such as accounting, planning and consolidation, receivables management, accounts payable, intercompany reconciliation, reporting and analytics, cash management, and more.
- A streamlined implementation: With Central Finance, the transition to SAP S/4HANA Finance is carried out without disruption to the organization's current system landscape.
- Data mapping and replication: Source systems are mapped to the Central Finance system so that all transactional data can be replicated to a centralized and consolidated finance environment to drive a common reporting structure. Users can drill back to the source system to view an original transaction, while the source systems continue transacting without any disruption.

Central Finance is an SAP S/4HANA Finance system that can act as a simplified single system landscape replicating transaction-level data from multiple systems without any major impact to the existing systems. The master data in Central Finance is harmonized into a unified structure from various source systems, and the organization can reap the benefits of faster processing, consolidation, and financial reporting from a single system, rather than reconciling data from multiple sources and then massaging the data for consolidation.

A.1.1 Key Benefits

Key finance processes for which Central Finance can be implemented and reap benefits include the following:

- Financial planning and forecasting
- Embedded consolidation
- Profitability management
- Cost management

- Financial reporting
- Intercompany reconciliation
- Month-end and year-end closing
- Cash and liquidity management
- Receivables management
- Dispute and collections management
- Invoice management
- Financial shared services

Outside of the finance LOB, the Central Finance platform offers many important benefits from an IT management standpoint:

- Creates a common reporting structure by mapping and harmonizing enterprise data such as profit center, cost center, chart of accounts, and so on from various systems, thus providing a single source of truth
- Brings about real-time replication of financial data from SAP and non-SAP source systems into the target Central Finance system
- Provides a platform for the future to seamlessly migrate and integrate any mergers and acquisitions with usual business functioning
- Enables similar tasks to be transferred to shared services for centralized processing, which increases organizational efficiency and reduces costs
- Helps functional people concentrate on more decision-making roles rather than transactional operation roles
- Increases transparency with a single source of truth and a common chart of accounts for legal, management, and consolidation purposes
- Provides a platform for faster closing with timely reporting, consolidation, and predictive analytics, for both managerial and statutory legal purposes
- Provides an enhanced UX with SAP Fiori apps so that users can work on any mobile device from anywhere
- Reduces the complexity and simplifies the future landscape of the organization; enables easy transition to SAP S/4HANA Finance without disruption to the current landscape
- Faster to execute with early benefits; doesn't require a "big bang" classic SAP implementation timeline and the related costs of implementation

A Central Finance

- Allows for nondisruptive adaptation of solutions and replacement of outdated applications
- Optimizes investments in new technology and sunsets multiple applications, reducing the higher maintenance cost of old legacy systems
- Reduces intervention of financial specialists and paper-based processes
- Reduces operating costs by enabling or consolidating shared service operations with centralized payments, improved closing-cycle management, and reduction of reconciliation effort

A.1.2 Central Finance Candidates

Many kinds of companies are going the Central Finance route, but it's proven to be especially popular with organizations that have a few characteristics in common:

- Organizations in a multi-instance, complex, disparate landscape environment looking to simplify to a single global instance for financial reporting. Central Finance eliminates the need to consolidate systems to achieve global financial reporting. It provides real-time consolidation by providing a single source for both legal and management consolidation and reporting.
- Organizations that are in a multi-instance or single-instance landscape and make frequent acquisitions for growth. The acquired companies can undergo a mapping to the centralized organizational structure, chart of accounts, and so on within a few weeks or months without undergoing years of long transformational projects.
- Organizations with complex interfaces and multiple versions of the chart of accounts with unstructured, unharmonized, and disparate use of organizational structures or master data can align to a single structure without undergoing a conversion.
- Organizations looking to centralize their finance processes with the simplification of the IT landscape and shared services function. Value is derived through standardization and harmonization of global data.
- Out-of-maintenance and highly customized systems that require expensive maintenance and upgrades and hinder the adoption of innovation due to system limitations. Organizations can use Central Finance to "reimplement" their current system.

- Organizations planning to implement SAP S/4HANA Finance can utilize Central Finance efficiently because it makes the move without disrupting the existing SAP and non-SAP systems in the ecosystem.

Before undertaking a Central Finance project, each organization should consider a few other program principles to help ensure successful implementation, as we'll discuss next.

A.1.3 Key Program Principles

For an organization to be successful in implementing the Central Finance scenario, it must adhere to the following program principles:

- **Get the leadership team engaged.**
  A Central Finance implementation is only successful when there's a rapid decision-making environment within an organization, enabled by active, in-person participation at the CFO and corporate controller levels.
- **Institute top-down decision-making.**
  Key design decisions should be driven by, determined, and agreed upon at the top level of the organization, which has decision-making authority for faster execution; final decisions should then be communicated from the top down for better alignment.
- **Gather line of business support.**
  All lines of business and functional areas should have a key stake, have buy-in, and support the key design decisions and overall global design.
- **Prioritize key design decisions.**
  The organization must prioritize the key design decisions that impact Central Finance during preparation for workshops, such as decisions about statutory and legal reporting, management reporting, centralized cash management, centralized payments, allocation strategy, and so on.
- **Perform data-profiling early.**
  A key component for success is to complete the data-profiling activities in legacy systems as early as possible, preferably prior to the start of Central Finance workshops so that the data profiling can expedite the mapping process as the organization moves to the next phase.

- **Define the end-state vision.**
  Always define and keep the end state in mind rather than stressing over short-term goals achieved by the Central Finance system and its functionalities.
- **Make key design decisions before starting program increments.**
  The key design decisions related to the foundational elements and organization structure need to be made at a very early stage so that the implementation timeline can be met.
- **Anticipate challenges during master data and system mapping.**
  These processes are often harder than expected, so the organization should provision adequate resources and time for mapping the master data so that data is replicated from the source to the Central Finance system without any major issues.
- **Assess the deployment timeline realistically.**
  Based on past SAP implementations or the timeline template required for SAP implementation, organizations generally provision for a lengthier timeline than required for Central Finance implementation. Central Finance is quite different and doesn't require the same timeline as a full-fledged SAP implementation. (This is good news!)
- **Deploy management reporting before financial reporting.**
  Based on the business case and if given a choice, management reporting should be deployed before financial reporting; this lets the organization test the waters of the new system and minimize the risk of financial reporting. This also allows the organization to take more risk on the deployment timeline because it doesn't impact the financial reporting and the transaction processing at the first instance.

Now that you understand some of the key benefits of Central Finance deployment and the business case for it, let's briefly look into the architecture and key configuration steps. The idea of this appendix is to provide an overview and understanding of what it takes to install Central Finance for migrating to SAP S/4HANA.

A.2 Architecture

The architecture for Central Finance will comprise the following data flow and mapping framework from both SAP and non-SAP systems.

You need to define the mapping strategy and mapping rules for deriving harmonized master data in the Central Finance system. All master data will originate from and likely be managed in SAP Master Data Governance (SAP MDG) and will then be replicated in the Central Finance system. You then follow the structured Central Finance mapping approach to reach a mature level of mapping for the initial load and for the real-time replication of transactional data from the heterogeneous source systems.

The Central Finance mapping flow is illustrated in Figure A.1. SAP Landscape Transformation replication server is used to replicate the real-time data from both SAP and non-SAP source systems to the Central Finance system. The transactional data is posted in both the source and the Central Finance system and is fully reconciled and harmonized after passing through the key-mapping and value-mapping rules. Key mappings are organizational unit data, typically comprising company code, customer, vendor, cost center, profit center, material, plant, and so on. Value mappings are mainly customizing values acting as attributes for the master record, typically comprising payment terms, payment methods, unit of measure, dunning area, and so on.

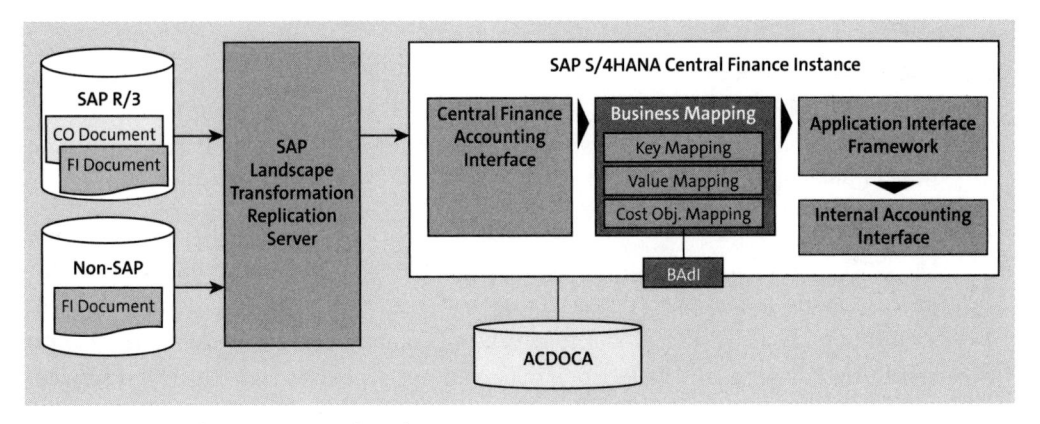

Figure A.1 Central Finance Mapping Flow

SAP MDG can be used for the creation and maintenance of master data elements, but you can also maintain the key-value mapping manually if SAP MDG is not used by your organization.

References

For more resources related to SAP Landscape Transformation replication server, see SAP Note 2154420: SAP LT Replication Server for SAP Central Finance.

A.3 New Capabilities

Central Finance has evolved over time. SAP has been focusing on this option and has offered new capabilities and enhancements in every release of SAP S/4HANA. Let's look at some of the recently incorporated new features and capabilities that Central Finance provides to users.

A.3.1 Open Items and Clearing

When the Central Finance product was launched, any open item that was created in the source system, such as accounts receivable debit and revenue credit entries, was replicated in the target Central Finance system and was technically cleared simultaneously. This resulted in an incorrect status in the two systems: the source system continued to reflect an open item until it was cleared, while the target system already reflected it as cleared. It also prevented having the Central Finance system as the centralized payment or reporting system because the open item was automatically set as cleared once it was replicated in the Central Finance system.

There has been lot of innovation and improvement in the functionality of Central Finance. Now, an open item is replicated from the source system to the Central Finance system using SAP Landscape Transformation and it remains an open item in the Central Finance system.

When the open item is cleared in the source system, it is again replicated through SAP Landscape Transformation and is cleared in the Central Finance system as well. This process helps reflect the correct status and real-time reporting and analysis of accounts receivables and accounts payables balances, using the SAP Fiori UX with centralized dispute- and collections-management processes and the shared services model, if required.

With the replication of clearing, some of the additional scenarios that can be leveraged in SAP Fiori using Central Finance include cash flow analysis, liquidity forecast, and KPIs such as aging analysis, overdue receivables, days payable outstanding, payment analysis, and so on.

However, this presents a limitation: all the payments should be carried out in the source system because Central Finance does not allow back posting to the source system. Many organizations want Central Finance to be the single centralized payment process system and want to implement a customized integration solution for clearing open items in Central Finance and then sending the same information to the source system so that the open item in the source system also clears. This makes Central Finance the system of record for all payment-related activities, including collections management. With shared services, users don't need to toggle between the source system and the Central Finance system to execute various functions.

A.3.2 Document Changes

Whenever an FI document is posted in the source system, it's replicated to the Central Finance system using SAP Landscape Transformation. If a document is changed or modified in the source system, the change is replicated to the Central Finance system and the same document is updated in the Central Finance system as well, reflecting all the changes made in the source system.

A.3.3 Cost Object Changes

Any changes to cost objects such as orders in the source system get replicated and updated in the Central Finance system. Check SAP Note 2308365 for further details about changes to cost object replication.

A.3.4 Simulation Run

Both business mapping and posting can now be simulated, and any errors can be analyzed before the actual initial load and document replication is executed.

A.3.5 Real-Time Consolidation

Consolidation is one of the key value propositions for implementing Central Finance. Although organizations still try to keep their existing systems, such as Hyperion, for consolidation, Central Finance provides an opportunity to consolidate within the SAP S/4HANA system.

With data harmonization and centralized mapping, a reduction in the number of interfaces and the complexity associated with them, increased flexibility to incorporate any business model changes, and ease of integration for any mergers and acquisitions, Central Finance becomes a good candidate to utilize the embedded consolidation functionality within SAP S/4HANA to support real-time consolidation. This minimizes the data-replication effort, reduces the closing-cycle time, and provides a real-time analysis of data.

A.4 Prerequisites

Before installing, configuring, and implementing Central Finance, you must ensure that all the prerequisite activities are performed and all relevant notes are applied either in the source system or the Central Finance system.

- Prerequisites in SAP source system
    - The Data Migration Server (DMIS) add-on must be installed with the latest support packages in the source system by applying SAP Note 2191214.
    - Authorization object SAP_IUUC_REPL_REMOTE must be assigned to the RFC user.
    - When a Finance or a Controlling document is posted in the SAP sender system, some additional data needs to be stored on a temporary basis and sent to the Central Finance system for replication. Refer to the notes listed in the following box to enable the document transfer through SAP Landscape Transformation.

> **References**
> Consult the following SAP Notes about the source system:
> - SAP Note 2111634: Enable Sender Systems for a Central Finance Scenario
> - SAP Note 2223621: Central Finance: Interface for Business Integration
> - SAP Note 2323494: Overview of Notes Relevant for Source System

- Prerequisites in SAP Landscape Transformation replication server
    - The DMIS add-on must be installed with the latest support packages in SAP Landscape Transformation replication server.
    - Establish an RFC connection between the SAP source system and the SAP Landscape Transformation replication server.
    - Authorization objects SAP_IUUC_REPL_ADMIN and SAP_MWB_PROJECT_MANAGER must be assigned to the configuration user.
- Prerequisites in the Central Finance system
    - Establish an RFC connection between the SAP source system and the Central Finance system.
    - Activate business function FINS_CFIN.
    - Create an RFC destination.
    - Define a logical system.

- Assign the logical system to the RFC.
- In the Central Finance system, refer to and implement the notes listed in the following box.

> **References**
>
> We recommend the following resources related to the Central Finance system:
>
> - SAP Note 2135027: Corrections and Improvements in FI
> - SAP Note 2142433: Corrections and Improvements in CO
> - SAP Note 2217711: Currency Handling Fix of CO Posting

A.5 Mapping

One of the major challenges of implementing Central Finance lies in harmonizing the master data from various source systems and subsequently mapping it so that the accounting data can flow from the source system and be posted in the Central Finance system.

For example, if a company code has been set up as US01 in the source system and it has been set up as 1001 in the Central Finance system, the correct mapping needs to be maintained so that the value US01 is translated to 1001 when posting in Central Finance. The mapping needs to be maintained for each source system; it could be set up as A001 in another source system, for example, which would also need to be mapped to 1001 in Central Finance. There is also a scenario in which you may need to change the cost object type during mapping because you may not want a detailed level of posting within Central Finance, or there might be a cost object type that may not be supported in Central Finance.

In Central Finance, we utilize three categories of mappings, as shown in Figure A.2:

1. **Key mapping**
   The mapping for business object identifiers is Web Dynpro–based maintenance and is carried out through SAP MDG; it includes items such as customer, vendor, material, and so on.
2. **Value mapping**
   The mapping for codes is configuration and is carried out through SAP MDG; it includes items such as company code, document type, payment method, and so on.

A   Central Finance

3. **Cost object mapping**

   The mapping for cost objects is handled through Customizing in Central Finance, for items such as production order, internal order, and so on.

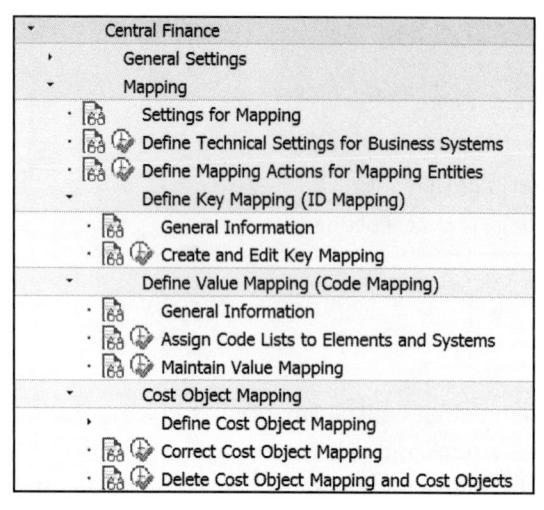

   ```
   ▼   Central Finance
     ▸   General Settings
     ▼   Mapping
       •   Settings for Mapping
       •   Define Technical Settings for Business Systems
       •   Define Mapping Actions for Mapping Entities
       ▼   Define Key Mapping (ID Mapping)
         •   General Information
         •   Create and Edit Key Mapping
       ▼   Define Value Mapping (Code Mapping)
         •   General Information
         •   Assign Code Lists to Elements and Systems
         •   Maintain Value Mapping
       ▼   Cost Object Mapping
         ▸   Define Cost Object Mapping
         •   Correct Cost Object Mapping
         •   Delete Cost Object Mapping and Cost Objects
   ```

   Figure A.2 Central Finance Mapping

In the **Define Mapping Actions for Mapping Entities** Customizing activity, you set the mapping action for each mapping entity and element to one of the following four settings, as shown in Figure A.3:

1. **Mapping Obligatory**

   Mapping of this field is mandatory in the target system.

2. **Map if Possible**

   If mapping isn't defined for this field, the value of this field from the source system is transferred to the target system during posting.

3. **Clear Data**

   The value of this field from the source system is cleared during posting in the target system.

4. **Keep Data**

   The value of this field is transferred to the target system during posting.

A.5 Mapping

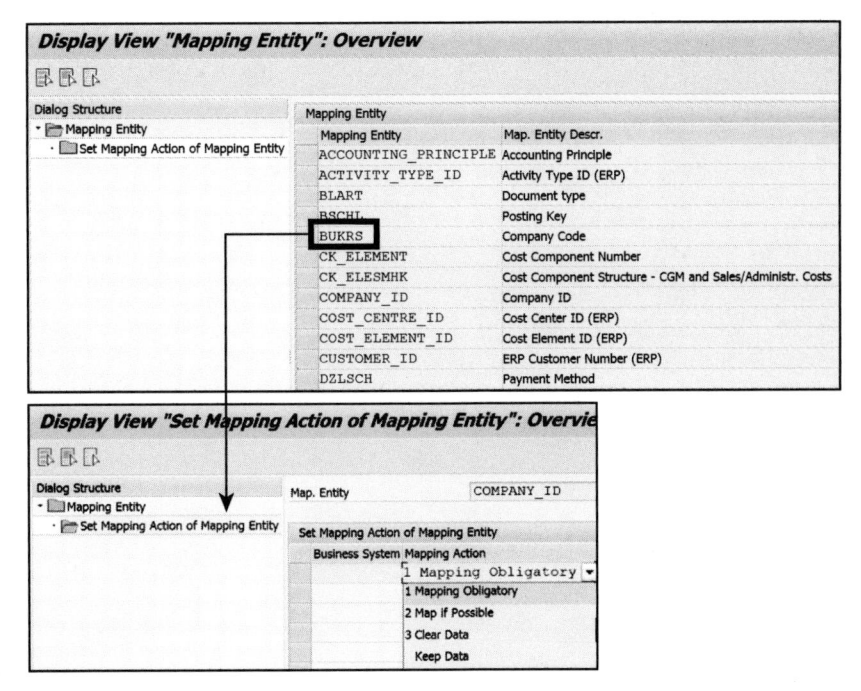

Figure A.3 Mapping Entity and Action

A.5.1 Define Key Mapping

Some business objects—such as customer, vendor, material, cost center, profit center, and general ledger account—are master data elements that are required in the transaction posting while replicating the data from the source systems. Key mappings in Central Finance comprise these objects. For example, key mapping of a customer ID is shown in Figure A.4. The first row displays the business object type, the business system of the Central Finance instance, the object ID type, and the ID of the object in the Central Finance system; the second row displays the business system of the source system and the mapping of the customer ID in the source system. Thus, the customer ID 10011000 in the source system is mapped to the customer ID C10011000 in the Central Finance system.

The same customer might exist with different IDs in various source systems that need to be mapped to a single customer ID in the Central Finance system so that, when the invoice is replicated, the system translates the correct customer ID before posting in Central Finance, creating a single, harmonized customer master record throughout the organization.

517

A   Central Finance

Key mappings can be displayed with the MDG_BS_WD_ANALYSE_IDM Web Dynpro application.

Key Mapping Customer : C10011000

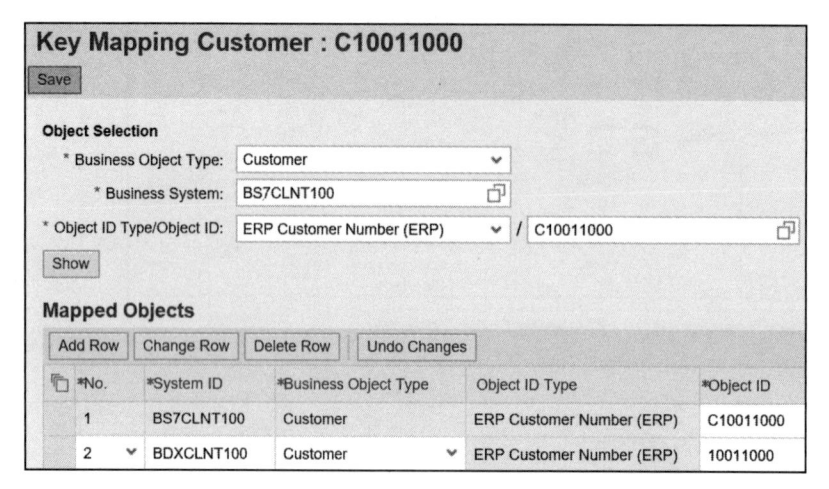

*No.	*System ID	*Business Object Type	Object ID Type	*Object ID
1	BS7CLNT100	Customer	ERP Customer Number (ERP)	C10011000
2	BDXCLNT100	Customer	ERP Customer Number (ERP)	10011000

Figure A.4 Key Mapping

A.5.2   Define Value Mapping

Some fields for accounting principle, document type, document type, company code, ledger, payment method, controlling area, and so on might be configured and used in the source system differently. These fields and codes need to be defined and configured for value mapping in the Customizing section of Central Finance.

In this Customizing activity, you can assign code lists to elements and systems; this is required for each global data type (GDT) to be mapped.

The following data must be specified for each of the sender systems as part of the mapping exercise (see Figure A.5):

- **Type**
  Specify the type configured for the mapping entity, such as a data element or a structure.

- **Global Data Type**
  Specify the global data type as the technical field name for the mapping entity.

- **Internal List ID**
  An internal list ID is required for those GDTs that have a context structure. For example, the dunning area (MABER) for GDT is mapped for each of the company codes. Thus, for company code 1001, the internal list ID is 1001 and the list ID is

MABER/1001. For the company code 1002, the internal list ID is 1002 and the list ID is MABER/1002.

- **Business System**
  Specify the business system of the source system.

- **List ID**
  Specify the same name as for the GDT; for example, use BUKRS if the GDT is also BUKRS. The only exception to this rule is when the GDT has a context structure; then, you concatenate the GDT and the value used for the internal list ID and separate the two values by a slash (/). For example, if the GDT is MABER and the internal list ID is 1001, use MABER/1001 for the list ID.

- **List Agency ID**
  Specify the business system of the source system.

- **List Version ID**
  Specify a value of 01.

Type		Global Data Type	Internal List ID	Business System	List ID	List Agency ID	List Version ID
DTEL	Data Element	BLART		AAECLNT200	BLART	AAECLNT200	01
DTEL	Data Element	BLART		BDECLNT200	BLART	BDECLNT200	01
DTEL	Data Element	BSCHL		AAECLNT200	BSCHL	AAECLNT200	01
DTEL	Data Element	BSCHL		BDECLNT200	BSCHL	BDECLNT200	01
DTEL	Data Element	BUKRS		AAECLNT200	BUKRS	AAECLNT200	01
DTEL	Data Element	BUKRS		BDECLNT200	BUKRS	BDECLNT200	01
DTEL	Data Element	FAGL_LDGRP		AAECLNT200	FAGL_LDGRP	AAECLNT200	01
DTEL	Data Element	FAGL_LDGRP		BDECLNT200	FAGL_LDGRP	BDECLNT200	01
DTEL	Data Element	FKBER		AAECLNT200	FKBER	AAECLNT200	01
DTEL	Data Element	FKBER		BDECLNT200	FKBER	BDECLNT200	01
DTEL	Data Element	KOKRS		AAECLNT200	KOKRS	AAECLNT200	01
DTEL	Data Element	KOKRS		BDECLNT200	KOKRS	BDECLNT200	01
DTEL	Data Element	MWSKZ		AAECLNT200	MWSKZ	AAECLNT200	01
DTEL	Data Element	MWSKZ		BDECLNT200	MWSKZ	BDECLNT200	01
DTEL	Data Element	RLDNR		AAECLNT200	RLDNR	AAECLNT200	01
DTEL	Data Element	RLDNR		BDECLNT200	RLDNR	BDECLNT200	01
DTEL	Data Element	VBUND		AAECLNT200	VBUND	AAECLNT200	01
TABL	Structure	MDGCO_MRP_T.		AAECLNT200	MDGCO_MRP_TYPE_CODE	AAECLNT200	01
TABL	Structure	MDGCO_MRP_T.		BDECLNT200	MDGCO_MRP_TYPE_CODE	BDECLNT200	01

Figure A.5 Assignment of Code to Elements

In the **Maintain Value Mapping** Customizing activity (see Figure A.6), you can configure mapping of all GDT fields based on the internal code value. Enter the value of the target Central Finance system and map to the external code value, specifying the value from the source system that needs to be mapped.

A Central Finance

If two or more values from the same source system need to be mapped to a single value in the Central Finance system, select the **Outbound Default** checkbox for any of the line items. In Figure A.6, company code ZCFI in the source system is mapped to company code 2002 in the Central Finance system.

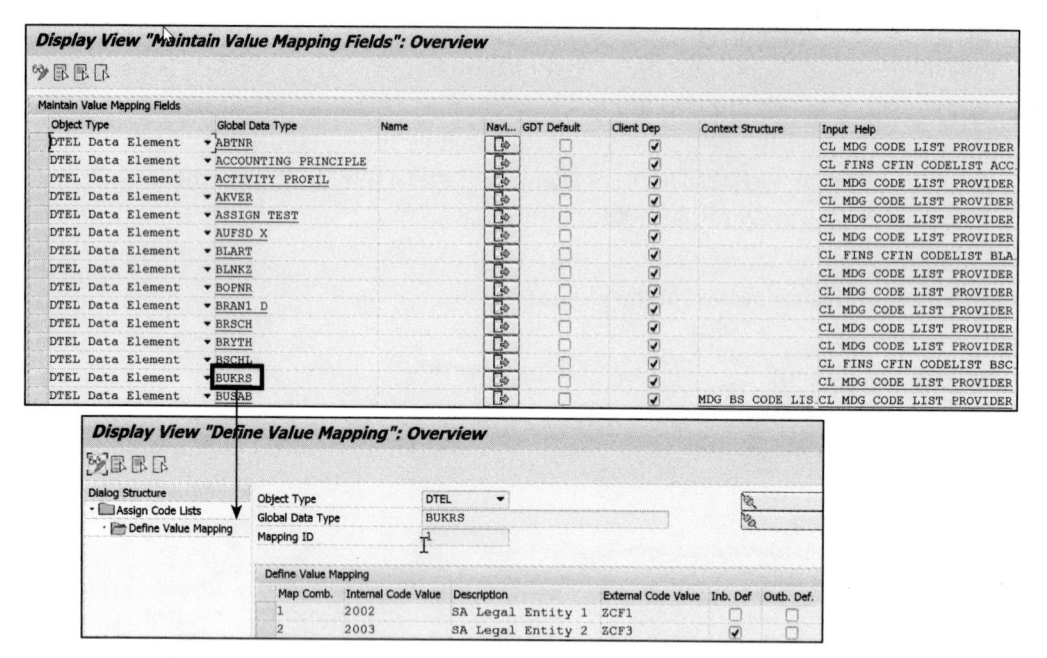

Figure A.6 Value Mapping

A.5.3 Define Cost Object Mapping

In this Customizing activity, you create scenarios to map the cost object category from the source system to the Central Finance system, as shown in Figure A.7. The mapping rules for scenarios need to be defined to assign a source cost object to a central cost object.

For each scenario identified, you need to define the source cost objects that need to be mapped to the central cost object based on the source characteristics. These cost objects are mainly used in the replication of transaction data—for example, internal order, production order, and so on. SAP provides commonly used fields that can be enhanced easily based on specific requirements.

A.5 Mapping

For replicating the CO documents from the source system to Central Finance system, function modules `FINS_CFIN_CO_CENTRAL_POSTING` and `FINS_CFIN_CO_POSTING_BULK` are used as the CO secondary posting interfaces.

Display View "Central Characteristic": Overview

Characteristic Name	Description	Derive From Source
AKSTL	Requesting cost center	✓
ASTKZ	Identifier for Statistical Order	✓
AUART	Order Type	☐
BUKRS	Company Code	✓
CYCLE	Cost center to which costs are actually	✓
GSBER	Business Area	✓
KOKRS	Controlling Area	✓
KOSTL	Cost Center for Basic Settlement	✓
KOSTV	Responsible cost center	✓
KSTAR	Settlement Cost Element	✓
KTEXT	Description	✓
PRCTR	Profit Center	✓
SAKNR	G/L Account for Basic Settlement	✓
TXJCD	Tax Jurisdiction	✓
WERKS	Plant	✓

Scenario: ZCFI_ION — Internal Order Scenario Mapping

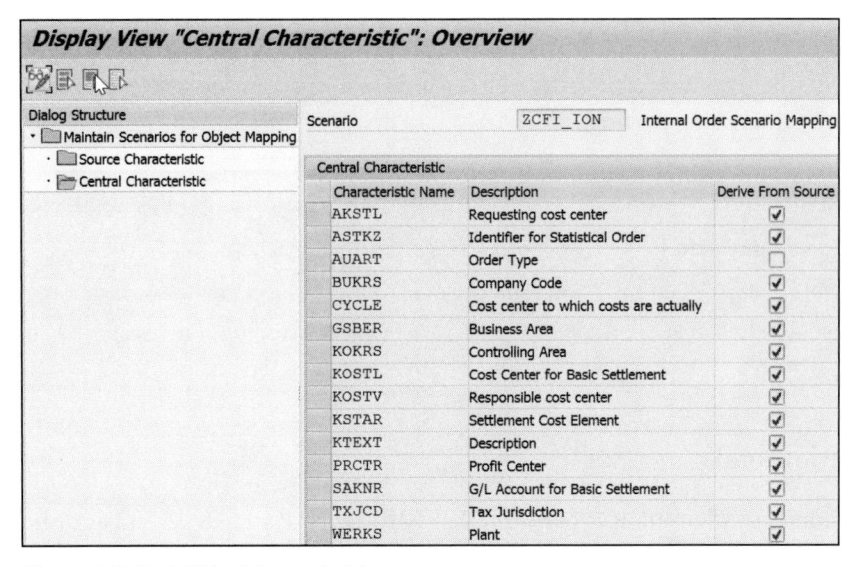

Figure A.7 Cost Object Scenario Mapping

A.5.4 Cost Object Changes

Table A.1 illustrates the cost object–mapping framework supported by Central Finance.

Cost Object in Source System	Cost Object in Central Finance System	Cardinality
Production order	Product cost collector/internal order	N:1/1:1
Product cost collector	Product cost collector	1:1
Internal order	Internal order	N:1/1:1
Service order	Service order/internal order	N:1/1:1
QM order	QM order/internal order	N:1/1:1

Table A.1 Cost Object–Mapping Framework

521

A Central Finance

When a production order is created in the source system, it's replicated as an internal order in the Central Finance system, as per the mapping set up in Central Finance. Whenever there are any changes to the order in the source system, all the changes to the attributes are replicated to the same order in the Central Finance system that was replicated initially. Thus, the integrity of the order in both systems is maintained, which subsequently allows the Central Finance system to act as the single source of truth for any financial reporting.

> **References**
>
> Some resources related to the cost object framework are listed here:
> - SAP Note 2308365: Central Finance: More Details of Cost Object Change Replication
> - SAP Note 2180924: Supported Scenarios in Cost Object Mapping Framework

A.6 Initial Load

The initial load configuration is performed in both the SAP source system and the Central Finance system to replicate the historical postings from the source system to the Central Finance system, as shown in Figure A.8. There are three different types of initial loads performed during the Central Finance implementation:

1. **Initial load of cost objects**
   This activity is performed to replicate cost objects from the source system to the Central Finance system using SAP Landscape Transformation. This activity should be performed to execute the initial load for FI and CO postings; accounting postings require cost objects during posting.

2. **Initial load of FI postings**
   This activity is performed to replicate historical financial postings from the source system. As a prerequisite, the master data in the Central Finance system and the proper mapping should be set up. You also need to specify the range of the period for which the balances need to be transferred and the range from which the line items need to be replicated.

3. **Initial load of CO and asset postings**
   This activity is performed to replicate only the CO postings, such as postings on secondary cost elements or CO-PA-specific postings from the source systems to

the Central Finance system. However, the secondary cost elements don't exist in the SAP S/4HANA Central Finance system: the mapping converts the secondary cost elements to the appropriate G/L accounts while replicating data to the Central Finance system.

In the Central Finance system, asset reconciliation accounts must be set as nonreconciliation balance sheet accounts via Transaction OAMK or must be mapped to a nonreconciliation balance sheet account.

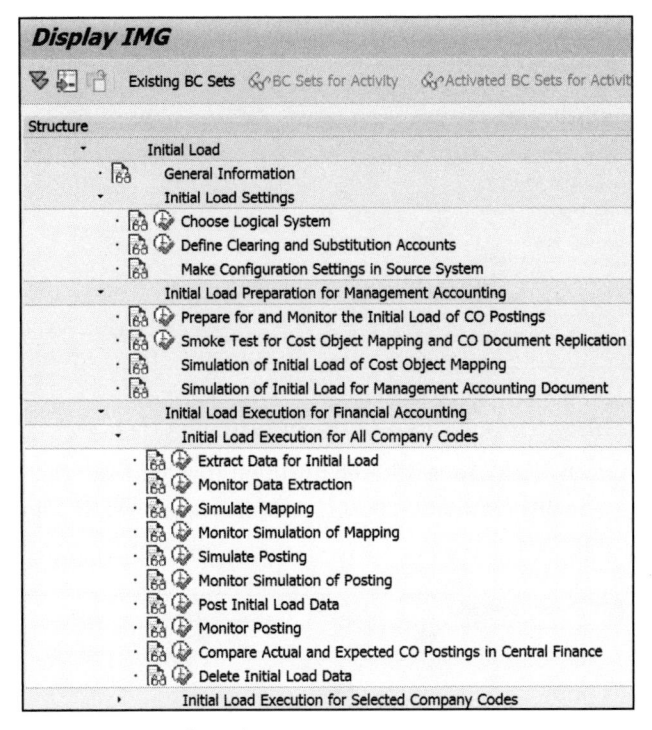

```
Display IMG
Existing BC Sets   BC Sets for Activity   Activated BC Sets for Activity
Structure
    • Initial Load
        • General Information
        • Initial Load Settings
            • Choose Logical System
            • Define Clearing and Substitution Accounts
            • Make Configuration Settings in Source System
        • Initial Load Preparation for Management Accounting
            • Prepare for and Monitor the Initial Load of CO Postings
            • Smoke Test for Cost Object Mapping and CO Document Replication
            • Simulation of Initial Load of Cost Object Mapping
            • Simulation of Initial Load for Management Accounting Document
        • Initial Load Execution for Financial Accounting
            • Initial Load Execution for All Company Codes
                • Extract Data for Initial Load
                • Monitor Data Extraction
                • Simulate Mapping
                • Monitor Simulation of Mapping
                • Simulate Posting
                • Monitor Simulation of Posting
                • Post Initial Load Data
                • Monitor Posting
                • Compare Actual and Expected CO Postings in Central Finance
                • Delete Initial Load Data
            • Initial Load Execution for Selected Company Codes
```

Figure A.8 Initial Load

Even if there's no requirement to replicate the historical data in Central Finance, the initial load execution is a mandatory step in which you run an "empty" initial load; that will activate the real-time replication of the documents going forward from the source system. Once the initial load is complete, the status in SAP Landscape Transformation will automatically change to **Replication**, as shown in Figure A.9.

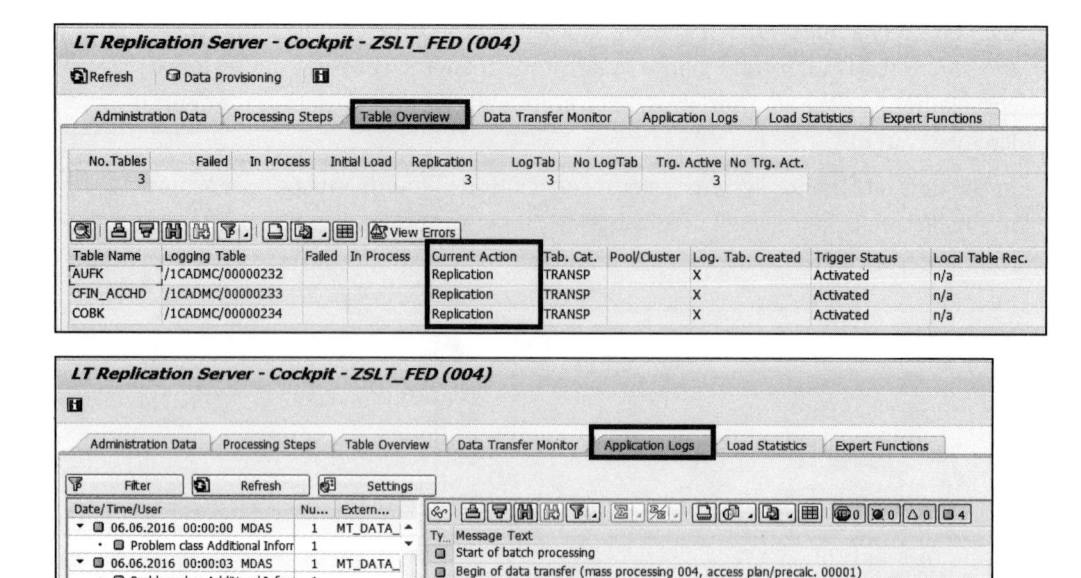

A Central Finance

Figure A.9 SAP Landscape Transformation Replication Server

In SAP Landscape Transformation, data can be filtered during initial load and real-time replication. The filter can be set up in table DMC_ACSPL_SELECT, as shown in Figure A.10.

Figure A.10 Filtering Data in SAP Landscape Transformation

A.6.1 Source System as SAP

Before you can do the initial load in the SAP source system, there are a few prerequisites to fulfill:

524

- Execute all scheduled jobs, and do not schedule any new jobs.
- Perform closing for periodic asset postings using program RAPERB2000.
- Execute the periodic depreciation posting run using program RAPOST2000.
- Check for update terminations in your system and correct any that you find.
- Lock all periods, apart from the current one, in Financial Accounting and Controlling (Plan/Actual).
- Carry out consistency checks: execute the FI consistency check using report RFINDEX.
- If you're using new General Ledger Accounting, execute reconciliation for the G/L and the subledgers. To do this, you can either run report TFC_COMPARE_VZ or use Transaction FAGLF03.
- If you're using new General Ledger Accounting, compare the ledgers. To do this, you can either run report RGUCOMP4 or use Transaction GCAC. Restrict the selection to the relevant company codes.
- Carry forward balances again for all currencies and all ledgers to make sure all balance carryforwards are complete and consistent. For account payables and account receivables, use report SAPF010. For GL accounting, use Transaction FAGLGVTR.

> **Expert Insight**
> Note that if you're replicating data from a non-SAP system, you must apply SAP Note 2300443: SAP LT Replication Server for SAP Central Finance—Legacy Source Systems.

A.6.2 Initial Load Execution in Central Finance

In Central Finance, the initial load is split into a sequence of steps that must be carried out in the same order. Each step must be complete before the next step can be started. The steps are as follows, in order:

1. Extract data for initial load (FINS_CFIN_LOAD1).
2. Monitor data extraction (FINS_CFIN_LOAD_MON1).
3. Simulate posting (FINS_CFIN_CJ5).
4. Post initial load data (FINS_CFIN_LOAD2).
5. Monitor posting (FINS_CFIN_MONI_CJ5).

A   Central Finance

Once the initial data is loaded in Central Finance, the post-load validation must be executed to audit the data and make sure it's been loaded correctly. You need to compare posting data from the Central Finance system against the sender system by running the following reports in the Central Finance system:

- The financial statements using report RFBILA00
- The totals report for cost centers using Transaction S_ALR_87013611
- The G/L account balances using report RFSSLD00
- The compact document journal using report RFBELJ00
- General ledger line items using report RFSOP000
- Actual and expected CO postings in Central Finance using report RFINS_CFIN_MATCH_FI_TO_CO

A.7   Error Handling

The Central Finance architecture comes with Application Interface Framework (AIF), which has error-correction and error-handling capability for some of the following common Central Finance error types and scenarios:

- Errors related to FI document replication, including errors with the new document and changes to the initial document posting
- Errors related to the CO document replication
- Errors related to cost object replication, including errors with new cost object posting and changes to the original cost object posting
- Errors encountered during the cost object initial load
- Errors encountered during the CO internal posting initial load

Note that a separate error-monitoring tool is used for errors encountered during the initial load of FI documents and balances. A single dashboard provides an overview and the statistics of all error types, which enhances the usability of the tool for error correction and quick remedial action, thereby increasing the productivity of users at the same time. Users can monitor all error messages and the status of any timeframe they would like to select and display. This setup provides the flexibility to assign error messages to SAP transaction codes, which makes it easier for the user responsible for fixing the errors to navigate to the correct transaction code and resolve the errors.

> **References**
>
> Some of the resources related to AIF are listed here:
>
> - SAP Note 1530212: SAP Application Interface Framework FAQ
> - SAP Note 2196783: Central Finance: Error handling with AIF
> - SAP Note 2202650: Central Finance: Error Handling in AIF for Replication of FI Documents
> - SAP Note 2202691: Central Finance: Error Handling in AIF for Replication of CO documents and Cost Objects

A.8 Key Lessons

Before we close this appendix on Central Finance, we offer the following key lessons gathered from implementing Central Finance at various organizations:

- Make sure you can justify the switch to SAP S/4HANA based on the business case evaluation of the whole value chain and application landscape.
- Keep in mind that there will be not one huge benefit, but instead numerous smaller benefits across all business functions and beyond the ERP application scope.
- Finding the right level of business audience for the evaluation workshops and getting their participation is critical to making an SAP S/4HANA roadmap exercise successful; demos from the preconfigured solutions are required and helpful to tell the user story.
- You should consider additional triggers in the business and IT (M&A, data center setup, shared services, hardware lifetime) during your analysis; such considerations will help you build your business case. Consider integrating "soft facts" like improvements to usability, user experience, and change management.
- Because SAP's functionality is being continuously enhanced, be prepared to react flexibly—even during the roadmap/implementation project phase. Central Finance is still evolving, with new functionalities being added with each new release. Because many improvements and additional functionalities are still on the development roadmap, establishing a close collaboration with SAP development is key to success.

- Assess your business efforts in detail and align them with business leadership to avoid potential bottlenecks during an implementation project. Be clear about business issues to be addressed and any expected benefits.
- It's essential to define the "to-be" data model early so the end goal is apparent to everyone.
- Master data management and mapping maintenance are key to success. SAP MDG configuration and settings are not always as easily changed as standard SAP functional configuration. Therefore, a missed requirement or misunderstood design element could jeopardize SAP MDG's ability to be ready for an integrated test phase.
- Anticipate that the initial data load will be technically complex; big data volumes require a certain runtime and a well-organized error-handling and error-resolution team.
- Weigh the options of upgrading support packs versus applying SAP Notes while considering the impacts to business and the amount of regression testing that needs to be performed.
- Lack of connectivity to systems like SAP Solution Manager and SAP GRC can prevent a team from fully implementing technical architecture or from performing user-provision services.

This appendix has introduced Central Finance as an implementation option for SAP S/4HANA Finance. More information on this topic is available in the E-Bite *SAP S/4HANA Finance: How Do I Get Started without Migrating?* (SAP PRESS, 2017, *www.sap-press.com/4364*).

Appendix B
Project Plan for SAP S/4HANA Finance Migration

This appendix provides a detailed project plan that you can reference, change, and customize based on your specific project requirements for migration to SAP S/4HANA Finance. In this project plan, the main tasks have been marked in bold with their subtasks outlined underneath. The duration mentioned for the individual tasks is based on a medium-size migration project; in this example, we'll imagine that it starts midway through 2018 and lasts for 205 days (from June 1, 2018, through March 11, 2019). You'll need to adjust these timelines based on the volume of transactions, complexity of the business processes, customization of the current system, and size of the organization, but all the tasks can still be used as a valid reference to jumpstart your migration project.

Task Name	Duration	Start	Finish	Program/Transaction/ SAP Notes
Project Planning	10 days	6/1/18	6/12/18	
Develop project charter	10 days	6/1/18	6/12/18	
Develop project plan with schedule and activities	5 days	6/8/18	6/12/18	
Prepare for kick-off	1 day	6/11/18	6/11/18	
Perform project kick-off	1 day	6/12/18	6/12/18	
Finalize resources: onsite/offshore	5 days	6/8/18	6/12/18	
Migration Planning	164 days	6/29/18	2/11/19	
Estimate downtime requirements	15 days	6/29/18	7/17/18	

B Project Plan for SAP S/4HANA Finance Migration

Task Name	Duration	Start	Finish	Program/Transaction/ SAP Notes
Validate downtime requirements	40 days	8/17/18	10/9/18	
Optimize downtime	45 days	10/12/18	12/11/18	
Perform downtime-optimization test	35 days	12/14/18	1/29/19	
Checklist for Migration	**10 days**	**6/15/18**	**6/26/18**	
Checklist Version	**1 day**	**6/15/18**	**6/15/18**	SAP Note 2157996
Fundamental Prerequisite	**5 days**	**6/15/18**	**6/19/18**	
Is SAP HANA currently being used?	5 days	6/15/18	6/19/18	SAP Note 2119188, http://help.sap.com/hana_platform
Is the current system on SAP ERP 6.0 EHP 7 or higher?	5 days	6/15/18	6/19/18	SAP Note 2119188, http://help.sap.com/erp_607
Software Update Manager (SUM)	5 days	6/15/18	6/19/18	SAP Note 2117481, http://service.sap.com/sltoolset • **Software Logistics Toolset 1.0 • SUM**
SAP HANA lifecycle manager/application lifecycle management	5 days	6/15/18	6/19/18	SAP Note 2117481
Administrator's Guide	5 days	6/15/18	6/19/18	http://help.sap.com/sfin200
Release Information Note (RIN)	5 days	6/15/18	6/19/18	SAP Note 2117481
Check restrictions	5 days	6/15/18	6/19/18	SAP Note 2127080

B Project Plan for SAP S/4HANA Finance Migration

Task Name	Duration	Start	Finish	Program/Transaction/SAP Notes
Perform new installation	5 days	6/15/18	6/19/18	New installations are recommended to use the installation package, immediately followed by using Maintenance Optimizer/SUM to upgrade to SAP S/4HANA Finance
Browser support	5 days	6/15/18	6/19/18	SAP Note 1971111
Current or Planned Application Coverage by SAP S/4HANA Finance	**5 days**	**6/15/18**	**6/19/18**	
Use Activity-Based Costing (CO-OM-ABC)	5 days	6/15/18	6/19/18	SAP Note 2119188
Use Lease Accounting Engine (LAE), Joint Venture Accounting (JVA), classic Real Estate Management (RE), etc.	5 days	6/15/18	6/19/18	SAP Note 1939592, SAP Note 1944871 (RE)
Use SAP Cash Management	5 days	6/15/18	6/19/18	SAP Note 1968568, SAP Note 2149337, SAP Note 2044295 (license info)
Use the general cost object and cost object hierarchies	5 days	6/15/18	6/19/18	SAP Note 2119188
Industry solutions used: perform business function set check	5 days	6/15/18	6/19/18	SAP Note 2119188

B Project Plan for SAP S/4HANA Finance Migration

Task Name	Duration	Start	Finish	Program/Transaction/SAP Notes
Industry solutions/compatible ERP: perform add-on check	5 days	6/15/18	6/19/18	SAP Note 2103558; refer to SAP Note 2035994 for details on how to handle the installation in case add-ons are not yet released for SAP S/4HANA Finance.
Installation Preparation	**5 days**	**6/15/18**	**6/19/18**	
Maintenance Optimizer ready	5 days	6/15/18	6/19/18	*https://wiki.scn.sap.com/wiki/display/SM/Maintenance+Tools%3A+Maintenance+Planner+and+Maintenance+Optimizer*
SUM ready	5 days	6/15/18	6/19/18	*http://service.sap.com/sltoolset* • **Software Logistics Toolset 1.0** • **SUM**
Perform license/visibility check	5 days	6/15/18	6/19/18	If you can't find the SAP ERP Financials (FI) add-on in the list, then consult this SAP internal Maintenance Optimizer Q&A: *https://wiki.scn.sap.com/wiki/display/SM/Maintenance+Optimizer+FAQ.*
Target stack XML created	5 days	6/15/18	6/19/18	
SAP HANA version	5 days	6/15/18	6/19/18	SAP Note 2117481

B Project Plan for SAP S/4HANA Finance Migration

Task Name	Duration	Start	Finish	Program/Transaction/SAP Notes
SAP Kernel	5 days	6/15/18	6/19/18	SAP Note 2117481
Installation Preparation (SAP HANA Live)	**2 days**	**6/18/18**	**6/19/18**	*http://help.sap.com/sfin200*
Migration Preparation	**5 days**	**6/22/18**	**6/26/18**	
Perform FI-AA preparation	5 days	6/22/18	6/26/18	SAP Note 1939592
Perform CO/FI customizing preparation	5 days	6/22/18	6/26/18	SAP Note 2129306
Perform general preparation for application data migration	5 days	6/22/18	6/26/18	*http://help.sap.com/sfin200*
Customer Code	**5 days**	**6/22/18**	**6/26/18**	
Modifications	5 days	6/22/18	6/26/18	
Customer code adaptations	5 days	6/22/18	6/26/18	SAP Note 1976487
Customer code adaptations	5 days	6/22/18	6/26/18	SAP Note 1946054; batch input programs for table AB01 are no longer supported in New Asset Accounting. If you're using customer-defined programs, you must convert these to Business Application Programming Interfaces (BAPIs).
Customer code adaptations	5 days	6/22/18	6/26/18	
Prepare to Apply Known Fixes	**5 days**	**6/22/18**	**6/26/18**	

B Project Plan for SAP S/4HANA Finance Migration

Task Name	Duration	Start	Finish	Program/Transaction/ SAP Notes
Perform data definition language statement (DDLS) corrections	5 days	6/22/18	6/26/18	
Error messages	5 days	6/22/18	6/26/18	SAP Note 2019282
Important corrections for installation/upgrade	5 days	6/22/18	6/26/18	SAP Note 2117481: section "Before the Installation or Upgrade of SAP S/4HANA Finance"
Important corrections for data migration	5 days	6/22/18	6/26/18	SAP Note 2117481: section "Migration Related Information"
Important corrections application functionality	5 days	6/22/18	6/26/18	SAP Note 2117481: section "Latest before Application Configuration and Testing"
Environment Clean-Up and Release Transports	30 days	6/29/18	8/7/18	
Sandbox Migration	60 days	6/29/18	9/18/18	
Environment ready	10 days	6/29/18	7/10/18	
Production system copy	5 days	7/6/18	7/10/18	
SAP Business Suite on HANA and SAP S/4HANA Finance Migration	20 days	7/13/18	8/7/18	
Preparation	5 days	7/13/18	7/17/18	
Enable the Customizing menu for FI	5 days	7/13/18	7/17/18	Transaction SA38 • RFAGL_SWAP_IMG_ NEW

B Project Plan for SAP S/4HANA Finance Migration

Task Name	Duration	Start	Finish	Program/Transaction/SAP Notes
Customize and activate FI-AA (New)	5 days	7/13/18	7/17/18	
Precheck Report for Migrating to FI-AA (New)	**5 days**	**7/13/18**	**7/17/18**	
RASFIN_MIGR_PRECHECK	5 days	7/13/18	7/17/18	Run special check report for FI-AA installed via SAP Note 1939592.
Check if new asset depreciation engine is active	5 days	7/13/18	7/17/18	SAP Note 965032
Differences between Old and New Depreciation Calculation	**5 days**	**7/13/18**	**7/17/18**	
Execute the periodic depreciation posting run	5 days	7/13/18	7/17/18	
Execute periodic Acquisition and Production Cost (APC) posting	5 days	7/13/18	7/17/18	
Execute year-end closing	5 days	7/13/18	7/17/18	
Reconcile SAP General Ledger (G/L) and subsidiary ledger using Report RAABST02	5 days	7/13/18	7/17/18	
Activate business function FI-AA, parallel valuation (FIN_AA_PARALLEL_VAL)	5 days	7/13/18	7/17/18	
Check if all relevant depreciation areas for parallel currencies exist	5 days	7/13/18	7/17/18	

535

B Project Plan for SAP S/4HANA Finance Migration

Task Name	Duration	Start	Finish	Program/Transaction/SAP Notes
For every additional currency type defined on the company code, set up corresponding depreciation area	5 days	7/13/18	7/17/18	
Consistency Checks before Installation and Migration	**5 days**	**7/13/18**	**7/17/18**	Transaction SA38 • RFINDEX_NACC SA38 • RAABST02 SA38 • RAABST01 GCAC SA38 • RM07MBST/ RM07MMFI
Consistency checks of the tables in G/L, AA, CO, ML	5 days	7/13/18	7/17/18	
Check to see if New G/L is active	5 days	7/13/18	7/17/18	
JVA not active	5 days	7/13/18	7/17/18	
LAE not active	5 days	7/13/18	7/17/18	
Classic RE not active	5 days	7/13/18	7/17/18	
Check sizing	5 days	7/13/18	7/17/18	
Check custom code and modifications	5 days	7/13/18	7/17/18	SAP Note 1976487
Handling Customer-Defined Fields and Interfaces	**5 days**	**7/13/18**	**7/17/18**	SE38
Check the consistency of the ledger, company code, and controlling area settings to determine if a migration to SAP S/4HANA Finance is possible	5 days	7/13/18	7/17/18	Transaction SA38 • RASFIN_MIGR_PRECHECK, SA38 • ZFINS_MIG_PRECHCK_CUST_SETTNGS, SAP Notes 1939592, 2129306

B Project Plan for SAP S/4HANA Finance Migration

Task Name	Duration	Start	Finish	Program/Transaction/ SAP Notes
Apply important bug fixes	5 days	7/13/18	7/17/18	Before you install SAP S/4HANA Finance, read RIN 2117481: SAP S/4HANA Finance for SAP Business Suite Powered by SAP HANA; apply the bug fixes that are described in this note.
Meet technical prerequisite by implementing SAP Notes to build and check reports	5 days	7/13/18	7/17/18	SAP Notes 1939592, 2105948
Run Reconciliation Reports to Ensure Consistent Data and Check for Errors.	5 days	7/13/18	7/17/18	Transaction SA38 • RFBILA00, RAGITT_ALV01, RAHAFA_ALV01, S_ALR_87013611, RKKBSELL, RFSSLD00, RFSOPO00, RFBELJ00, RFKUML00, RFKOPO00, RFKUML00, RFKOPO00, RFDAUB00 GR55 • 1SIP
Reconcile Asset Accounting with G/L	5 days	7/13/18	7/17/18	ABST2
Execute the reconciliation for the G/L and the AP/AR subledgers using Report TFC_COMPARE_VZ	5 days	7/13/18	7/17/18	SAPF190, TFC_COMPARE_VZ
Reconcile Materials Management (MM) with the G/L using Reports RM07MBST and RM07MMFI	5 days	7/13/18	7/17/18	RM07MBST, RM07MMFI

537

B Project Plan for SAP S/4HANA Finance Migration

Task Name	Duration	Start	Finish	Program/Transaction/SAP Notes
Reconcile ledgers	5 days	7/13/18	7/17/18	GCAC
Check consistency between indices and documents by executing Report RFINDEX_NACC	5 days	7/13/18	7/17/18	RFINDEX_NACC
Check FI documents with FI balances for all fiscal years without archived data	5 days	7/13/18	7/17/18	F.03, FAGLF03
Execute a delta upload of account-based Profitability Analysis (CO-PA) with a delta load to SAP Business Warehouse (SAP BW)	5 days	7/13/18	7/17/18	
Perform Period-End Closing Activities	5 days	7/13/18	7/17/18	Transaction SA38 • RMMMPERI SA38 • RAPERB2000 SA38 • RAPOST2000 FAGLGVTR, AJRW, F.07, SAPF100 SA38 • SAPLOF00
Post all held documents in the system	5 days	7/13/18	7/17/18	
Perform period-end closing activity in Asset Accounting periodic asset posting	5 days	7/13/18	7/17/18	RAPERB2000
Perform period-end closing activity in Asset Accounting depreciation run	5 days	7/13/18	7/17/18	RAPOST2000
Perform Asset Accounting year-end closing for previous fiscal year	5 days	7/13/18	7/17/18	AJAB

Task Name	Duration	Start	Finish	Program/Transaction/SAP Notes
Ensure all balances are carried forward for the current fiscal year: accounts	5 days	7/13/18	7/17/18	FAGLGVTR
Ensure all balances are carried forward for the current fiscal year: Accounts Receivable/Accounts Payable (AR/AP)	5 days	7/13/18	7/17/18	F.07
Ensure all balances are carried forward for the current fiscal year: assets	5 days	7/13/18	7/17/18	AJRW
Lock Asset Accounting via posting periods to avoid further asset transactions	5 days	7/13/18	7/17/18	OB52
Lock the current and previous periods in MM (Program RMMMPERI)	5 days	7/13/18	7/17/18	
Close all fiscal years except the current fiscal year using Program RAJABS00	5 days	7/13/18	7/17/18	
Reset the valuations for all periods in the current fiscal year using Program FAGL_FCV	5 days	7/13/18	7/17/18	FAGL_FC_VAL
Initialize valuation differences from currency valuation if using classic G/L; field BSEG_BDIFF in open items must be empty over all years	5 days	7/13/18	7/17/18	
Lock the periods in FI (program SAPLOF00)	5 days	7/13/18	7/17/18	OB52

B Project Plan for SAP S/4HANA Finance Migration

Task Name	Duration	Start	Finish	Program/Transaction/ SAP Notes
Lock the periods in CO (plan/actual; program SAPMKCSP)	5 days	7/13/18	7/17/18	OKP1
Lock all users in the system who don't have any tasks associated with the migration	1 day	7/17/18	7/17/18	
Reports and Tables for Comparison Purpose	**5 days**	**7/13/18**	**7/17/18**	
Execute and Save Financial Reports to Allow Comparison of Financial Reports after Migration	**5 days**	**7/13/18**	**7/17/18**	
Ledger comparison	5 days	7/13/18	7/17/18	GCAC
Financial statements	5 days	7/13/18	7/17/18	RFBILA00
Asset history sheet	5 days	7/13/18	7/17/18	Transaction S_ALR_87011990, SE38 • **RAGITT_ALV01**
Depreciation run for planned depreciations	5 days	7/13/18	7/17/18	Transaction S_ALR_87012026, SE38 • **RAHAFA_ALV01**
Total report for cost centers	5 days	7/13/18	7/17/18	S_ALR_87013611
Sales order selection	5 days	7/13/18	7/17/18	RKKBSELL
G/L account balance list	5 days	7/13/18	7/17/18	RFSSLD00
G/L line item list	5 days	7/13/18	7/17/18	Transaction S_ALR_87012332, SE38 • **RFSOPO00**
Compact Document Journal	5 days	7/13/18	7/17/18	RFBELJ00

Task Name	Duration	Start	Finish	Program/Transaction/ SAP Notes
Run and download list of recurring line items	5 days	7/13/18	7/17/18	S_ALR_87012346
Vendor sales	5 days	7/13/18	7/17/18	Transaction S_ALR_87012093, SE38 • RFKUML00
Vendor open item list	5 days	7/13/18	7/17/18	RFKEPL00
Customer sales	5 days	7/13/18	7/17/18	RFDUML00
Customer open item list	5 days	7/13/18	7/17/18	RFDEPL00
Customer recurring entry	5 days	7/13/18	7/17/18	RFDAUB00
Cost Centers: actual/plan/variance	5 days	7/13/18	7/17/18	GR55
Order: actual/plan/variance	5 days	7/13/18	7/17/18	S_ALR_87012993
Display FI Table before Migration for Comparison Purposes after SAP S/4HANA Finance Is Installed	5 days	7/13/18	7/17/18	
Check the number of entries in table FAGLFLEXT	5 days	7/13/18	7/17/18	Transaction SE16N • FAGLFLEXT
Check the number of entries in table GLT0	5 days	7/13/18	7/17/18	Transaction SE16N • GLT0
Check the number of entries in table BSEG where FI line items are stored	5 days	7/13/18	7/17/18	Transaction SE16N • BSEG
Installation	**5 days**	**7/20/18**	**7/24/18**	
Prepare installation or upgrade	5 days	7/20/18	7/24/18	SUM, Maintenance Optimizer

B Project Plan for SAP S/4HANA Finance Migration

Task Name	Duration	Start	Finish	Program/Transaction/SAP Notes
Create backup tables for the totals and index tables	5 days	7/20/18	7/24/18	
Save the totals and index tables in backup tables	5 days	7/20/18	7/24/18	
Run check reports	5 days	7/20/18	7/24/18	
Rename index and total tables into tables *BCK for compatibility views	5 days	7/20/18	7/24/18	
Delete the original totals and index tables	5 days	7/20/18	7/24/18	
Totals tables such as GLT0 or COSS are empty	5 days	7/20/18	7/24/18	
Import and activate new programs	5 days	7/20/18	7/24/18	
Install all hardware components, web services, and servers	5 days	7/20/18	7/24/18	
Install all technical patches as recommended by SAP	5 days	7/20/18	7/24/18	
Migration from any database to SAP HANA with SUM and the database migration option (DMO)	5 days	7/20/18	7/24/18	
Install SAP S/4HANA	5 days	7/20/18	7/24/18	SUM
Deploy the SAP HANA content using SAP HANA application lifecycle management	5 days	7/20/18	7/24/18	http://help.sap.com/saphelp_hanaplatform/helpdata/en/9a/012d6438764459a581e6af55a87c46/content.htm

B Project Plan for SAP S/4HANA Finance Migration

Task Name	Duration	Start	Finish	Program/Transaction/ SAP Notes
Activate the FI Extension (EA-FIN)	5 days	7/20/18	7/24/18	Activate the FI Extension (EA-FIN) SFW Switch in Transaction SFW5 (Switch Framework).
Activate additional business functions	5 days	7/20/18	7/24/18	SFW5
Prepare Data Migration and Customization	**5 days**	**7/27/18**	**7/31/18**	
Customizing the New G/L	**5 days**	**7/27/18**	**7/31/18**	SAP Customizing Implementation Guide • Migration to SAP S/4HANA Finance • Preparations and Migration of Customizing • Preparations and Migration of Customizing for General Ledger
Activate the new G/L when using the classic G/L	5 days	7/27/18	7/31/18	SA38 • RFAGL_SWAP_MENU_NEW
Fiscal year variants of all active controlling areas and their assigned company codes must be the same	5 days	7/27/18	7/31/18	
Migrate G/L customizing	5 days	7/27/18	7/31/18	
Accounting principles and valuation areas need to be defined if coming from classic G/L	5 days	7/27/18	7/31/18	
Assign accounting principles to ledger groups; should be in place for the new G/L	5 days	7/27/18	7/31/18	

543

B   Project Plan for SAP S/4HANA Finance Migration

Task Name	Duration	Start	Finish	Program/Transaction/ SAP Notes
Define valuation areas and assign them to accounting principles	5 days	7/27/18	7/31/18	
Assign accounting principles to the ledger per company code	5 days	7/27/18	7/31/18	
The leading ledger must always be assigned to the CO version 0	5 days	7/27/18	7/31/18	
Define document types for postings in CO	5 days	7/27/18	7/31/18	
Define document type mapping variants for CO business transactions	5 days	7/27/18	7/31/18	
Enter both document type and ledger group in CO transactions	5 days	7/27/18	7/31/18	
Check and define default values for postings in CO	5 days	7/27/18	7/31/18	
Define offsetting account determination type: highest amount	5 days	7/27/18	7/31/18	
Define source ledger for migration of balances	5 days	7/27/18	7/31/18	
Execute consistency check for G/L settings	5 days	7/27/18	7/31/18	
Activate business functions FIN_GL_CI_1, FIN_GL_CI_2, and FIN_GL_CI_3	5 days	7/27/18	7/31/18	

B Project Plan for SAP S/4HANA Finance Migration

Task Name	Duration	Start	Finish	Program/Transaction/SAP Notes
Checking the Prerequisites for Activating New Asset Accounting	5 days	7/27/18	7/31/18	Transaction SPRO • Asset Accounting (New) • Migration: Asset Accounting (New) • Migration for New Asset Accounting • Check Prerequisites for Activating Asset Accounting (New)
Run a special check report for FI-AA installed via SAP Note 1939592	5 days	7/27/18	7/31/18	RASFIN_MIGR_PRECHECK
Activation of new Asset Accounting	5 days	7/27/18	7/31/18	Transaction SPRO • Asset Accounting (New) • Migration: Asset Accounting (New) • Activate New Asset Accounting
Customizing New Asset Accounting	5 days	7/27/18	7/31/18	
Set new Asset Accounting activation status to **In Preparation**	5 days	7/27/18	7/31/18	Transaction SPRO • Asset Accounting (New) • Migration: Asset Accounting (New) • Activate New Asset Accounting
Migrate every active chart of depreciation, preferably manually	5 days	7/27/18	7/31/18	
Manual Migration of Chart of Depreciation Checklist	5 days	7/27/18	7/31/18	

B Project Plan for SAP S/4HANA Finance Migration

Task Name	Duration	Start	Finish	Program/Transaction/ SAP Notes
Check which depreciation plans are active/need to be migrated	5 days	7/27/18	7/31/18	
Are accounting principles set up?	5 days	7/27/18	7/31/18	
Are ledgers and ledger groups set up?	5 days	7/27/18	7/31/18	
Check assignment of accounting principles to ledger groups	5 days	7/27/18	7/31/18	
Setup of Depreciation Areas	**5 days**	**7/27/18**	**7/31/18**	
Are accounting principles and ledger groups assigned to each depreciation area?	5 days	7/27/18	7/31/18	
Is the posting indicator for each depreciation area correct?	5 days	7/27/18	7/31/18	
Is the posting indicator for adoption of APC values correct?	5 days	7/27/18	7/31/18	
Is the posting indicator for adoption of depreciation terms correct?	5 days	7/27/18	7/31/18	
Check currency type of a depreciation area for parallel currency	5 days	7/27/18	7/31/18	
Use parallel valuation approach: account or ledger	5 days	7/27/18	7/31/18	

Task Name	Duration	Start	Finish	Program/Transaction/ SAP Notes
Execute migration report for depreciation plan: prefer manual	5 days	7/27/18	7/31/18	FAA_CHECK_MIG2SFIN
Adapt value takeover and parameter takeover	5 days	7/27/18	7/31/18	
Define asset balance sheet accounts of parallel valuation as reconciliation accounts	5 days	7/27/18	7/31/18	
Define new technical clearing account for integrated asset acquisition	5 days	7/27/18	7/31/18	
Define depreciation area for quantity update	5 days	7/27/18	7/31/18	
Specify alternative document type for integrated transactions	5 days	7/27/18	7/31/18	
Perform revenue distribution for retirement by APC or net book value (preferred)	5 days	7/27/18	7/31/18	
Post net book value instead of gain/loss	5 days	7/27/18	7/31/18	
No restriction of transaction types to depreciation areas	5 days	7/27/18	7/31/18	
Display migration report	5 days	7/27/18	7/31/18	
Set new Asset Accounting activation status to **Active**	5 days	7/27/18	7/31/18	
Open posting period after finishing migration to table ACDOCA	5 days	7/27/18	7/31/18	

B   Project Plan for SAP S/4HANA Finance Migration

Task Name	Duration	Start	Finish	Program/Transaction/SAP Notes
Preparations and Migration of Customizing for CO	**5 days**	**7/27/18**	**7/31/18**	**SAP Customizing Implementation Guide • Conversion of Accounting to SAP S/4HANA • Preparations and Migration of Customizing • Preparations and Migration of Customizing for Controlling**
Execute SAP BW delta extraction for account-based CO-PA	5 days	7/27/18	7/31/18	
Delete settings for the change of profitability segment characteristics	5 days	7/27/18	7/31/18	SPRO
Maintain operating concern	5 days	7/27/18	7/31/18	SPRO
Execute program to add fields to new table ACDOCA Universal Journal entry line items	5 days	7/27/18	7/31/18	SA38
Check background job completion status and log	5 days	7/27/18	7/31/18	SM37
Assign controlling area to operating concern	5 days	7/27/18	7/31/18	SPRO
Define and activate account-based CO-PA	5 days	7/27/18	7/31/18	Costing-based CO-PA is still available, and you can use both types of CO-PA in parallel. However, account-based CO-PA is the default solution.
Migration	**5 days**	**8/3/18**	**8/7/18**	

B Project Plan for SAP S/4HANA Finance Migration

Task Name	Duration	Start	Finish	Program/Transaction/ SAP Notes
Technical Migration	**5 days**	**8/3/18**	**8/7/18**	
Execute upgrade in the source system	5 days	8/3/18	8/7/18	
Implement SAP Notes	5 days	8/3/18	8/7/18	
Start of downtime phase: S11 to HS1	5 days	8/3/18	8/7/18	
Transactions SPDD/SPAU: development and application	5 days	8/3/18	8/7/18	
Transactions SPDD/SPAU: SAP Basis	5 days	8/3/18	8/7/18	
Distribute temporary GUI to IT teams	5 days	8/3/18	8/7/18	
Application SPAU	5 days	8/3/18	8/7/18	
Migrate application data	5 days	8/3/18	8/7/18	
Activate SAP S/4HANA installation	5 days	8/3/18	8/7/18	
Apply SAP Notes for SAP S/4HANA	5 days	8/3/18	8/7/18	
Finalize upgrade	5 days	8/3/18	8/7/18	
Implement SAP Notes	5 days	8/3/18	8/7/18	
Migrate primary application server	5 days	8/3/18	8/7/18	
Data Migration	**5 days**	**8/3/18**	**8/7/18**	
Regenerate Core Data Services (CDS) views and field mapping	5 days	8/3/18	8/7/18	**Transaction SPRO • Conversion of Accounting to SAP S/4HANA • Data Migration • Regenerate CDS Views and Field Mapping**

Task Name	Duration	Start	Finish	Program/Transaction/ SAP Notes
Perform new G/L data migration	5 days	8/3/18	8/7/18	
Regenerate CO-PA operating concern	5 days	8/3/18	8/7/18	
Perform consistency checks on data	5 days	8/3/18	8/7/18	
Perform SAP Smart Financials migration: Fill delta tables, fill table for AP/AR balances carried forward, perform initial balance carryforward, and link line items between CO and FI	5 days	8/3/18	8/7/18	
Perform migration of cost elements	5 days	8/3/18	8/7/18	Transaction SPRO • Conversion of Accounting to SAP S/4HANA • Data Migration • Documentation of Data Migration • Migration of Cost Elements
Perform technical check of transaction data	5 days	8/3/18	8/7/18	Transaction SPRO • Conversion of Accounting to SAP S/4HANA • Data Migration • Documentation of Data Migration • Technical Check of Transaction Data
Enrich data	5 days	8/3/18	8/7/18	Transaction SPRO • Conversion of Accounting to SAP S/4HANA • Data Migration • Documentation of Data Migration • Enrichment of Data

Task Name	Duration	Start	Finish	Program/Transaction/ SAP Notes
Perform migration of line items into new data structure	5 days	8/3/18	8/7/18	Transaction SPRO • Conversion of Accounting to SAP S/4HANA • Data Migration • Documentation of Data Migration • Migration of Line Items
Perform migration of balances	5 days	8/3/18	8/7/18	Transaction SPRO • Conversion of Accounting to SAP S/4HANA • Data Migration • Documentation of Data Migration • Migration of Balances
Migrate transaction data: documents, balances, and depreciation values	5 days	8/3/18	8/7/18	Transaction SPRO • Conversion of Accounting to SAP S/4HANA • Data Migration • Documentation of Data Migration • Calculation of Depreciation and Totals Values
Migrate house bank accounts	5 days	8/3/18	8/7/18	FCLM_BAM_ MIGRATION
Complete the migration	5 days	8/3/18	8/7/18	Transaction SPRO • Conversion of Accounting to SAP S/4HANA • Data Migration • Complete Migration
Postmigration	**5 days**	**8/3/18**	**8/7/18**	
Open the periods in FI and CO	5 days	8/3/18	8/7/18	
Run reconciliation reports to check data consistency	5 days	8/3/18	8/7/18	Transaction SA38 • **RAPERB2000 SA38** • **RAPOST2000**

Task Name	Duration	Start	Finish	Program/Transaction/ SAP Notes
Perform process tests to ensure successful migration	5 days	8/3/18	8/7/18	
Transfer application indexes	5 days	8/3/18	8/7/18	Transaction SPRO • Conversion of Accounting to SAP S/4HANA • Activities after Migration • Transfer Application Indexes
Display status of transfer of application indexes	5 days	8/3/18	8/7/18	
Fill due dates in FI documents	5 days	8/3/18	8/7/18	Transaction SPRO • Conversion of Accounting to SAP S/4HANA • Activities after Migration • Fill Due Dates in FI Documents
Display status of filling in due dates into FI documents	5 days	8/3/18	8/7/18	
Fill the offsetting account in FI documents	5 days	8/3/18	8/7/18	Transaction SPRO • Conversion of Accounting to SAP S/4HANA • Activities after Migration • Fill the Offsetting Account in FI Documents
Display status of filling the offsetting account in FI documents	5 days	8/3/18	8/7/18	

B Project Plan for SAP S/4HANA Finance Migration

Task Name	Duration	Start	Finish	Program/Transaction/ SAP Notes
Set the Migration Completed indicator	5 days	8/3/18	8/7/18	Transaction SPRO • Conversion of Accounting to SAP S/4HANA • Data Migration • Complete Migration • Set Migration to Completed
Prepare for start	5 days	8/3/18	8/7/18	Unblock users' open periods
Set up data aging	5 days	8/3/18	8/7/18	Transaction SPRO • Financial Accounting (New) • Financial Accounting Global Settings (New) • Tools • Data Aging • Data Aging for Accounting Documents
Execute balance carryforward	5 days	8/3/18	8/7/18	
Data Checks	**5 days**	**8/3/18**	**8/7/18**	
Execute SAP HANA-optimized report transaction	5 days	8/3/18	8/7/18	
Check financial statement	5 days	8/3/18	8/7/18	S_ALR_87012284
Display obsolete FI tables FAGLFLEXT and GLT0 to verify that they are now only views	5 days	8/3/18	8/7/18	SE16N
Display/change items	5 days	8/3/18	8/7/18	FAGLL03
Check G/L line item transaction	5 days	8/3/18	8/7/18	FBL3N

553

B   Project Plan for SAP S/4HANA Finance Migration

Task Name	Duration	Start	Finish	Program/Transaction/ SAP Notes
Check G/L account line item	5 days	8/3/18	8/7/18	FBL3H
Check vendor line item	5 days	8/3/18	8/7/18	FBL1H
SAP HANA Infrastructure Ready	**5 days**	**7/20/18**	**7/24/18**	
Ensure all the technical infrastructure is available for SAP HANA installation	5 days	7/20/18	7/24/18	
Configure and install SAP HANA database in SAP system	5 days	7/20/18	7/24/18	
HANA-tization	**20 days**	**8/10/18**	**9/4/18**	SAP Note 1976487
Perform DB migration—Native SQL, DB Hints, and ABAP Database Connectivity (ADBC)	20 days	8/10/18	9/4/18	Transaction CODE_SCANNER
Perform depooling/ declustering: sorting behavior	20 days	8/10/18	9/4/18	New features in Code Inspector must be executed after upgrade but before migration.
Perform depooling/ declustering: Use of physical cluster/pool	20 days	8/10/18	9/4/18	Usage is very rare. Manual analysis and testing are required.
SAP HANA architecture: Perform sorting behavior of transparent table	20 days	8/10/18	9/4/18	Transparent DB tables: ■ Rely on not guaranteed "default" sorting of DB content ■ Direct access and analysis of technical DB index information

B Project Plan for SAP S/4HANA Finance Migration

Task Name	Duration	Start	Finish	Program/Transaction/SAP Notes
SAP HANA architecture: Perform direct access/ analysis of technical index information	20 days	8/10/18	9/4/18	CODE_SCANNER
Run check on custom code	20 days	8/10/18	9/4/18	SAP Note 1976487
Testing in Sandbox	**15 days**	**8/31/18**	**9/18/18**	
Execute FI unit test of basic functionality and postings	15 days	8/31/18	9/18/18	
Execute integration test to check the functionality and FI integration postings with other modules	15 days	8/31/18	9/18/18	
Execute regression testing to check if the existing functionality prior to SAP S/4HANA Finance installation works	15 days	8/31/18	9/18/18	
Development Migration and Unit Testing	**70 days**	**7/13/18**	**10/16/18**	
Environment ready	20 days	7/13/18	8/7/18	
Development system ready	5 days	8/10/18	8/14/18	
SAP Business Suite on HANA and SAP S/4HANA Finance Migration	**25 days**	**8/17/18**	**9/18/18**	
HANA-tization	**10 days**	**9/21/18**	**10/2/18**	
Migration Unit Test	**10 days**	**10/5/18**	**10/16/18**	
Integration Test 1: Migration and Test	**50 days**	**9/7/18**	**11/13/18**	

555

B Project Plan for SAP S/4HANA Finance Migration

Task Name	Duration	Start	Finish	Program/Transaction/SAP Notes
Environment ready	15 days	9/7/18	9/25/18	
Production system copy	5 days	9/21/18	9/25/18	
SAP Business Suite on HANA and SAP S/4HANA Finance Migration	15 days	9/28/18	10/16/18	
Integration Test 1	20 days	10/19/18	11/13/18	
Runbook	130 days	7/13/18	1/8/19	
Runbook draft	85 days	7/13/18	11/6/18	
Runbook test and enhancement	45 days	11/9/18	1/8/19	
Integration Test 2: Migration and Test	40 days	10/12/18	12/4/18	
Environment ready	5 days	10/12/18	10/16/18	
Production system copy	5 days	10/12/18	10/16/18	
SAP Business Suite on HANA and SAP S/4HANA Finance Migration	15 days	10/19/18	11/6/18	
Integration Test 2	20 days	11/9/18	12/4/18	
Performance Testing	20 days	11/23/18	12/18/18	
User Acceptance Testing (UAT): Migration and Test	55 days	11/9/18	1/22/19	
Environment ready	5 days	11/9/18	11/13/18	
Production system copy	5 days	11/9/18	11/13/18	
SAP Business Suite on HANA and SAP S/4HANA Finance Migration	10 days	12/7/18	12/18/18	
UAT	15 days	1/4/19	1/22/19	

B Project Plan for SAP S/4HANA Finance Migration

Task Name	Duration	Start	Finish	Program/Transaction/SAP Notes
Mock Cutover 1	25 days	12/14/18	1/15/19	
Environment ready	5 days	12/14/18	12/18/18	
Production system copy	5 days	12/14/18	12/18/18	
SAP Business Suite on HANA and SAP S/4HANA Finance Migration	5 days	1/4/19	1/8/19	
Consistency Check	5 days	1/11/19	1/15/19	
Mock Cutover 2: Real Time	10 days	1/18/19	1/29/19	
Environment ready	5 days	1/18/19	1/22/19	
Production system copy	5 days	1/18/19	1/22/19	
SAP Business Suite on HANA and SAP S/4HANA Finance Migration	5 days	1/25/19	1/29/19	
Consistency Check	5 days	1/25/19	1/29/19	
Mock Cutover 3: Real Time	10 days	1/18/19	1/29/19	
Environment ready	5 days	1/18/19	1/22/19	
Production system copy	5 days	1/18/19	1/22/19	
SAP Business Suite on HANA and SAP S/4HANA Finance Migration	5 days	1/25/19	1/29/19	
Consistency Check	5 days	1/25/19	1/29/19	
Training	75 days	10/19/18	1/29/19	
Train the trainer	45 days	10/19/18	12/18/18	
End user training	20 days	1/4/19	1/29/19	
Cutover	120 days	8/24/18	2/5/19	
Planning	65 days	8/24/18	11/20/18	

557

B Project Plan for SAP S/4HANA Finance Migration

Task Name	Duration	Start	Finish	Program/Transaction/ SAP Notes
Test	50 days	11/23/18	1/29/19	
Ramp-down and actual cutover	5 days	2/1/19	2/5/19	
Go-Live	5 days	2/8/19	2/12/19	
Post-Go-Live Support	20 days	2/15/19	3/11/19	

Appendix C
The Author

Anup Maheshwari is a proficient SAP S/4HANA Finance professional and business and digital transformation thought leader with 20 years of IT and business consulting experience in managing and delivering complex SAP projects. Anup is currently working as a principal director at Accenture and is an adjunct professor at the University of Texas at Dallas, an SAP University Alliances program.

Anup has led design, migration, and implementation teams at multiple global deployments of SAP S/4HANA Finance. He has successfully led multiple sales pursuits and managed more than 12 full lifecycle and global roll-out SAP implementation projects across North America, Europe, and Asia Pacific.

As a trusted business advisor, Anup has been responsible for defining the strategy, roadmap, design, and solutioning of implementing SAP S/4HANA Finance; driving design validation workshops; proposing best business practices as a subject matter expertise; managing the end-to-end delivery from architecture, configuration, solution building, development, test strategy, and execution; collaborating with clients to improve their business performance, drive shareholder value, and create a competitive advantage by helping them solve complex business problems.

Anup's SAP functional experience includes SAP S/4HANA Finance, Central Finance, application of artificial intelligence and cloud computing to SAP S/4HANA business processes, SAP Fiori design, Cash Management, SAP BPC for SAP S/4HANA Finance, and Financial Supply Chain Management.

Anup has an MBA and MS in project management from The George Washington University. He is a Stanford Certified Project Manager and a PMI Certified Project Management Professional (PMP). Anup also has an Enterprise Architect Certificate from Carnegie Mellon University. He is a Chartered Financial Analyst and a Certified SAP Consultant.

You can reach Anup Maheshwari at *anupmah@gmail.com*.

Index

A

ABAP 64, 128, 473
   backend server 469
   frontend server 468
ABAP Development Tools (ADT) 117, 127
ABAP Workbench 429
Account assignment 266
Account determination 145, 365
Account-based CO-PA 60
Accounting 32
Accounting principle 140, 190, 193
Accounting principle document 196
Accounts Payable (AP) 38, 76, 79
Accounts payable accountant 483
Accounts Payable Manager app 497
Accounts Receivable (AR) 38, 76, 79
Accounts receivable accountant 485
Acquisition and production cost (APC) 67, 190, 193, 205
   transaction 188
   value 81, 188
Activation 95
Activation log 448
Activity-based costing (ABC) 54
Administrator's Guide for SAP S/4HANA 63, 111
Adopt authorizations 268
Aggregate table 110
Allocation 213–214
Analytic view 128
Appendix ledger 154–155, 161
Application index 318
   transfer 317
Application index table 110
Application Interface Framework (AIF) 526
Application Link Enabling (ALE) 155
Application Linking and Embedding (ALE) ... 65
Approval pattern 247–249
Architecture 36
Asset 194
   acquisition 196

Asset (Cont.)
   retirement 183
   value 188
Asset Accounting (classic FI-AA) 76, 177
Assigned ledgers 68
Attribute view 128
Authorization profile 269
Automatic payment 348

B

Balance carryforward 84, 169, 322
Balance sheet 188
   account 91, 265, 323
Bank account
   closure 412
   master data 242–243, 340, 362
   number mapping 304
   technical ID 242
   type 243–244
Bank Account Management 242, 304, 337, 344, 352, 354, 363, 412
Bank clearing account 372
   account determination 365
Bank directory 341
Bank master data 415
Bank statement 246
Bank statement monitor 350
Bank subaccount 372
Batch job 94
Budget control system (PSM-FM-BCS) 62
Business Add-In (BAdI) 304
Business Application Programming Interface (BAPI) 64
Business Configuration Sets (BC Sets) 71
Business function 68, 131, 147, 424
   DAAG_DATA_AGING 317
   EA-FIN 70
   FI-G/L 65
   FIN_AA_CI_1 72
   FIN_AA_PARALLEL_VAL 68–69, 184
   FIN_CO_CCMGMT 424

561

Index

Business function (Cont.)
   FIN_CO_CCPLAN 424
   FIN_CO_ORPLAN 424
   FIN_FSCM_CLM 339
   FIN_GL_CI_1 148
   FIN_GL_CI_2 148
   FIN_GL_CI_3 148
   FIN_GL_DISTR_SCEN_1 65
   OPS_PS_CI_1 424
Business function/switch concept 117
Business Object Repository (BOR) 359
Business unit 229

C

Cash concentration 363
Cash Journal 224
Cash manager 493
Cash Operations 337, 366
Cash pool 363
Cash Position 415
Central Finance 46, 108, 155, 505, 510
   architecture 510
   business case 505
   data mapping 515
   error handling 526
   initial data load 522, 525
   system prerequisites 514
CFO 30, 500
Change and Transport System (CTS) 428
Change management 40, 332
Change request number range 242
Chart of accounts 266
Chart of depreciation 178–179, 185, 192, 202
   migration 178
Charts 479
Checklist 108
Classic G/L 146, 149
Clearing 512
Clearing account 364–365
Clone system 311
Closing process 205
Cluster table 128
Cluster/pool table 124
Code Inspector 126–127
Code pushdown 126

Company code 96, 136, 139, 141–142, 158, 177, 193, 222, 245
Compatibility view 235, 302
Compliance capabilities 329
Compliance management 33
Concur 29
Consistency check 76, 131, 147, 159, 262
Consumer and Mortgage Loans (CML) 388
Content bundle 444
Control parameter 190
Controller 488
Controlling 37, 54, 107, 131, 196, 207, 234, 424
   area 95, 136, 146, 230
   business transaction 143
   document 276
   document migration 216
   historic plan data 425
   posting 214
   transactional data 277
   version 141
Core Data Services (CDS) view 117, 236, 253
Cost center 199, 236, 267
Cost Center Accounting 237
Cost center report 239
Cost element 236, 262, 264, 425
Cost manager 495
Cost object 112
   changes 513
   hierarchy 112
   mapping 516, 520
Cost of goods sold (COGS) 228–229, 330
Create Manual Payment app 485
Credit exposure data 323
Credit limit check 167
Credit management 167
Credit management data 323
Currency 68
   conversion 408
   new settings 131, 134, 214
   type 134
Custom code 42, 44, 64, 117
Custom Development Management Cockpit (CDMC) 127
Customer master data 166

Index

D

Data aging 36
Data cleansing 41
Data consistency 76, 316
Data definition language (DDL) 117, 253
Data definition language statement
   (DDLS) 117
   views 117
Data Dictionary (DDIC) 40, 64, 151, 254, 434
Data migration 39
Data model 117
Data replication 507
Data structure 218, 285
Data Warehousing Workbench 431, 457
Database footprint 329
Database migration option (DMO) 40, 110
Database size 58
Database table 123
DataSource 443
Days sales outstanding (DSO) 465
Days Sales Outstanding app 499
Declustering 125
Default ledger group 144, 222
Delta CO totals 289
Delta migration 313
Deployment scenarios 108
Depooling 125
Depreciation 81, 87–88, 296
   area 67, 175, 178, 180, 186, 189–191, 202
   calculation 74
   depreciation calculation program
     (DCP) 177
   terms 190, 203
Depreciation run 317
   posting 199
Depreciation value 297
   initial 299
Display Customer Balances app 487–488
Display log 302
Document changes 513
Document migration status 286
Document number 152, 258
Document number range 86
Document posting 163
Document splitting 43
Document summarization 153, 159
Document type 79, 131, 142, 163
Due date 318
Duplicate entry 288

E

EDI 412
EHP 7 .... 40, 45, 109
End-of-day statement 246
Enhancement Package Installer (EHPI) 113
Enrich transactional data 281
Enterprise extension 71
   EA-FIN 71, 73
Enterprise risk 33
Error 257, 278
Error log 210
Error message 210, 299, 453
Extension ledger 136

F

FI-CO reconciliations 33
Field
   FDTAG 383
   HBKID 391
   HKTID 391
Financial close 32, 35
Financial operations source application 389
Fiscal year 145
   change 75, 81
   variant 131, 133, 196
Flexible Real Estate Management (RE-FX) 62
Flow category 368
Flow level 368
Flow type 368, 370
Foreign currency valuation 92
Function module
   RS_MANDT_UNIQUE_SET 432
Functional account 244
Funds Management (PSM-FM) 62

G

G/L accountant 480
General Availability Care program 116

563

Index

General Ledger (G/L) 36–37, 42, 54, 76, 131, 146, 149, 179, 188, 425
   account 214, 262, 264, 330
   account mapping 216
   allocation 301
   Customizing 135
   document 276
   migration 39, 218
   summary table 302
General Ledger Accounting 38, 65, 76, 145, 148, 188, 194–195, 224, 229, 234, 296
Generally accepted accounting principles (GAAP) 70
Goods receipt/invoice receipt (GR/IR) 317
Graphical calculation view 128
Greenfield implementation 45, 53

H

HANA-tization 123
   tools 125
Held document 88
House bank 391
House bank account 304

I

Import and Export Bank Accounts tool 305
Import method 246
Income statement 230
Index table 44
Industry solution 112
InfoCube 425
InfoObject 425, 442
InfoProvider 425
Installation 107
Integrated asset acquisition 204
Intercompany reconciliation 169, 329
International Financial Reporting Standards (IFRS) 70
Internet Communication Framework (ICF) 452
Internet Communication Manager (ICM) 452
Invoice verification 483, 486

J

Job BI_TCO_ACTIVATION 434, 439
Joint Venture Accounting (JVA) 54, 62
Journal entry 152, 216

K

Key mapping 515, 517
Key performance indicator (KPI) 32, 465

L

Landscape Management Database (LMDB) 119
Leading ledger 136–137, 141, 160, 165, 222
Lease Accounting Engine (LAE) 54, 62
Ledger assignment 141
Ledger comparison report 84
Ledger definition 160
Ledger group 76, 138–140, 144, 175, 278
Liquidity forecast 415
Liquidity item 378, 409
Liquidity item hierarchy 380
Liquidity planning 404
Liquidity planning type 409

M

Maintenance Optimizer 109–110, 113, 116
Maintenance Planner 63, 66, 116, 118
Manage Bank Accounts app 495
Mapping 254
Mapping variant 222
Material Ledger (ML) 61, 211, 217–219, 227
Materials Management (MM) 76
Migrated documents check 283
Migration 91, 278
   cost element 261
   cost elements 265
   data 251
   data view 254
   house bank account 304, 342
   log 193
   phases 47

Index

Migration of balances 131, 217, 289–291
   check 292
   display status 293
Month-end depreciation run 195
Multidimensional reporting 328
Multi-instance environment 508
My Spend app 496

N

Near-zero downtime (NZDT) 251, 311
Net book value 183
New Asset Accounting 35, 42–43, 54,
   66–67, 175
   activation 204
Nonleading ledger 154, 160
Nonoperating expense 265
Nonsequential signatory pattern 248
Nonstatistical line item 195
Number range 79, 242
   interval 242

O

OData services 469
Offsetting account 145, 320
One Exposure from Operations 381, 385
Open items 512
Operating account 244
Operating concern 207, 209
Operational data providers (ODP) 433
Operational entry document 196
Optimization 126
Overdraft Limit tab 245
Overdue Payables app 497

P

Parallel accounting 43
Parallel currency 92, 179
Parallel ledger 72
Parallel valuation 179, 184
Partitioning 252
Payment approval 344
Payment behavior 323
Payment grouping 346

Payment request 373
Performance expectations 58
Performance statistics 126
Period control 87
Period-end closing 86, 168
Periodic depreciation posting run 73
Plan data 202
Planned depreciation 169
Planned depreciation value 194
Planned status 69
Planning group 382–383
Planning level 376, 382
Planning modeler 456–457
Planning query 449
Planning unit 406
   hierarchy 406–407
Planning view 401
Post General Journal Entries app 482
Posting value 143
Postmigration activity 315
Preparation 53
Prima nota 154
Primary cost 265
Primary cost element 221, 262
Prior period 92
Product Cost Controlling (CO-PC) 112
Product System Editor 119
Production variance 229
Profit and loss (P&L) 213
   account 236
Profit Center Accounting 54, 234, 237
Profit center planning 236
Profit Centers—Actuals app 492
Profitability Analysis (CO-PA) 60, 207, 213,
   317, 327
   account-based 208, 229
   costing-based 229
   distributed 233
Profitability characteristic 229
Profitability segment 207, 286
Program
   FAA_DEPRECIATION_CALCULATE 297
   FAA_DEPRECIATION_POST 74
   *FCO_ADD_COPA_FIELD_TO_*
     ACDOCA 231
   FINS_MIG_PRECHCK_CUST_SETTNGS 95

565

Index

Program (Cont.)
   FINS_MIGRATION_START 313
   General Ledger Line Items List 98
   RAABST01 80
   RAABST02 80
   RAGITT_ALV01 100
   RAHAFA_ALV01 101
   RAJABS00 .... 75, 88
   RAPOST2000 88
   RASFIN_MIGR_PRECHECK 66, 94, 177
   RFAGL_SWAP_IMG_NEW 133
   RFAGL_SWAP_MENU_NEW 133
   RFBELJ00 99
   RFBILA00 96
   RFDAUB00 105
   RFDEPL00 103
   RFDUML00 103
   RFINDEX_NACC 77
   RFKEPL00 101
   RFKUML00 101
   RFNRIV20 86
   RFSOPO00 98
   RFSSLD00 98
   RFTMPBLD 88
   RGUCOMP4 84
   RKKBSELL 96
   RM07MBST 82
   RM07MMFI 82
   RMMMPERI 87
Project plan 529

Q

Questionnaire 55

R

Read access 255
Real Estate Management 54, 62
Real-time consolidation 513
Real-time integration 136
Reconciliation 96, 278, 309
   ledger 84, 165, 324
Reconciliation report 316
Reference data source 408
Relational database management system
   (RDBMS) 39–40

Remote function call (RFC) 446, 471
Report 239, 316
   FINS_MIGRATION_STATUS 255
   FQME_BANK_CASH_BAL_IMPORT 387
   PFCG_TIME_DEPENDENCY 274
   RAPERB2000 74
   RSICF_SERVICE_ACTIVATION 452
   RVKRED09 324
Report hierarchy 225
Reporting 195, 507
Representative ledger 139, 144
Restrictions 53
Role 269
   FUCN_GL_ACCOUNTANT 268
   SAP_BW_BI_ADMINISTRATOR 441
   SAP_SFIN_ACC_PLANNING 425
   SAP_SFIN_CASH_MANAGER 339
Root cause 278
Rule
   FCLM_CASHMGR 359
   FCLM_CASHSYSCOLL 360
   FCLM_REVWOR 360

S

SAP Add-On Installation Tool (SAINT) 110
SAP Ariba Network 29
SAP Bank Communication Management ... 344
SAP BPC for SAP S/4HANA Finance 61, 236,
   401, 412, 422–423
SAP BPC Web Client 423
SAP Business Client 120, 224, 237,
   410–411, 423
SAP Business Explorer 430
SAP Business Suite 38, 40, 68
SAP Business Suite on SAP HANA 465
SAP Business Warehouse (SAP BW) 56,
   207–208, 406, 421
   client 432–433
   embedded 431
   namespace 437
SAP Business Workflow 244
SAP BusinessObjects BI Content Activation
   Workbench 445
SAP BusinessObjects BI Content bundle 442
SAP BusinessObjects Business Intelligence
   (BI) 396, 426, 468

566

Index

SAP BusinessObjects Design Studio 494
SAP Cash and Liquidity Management ... 61, 304
SAP Cash Management 35, 42, 54, 112, 250, 337, 382, 389, 415, 500
SAP Cloud Platform 29
SAP Credit Management 167
SAP DataSource 430
SAP ERP 56–57
SAP ERP 6.0 38
 EHP 7 .... 40, 45, 109
SAP ERP Financials ... 37, 74, 107, 112, 117, 133, 179, 207, 213, 315, 328, 466
SAP ERP Financials Extension (EA-FIN) 177
SAP ERP HCM Organizational Management 274
SAP Extended Warehouse Management (SAP EWM) 114
SAP Financial Closing cockpit 169, 172
SAP Fiori 29, 59, 108, 423, 461, 465
 analytical app 465
 apps 30, 472
 architecture 467
 dashboard for Cash Manager 494
 fact sheet app 465
 project phases 466
 transactional app 465
SAP Fiori launchpad 468, 473
SAP Gateway 115, 120, 468, 470
SAP GUI 59, 420
SAP HANA 31, 59, 108, 125, 232, 461
 artifact 127
 database 29
 database migration 46
 integration 232
 modeling 128
SAP HANA application lifecycle management 111, 123
SAP HANA Extended Application Services Advanced 468
SAP HANA lifecycle manager 111
SAP HANA Live 30, 123
 packages 111
SAP Landscape Transformation 511
 replication server 108, 511
SAP Liquidity Management 338, 395
SAP List Viewer (ALV) 128
SAP Master Data Governance (MDG) 511

SAP Mobile Platform 116, 467
SAP NetWeaver 110, 116, 423
SAP NetWeaver 7.40 109
SAP NetWeaver ABAP 40
SAP NetWeaver Enterprise Search 472
SAP Note 121
SAP Process Integration (SAP PI) 469
SAP S/4HANA Finance 38, 175, 412
SAP Smart Business 60, 111, 115, 496, 498
 KPIs 478
SAP Smart Business mobile UI 36
SAP Treasury and Risk Management 33, 365
SAP Web Dispatcher 468, 472
Scale-out 41
Scale-up 41
Secondary cost 265
Secondary cost element 214, 236
Secure Sockets Layer (SSL) 471
Segment reporting 43
Segment-level characteristics 233
Sensitive field 244
Sequential approval pattern 248
Signatories tab 245
Signatory approval 349
Signatory control 246
Signatory group 246
Signature method 349
Simulation run 513
Single signature 247
Single Sign-On (SSO) 473
Single source of truth 506
Sizing 66
Software Update Manager (SUM) 40, 63, 66, 110, 119
Sorting behavior 125
Source ledger 131, 145
SQL 64
SQL Monitor 127
SQL Performance Tuning Worklist 127
Stack calculation 109
Standard ledger 136
Statistical data 202
Subledger 82, 89, 291
 reconciliation 79
Substitution rule 146
Support Package Manager (SPAM) 113
Switch Framework 428

567

Switch PARALLEL_VAL 185
System landscape 56, 506
System review 55

T

Table 201, 238
   ACDOCA 37, 64, 149, 215, 252, 262, 287
   ANLC 194
   ANLP 194
   BKPF 76, 149
   BNKA 341
   BSAD 77
   BSAD_BCK 259
   BSAK 77
   BSAS 77
   BSAS_BCK 259
   BSEG 65, 77, 150, 159, 287
   BSID 77
   BSID_BCK 258
   BSIK 77
   BSIS 77
   BSIS_BCK 259
   FAAT_DOC_IT 194
   FAAT_PLAN_VALUES 194–195
   FAGLFLEXA 151, 153
   FAGLFLEXT 151, 302
   FAGLFLEXT_BCK 151, 293, 295
   FCLM_BAM_ACLINK2 342
   FCLM_BAM_AMD 415
   FDES 388
   FQM_FLOW 376, 388
   FQMI_FLOW_CAT 368
   GLT0 78
   HRRP_DIRECTORY 226
   HRRP_NODE 226
   MLHD 154
   MLIT 154
   RSADMINA 432
   T012K 342
Table index 76
Table join 41
Target ledger 145
Technical clearing account 180, 204
Test run 302

Transaction 127, 169, 200, 219, 237, 270
   AB01 198
   ABLDT 198
   AFAB 81
   AFAR 298
   AJAB 75, 81
   AJRW 75, 81, 90
   AS91 .... 198, 205
   ASKB 81
   AW01 73
   AW01_AFAR 73
   BAUP 341
   BSANLY_BI_ACTIVATION 443
   CODE_SCANNER 124
   F.07 90
   F111 365
   FAGLF03 79
   FAGLGVTR 84, 89, 156
   FB01 154
   FB01L 161
   FB50 .... 88, 154
   FB60 154
   FB70 154
   FBB1 161
   FBICS3 329
   FBL3H 237
   FF7A 415
   FI01 340
   FI12_HBANK 342, 415
   FINS_CUST_CONS_CHK 147, 159
   FINS_MASS_DATA_MASTER 286, 290
   FINS_MASS_DATA_MONITOR 286
   FINS_MIG_DAA 266
   FINS_MIG_DUE 318
   FINS_MIG_GCM 264
   FINS_MIG_GKONT 320
   FINS_MIG_INIT_COLD 317
   FINS_MIG_LEDGER_CUST 135
   FINS_MIG_MONITOR 282
   FINS_MIG_MONITOR_AFA 298
   FINS_MIG_MONITOR_CLD 318
   FINS_MIG_MONITOR_DAA 267
   FINS_MIG_MONITOR_DUE 319
   FINS_MIG_MONITOR_GCM 265
   FINS_MIG_MONITOR_GKO 321
   FINS_MIG_MONITOR_RC0 257

Index

Transaction (Cont.)
 FINS_MIG_MONITOR_RC1 276
 FINS_MIG_MONITOR_RC2 284
 FINS_MIG_MONITOR_RC3 288
 FINS_MIG_MONITOR_RC4 293
 FINS_MIG_MONITOR_RC5 299
 FINS_MIG_STATUS 313
 FINS_MIGRATION 281
 FINS_RECON_RC0 256
 FINS_RECON_RC1 275
 FINS_RECON_RC3 288
 FINS_RECON_RC5 298
 FLQC0 381
 FLQC15 381
 FLQQA1 381
 FLQQA5 381
 for reports 328
 FQM_ACTIVATE 389
 FQM_INITIALIZE 394
 FQM_UPD_FLOW_TYPE 393
 FQM_UPD_LITEM 392
 FQM21 .... 375, 387
 FS00 .... 182, 221, 264, 269
 GCA9 303
 GCAC 84, 309
 GR55 316
 KA01 221
 KA06 221
 KB11 .... 152, 161
 KB11 and KB41 216
 KB41 .... 152, 161
 KEA0 150
 KEA5 150
 KP06 237
 LMDB 113
 MR21 154
 NWBC 305, 343, 410
 OBH2 86
 OXK3 150
 PFCG 268, 471
 PPOCE 354
 PPOMW 354
 RSA1 .... 406, 439, 442
 RSA5 443
 RSD1 441
 RSOR 445

Transaction (Cont.)
 RSPLAN 456
 RSRTS_ACTIVATE_R3IS 396
 RSTCO_ADMIN 439
 S_ALR_87012993 106
 S_ALR_87013611 105
 SA38 ... 80, 82, 84, 86, 88, 94–95, 133, 255, 324
 SAPF190 79
 SAT 126–127
 SE30 127
 SFW5 .... 69, 71–73
 SICF 453
 SLG1 .... 322, 343
 SM30 428
 SM37 322
 SMSY 115
 SPDD/SPAU 117
 SPRO 70, 435, 444
 SQLM 126
 STC01 469–470
 SU01 471
 SWDD 359
 SWETYPV 352
 SWLT 126
 UKM_BP 167
 UKM_MY_DCDS 167
Transaction currency 147
Transaction type 184
Transactional data 147, 257, 274–275, 387
Transfer rule 188, 202
Transport Layer Security 468

U

Unicode 57
Universal Journal 31, 33–34, 36, 147,
 149–150, 159, 213, 217, 251, 255, 331–332
User experience (UX) 29, 421, 465
User interface (UI) 30, 419
User screen 474

V

Valuating part 204
Valuation 92
Valuation area 227–228

Index

Value mapping 515, 518
Value transfer 179
Value type 236
Vendor master data 166
Virtual data model (VDM) 123

W

Web Dynpro 305, 451, 481, 488, 493
   report 239

Work in Process (WIP) 330
Workflow 352
   custom 359
   template 360
Workflow, report, interface, conversion,
   enhancement, and form (WRICEF) 60, 332

Y

Year-end closing 41, 81, 87

- Master the profitability analysis functionality in SAP S/4HANA Finance
- Set up your value flows, reporting, and planning processes
- Learn how to migrate your profitability analysis data from SAP ERP to SAP S/4HANA

Kathrin Schmalzing

CO-PA in SAP S/4HANA Finance

Business Processes, Functionality, and Configuration

SAP S/4HANA Finance has transformed the CO-PA landscape! Learn about the updates and developments to profitability analysis in SAP S/4HANA Finance, and then configure your new system with step-by-step instructions and screenshots. Start with the basics: master data, actual value flow, and data enrichment. Then learn how to migrate your existing SAP ERP data into SAP S/4HANA Finance. The future of CO-PA with SAP is here!

337 pages, pub. 10/2017
E-Book: $79.99 | **Print:** $89.95 | **Bundle:** $99.99

www.sap-press.com/4383

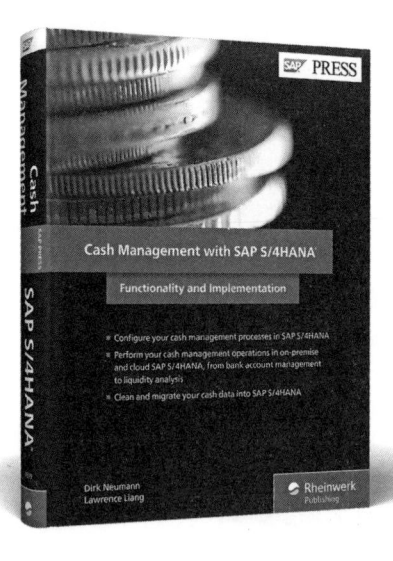

- Configure your cash management processes in SAP S/4HANA
- Perform your cash management operations in on-premise and cloud SAP S/4HANA, from bank account management to liquidity analysis
- Clean and migrate your cash data into SAP S/4HANA

Dirk Neumann, Lawrence Liang

Cash Management with SAP S/4HANA

Functionality and Implementation

Get greater insight into your cash operations with this comprehensive guide to cash management in SAP S/4HANA! Start by configuring bank account management (BAM), cash positioning, and liquidity management. Then perform your key processes: maintaining banks, processing cash transactions, forecasting liquidity, and more. Choose your deployment model, dive into the new One Exposure from Operations data model, and see what it takes to migrate your cash data. Cash in on SAP S/4HANA!

477 pages, pub. 10/2017
E-Book: $79.99 | **Print:** $89.95 | **Bundle:** $99.99

www.sap-press.com/4479

- Manage your financial consolidation with Real-Time Consolidation (RTC) in SAP S/4HANA

- Set up and perform currency translation, intercompany elimination, and consolidation of investments

- Create standard and ad-hoc consolidation reports

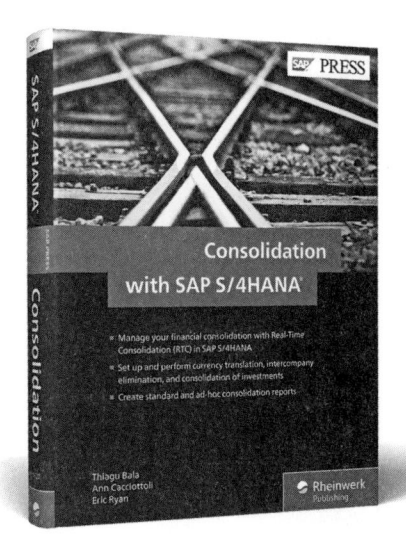

Bala, Cacciottoli, Ryan

Consolidation with SAP S/4HANA

Real-Time Consolidation is ready, and your comprehensive SAP S/4HANA consolidation guide is here! Explore the architecture of SAP S/4HANA and how table ACDOCC changes your landscape; then follow step-by-step instructions for activating and configuring the key consolidation models. Check out currency translation, intercompany elimination, reporting, and data migration from SAP BPC. Finally—details about consolidation with SAP S/4HANA, all in one place!

approx. 425 pages, avail. 04/2018
E-Book: $89.99 | **Print:** $99.95 | **Bundle:** $109.99

www.sap-press.com/4532

Rheinwerk Publishing

- Learn what SAP S/4HANA offers your company for financials and logistics
- Get the scoop on SAP S/4HANA deployment options, implementation, extensibility, and more
- Consult SAP S/4HANA customer case studies

Bardhan, Baumgartl, Chaadaev, Choi, Dudgeon, Lahiri, Meijerink, Worsley-Tonks

SAP S/4HANA

An Introduction

Moving your business to SAP S/4HANA or wondering if it's right for you? From finance to logistics, from on-premise to cloud implementations, and from industry solutions to reporting, see what SAP S/4HANA can offer! Understand its architecture, adoption scenarios, and how SAP Activate can expedite your transformation. Learn about all-new functionality for warehousing, manufacturing, procurement, and more. Up to date for release 1709!

511 pages, 2nd edition, pub. 10/2017
E-Book: $59.99 | **Print:** $69.95 | **Bundle:** $79.99

www.sap-press.com/4499

www.sap-press.com

- Learn what SAP S/4HANA Finance is—and what it can do for you
- Understand the technical foundation of SAP S/4HANA
- Explore your SAP S/4HANA Finance deployment options: on-premise, cloud, and hybrid

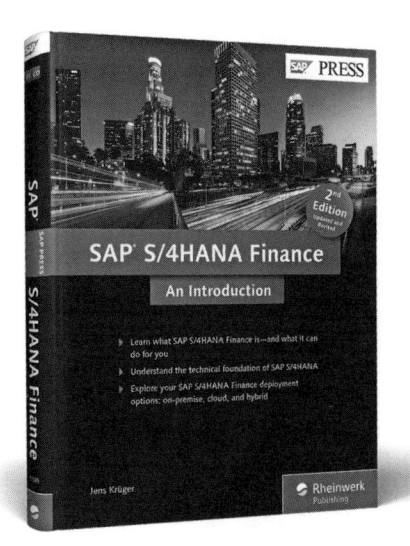

Jens Krüger

SAP S/4HANA Finance

An Introduction

It's high time you got to know SAP S/4HANA Finance. Learn what SAP S/4HANA Finance can do, what it offers your organization, and how it fits into the SAP S/4HANA landscape. Explore critical finance functionality, from cash management to profitability analysis, and consider your deployment options. Lay the groundwork for your SAP S/4HANA Finance future!

411 pages, 2nd edition, pub. 02/2016
E-Book: $59.99 | **Print:** $69.95 | **Bundle:** $79.99

www.sap-press.com/4122

Rheinwerk Publishing

- Learn what SAP S/4HANA Cloud is and how it runs your business
- Understand its use cases, from startups to large enterprises
- Explore the best practices for a cloud ERP: finance, manufacturing, and more

Michael Jolton, Yosh Eisbart

SAP S/4HANA Cloud

Use Cases, Functionality, and Extensibility

Is SAP S/4HANA Cloud right for you? Get the scoop on SAP S/4HANA Cloud, from implementation to extensibility. Find answers to your questions about use cases, costs, and maintenance requirements. Then dive into SAP S/4HANA Cloud's core processes: finance, inventory, production, sales, and more. Learn how you can tailor the system to grow with your business. Get the SAP S/4HANA Cloud big picture!

334 pages, pub. 09/2017
E-Book: $59.99 | **Print:** $69.95 | **Bundle:** $79.99

www.sap-press.com/4498

www.sap-press.com

Interested in reading more?

Please visit our website for all new book
and e-book releases from SAP PRESS.

www.sap-press.com